# IFIP Advances in Information and Communication Technology 368

# IFIP – The International Federation for Information Processing

IFIP was founded in 1960 under the auspices of UNESCO, following the First World Computer Congress held in Paris the previous year. An umbrella organization for societies working in information processing, IFIP's aim is two-fold: to support information processing within ist member countries and to encourage technology transfer to developing nations. As ist mission statement clearly states,

> *IFIP's mission is to be the leading, truly international, apolitical organization which encourages and assists in the development, exploitation and application of information technology for the benefit of all people.*

IFIP is a non-profitmaking organization, run almost solely by 2500 volunteers. It operates through a number of technical committees, which organize events and publications. IFIP's events range from an international congress to local seminars, but the most important are:

- The IFIP World Computer Congress, held every second year;
- Open conferences;
- Working conferences.

The flagship event is the IFIP World Computer Congress, at which both invited and contributed papers are presented. Contributed papers are rigorously refereed and the rejection rate is high.

As with the Congress, participation in the open conferences is open to all and papers may be invited or submitted. Again, submitted papers are stringently refereed.

The working conferences are structured differently. They are usually run by a working group and attendance is small and by invitation only. Their purpose is to create an atmosphere conducive to innovation and development. Refereeing is less rigorous and papers are subjected to extensive group discussion.

Publications arising from IFIP events vary. The papers presented at the IFIP World Computer Congress and at open conferences are published as conference proceedings, while the results of the working conferences are often published as collections of selected and edited papers.

Any national society whose primary activity is in information may apply to become a full member of IFIP, although full membership is restricted to one society per country. Full members are entitled to vote at the annual General Assembly, National societies preferring a less committed involvement may apply for associate or corresponding membership. Associate members enjoy the same benefits as full members, but without voting rights. Corresponding members are not represented in IFIP bodies. Affiliated membership is open to non-national societies, and individual and honorary membership schemes are also offered.

Daoliang Li  Yingyi Chen (Eds.)

# Computer and Computing Technologies in Agriculture V

5th IFIP TC 5/SIG 5.1 Conference, CCTA 2011
Beijing, China, October 29-31, 2011
Proceedings, Part I

 Springer

Volume Editors

Daoliang Li
Yingyi Chen
China Agricultural University
China-EU Center for Information & Communication Technologies (CICTA)
17 Tsinghua East Road, P.O. Box 121, Beijing, 100083, P.R. China
E-mail: {dliangl, chenyingyi}@cau.edu.cn

ISSN 1868-4238                          e-ISSN 1868-422X
ISBN 978-3-642-27280-6                  e-ISBN 978-3-642-27281-3
DOI 10.1007/978-3-642-27281-3
Springer Heidelberg Dordrecht London New York

Library of Congress Control Number: 2011944691

CR Subject Classification (1998): I.2.11, H.3-4, C.3, I.4, C.2, D.2

*Typesetting:* Camera-ready by author, data conversion by Scientific Publishing Services, Chennai, India

Printed on acid-free paper

Springer is part of Springer Science+Business Media (www.springer.com)

# Preface

I would like to express my sincere thanks to all authors who submitted research papers to support the 5th International Conference on Computer and Computing Technologies in Agriculture (CCTA 2011) held in Beijing, China, during October 29–31, 2011.

This conference was hosted by China Agricultural University; the IFIP TC5 Special Interest Group (SIG) on Advanced Information Processing for Agriculture (AIPA); National Natural Science Foundation of China; and China-EU Centre for Information and Communication Technologies (CICTA).

Proper scale management is not only a necessary approach in agro-modernization and agro-industrialization but also required for the development of agricultural productivity. Therefore, the application of different technologies in agriculture has become especially important. 'Informatized agriculture' and the 'Internet of Things' are hot research topics in many countries aiming to scientifically manage agriculture to yield high incomes with low costs. CICTA covers the research and development of advanced and practical technologies applied to agriculture and promotes international communication and cooperation; it has successfully held five International Conferences on Computer and Computing Technologies in Agriculture since 2007.

The topics of CCTA 2011 covered a wide range of the interesting theory and applications of all kinds of technology in agriculture, including the Internet of Things; simulation models and decision-support systems for agricultural production; agricultural product quality testing; traceability and e-commerce technology; the application of information and communication technology in agriculture; and universal information service technology and service system development in rural areas.

We selected the 189 best papers among all those submitted to CCTA 2011 for these proceedings. The papers are divided into three themes. It is always exciting to have experts, professionals and scholars with creative contributions getting together and sharing some inspiring ideas and hopefully accomplishing great developments in high-demand technologies.

Finally, I would like also to express my sincere thanks to all authors, speakers, Session Chairs and attendees, from home and abroad, for their active participation and support of this conference.

October 2011 Daoliang Li

# Conference Organization

## Sponsors

China Agricultural University
The IFIP TC5 Special Interest Group (SIG) on Advanced Information
  Processing for Agriculture(AIPA)
National Natural Science Foundation of China

## Organizers

China-EU Center for Information and Communication Technologies in
  Agriculture (CICTA)

## Chair

Daoliang Li

## Conference Secretariat

Lingling Gao

# Table of Contents – Part I

## Decision Support Systems, Intelligent Systems and Artificial Intelligence Applications

# Table of Contents – Part II

## GIS, GPS, RS and Precision Farming

# Table of Contents – Part III

## Simulation, Optimization, Monitoring and Control Technology

# Impact of Regional Industries on Logistics Demand with Improved Grey Analysis

Wenqin Cao[1,2], Haiyan Zhu[3],
and Bin Li[4]

[1] School of Science, Nanchang University,
Nanchang, Jiangxi 330031, China
[2] School of Mechatronics Engineering, East China Jiaotong University,
Nanchang, Jiangxi 330013, China
[3] School of Railway Tracks and Transportation,
East China Jiaotong University,
Nanchang, Jiangxi 330013, China
[4] Institute of Technology East China Jiaotong University,
Nanchang, Jiangxi 330100, China
bessie2310@163.com

**Abstract.** An improved Grey Relational Analysis (GRA) is used to quantitatively investigate the impact of Jiangxi Province regional economy on local logistics demand. The grey characteristics of data from regional economy and logistics is studied, which shows GRA is applicable; then a multi-sequence GRA is proposed, which generates total 4 groups of grey relational sequence from three indices of industrial added value and logistics demand based on GRA. Finally statement and explanation are given based on the Jiangxi Provincial industrial situation.

**Keywords:** Logistics Demand, Grey System, Grey Rational Analysis (GRA), Industry.

## 1    Introduction

The planning of regional logistics industry is influenced by multiple complex factors. However, the main factor is always depended on the development of local industries, so an analytical model for relationship between these factors is hard to setup [1]. Hence a study to the development of local economy and its impact on logistics industry will lay the milestone to the logistics planning.

The level of regional economical development, industrial structure, industrial distribution and industrial upgrading has direct impact on the demand and the level of regional logistics [2]. So in this paper, the gray relational theory is used to analyze the impact of Jiangxi provincial regional economy on the local logistics demand from a quantitative respective [4].

D. Li and Y. Chen (Eds.): CCTA 2011, Part I, IFIP AICT 368, pp. 1–7, 2012.

# 2     Applicability of Grey Relational Analysis and Its Improvement

## 2.1     Applicability of Grey Relational Analysis

The Grey System theory proposed by Deng (1982) has been proven to be useful for dealing with poor, incomplete and uncertain information system called grey system. The Grey System theory is aimed at problems with no experience and insufficient, uncertainty data, which fuzzy mathematics, statistics and probability theory can not solve[4]. Grey Relational Analysis (GRA) is part of Grey System theory, which is suitable for solving problems with complicated interrelationships between multiple factors and variables [5-7]. GRA is to establish gray correlation model to make grey relationship whose operating mechanism and the physical prototype is not clear or non-existent quantification, sequence and obvious. GRA can define system or factor boundary, analyze influence of system and behavior, distinguish primary and secondary factors, identify patterns and so on [8]. Technical connotation of GRA is to obtain difference from variable sequences; establish space of difference; establish and calculate comparison measure of differences, called gray relational grade; establish sequence relationship between factors.

Data of logistics demand is regarded as grey because the statistical data relating with regional logistics demand is not complete for historical reasons, at the same time these statistical data have its flaws ( such as inaccurate, incomplete, estimation, etc.) [9]. Furthermore, socio-economic system is an open system influenced by complexity factors, which is stochastic interacting with after-effect processes and uncertain relationship. The mathematical model for relationship between various economic factors and logistics demand has not been established. Above all, it proves that the relationship between industries and logistics demand shows significant grey characteristic.

## 2.2     Variable Definition

Variable definition is the first step of grey theory application. In the logistics field, almost all goods need transportation, and transportation is first one of the seven logistics activities. So the freight traffic data from the transportation field can be an indicator as logistics demand when logistics demand has no systematic statistics, and be regarded as a reference sequence of GRA model [10]. The scale and level of regional economy directly impact on logistics demand. The statistical Industrial Added Value (IAV) of primary industry, secondary industry and tertiary industry can indicate industrial structure, as compared sequence of GRA model. In our study, the time span of variable data is eight years from 2003 to 2010.

## 2.3     Improved GRA Based on Multi-group Grey Relational Grade

Past research just used only one group of grey relational grade to analyze the degree of influence, because the operational mechanism of grey system was assumed certain and unchanged [11]. However, the economy of Jiangxi Province is in the rapid development stage; structure of three industries is adjusted in wider margin variation by years [12]. So model of economic operation is uncertain and variable, which cause relative degree of three factors impact on freight traffic changing. If using only one group of gray relational grade, these changes can not be expressed. The paper introduces multi-group GRA which establishes eight grey relational matrixes, but not just traditional one.

Every sequence of matrix is made of variable data of five consecutive years of 2003 to 2010 by consecutively rolling, that is to say data of year 2003~2007 as group 1, data of year 2004~2008 as group 2,…, and data of year 2006~2010 as group 4 [13]. Finally four groups of grey relational sequence can be gained based on GRA. By horizontal comparison, changes can be grasped dynamically, so analysis is more complete and reliable.

## 3    Grey Relational Model and Data Analysis

### 3.1    Source Data and Eight Groups of Matrix

Variable data is from Jiangxi Statistical Yearbooks. Considering inflation, Industrial Added Value (IAV) of three industries is calculated at 2003 constant prices. All source data is showed in table 1, eight groups of matrix is showed in table 2, which reference sequence is $y_0$ and the comparison sequence is $y_i$.

**Table 1.** Added value of three industries and freight traffic from year 2003 to 2010 in jiangxi province

| Year | Freight Traffic (10000 tons) , $y_0$ | IAV of primary industry (RMB 100 million), $y_1$ | IAV of Secondary industry (RMB 100 million) $y_2$ | IAV of Tertiary industry (RMB 100 million) $y_3$ |
|------|------|------|------|------|
| 2003 | 27709 | 560 | 1227 | 1043 |
| 2004 | 31924 | 605 | 1455 | 1143 |
| 2005 | 33996 | 644 | 1704 | 1267 |
| 2006 | 37517 | 686 | 1982 | 1392 |
| 2007 | 40046 | 720 | 2325 | 1541 |
| 2008 | 43011 | 755 | 2711 | 1697 |
| 2009 | 46237 | 787 | 2968 | 1848 |
| 2010 | 54190 | 818 | 3511 | 2047 |

Notes: Data of IAV in this table are calculated at 2003 constant prices, which is from Jiangxi Statistical Yearbooks.

**Table 2.** Four groups of matrix

| Group1 (Year 2003~2007) | $Y_0(k)=(27709,31924,33996,37517,40046);\ Y_1(k)=(560,605,644,686,720)$ $Y_2(k)=\ (1227,1455,1704,1982,2325;\ Y_3(k)=(1043,1143,1267,1392,1541)$ |
|---|---|
| Group2 (Year 2004~2008) | $Y_0(k)=(31924,33996,37517,40046,43011);\ Y_1(k)=(605,644,686,720,755)$ $Y_2(k)=\ (1455,1704,1982,2325,2711;\ Y_3(k)=(1143,1267,1392,1541,1697)$ |
| Group3 (Year 2005~2009) | $Y_0(k)=(33996,37517,40046,43011,46237);\ Y_1(k)=(644,686,720,755,787)$ $Y_2(k)=\ (1704,1982,2325,2711,2968;\ Y_3(k)=(1267,1392,1541,1697,1848)$ |
| Group4 (Year 2006~2010) | $Y_0(k)=(37517,40046,43011,46237,54190);\ Y_1(k)=(686,720,755,787,818)$ $Y_2(k)=\ (1982,2325,2711,2968,3511;\ Y_3(k)=(1392,1541,1697,1848,2047)$ |

## 3.2    Calculation of Grey Relational Grade

1. Data dimensionless
Source data should be made dimensionless in order to ensure the accuracy of gray correlation calculation, because of their unified units and large difference in value. The three methods commonly used for dimensionless are interval-based method, mean method and initial value method. The initial value method is used as follows:

$$x_{ik} = \frac{y_i(k)}{y_i(1)} \qquad k = 1,2,\cdots,n\ i = 0,1,2,\cdots,m \tag{1}$$

2. Consideration of grey relational grade
Absolute difference is expressed by Eq (2)

$$\Delta = \left\{ \Delta_{0i}(k) \mid k=1,2,...n, i=0,1,2,...m \right\} \tag{2}$$

Environmental parameters are expressed by Eq (3)

$$M = \max_i \max_k \Delta_{0i}(k), \quad m = \min_i \min_k \Delta_{0i}(k) \tag{3}$$

The grey rational coefficient at point k is defined by Eq (4)

$$\gamma(x_{0k}, x_{ik}) = \frac{m + \xi M}{\Delta_{0i}(k) + \xi M}, k = 1,2,...n; i = 1,2,...m; \tag{4}$$

In Deng's study (1989), the general grey relational grade is expressed by Eq (5)

$$\gamma(x_0, x_i) = \frac{1}{n} \sum_{k=1}^{n} \gamma(x_{0k}, x_{ik}) \tag{5}$$

The $\zeta$ is a distinguishing factor, which is set to be 0.5 generally.

Here we adopt the grade computation, and finally the eight groups of grey relational sequence of three industries impact on freight traffic is showed in table 3, which is retained three decimal.

**Table 3.** Eight groups of grey relational sequence of three industries impact on freight traffic

| Group Year | Group 1 (2003~2007) | Group 2 (2004~2008) | Group 3 (2005~2009) | Group 4 (2006~2010) |
|---|---|---|---|---|
| Primary industry | 0.745 | 0.877 | 0.769 | 0.749 |
| Secondary industry | 0.649 | 0.610 | 0.594 | 0.550 |
| Tertiary industry | 0.910 | 0.820 | 0.837 | 0.799 |

### 3.3 Grey Relational Sequence Analysis

The higher value of the grey relational grade represents the stronger relational degree between the reference sequence and the given sequence. Table 3 shows that descending order of grey relational coefficient is the primary industry, tertiary industry and secondary industry.

Jiangxi is a granary province, whose Primary industry is developed with a rural population of 32 million, accounting for about 77% of the total population. Jaingxi allocates to the state 8 to 10 billion kilograms of grain annually, is one of the few provinces with grains output surplus [14].

Jiangxi's future policy and strategies on the Primary industry is to reinforce eco-agricultural construction, whose essential content is to vigorously develop harmless agriculture, green food and organic food. So freight traffic of agricultural produce will still increase [15]. In generally, the agricultural produce's price is low, so its contribution to IAV is limited in the past few years. At the same, outsourcing logistics of Primary industry accounted for a large proportion. From 1998 to 2008, although the IAV from the Primary industries accounted for small proportion of GDP (about 20%), The Primary industry has the greatest impact on the freight transportation.

The relationship between the tertiary industry and freight traffic is becoming closer. Rapid development of modern logistics industry raises the level and quality of logistics services effectively, which facilitates the logistics outsourcing in turn [16]. Such virtuous circle makes industrial transport, post and telecommunication industries increase year by year, accounting about 40% of the tertiary industry.

Although IAV of the secondary industry accounts large proportion of GDP between year 1998 and 2006, about 35 ~ 45%, its gray relational grade is the smallest of the three factors.

With the level of technology improvement, IAV of the secondary industry accounts for a large proportion of production value, and IAV per unit is high. The proportion of logistics outsourcing is low in industrial enterprises.

## 4     Conclusions

The grey rational grades of economic indicators and freight traffic in different province are different because of the different types of provinces and its different economics stages of evolution.

The improved GRA can be referred to analyze the main factors influencing logistics demand, which will be used to improve logistics industry and coordinate the development of regional economics. It is difficult to establish the physical prototype because of less scientific theory and practice for regional logistics development and planning guidance and more conditions with complex relationship. In the past, regional economic factors and their impact on logistics are limited to qualitative analysis, which is subjectively appraisal, lack of data support. GRA can rule out subjectivity and arbitrariness at a certain extent, which make traditional approach quantitative, scientific and artificial intelligence. Conclusion based on GRA is more comprehensive, objective and impartial.

Further study is considered to the amendment of statistical data. Some Statistical data has its own shortcomings, data of freight traffic has big jump in some years. So further study need revising statistical data to include the strange data and vacancy data to make them more realistic. Then it needs more qualitative method. Many other factors which are eliminated in the model should be analyzed with more qualitative method.

**Acknowledgments.** The paper is one of the results of project, Reverse Logistics Network Design for Jiangxi Province Based on Circular Economy (GL1114) supported by the provincial education department of Jiangxi, and assisted by key laboratory of conveyance and equipment, ministry of education.

# References

1. Cao, W.-Q.: Logistics demand forecast for urban logistics planning. Master thesis of South China University of technology (2005)
2. Deng, J.: Control problems of grey systems. Systems and Control Letters 1, 288–294 (1982)
3. Williamson, O.E.: Economics and Organization: A Primer. California Management Review 38, 131–146 (1996)
4. Statistic bureau of Jiangxi, Jiangxi statistical yearbook 2009. China Statistics Press (2009)
5. Hibiki, N., Sueyoshi, T.: DEA sensitivity analysis by changing a reference set: regional contribution to Japanese industrial development. Omega 27, 139–153 (1999)
6. Wu, H.H.: A comparative study of using grey relational analysis in multiple attribute decision making problems. Quality Engineering 15, 209–217 (2002-2003)
7. Deng, J.L.: Introduction to grey system theory. The Journal of Grey System 1(1), 1–24 (1989)
8. Yeh, Y.-L., Chen, T.-C.: Application of grey correlation analysis for evaluating the artificial lake site in Pingtung Plain, Taiwan, NRC Annual Report 2003-2004, 56–64 (2004)
9. Wen, K.L.: The cardinal form of grey relational grade. Journal of The Chinese Grey System Association 2(2), 117–133 (1999)
10. Wu, H.J., Chen, C.B.: An alternative form for grey relational grades. The Journal of Grey System 11(1), 7–12 (1999)
11. Lin, C.L.: Use of the Taguchi Method and Grey Relational Analysis to Optimize Turning Operations with Multiple Performance Characteristics. Materials and Manufacturing Processes 19(2), 209–220 (2004)

12. Lin, Y.-H., Wang, J.-S., Pai, P.-F.: A Grey Prediction Model With Factor, Analysis Technique. Journal of the Chinese Institute of Industrial Engineers 21(6), 535–542 (2004)
13. Chen, W.-H.: A Grey-Based Approach For Distribution Network Reconfiguration. Journal of the Chinese Institute of Engineers 28(5), 795–802 (2005)
14. Chang, J.-C., Lu, H.-C.: Backing Up a Simulated Truck Via Grey Relational Analysis. Journal of the Chinese Institute of Engineers 24(6), 745–752 (2001)
15. Deng, J.L.: Introduction to Grey System Theory. The Journal of Grey System 1, 1–24 (1989)
16. Kuo, Y., Yang, T., Huang, G.-W.: The Use of Grey Relational Analysis in Solving Facilities Layout Design Problem. In: The 36th CIE Conference on Computers & Industrial Engineering, pp. 1101–1110 (2005)

# Research on the Shape of Wheat Kernels Based on Fourier Describer

Wei Xiao[1], Qinghai Li[1,2], and Longzhe Quan[3,*]

[1] Wenzhou Vocational & Technical College.325035 Wenzhou, P.R. China
[2] Zhejiang industry&Trade Vocational College.325003 Wenzhou, P.R. China
68890105@qq.com
[3] College of Engineering, Northeast Agricultural University, 150030 Harbin, P.R. China
quanlongzhe@163.com

**Abstract.** The shape of wheat kernels is one of the most important criterions for quality inspection and grading. This paper has used Fourier describer to describe the three views of wheat shape accurately and has had a counter-construction operation.Also it verified this method for describing the shape, small but complex. Finally, the appropriate characteristic parameters were selected, and the BP-network was used to classify the four varieties wheat kernels. This method deserves a recognition rate of 98%~99%.

**Keywords:** machine vision, wheat kernel, Fourier describer, pattern recognition, BP-network.

## 1    Introduction

Seed identification, which can keep economic order, increase farmers' income and promote economic growth, is always one important issue in the area of agriculture.They can also help us understand kinds of seeds better. There have been more studies on appearance characteristics of wheat kernels with machine vision at home and abroad, which have gained approving effect [1-6]. However, it was difficult to describe the wheat kernel shape accurately with traditional description methods because the views of wheat shape are too complex. On the other side, traditional description methods need more parameters, which would go against the pattern classification, while the Fourier describer can describe the shape of wheat kernel more precisely with fewer parameters, and set a reliable foundation for the pattern classification.So this paper will classify the four varieties of wheat kernels with the method of Fourier describer.

## 2    Acquisition of Kernel Edge Coordinates

### 2.1    Preprocessing of the Three-Dimensional Images of Wheat Kernel

By using digital image processing techniques, such as image denoising, image segmentation, image transformation and image edge detection, the edges of wheat kernel image can be detected.

---

* Corresponding author.

D. Li and Y. Chen (Eds.): CCTA 2011, Part I, IFIP AICT 368, pp. 8–15, 2012.

**Fig. 1.** The front view of wheat kernel

**Fig. 2.** The side view of wheat kernel

**Fig. 3.** The top view of wheat kernel

Fig.1, Fig.2, Fig.3 have presented respectively the color images, binary images and marginal detection images of each view of wheat kernel. Better marginal detection can set a firm foundation for the follow-up Fourier describer.

## 2.2    Acquisition of Kernel Marginal Coordinates

At First, before doing Fourier describer of kernel shape, the coordinates on marginal images should be ensured, namely, determining each pixel's position in the images.

| $(x-1, y+1)$ | $(x, y+1)$ | $(x-1, y+1)$ |
|---|---|---|
| $(x-1, y)$ | $(x, y)$ | $(x+1, y)$ |
| $(x-1, y-1)$ | $(x, y-1)$ | $(x+1, y-1)$ |

**Fig. 4.** The relation of every pixel coordinatesin eight connected domains

According to Fig.4, any relational pixel point coordinate can be determined if center pixel coordinates (x, y) were known in eight connected domains. Similarly, nearby pixels coordinates can be identified by the edge of a known pixel coordinate. And so, each pixel coordinates can be obtained.

# 3        Determination of Edge Spread Vector and Phase Angle

Spread vector is an indispensable condition for Fourier describer, and phase angle is the essential condition of the counter- construction of kernel shape.

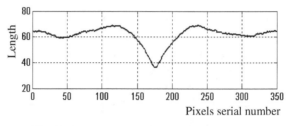

**Fig. 5.** The edge curve of wheat kernel image

We need to calculate the distance from every edge pixel to the centroid and get a length sequence base on the centroid of wheat kernel. That is the unfolded of edge vector (as shown in Fig.5).

$$l_k = \sqrt{(x_k - x^*)^2 + (y_k - y^*)^2} \qquad (1)$$

Where: $l_k$ --The distance from the kth edge pixel to the centroid ;

$x_i$, $y_i$ --Every edge pixel's coordinate;

$x^*$, $y^*$ --The centroid of contour curve of wheat kernel.

The edge pixel coordinates cannot be determined with only the value of $l_k$ when making the counter-construction. The phase angle ( $\theta_k$ ) of every pixel's should also be identified.

$$\theta_k = \arctan(\frac{y_k - y_k^*}{x_k - x_k^*}) \qquad (2)$$

# 4        The Discrete Fourier Descriptor to the Vector of Wheat Shape

Fourier transformation is a familiar kind of linear transformation, which can simplify the dimensions of 2-D boundary data easily [7].

## 4.1        The Fourier Transformation and Counter Transformation on the Vector of Wheat Shape

N-D vector of wheat shape can be acquired with its edge, which consists of N pixels, and it is transformed in the way of discrete Fourier transformation:

$$L(\omega) = \frac{1}{N}\sum_{k=0}^{N-1} l_k \exp[-j2\pi\omega k/N] \quad \omega=0,1,\cdots,N-1 \tag{3}$$

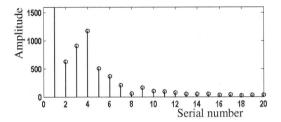

**Fig. 6.** The Fourier transformation sequence of wheat edge curve

In the expression above, $L(\omega)$ is the Fourier transformation sequence of marginal vector. From the Fig.6, we can conclude that major information about the wheat shape was well reflected by the first few larger numbers, rather than the last smaller numbers, which were supposed to the secondary information or noise.

Counter- transformation about $L(\omega)$ :

$$l_k = \sum_{\omega=0}^{N-1} L(\omega)\exp[j2\pi\omega k/N] \quad k=0,1,\cdots,N-1 \tag{4}$$

**Table 1.** Data errors

| Error | M=1 | M=2 | M=3 | M=4 | M=5 | M=6 |
|-------|-----|-----|-----|-----|-----|-----|
| Front | 4.04 | 2.43 | 2.34 | 1.23 | 0.88 | 0.73 |
| Size | 8.96 | 8.92 | 1.89 | 1.65 | 0.83 | 0.73 |
| Top | 8.68 | 8.67 | 0.95 | 0.74 | 8.68 | 8.67 |

The marginal vector can be reciprocal converted between length field and frequency domain with the expression (4) and (5). Discrete Fourier transformation is a reversible linear transformation, so there is no information wastage in this process. However, it is unprofitable to describe wheat shape with entire Fourier transformation sequences for pattern classifying. Thus, the wheat shape can be described precisely; characteristic parameters can be simplified by the first few components including larger information. A vector $\hat{l}_k$ , similar with $l_k$ , can be obtained with the help of counter- transformation on parts of Fourier transformation coefficients.

$$\hat{l}_k = \sum_{\omega=0}^{M-1} L(\omega)\exp[j2\pi\omega k/N] \, k=0,1,\cdots,N-1 \tag{5}$$

Where: M-- the number of Fourier transformation values.

## 4.2    Counter- Construction of Kernel Shape

A group of proximate edge pixel coordinates vector can be counter –constructed through approximate vector $\hat{l}_k$ and phase angle vector $\theta_k$ [7~9].

$$\begin{cases} \hat{x}_k = x^* + \hat{l}_k \cos\theta_k \\ \hat{y}_k = y^* + \hat{l}_k \sin\theta_k \end{cases} \qquad (6)$$

Where: $\hat{x}_k, \hat{y}_k$ --proximate edge pixel coordinates.

By means of analyzing the level of similarity between $(x_k, y_k)$ and $(\hat{x}_k, \hat{y}_k)$, the describing ability of each component for kernel shape can be represented which could underlie the determination of characteristic model.That can be seen from the Fig.7,Fig.8, the larger the value of M, the better the counter- construction. However, if the value of M is too large, description model will become confused(as shown in Table 1). Thus,according to the specific circumstance, it is necessary to choose the appropriate M value.

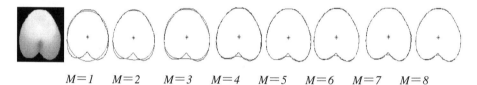

M=1    M=2    M=3    M=4    M=5    M=6    M=7    M=8

**Fig. 7.**   The counter- construction image of wheat in front view image

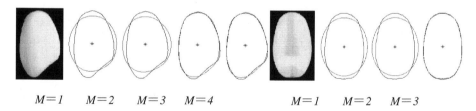

M=1    M=2    M=3    M=4                M=1    M=2    M=3

**Fig. 8.** The counter- construction image of wheat side view and top view image

## 4.3    Error Analysis of Counter- Construction of Kernel Shape

The relationship between error of counter-construction of each M can be figured out through the Fourier describer of 300 wheat kernels' 3-D views of four varieties.

According to the research, the average error between similar kernel shape and original one were less than 2 pixels that do not affect the pattern discrimination. Thus, choosing the first four of the Fourier transformation, can describe the front view of kernel shape and serve as the judgment characters. Likewise, the first three were chosen for the side view and so were the top view.

Evaluation mode of 3-D wheat kernel consists of following parts: (1) The first four ($f_1, f_2, f_3, f_4$) in Fourier transformation of front view image; (2) The first three ($s_1, s_2, s_3$) in side view image; (3) The first three ($t_1, t_2, t_3$) in top view image.

## 5    Examples of Application

In this paper, four varieties of 300 wheat kernels (Dong nong99-6501(variety A), Dong97-3821(variety B), Dong97-4056(variety C), Long94-4083(variety D)) have been made pattern classification. Specifically, all varieties of wheat have been classified with the help of BP network method, and characteristic parameters of 3-D shape of wheat kernels have respectively extracted.

### 5.1    Data Normalization

As Table 2 shown, normalized treatment should be taken among these datas, as some orders of magnitude exit in characteristic modes.

$$n_i = \frac{o_i - o_{min}}{o_{max} - o_{min}} \tag{7}$$

Where: $o_i$ — feature data; $n_i$ — normalized data;

**Table 2.** The mean judgment pattern values of four varieties of wheat kernel image

|   | $f_1$ | $f_2$ | $f_3$ | $f_4$ | $s_1$ | $s_2$ | $s_3$ | $t_1$ | $t_2$ | $t_3$ | out |
|---|-------|-------|-------|-------|-------|-------|-------|-------|-------|-------|-----|
| A | 2.255 | 0.063 | 0.091 | 0.118 | 0.337 | 0.061 | 0.679 | 4.881 | 0.003 | 0.01 | 1 |
| B | 2.070 | 0.047 | 0.078 | 0.092 | 4.387 | 0.047 | 0.806 | 5.144 | 0.014 | 0.93 | 2 |
| C | 1.998 | 0.049 | 0.127 | 0.076 | 4.954 | 0.036 | 1.079 | 5.980 | 0.016 | 1.12 | 3 |
| D | 2.174 | 0.055 | 0.044 | 0.093 | 4.693 | 0.075 | 0.809 | 5.224 | 0.016 | 0.91 | 4 |

### 5.2    Network Design

With the neural network toolbox in MATLAB, a 3-layer neural network was designed [9]. The input includes 10 neurons and the transfer function is "pureline()". The middle layer contains 15 neurons and the transfer function is tansig(). The output consists 1 neuron and the transfer function is pureline(). The input datas was normalized which belong to each characteristic pattern, and the number 1, 2, 3, 4 are labled as the varieties of wheat kernels in the output datas.

## 5.3    Network Simulation

Take 250 wheat kernels as the training samples, and put them in the course of neural network training, a good effect was achieved (Fig.9). The other 50 wheat kernels serve as test samples that used to test the constructed network. The recognition correct rate of nerve network is presented in the Table 3.

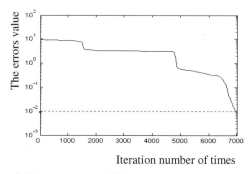

Iteration number of times

**Fig. 9.** The error curve of BP neural network learning

**Table 3.** The Recognition correct rate of nerve network

| Classification Accuracy | A | B | C | D |
|---|---|---|---|---|
| Training sample | 100% | 100% | 100% | 100% |
| Examination sample | 96% | 94% | 90% | 92% |
| Overall sample | 99.3% | 99% | 98.3% | 98.7% |

# 6    Conclusion

In this paper, the Fourier descriptor was used to further describe the 3-D shape of wheat kernels only with several appropriate characteristic parameters and a satisfactory result was obtained. In particular, the counter-construction of wheat shape was achieved by means of the transformation coefficients of the vector of the wheat.

A better description pattern was determined to discribe the shape of wheat kernels by use of the statistical error analysis, simultaneously, the classification of four varieties of wheat shape was come true by means of BP nerve network.

It is thus clear that, irregular shape of wheat kernels can described precisely by the Fourier describer; meanwhile, it can distinguish the delicate different shape between wheat kernels. What is more, by the use of the counter-construction method, the capacity to describe the wheat shape got a good validation. In conclusion, this method has laid the wide foundation for application in detecting and classifying of grain kinds of agricultural products.

# References

1. Yang, J.-Z., Hao, J.-P., Du, T.-Q., Cui, F.-Z., Sang, S.-P.: Discrimination of Numerous Maize Cultivars Based on Seed Image Process. Acta Agronomica Sinica 34(6), 1069–1073 (2008)
2. Zha, J., Chen, Y.: Recognition System for Corn Species by Exterior Parameters. Transactions of the Chinese Society for Agricultural Machinery 35(6), 115–118 (2004)
3. Cheng, F., Liu, Z.Y., Ying, Y.B.: Machine vision analysis of characteristics and image information base construction for hybrid rice seed. Rice Science 12(1), 13–18 (2005)
4. Dubey, B.P., Bhagwat, S.G., Shouche, S.P., Sainis, J.K.: Potential of artificial neural networks in varietals identification using morphometry of wheat grains. Biosyst. Eng. 95, 61–67 (2006)
5. Yang, G.H., Ouyang, Y.Q., Li, X., Luo, X.N., Wang, C.L.: Primary valuations in morphologic traits of foreign outstanding germplasmsn maize. Seeds 25(9), 100–102 (2006)
6. Hao, J.-P., Yang, J.-Z., Du, T.-Q., Cui, F.-Z., Sang, S.-P.: A Study on Basic Morphologic Information and Classification of Maize Cultivars Based on Seed Image Process. Scientia Agricultura Sinica 41(4), 994–1002 (2008)
7. Ying, Y., Rao, X.: Application of Machine Vision Technique to Quality Automatic Identification of Agricultural Products. Fundamental and Applied Research (2000)
8. Nelson, S.O.: Dimensional and Density Data for Seeds of Cereal Grain and Other Crops. Transactions of ASAE 45(1), 165–170 (2002)
9. Lurk, W., et al.: Video monitoring of pulverized coal injection in blast furnace. IEEE Transactions on Industry Applications 38, 571–576 (2002)

# Research on Knowledge Acquisition of Motorcycle Intelligent Design System Based on Rough Set

Rong Dai and Xiangmin Duan

College of Engineering and Technology, Southwest University, Chongqing, China
dai_yun2002@sina.com

**Abstract.** In the intelligent design of motorcycle, a large number of data in the simulation or physical experiment are almost not utilized to guide our design and make decision for the design, so rough set theory is introduced to the intelligent design of motorcycle. Then, aim at experimental data of the engine piston performance, rough set theory is used. An attribute reduction algorithm of decision table based on discernibility matrix and heuristic value reduction algorithm are adopted. Knowledge is extracted from the data of performance experiment of the engine piston, in order to enrich knowledge base in motorcycle intelligent design system.

**Keywords:** Motorcycle, intelligent design, rough set, attribute reduction, value reduction.

## 1    Introduction

Simulation analysis and physical testing are adopted to carry out research on the machine performance, but most of these tools are only as a verification of design result and are the lack of guidance and decision-making for design; At the same time, the results of test and analysis are mostly shown in the charts, graphs, etc., and interpretation and evaluation of results are lacked, so that the guiding role of the test and analysis for design has not been fully realized. With the simulation analysis and experimental research carried out, and a large amount of raw data about performance are accumulated, how to quickly extract valuable knowledge of motorcycle performance evaluation from a mass of data for guiding designer is a very urgent and meaningful questions.

Based on the above requirements, for the motorcycle engine piston test data and simulation features, rough set method is introduced. Knowledge acquisition based rough set is proposed. Experts level domain knowledge can be accessed to through processing and extraction of results on test and simulation analysis.

There are two main ways in the knowledge acquisition: First is obtained from experts in the field of expertise, and the second is directly accessed from the text or database. Expert domain knowledge for knowledge acquisition is got by artificial methods, and it will be inputted directly into the knowledge base. To acquire knowledge from text has two ways: One is to extract directly concepts and relationships from the text automatically. However, a fully automated approach is not always effective, because the text is often ambiguous, irregular knowledge. Therefore,

D. Li and Y. Chen (Eds.): CCTA 2011, Part I, IFIP AICT 368, pp. 16–27, 2012.

if the machine does not have a certain amount of "background knowledge", the realization of fully automated access is not realistic. The second way is semi-automatic method, which requires the necessary knowledge engineer intervention [1-5].

## 2    Rough Set Theory

**Definition 1.** A decision table is an information system $S=<U,\ R,\ V,\ f>$, $R=C\cup D$ is a set of properties, subset C and D are respectively called condition attributes set and the result attribute set, $D \neq \varnothing$. If the result attribute set $D=\{d_1,d_2,\ldots,d_n\}$, the decision table can be decomposed into n different single decision-making table$\{S_1,S_2,\ldots,S_n\}$, where $S_i=<U,\ R_i,\ V_i,\ f_i>$, U is the domain, $R_i=C\cup\{d_i\}$ is a set of properties, subset C and subset $\{d_i\}$ are respectively called condition attributes set and the result attributes set, $V_i=\bigcup_{r\in R_i}V_r$ is the set of attribute values , $V_r$ indicates attribute values range of the property $r\in R_i$, that is the range of attribute r, $f_i : U \times R_i \to V_i$ is an information function.

**Definition 2.** On the knowledge representation system $S= (U, A, V, f)$, $P \subseteq A$, the indiscernibility          relationship          of          attribute          sets          P is $ind(P)=\{(X,Y)\in (U\times U)|\forall a\in P, f(x,a)=f(y,a)\}$ .   Indiscernibility relation ind (P) is the equivalence relation on U, all the equivalence classes is educed by ind (P), denoted by U / P, which constitutes a partition of the domain U.

**Definition 3.** Knowledge representation system $S=(U,C\cup D,V,f)$, $\forall a\in C$ , if $POS_{ind(C)}(ind(D)) = Pos_{ind(c-\{a\})}(ind(D))$, a is called unnecessary in C on D, otherwise, and is known as necessary in C on D. $POS_{ind(C)}(ind(D))$ is the set of all objects that are correctly classified to the every equivalence class U / D, namely equivalence class on the positive region of $ind(C)$ is derived from $ind(D)$. If each attribute of C is necessary, C is independent to D.

**Definition 4.** knowledge representation system $S= (U,\ C\ U\ D,V,\ f)$, $B \subseteq C$, if $pos_{ind(B)}(ind(D)) = Pos_{ind(C)}(ind(D))$ , and B is independent to D, B is called reduction with C relative to D, and is denoted $red_D(C)$. It should be noted that reduction of C is not the only. the intersection of all D reduction in C is D core of C, which is denoted by core $D\ (C) = \cap$ redD $(C)$ .

**Definition 5.** The decision table system $S=<U,\ R,\ V,\ f>$, $R=P\cup D$ is a set of attributes, the subset P = {ai | i = 1, ..., m} and D = {d}, respectively, is called the condition attribute set and decision attribute set, $U=\{x_1,x_2,\ldots,x_n\}$ is the domain, $a_i(x_j)$ is the value the property $a_i$ in the sample $x_j$. $C_D(i,\ j)$ is the element of column i row j in the identification matrix, the identification matrix can be defined as follows:

$$C_D(i,j)=\begin{cases}\{a_k\mid a_k\in P\wedge a_k(x_i)\neq a_k(x_j)\},d(x_i)\neq d(x_j)\\ 0,d(x_i)=d(x_j)\end{cases} \tag{1}$$

Where i, j = 1, ..., n.

## 2.1    Attribute Reduction Algorithm

Based on the concept of discernibility matrix of decision table, we can get the following attribute reduction algorithm through discernibility matrix and logical operation [5].

1) The discernibility matrix of decision table is calculated $C_D$;
2) The corresponding logic expressions $L_{ij}$ is established by using $C_{ij}(C_{ij}\neq0,\ C_{ij}\neq\varnothing)$ in the discernibility matrix.

$$L_{ij} = \underset{a_i \in C_{ij}}{V}\ a_i \tag{2}$$

3) When all the disjunction logical expression $L_{ij}$ are conjunctive, CNF L can be got:

$$L = \underset{C_{ij}\neq0,C_{ij}\neq\varnothing}{\wedge}L_{ij} \tag{3}$$

4) L is converted to disjunctive normal form:

$$L' = \underset{i}{\vee} L_i \tag{4}$$

5) Attribute reduction results output. Each conjunction entry of disjunctive normal form corresponds to attribute reduction result. The attributes that each conjunction item contains compose a set of condition attributes after being reduced.

Process can be seen from the above, disjunction logical expression $L_{ij}$ created in step 2 of the algorithm is a lot, which will result in increasing the computational time when logical formulation is reduced. Therefore, certain measures need to be taken to further streamline the process of attribute reduction. It can be found through the discernibility matrix that, if there is a matrix element, its value is a collection of element containing a single attribute, it indicates that the necessary attribute is to distinguish between the matrix elements corresponding to two samples, and is the only distinction between the two sample properties. The collection of the attributes included these elements in discernibility matrix is actually the relative attribute nuclear of deciding-table system. So first of all, these attributes can be removed, but the value of the matrix element containing the nuclear attributes will be change to 0 to get a new matrix, and then in the new basis matrix, the algorithm 2,3,4 step can be implemented. Disjunctive logic expressions can be given. Finally the result of attribute reduction can be got through adding all the nuclear attributes to each conjunction item in disjunctive normal formal.

## 2.2    Value Reduction Algorithm of Decision Table

Through attribute reduction, the unnecessary attributes for decision-making in the decision tables can be omitted, then a simplified decision table can be achieved. This is beneficial to found the attributes that play role in decision-making classification. However, the attribute reduction is, to some extent, to remove the redundant attribute in the decision table, but not fully remove redundant information in the decision table. Therefore, the decision table needs to be further processed to be more streamlined decision-making table, i.e. reduction of decision table values.

Heuristic value reduction algorithm:

Input: Information system T (assuming the system has only one decision attribute)
Output: a value reduction T' of T.

1) The condition attributes of information table are inspected by column. If you remove the column, conflict of the records occurs, then keep the value of the property of conflict records; Otherwise, if there are duplicate records, the property value of duplicate records will be recorded as "*"; For other records, the property value is marked "?";

2) Possible duplicate records are deleted, and each record containing the mark "?" is examined. If the property value that is not marked can make decision, it will mark from"?" To "*"; Otherwise, it will mark from"?" to the original property value; if all the condition attributes of a record are mark, the mark "?" was changed to the original property value;

3) Remove record that all condition attributes are marked "*" , and possible duplication records after removing;

4) If only one condition attribute values between the two records are different, and the property of a record is marked as "*", then if the property value that is not mark can determine the decision-making for the record, then delete the other one record; Otherwise, delete the record.

After a new information table is obtained through the reduction, all the property values are the core of table, every record corresponds to a decision rule respectively.

# 3    Knowledge Acquisition of Engine Piston Performance Based on Rough Set

In the motorcycle intelligent design system, the knowledge acquisition will have access to expert experience, book knowledge processed and abstracted into knowledge base. By operation of the system ,the knowledge is constantly improved and modified. While the potential knowledge is identified and extracted from the large amount of simulation analysis and experimental test results, revealing the inherent law that the implicate in the data, so as to provide decision support for development and design, CAE technology and physical test are to achieve position from design verification to the design guidance and design decisions.

From the reference [6] section 6.3.1, study of orthogonal testing on piston performance shows that, orthogonal design method to ensure that the various levels of each factor mix respectively once in the test, so orthogonal table used is completely the indiscernibility relationship collection. Since rough set theory emphasize the indiscernibility relation between objects of the collection, in order to use rough set theory to acquire knowledge, combined with reference [6], Chapter 6, the forecasting method of neural network, the results of orthogonal test in the table 6.2    are extended analyze. Through random combination of multiple experimental conditions and  the BP network [7], the prediction results are obtained in Table 1. At the same time equidistant partitioning algorithm is used, the test conditions and test results are processed,   the results are shown in Table 2.

**Table 1.** Results of Piston Orthogonal Experimental Analysis & Results of BP Neural Network

| No. | A | B | C | D | E | friction power /kw | power /kw | fuel consumption (g/kw.h) | Noise dB(A) |
|-----|---|---|---|---|---|------|------|------|------|
| 1 | 1 | 1 | 1 | 1 | 1 | 2.93 | 64.04 | 259.3 | 108.1 |
| 2 | 1 | 2 | 2 | 2 | 2 | 2.68 | 64.17 | 259.2 | 108.2 |
| 3 | 1 | 3 | 3 | 3 | 3 | 2.4 | 64.1 | 259.5 | 106.8 |
| 4 | 1 | 4 | 4 | 4 | 4 | 2.33 | 63.02 | 259.5 | 108.2 |
| 5 | 2 | 1 | 2 | 3 | 4 | 3.04 | 64.06 | 259.6 | 108.1 |
| 6 | 2 | 2 | 1 | 4 | 3 | 2.93 | 64.07 | 259.7 | 108.5 |
| 7 | 2 | 3 | 4 | 1 | 2 | 2.43 | 65.02 | 258.5 | 108 |
| 8 | 2 | 4 | 3 | 2 | 1 | 2.17 | 6.3.85 | 259.1 | 108.2 |
| 9 | 3 | 1 | 3 | 4 | 2 | 2.52 | 64.02 | 259.6 | 108.3 |
| 10 | 3 | 2 | 4 | 3 | 1 | 2.36 | 63.99 | 259.6 | 108.2 |
| 11 | 3 | 3 | 1 | 2 | 4 | 2.23 | 64.37 | 259 | 108.1 |
| 12 | 3 | 4 | 2 | 1 | 3 | 1.92 | 64.18 | 259.2 | 108.4 |
| 13 | 4 | 1 | 4 | 2 | 3 | 1.77 | 63.78 | 260.6 | 107.6 |
| 14 | 4 | 2 | 3 | 1 | 4 | 1.7 | 63.78 | 259.2 | 108.2 |
| 15 | 4 | 3 | 2 | 4 | 1 | 1.61 | 64.19 | 259.5 | 108.6 |
| 16 | 4 | 4 | 1 | 3 | 2 | 1.41 | 64.09 | 259.5 | 109.2 |
| 17 | 1 | 2 | 3 | 3 | 2 | 2.76 | 64.26 | 259.49 | 106.99 |
| 18 | 2 | 3 | 3 | 2 | 4 | 2.18 | 63.76 | 259 | 107.24 |
| 19 | 3 | 2 | 2 | 2 | 4 | 1.85 | 64.14 | 259.05 | 108.24 |
| 20 | 4 | 2 | 4 | 2 | 3 | 1.64 | 64.15 | 259.73 | 107.83 |
| 21 | 1 | 3 | 2 | 2 | 2 | 2.34 | 63.948 | 259.22 | 107.68 |
| 22 | 3 | 4 | 4 | 4 | 4 | 1.59 | 63.052 | 259.43 | 108.98 |
| 23 | 2 | 4 | 3 | 3 | 1 | 2.07 | 63.80 | 259.35 | 107.54 |

**Table 2.** Decision Table System of Piston Performance

| U | Condition attribute | | | | | Decision attribute |
|---|---|---|---|---|---|---|
| | Materials piston skirt and cylinder liner clearance $a$ | piston head and liner clearance $b$ | piston pin offset $c$ | piston skirt length $d$ | liner surface roughness RMS $e$ | friction power f |
| 1 | -2 | -2 | -2 | -2 | -2 | 2 |
| 2 | -2 | -1 | -1 | -1 | -1 | 1 |
| 3 | -2 | 1 | 1 | 1 | 1 | 1 |
| 4 | -2 | 2 | 2 | 2 | 2 | 0 |
| 5 | -1 | -2 | -1 | 1 | 2 | 2 |
| 6 | -1 | -1 | -2 | 2 | 1 | 2 |
| 7 | -1 | 1 | 2 | -2 | -1 | 1 |
| 8 | -1 | 2 | 1 | -1 | -2 | 0 |
| 9 | 1 | -2 | 1 | 2 | -1 | 1 |
| 10 | 1 | -1 | 2 | 1 | -2 | 0 |
| 11 | 1 | 1 | -2 | -1 | 2 | 0 |
| 12 | 1 | 2 | -1 | -2 | 1 | -1 |
| 13 | 2 | -2 | 2 | -1 | 1 | -1 |
| 14 | 2 | -1 | 1 | -2 | 2 | -2 |
| 15 | 2 | 1 | -1 | 2 | -2 | -2 |
| 16 | 2 | 2 | -2 | 1 | -1 | -2 |
| 17 | -2 | -1 | 1 | 1 | -1 | 2 |
| 18 | -1 | 1 | 1 | -1 | 2 | 0 |
| 19 | 1 | -1 | -1 | -1 | 2 | -1 |
| 20 | 2 | -1 | 2 | -1 | 1 | -2 |
| 21 | -2 | 1 | -1 | -1 | -1 | 0 |
| 22 | 1 | 2 | 2 | 2 | 2 | -2 |
| 23 | -1 | 2 | 1 | 1 | -2 | 0 |

Because there are five conditions property, set up materials piston skirt and cylinder liner clearance A, the domain is X = [10,140], the X is divided into 5 grades, ie X = {-2, -1,0,1 , 2}. Also set up the domain B of piston head and cylinder liner clearance, the domain is Y = [40,340], is divided into five grades, namely, Y = {-2, -1, 0, 1, 2}. Also set up the piston pin offset C , the domain Z = [0.05, 1.55], divided into 5 grades, ie Z = {-2, -1,0,1,2}. Set up the piston skirt length D, the domain W = [40, 61], is divided into five grades, namely, W = {-2, -1,0,1,2}. the domain of E liner surface roughness RMS is V = [0.1,9.10], divided into 5 grades, ie V = {-2, -1,0,1,2}, the domain of friction power F is U = [1.41,3.04], divided into five grades, namely U = {-2, -1,0,1,2}.

As can be seen from Table 1, there are four decision attribute in the table, belong to more decision-making. Therefore, according to the method described by definition 1, Table 1 is divided into four equivalent of a single decision table by the decision attribute, that is, the condition attributes of the four tables are identical, decision-making is not same. Namely, condition attributes such as the friction power, power, fuel consumption, noise, and the decision attribute for the friction power, this single decision table is shown in Table 2.  Analysis shows that, when Table 1 is converted to four single decision tables, the table has not duplicate records in the condition attributes, so objects of a single decision-making table are still 23. The single decision table aiming to friction power is as an example that all data are analyzed and processed, and extracted the rule.

## 3.1    Attribute Reduction

When the decision attribute is "f = friction power", so that Q = decision attribute set = {f}, P = condition attribute set = {a, b, c, d, e}, then

$IND(P)$={{1},{2},{3},{4},{5},{6},{7},{8},{9},{10},{11},{12},{13},{14},{15}, {16},{17},{18},{19},{20},{21},{22},{23}},
$IND(Q)$={{1,5,6,17},{2,3,7,9},{4,8,10,11,18,21,23},{12,13,19},{14,15,16,20,22}},
$POS_P(Q)=U$.

The domain U is consistent with P relative to Q, which shows that the decision table decision table is completely determined, the table does not contain inconsistent information.

$IND(P\backslash\{a\})$={{1},{2},{3},{4,22},{5},{6},{7},{8},{9},{10},{11},{12},{13},{14}, {15},{16},{17},{18},{19},{20},{21},{22},{23}}
$POS_{(P\backslash\{a\})}(Q)$={1,2,3,5,6,7,8,9,10,11,12,13,14,15,16,17,18,19,20,21,23}

Similarly:

$POS_{(P\backslash\{b\})}(Q)$={1,3,4,5,6,7,8,9,10,11,12,13,14,15,16,17,18,19,20,22,23}
$POS_{(P\backslash\{c\})}(Q)=U=POS_P(Q)$
$POS_{(P\backslash\{d\})}(Q)=U=POS_P(Q)$
$POS_{(P\backslash\{e\})}(Q)=U=POS_P(Q)$

It can be seen that, attributes c, d, e may be omitted relatively to the decision attribute f, but it can not be omitted at same time. The properties a and b that are relative to the decision attribute f can not be deleted, so

$CORE_Q(P)$={a,  b}

**Table 3.** Identification Matrix Revised by Core Attributes

```
0 0 0 0 0 0 0 0 0 0 0 0 0 0 0 0 0   0   0 0 0   0 0
  0 0 0 0 0 0 0 0 0 0 0 0 0 0 0 0 cd  0   0 0 0   0 0
    0 0 0 0 0 0 0 0 0 0 0 0 0 0 0   0   0 0 cde  0 0
      0 0 0 0 0 0 0 0 0 0 0 0 0 0   0   0 0 0   0 0
        0 0 0 0 0 0 0 0 0 0 0 0 0   0   0 0 0   0 0
          0 0 0 0 0 0 0 0 0 0 0 0   0   0 0 0   0 0
            0 0 0 0 0 0 0 0 0 0 cde  0 0 0   0 0
              0 0 0 0 0 0 0 0 0   0   0 0 0   0 0
                0 0 0 0 0 0 0 0   0   0 0 0   0 0
                  0 0 0 0 0 0 0   0 cde 0   0       0
                    0 0 0 0 0 0 0   0   0 0 0   0 0
                      0 0 0 0 0 0   0   0 0 0 cde 0
                        0 0 0 0 0   0   0 0 0   0 0
                          0 0 0 0   0   0 0 0   0 0
                            0 0 0   0   0 0 0   0 0
                              0 0   0   0 0 0   0 0
                                0   0   0 0 0   0 0
                                  0   0 0 0 0   0 0
                                    0 0 0 0 0   0 0
                                      0 0 0 0   0 0
                                        0 0 0   0 0
                                          0 0   0 0
                                            0   0 0
                                              0 0
                                                0
```

The property c, d and e are the relative properties nuclear of the decision-making table. According to 2.1 section, attribute reduction algorithm based on discernibility matrix and logical operation, when discernibility matrix of decision-making table is calculated, these two properties can be removed first, while at the time the value of the elements that contains the nuclear attribute in the matrix will rewritten to 0 , then obtained a new matrix. New matrix of which elements are modified is showed in Table 3.

According to Table 3, CNF L can be got.

$$L=(c\lor d\lor e)\land(c\lor d) \tag{5}$$

After simplification, disjunctive CNF L ' was obtained.

$$L'=c\lor d \tag{6}$$

After the nuclear properties are added to conjunctive items, reduction results $(a\land b\land c)\lor(a\land b\land d)$  can be obtained, i.e. producing two new decision table, attributes in the table are respectively as a, b, c and a, b, d. Reduction results obtained $(a\land b\land c)$ as new decision-making table is treated.

**Table 4.** Attribute Reduction Result of   Friction Power

| U | condition attribute | | | decision attribute | U | condition attribute | | | decision attribute |
|---|---|---|---|---|---|---|---|---|---|
| | Materials piston skirt and cylinder liner clearance (a) | piston head and cylinder liner clearance (b) | eccentricity of piston pin (c) | friction power (f) | | Materials piston skirt and cylinder liner clearance (a) | piston head and cylinder liner clearance (b) | eccentricity of piston pin (c) | friction power (f) |
| 1 | -2 | -2 | -2 | 2 | 12 | 1 | 2 | -1 | -1 |
| 2 | -2 | -1 | -1 | 1 | 13 | 2 | -2 | 2 | -1 |
| 3 | -2 | 1 | 1 | 1 | 14 | 2 | -1 | 1 | -2 |
| 4 | -2 | 2 | 2 | 0 | 15 | 2 | 1 | -1 | -2 |
| 5 | -1 | -2 | -1 | 2 | 16 | 2 | 2 | -2 | -2 |
| 6 | -1 | -1 | -2 | 2 | 17 | -2 | -1 | 1 | 2 |
| 7 | -1 | 1 | 2 | 1 | 18 | -1 | 1 | 1 | 0 |
| 8 | -1 | 2 | 1 | 0 | 19 | 1 | -1 | -1 | -1 |
| 9 | 1 | -2 | 1 | 1 | 20 | 2 | -1 | 2 | -2 |
| 10 | 1 | -1 | 2 | 0 | 21 | -2 | 1 | -1 | 0 |
| 11 | 1 | 1 | -2 | 0 | 22 | 1 | 2 | 2 | -2 |

## 3.2    Value Reduction

The new decision Table 4 is got from the reduction result $(a \wedge b \wedge c)$ . By analyzing the data in the table,   the table does not contain inconsistent information. However, when value reduction algorithm is carried out, there will be inconsistencies between samples. Therefore decision-making rules are treated as follows. That is part of the decision rules for inconsistency, assuming it can not be simplified, the value of these attributes is fully retained. For the consistent part of the decision-making rule, and inconsistent part of it together, and then only to examine whether the property value of the same part of the decision rule may be eliminated. If you eliminate the value of some properties, its positive field changes, or data table becomes inconsistent, then the property can not be omitted. Thus, data tables that may be consistent and inconsistent are handled by a unified approach. According to the above approach, the value reduction resulting are shown in Table 5, each row of which represents a decision rule.

Decision attribute value f is discretized into five zones, namely the information system has five concepts. Based on the reduction results of Table 5, some of rules are analyzed as follows.

**Table 5.** Value Reduction Results of Vriction Power

| R | Materials piston skirt and cylinder liner clearance (a) | piston head and cylinder liner clearance (b) | eccentricity of piston pin (c) | friction power (f) | R | Materials piston skirt and cylinder liner clearance (a) | piston head and cylinder liner clearance (b) | eccentricity of piston pin (c) | friction power (f) |
|---|---|---|---|---|---|---|---|---|---|
| | condition attribute | | | decision attribute | | condition attribute | | | decision attribute |
| 1 | -2 | -2 | -2 | 2 | 10 | 1 | — | -1 | -1 |
| 2 | -2 | -1 | -1 | 1 | 11 | 2 | -2 | — | -1 |
| 3 | -2 | 1 | 1 | 1 | 12 | 2 | -1 | — | -2 |
| 4 | -2 | 2 | 2 | 0 * | 13 | 2 | 1 | — | -2 |
| 5 | -1 | — | 2 | 1 | 14 | 2 | 2 | — | -2 |
| 6 | -1 | — | 1 | 0 | 15 | -2 | -1 | 1 | 2 |
| 7 | 1 | -2 | — | 1 | 16 | -2 | 1 | -1 | 0 |
| 8 | 1 | -1 | 2 | 0 | 17 | 1 | 2 | 2 | -2 |
| 9 | 1 | 1 | — | 0 | | | | | |

A rule of the concept R=2 is

$(114 < a \leq 140) \wedge (100 < b \leq 160) \longrightarrow (r = -2)$  |1

This rule covers 40% samples of the concepts r=-2 in Table 1. Its meaning is: If the clearance value between piston skirt and cylinder material is among 114~140μm, and the clearance value between piston head and cylinder is among 100~160μm, the friction power value is among 1.41 ~ 1.736kw, its credibility is equal to 1.

A rule of the concept R=-1 is

$(88 < a \leq 114) \wedge (0.35 < c \leq 0.65) \rightarrow (r = -1)$ | 1

This rule covers 66.7% samples of the concepts r=-1 in Table 1. Its meaning is: If the clearance value between piston skirt and cylinder material is among 88~140μm, and the eccentricity of piston pin is among 0.35~0.65μm, the friction power value is among 1.736 ~ 2.062kw, its credibility is equal to 1.

A rule of the concept R=0 is

$(10 < a \leq 36) \wedge (280 < b \leq 340) \wedge (1.25 < c \leq 1.55) \longrightarrow (r = 0)$  |1

This rule covers 16.7% samples of the concepts r=0 in Table 1. Its meaning is: If the clearance value between piston skirt and cylinder material is among 10~36μm, and the clearance value between piston head and cylinder is among 280~340μm, and the eccentricity of piston pin is among 1.25~1.55µm, the friction power value is among 2.062 ~ 2.388kw, its credibility is equal to 1.

A rule of the concept R=1 is

$$(10 < a \leq 36) \wedge (100 < b \leq 160) \wedge (0.35 < b \leq 0.65) \longrightarrow (r=1) \quad |1$$

This rule covers 25% samples of the concepts r=1 in Table 1. Its meaning is: If the clearance value between piston skirt and cylinder material is among 10~36µm, and the clearance value between piston head and cylinder is among 100~160µm, and the eccentricity of piston pin is among 0.35~0.65µm, the friction power value is among 2.388~2.714kw, its credibility is equal to 1.

A rule of the concept R=2 is

$$(10 < a \leq 36) \wedge (40 < b \leq 100) \wedge (0.05 < b \leq 0.35) \longrightarrow (r=2) \quad |1$$

This rule covers 25% samples of the concepts r=2 in Table 1. Its meaning is: If the clearance value between piston skirt and cylinder material is among 10~36µm, and the clearance value between piston head and cylinder is among 40~100µm, and the eccentricity of piston pin is among 0.05~0.35µm, the friction power value is among 2.714~3.04kw, its credibility is equal to 1.

# 4     Conclusion

The rough set method is adopted to identify and extract the potential knowledge from the experiment result, and the inherent laws implication behind these data are revealed. The results show that rough set theory is adopt to acquire knowledge, not only the attributes that have important influence on decision-making information can be found, but also redundant information of information table may be deleted. Thus the final decision table has not only the simplified  information, but also not affect the original decision table information. Using the extracted knowledge, reasoning process of neural network can be explained, and it can provide decision support for the designer, improving the intelligence level of intelligent design system.

**Acknowledgement.** This work is supported by "the Fundamental Research Funds for the Central Universities."(N0.XDJK2009C005) and supported by "the Doctoral Fund of Southwest University"(N0.SWU109043).

# References

1. Joo, H.P., Poong, H.S.: An integrated knowledge base development tool for knowledge acquisition and verification for NPP dynamic alarm processing systems. Annals of Nuclear Energy 29, 447–463 (2002)
2. Shao, X.Y., Zhang, G.J., et al.: Application of ID3 algorithm in knowledge acquisition for tolerance design. Journal of Materials Processing Technology 117, 66–74 (2001)
3. Wang, L., Wu, J., Huang, D.: Attribute reduction algorithm for decision table based on relative discernibility matrix. Computer Engineering and Design 31(11), 2536–2538, 2542 (2010)

4. Hullermeier, E.: Fuzzy sets in machine learning and data mining. Applied Soft Computing 11(2), 1493–1505 (2011)
5. Feng, L., Wang, G.Y., Li, X.X.: Knowledge acquisition in vague objective information systems based on rough sets. Expert Systems 27(2), 129–142 (2010)
6. Dai, R.: Research on Key Technologies of Motorcycle Intelligent Design Based on Soft Computing. Chongqing University, Chongqing (2009)
7. Dai, R.: Performance forecasting of piston element in motorcycle engine based on BP neural network. In: Li, D., Liu, Y., Chen, Y. (eds.) CCTA 2010, Part II. IFIP AICT, vol. 345, pp. 148–157. Springer, Heidelberg (2011)

# Research on the Common Causes of Defects and Their Prevention Measures for RCF-Type PCB Mills Production

Heying Wu and Haiyan Zhu

School of Railway Tracks and Transportation, East China Jiaotong University,
Nanchang, Jiangxi 330013, China
{Heying Wu,wuhy001}@163.com

**Abstract.** Blade-type error, edge collapse cutaway, micro missing, four kinds of defect for RCF-type PCB mill production are deeply analyzed and their preventions measures are given detailed according to the author's many year's practice. These measures have been practiced and achieved good results. The research results can increase pass rate of such tools in the production and reduce production costs obviously, and owns with a special important using values and widely promoted significance.

**Keywords:** PCB mills, Blade-type errors, Edge collapse, Missing angle, Micro missing.

## 1    Introduction

Printed Circuit Board (PCB) is an important part of electronic component. PCB mills are used to process various products of printed circuit board for notebook computers and mobile phone plants. With the current rapid development of CNC machine tool technology, the production and the process technologies of PCB milling are also making progress. Through investigation, most domestic and foreign enterprises have adopted the high cost of CNC grinder to produce PCB milling. However, in spite of the performance of advanced CNC grinding machine, the production process of PCB mills will inevitably lead to a variety of defects because of its production technology, poor management and CNC machine tool comprehensive factors of failure and so on. In order to improve the rate of qualified products and reduce production costs, it is necessary to further study the causes of defects and effective measures of the PCB mills in its production process.

## 2    Type of PCB Mills

The following describes the common of four major categories PCB mills all over the world, they have accounted for above 90% of all the printed circuit board tools, and will have huge potential market and development prospects [1]. All the pictures in this paper are filmed by author himself during the production research process.

D. Li and Y. Chen (Eds.): CCTA 2011, Part I, IFIP AICT 368, pp. 28–34, 2012.
© IFIP International Federation for Information Processing 2012

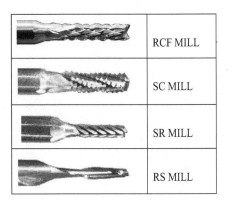

**Fig. 1.** Four types of PCB mills

## 2.1    RCF Mill (Diamond Mesh Type Mills)

This kind of mill is the most common type of cutting for milling printed circuit board outside, with diamond-shaped blade, chip up along the trench discharge, effective chip removal with a large cutting force and the characteristics of higher life expectancy. Its front-end tools will be designed to various structures and parameters according to the productive required, however, the shape of a swallowtail is the main designed structure to facilitate cutting materials.

## 2.2    SC Mill (Spiral Mills with Broken Bits Slot)

SC Mill is called spiral mills with broken bits slot, its right spiral cutter blade as the main body, with multiple right-spiral grooves and the thin edge cutting edge grooves, and the spiral grooves with a good chip removal performance, especially suitable for processing of paper substrates and CEM-3 products.

## 2.3    SR Mill (Consecutive Mills with Multi-edges)

SR Mill is called consecutive mills with multi-edges, has multi-right spiral cutting edges without chip-breaker grooves, which is mainly used for PCB terminal notch processing. If the high accuracy is required, it can be designed to the right spiral and the left spiral types, which is mainly based on the process precision and the product categories.

## 2.4    RS Mill (Consecutive Milling with Two Edges under Cut)

RS Mill is called consecutive milling with two edges under cut. This kind of mill has two left helical cutting edges and large junk slots, and suitable for precision milling. With excellent functions of machining surface precision and preventing flash. This under-cut mill is required to pay special attention to its downward chip removal direction.

# 3     Common Causes of Defect and Their Preventive Measures for Producing RCF-Type PCB Mills

In the above described the types of PCB mills, not only is the RCF-type milling cutter the most commonly used in processing printed circuit board, but also is the largest number of production in the enterprises. But the defects produced in the production process would decline the rate of finished products, which can lead to an increased production costs, and to market competition pressure of enterprises [2]. Therefore, it is necessary to further study and analysis the causes of defects and their preventive measures during the produce milling cutters in enterprises. The author has years' enterprise's production line experience of RCF type PCB milling. The following will analyze the common defect types, causes and preventive measures in the process of milling cutter production.

## 3.1     Defects 、 Causes and Measures of Blade-Type Errors

### 3.1.1     Blade-Type Errors

Blade-type error refers to the milling edge geometry and the geometric shape of drawings required exist one or several differences [3]. As shown in Figure 2 (a), the difference between the milling cutter and the drawing is that the former is less a L-edge, the drawings require RCF milling cutter has six Left- edges, but only has five Left-edges in the actual process of production, which must cause the milling cutter to waste product. Similarly, there exists such phenomena that the milling cutters are less one or several Right-edges, or while both on the left and right edges are less one or several edges in the milling cutters production, or vice versa. As shown in Figure 2 (b), the milling cutter has no fish tail, which would also cause it to waste product.

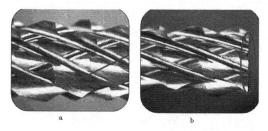

a                                    b

**Fig. 2.** Blade-type errors with (a) Less a left spiral edge and (b) Without fish tail

### 3.1.2     Causes of Blade-Type Errors

The main reasons for this defect are as follows: First, the operators are not strictly implemented the technological process of production, for example the technology workers look at drawings with mistakes cause to count the wrong edges, and then lead to set the wrong edges parameters of programs. Second, the machine operators have not checked the products, the milling cutters, carefully by themselves. Besides, the quality inspection workers have not timely feedback the defects to production sites, which lead a lot of such defect to occur. Finally, the technical personnel who did not perform their duties at the production site, they did not comply with the related requirements of production process, not strictly random in proportion to the production machine products, leading to these defects are ignored. However, the milling cutter has not the fish tail because of programmers forgot to compile the fish tail program, which causes CNC machine does not carry out the production process.

### 3.1.3    Preventive Measures

First, all the programmers, the technical personnel and the production operators must master the production drawings thoroughly and review them carefully, especially should rigorous review and check each parameter of the trial products. If there were parameters not comfort to the drawings, then the corresponding correction should to be done immediately, and eliminate such defects in the bud state effectively. Second, the machine operators and production technology workers should check the some proportion products made by machines randomly in accordance with of the production process. If any parameter surpasses the tolerance range, an immediate correction to the processing program parameter, to eliminate the edge flaws of products.

**Fig. 3.** Edge collapse with (a) Front end edge collapse and (b) Fish tail edge collapse

### 3.2    Edge Collapse

### 3.2.1    Causes of Edge Collapse

Edge collapse means a edge gap is greater than or equal to1/2 values of the edge depth or edge width, or the fish tail has the phenomena of serious damage and many edges missing.

Through analyzing, we know that the carbide is a common tool material, and its major shortcoming of mechanical property is brittle, if there is little impact or vibration, it would prone to cause the destruction phenomenon of break off, flaking and collapse[4]. Therefore, the edge collapse defect is produced mainly by the following several reasons:

(1) Due to the unloading robot and the yard lumber holes beyond the tolerance range in the horizontal direction during the robots of CNC grinding unload mills to the yard lumber, resulting in a collision causes mills produce edge collapse defect.

(2) It is very easily leads to serious collision among mills, or with other objects while workers are taking, attiring or checking mills during all the production processes.

(3) The cutting grinding wheel edge has bumps lacks, which causes mills load uneven forces and thus produces edge collapse in machining the spiral grooves process.

(4) The grinding wheel surface is blocked by chips, which can increase friction force between the grinding wheel and the mills.

### 3.2.2    Preventive Measures

(1) Adjust the tolerance level accuracy between the unloading robot and the yard lumber holes in the horizontal movement direction to ensure that the both at work can not interference with each other.

(2) Mills can not be collided in all aspects of the production.

(3) In order to prevent collapse defect occurs in grinding wheel's edge, it is necessary regularly to test grinding wheel's working status and processing geometric parameters, which can   ensure the wheel meets machining requirements.

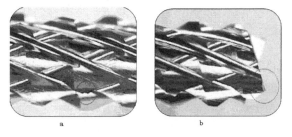

a                                    b

**Fig. 4.** Missing angle with (a) Middle edge missing angle and (b) Fish tail edge missing angle

### 3.3    Missing Angle

Missing angle means a edge gap is more than 1/4 and less than 1/2 values of the edge depth or edge width. The extent of this defect is much slither than the edge collapse defect. However, its causes are identical with the edge collapse. Therefore, its preventive measures are consistent with the edge collapse.

### 3.4    Micro Missing

Micro missing refers to a row of micro saw teeth are presented on edges. And it can be discovered by eyes observed carefully in compare with the edge collapse and the micro missing [5]. However, this defect is quite easy to be discovered if it is placed under the 20 or 30 times microscopes. So the defect judgment standards main rely on its appearance.

The main cause of micro missing is the surface of grinding wheel is too rough, resulting in a series of continuous micro saw teeth are generated on the milling edges by the grinding wheel's abrasives during the cutting process; another main cause is the initial speed of grinding wheel is too fast after finishing the wheel [6]. This defect can cause the result is that a serials of ripple type of cutting edges will present on products' surface, which can undoubtedly affect the quality of the PCB processing.

Preventive measures: First, The just repaired wheel should be slight grinded again by the whetstone wheel with micro size abrasives to further increase the grinding wheel surface's finish. Second, set the wheel with low-speed to grind in the beginning, and then gradually increase the speed to prevent the micro-missing of mill edges. Third, change the grinding wheel's rotation can reduce such defect according to certain rules in processing.

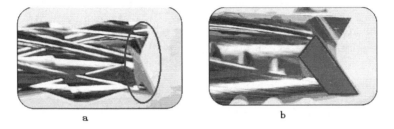

a                                      b

**Fig. 5.** Irregular fish tails with (a) Fish tail is asymmetry and (b) Moon surface arc

Fish tail is the most critical part to determine mill to process, and its geometric size and shape can directly affect the quality of PCB products and the life of itself. The judgment standards include the fish-tail's shape asymmetry and the moon surface arc and so on.

The main cause of this defect as follows: First, the aperture grinding wheel has not located in the fish-tail axis center while processing, which can make the fish-tail edge points exist a height difference and the geometry size is asymmetrical [7].

## 4    Conclusions

This paper at first introduced the most common types of PCB mills that produced by domestic and foreign enterprises. And then combined with the author's many years' front-line production practice learned in enterprise, in-depth study various definitions and types of defects of the RCF-type PCB mills, and shows with the corresponding defective photographs to explain the meaning of various defects clearly. Besides, this paper has also studied the common causes of each defect and proposed the practical and feasible preventive measures. These measures have been practiced and achieved good results, which has advantage of improving the rate of finished products and reducing productive costs, and owns with a very important applicable value and widely promoted significance.

## References

1. Yan, X.L.: Circuit board machining technology, World electronic technology (2006)
2. Xu, D.W.: Operation technique and examples of machining production line. Shanghai Science and Technology Publishing Press (2008)

3. Park, J.-B.: Evaluation of mach inability in the micro end milling of printed circuit boards. Professional Engineering Publishing 223(11), 1465–1474 (2009)
4. Hinds, B.K., Treanor, M.: Drilling of printed circuit boards: factors limiting the use of smaller drill sizes. Proc. IMechE, Part B: J. Engineering Manufacture 214(B1), 35–45 (2000)
5. Chae, J., Park, S.S., Freiheit, T.: Investigation of micro-cutting operations. Int. J. Mach. Tools Mf. 46(3-4), 313–332 (2006)
6. Yang, Z., Li, W., Chen, Y., Wang, L.: Study for increasing micro-mill reliability by vibrating milling. Reliab. Engng. Syst. Safety 6, 229–233 (1998)
7. Jun, M.B.G., DeVor, R.E., Kapoor, S.G.: Investigation of the dynamics of micro end milling – Part II: model validation and interpretation. ASME, J. Manuf. Sci. Engng. 128, 901–912 (2006)

# Implementation of Business Process Reengineering Based on Workflow Management

Wen Yang[1] and Hongjiang Chen[2]

[1] School of Mechanical and Electrical Engineer,
Jiangxi Science & Technology Normal University,
Nanchang, Jiangxi 330013, P.R. China
[2] School of Mechanical and Electrical Engineer,
Jiangxi Science & Technology Normal University,
Nanchang, Jiangxi 330013, P.R. China
{Wen Yang,Hongjiang Chen,hongjiangc}@163.com

**Abstract.** To achieve better performance of BPR, workflow management is integrated with BPR based on the core idea and steps of BPR. Main problems of hotel business process are studied, at the same the characteristics and advantages of WFM are introduced, which show that WFM is sound. Then BPR case of a five-star hotel in Guangzhou which adopts the WFM workflow is proposed. The rent and service charge processes are analyzed; the collaborative workflow and its new process after reengineering are also given, which achieve better results.

**Keywords:** Business Process (BP), Business Process Reengineering (BPR), Workflow Management (WFM), Workflow Management System (WFMS).

## 1 Introduction

Customer, competition, change and the theme of external environment make the service of hotel more flexible and comprehensive, which change management from occupation-center to process-centric. Business Process Reengineering (BPR), firstly introduced by Hammer, has become a powerful way to continuously optimize business process (BP) and improve hotel's core competitiveness [1]. Now many organizations have implemented BPR for improving their performances [2]. Yet it is lack of effective implementation tools, which makes it very difficult to achieve desired results. Workflow technology can strengthen the control of BP and enhance BP's flexibility and applicability through modeling, analysis and improvement, which can avoid failure effectively in the application of new processes caused by human and resource factors [3]. Workflow technology is the core technology for integration of the implementation of BPR, management and technology.

D. Li and Y. Chen (Eds.): CCTA 2011, Part I, IFIP AICT 368, pp. 35–40, 2012.

## 2     BPR of Hotel

### 2.1     Main Problems of Hotel Business Process

To meet the competition, modern hotel management is required to not only good and efficient service, but also is expected to achieve maximum profits and more flexibility. Hotel operating activities is to including forecast, decision-making, control, responsibility assessment and evaluation of the entire management process and so on. Though the hotel management developed quiet well in the past years, there are still a lot of problems to overcome.

According to the statistics, about 70% of activity in an organization is related with the process activity [4], so BP plays an important role in organization efficiency. However, BP is divided into a variety of simple tasks in the way of dividing traditional labor. Each unit is subject to its senior official, but not responsible for customer directly, which don't work to solve problems and improve their work. For example, changing requests of the scheduled banquet is quiet time-consuming and involves several departments. Therefore, it is urgent to change the organizational structure from the traditional way to the market-oriented, ie. task-oriented to process-oriented.

Most hotels have introduced corresponding information systems such as marketing system, financial system, and so on [5]. But these systems are often only authorized to the respective department to specific issues and work well in the internal management. Yet they are not market-oriented and customer-oriented. Secondly, each BP change may causes significant changes in program structure, because these BP have been coded with software programs. Furthermore, the resource utilization's rate is low. In addition, they are very difficult to modify the process reengineering, because these systems are developed by different software corporations.

The hotel's BPR should be customer-oriented, integrating with key BP, reducing non-value-added chain and complex chain of operational steps.

### 2.2     BPR Based on Workflow Management

BPR, re-thinking and re-engineering business process [6] delivers a lot of changes to organizational structure and business processes, which risks a lot at the same. Now the BPR works not well, which were reported 70% projects fail to achieve the desired objectives and even flat failure [7]. To build up its practical implementation, it's should be further explored and improved.

Workflow management (WFM) is a fast evolving technology, which is used in a variety of industrial processes. Workflow is concerned with the automation of procedure, whose documents, information or tasks are passed between participants according to a defined set of rules to achieve an overall business goal. A Workflow Management System (WFMS) defines, creates and manages the execution of workflows based on software, which is able to interpret the process definition, interact with workflow participants and invoke the use of IT tools and applications where required [WfMC99a] [8]. The evolution of WFM concentrates on the automation of business processes where interactions of human and machine-based activities play a major role. Within workflows, information or tasks are passed among participants in a way that is governed by rules or procedures.

Workflow is often associated with BPR, which is concerned with the assessment, analysis, modeling, definition and subsequent operational implementation of the core BP of an organization (or other business entity) [9]. Although not all BPR activities result in workflow implementations, workflow technology is often an appropriate solution as it provides separation of the business procedure logic and its IT operational support, enabling subsequent changes to be incorporated into the procedural rules defining the BP. Figure 1 shows the basic characteristics of WFMS and relationships between these main functions (WfMC95).

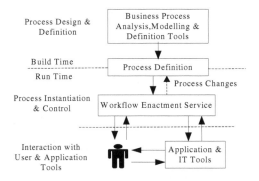

**Fig. 1.** Workflow system characteristics

At the highest level, all WFM systems may be characterized as providing support in three functional areas. The Build-time functions are concerned with defining, and possibly modeling the workflow process and its constituent activities. The Run-time control functions are concerned with managing the workflow processes in an operational environment and sequencing the various activities to be handled as part of each process. The Run-time interactions are concerned with human users and IT application tools for processing the various activities [10].

# 3   An Implementation Case

## 3.1   Analysis for Information Exchange of a Hotel Business

In this paper, a case for a five-star hotel in Guangzhou sets out the application of BPR based on WFMS in the hotel industry. Information data exchange and sharing process of the hotel based on workflow management system is shown in figure 2.

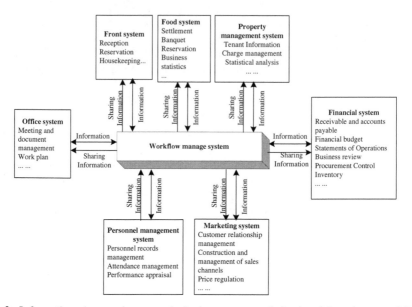

**Fig. 2.** Information data exchange and sharing process of the hotel based on workflow management system

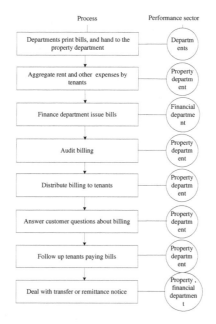

**Fig. 3.** Old process of rent and service charge

## 3.2     Analysis of Rent and Service Charge Process

BPR of rent and service charge process in the hotel as an example is to elaborate for the space limitation. Processes for rent and service charge involve nearly all departments and consumption points. If they can be effectively improved, hotel can significantly improve efficiency, enhance customer satisfaction and its image, and provide data to support marketing.

Figure 3, an old process of rent and service charge, indicates some inadequacy which are more review and transmission of documents between various departments, more heavy workload and error-prone, isolation between property management systems and financial management systems, repeating input of information, low work efficiency, and delayed analysis of relevant business data, and so on.

## 3.3     BPR of Rent and Service Charge Process

To connect data interface of property management system, consumption point and financial management system, the workflow system is developed based on WFM. Without changing the existing application software, the information can be automatically transmitted to the relevant application software according to the pre-defined rules. Consumption data can automatically transfer to property and financial management systems with the WFM, and can be analyzed and gathered in time.

The platform of collaborative workflow and its new process after reengineering are shown as Fig.4.

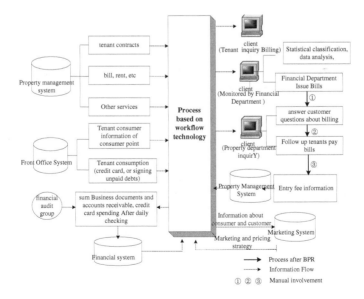

**Fig. 4.** Flow of mechanism and platform for collaborative workflow and its new process after reengineering

The BPR based on workflow technology can optimize processes of the rents and service charge, coordinate the work of various departments, and transfer the information to the related departments. At the same time, all application software and their business processes, such as property management system and financial management system, are systematically integrated and implemented automatically, which greatly Shorten the execution time, eliminate redundancy non-value process. Financial department, property department and marketing department can jointly develop marketing programs by real-time tracking consumer information and consumer trends. Furthermore the BPR can avoid human factors and resource affecting the implementation of new processes, so that the overall process can achieve optimal.

# 4      Conclusions

To optimize the business processes, BPR based on WFMS is simulated in this paper. The Simulation results show that BPR is more effective and flexible.

**Acknowledgments.** The paper is one of the results of project, the Project of BPR and Information Network System in the Garden Hotel, supported by Guangzhou Garden Hotel.

# References

[1]    Hammer, M.: Harvard Business Review (July/August 1990)
[2]    Worley, J.H., Castillo, G.R., Geneste, L., Grabot, B.: Computers in Industry, vol. 49 (2002)
[3]    Workflow Management Coalition, Terminology and Glossary, Document Number WFMC-TC-1011, Issue 3.0 (1999)
[4]    Lawrence, P. (ed.): Workflow Handbook. Wiley, New York (1997)
[5]    Cheung, Y., Bal, J.: Process analysis techniques and tools for business improvements. Business Process Management Journal 4(4), 274–290 (1998)
[6]    Eatock, J., Serrano, A., Giaglis, G.M., Paul, R.J.: A Case Study on Integrating Business and Network Simulation for Business Process Redesign. In: The Proceedings of the 4th United Kingdom Simulation Society Conference, Cambridge, pp. 114–118 (1999)
[7]    Hansen, G.: Automating Business Process Reengineering, p. 40. Prentice-Hall (1994)
[8]    Hammer, M., Champy, J.: Reengineering the Corporation: A Manifesto for Business Revolution. Harper Collins, London (1993)
[9]    Hayes, J.G., Peyrovian, E., Sarin, S., Schmidt, M.T., Swenson, K.D., Weber, R.: Workflow Interoperability Standards for the Internet. IEEE Internet Computing 4(3), 37–45 (2000)
[10]   Workflow Management Coalition, The Workflow Reference Model, Document Number TC00-1003

# Design of Labour Agency Platform Based on Agent Technology of JADE[*]

Xiaobin Qiu[**], Nan Zhou, and Xin Wang

Network Center, China Agriculture University, Beijing 100083, P.R. China
qxb@cau.edu.cn

**Abstract.** Ordinary labour agency system provides services for clients with a data center which comprises single or multi servers according to the scale. And each server provides service of regular function. Therefore problems in security, load balance and extendibility may be involved. In this paper, a labour agency platform using an agent technology called JADE was designed, which effectively solved the problem of normal systems.

**Keywords:** labour agency, multi-agent, JADE.

## 1 Introduction

With the rapid development of network, labour agency system gradually becomes the main approach to gaining the labour information for both employers and employees, and gives departments in charge prop for formulating policies. Ordinary labor agency system mainly provides information. Employers and employees obtain their required information by key word query, etc. The matching accuracy is in mass shortage. In order to solve problems of the Information Island, systems are generally composed of one or more servers to constitute a large system center platform to provide customer service. As the system volume turns larger, some disadvantages emerge in the structure, such as security and robustness. Due to the unitary center, once the system is attacked or broken down, the whole system will collapse. In addition, database load is also a bottleneck of the whole system.

This paper adopts JADE (Java Agent Development Environment, referred to JADE) for labour agency system based on multi-agent framework design, which effectively solves the above problems through multi-agent technology.

## 2 Agent and JADE

Agent refers to an entity which stays in specific environment with independent behavior and can interact with other agent at high-level. Agent technology supports analyzing, modeling, structuring  and deploying the system by abstract concept and

---

[*]"The 11th five-year plan" National science and technology support projects (2006BAJ07B07).

[**] Corresponding author.

D. Li and Y. Chen (Eds.): CCTA 2011, Part I, IFIP AICT 368, pp. 41–45, 2012.

design concept of agent. As it provides high-level abstractions and natural modeling method to simplify the system development and control complexity, and especially because software agent can effectively adapt to dynamic open environment, in recent years research in this area acquires widespread attention among many mainstream computer information research fields.

JADE is a software architecture which is fully parsed by Java. It is also an agent platform architecture which completely follows the standard of FIPA(Foundation for Intelligent Physical Agent). Its platform architecture as shown in Fig. 1, includes AMS(Agent Management System), DF(Directory Facilitator) and MTS(Message Transport System).

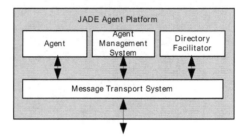

**Fig. 1.** Agent platform architecture

Each agent in JADE is a self-governing entity, which has the cooperation ability and the communication ability. External cannot obtain the quote, namely, agent attributes cannot be accessed directly by external, and agent's behavior cannot be designated directly by external too. The specific task of creating agent is completed only by the container. The returned results are encapsulated agents. A container is a Java virtual machine. Same containers can accommodate multiple agents, and each container must register to a main container. JADE platform, when activated, will immediately creates the AMS Agent and the DF Agent, meanwhile it will set MTS module to allow communication between each other.

## 3    System Framework

Ordinary labour agency system usually includes a recruitment management subsystem, a job management subsystem and an information release subsystem. All functions which every labour service agency uses are completely the same. When using agent, each system can provide personalized functions in the main function consistent circumstance according to the agent requirements. For instance several labor agency systems can be deployed in a platform, namely, system 1, system 2, etc. All these systems may have the same functions or some personalized functions, but all interfaces must be completely consistent in order to provide a uniform service. These systems are equal between statuses. A system can work with other systems, or work alone while not suffered from any other system's influence. Platform structure is shown as Fig. 2.

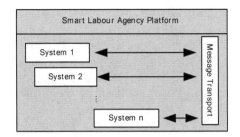

**Fig. 2.** Labour agency platform architecture

The function of each system platform is complete. All systems unite each other by agency communication channels. For users, it appears like one system. Consequently, not only every system on the platform has complete function, but also there is not any coupling between systems. Safety and extendibility of platform can be improved effectively.

In the design of labour agency platform, each system mainly includes a system management agent, a recruitment agent, a job agent, a recruitment broker agent and a job broker agent. System function structure is shown as Fig. 3.

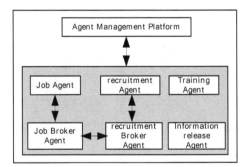

**Fig. 3.** Functions of the system platform

System management agent is responsible for managing the entire system agents. When a job seeker arrives, system management agent will start the job agent and the job broker agent to serve it. Job agent manages the basic information of job seeker. Job broker agent is primarily responsible for job seekers offering the right candidates. In the same way, when an interviewer comes, system management agent will start the recruitment agent and the recruitment broker agent to serve it. Job broker agent and recruitment broker agent is in the many-to-many relationships. When a job broker agent inquires a recruitment position, multiple recruitment broker agents can provide recruitment posts for it. And it chooses the most suitable one for its recruitment broker agent.

# 4     System Implementation

The system is implemented by mature technology and extensive JADE. JADE manages agents by containers. Containers can be in one computer or in multiple computer hosts, but a JADE platform has only one main container. Any other containers are agent containers. Every container includes all kinds of agent of the system. There are four objects in the labour agency system, which are JobSeekerAgent, JobSeekerBrokerAgent, JobInforAgent and JobInforBrokerAgent. All these objects are inherited from jade.core.Agent. So they have all basic methods of the superclass, including setup(), addBehaviour(Behaviour b), removeBehaviour(Behaviour b), send(ACLMessage msg) and receive(). System realization model is shown as Fig. 4.

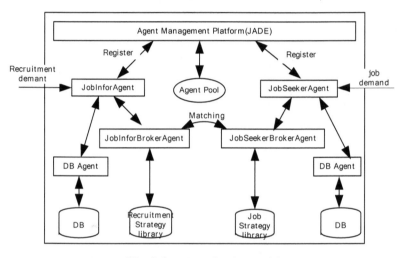

**Fig. 4.** System realization model

Agent management platform is responsible for creating agent and managing the agent pool. JobInfoAgent and JobSeekerAgent are responsible for receiving the needs of users and paying the broker agent. Broker agent performs match and returns results according to the strategy library. To demonstrate the working process of the system implementation, an example of seeking a job launched by a job seeker is given below. The recruitment process is similar.

When JobSeekerAgent obtains demand, it sends messages to all actived.recruitment agents, with the message type CFP.The content is job intension including salary requirement, site requirement, position requirement, etc. The purpose is to let recruitment agent send their recruitment information. Recruitment agent detects CFP message, inquires, starts recruitment broker agent and sends PROPOSE message to recruitment agent, if there is information matching the requirements. The content of message is recruitment information. When job agent detects PROPOSE message, job agent will start the job broker agent, create a list of job agents and send the list as a parameter to the job broker agent. Job broker agent performs matching with recruitment broker agents according to related conditions. If matched, job broker agent will send an ACCEPT message to the recruitment broker agent, or send a REJECT message to it. The agent which detects the ACCEPT message is the recruitment agent selected by job broker agent. The recruitment agent sends an OK message whose content is the information of matching successfully. Job agent detects the OK message, confirms the success of the employment and notifies users. If match fails, the process will start again.

## 5    Conclusions

Labour agency system is implemented by multi-agent with JADE. It can effectively improve the platform for safety and expansibility, and can implement load balance better than other systems. Not only can JADE implement multi-agent in one machine, but also in multi machines and can be deployed distributedly. Currently the implementation is in only two machines due to the actual platform situation. The improvement of the system can mainly be in the efficiency of system strategy and the further promotion in the future.

## References

1. Ye, R., Yang, X.: Multi-agent web services aggregation driven by requirement in JADE. In: Proceedings - 1st International Symposium on Computer Network and Multimedia Technology, CNMT 2009 (2009)
2. Bellifemine, F.: JADE a FIPA2000 compliant agent development environment. In: Proceedings of the International Conference on Autonomous Agents (2001)
3. Chmiel, K.: Efficiency of JADE agent platform. Scientific Programming (2005)
4. Mundle, S.: JADE based Multi Agent System for mobile computing for Cellular networks. In: Proceedings of the International Conference on Advances in Computing, Communication and Control, ICAC3 2009 (2009)
5. Vila, X., Schuster, A., Riera, A.: Security for a Multi-Agent System based on JADE. Computers & Security 26, 391–400 (2007)
6. Su, C.-J., Wu, C.-Y.: JADE implemented mobile multi-agent based, distributed information platform for pervasive health care monitoring. Applied Soft Computing 11, 315–325 (2011)
7. Bellifemine, F., Caire, G., Poggi, A., Rimassa, G.: JADE: A software framework for developing multi-agent applications. Information and Software Technology 50, 10–21 (2008)

# GIS-Based Regional Agricultural Economic Information Query and Analysis System

Yan Xue and Yeping Zhu

Laboratory of Digital Agricultural Early-warning Technology of Ministry
of Agriculture of China,
Institute of Agricultural Information, CAAS, 100081 Beijing, China
Xueyan@mail.caas.net.cn

**Abstract.** GIS-based "Regional Agricultural Economic Information Query and Analysis System" built on spatial attribute characteristics of statistical information implements dynamic information query, dynamic generation of statistical charts and tables, and dynamic generation of spatial distribution map with geographic attributes and specialized charts, and provides a solid basis for researching geographic distribution of agricultural economic information, analyzing issues concerning the agriculture, countryside and farmers from micro and macro perspective, and making macro decisions scientifically and rationally. This paper provides the system architecture design and related function demonstration, and discusses further development direction of the system.

**Keywords:** GIS, Agricultural Economic, Information Query.

## 1    Introduction

Fast growth of the information age poses higher requirements on statistical data informatization - requiring the integration of statistical data and spatial information resources to provide comprehensive and deep statistical analysis, as well as more timely and complete information services. Hence, with the fast development of social informatization and geographic space technology, the integration of statistical information and geographic space information resources has become an important part in the construction of statistical data system.[1-2]

Geographic Information System (GIS) is a computer system capable of collecting, storing, managing, analyzing, displaying and applying the data related to spatial geographic distribution on entire or part of the earth surface, and it is a universal technology for analyzing and handling massive geographic data.[3-4] GIS is an emerging frontier discipline incorporating the computer science, geography, surveying and telemetry, environmental science, urban science, spatial science, information science and management science. GIS has experienced amazing progress over the past 30 years with improving functions, increasingly showing its powerful vitality and

D. Li and Y. Chen (Eds.): CCTA 2011, Part I, IFIP AICT 368, pp. 46–53, 2012.
© IFIP International Federation for Information Processing 2012

bright prospect. At present, GIS has been widely applied in many areas including city planning, transportation, agricultural production, natural resource investigation, ecologic environment assessment, facilities management, etc..[5-6]

Since 1980s, "Rural Economic Information Database" that focuses on agricultural and rural economic statistical information has covered agricultural economic information with spatial implication in Chinese counties involving the population, farmland, crop production, etc. Since then, it has been primarily used in government agencies and research institutions, while "Regional Agricultural Economic Information Query and Analysis System" built on data resources closely related to this geographic information implements dynamic information query, dynamic generation of statistical charts and tables, and dynamic generation of spatial distribution map with geographic attributes and specialized charts by utilizing the database technology and GIS technology, and provides a solid basis for researching geographic distribution of agricultural economic information, analyzing issues concerning the agriculture, countryside and farmers from micro and macro perspective, and making macro decisions scientifically and rationally.

## 2    System Design Objective

To research, analyze, design and develop functions of "Regional Agricultural Economic Information Query and Analysis System" based on the database and GIS technologies, the system should realize the following main objectives:

1  To research visualized query and management of statistical information; provide such functions as information display, query and retrieval.
2  To implement statistical information analysis by utilizing spatial information analysis technology, so as to provide the analysis of agricultural economic information with spatial attributes for agricultural managers and decision makers.
3  To encapsulate system functions as GIS component objects and business logic component objects by utilizing the component technology, and implement the system integration by connecting the component objects to make the system scalable.
4  As critical information resource of the country, the confidentiality and security of rural economic statistical data are of very importance. Strict encryption management mechanism shall be established for the system to guarantee the database security.

## 3    System Function Structure

Following the principle of top-down and gradual refinement structure design, the system function analysis and module division are undertaken by combining structured

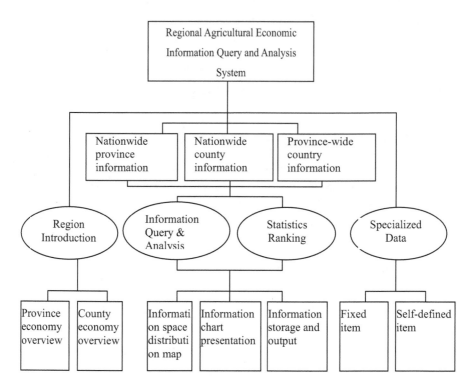

**Fig. 1.** System Function Structure

method and prototyping method according to different business requirements of the users. "Regional Agricultural Economic Information Query and Analysis System" consists of four modules: Region Introduction, Information Query and Analysis, Statistics Ranking and Specialized Data. The province information displayed in Region Introduction section presents main indicators like general information, economic and social development, agricultural and rural economy of the region by clicking on the map and opening different windows; the county information provides agricultural and rural economy information of each region by means of county-wide search, and marks the location of this county on the map. Information Query & Analysis and Statistics Ranking modules provide nationwide province and county information query, statistics and analysis in the form of spatial distribution map and chart. In Specialized Data module, the system is preconfigured with advantageous industry zone of agricultural products, regional layout of unique agricultural products and nationwide agricultural product trading market through which specialized distribution map can be created by means of the query. At the same time, self-defined topic is designed, allowing the user to create the specialized item and form the specialized item distribution map as needed. Related information displayed in above modules can be saved, printed or output in file.

# 4    Realization and Presentation of System Function

The system can run on WinddowXP/2000 or higher. In order to ensure the system operation and background data security, the encryption lock shall be used during the software operation.

This system takes full advantages of powerful graphic presentation capability of GIS platform to provide numerous view presentation means and present the information queried and analyzed on geographic map by means of "What You See Is What You Get", allowing the user to have a visualized perception and operation platform.

## 4.1    Region Introduction

This module presents agricultural and rural economic information of each province or county. In general, there are two options for selecting the information to be displayed: by clicking on related icon in the window, for example: clicking on the location of the region on the map to display related information of this region, or by inputting the name of the region to be displayed in relative window, then the system will search automatically and display all information of this icon in the database. Currently, there are 31 provinces, municipalities and autonomous regions, as well as over 2800 cities and counties in China, hence, this system displays related information of each province by clicking on the location of each province (see Figure 2), and displays the information of each county through the county search function by inputting the county name (see Figure 3).

**Fig. 2.** Displays information of each province

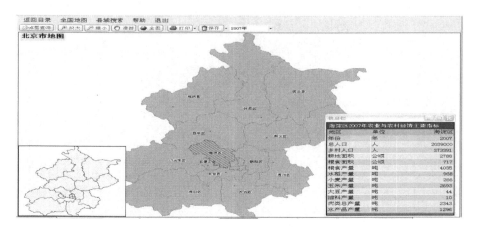

**Fig. 3.** Displays information of each county

## 4.2    Information Query and Analysis

For users, it is especially important to capture, seize and analyze related information anytime as needed. This module provides the province or county query result in the form of the map and table quickly by clicking the year and region easily and quickly (see Figures 4 and 5), and displays the data change in the form of the chart for the purpose of analyzing agricultural and rural economic information (see Figure 5).

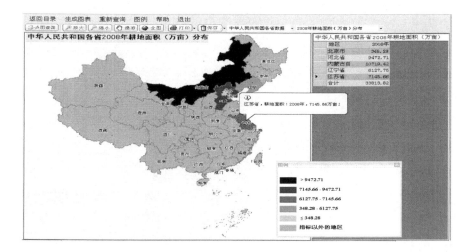

**Fig. 4.** The province query result

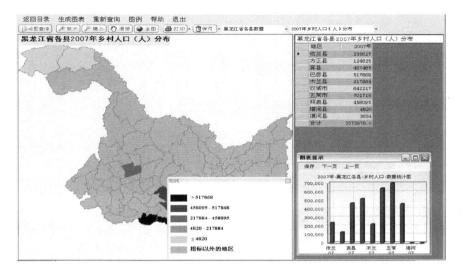

**Fig. 5.** The county query result

## 4.3    Statistics Ranking

This module is designed to meet conventional demand of users for the utilization of agricultural economic information. Through this platform, the users can view statistics ranking of hot regions or important agricultural economic indicators they concern (see Figure 6).

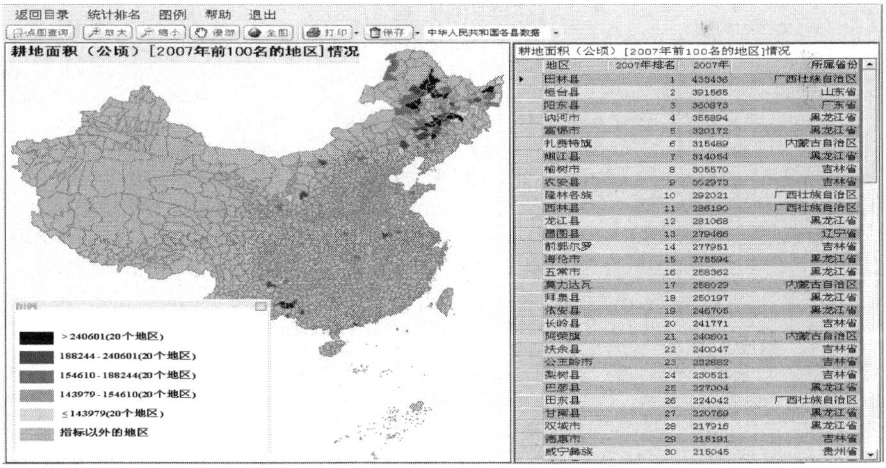

**Fig. 6.** Statistics Ranking

## 4.4    Specialized Data

This module is mainly used by decision making department of the government and macro researchers. In this module, the system has provided the information of agricultural production and agricultural product market distribution in the country, and can display, search, locate on the map and output relative specialized information easily as needed (see Figure 7). In addition, the system is designed to provide self-defined topic function, enabling the user to design different specialized data at will and create the specialized data distribution chart to respond to instant or urgent event, and understand related agricultural and rural economic information of different regions in real time.

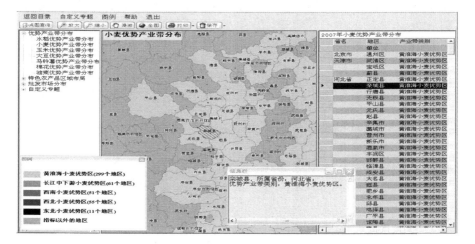

**Fig. 7.** Specialized Data

## 5    Conclusion and Discussion

"Regional Agricultural Economic Information Query and Analysis System" takes full advantages of spatial data organization capability and spatial analysis capability of GIS technology. It can not only provide scientific and accurate basic agricultural economic data timely, accurately and comprehensively, but also lay a solid foundation for drilling down and analyzing the data of different years and different indicators, improving the data management, development and utilization level, driving the systematic management and sharing of basic data, and realizing the resource management informatization. The system has been used by related government agencies and agricultural statisticians. The result shows that the system function design accords with the work characteristics of users, and provides scientific and effective means and methods for improving the productivity and realizing the value of the data.

Of course, the system function needs further enrichment and improvement, for example, further researching and realizing and deep mining of basic data by utilizing the modeling technique, GIS route analysis and buffer analysis.

# References

1. Li, J., Zeng, L.: Application of Geospatial Information and Technology in E-Government, pp. 2–10. Publishing House of Electronics Industry, Beijing (2005)
2. Zhang, J., Li, X., Wang, Y.: Technology of Rural Socio-Economic Statistical System Based on GIS. Computer System Application 19(9) (2010)
3. Zhu, Y., Chen, S., Wang, X.: Development and Application of GIS in Precision Agriculture. Journal of Agricultural Mechanization Research (5), 179–180 (2007)
4. Rao, W., Zhang, J., Xiao, H., et al.: Review on Present Situation of GIS Application in Agriculture. Yunnan Geographic Environment Research 16(2), 13–17 (2004)
5. Sun, C., Yuan, D., Wang, Y.: Application and Advance of Geographic Information System in Agriculture. Acta Agriculturae Shanghai 20(3), 99–101 (2004)
6. Chen, C.: Investigation and Analysis on Present Situation of GIS Technology in China. Science of Surveying and Mapping (1), 26–34 (1996)

# Research on Static Decoupling Method
# of Non-Gyro Micro Inertial Measurement Unit

Mingli Ding, Dongmei Yang, Jindong Zhao, and Lili Zhuang

Dept. of Automatic Test and Control, Harbin Institute of Technology,
150001 Harbin, China
dingmingli2006@gmail.com

**Abstract.** In a non-gyro micro inertial measurement unit (NGMIMU), the coupling error reduces the system measurement precision obviously. Based on the definition of the coupling error, a new static decoupling method applied total least squares (TLS) algorithm is proposed. TLS considers not only the error of accelerometer output, but also the calibrating error of the input signal arising from the couple factor. Based on TLS, the solution of the coupling coefficient equation has the characteristic of minimum norm to the input and output values. In the navigation parameter estimation, according to the relationship of the accelerometer input and output value, the accurate estimated input value can be acquired through fitting the couple coefficient matrix using TLS and reconstructing the input value using Moore-Penrose generalized inverse matrix. A simulation case for estimating angle rate is investigated by this approach. The results show that the ratio of decoupling error is less than 8% and verify the feasibility of the static decoupling method.

**Keywords:** Non-gyro micro measurement unit (NGMIMU), decoupling, total least squares (TLS).

## 1    Introduction

Most current micro inertial measurement units (MIMU) use linear accelerometers and gyroscopes to sense linear the acceleration and angular rate of a moving body respectively. In a non-gyro micro inertial measurement unit (NGMIMU)[1-6], accelerometers are not only used to acquire the linear acceleration, but also replace gyroscopes to compute the angular rate according to their positions in three-dimension space. NGMIMU has the advantages of anti-high g value shock, low power consumption, small volume and low cost. It can be applied to some specific occasions such as tactic missiles, intelligent bombs and so on.

A generalized definition of couple is that the response of an actuation includes the additional information about the other actuation which would not affect the response. In a NGMIMU system, the couple defines that the output of a single-axis accelerometer contains the additional information of the other accelerometer in other direction.

D. Li and Y. Chen (Eds.): CCTA 2011, Part I, IFIP AICT 368, pp. 54–64, 2012.
© IFIP International Federation for Information Processing 2012

The static couple indicates that the coupling degree is fixed whether the measuring time and measuring conditions change or not. We use the coupling coefficient to denote the coupling degree. The static couple mainly arises from the following reasons: a. the sensing axis of the accelerometer produces a deviation due to the low precision of the accelerometer itself; b. the low machining precision of the rigid body which bears the weigh of the accelerometer; c. the low mounting precision of the accelerometer; d. it is difficult to realize in physics that all the accelerometers mount at one point on the rigid body when some algorithms are expected. When the accelerometer coupling error is small, the measurement value of the angular rate will distort seriously. So the study of the decoupling method is expected urgently. The key problem of the static decoupling method is to estimate the coupling coefficient. The traditional least squares algorithm could not acquire the ideal estimation precision for it considers only the output error of the accelerometer.

In this paper, Total Least Squares algorithm-TLS[7-9] is applied in the novel static decoupling method. This method reconstructs the linear calibrating input signal under the condition that there exist errors not only in the input signal but also in the output signal. The signal reconstructing has two steps: step 1. fitting the couple coefficient matrix by using TLS, step 2. reconstructing the calibrating signal by using Moore-Penrose generalized inverse matrix.

## 2      Accelerometer Output Equation

As all know, the precession of gyroscopes can be used to measure the angular rate. Based on this principle, MIMU measures the angular rate of a moving body. The angle value can be obtained by integrating the angular rate with given initial conditions. With this angle value and the linear acceleration values in three directions, the current posture of the moving body can be estimated.

NGMIMU uses linear accelerometers to measure the angular acceleration of the body, and the relationship between the linear acceleration $a$ and the angular acceleration $\dot{\omega}$ is

$$a = r \times \dot{\omega} \ . \tag{1}$$

The angular rate in a certain direction can be calculated by using the linear acceleration between two points. To obtain the linear and angular motion parameters of a moving body in three-dimension space, the accelerometers need to be appropriately distributed on the moving body and the analysis of the accelerometer outputs is needed.

An inertial frame and a rotating moving body frame are exhibited in Fig. 1, where $b$ represents the moving body frame and $I$ the inertial frame. An inertial frame and a rotating moving body frame are exhibited in Fig. 1, where $b$ represents the moving body frame and $I$ the inertial frame.

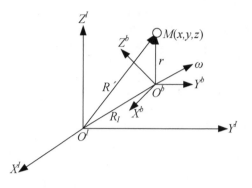

**Fig. 1.** Geometry of body frame (b) and inertial frame (I)

The acceleration of point $M$ is given by

$$a = \ddot{R}_I + \ddot{r}_b + \dot{\omega} \times r + 2\omega \times \dot{r}_b + \omega \times (\omega \times r), \qquad (2)$$

where $\ddot{r}_b$ is the acceleration of point $M$ relative to body frame. $\ddot{R}_I$ is the inertial acceleration of $O^b$ relative to $O^I$. $2\omega \times \dot{r}_b$ is known as the Coriolis acceleration, $\omega \times (\omega \times r)$ represents a centripetal acceleration, and $\dot{\omega} \times r$ is the tangential acceleration owing to angular acceleration of the rotating frame.

If $M$ is fixed in the $b$ frame, the terms $\dot{r}_b$ and $\ddot{r}_b$ vanish. And (2) can be rewritten as

$$a = \ddot{R}_I + \dot{\omega} \times r + \omega \times (\omega \times r). \qquad (3)$$

Thus the accelerometers rigidly mounted at location $r_i$ on the body with sensing direction $\theta_i$ produce $A_i$ as outputs.

$$A_i = [\ddot{R}_I + \dot{\Omega}r_i + \Omega\Omega r_i] \cdot \theta_i \qquad (i = 1, 2, \ldots, N), \qquad (4)$$

where

$$\Omega = \begin{bmatrix} 0 & -\omega_z & \omega_y \\ \omega_z & 0 & -\omega_x \\ -\omega_y & \omega_x & 0 \end{bmatrix}, \quad \ddot{R}_I = \begin{bmatrix} \ddot{R}_{Ix} \\ \ddot{R}_{Iy} \\ \ddot{R}_{Iz} \end{bmatrix}. \qquad (5)$$

In (5), $\omega_x$, $\omega_y$ and $\omega_z$ represent the angular rate along x, y and z axis respectively; $\ddot{R}_{Ix}$, $\ddot{R}_{Iy}$ and $\ddot{R}_{Iy}$ represent the linear acceleration along x, y and z axis respectively.

Considering $N$ accelerometer distributed at locations $r_1, \ldots, r_N$ with sensing directions $\theta_1, \ldots, \theta_N$ respectively. The pair $(r_i, \theta_i)$ is express in the body frame.

Let $\omega = \begin{bmatrix} \omega_x & \omega_y & \omega_z \end{bmatrix}^T$. Considering the skew-symmetric vector $\Omega$, for any $N = \begin{bmatrix} n_x & n_y & n_z \end{bmatrix}^T$, we have

$$\Omega \cdot N = \begin{bmatrix} 0 & -\omega_z & \omega_y \\ \omega_z & 0 & -\omega_x \\ -\omega_y & \omega_x & 0 \end{bmatrix} \begin{bmatrix} n_x \\ n_y \\ n_z \end{bmatrix} = \begin{bmatrix} \omega_y n_z - \omega_z n_y \\ \omega_z n_x - \omega_x n_z \\ \omega_x n_y - \omega_y n_x \end{bmatrix} = \omega \times N . \tag{6}$$

Using (4) and $\omega \leftrightarrow \Omega$, we have

$$\begin{aligned} A_i &= (\ddot{R}_I + \dot{\Omega} r_i + \Omega\Omega\, r_i) \cdot \theta_i \\ &= \theta_i^T \ddot{R}_I + (r_i \times \theta_i)^T \dot{\omega} + \theta_i^T \Omega^2 r_i \\ &= \begin{bmatrix} (r_i \times \theta_i)^T & \theta_i^T \end{bmatrix} \begin{bmatrix} \dot{\omega} \\ \ddot{R}_I \end{bmatrix} + \theta_i^T \Omega^2 r_i . \end{aligned} \tag{7}$$

## 3    Analysis of Static Couple of NGMIMU

### 3.1    Nine-Accelerometer Configuration

The study of the decoupling method is based on the nine-accelerometer configuration of NGMIMU in [6]. The locations and the sensing directions of the nine accelerometers in the body frame are shown in Fig.2. Each arrow in Fig. 2 points to the sensing direction of each accelerometer.

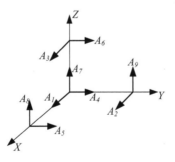

Fig. 2. Nine-accelerometer NGMIMU configuration

The locations of the nine accelerometers are

$$[r_1, \cdots, r_9] = l \begin{bmatrix} 0 & 0 & 0 & 0 & 1 & 0 & 0 & 1 & 0 \\ 0 & 1 & 0 & 0 & 0 & 0 & 0 & 0 & 1 \\ 0 & 0 & 1 & 0 & 0 & 1 & 0 & 0 & 0 \end{bmatrix}, \tag{8}$$

where $l$ is the distance between the accelerometer and the origin of the body frame. The sensing directions are

$$[\theta_1,\cdots,\theta_9]=\begin{bmatrix} 1 & 1 & 1 & 0 & 0 & 0 & 0 & 0 & 0 \\ 0 & 0 & 0 & 1 & 1 & 1 & 0 & 0 & 0 \\ 0 & 0 & 0 & 0 & 0 & 0 & 1 & 1 & 1 \end{bmatrix}. \tag{9}$$

It is easy to obtain

$$[r_1\times\theta_1,\cdots,r_1\times\theta_1]=l\begin{bmatrix} 0 & 0 & 0 & 0 & 0 & -1 & 0 & 0 & 1 \\ 0 & 0 & 1 & 0 & 0 & 0 & 0 & -1 & 0 \\ 0 & -1 & 0 & 0 & 1 & 0 & 0 & 0 & 0 \end{bmatrix}. \tag{10}$$

Using (7), the accelerometer output equation can be acquired as

$$A_i = \begin{bmatrix} 0 & 0 & 0 & 1 & 0 & 0 \\ 0 & 0 & -l & 1 & 0 & 0 \\ 0 & l & 0 & 1 & 0 & 0 \\ 0 & 0 & 0 & 0 & 1 & 0 \\ 0 & 0 & l & 0 & 1 & 0 \\ -l & 0 & 0 & 0 & 1 & 0 \\ 0 & 0 & 0 & 0 & 0 & 1 \\ 0 & -l & 0 & 0 & 0 & 1 \\ l & 0 & 0 & 0 & 0 & 1 \end{bmatrix}\begin{bmatrix} \dot{\omega}_x \\ \dot{\omega}_y \\ \dot{\omega}_z \\ \ddot{R}_{Ix} \\ \ddot{R}_{Iy} \\ \ddot{R}_{Iz} \end{bmatrix} + \begin{bmatrix} 0 & 0 & 0 & 0 & 0 & 0 \\ 0 & 0 & 0 & 0 & 0 & l \\ 0 & 0 & 0 & 0 & l & 0 \\ 0 & 0 & 0 & 0 & 0 & 0 \\ 0 & 0 & 0 & 0 & 0 & l \\ 0 & 0 & 0 & l & 0 & 0 \\ 0 & 0 & 0 & 0 & 0 & 0 \\ 0 & 0 & 0 & 0 & l & 0 \\ 0 & 0 & 0 & l & 0 & 0 \end{bmatrix}\begin{bmatrix} \omega_x^2 \\ \omega_y^2 \\ \omega_z^2 \\ \omega_y\omega_z \\ \omega_x\omega_z \\ \omega_x\omega_y \end{bmatrix}. \tag{11}$$

With (11), the linear expressions are

$$\dot{\omega}_x = \frac{1}{2l}(A_4 + A_9 - A_6 - A_7), \tag{12a}$$

$$\dot{\omega}_y = \frac{1}{2l}(A_3 + A_7 - A_1 - A_8), \tag{12b}$$

$$\dot{\omega}_z = \frac{1}{2l}(A_1 + A_5 - A_2 - A_4), \tag{12c}$$

## 3.2 Analysis of Static Coupling Error

In (12), the angular accelerations are all expressed as the linear combinations of the accelerometer outputs. The conventional algorithm computes the angular rate as the time integration of the equations in (12), and gets the rotation matrix of the body frame with respect to earth frame by using a numerical solution, then calculates the posture parameters of the moving body by using the relationship of the elements in the rotation matrix.

According to the definition of the couple and the reasons for the static coupling error, the static couple of the accelerometer can be regarded as the situation that there is a small angle between the sensing direction of the accelerometer and the body coordinate axis as shown in Fig. 3.

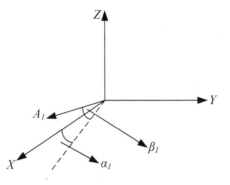

**Fig. 3.** Real location of accelerometer

For being simple and convenient, the cross coupling problem of $A_1$, $A_4$ and $A_7$ is specially discussed here. In an idea case, $A_1$, $A_4$ and $A_7$ are the three accelerometer outputs which are perpendicular each other in the configuration. But due to the static coupling error, the outputs of the accelerometer $A_1$ includes the additional acceleration information from the other two accelerometer $A_4$, $A_7$. $A_4$ and $A_7$ have the similar case. Obviously the computed angular rate has the coupling error and will bring the posture error to the navigation parameters. Assume that the angles between $A_1$, $A_4$, $A_7$ and the horizontal direction of the coordinate axis where the corresponding accelerometer locates are $\alpha_1$, $\alpha_4$, $\alpha_7$, respectively, the altitude angles are $\beta_1$, $\beta_4$, $\beta_7$, respectively. The real accelerometers outputs are

$$A_1 = A_x \cos \alpha_1 \cos \beta_1 + A_y \sin \alpha_1 \cos \beta_1 + A_z \sin \beta_1 + C_1 , \tag{13a}$$

$$A_4 = A_x \sin \beta_2 + A_y \cos \alpha_2 \cos \beta_2 + A_z \sin \alpha_2 \cos \beta_2 + C_2 , \tag{13b}$$

$$A_7 = A_x \sin \alpha_3 \cos \beta_3 + A_y \sin \beta_3 + A_z \cos \alpha_3 \cos \beta_3 + C_3 . \tag{13c}$$

where $A_x$, $A_y$, $A_z$ are the real accelerations in three directions. In the course of decoupling, we replace them by the setting input signal calibrated, which all include the calibrating errors. In (13), $C_1$, $C_2$, $C_3$ are the static zero drift errors of the accelerometers respectively. From (13a), we arrive that $A_1$ includes two real output components of the two accelerometers which are perpendicular with x axial, and $A_4$ and $A_7$ have the similar outputs. Based above, it is found that there exists errors not only in the calibrating values of the accelerometers $A_x$, $A_y$, $A_z$, but also in the accelerometers outputs $A_1$, $A_4$, $A_7$. In order to increase the estimation precision of the NGMIMU system, the decoupling method to the corresponding coupling error should be carried on.

# 4    Static Decoupling Method

## 4.1    Total-Least Squares Algorithm-TLS

Consider the equation

$$Ax = b, \tag{14}$$

where $A \in R^{m \times n}$, $x \in R^n$, $b \in R^m$, $m \geq n$. Calculating (14) by using the Least Squares algorithm is equivalent to seek the solution $x_{LS}$ which fulfills $\|e\|_2 = \|b - Ax_{LS}\|_2 = \min_x \|b - Ax\|_2$. It is obvious that the calculation is based on the assumption that the vector $b$ has a deviation $\Delta b$ and the coefficient matrix $A$ has no deviation, (14) becomes

$$Ax = b + \Delta b. \tag{15}$$

But in fact, $A$ is often formed by the input signal and the output signal of the system which inevitably have errors. So the best prediction method is to consider the deviations both in $A$ and $b$. This is the key point of the TLS.

Assume $A$ and $b$ have the deviation errors $E$ and $e$ at the same time, (14) can be rewritten as

$$(A + E)x = b + e. \tag{16}$$

Now we calculate (16) by using TLS. Change (16) into

$$(B + D)z = 0, \tag{17}$$

where $B = [-b : A]$, $D = [-e : E]$, $z = \begin{bmatrix} 1 \\ x \end{bmatrix}$. So the solution of (17) can be express as to find a vector $z$ such that

$$\|D\|_2 = \min, (b + e) \in range(A + E), \tag{18}$$

where $\|D\|_2 = \left( \sum_{i=1}^{m} \sum_{j=1}^{n} d_{ij}^2 \right)^{\frac{1}{2}}$. And to the given function (17), TLS can find a vector $x_{TLS}$ such as the following consistency equation

$$(b + e) \in range(A + E), \tag{19}$$

where $\hat{A}$ and $b_{TLS}$ are defined by the optimizing problem which is express as $\min\limits_{x}\left\|[A,b]-\left[\hat{A},b_{TLS}\right]\right\|_2$ . It is obvious that the TLS solution has the minimum norm with respect to $A$ and $b$ simultaneously.

Let singular value decomposition (SVD) of matrix $B$ be $B=USV^*$, where $U$ is an unitary matrix with size $m\times m$ , $V$ is an unitary matrix with size $n\times n$, $V^*$ is the associate matrix of $V$ , $S$ is an diagonal matrix with size $m\times n$ and the elements in its leading diagonal is non-negative.

## 4.2    Analysis of the Decoupling Method

Basing the analysis in 3.2, (13) can be expressed by

$$H\cdot A_{IN}=A_{out},\qquad(20)$$

where $H$ is the coupling coefficient matrix and its value is $\begin{bmatrix}\cos\alpha_1\cos\beta_1 & \sin\alpha_1\cos\beta_1 & \sin\beta_1 & C_1\\ \sin\beta_2 & \cos\alpha_2\cos\beta_2 & \sin\alpha_2\cos\beta_2 & C_2\\ \sin\alpha_3\cos\beta_3 & \sin\beta_3 & \cos\alpha_3\cos\beta_3 & C_3\end{bmatrix}$, $A_{IN}$ is the calibrating matrix of the accelerometer input and is express by $\begin{bmatrix}A_x & A_y & A_z & 1\end{bmatrix}^T$ , $A_{out}$ is the accelerometer output matrix and is express by $\begin{bmatrix}A_1 & A_4 & A_7\end{bmatrix}^T$ .

If we measure the system $m$ times, we get $\left(A_{xk},A_{yk},A_{zk},A_{1k},A_{4k},A_{7k}\right), k=1,\ldots\ldots,m$ from (20). First consider to fit the first row of $H$ and substitute the measured data into (20), and we get

$$\begin{bmatrix}A_{11}\\ \vdots\\ A_{1m}\end{bmatrix}=\begin{bmatrix}A_{x1} & A_{y1} & A_{z1} & 1\\ \vdots & \vdots & \vdots & \vdots\\ A_{xm} & A_{ym} & A_{zm} & 1\end{bmatrix}\begin{bmatrix}\cos\alpha_1\cos\beta_1\\ \sin\alpha_1\cos\beta_1\\ \sin\beta_1\\ C_1\end{bmatrix}.\qquad(21)$$

The solution of the linear equation is the first row of the coupling coefficient matrix. But for that both of the calibrating matrix $A_{IN}$ of the accelerometer input and the accelerometer output matrix $A_{out}$ have errors, we can not arrive the solution with high precision by using the traditional method. While using TLS, the solution to (21) has the minimum norm to $A_{IN}$ and $A_{out}$ simultaneously by using TLS. We also can find the TLS solution of the second and third row of $H$ by using the same method. Now we reconstruct the input signal $\begin{bmatrix}A_x & A_y & A_z\end{bmatrix}^T$ based on the output signal $\begin{bmatrix}A_1 & A_4 & A_7\end{bmatrix}^T$ .

For that the coupling coefficient matrix $H_{TLS}$ is acquired, there exists an input signal with respect to the measured output signal fulfill (20), namely

$$\begin{bmatrix} A_1 \\ A_4 \\ A_7 \end{bmatrix} = H_{TLS} \begin{bmatrix} A_x \\ A_y \\ A_z \\ 1 \end{bmatrix}.$$
(22)

With the characteristic of the Moore-Penrose generalized inverse matrix , we get

$$\begin{bmatrix} A_x \\ A_y \\ A_z \\ 1 \end{bmatrix} = H_{TLS}^{+} \begin{bmatrix} A_1 \\ A_4 \\ A_7 \end{bmatrix},$$
(22)

where $H_{TLS}^{+}$ is the generalized inverse matrix with respect to $H_{TLS}$. Using (23), the accelerometer output signal $\begin{bmatrix} A_x & A_y & A_z \end{bmatrix}^T$ can be reconstructed. Replacing $\begin{bmatrix} A_1 & A_4 & A_7 \end{bmatrix}^T$ by $\begin{bmatrix} A_x & A_y & A_z \end{bmatrix}^T$ and substituting $\begin{bmatrix} A_x & A_y & A_z \end{bmatrix}^T$ into (14), we can get the angular acceleration without coupling error.

## 5    Simulation Results

After analyzing the static decoupling method to the accelerometer of the NGMIMU system mentioned above using TLS, simulations of the system with different coupling angles are performed respectively in this section. Table 1 and Table 2 illustrate the measured results and the output values of the angular rate after decoupling by using the method in this paper with different sampling numbers, respectively.

In the simulation, the initial conditions in position, velocity, posture angle and angular rate are $x(0) = 0$ m, $y(0) = 0$ m, $z(0) = 0$ m, $v_x(0) = 0$ m/s, $v_y(0) = 0$ m/s, $v_z(0) = 0$ m/s, $\alpha_x = 0$ rad, $\alpha_y = 0$ rad, $\alpha_z = \pi/3$ rad, $\omega_x(0) = 0$ rad/s, $\omega_y(0) = 0$ rad/s, $\omega_z(0) = 0$ rad/s respectively. The accelerometer static bias is $10^{-5}$g. The sampling time is 10ms. Fig. 4 is curve of the decoupling error at different coupling error.

**Table 1.** Decoupling results when coupling error is 0.001rad

| Sampling number N | Real value $\omega_z$ (rad/s) | Before decouping $\omega_{z\,c}$(rad/s) | After decoupling $\omega_{zdc}$ (rad/s) | Decoupling error (%) |
|---|---|---|---|---|
| 10 | 0.000499 | 0.000815 | 0.000548 | 9.82 |
| 50 | 0.002397 | 0.003683 | 0.002550 | 6.38 |
| 100 | 0.004207 | 0.006736 | 0.004452 | 5.82 |
| 150 | 0.004987 | 0.008811 | 0.005243 | 5.13 |
| 200 | 0.004564 | 0.009722 | 0.004769 | 4.49 |
| 300 | 0.000756 | 0.034278 | 0.000801 | 5.95 |
| 400 | -0.003784 | 0.039546 | -0.003626 | 3.25 |
| 500 | -0.004794 | 0.048781 | -0.004648 | 3.05 |

**Table 2.** Decoupling results when coupling error is 0.005rad

| Sampling number N | Real value $\omega_z$ (rad/s) | Before decoupling $\omega_{z\_c}$ (rad/s) | After decoupling $\omega_{zdc}$ (rad/s) | Decoupling error (%) |
|---|---|---|---|---|
| 10 | 0.000499 | 0.001879 | 0.000574 | 15.03 |
| 50 | 0.002397 | 0.008616 | 0.002605 | 8.67 |
| 100 | 0.004207 | 0.016490 | 0.004549 | 8.13 |
| 150 | 0.004987 | 0.022333 | 0.005385 | 7.98 |
| 200 | 0.004564 | 0.028845 | 0.004921 | 7.82 |
| 300 | 0.000756 | 0.036292 | 0.000825 | 9.12 |
| 400 | -0.003784 | 0.043270 | -0.003563 | 5.84 |
| 500 | -0.004794 | 0.056988 | -0.004577 | 4.53 |

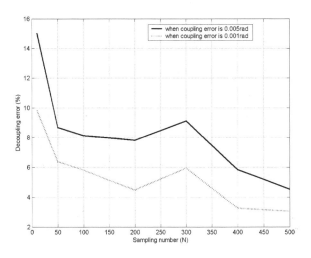

**Fig. 4.** Curves of decoupling error

From Table 1, Table 2 and Fig. 4, it is obvious that the value of the angular rate before decoupling distorts seriously no matter what the coupling angle is. Under the situation of the same coupling angle, with the increasing of the sampling numbers, the decoupling error ratio ( $\dfrac{|\omega_{zh} - \omega_z|}{|\omega_z|} \times 100\%$ ) is smaller and smaller. The value of the decoupling error ratio is smaller than 8% and near to 0. The increasing estimating precision is due to the increasing sampling points which fit the coupling coefficient matrix correctly. Comparing Tab.1 and Tab.2, it is obvious that the decoupling error ratio in Tab.1 is less than that in Tab.2. The reason is that the larger the coupling angle is, the serious the distortion degree of the accelerometer is. The simulation results show that the static decoupling method can reconstruct the input signal with high precision effectively.

# 6    Conclusions

The static coupling error is one of the main system errors which seriously affect the estimating precision when the navigation calculation is being carrying on to a NGMIMU system. The decoupling problem can be transform into a problem of solving an equation by changing the system mathematics model with coupling error into a format like $AX = b$. In this paper, the decoupling method by using TLS and Moore-Penrose generalized inverse matrix considers not only the error of the accelerometer output but also the error of the input signal for calibrating the system. The method highly improves the estimating precision of the coupling coefficient and the reconstructing precision of the input signal. And it is necessary to be home in on the analysis of the dynamic coupling error with nonlinear characteristic in further research.

**Acknowledgments.** This work is supported by "the National Natural Science Foundation of China" (Grant No. 60901042 and No. 61171189) and "the Fundamental Research Funds for Central Universities" (Grant No. HIT. NSRIF. 2010105).

# References

1. Schuler, A.R.: Measuring Rotational Motion with Linear Accelerometers. IEEE Trans. on AES 3(3), 465–472 (1967)
2. Merhav, S.J.: A Nongyroscopic Inertial Measurement Unit. J. Guidance 5(3), 227–235 (1982)
3. Tan, C.-W., Park, S.: Design of Gyroscope-free Navigation Systems. In: 2001 Proceedings of Intelligent Transportation Systems, pp. 286–291 (2001)
4. Lee, S.C., Huang, Y.C.: Innovative Estimation Method with Measurement Likelihood for All-accelerometer Type Inertial Navigation System. IEEE Trans. on AES 38(1), 339–346 (2002)
5. Kao, C.F., Chen, T.L.: Design and Analysis of an Orientation Estimation System Using Coplanar Gyro-free Inertial Measurement Unit and Magnetic Sensors. Sensor and Actuators A 144, 251–262 (2008)
6. Wang, J., Wang, Q., Sun, S.: Optimum technology for non-gyro micro inertial measuring unit. Jounal of Harbin Institute of Technology 34(5), 632–635 (2003)
7. Valaee, S., Champagne, B., Kabal, P.: Localization of Wideband Signals Using Least-Squaress and Total Least-Squaress Approaches. IEEE Trans. on Signal Processing 47(5), 1213–1222 (1999)
8. Kubus, D., Kroger, T., Wahl, F.M.: On-line estimation of inertial parameters using a recursive total least-squares approach. In: Proceedings of International Conference on Intelligent Robots and Systems, pp. 3845–3852 (2008)
9. Yang, K., An, J., Bu, X., Sun, G.: Constrained Total Least-Squares Location Algorithm Using Time-Difference-of-Arrival Measurements. IEEE Trans. on Vehicular Technology 59(3), 1558–1562 (2010)

# Object Recognition on Cotton Harvesting Robot Using Human Visual System

Yong Wang[1], Xiaorong Zhu[2], Yongxing Jia[1], and Changying Ji[3,*]

[1] College of Science, PLA University of Science and Technology, 210003, Nanjing, China
[2] College of Telecommunications and Information Engineering,
Nanjing University of Posts and Telecommunications, 210003, Nanjing, China
[3] College of Engineering, Nanjing Agricultural University, 210031, Nanjing, China
njwy1978@126.com, chyji@njau.edu.cn

**Abstract.** Object recognition is one of the hottest issues in the field of vision system for harvesting robot. How efficiently and accurately to remove the background and get the object in image is the key research. The attention mechanisms of human visual system (HVS) can be segmented an image into the region of interesting (ROI) which is considered important and the background which is less important, and recognized the object from ROI using the local information. In this paper, an algorithm based on the characteristic of HVS is proposed. In algorithm, the image was partitioned into many blocks of equal size. ROI was got through calculating the factor of weight of each sub-block image, and the object was extracted by segmenting the ROI. Experiment results show that the algorithm can be recognized the object efficiently and accurately. A new method for vision system of harvesting robot is provided.

**Keywords:** attention mechanisms, human visual system, cotton, object recognition.

## 1 Introduction

Two main tasks of harvesting robot are to recognize and locate the object and to harvest the object without damaging. The first task recognize and locate the object is the key task. This task determined how the harvesting task can implement smoothly. The principal objective in the first task is to extract the object which was interesting from the image, in order to prepare for subsequent image processing steps. Nowadays, there are many methods for object reorganization, such as using the color difference between object and background. Some researchers use color difference (R-G) and color difference ratio (R-G)/(G-B) to recognize the apples[1-3]. The experiment results showed this method can eliminate the inferences of shade, backlighting and soil. The recognition rate reaches above 90%. Others use the spectral reflection ration of

---

* This work is supported by the Natural Science Foundation of China(No.61001078), China Postdoctoral Science Foundation(2010047065), the Postdoctoral Science Foundation of Jiangsu Province(0902005C), Youth Foundation of College of Science(QNDZ200905).

D. Li and Y. Chen (Eds.): CCTA 2011, Part I, IFIP AICT 368, pp. 65–71, 2012.
© IFIP International Federation for Information Processing 2012

different parts of the crop[4,5]. These methods have a good effect for recognizing object. However, there is no considering the biological visual characteristics, especial the characteristics of human vision, to recognize the object. The human eyes were formed a unique visual characters in the long evolutionary history. The human eyes can recognize the target accurately and quickly in the complex environment. So many researchers are interesting in the biological vision. Liu Changqin[6] present a model of motion direction detection based on the characteristics of sustained-transient cell of biological vision, and simulated on the computer. The experiment results show this model can recognize the motion direction of object. Song Nong[7] developed an auto target recognition algorithm employing attention mechanisms with bottom-up and top-down control strategies. The experiment results show the objects for detection using the algorithm is effectively. Other researchers[8-13] present their own algorithms for image process based on the research of biological vision. Therefore, the bionic vision will be a hottest field for the future research[14-15]. This paper developed an algorithm for cotton recognition using the characteristic of attention mechanisms of HVS.

The rest of the paper is organized as follows. In Section 2 we introduce the materials of experiment throughout the paper. In Section 3 an algorithm using four factors of attention mechanisms of HVS can be found. We present some experiment results in Section 4. Finally, we conclude the paper in Section 5.

## 2     Materials

This subject is Suman-12 which was in mature period Jiangpu farm of Nanjing Agricultural University. The color images in the outside were acquired by a digital color CCD camera WAT-231S in October. The image acquisition card is Matrox Meter-II/Standards. The color signals from WAT-231s were transferred by the image acquisition card as a 24-bit RGB color image and processed using Lenovo X200 Computer, the CPU is Intel Core2 Duo 2.4GHz, the memory is 2GB, and OS is Windows XP. The color images were taken at the time from 10:00 AM to 4:00 PM. These images were taken under sunny and cloudy weather. So the machine vision system is composed of a color CCD camera to acquire the cotton image, the image acquired card to transferred the analog signal to digital signal, and the PC to process the acquired image. The machine vision is shown as Figure 1.

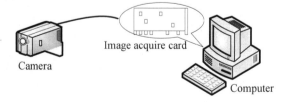

**Fig. 1.** Composition of machine vision

# 3    Principal of Human Visual System

We are interesting of the rapid change of image when we observed. It is so called the attention mechanisms. The rapid change area is called the region of interesting (ROI). To extract the ROI, the main factor affected human eyes are to be considered, such as the impact factor of brightness, contrast, sharpness and location. To calculate the effect of four factors mentioned above. First the image was blocked sub-image by equal space. Set the size of each block is $m$ and $n$, and then calculated the impact factor of each block, obtained the weight factor $\omega$ of each blocks through normalization. Finally, the background was removed and ROI was remained based on the value of weight factor of $\omega$.

## 3.1    Brightness Factor

Brightness factor describes the sensitivity level of human eyes to light. It is measured through Weber-Fechner law that is the relationship between the physical magnitude of stimuli and the percered intensity of the stimuli is the logarithm. This kind of relationship can be expressed as Equation (1):

$$s = k \lg \frac{I}{I_0} \,.$$

(1)

where $k$ is the constant factor, $I$ is the mean brightness of each block, $I_0$ is the absolute threshold, generally taken the maximum brightness value of each block.

## 3.2    Contrast Factor

Contrast factor describes the sensitivity level of human eyes to changed detail in image which can be expressed by variance. It can be expressed as Equation (2):

$$d = \sqrt{\frac{1}{m \times n} \sum_{i=1}^{m} \sum_{j=1}^{n} f^2(i, j) - \left[ \frac{1}{m \times n} \sum_{i=1}^{m} \sum_{j=1}^{n} f(i, j) \right]^2} \,.$$

(2)

where $f(i, j)$ is the gray value of pixel$(i, j)$.

## 3.3    Sharpness Factor

Sharpness factor describes the resolution of human vision. It can be expressed through the gradient. It can be written as Equation (3):

$$k = \frac{\sum_{i=1}^{m} \sum_{j=1}^{n} \sqrt{\nabla^2 f_H(i, j) + \nabla^2 f_V(i, j)}}{m \times n} \,.$$

(3)

where $f_H(i, j)$ and $f_V(i, j)$ is the horizontal and vertical gradient, respectively. Combining the horizontal and vertical gradient yields the spatial gradient.

## 3.4    Location Factor

Location factor describes the degree of interest in the different parts of image. It can be express as Equation (4):

$$r = 1 - (1 - B) \frac{\sqrt{(x_{i0} - x_c)^2 + (y_{i0} - y_c)^2}}{r_{max}} . \tag{4}$$

where $B$ is the basic weight value, the range value is [0, 0.5], $x_c$, $y_c$ is, respectively, the center coordinate of original image, $x_{c0}$, $y_{c0}$ is the center coordinate of each block image, respectively, and $r_{max}$ is the maximum distance from each point to the center coordinate of original image.

## 3.5    Weight Factor

The four factors of each sub-block were considered, $\omega_i$ was used to evaluate the importance of each sub-block. $\omega_i$ is expressed as Equation (5):

$$\omega_i = \sqrt{s^2 \times d^2 \times k^2 \times r^2} . \tag{5}$$

In order to decrease the influence of the absolute error of $\omega_i$, the $\omega_i$ was progressed by normalized. The weight vector of $\omega$ is expressed as Equation (6):

$$\omega = \frac{\omega_i}{\sum\limits_{i=1}^{N} \omega_i} . \tag{6}$$

where $N$ is the number of block.

Now, the importance of each block can be expressed by the vector of $\omega$. It is matched with the characteristic of human eyes. We call it as weight factor. If the value of $\omega$ is smaller than threshold, then the gray value was become zero, otherwise, the gray value is no changed. Then ROI can be extract through all the vector $\omega$. The object of interesting can be got through segmenting ROI. The formula is expressed as Equation (7):

$$I = \begin{cases} I_i, & \omega > T \\ 0, & \omega < T \end{cases} \quad i = 1, 2, \cdots N . \tag{7}$$

where $T$ is the threshold, $N$ is the number of blocks.

Figure 2 shows the cotton recognition algorithm which was mentioned above. The process starts with the factor functions for segmentation. After segmenting the image, a low pass filter was conducted to remove noise. Then the features of object were labeled, such as area, perimeter, etc, from the binary image. These features were used to locate the cotton in 3-dimension space.

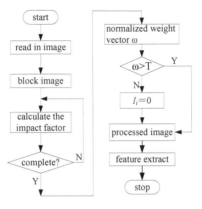

**Fig. 2.** Cotton recognition algorithm

# 4    Experiments and Analysis

To check how effective the proposed method is extracting object in actual image, several experiments were conducted using sample color images under natural environment. Experiment results are shown in Figure 3.

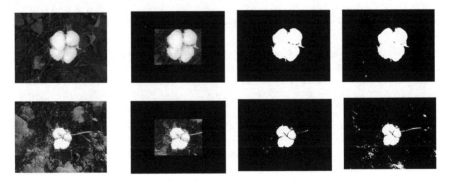

(a)Original image       (b)ROI image   (c)recognition with ROI   (d)recognition without ROI

**Fig. 3.** Experimental results

It can be seen that almost all the interesting object could be recognized by the proposed method. However, the number of sub-block images is changed by manually. Under cloudy weather, the segmentation achieved good results when the number of sub-block images is 4×4. The object segmentation will be failure when the number of sub-block image is too many, for extraction of ROI is incomplete. Otherwise, the segmentation will be failure because too many background joining in ROI. Therefore, the number of sub-block will be changed interactive in order to achieve good results.

It can be seen from the experimental results. The segmentation results under cloudy weather are better than sunny weather. The brightness of leaves and ground closed to the cotton fruit under sunny weather that lead to mistake between leaves and fruit. There is spot noise after segmentation. It needs further process to remove the noise.

## 5    Conclusions

We proposed an algorithm to detect the object. The algorithm is based on the attention mechanism of human vision so that some experiments were conducted to investigate how effective and accurate it is. The experiment results show that the algorithm is effective and accurately at extracting the object present in complex scene. However, the accurate of detection is better under cloudy weather than sunny weather. Under the sunny weather, there is spot noise after the recognition of ROI. It needs further process to extract the object.

## References

1. Si, Y., Qiao, J., Liu, G., et al.: Recognition and shape feature extraction of apples based on machine vision. Transaction of the Chinese Society for Agricultural Machinery 40(8), 161–165 (2009)
2. Yang, X., Duan, J., Gao, D., et al.: Research on Lane Detection Based on Improved Hough Transform. Computer Measurement and Control 18(2), 292–295 (2010)
3. Wang, Y., Shen, M., Ji, C.: Using Color Data and Shape properties for Cotton Fruit Recognition. Transaction of the Chinese Society for Agricultural Machinery 38(2), 77–79 (2007)
4. Yuan, T., Zhang, J., Li, W., et al.: Feature Acquisition of Cucumber Fruit in Unstructured Environment Using Machine Vision. Transaction of the Chinese Society for Agricultural Machinery 40(8), 170–174 (2009)
5. Henten, E.J., Hemming, J., Tuijl, B.J., et al.: An autonomous robot for harvesting cucumbers in greenhouse. Autonomous Robots 13(3), 241–258 (2002)
6. Liu, C., Wang, Z.: A model of Motion Direction Detection based on Biological Vision. Computer Simulation 23(8), 181–183 (2006)
7. Sang, N., Li, Z., Zhang, T.: Applications of human visual attention mechanisms in object detection. Infrared and Laser Engineering 33(1), 38–42 (2004)
8. Kang, M., Li, Y.: An Adaptive Image Enhancement Algorithm based on Human Visual properties. Opto-Electronic Engineering 36(7), 71–77 (2009)
9. Kang, M., Wang, B.: An Adaptive Color Image Enhancement Algorithm Based on Human Visual Properties. Acta Optical Sinica 29(11), 3018–3024 (2009)
10. Liu, L., Zhou, G.: Application of human visual system in extraction of plant leaf image. Computer Engineering and Applications 45(19), 22–26 (2009)
11. Saghri, J.A., Cheatham, P.S., Habibi, H.: Image quality measure based on a human visual system model. Optical Engineering 28(7), 813–818 (1989)

12. Cao, J., Wang, W., Han, F., et al.: Research on Target Recognition Technology based on Local Feature. Computer Engineering 36(10), 203–205 (2010)
13. Yang, W., Zhao, Y., Xu, D.: Method of image quality assessment based on human visual system and structural similarity. Journal of Beijing University of Aeronautics and Astronautics 34(1), 1–4 (2008)
14. Liu, W., Yuan, X.: Study on Biological Vision. China Safety Science Journal 10(6), 51–56 (2000)
15. Yao, X., Lu, T., Hu, H.: Object Recognition Models Based on Primitive Visual Cortices: A Review. Pattern Recognition and Artificial Intelligence 22(4), 581–588 (2001)

# The Design of Greenhouse Environment Control System Based on Variable Universe Fuzzy Control Algorithm

Haiyan He and Heru Xue[*]

College of computer & information Engineering,
Inner Mongolia Agricultural University,
Hohhot, Inner Mongolia, P.R. China
hehaiyan808@sina.com, xuehr@imau.edu.cn

**Abstract.** Greenhouse environment has the characteristics such as multiple-input, multiple-output, nonlinearity, and difficulties of establishing its accurate mathematical model. Therefore, in order to make the greenhouse environment control more effective and accurate, an expert system of variable universe fuzzy control based on BP neural network has been proposed. In this method an appropriate universe is selected according to the error and the changing rate of error to overcome the effect for greenhouse control when the error is too large or too small. The paper introduces the design of greenhouse environment control system based on variable universe fuzzy control in details, and presents the main control parameters.

**Keywords:** fuzzy control, variable universe, greenhouse environment control, expert system, BP neural network.

## 1 Introduction

Greenhouse environment control can increase crop yield, improve quality, adjust the production cycle and improve the economic efficiency, if we can make full use of natural resources and change environmental factors (e.g. the temperature, humidity, light intensity, $CO_2$ concentration, etc.) to obtain the optimum condition of crop growth[1]. The current greenhouse environment controlling system has a lot of shortcomings, especially great influence on the control accuracy of the controlling algorithm. Only reasonable control algorithm can make the comprehensive factor of greenhouse environment achieve optimal control effect, and make the greenhouse system achieve intelligent level.

There are a lot of algorithms about greenhouse environment control, such as PID control algorithm, the fuzzy control algorithm, the neural network control algorithm, etc. However, these algorithms have their shortcomings. PID control algorithm needs to build accurate mathematical model and it is difficult to build accurate mathematical

---

[*] Corresponding author.

D. Li and Y. Chen (Eds.): CCTA 2011, Part I, IFIP AICT 368, pp. 72–78, 2012.

model for the multivariable and complex greenhouse environment. With inaccurate model, the entire greenhouse environment control system will be directly affected, even some errors occur in the system. Fuzzy control doesn't need accurate mathematical model. Computer is used to achieve the control which people complete with natural language. But there are very high requirements on membership functions selection and expert knowledge. If not taken carefully, it will be inaccurate and lead to the influence of greenhouse crop growth.

In this paper, the variable universe fuzzy control based on BP neural network is used in greenhouse environment control system, which has strong dynamic prediction functions and decision-making explained ability.

## 2     Variable Universe Fuzzy Control Based on BP Neural Network

### 2.1     Fuzzy Control

Fuzzy control doesn't need accurate mathematical model. Computer is used to achieve the control which people complete with natural language. The control algorithm puts all environmental parameters together, then realizes fuzzy control. The block diagram of the principle of fuzzy control system is shown as fig.1 [2].

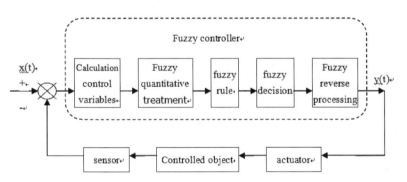

**Fig. 1.** The block diagram of principle of fuzzy control system

### 2.2     Variable Universe Fuzzy Control

In greenhouse environment control process, greenhouse environment is a multivariable nonlinear system, which is difficult to establish the mathematical model. Using the fuzzy control doesn't need to build accurate mathematical model, but the initial variable universe has great effect on the accuracy of control system. As a result, Variable Universe Fuzzy Control can solve the problem of selecting initial universe.

On the premise of fuzzy division unchanged in the variable universe, Variable Universe shrinks with error decrease, and expands with error increase. Through the changing of universe, it makes the initial rule which experts concluded a more effective new rule. On the surface, the number of rules has not changed, but the rules are more precise because the universe changes, equivalent to increase of the number of rules, and improvement of the accuracy of control [3]. The change of domain is shown as fig.2.

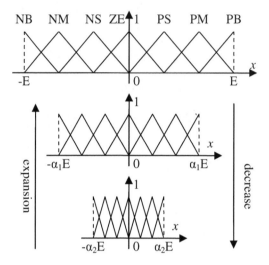

**Fig. 2.** Change of universe chart

## 2.3    BP Neural Network

The BP neural network is Error Back Propagation network. It consists of three parts: input layer, hidden layer and output layer. The BP neural network, which realizes adjustable factor function of universe, is a three-layer forward network composed of a binary input and a triple output. The network's input node is error $e$ and error rate $ec$, and the output node is adjustable factors of systematology universe, $\alpha1,\alpha2,\beta$. The structure of BP neural network is shown as fig.3 [4].

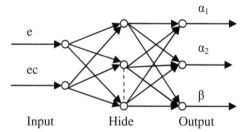

**Fig. 3.** BP neural network structure chart

## 2.4    Variable Universe Fuzzy Control Based on BP Neural Network

Variable universe fuzzy control based on BP neural network is composed of fuzzy control by fuzzy control technology and the BP neural network. It combines fuzzy reasoning ability of linguistic expression with the BP neural network self-learning ability. The BP neural network describes the telescopic change. In system control process, the BP neural network computes out suitable factor. Fuzzy control change universe achieves better control effect according to the suitable factor. The structure of variable universe fuzzy control based on BP neural network is shown as fig.4 [5-6].

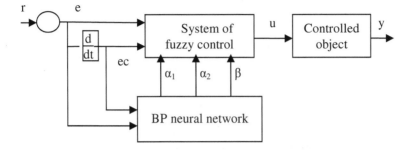

**Fig. 4.** Structure chart of variable universe fuzzy control based on BP Neural Network

# 3    Controlling System Design

### 3.1    Structure of Control System

Indoor/outdoor sensor array collects real-time environmental data, such as temperature, humidity and so on. The data are analyzed by variable universe fuzzy control based on BP neural network system, and control decision is obtained, then the control part is notified to perform corresponding action. Control system structure is shown as fig.5 [7].

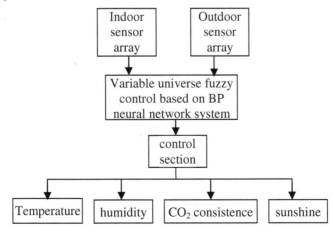

**Fig. 5.** Control system structure chart

## 3.2    Control System Process

Greenhouse system is a big lag and nonlinear systems, so we need to constantly detect greenhouse system control parameters, and adjust the execution time of each execute equipment, which makes greenhouse always maintain the best environment for crop growth. Control system process is shown as fig.6 [8].

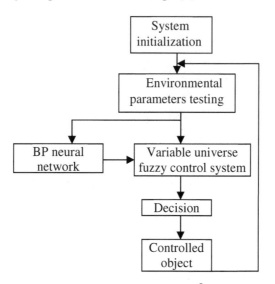

**Fig. 6.** Control system process chart

## 3.3    Control System Parameter Design

### 3.3.1    Variable Universe Fuzzy Control Design

Error $e$ basic universe $[-4, +4]$;

Error rate $ec$ basic universe $[-2, +2]$;

Output U basic universe $[-1, 1]$; Controlled variable of output is described by four fuzzy states, for instance PB, PM, PS, ZO.

The principle of selecting controlled variables: When the error is big, we should primarily choose controlled variable to eliminate error as soon as possible; when the

**Table 1.** Fuzzy control rule

| E | EC | | | | | | |
|---|----|----|----|----|----|----|----|
|   | NB | NM | NS | ZO | PS | PM | PB |
| NB | PB | PB | PB | PM | PS | ZO | ZO |
| NM | PB | PB | PM | PM | PS | ZO | ZO |
| NS | PB | PB | PM | PS | ZO | NS | NM |
| ZO | PM | PM | PS | ZO | NS | NM | NM |
| PS | PM | PS | ZO | NS | NM | NM | NM |
| PM | PM | ZO | ZO | NM | NM | NM | NM |
| PZ | PS | ZO | ZO | NB | NB | NB | NB |

error is less, we should avoid overshooting while selecting controlled variables, and ensure the stability of the system.

We choose triangle membership Functions, due to variable universe fuzzy control having low requirement to membership function, which is denoted by three parameters (a, b, c):

$$u(x) = \begin{cases} 0 & x <= a \\ \dfrac{x-a}{b-a} & a < x <= b \\ \dfrac{x-b}{c-b} & b < x <= c \\ 1 & x >= c \end{cases}$$

### 3.3.2    BP Neural Network Design

There are 2 input nodes, 3 output nodes, 7 hidden layer nodes. Learning rate $\eta$ is 0.4, momentum factor is 0.1 and mean square error is 0.01.

## 4    Output Results Comparison

Variable universe fuzzy control which is based on BP neural network, according to the size of the error and error rate, chooses suitable universe to control. It solves the improper selection problem of initial universe to obtain more accurate control. The following is a comparison of output between fuzzy control and variable universe fuzzy control based on BP neural network (e.g. temperature).

**Table 2.** Output comparison

| Error | Error rate | variable universe fuzzy control | | fuzzy control | |
|---|---|---|---|---|---|
| | | Output U | Input energy (W) | Output U | Input energy (W) |
| -3.5 | -1 | 5.00 | $4.8\times10^5$ | 6.00 | $4.8\times10^5$ |
| -2.2 | -1.2 | 4.28 | $3.2\times10^5$ | 6.00 | $4.8\times10^5$ |
| -2.5 | -0.8 | 4.58 | $4.8\times10^5$ | 5.20 | $4.8\times10^5$ |
| -2.0 | -0.5 | 4.00 | $3.2\times10^5$ | 4.00 | $3.2\times10^5$ |
| -1.8 | -1.2 | 3.50 | $3.2\times10^5$ | 6.00 | $4.8\times10^5$ |
| -1.5 | -0.8 | 3.00 | $1.6\times10^5$ | 5.20 | $4.8\times10^5$ |
| -1.2 | -0.7 | 2.70 | $1.6\times10^5$ | 4.80 | $4.8\times10^5$ |
| -0.8 | -0.3 | 1.82 | $1.6\times10^5$ | 2.66 | $1.6\times10^5$ |
| -0.3 | -0.1 | 0.70 | 0 | 1.16 | $1.6\times10^5$ |

It is very important for the rational choice of suitable factor for input and output variables of the fuzzy control. Suitable factors α1 and α2 are the different weight of error and the error rate of input variable. So it has great influence on the dynamic performance of the control system. Variable universe fuzzy control based on BP neural network has solved this problem. It gives suitable factor which adapts with error and error rate by the BP neural network. It makes the control more accurate, and won't make the responding time too long or overshoot the phenomenon.

As shown in chart 2, When the error and error rate is (-2.2, -1.2)、(-1.5,-0.5)、(-1.2,-0.7), fuzzy control output (U = 6) reaches the highest level (4.8×105W) . Big energy input may cause overshooting and make the concussion intensified. Therefore, fuzzy control variable universe based on BP neural network is better than fuzzy control. For a multivariate and nonlinear greenhouse environment system with delay phenomenon, variable universe is more suitable.

# 5    Conclusion

As stated previously, variable universe fuzzy control based on BP neural network is more suitable for greenhouse environment control. The system can gain better control effect than general control system. If we ascertain the change rule of real-time of universe. In addition, variable universe fuzzy control based on BP neural network also does not need too much expert knowledge, which makes the establishment of the greenhouse environment control system easier.

**Acknowledgements.** This study has been funded by Research projects (ZN201010 and NDPYTD2010-9).

# References

1. Li, X., Yang, M., Yang, R.: Modern greenhouse environment intelligent control development present situation and prospect. Journal of Agricultural Mechanization Research (4), 9–12 (April 2008)
2. Zhao, Y.: Study on the expert system of greenhouse intelligent control. Kunming polytechnic university (March 2007)
3. Li, L.: Study on variable universe fuzzy control algorithm. University of electronic science and technology (May 2008)
4. Zhang, H., Chen, P., Liu, X., Yu, Z.: The expert system based on neural network in the application of greenhouse control. Journal of Chengdu University Of Information Technology 25(3), 260–263 (2010)
5. Hayashi, Y., Buckley, J.J., Czogala, E.: Fuzzy expert systems versus neural networks. In: Proc. of Int. Joint Conf. on Neural Networks, Baltimore, MD, June 7-11, vol. 2, pp. 720–762 (1992)
6. Wang, L.-X.: Adaptive Fuzzy Systems and Control. Prentice-Hall, Englewood-Cliffs (1994)
7. Mamdani, E.H.: Application of Fuzzy Algorithms for Control of a Simple Dynamic Plant. Proc. IEE 121(12), 1585–1588 (1974)
8. Cai, C.: Study on intelligent greenhouse environment control system. Journal of Chongqing Institute of Technology 21(10), 105–107 (2007)

# Research on Decoupling Control in Temperature and Humidity Control Systems

Weiming Cai, Songming Zhu, Huinong He[*], Zhangying Ye, and Fang Zhu

College of Biosystems Engineering and Food Science,
Zhejiang University, Hangzhou 310058, China
nnhe@mail.hz.zj.cn

**Abstract.** Temperature and humidity are two highly coupled variables in a control system, which need to be decoupled for effective control. Moreover, the coupling problem may get more severe and the two control loops may produce a strong interference to each other that can cause system instability when the humidity is measured by dry-and-wet bulb method. In this study, a control method based on fuzzy-neural-network was studied for solving the coupling problem. The shape of membership function can be adjusted in time by using a wavelet basis as the fuzzy membership function. An effective real-time decoupling control system for temperature and humidity could be realized by neural network fuzzy inference. Decoupling control tests were conducted in a control room with 1.6 m × 1.0 m × 4.0 m. The results show that the performance of the control system on dynamic response speed, stability, and anti-jamming have been improved after decoupling.

**Keywords:** Dry-and-wet Bulb Method, Coupling Problems, Fuzzy Neural Network, Wavelet Basis, Temperature and Humidity.

## 1 Introduction

Coupling problems widely exist in nonlinear time-varying systems with multiple inputs and outputs. One of the major technical difficulties in designing a measurement and control system is to control the coupling objects effectively [1]. The objects need to be decoupled for effective control. Most of traditional method of decoupling control is built on the basis of a mathematical model, however, it is hard to establish accurate mathematical model for many production process [2]. As a kind of multivariable nonlinear system, control systems of temperature and humidity are widely embedded in many products such as temperature and humidity environmental chambers, drying box of agricultural products, food processing ovens, etc [3-5]. The performance of those products mainly depends on the control veracity of temperature and humidity, however, there is coupling between the two variables, and it is very difficult to improve the accuracy for the needs of high quality products by using

---

[*] Corresponding author.

D. Li and Y. Chen (Eds.): CCTA 2011, Part I, IFIP AICT 368, pp. 79–89, 2012.

traditional control methods [6]. Decoupling Control has been already proved to be a key technique for building temperature and humidity control systems for high quality products.

In recent years, fuzzy neural network provides a new way to solve problems that can't be done by traditional methods in the field of control [7]. Fuzzy control does not require precise mathematical description of the control object in achieving good control of the system, however, factors such as nonlinear, time-varying and random interference of the system may result in inappropriate or incomplete fuzzy control rules which will affect control performance [8, 9]. Neural network has good capacities in nonlinear processing, self-learning, self-organizing, and adaptability although it needs long training time and its dynamic characteristics are not ideal [10]. Fuzzy neural network is the combination of fuzzy control and neural network, and it can not only integrate the merits of both fuzzy control and neural network, but also can overcome their shortcomings. Therefore, this new method makes it possible to build higher precision control systems in products with coupling problems.

Nowadays, products with core of temperature and humidity control system such as environmental chambers are widely used in agriculture, aerospace, military, electronics, and other fields. It is the objective of many scientists and engineers to improve the performance of those products and to meet the requirements for higher accuracy in control process. In order to look for a new way in designing high quality temperature and humidity control systems, a novel method was proposed to improve the decoupling effects in a temperature and humidity control system in the paper.

## 2    Coupling in Temperature and Humidity Control Systems

The temperature and humidity will have effect on each other in an environment; changes from temperature will result in humidity fluctuating, and the temperature will also get a certain influence from humidity variety.

Relative humidity (RH) is usually measured by dry-and-wet bulb method: To detect air temperature by a thermal resistance sensor, namely the dry-bulb temperature; and to detect the temperature of the veil kit soaked in distilled water by a same thermal resistance sensor, namely the wet-bulb temperature. The mathematical formula can be derived through the heat transfer theory and thermodynamic theory as follows:

$$X_h = \frac{E_s - NP\left(T_g - T_s\right)}{E_g} \times 100 \tag{1}$$

Where: $X_h$ is the relative humidity %; $E_s$ is the saturated water pressure under wet-bulb temperature; $E_g$ is the saturated vapor pressure under dry bulb temperature; $N$ is a constant related with wind speed; $P$ is atmospheric pressure; $T_g$ is the dry-bulb temperature ; $T_s$ is the wet-bulb temperature.

The control of temperature and humidity is generally based on the principle of balances on temperature and humidity. Customarily, temperature homeostasis is realized through heating by a heater and refrigerating by a cooler or adding cold air; simultaneously, the humidifier (usually produced by heating steam) is work together with a dehumidifier (Generally by cooling and dehumidification condensation through the heat exchanger) for achieving dynamic equilibrium of humidity.

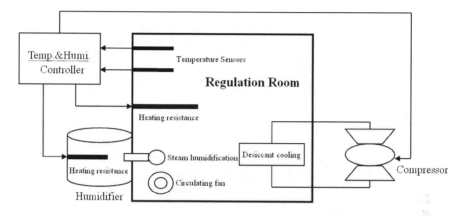

**Fig. 1.** Schematic diagram of measurement and control for room temperature and humidity

However, this kind of method for temperature and humidity monitoring and control may produce coupling problem. As Fig.1 show, the temperature of dry bulb will decrease quicker than the wet bulb when the temperature in the regulation room drops for some reason; consequently, by formula (1), the measurement value of relative humidity will increase although the actual humidity in the room has not changed. Then, the humidity control loop will start to work for adjusting the humidity falsely. It might be called systematic error which is brought by the measured value of the relative humidity [11], and will exacerbate the coupling effect between the temperature and humidity in the room. Therefore, coupling problems may get more severe and the two control loops may produce a stronger interference to each other that can cause system instability when the humidity variable parameter is measured by dry-and-wet bulb method although it is the most popular way in humidity measurement.

# 3    Principles and Methods

## 3.1    Control Systems of Temperature and Humidity

Input and output control systems for temperature and humidity can be described as follows:

$$\begin{bmatrix} Y_t(k) \\ Y_h(k) \end{bmatrix} = P[X_t(k), X_t(k-1), X_h(k), X_h(k-1), Y_t(k-1), Y_h(k-1)] + \begin{bmatrix} T_t(k) \\ T_h(k) \end{bmatrix} \tag{2}$$

Where: $Y_t$ is the output of temperature, $Y_h$ is the output of humidity; $X_t$ is the input of temperature, $X_h$ is the input of humidity; $T_t$ is the system disturbance and measurement noise of temperature, $T_h$ is the system disturbance and measurement noise of humidity.

## 3.2    The Method of Wavelet

A wavelet is a mathematical function used to divide a given function or continuous-time signal into different scale components [12]. Usually, one can assign a frequency range to each scale component. Each scale component can then be studied with a resolution that matches its scale. A wavelet transform is the representation of a function by wavelets. The wavelets are scaled and translated copies (known as "daughter wavelets") of a finite-length or fast-decaying oscillating waveform (known as the "mother wavelet"). Wavelet transforms have advantages over traditional Fourier transforms for representing functions that have discontinuities and sharp peaks, and for accurately deconstructing and reconstructing finite, non-periodic or non-stationary signals. Information can be effectively extracted from signals by wavelet transform, which is a good way for local analysis [13]. Continuous wavelet transform is a waveform transform that obtain continuous values through scaling parameter $a$ and translating parameter $b$. In practical applications, $a$ and $b$ will be discretized and all the discrete wavelet form a function group which can be used as a base function.

For the advantages of wavelet described above, Wavelet basis [14, 15] was used as the membership function of fuzzy neural network in our study, and it can be expressed as follows:

$$H_{a,b} = H\left[ \frac{(x-a)}{b} \right] \tag{3}$$

Where: $a$ is the expansion factor; $b$ is the translation factor. The base expression of mother wavelet $H\ (\bullet)$ is as follows:

$$H(x) = e^{\left(-x^2/2\right)} \cdot \cos(x/2) \tag{4}$$

## 3.3    Decoupling Control Based on Fuzzy Neural Network

The decoupling control structure of temperature and humidity based on fuzzy neural network (shown in Fig. 2) is consists of four layers, which includes an input layer, a fuzzy layer, a fuzzy rules layer and an output layer.

(a) Input layer: Changes of temperature and humidity $(X_t, X_h)$ will be put into the neural network, and the input value of each neuron will be converted to the fuzzy domain [-1, 1].

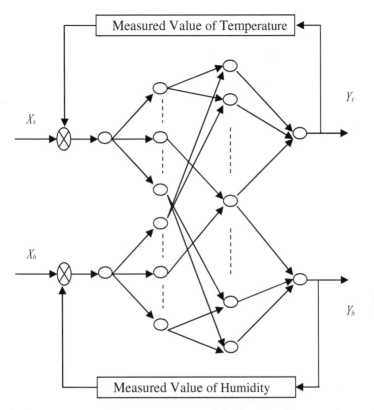

**Fig. 2.** Control structure of temperature and humidity based on fuzzy neural network

(b) Fuzzy layer: Fuzzy variables will be obtained from the inputs; and wavelets are used as the fuzzy membership function in our study. The affiliation between the inputs and the fuzzy linguistic variables is as follows:

$$H_{ij}(x_i) = e^{\left(-(x_i-b_{ij})^2 / 2a_{ij}^2\right)} \cdot \cos\left[(x_i - b_{ij}) / 2a_{ij}\right] \qquad (5)$$

Where: $i = 1, 2; j = 1, 2 \dots N$; $a_{ij}$, $b_{ij}$ are the corresponding dilation factor and translation factor.

(c) Fuzzy rules layer: each neuron represents a fuzzy rule, which will export the corresponding fitness of rules.

(d) Output layer: Defuzzfication will be achieved, and the output will be normalized in this layer.

## 4    Results and Discussion

In order to see the validity of the control method in our study, test works were done in a control box with the dimensions of 1.6m × 1.0m × 4.0m, and the total power of the control box is about 16.5kw; as shown in Fig.1, the control box is made up of heater, evaporator, compressor, circulating, and Temp.&Humi. Controller.

Fig.3 shows a response curve of temperature and relative humidity before and after decoupling when the set value of temperature is changed from 37 °C to 28 °C and humidity is changed from 60% to 82% in our test work; Fig.3a and Fig.3b are the response curves before and after decoupling respectively. From Fig.3a, it can be observed the temperature reached the predetermined value (28 °C) after about 14 minutes but the humidity still not reached a steady state half an hour later, and the overshoot is more than 7%RH; The change of temperature and humidity has brought

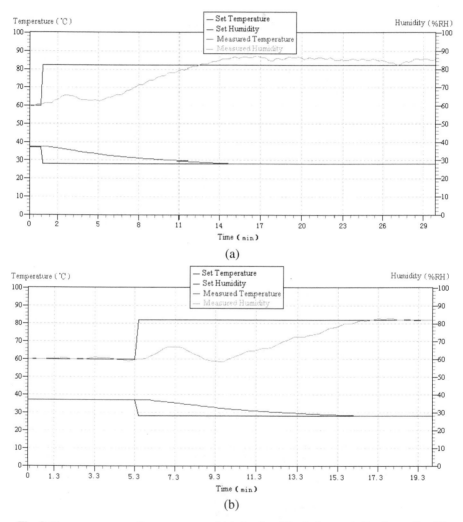

(a)

(b)

**Fig. 3.** Response curves of temperature and relative humidity before and after decoupling(1)

more serious coupling to the humidity control. From Fig.3b, we can find the temperature and humidity reached the predetermined value after about 11 minutes; the overshoot of humidity is less than 1%, and the overshoot of temperature is less than 1 °C. This shows that the decoupling control is successful by the way of fuzzy neural network in the changed process. In addition, from Fig.3a and Fig.3b, it can also be found that the time needed for reaching the setting value is 1 minute shorter after decoupling, which suggesting that the changes of humidity can also have effect on temperature control.

Fig.4 shows another response curve of temperature and relative humidity before and after decoupling when the humidity is not changed(60%RH) but the set value of temperature is changed from 50 °C to 40 °C; Fig.4a and Fig.4b are the response curves before and after decoupling respectively. From Fig.4, It can be found that the temperature reached the set value(40°C) after about 6 minutes under decoupling control (see Fig.4b) and the change of humidity caused by temperature also returned to the original(60% RH); However, without decoupling, it took more than 15 minutes for the humidity returning its original value as the measured value of humidity rose because of temperature dropped. This further shows that the system achieved a good control effect by the way of fuzzy neural network and the response speed has also been improved a lot. In addition, from Fig.4a, at about the 6$^{th}$ minute, we can notice that there is a short time interval in which the measured value of humidity is lower than its set value from the; it is because that the control loop of humidity took effect falsely as the drop of temperature resulted in the measured value of humidity increased (detail reason is included in the second part of this paper); however, the coupling problems does not exit any more when decoupling control was used according to Fig.4b.

Fig.5 shows variations of temperature and relative humidity when the measured temperature value fell because of disturbance from the outside world; Fig.5a and Fig.5b are the variations of temperature and relative humidity before and after decoupling respectively. From Fig.5a, it can be found that the measured value of the temperature was suddenly decreased about 14°C at the 2$^{nd}$ minute(From 60°C to 46°C) for outside interference; it took more than 7 minutes for the humidity return to steady state although the temperature recovered to 60 °C about 1.5 minutes later as the temperature control loop took effect. From Fig.5b, the measured value of the temperature was suddenly decreased about 18°C (From 60°C to 42°C) at the first minute for outside interference; It only spent about 2 minutes for the humidity recover from the interference and recover time of the temperature is less than 1 minute although the interference is more serious compare to Fig.5a. Comparing Fig.5a and Fig.5b, It can be indicated that changes in temperature had brought a greater impact on humidity control; therefore, for achieving a humidity control loop with high anti-jamming capability, we should find good ways to decrease the coupling effect from temperature changes, which is a most important factor that should be considered in designing control systems of temperature and humidity.

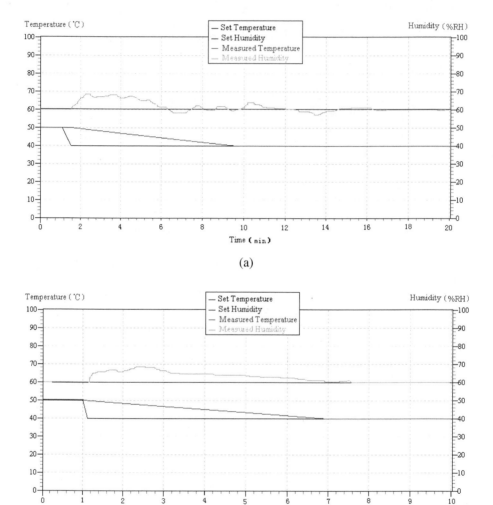

(a)

(b)

**Fig. 4.** Response curves of temperature and relative humidity before and after decoupling(2)

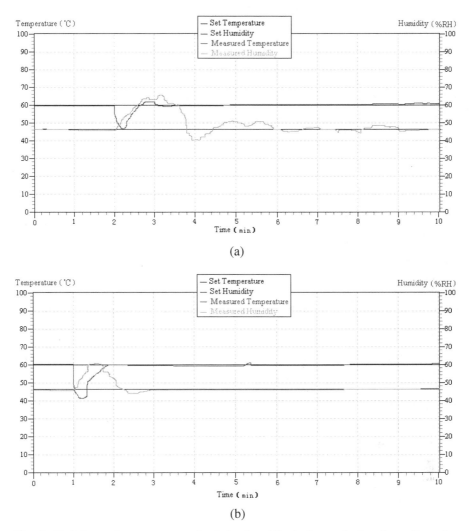

**Fig. 5.** Variations of temperature and relative humidity before and after decoupling when measured values of temperature fall

Usually, there is coupling in measurement and control systems of temperature and humidity; the change of temperature and humidity can take effect on each other's control loop. Systematic error caused by the coupling described in the second part of this paper is one of the main factors in the performance of control systems, which can reduce the anti-interference ability. Therefore, it is very important to find a way to solve the coupling problem. The fuzzy neural network was used for its good performance of local anomaly identification. Fig.3, Fig.4, and Fig.5 show that the method tried in this paper has achieved good decoupling effect; the decoupling control systems has a strong anti-interference ability, fast response, smaller overshoot, and high stability.

## 5    Conclusions

Systematic error brought by the measured value of relative humidity is unavoidable, which will exacerbate the coupling effect in measurement and control systems for temperature and humidity. Fortunately, there are some decoupling ways to reduce the effect of errors and improve control precise. Most of traditional method of decoupling control is built on the basis of mathematical models; coupling from measured value errors could be reduced by mathematical compensation, however, the humidity and the temperature themselves are a pair of coupled variables, which also need to be decoupled. Moreover, it is hard to establish accurate mathematical model for many production process. Whereas fuzzy neural network can provide new ways in decoupling control, which does not require precise mathematical description of control objects.

The membership function is a generalization of the indicator function in classical sets, which were introduced by Zadeh in the first paper on fuzzy sets (1965). In fuzzy logic, it represents the degree of truth as an extension of valuation. One of the most important factors on the effect of the fuzzy neural network is the membership function we chose. Our primarily study shows that it is a good choice to put wavelet basis as the membership function of fuzzy neural network for decoupling control.

This study provided scientific analysis on coupling problems of measurement and control systems for temperature and humidity, which is important for better understanding coupling problems in control process for this kind of system, and thus improving decoupling ways for control loops. Although more experiments should be done in different type of environment to further confirm our decoupling way, the research offered a novel try in designing high quality temperature and humidity control systems on technical theory and engineering design. Following this work, further verification experiment and scientific evaluation will be done in the future.

**Acknowledgments.** Research grant support from the Key Laboratory of Eco-Agricultural Environmental Engineering and Intelligent Equipment of China Agricultural Ministry (Grant Number: 588040*172210214[2]) is acknowledged.

## References

1. Tan, K.K., Lee, T.H., Ferdous, R.: Online relay automatic tuning of multi-loop PI controllers. Intelligent Automation and Soft Computing 9(3), 155–167 (2003)
2. Kim, Y.T.: Independent joint adaptive fuzzy control of robot manipulator. Intelligent Automation and Soft Computing 11(1), 21–32 (2005)
3. Putranto, A., Chen, X.D., Devahastin, S., Xiao, Z.Y., Webley, P.A.: Application of the reaction engineering approach (REA) for modeling intermittent drying under time-varying humidity and temperature. Chemical Engineering Science 66(10), 2149–2156 (2011)
4. Jin, T.X., Li, G.L., Gong, Y., Lu, Y.L., Shi, Y.: Modelling evaporation-boiling phenomena during vacuum cooling of cooked meat. Intelligent Automation and Soft Computing 16(6), 1119–1133 (2010)

5. Varela, A.C., Mendoza, O.B.: Design and implementation of a strategy of predictive control of paddy rice drying. Revista Facultad Dd Ingenteria-universidad Dd Antioquia (56), 78–86 (2010)
6. Schoen, C.: A new empirical model of the temperature-humidity index. Journal of Applied Meteorology 44(9), 1413–1420 (2005)
7. Lin, T.C., Chen, M.C.: Adaptive hybrid type-2 intelligent sliding mode control for uncertain nonlinear multivariable dynamical systems. Fuzzy Sets and Systems 171(1), 44–71 (2011)
8. Ren, M.L., Wang, B.D., Liang, Q.H., Fu, G.T.: Classified real-time flood forecasting by coupling fuzzy clustering and neural network. International Journal of Sediment Research 25(2), 134–148 (2010)
9. Soyguder, S., Alli, H.: Fuzzy adaptive control for the actuators position control and modeling of an expert system. Expert Systems with Applications 37(3), 2072–2080 (2010)
10. Mahdavi, N., Menhaj, M.B.: A New Set of Sufficient Conditions Based on Coupling Parameters for Synchronization of Hopfield like Chaotic Neural Networks. International Journal of Control Automation and Systema 9(1), 104–111 (2011)
11. Singh, B., Kishan, H., Singh, Y.P.: Calibration of special relative humidity and temperature (RHT) sensors and evaluation and expression of uncertainty in the measurement. Mapan-journal of Metrology Society of India 23(2), 115–121 (2008)
12. Jin, N., Liu, D.R.: Wavelet basis function neural networks for sequential learning. IEEE Transaction on Neural Networks 19(3), 523–528 (2008)
13. Yilmaz, S., Oysal, Y.: Fuzzy Wavelet Neural Network Models for Prediction and Identification of Dynamical Systems. IEEE Transaction on Neural Networks 21(10), 1599–1609 (2010)
14. Li, J., Zhang, W.: The Performance Analysis of Several Wavelet Bases in Applications (I). Journal of Chongqing University (Natural Science Edition) 21(2), 111–116 (1998) (in Chinese)
15. Li, J., Zhang, W.: The Performance Analysis of Several Wavelet Bases in Applications (II). Journal of Chongqing University (Natural Science Edition) 21(4), 39–43 (1998) (in Chinese)

# Visualization of Virtual Plants Growth Based on Open L-System

Yingying Liu, Juan Pan, Li Yang, Xiaodong Zhu, and Na Zhang[*]

Department of Computer and Information Engineering,
Beijing University of Agriculture, Beijing, P.R. China 102206
liuyingying@bac.edu.cn

**Abstract.** Based on the improvement of Open L-system, this paper presents a four-layer model of plant growth visualization. Take Radix Isatidis for example, the paper carries on morphologic model of its base leaves growing period and eco-physiological model about temperature and growth rate. The prototype system design and development are also discussed on the base of this four-layer model. The results show that the four-layer model solves the combination of the plant morphologic model and eco-physiological model, with some reference value and practical significance.

**Keywords:** virtual plant, Open L-system, modeling, visualization.

## 1 Introduction

Virtual plants center on the research of plant individual, establish three-dimensional model with a focus on the research of plant morphology and visually reflect the physiological and ecological characteristics of crops. [1].

Many scholars at home and abroad have done a great deal researches about morphologic and eco-physiological modeling of virtual plants and have made great progress. But there is still an urgent need for researchers to solve many problems. One of the key issues is to systematically and organically integrate morphologic model and eco-physiological model into growth model. [2] Based on the improvement of Open L-system, this paper puts forward the four-layer model and focuses on solving the combination of the plant morphologic model and eco-physiological model.

## 2 Analysis and Improvement of Open L-System

### 2.1 About Open L-System

Lindenmayer system [3] was designed by Aristid Lindenmayer in 1968 to simulate biological forms, named after himself, and was called L-system for short. L-system is more suitable for the description of fractal phenomenon and also suitable for the

---

[*] Corresponding author.

D. Li and Y. Chen (Eds.): CCTA 2011, Part I, IFIP AICT 368, pp. 90–96, 2012.

description of plant morphology. Based on the original L-system (determinacy OL-system, random L-system, parameter L-system and so on), Open L-system builds an interactive information mode between plants and external conditions by introducing the function expression $E(x1,x2,\ldots, xn)$.

Open L-system is usually regarded as an ordered six-tuple shown in formula (1) as followed [4].

$$G= (V, \ \Sigma, \ \prod, \ E, \ \omega, \ P) \ . \tag{1}$$

In which, V is character set of system; $\Sigma$ is formal parameter set; $\prod$ is random probability effect function set, it matches the probability that each production is applied, the sum of each function value is one; E is the information transfer function to transfer information between plants and condition; $\omega$ is called axiom component of non-empty character; P is a finite production set.

## 2.2    Defect Analysis

After analyzing how the open L-system works, the author thinks that the open L-system has some insufficient s summed up as follows [5].

**Inherited Defect.** Open L-system inherits the fundamental features of L-system like other L-systems, so it is necessary for users to know well character string rewrite rules and have the skill of converting the rules of plant development into complex productions.   Representing geometric construction as well as topological structure of plants in this formal language, especially describing the extremely complicated process of growth makes the production more difficult to comprehend, and it is a trouble for the researchers.

**Extensional Defect.** Open L-system integrates the processing information such as calculating functions for interacting with external environment, so the indigestible L-system becomes more complicated. From the perspective of software engineering it reduces the expandability of the software to a great degree, and it doesn't correspond with modularization principle. It's a taboo that the whole program need modify when processing functions change or development parameters vary.

## 2.3    Improvement Research

Based on the analysis above, the improvement research is focused on "slimming" that mainly reflects in the following two aspects.

**Optimizing and Simplifying the Character Set.** It is the first step to optimize V in formula (1). When the research object is one specific plant it is reasonable to keep necessary expression symbols and cut down those unnecessary according the growth rules. For example, for the visualization of Radix Isatidis base leaf growth, it's a good idea to keep those basic symbols such as rotation angle, increase and decrease angle, beginning of one leaf, end of one leaf, drawing a leaf and returning to origin.

**Splitting the Interactive Processing Units off.** The next modification is to slip the E and $\prod$ in formula (1) off the open L-system and put them into another modular. So the open L-system is transformed as formula (2).

$$G= (V, \Sigma, \omega, P) \tag{2}$$

The formal parameters in $\Sigma$ are interfaces between morphogenetic model and eco-physiological model. Eco-physiological model processes growth parameters in give condition according to some growth rules even agricultural expert system. Then those parameters are transferred to open L-system as new plants morphological parameters, so L-system can rewrite character string according to new parameters to represent new state that plants interact with environment.

Some advantages can be manifested by handling in this way.

1. The complexity of open L-system is lower.
2. The degree of coupling between morphogenesis model and eco-physiological model is reduced and the expandability of software is increased.
3. Visualization modular and interactive modular can be parallel processed, so the performance of the system can be improved.

# 3      Four-Layer Model Architecture

Followed the research results above, one integrated framework for virtual plant growth visualization system is presented with the purpose of combination of morphogenetic model and eco-physiological model as shown in fig.1. In this framework, one middle layer is introduced besides the eco-physiological layer, morphological layer and visualization layer. Like OSI/RM or TCP/IP network architecture, layers in the framework coordinate each other in C/S way.

## 3.1      Eco-physiological Layer

Eco-physiological layer mainly imitates the interaction between plants and environments, such as the effect of temperature, humidity or photometric quantity on plant growth and it can also deal with the competition mechanism of plant themselves and feedback to environment from plant. This layer receives the data processed by the middle layer or feedback from plant, and then through plant growth mechanism model even expert system it computes the specific parameters for plant growth. The parameters are transferred to the middle layer later, and then should be transferred to morphological layer, so the interaction between plant and environment can be obtained.

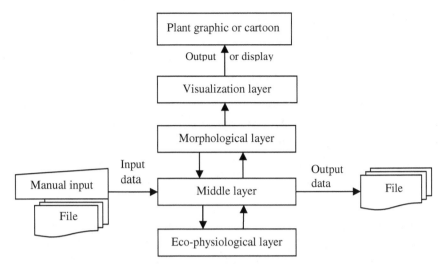

**Fig. 1.** Four-layer model architecture for virtual plant growth visualization system

### 3.2 Morphogenetic Layer

Based on open L-system, the morphogenetic layer represents the topological and geometric structure by character strings and productions. The interface of plant and environment is held as parameters in the open L-system improved and the middle layer will transfer the parameters processed by the eco-physiological layer through the interface, so eco-physiological model and morphogenetic model integrate well.

### 3.3 Visualization Layer

On the basic of the data processed by morphogenetic layer the visualization layer takes advantage of computer graphics techniques such as geometrical processing, lighting, texture and rendering to show the plant growth in three-dimensional visualization way.

### 3.4 Middle Layer

The middle layer plays a certain role in the nexus. It transfers the definite parameters between morphogenetic layer and eco-physiological layer. Meanwhile, the middle layer is charged with an important mission to receive extern data or output and store data in file or database which is convenient for statistic and analysis later.

## 4    Implementation and Results

Design and Implementation of one proto software are discussed in the following section. Radix Isatidis is taken as research object in this software which validates the feasibility of four-layer model. The focus is only on the base leaf growth stage of Radix Isatidis in consideration of operability.

## 4.1    Design of Eco-physiological Layer

It is "accumulated temperature method" that was adopted to map the leaf count and temperature .For one single leaf, normality model and "clock model" were introduced to define the function of growth rate and temperature as shown in formula (3).

$$V(D) = \left(\frac{T - T\min}{To - T\min}\right)^{-2}\left(\frac{T\max - T}{T\max - To}\right)^{-2\left(\frac{T\max - T0}{To - T\min}\right)}\frac{1}{11\sqrt{2\pi}}\text{EXP}(-\frac{(D-11)^2}{2\times 6.65^2}) \tag{3}$$

In which T=average temperature of one day; Tmin=0, the min temperature that base leaf can live; Tmax=35, the max temperature that base leaf can live; To=17, the temperature best fit base leaf; P=-2, impact factor; D =days.

Furthermore, the functions between growth rate and growth parameters such as length, width, stretch, crimp and color are also defined. Due to space limitations, these elements do not go into details.

## 4.2    Process of Morphogenetic Layer

Based on NURBS the whole base leaf model is built, and the specific leaf appearance was played by a 7×7×3 parameterized array shown as formula(4), formula(5) and formula(6). This method ensures the blade fluency and clear biological significance.

$$c[i][j][0] = (j-3)\frac{iw}{6} \tag{4}$$

$$c[i][j][1] = \frac{iw}{2}\tan(\frac{1}{3}(\frac{\pi}{2} - \frac{AC\pi}{360})ABS(j-3)) \tag{5}$$

$$c[i][j][1] = (L - L\text{stalk})\frac{i}{6} \tag{6}$$

In addition, basic characters and productions were also defined. As the space is limited, relevant information is leaved out.

## 4.3    Design of Middle Layer

First, both file and database as I/O manner are introduced in this software. The data in database is stored in table, and each table is correlative. The conceptual structure of database is shown as table1.

On the other hand, parallel processing and multithreading technologies are adopted in the software to display morphology results and compute physiological results in parallel. Then parameters are processed into a suitable form, and then transferred between morphology layer and eco-physiological layer.

**Table 1.** The conceptual structure of database

| Name of relation | Attributes | Key |
| --- | --- | --- |
| day | dayid,min,max,s,phaseid | dayid |
| phase | phaseid,s | phaseid |
| topology | dayid,baseleaf,stemleaf,branch,flower,fruit | dayid |
| baseleaf | dayid,leafid,days,len,wid,as,ac,r,g,b | dayid,leafid |

### 4.4    Visualization Technology

Based on VC++ development platform, twenty-seven classes are defined and implemented. One single Radix Isatidis is drawn according to the hierarchical model based on matrix stack and transformation of open GL. Relevant functions about illumination of open GL are adopted to achieve the illumination and color change.

The prototype system interface is similar to VC style shown as fig.2. Besides the menu and tool bar above, left part is control area concluding three switchable areas that display the parameters of static status display, dynamic display and group display and the right part is graphic display area.

## 5    Conclusion and Discussion

The prototype system shows that the four-layer model can well solve the combination of morphology model and eco-physiological model. The four-layer model that encapsulates the eco-physiological model in another layer instead of open L-system, so it is coupling efficiency, scalable and easy to be modified and restructured. In the background of the agriculture and forestry application software, it has certain reference value and practical value.

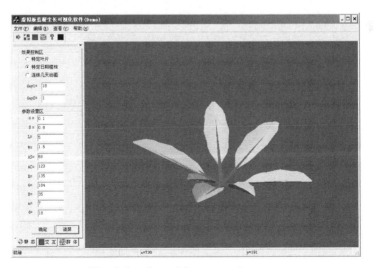

**Fig. 2.** Interface of the proto software

This paper is just a try and exploration in a smaller range and further research work is required. Based on perfecting morphology model and eco-physiological model, phototropism of plants, collision detection and realistic graphics generation need to be considered in the following research. In addition, agricultural experts system can consider to be combined, so they will complement each other and guide agricultural production in a better way.

## References

1. Zhou, S.Q.: Virtual plants modeling and visualization. Electronic Industry Press, Beijing (2008) (in Chinese)
2. Hu, B.G., Zhao, X., Yan, H.P., de Reffye, P., Blaise, F., Xiong, F.L., Wang, Y.M.: Plant development model and visualization—review and prospect. Acta 27(6), 816–835 (2001) (in Chinese)
3. Room, P., Hanan, J., Prusinkiewicz, P.: Virtual plants: new perspectives for ecologists, pathologists and agricultural scientists. Trends in Plant Science 1(1), 33–38 (1996)
4. Prusinkiewicz, P.: Modeling plant growth and development. Current Opinion in Plant Biology 7, 79–83 (2004)
5. Liu, Y.Y.: Visualization of Virtual Plants Development Based on Open L System. North China Electric Power University, Beijing (2009) (in Chinese)

# Research on Navel Orange Safety Production Information Management System

Huoguo Zheng[1,2], Shihong Liu[1,2], Liping Zheng[3], and Jiayou Zhong[3]

[1] Key Laboratory of Digital Agricultural Early-warning Technology of Ministry of Agriculture,
The People's Republic of China, Beijing 100081, Beijing, China
[2] Agricultural Information Institute of Chinese Academy of Agriculture Science,
Beijing 100081, Beijing, China
[3] Agricultural Information Institute of Jiangxi Academy of Agriculture Science,
Nanchang 330200, Jiangxi, China
huoguo@caas.net.cn, lius@mail.caas.net.cn, lsny@163.com,
zjyou666@vip.163.com

**Abstract.** To deal with the incident, and guarantee the quality safety of navel orange, traceability system are used to record the information from tree planting to fruit sale. Navel orange safety production information management system, which manages the whole process from tree planting to circulation, achieves the entire information management except sale step of the navel orange food chain, is the core and foundation of navel orange traceability system. This paper discusses the basic function of navel orange safety production information management system based on analyses the whole business process, design the main function modules of the system according to GAP(Good Agricultural Practice), implement the system with the strategy of RBAC(Role Based Access Control based).

**Keywords:** navel orange, safety production information management system, GAP, RBAC.

## 1 Introduction

Navel orange is one of characteristic agricultural products in the middle of china. Gannan is the advantageous product area of navel orange determined by ministry of Agriculture in China. Gannan is the famous base for navel orange, where is known as "town of navel orange in China". Many counties have taken navel orange as an important tool for local farmer income. The navel orange produced in gannan has many unique features, such as large shaped, bright color, crisp flesh and good taste.

However, the incidents occurred in recently years, such as "dyeing navel orange" in Hong Kong in 2004, "bactrocera minax" in guangyuan city in 2008, Sichuan province, have damaged the orange industry in south of china. For example, The "dyeing navel orange" incident made 70% order in Hong Kong cancellation, the price of navel orange fell sharply in 2004. In 2008, affected by the "bactrocera minax" incident, all of the consumers don't want to buy navel orange in china. These events cause severe economic losses to fruit growers.

D. Li and Y. Chen (Eds.): CCTA 2011, Part I, IFIP AICT 368, pp. 97–103, 2012.
© IFIP International Federation for Information Processing 2012

To deal with the incident, and guarantee the quality safety of navel orange, traceability system are used to record the information from tree planting to fruit sale, which also called "management from orchard to table" [1]. There are three main meaning to construct traceability system: one is to make consumers know the quality safety conditions of the product they bought, the second is standardized production process of enterprises ,ensure the quality safety of products produced, and the third is to find the root causes when the food safety issues happened [2].

Navel orange safety production information management system, which manages the whole process from tree planting to circulation, achieves the entire information management except sale step of the navel orange food chain. It provides the safety information for consumer-oriented traceability system, and is the core and foundation of navel orange traceability system.

This paper point out the basic functions and modules of the navel orange safety production system based on business processes analysis, indicate the information the system should be recorded, then implementation the system according to the GAP(Good Agricultural Practice).

## 2     Navel Orange Safety Production System Analysis

### 2.1     Navel Orange Production Process Analysis

Generally, from tree planting to bear fruits need 2-3 years for navel orange tree. And it need 280-300 days from blooming to outcome when the navel tree is in produce fruiting period. A lot of operations should be taken from navel orange tree planting to fruit sales [3].

There are 9 main steps from navel orange tree planting to navel orange fruit transportation: orchard selection, tree planting, irrigation and fertilization, insects and disease control, fruit picking, washing and packing, storage and transportation (shown as Fig. 1).

### 2.2     System Function Analysis

For the navel orange safety production information management system, which functions include two aspects: the first is achieve the core business process management from fruit tree planting to transportation, including orchard management, production management, harvesting management, process management, and the second aspect is related to personnel management for system, such as user management, permissions management.

Essentially, the core of navel orange safety production information management system is to manage the information about production and processing affect the quality and safety of navel orange. The information the system manage can be divided into three kinds:

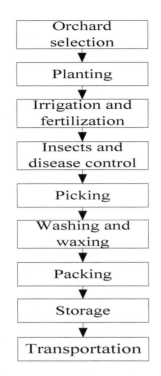

**Fig. 1.** 9 main steps from orchard to market of navel orange

The first type information is the quality safety information during navel orange production, including producing area conditions information (such as detection information of the origin water, soil and air); production process information (such as irrigation and fertilization information, major climate disaster information, diseases and insect pests, pesticide use information); information about picking and post-picking measures; cleanser, disinfectant, wax information during the process; packing information, storage surrounding information (such as place, temperature and sanitary condition), information about transportation.

The second type information is the information about organization, company and related personnel involved navel orange planting and processing, including ownership of the orchard, manager and worker of the orchard, processing company and worker of the company, transportation enterprise and vehicle.

The third type information is the user information of the navel orange safety production information management system, including basic information of the system user, login name, password, and the information of the user's role permissions. These users can log into the system, view information, input and maintain information within limits of authority. The user maybe the person himself mentioned above, such as ownership, manager or worker of the orchard, he also can be others who has the rights of operator or transporter.

# 3    Design of Navel Orange Safety Production Information Management System

## 3.1    Principles of System Design

Navel orange safety production information management system was designed based on the principle of GAP (Good Agricultural Practices).

Good Agricultural Practices are a collection of principles to apply for farm production and post-production processes, resulting in safe and healthy food, while taking into account economical, social and environmental sustainability. GAPs can be applied to a wide range of farming systems and at different scales. They are applied through sustainable agricultural methods, such as integrated pest management, integrated fertilizer management and conservation agriculture. It relies on four principles: economically and efficiently produce sufficient (food security), safe (food safety) and nutritious food (food quality); sustain and enhance natural resources; maintain viable farming enterprises and contribute to sustainable livelihoods; meet cultural and social demands of society.

As for navel orange safety production information management system, GAP is applied to control the common quality safety hazard in planting, harvest, cleaning, packing and transportation. For example, worker will be guide to use environmentally friendly manure, low-toxic low residue of pesticides.

## 3.2    System Function Module Design

In order to manage the information related to quality and safety from navel tree planting to fruit transportation, the function of navel orange safety production information management system should include at least the following 7 modules: system user management, navel orange standards management, orchard management, production control, picking management, processing management, storage and transportation management (shown as Fig 2).

In system user management, the information about user basic information such as login name, password and the information about authority was managed. There are two kinds of standards in standards management module: origin environmental standard such as water, air and soil quality standard; navel orange quality standard. The information of location and surrounding of the orchard, the quality information of irrigation water, soil and air of the orchard, and the information of orchard employee was recorded in the orchard management module. In the production control module, basic information and use information of inputs such as chemical fertilizers, pesticides, herbicides, and the information of diseases and insect was controlled [4]. The function of picking management module includes picking process information and treatment measures information of post-harvest. There are three kinds of information should be managed in processing management: enterprise information, processing information (detergent, disinfectants, and keeping fresh agent) and packing information. In the final step of safety production, storage and transportation information will be saved.

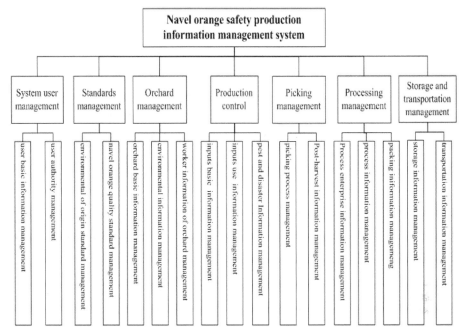

**Fig. 2.** Function modules of the system

# 4 Implementation of Navel Orange Safety Production Information Management System

## 4.1 Implementation of User Access Authority Control

There are many kinds of users in navel orange safety production information management system: system administrator, system operators, orchard owners, orchard workers, processing company managers, processing workers, managers of transportation enterprises, transporters. These different sorts of users have different permissions, such as system administrator has all right of the system; system operators have part right of the system administrator; an orchard owner can manage all orchards information belonging to him, but an orchard worker can only control the data of the exact orchard he have the right.

To facilitate the management, strategy of RBAC (Role Based Access Control based) is applied in this system. Different sorts of users are endowed with different permissions, each specific user can only have rights in their operations within. The workflow of loading the access and data control permissions is shown in Fig 3.

## 4.2 Implementation of the System

Navel orange safety production information system is achieved based on B/S model. Eight sort of users can login the system via one entry. The system can manage the

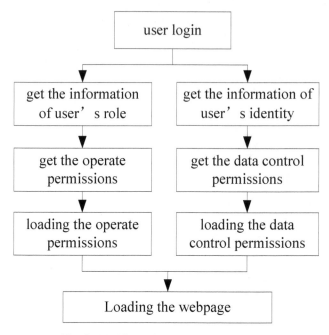

**Fig. 3.** Workflow of loading the permissions

information from navel tree planting to fruit transportation for many orchards, which is the foundation, and is also the core of navel orange quality safety traceability system. In the packing information management module, navel orange traceability code is generated according to the orchard code and packing batch code, by means of navel orange traceability code, consumers can get the quality safety information through the safety production information management system. The webpage of the system is shown in Fig 4.

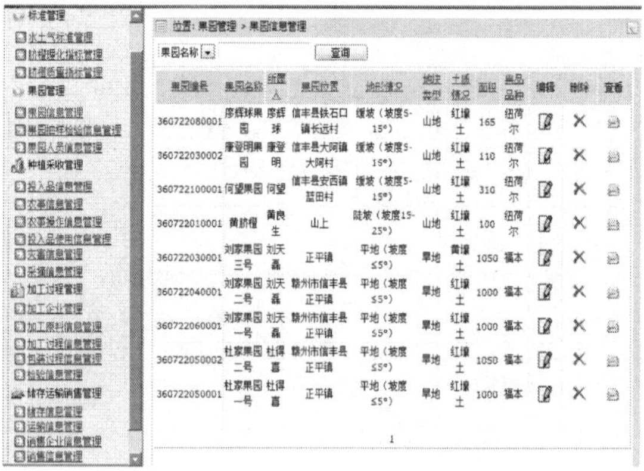

**Fig. 4.** Webpage of the system

# 5      Conclusion

This paper discusses the basic function of navel orange safety production information management system based on analyses the business process from orchard selection to navel orange fruit transportation. Then introduce the principles of system design, and figure out the 7 main function modules of this system. In the end of this article, the RBAC strategy is mentioned to manage eight sorts user of navel orange safety production information management system. Navel orange safety production information management system is the core of navel orange quality safety traceability system. This study makes the navel orange traceability system construction possible.

**Acknowledgements.** This study is supported by The National Science and Technology Support Programme (2009BADC4B04).

# References

1. Fan, H., Feng, Z., Yang, L., Ren, A.: Appliance and Discussion of Traceability System in Food Chain. Ecological Economy 17(4), 30–33 (2007)
2. Zhou, Y., Geng, X.: Application of Traceability in Food Safety. Research of Agricultural Modernization (06) (2002)
3. NY/T 977-2006.Technological regulation of navel orange cultivation in south jiangxi-south hunan-north guangxi. Publisher of China Standards (2006)
4. Zheng, H., Meng, X., Liu, S.: The Study on Navel Orange Traceability Chain. IFIP AICT, pp. 179–185 (2010)
5. Xu, J.: Agricultural product supply chain—Guarantee food safety. China Logistics & Purchasing (07) (2005)
6. Liu, Y., Chen, L.: Traceability Production System of Beef in EU and USA, food science, vol. (8), pp. 182–185 (2003)
7. Yu, H., An, Y.: Theoretical discussion of implementation Traceability System in food supply chain. Agricultural Quality and Standards (03) (2005)
8. Zhang, G., Chen, G.: Food safety and Traceability System. China Logistics & Purchasing (14) (2005)

# Rice Kernel Shape Description Using an Improved Fourier Descriptor[*]

Hua Gao, Yaqin Wang[**], Guangmei Zhang, Pingju Ge, and Yong Liang

College of Information Science & Engineering, Shandong Agricultural University,
No. 61 Daizong Road, Taian, Shandong 271018, China
{wyq,gaoh}@sdau.edu.cn

**Abstract.** A Fourier descriptor is one of the best methods for describing object boundaries, but there are limitations in describing the boundary of rice kernels using traditional Fourier descriptors. An innovative approach was developed to describe rice kernel boundaries by improving a traditional Fourier descriptor. This radius Fourier descriptor (RFD) uses a radius set for rice kernel images as its basis function, and uses amplitude spectrum of Fourier transform for the radius set as its descriptor. This method only retains the first 9 components of RFD, which is simple and the dimension of the feature vector can be reduced greatly without concern for the initial starting point on the contour. The method was validated in terms of area computation, variety distance calculation, shape description, and detection of broken kernels using a backpropagation (BP) neural network for several varieties of rice kernels. The detection accuracy for whole rice kernels of different samples was 96%-100% and for broken rice kernels was 96.5%.

**Keywords:** Image processing, Radius set, Rice kernel shape description, Radius Fourier descriptor.

## 1    Introduction

The shape of rice kernels is a basic parameter for quality assessment and classification of rice[1-2]. According to GB 1354-1986, the main parameters for rice quality assessment include machining precision, grain integrity, impurities, and broken rice rate. These parameters are related to kernel shape directly or indirectly. To realize detection of rice parameters using machine vision, one of the major challenges is to find a method to effectively and accurately describe rice shape features and discriminate whole rice kernels. At present, there are several parameters used to describe the kernel shape of agricultural products[3-4], including area, eccentric

---

[*] Supported by the Innovation and Technology Fund of Shandong Agricultural University of China under Grant No.23660. First author: Hua Gao, 1963, Male, Professor. Research interests: Image processing, Precision agriculture.
[**] Corresponding author.

D. Li and Y. Chen (Eds.): CCTA 2011, Part I, IFIP AICT 368, pp. 104–114, 2012.

moment, elongation, inertial center, aspect ratio, flakiness ratio, sphericity, roundness and Fourier descriptors. While for shape-based pattern recognition technique, moment invariant[5] and Fourier descriptor [6-8] are two major image recognition methods.

Experimental tests indicated that coordinate sequences for object contours based on a Fourier descriptor had the best shape recognition ability. Kauppien and Sepanen compared auto regressive and Fourier based descriptors in 2D shape classification [6]. Wei et al. reviewed on shape representation techniques and their applications in image retrieval[9]. Zhang and Lu classified and reviewed some important shape representation and description techniques[10]. However, traditional descriptors use Fourier transforms of a series of coordinate pairs for a shape boundary. According to the properties of the Fourier transform, a traditional Fourier descriptor is related to boundary scale, direction, and starting position of the curve, resulting in many limitations in describing rice shape boundaries. According to the periodicity of Fourier transform, when the original function of a Fourier transform shifts, the phase spectrum of Fourier transform will change, but the amplitude spectrum of Fourier transform will not change. In this paper, the amplitude of Fourier transform coefficient for a boundary radius set is used as a descriptor to describe rice kernel shape. This descriptor is named as Radius Fourier Descriptor (RFD). The rotation of rice kernel, corresponding to the shift of radius set, affects phase spectrum only, but does not affect amplitude spectrum. Therefore, it is rotation invariant to describe rice kernel shape using the RFD.

## 2     Materials and Methods

### 2.1     Image Acquisition

Several varieties of whole rice kernels and broken ones, including Dongbei long grain rice, Meihe rice, and Thai jasmine rice were taken as experimental objects. The original rice kernel images were acquired on a fixed image collection bench in this research. The surface of the image collection bench was covered with black cloth. A lighting chamber comprising a metal cylinder of 60 cm in diameter and 60 cm in height contained four 10-W ordinary fluorescent lamps installed symmetrically. The internal wall of the chamber was painted white to yield equal diffuse reflection. The test camera (Canon A580), fixed with a homemade arm with adjustable position and height, had a resolution of 3264×2448 and was placed at the center of the chamber, 50 cm above the bench. Part of the original rice kernel images were shown in Fig. 1. To determine the boundary of every rice kernel, several preprocessing steps including image filtering, binarization and segmentation[11] were carried out. Fig. 2 was the segmentation result of Fig. 1a. Based on the segmentation result, the boundary of every rice kernel was obtained. Fig. 3 was the boundary image of five touched kernels on the top-left corner of Fig. 2.

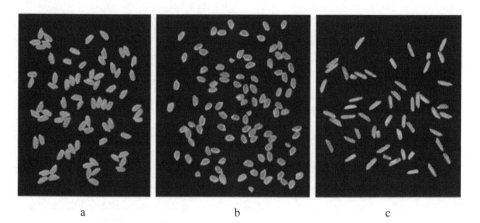

**Fig. 1.** Rice kernel images: (a) Dongbei long grain rice; (b) Meihe rice; (c) Thai jasmine rice

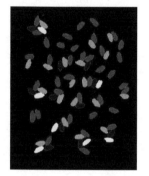

**Fig. 2.** The segmentation result of Fig. 1a    **Fig. 3.** The boundary of the five touched kernels on the top-left corner of Fig. 2

## 2.2    Fourier Descriptor

Position information for boundary points is vital in defining image boundaries, whereas gray information can be neglected in this study. A normalized boundary is a closed curve, so the boundary can be regarded as a curve y=f(x) consisting of a set of points in the regular x–y Cartesian coordinate system. A large amount of data is needed to totally describe such a curve in the spatial domain, resulting in complicated feature extraction. Thus, a boundary can be described in the frequency domain using a Fourier transform in a method known as a Fourier descriptor[8]. Traditional Fourier descriptor is related to boundary scale, direction, and start point position of curve, which result in many limitations for describing rice boundary with traditional Fourier descriptor. The amplitude of Fourier transform coefficient for a boundary radius set is used as a descriptor to describe rice kernel shape. This method can describe rice kernel shape accurately, and it is rotation invariant. Without concern for the start point of boundary when calculating, the method is simple to process and has a small amount of data.

If Fourier transformation is performed using $y=f(x)$ directly, the transform result will depend on the specific coordinates of $x$ and $y$, which cannot satisfy shift and rotation invariability requirements[12]. Thus, the RFD was introduced to satisfy these requirements.

**Definition 1.** Suppose that a closed image boundary is a set $B$ consisting of $M$ boundary points and $b_j(x_j, y_j)$ is any point on the boundary. The center point of the boundary, $p_o(x_o, y_o)$, can then be defined as:

$$x_o = \sum_{j=0}^{M-1} x_j / M , \quad y_o = \sum_{j=0}^{M-1} y_j / M \quad , \quad b_j(x_j, y_j) \in B .$$  (1)

**Definition 2.** As shown in Fig. 4, $N$ radial lines were constructed from $p_o$ to object image boundary with equal angle interval of $2\pi/N$. Let $b_i(x_i, y_i)$ be the intersection point of the radial lines and the object boundary, where $i=0,1,2,...,N-1$. The radius descriptor of the object can then be defined as radius set $R=[r_0,r_1,...r_{N-1}]$, where:

$$r_i = \sqrt{(x_o - x_i)^2 + (y_o - y_i)^2} .$$  (2)

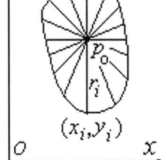

**Fig. 4.** Diagram showing calculation of the radius descriptor $R$

Because of the rigidity characteristic of rice kernel, it is impossible to produce deep hole on the fracture surface of rice kernel after breaking. Therefore, radial lines from the mass center intersect a rice boundary only once either for intact grains or for broken ones.

**Definition 3.** The discrete Fourier transform for $R$ is described by the equation:

$$F_r(u) = \frac{1}{\sqrt{N}} \sum_{i=0}^{N-1} r_i \exp[-j\frac{2\pi u i}{N}]$$  (3)

$$|F_r(u)| = \sqrt{R^2(u) + I^2(u)} \tag{4}$$

Where $j^2 = -1$. $R(u)$ is the real part of $Fr(u)$, and $I(u)$ is the imaginary part of $Fr(u)$. And $|F_r(u)|$ is defined as the RFD of the object boundary. According to the process of FFT algorithm, the value of $N$ is 2 to the power of n (n is an integer). It is usually not necessary to represent rice kernel shape with very high precision in practical applications, so the value of $N$ is not necessary to be too big (the bigger the value of $N$, the more accurate the description). Experimental test indicated that 32 or 64 of $N$ can express the detail of rice kernel shape accurately. The value of $N$ is set to 32 in this research.

According to the periodicity of Fourier transform, when the original function of a Fourier transform shifts, the phase spectrum of Fourier transform will change, but not the amplitude spectrum. Therefore, the amplitude spectrum of RFD is rotation invariant.

## 2.3    RFD Calculation

The first step in RFD calculation is to find the boundary center point $p_o$ and then the intersection point $b_i(x_i, y_i)$ of the radial lines and the boundary, with $2\pi/N$ as the interval angle. Because of the discreteness of digital images, many radial lines might not intersect with the boundary so the coordinates of a virtual intersection point coordinates must be obtained by interpolation. The specific algorithm proposed in this paper is as follows.

(1) Rice image boundary: The original rice image was processed via filtering, segmentation and binarization to obtain a binary image. Then the 8-neighbour boundary of the rice kernel was obtained using a morphological method:

$$B = A - (A \Theta E) \tag{5}$$

Where $A$ is the binary image, $E = \begin{vmatrix} 0 & 1 & 0 \\ 1 & 1 & 1 \\ 0 & 1 & 0 \end{vmatrix}$ is a structural erosion element,

and operator "$-$" stands for the subtraction operation, and "$\Theta$" stands for the erosion operation.

(2) Coordinates of the boundary center $p_o$: For any point on the boundary as the starting point, each point was traversed along the boundary from the start until the point was reached again. The average of all traverse points was calculated using Eq. (1) to yield the coordinates of $p_o(x_o, y_o)$.

(3) Similar circle radius:

   (i)    Find the first boundary point $b_0$ along the straight line $y = x_o$ from $p_o(x_o, y_o)$ and traverse every point $b_j(x_j, y_j)$ on the boundary to calculate the angle $\varphi_j$:

$$\phi_j = \arccos\left(\frac{\left|x_j - x_o\right|}{\sqrt{\left(x_j - x_o\right)^2 + \left(y_j - y_o\right)^2}}\right) \tag{6}$$

(ii)      Confirm an intersection point for the radius and boundary, $b_i$ ($i=0,1,2,...N-1$). If $\varphi_j=i*2\pi/N$, point $b_j$ is an intersection point for a similar circle radius and the boundary. If $\varphi_j<i*2\pi/N$, find the next point $b_{j+1}$. If $\varphi_j>i*2\pi/N$, the coordinates of $b_i$ can be calculated according to:

$$x_i = x_{j-1} \times \frac{2\pi i / N - \phi_{j-1}}{\phi_j - \phi_{j-1}} + x_j \times \frac{\phi_j - 2\pi i / N}{\phi_j - \phi_{j-1}}$$
$$y_i = y_{j-1} \times \frac{2\pi i / N - \phi_{j-1}}{\phi_j - \phi_{j-1}} + y_j \times \frac{\phi_j - 2\pi i / N}{\phi_j - \phi_{j-1}} \tag{7}$$

(iii)      Obtain $R$ by calculating $r_i$ according to Eq. (2).

(4) Fourier transform for $R$: According to Eq. (3), all calculations require $N^2$ multiplications and $N(N-1)$ additions so the computational workload increases greatly with $N$. To improve the computational efficiency, a fast Fourier transform (FFT) was used for practical application:

$$\begin{bmatrix} F_r(0) \\ \vdots \\ F_r(N-1) \end{bmatrix} = \begin{bmatrix} w_{0,0} & \cdots & w_{0,N-1} \\ \vdots & \ddots & \vdots \\ w_{N-1,0} & \cdots & w_{N-1,N-1} \end{bmatrix} \begin{bmatrix} r_0 \\ \vdots \\ r_{N-1} \end{bmatrix} \tag{8}$$

Where $w_{i,u} = \dfrac{1}{\sqrt{N}} e^{-j2\pi\frac{iu}{N}}$.

The computational complexity can be reduced to $N\log_2(N)$ when using FFT for $N=2^n$, otherwise zero should be added.

## 2.4      RFD Intercept

The Fourier transform is a reversible linear integral transform (Eqs. (3) and (4)). Therefore, the radius descriptor $r_i$ can be restored by the Fourier descriptor $F_r(u)$. If all the coefficients of the Fourier transform were chosen as the boundary description feature, the dimension of the feature vector would be too high and the computational workload would be excessive, even though no contour information would be lost. Such high precision is usually not necessary in practical applications. Therefore, selective interception for the Fourier transform coefficient is essential.

$F_r(u)$ is a sequence of $N$ frequency points and has conjugate symmetry with Nyquist frequency $n=N/2+1$ as its center. Therefore, only half of the $F_r(u)$ points ($N/2$) are required for spectral analysis.

Because the power of Fourier spectrum mainly focuses on the low-frequency components, the fundamental shape of rice kernel can be described with small amount of low-frequency components. Experiments have been done to test how many components should be reserved to restore the rice kernel shape. Fig.5 shows the restoration of rice kernel shape with different number of components, such as 3, 5, 7, and 9 components. Test result indicated that the first 9 components of RDF could restore the contours of object almost without distortion[13]. Therefore, only the first 9 components of RFD (that is the first 9 low-frequency coefficients of DFT) are required for rice shape description.

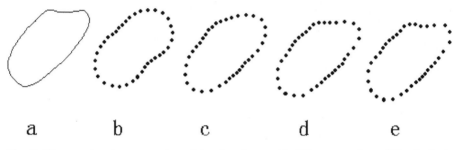

a          b          c          d          e

**Fig. 5.** Diagram showing restoration of the rice shape with different number of Fourier low-frequency components: (a) original image; (b) restoration with 3 components; (c) restoration with 5 components; (d) restoration with 7 components; and (e) restoration with 9 components

## 3     Results and Analysis

According to the physical meaning of Fourier transform, each component of the descriptor represents a specific meaning of rice shape. That is, $F_r(0)$ includes the scale information, $F_r(1)$ includes the circularity information, $F_r(2)$ includes the length information, $F_r(3)$ includes the triangularity information, $F_r(4)$ includes the rectangularity information, $F_r(5)$ includes the pentagon information, $F_r(6)$ includes the hexagon information, and so on. Each kind of information can be used to perform shape calculation and recognition for different kind of applications. For example, $F_r(0)$ could calculate area approximately, and the first 9 components could detect rice variety and broken rice kernel. Especially, with the development of neural network, reliable classification and recognition can be finished only through appropriate discipline without regard for the meaning of components of Fourier descriptor.

To verify the usability of the RFD, experiments were carried out on some whole rice kernels and broken ones of China Dongbei long grain rice, Meihe rice and Thai jasmine rice. Results for kernel area, variety distance computation, and rice variety and broken kernel detection using RFD are discussed in the following sections.

## 3.1    Computation of Kernel Area

According to the characteristic of Fourier transform, the first coefficient of Fourier transform reflects the scale information of image. If we take the rice kernel image as a similar circle, we can use $r_a = F_r(0)/N$ representing rice kernel radius approximately. Therefore, we can use the formula $S = k\pi r_a^2$ to approximately express the area of the enclosed region, where $k$ is an adjustment coefficient that can be set to different values for different objects according to experience. Table 1 lists the kernel area results for sample rice kernels. The actual area was obtained using a pixel statistical method. The unit of measurement would be size instead of pixels in practical applications.

**Table 1.** Calculation result of rice kernel area

| Sample | Number | Average area (pixels) | | | |
|---|---|---|---|---|---|
| | | Calculated | Actual | Error | STDEV |
| Broken kernels | 50 | 2538 | 2446 | 238 | 213(8.71%) |
| Whole kernels of Dongbei long grain rice | 50 | 4636 | 4600 | 194 | 205(4.46%) |
| Whole kernels of Meihe rice | 50 | 4516 | 4497 | 167 | 151(3.36%) |
| Whole kernels of Thai jasmine rice | 50 | 4589 | 4551 | 199 | 211(4.64%) |

## 3.2    Shape Similarity

The basis function of the Fourier transform is a set of orthogonal normalization functions. Its transform coefficient is determined by the inner product of the input function (image) and its basis function and is a measure of the similarity of the input and basis functions. Therefore, the distance for RFD spectral vectors can be used to measure the similarity of two contours. To compare rice kernels of different size and resolution, a normalization procedure should be applied to $F_r(u)$ according to:

$$F_{rs}(u) = \frac{F_r(u)}{r_a} \tag{9}$$

The normalized RFD is scale invariance and is only associated with the contour shape and is not related to the size of the rice kernel. Therefore, the distance between the normalized Fourier spectrum vectors for two contours can be used as variety distance for rice variety and broken kernel classification and differentiation. For easy classification, the Euclidean distance $\delta(x_k, x_l)$ is used to describe the contour similarity for rice kernels $x_k$ and $x_l$:

$$\delta(x_k, x_l) = \left[ \sum_{i=1}^{m} \left( \left| F_{rsk}(i) \right| - \left| F_{rsl}(i) \right| \right)^2 \right]^{\frac{1}{2}} \tag{10}$$

Where $m$ is the number of components of the Fourier descriptor. The smaller the $\delta(x_k, x_l)$, the smaller the difference between two rice kernels and the greater their similarity. If $\delta(x_k, x_l) = 0$, the two kernels are identical. Data on shape similarity for different rice samples are listed in Table 2.

**Table 2.** Shape similarity for rice kernels

| Comparison | Number | Average similarity | Variance |
|---|---|---|---|
| Whole Dongbei long grain rice kernels | 50 | 0.027790 | 0.000558 |
| Whole Meihe rice kernels | 50 | 0.026923 | 0.000498 |
| Whole Thai jasmine rice kernels | 50 | 0.028462 | 0.000689 |
| Whole Dongbei long grain rice and Meihe rice kernels | 100 | 0.068235 | 0.000998 |
| Whole Dongbei long grain rice and Thai jasmine rice kernels | 100 | 0.078534 | 0.001521 |
| Whole Thai jasmine rice and Meihe rice kernels | 100 | 0.080236 | 0.001598 |
| Broken kernels | 50 | 0.054914 | 0.001045 |
| Whole and broken kernels[*] | 200 | 0.057136 | 0.001461 |
| Whole and broken kernels[**] | 150+50 | 0.076235 | 0.001416 |

Notes: *The comparison sample is the mixture of whole and broken kernels. **The comparison sample is a group of whole kernels and a group of broken kernels, which means that each whole kernel is compared with every broken kernel and each individual in the group of broken kernels is compared with every individual in the group of whole kernels.

We can see from table 2 that there are significant differences in similarity among different varieties of rice kernels as well as between whole rice kernels and broken rice kernels. Therefore, they can be classified and recognized in theory. We have used artificial neural network to recognize rice kernels with high efficiency.

### 3.3    Recognition of Rice Kernels Using an Artificial Neural Network

A BP neural network was used as the classifier. The network structure has three layers: an input layer, a hidden layer, and an output layer. There are nine nodes in the input layer, corresponding to the first nine RFD components. There are two nodes in the output layer, considering network expansibility. Suppose that an output of 00 denotes a standard rice kernel and an output of 11 denotes a broken kernel. Experimental tests revealed that there can be four hidden nodes, Tansig can be used for the activation function, and the YPROP algorithm can be used to deal with the problem of low convergence speed.

A sample of 200 rice kernels (150 whole and 50 broken) was used to train the network and then to determine the network weight value. Another sample of 800 rice kernels (600 whole and 200 broken) were used as test samples for classification. The test results are presented in Table 3.

**Table 3.** Detection of broken rice using a BP neural network

| Sample | Number | Number detected | Accuracy (%) |
|---|---|---|---|
| Whole Dongbei long grain rice kernels | 200 | 196 | 98 |
| Whole Meihe rice kernels | 200 | 192 | 96 |
| Whole Thai jasmine rice kernels | 200 | 200 | 100 |
| Broken rice kernels | 200 | 193 | 96.5 |

# 4    Conclusions

In this research we developed an improved Fourier descriptor, a radius Fourier descriptor. Experimental test indicated that this RFD includes almost all the shape information of rice kernel. It is evident that we can calculate rice kernel area and differentiate rice variety and broken kernels using RFD. As a result, only using the first 9 RFD components we can reproduce rice contours without distortion and retain almost all of the feature information. Without concern for the initial starting point on the contour, this method is simple and the dimension of the feature vector can be reduced greatly. Taking China Dongbei long grain rice, Meihe rice, and Thai jasmine rice as examples, area of rice kernels and variety distance between different rice samples were calculated and a backpropagation neural network was tested for detection of broken rice kernels. The detection accuracy for whole rice kernels of different samples was 96%-100% and for broken rice kernels was 96.5%. Combined with backpropagation neural network, we can classify rice variety accurately. Moreover, the RFD has the following advantages for describing the contours of rice kernels:

1. Uniqueness: the Fourier transform is a one-to-one mapping and one descriptor set corresponds to one boundary contour image.
2. Shift invariance: The transform coefficient of the RFD relies only on the boundary shape and is not related to the image position.
3. Rotation invariance: Image rotation only changes the phase spectrum of descriptor and the power spectrum does not change.
4. Scale invariance: The descriptor is scale-invariant after normalization.
5. Precise description: An image boundary can be totally restored using the RFD, which is impossible using other boundary description methods.
6. Low dimensionality of the feature vector: Fewer components are required to describe the boundary and the Euclidean distance is used for easy classification.

The RFD provides a means to analyze the shape of rice kernels in the frequency domain. It also provides a reference scheme for shape analysis of other agricultural products. For example, it has practical significance for quality assessment, classification and recognition of fruit, vegetables, seeds and other agricultural products.

Known limitations: when the RFD, which using amplitude spectrum of Fourier transform to describe rice shape, is used to do rice variety recognition, some preparation should be done in advance. If using variety distance, the average of standard rice kernels' descriptor should be calculated for statistics; if using artificial neural network, the standard sample should be used for training.

**Acknowledgments.** This research was partially supported by the Innovation and Technology Fund of Shandong Agricultural University of China, the Provincial Scholarship Fund of Shandong, China. The authors would like to thank the anonymous reviewers for the many useful observations that greatly contributed to improve the overall quality of the paper.

# References

1. Ren, X.Z., Ma, X.Y.: Research advances of agricultural product grain shape identification and current situation of its application in the engineering field. Trans. Chin. Soc. Agric. Eng. 20(3), 276–280 (2004) (in Chinese)
2. Wang, F.J.: Rice Quality Detection Based on Digital Image Processing. Journal of Anhui Agricultural Sciences 38(22), 11998–11999, 12056 (2010) (in Chinese)
3. Shi, L.J., Wen, Y.X., Mou, T.M., Xu, J.Y.: Application Progress of Machine Vision Technology in Grain Detection. Hubei Agricultural Science 48(6), 1514–1518 (2009) (in Chinese)
4. Kilic, K., Boyaci, I.H., Koksel, H.: A classification system for beans using computer vision system and artificial neural networks. Journal of Food Engineering 78(3), 897–904 (2007)
5. Wang, B.T., Sun, J.A., Cai, A.N.: Relative moments and their applications to geometric shape recognition. Journal of Image and Graphics 6(3), 296–300 (2001) (in Chinese)
6. Nii, K., Kawabata, S.: Assessment of the Association between the Three-dimensional Shape of the Corolla and Two-dimensional Shapes of Petals Using Fourier Descriptors and Principal Component Analysis in Eustoma grandiflorum. Journal of the Japanese Society for Horticultural 80(2), 200–205 (2011)
7. Suzuki, K., Zheng, Z.Y., Tamura, Y.: Establishment of a Quantitative Evaluation Method of Rice Plant Type Using P-type Fourier Descriptors. Plant Production Science 14(2), 105–110 (2011)
8. Zhao, S.Q., Ding, W.M., Liu, D.Y.: Rice Hopper Shape Recognition Based on Fourier Descriptors. Transactions of the Chinese Society for Agricultural Machinery 40(8), 181–184, 160 (2009)
9. Wei, Y., He, Y.W., Ni, H.F., Zhang, W.: Review on shape representation techniques and their applications in image retrieval. Systems Engineering and Electronics 31(7), 1755–1762 (2009)
10. Zhang, D.S., Lu, G.J.: Review of shape representation and description techniques. Pattern Recognition 37, 1–19 (2004)
11. Ling, Y., Wang, Y.M., Sun, M., Zhang, X.C.: Application of watershed algorithm to paddy image segmentation. Trans. Chin. Soc. Agric. Mach. 36(3), 95–98 (2005) (in Chinese)
12. Gao, H., Wang, Y.Q.: Study on the shape classification of farm produce based on computer vision. Comput. Eng. Appl. (14), 227-229 (2004) (in Chinese)
13. Wang, Y.Q., Gao, H.: Research on the feature description of similar round object. Computer Engineering 30(1), 158–169, 162 (2004) (in Chinese)

# Traceability System of Pig-Raising Process and Quality Safety on 3G

Benhai Xiong[1,2,*], Qingyao Luo[1,2], Liang Yang[1,2], and Jiayi Pan[1,2]

[1] Institute of Animal Science, Chinese Academy of Agricultural Sciences,
Beijing 100193, China
[2] Satte Key Laboratory of Animal Nutrition, Beijing 100193, China

**Abstract.** In view of existed not flexibility and low efficiency in establishing feeding file of large-scale farms or farmer farms of pigs, by adopting intelligent PDA or mobile phone as application platform, combining with .Net 2005 language and SQL Server 2005 CE database as well as TD-SCDMA wireless wide band communication linking Internet as data transmission method, this study suggested data criterions on feeding process information collection of pigs, and developed a mobile PDA or phone system to track swine feeding process data, such as operators and main inputs, and to trace pork quality safety. The running of the system shows that it realized all kinds of data collecting and wireless submission including ear tag wearing and movements, immunity events, feeds and veterinary drugs used as well as casual inspection data, and also achieved remote data maintaining for pig's feeding files and deepness inquiry to pork quality. The system not only makes up a deficiency from table data recording system for feeding file setting of a large-scale swine farm, but also is a kind of effective solution for farmer farm to set up swine feeding files. Furthermore, the system is a kind of mobile and convenient supervising tool to service official veterinarian to carry out their work. Finally, with the TD-SCDMA technology prevalence and communication fee decrease, the system will take part in a important role in constructing Chinese pork quality safety traceability system.

**Keywords:** Intelligent PDA, 3G, Live pigs, Feeding files, Quality traceability.

## 1    Introduction

Since a case of the Bovine spongiform encephalopathy（BSE） occurred in Britain in 1986, zoonoses such as BSE , highly pathogenic avian influenza (HPAI) and food quality safety problems such as Sudan red powder, melamine milk and Clenbuterol pork happened occasionally and so have been paid wide attention[1]. The case of Shuanghui Clenbuterol pork[2], reported by the CCTV on March 15,2010, showed again great potential problems for the food safety and the importance of supervision and traceability of animal product quality. Early in this century, some developed countries and regions set up trade barriers such as technical regulations, standards and conformity assessment procedures on the advantage of science and technology,

---

* Corresponding author.

D. Li and Y. Chen (Eds.): CCTA 2011, Part I, IFIP AICT 368, pp. 115–123, 2012.

management and environmental protection and established new threshold for Chinese export, especially for animal product export. From 1 January 2002, the European Union (EU) legislation ((EC) No 178/2002) require that all products sold in shops must have traceability labels, including the country of birth, fattening, slaughter, slaughterhouse ID, segmentation packaging country , segmentation grant No, whether European Union membership is and so on. Canada began to construct traceability system for individual identification, move and premises identification about cattle, sheep and swine as the earliest as 2001, developed the first traceability system in 2003, respectively published the first edition (Can-Trance standard) in 2003, and second edition of the agricultural traceability standard based on EAN.UCC information identification and bar code traceability system in 2006. These standards for all the food in Canada are not mandatory. U.S. introduced the biological invasion movement framework in 2002 and all foods sold in the United States, including US and other country food, must been registered in the U.S. food and drug administration (FDA). Importers and processors have the obligation to record information about their middle suppliers and buyers for 2 years at least, and must copy the records in order to accept the FDA investigation. Subsequently in 2007, FDA also announced food protection plan (FPP) to improve food security and strengthen traceability in the food processing and distribution processes[3,4,5].

In China, animal product quality traceability system began with animal epidemic prevention system led by the ministry of agriculture in 2002[3]. After the animal husbandry and law enacted in 2005, "the Administrative Rules on identification and rearing files for animal and poultry" was issued by the Ministry of Agriculture[6] and put in effect on July 1,2006. The rules proposed specific norms for identification and rearing files in pig-rearing link. Then, State council of China issued "the administrative regulations on pig slaughter"[7] on May 1, 2008 and took effect on August 1, 2008, which  mainly provides legal base for supervising pig-slaughtering link by commerce departments according to law.

3G is able to provide high-speed data business and is the new generation mobile communication combining with wireless communication, multimedia communication technologies. TD-SCDMA is a 3G technology standard proposed by China based on international cooperation[8]. The technology convergence of wireless 3G network data transmission and international Internet system provide new technology means for expanding safety supervision and quality traceability for pig and products.

By the means of 3G technologies and PDA or mobile intelligent system, this study attempts to develop the mobile data collection and transmit system for main inputs in pig-producing link, and mobile terminal for government supervision and traceability enquiry, and provide technical reserves for exploring whole tracking and traceability solution in different pig-rearing models and network environments

# 2     Materials and Methods

## 2.1     Research Object

This study takes commercial pig-raising farms or household farmers as the research model, pig individual and pork end-product as the research object in order to study data collection solution in pig-raising link and traceability inquires on end product.

## 2.2    Individual Code and Ear Tag for Pig

According to the administrative rule, a pig must have a unique logo code, which consists of 15 digit code. The first digit represents the category of animal, for example, 1 represents pig; Then the subsequent 6 digits represent administrative district code in where pig farms are located, corresponding with GB T2260-1999[9]; the next eight digits from the 8th to the 15th is pig individual No in the same district.

## 2.3    Data Standards for Pig-Raising Process

In the pig-raising link, the required collection information includes responsible body information including pig-raising farm or farmer, pig individual identification, main inputs (feed, veterinary drugs, vaccine) and supervision test such as test results for Clenbuterol. As the space is limited, only part data standards listed in the study are respectively for responsible body (table 1), pig identification (table 2), vaccine (table 3), supervision and inspection (table 4). Mobile data collection in the raising link also based on the data standards.

**Table 1.** Base information for farm

| Name | Field Name | type | Length | IsNull |
|------|-----------|------|--------|--------|
| Owner ID | FARM_ID | string | 20 | not |
| Owner | FARM _NAME | string | 50 | |
| Farm type | FARM _TYPE | string | 10 | |
| Address | FARM_ADDR | string | 100 | |
| legal representative | LEGAL_PERSON | string | 20 | |
| Record date | RECORD_DATE | date | 8 | |
| communication Address | ADDR | string | 100 | |
| Post code | POSTAL_CODE | string | 6 | |
| telephone | TEL | string | 20 | |
| fax | FAX | string | 20 | |

**Table 2.** Individual data for swine

| Name | Field Name | type | Length | IsNull |
|------|-----------|------|--------|--------|
| Owner | FARM_NAME | string | 50 | not |
| Animal type | BREED_TYPE | string | 20 | not |
| Pigsty | PEN_No | number | 10 | |
| Use | PURPOSE | string | 10 | |
| Ear tag digit | EAG_No | number | 2 | |
| County | REGION | string | 40 | not |
| Ear tag ID | PIG_ID | string | 15 | |
| Buy date | BUY_DATE | date | 8 | |
| note | NOTE | string | 50 | |

**Table 3.** Data of used vaccine

| Name | Field Name | type | Length | IsNull |
|------|-----------|------|--------|--------|
| Ear tag ID | PIG_ID | string | 15 | not |
| Vaccine name | VACCINE_NAME | string | 50 | not |
| source | VACCINE _SOURCE | string | 50 | |
| batch | VACCINE_BATCH | string | 50 | |
| method | IMMUN_METHOD | string | 50 | |
| Beginning date | IMMUN_DATE | date | 8 | |
| End date | IMMUN_DATE | date | 8 | |
| person | IMMUN_PERSON | string | 10 | |
| note | NOTE | string | 50 | |

**Table 4.** Data of supervision

| Name | Field Name | type | Length | IsNull |
|---|---|---|---|---|
| Ear tag ID | PIG_ID | string | 15 | Not |
| No | CHECH_ID | string | 20 | |
| item | CHECH_ITEM | string | 30 | Not |
| Method | CHECH_METHOD | string | 20 | |
| Result | CHECH_RESULT | string | 10 | Not |
| date | CHECK_DATE | date | 20 | |
| Unit | CHECK_UNIT | string | 50 | |
| Person | CHECH_PERSON | string | 20 | |
| note | NOTE | string | 50 | |

### 2.4    Development Environment

System development adopts Microsoft Visual Studio, Windows mobile 6.0 SDK, SQL mobile 2005, Visual c #, Microsoft ActiveSync 4.5[10,11]. A PDA or smart phone collect, submit the collected data to the Tianjin pork quality traceability central database constructed by XiongBenHai (2009)[12], or modify and query uploaded data remotely.

### 2.5    Technical Route of System Development

As shown in Fig 1, system models contain user management model solving user extent to different data use, raising files model including collection and transmission of data, supervision and inspection model for official vet to treat test results for hormone, sulfonamides and heavy metal residues for marketing pigs and for government easily to know sampling supervision results, tracing inquiry model to provide different levels of query service for government supervision department and consumers.

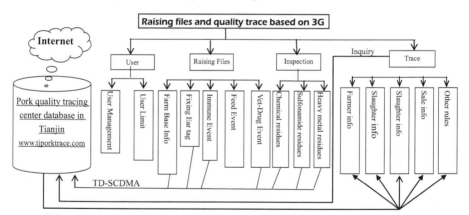

**Fig. 1.** Function structure of embed system on pig feeding process data collection and final product quality inquiry

## 3    Results and Analysis

According to pig identification code, data collection standards, hardware and software development environments and technology framework of system function design suggested from 2.1 to 2.5, mobile construction of pig-raising files and traceability inquiry system based on intelligent PDA or phone is developed. Main results are as follows:

## 3.1    Collection of Pig Individual Identification

Fig 2 showed the running interface for fixing ear-tag, 15-digit code can be not only manually typed in and also scanned by PDA in batches. Considering PDA's memory capacity, the max number of reading or inputting ear-tag is 20 every operation. Collecting data can save in the mobile client or IC card in .txt file format in order to subsequent data treatment, also synchronize to PC or directly submit to remote pork quality traceability center database by GPRS (2G) or TD-SCDMA(3G).

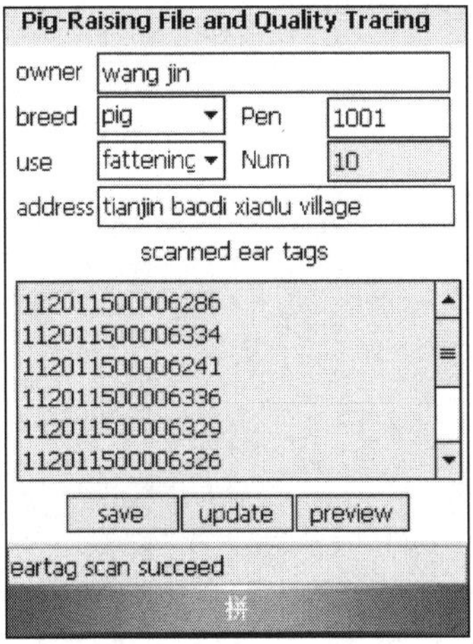

**Fig. 2.** Tag wearing, data collection and submission for pig

## 3.2    Collection of Pig Immunity Event

Fig 3 shows treatment model for pig immune event. After ear tag number is inputted or scanned, immune information is inputted. Of which used vaccine information is stored in the system database and can selected in the running period and reduced cumbersome text-entry. Inputting data generally submits to remote center database.

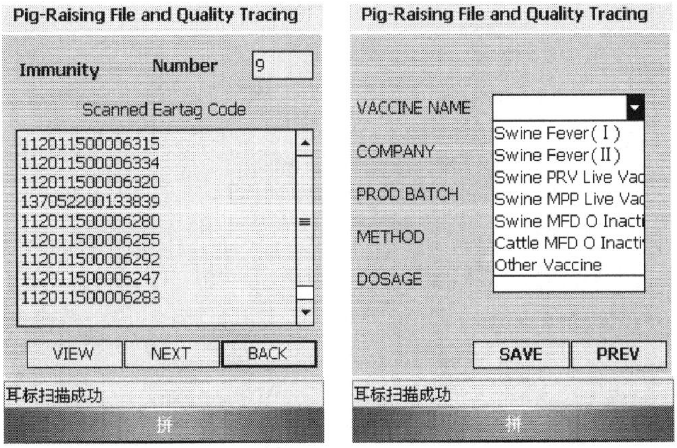

**Fig. 3.** Immunity events and data collecting for pigs

### 3.3    Collection and Transmission of Sampling Test Result by Official Supervisor

Sampling inspection for residual toxic and harmful substance in body of pigs for sale is an important part to ensure pork quality safety. In general, official supervisors assigned by animal epidemic prevention and supervision department are in charge of sampling inspection in links of pig production, pig slaughter and pig distribution. At present, main inspective items are respectively Clenbuterol, sulfonamides and drugs residues. When accessing to data collection interface like Fig 4, users must pass limit confirmation and then can collect and transmit data. The input interface of inspection result in the right does not present until one or one batch ear tag code is inputted. Furthermore, the device system date on the mobile client is also uploaded as the sampling inspection date when the data is saved or uploaded.

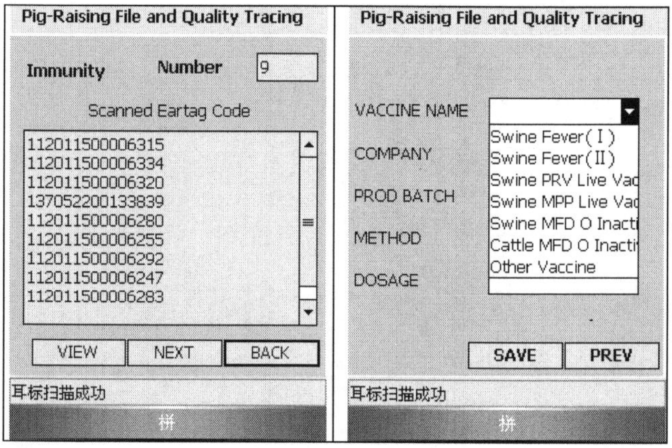

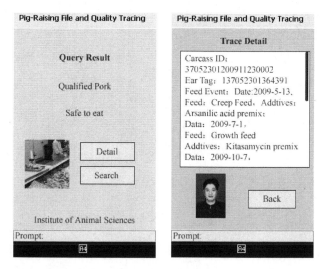

**Fig. 4.** Sampling inspection data collecting and submission for pigs

**Fig. 5.** Output of traceability inquiry results based on 3G system

### 3.4    Mobile Inquiry of Carved Pork

As shown in Fig 5, by tracing model running on PDA, input 20-digit traceability code on the package ("37052301200912300002") and then receive the inquiry result. Regarding to 3G communication ability, the image transmission function is designed in the systematic inquiry interface, for example, sale image, official supervisor's image. More detail information also includes different inputs information.

## 4    Discussion

China is a big pig producing country, the number of pigs for sale reaches up to 640 million in 2009, pork production up to 48 890 thousand tons, both rank the first in the world[13]. But for pig production mode, both large sized commercial production and small scale backyard production will exist in a rather long period. How to build effect pork quality traceability system from pig production to consumer dinning-table is heavy responsibility for consumers' right and food safety despite of a difficult task. Therefore, exploring different modes of tracking and tracing technology solution of pork production for different requirement environments should prepare for a rainy day.

Normally, because producing number in large-scale commercial farms is big, their production and management are also standard, hardware and software in the information technology application is better than small-size farms and backyard farmers, pig-raising files data in raising process is collected by computer record and internet transmit system, batch data treatment is able to be accomplished[12]. Nevertheless, if there is the communication signal of GPRS or 3G within farm, the mobile data collection system is able to be used for recording part key data and modifying data in the center database by farmer technician or area official vet, especially fro sampling inspection information for pigs raised or for sale. In fact, the raising files for commercial farmers is conducted by farmer technicians and supervised by area official vet at present. The mobile system provides a mobile supervision means for supervisors.

Next, for free-range pig-raising farmers, constructing computer data recording and internet transmit system is not practical, so the mobile data collection solution is improved from that of 2009 based on GPRS technology [14]. Free-range farmer raising files on the remote server can be established for certain quality farmers with proper training and area official vet's help. Obviously, establishing pig-raising electronic files by this system is simpler than that based on computer, without warning function for feed additives and veterinary drugs' withdrawal period. But, it can meet general traceability requirement of consumers.

For the end product traceability, traceability inquiry based on 3G has obvious advantages comparing to that on GPRS technology developed by Xiong (2009), this study introduces image's inquiry and view (Fig 4). At present, although just trying to display supervisor and sale scene pictures, as supervision ticketing in deferent traceability points are put into effect in the future, they are directly viewed in relative links, especially for ticketing of illegal drugs in order to meet traceability right for high-grade consumers. Obviously, all these need 3G technology. With the rapid development of 3G technology, continuously increasing effective area and deducing charges, 3G technology application of the mobile traceability inquires will be more and more.

# 5    Conclusion

Tracking and traceability for the whole production process of pig and pork products is a focused issue widely concerned by governments at all levels and consumers at present and in a quite long time period and is also a test of government ability for people. This study showed that using smart PDA or phone, 3G wireless wide band network communication technology as well with internet, provide a solution of Chinese pig-raising information in the process of pig production, which includes mobile collection and transmit solution for farm manager and pig individual ID, main inputs in pig production, multimedia traceability solution such as that of image and text based on 3G. The developed system has been applied in Tianjin pork quality traceability network platform and application effects achieve the systematic design goal. The study is supplement for constructing pig-raising electronic files in commercial farms and may be a whole solution for free-range pig-raising farmers and can meet for high level consumers' right. As the rapid development of TD-SCDMA network service and decrease of service fee, data tracking and quality traceability in the whole pig production based on 3G technologies will be vast potential for future development.

**Acknowledgements.** Funding were provided by the national high technology research and development program of China (863 Program) (2006AA10Z266), Tianjin municipal science & technology Innovation fund (06FZZDNC0100) and the national science & technology program (2009ZX03001-019).

# References

1. Lu, C.H., Wang, C.J., Hu, Y.N.: Animals and their Products Identification Technologies as well as Traceability Management, pp. 46–47. Chinese Agricultural Science & Technology Press, Beijing (2007) (in Chinese)
2. CCTV.: Special View: Clenbuterol pork into Shuanghui (2011),
   http://stock.jrj.com.cn/2011/03/1618499472023-1.shtml
   (in Chinese)
3. http://www.foodsafetynetwork.ca/aspx/public/
   publication_detail.aspx?id=80:foodTraceability(2011)
4. U.S. Food and Drug Administration.: FDA Food Protection Plan six-month summary (2008). Retrieved from, http://www.fda.gov/oc/initiatives/
   advance/food/progressreport.html (2010)
5. United States Department of Agriculture(USDA): Marketing and Regulatory Programs Animal and Plant Health Inspection Service. National Animal Identification System (NAIS)- Technical Supplement to Draft Program Standards,
   http://animalid.aphis.usda.gov/nais

6. Decree No 67 of the Ministry of Agriculture, China.: The administrative rule on identification and farming files of livestock and poultry (2006) (in Chinese), http://www.agri.gov.cn/blgg/t20060628_638621.htm

7. Decree No 525 of the State Council of China.: Administrative rule on pig slaughter (2010), http://www.gov.cn/zwgk/2008-05/30/content_1000067.htm (in Chinese)

8. Fan T.H.: Development study for wide wireless communication technology: Chinese high technology enterprises 5, 63–67 (2004) (in Chinese)

9. National Bureau of Statistics of China.: Administrative districts code for the People's Republic of China (2006) (in Chinese), http://www.stats.gov.cn/tjbz/xzqhdm/t20070411_402397928.htm

10. Fu, X., Qi, N., Xu, J.: Windows Mobile telephone application and development. Posts & Telecom Press, Beijing (2005) (in Chinese)

11. Luan, C.H., Wang, M.: The design and study of the embedded internet based on GPRS. Microcomputer Information 17(22), 94–96 (2006) (in Chinese)

12. Xiong, B.H., Lin, Z.H.: A Solution on Pork Quality Safety Production Traceability from Farm to Dining Table-Taking Tianjin City as an Example. Agricultural Sciences in China 42(1), 230–237 (2009) (in Chinese)

13. Gao, H.B.: Animal almanac of China. China Agriculture Press, Beijing (2008) (in Chinese)

14. Xiong, B.H., Fu, R.T., Lin, Z.H.: Identification of Swine Individuals and Construction of Traceability System under Free-range Pig-rearing System. Transactions of the CSAE 25(3), 98–102 (2009) (in Chinese)

# An Audio Generator System for Experimental Studies on Acoustic Biology

Weiming Cai, Huinong He, and Songming Zhu*

College of Biosystems Engineering and Food Science, Zhejiang University,
Hangzhou 310058, China
zhusm@zju.edu.cn

**Abstract.** There are studies indicate that audible sound wave could have effects on propagation growth through catalyzing hearing sense organs, which would bring a series of physiological and biological chemistry reaction. The sound-pressure level and frequency are important factors in propagation growth. In this study, an experimental system of audio generator was developed for investigating sound wave effect on propagation growth promotion, and an embedded development platform based on ARM+DSP+FPGA was built for the system. The DDFS（Direct Digital Frequency Synthesis）method was used to make various waveforms in the system. A feedback analysis networks was added in the system for reliable output of sound waves. Results show that the audio generator system can produce sound waves with frequency of 20 Hz~20,000Hz accurately and make octave analysis of the sound in experimental environments. The new-type audio generator system will facilitate scientific researches on the field of acoustic biology.

**Keywords:** Audio Generator System, Acoustic Biology, ARM+DSP+FPGA, DDFS, Sound Wave.

## 1 Introduction

Audible sound, as a sort of sound waves, whose frequency is between 20Hz and 20,000Hz, widely exists in natural environment. In recent years, there have been studies relating to sound and the growth and health of plants or animals, including human beings (Chabris, 1999; Creath and Schwartz, 2004; Collins and Foreman, 2001). It has been hypothesized that sound increases growth in plants, and some companies even use a growth system that incorporates sound to try to increase growth. Studies have been done on the use of music to improve crop yield and quality in plants such as tomato plants (Hou and Mooneyham, 1999), barley (Xiao, 1991), and vegetables (Hou et al., 2009); Hou et al. (2009) used audible sound waves to stimulate more than 50 different crops, and achieved remarkable effects. This field of science is known as acoustic biology. Up to now, why plants or animals are subjected to sound waves in order to improve crop yield, quality, and animal health is still

---

* Corresponding author.

D. Li and Y. Chen (Eds.): CCTA 2011, Part I, IFIP AICT 368, pp. 124–132, 2012.

unknown. Not much study was done in this area, as there was a lack of precise instruments to facilitate propagation growth studies in the acoustic biology field as well as a lack of proven scientific theories in this area.

Direct digital frequency synthesis (DDFS) is a method of producing an analog arbitrary waveform (Jeng et al., 2010; Chen and Chau, 2010). The operations within DDFS devices are primarily digital; it can offer faster switching between output frequencies, operation over a broader spectrum of frequencies and better frequency resolution than traditional ways (Shmelev, 2006; Shen, 2010). A practical DDFS system is often realized in hardware platform. ARM+DSP+FPGA is a new-type platform for complex system development, algorithm verification, prototype trial-manufacture, and prototype evaluation (e.g. multimedia processing system, digital communication system, and high performance instrument prototype development), and it haven't been used to design audio generator before, although it is ideal for us to perform high performance system verification and instrument development.

Therefore, in order to offer a scientific research instrument for the study of sound wave effect on propagation growth promotion in the field of acoustic biology and explore a new way in making high-performance audio generators, a new-type audio generator system based on ARM+DSP+FPGA and Technology of DDFS was proposed in the paper.

## 2     Principles and Methods

### 2.1     Technology of Direct Digital Frequency Synthesis (DDFS)

A basic Direct Digital Frequency Synthesizer consists of a phase accumulator, phase-to-amplitude converter (a Waveform Memory), a Digital-to-Analog Converter and filter as shown in Fig. 1.

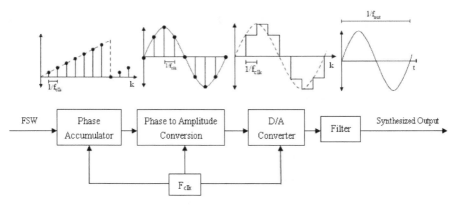

**Fig. 1.** Block diagram of DDFS

The frequency of synthesized output depends on three variables: a reference-clock frequency $F_{clk}$ and a binary number programmed into the phase register (frequency setting word *d*), the length of accumulator *k*. When a sine signal is recorded in the waveform memory, the phase accumulator computes a phase (angle) address for the waveform memory, which outputs the digital value of amplitude (phase angle) to the DAC. The DAC, in turn, converts the number to a corresponding value of analog voltage or current. To generate a fixed-frequency sine wave, a constant value (the phase increment determined by the binary number *d*) is added to the phase accumulator with each clock cycle. When the phase increment is large, the phase accumulator will step quickly through the sine record in the waveform memory and thus generate a high frequency sine wave. When the phase increment is small, the phase accumulator will take many more steps, accordingly generating a slower waveform.

If $F_{clk}$ is the clock frequency, then the frequency of the output sine wave can be described as follows:

$$F_{out} = \frac{d * F_{clk}}{2^k} \qquad 2^{k-1} > d \geq 1 \qquad (1)$$

Where: $F_{out}$ is the output frequency of DDFS; *d* is the frequency setting word; *n* (in bits) is the length of the phase accumulator; $F_{clk}$ is the system clock frequency.

Equation (1) is known as the tuning equation of DDFS. Any change to the value of *d* results in immediate and phase-continuous changes in the output frequency. In a DDFS, no loop settling time is incurred as in the case of a PLL. As the output frequency is increased, the number of samples per cycle decreases. According to sampling theory, at least two samples per cycle are required to reconstruct the output waveform; the maximum fundamental output frequency of a DDFS is $2F_{clk}$. However, for practical applications, the output frequency is limited to somewhat less than that for improving the quality of the reconstructed waveform and permitting filtering on the output.

## 2.2     Audio Generator Based on ARM+DSP+FPGA and DDFS

An embedded development platform based on ARM, DSP, and FPGA was set up for the design of audio generator system. As shown in Fig. 2, the embedded development platform consists of a C6-Integra DSP+ARM Processor OMAP-L137, a Xilinx Spartan™-3A FPGA Platform--XC3S50A, a D/A converter CS4341, an A/D converter AK5350, sound sensor, User interface (LCD and Touch screen), Communication interface (USB and RS-232), and so on.

The OMAP-L137 C6-Integra™ (Texas Instruments Incorporated, 2010) is a processor of low-power applications based on an ARM926EJ-S and a C674x DSP core, and it enables us to quickly bring to devices featuring robust operating systems support, rich user interfaces, and high processing performance through the maximum flexibility of fully integrated mixed processor solutions. The ARM926EJ-S is a 32-bit RISC processor core that performs 32-bit or 16-bit instructions and processes 32-bit, 16-bit, or 8-bit data, and the core uses pipelining so that all parts of the processor and

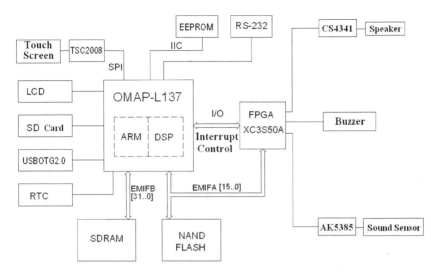

**Fig. 2.** Schematic diagram of embedded platform for audio generator design

memory system can operate continuously. The OMAP-L137 DSP core uses a two-level cache-based architecture: the Level 1 program cache (L1P) is a 32KB direct mapped cache and the Level 1 data cache (L1D) is a 32KB 2-way set-associative cache; the Level 2 program cache (L2P) consists of a 256KB memory space that is shared between program and data space. L2 memory can be configured as mapped memory, cache, or combinations of the two. Although the DSP L2 is accessible by ARM and other hosts in the system, an additional 128KB RAM shared memory is available for use by other hosts without affecting DSP performance. In our design, the functions such as User interface, frequency setting control for the DDFS system, feedback analysis for output sound waves are mainly depend on the OMAP-L137 processor, which is one of the cores in the design of audio generator.

The Spartan-3A FPGA XC3S50A (Xilinx, 2007) is one of programmable chips with 1.4M system gates, and 502 I/Os, with density migration. The phase accumulator and phase to amplitude conversion of DDFS is realized through programming in the FPGA; the FPGA also was used to the data communications and external state control in our design.

The CS4341 is a complete stereo digital-to-analog system including digital interpolation, fourth-order Delta-Sigma digital-to-analog conversion, digital de-emphasis and switched capacitor analog filtering. The advantages of this architecture include: ideal differential linearity, no distortion mechanisms due to resistor matching errors, no linearity drift over time and temperature and a high tolerance to clock jitter. The CS4341 can accept data at audio sample rates from 4 kHz to 100 kHz. There is a filter in the inner of CS4341. So it is not necessary for us to design additional filter for the DDFS module.

The AK5385A is a 24 bit, 192 kHz sampling 2ch A/D converter for high-end audio system. The modulator in the AK5385A uses the Enhanced Dual Bit architecture and the AK5385A realizes high accuracy and low cost. The AK5385A performs 114dB dynamic range, which can meet the dynamic range from 0 dB to 110dB of our design requirement. By using a sound pressure sensor, the A/D converter and programming in the OMAP-L137 (the sound analysis are mainly made by the C674x DSP core), the feedback analysis network can be accomplished.

# 3     Results and Discussion

In order to see whether the accomplished audio generator system can satisfy the demand of studies of sound wave effect on propagation growth promotion, a series of tests were conducted.

Fig. 3 is the time domain signal graph of sound wave detected by the feedback block of the accomplished audio generator system when a sine wave with frequency of 1000Hz was inputted from the User interface of the generator. The generator system can produce sound wave signals with frequencies range from 20Hz to 20,000Hz for the speaker.

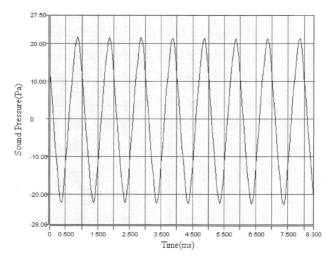

**Fig. 3.** Time domain signal graph of 1000Hz sound wave

Natural sound such as cricket sound may have effect on propagation growth according to many studies (Chabris, 1999; Creath and Schwartz, 2004; Collins and Foreman, 2001; Hou et al., 2009). The generator can simulate the cricket or other insects' or birds' sound for the studies and the sound frequency can also be analyzed by the generator. Fig.4 is the time domain signal graph of sound wave detected by the feedback block of the accomplished audio generator when cricket sound wave was inputted from the User interface of the generator.

Sound-level measurements offer a conventional way to measure sound but do not contain frequency information, making it difficult to compare different sounds effect in our research. Octave analysis filters the signal and measures the energy at the

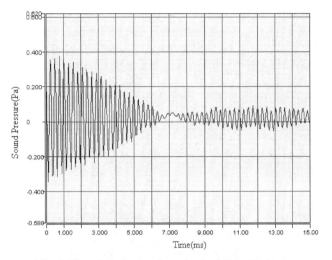

**Fig. 4.** Time domain signal graph of cricket sound wave

output to provide useful frequency information. With fractional-octave analysis, we can select a frequency resolution that is well adapted to the signal of interest. In a word, Octave analysis is a valuable tool for visual inspection and comparison during our researches. The new-type audio generator system offer octave analysis of output sound both for the output regulation and frequency information.

Some octave analysis was made by the generator system when the test work was conducted. The results can be seen in Figs. 5-8.

Fig. 5 shows the octave analysis chart of background noise in our testing environment. The background noise is also a factor in the research on propagation growth. So it will give us deeper understanding on the grow environment and help to explore growth promotion secrets to analysis background noise.

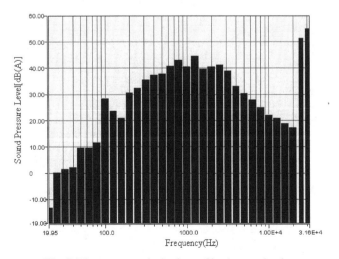

**Fig. 5.** The octave analysis chart of background noise

Fig. 6 is the octave analysis chart of cricket sound. Through the octave analysis on cricket sound, we can find that frequencies around 4000Hz are main frequency components in cricket sound. This offers us a scientific way in study of insects' sound effect on propagation growth.

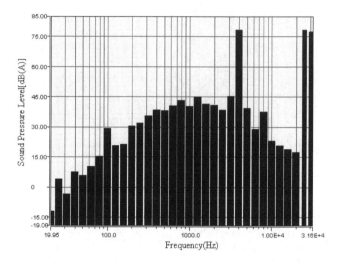

**Fig. 6.** The octave analysis chart of cricket sound

Fig. 7 shows the octave analysis chart of thrush sound. Through the octave analysis on thrush sound, it can be found that frequencies around 2000Hz are main frequency components in thrush sound. This offers us a scientific way in study of birds' sound effect on propagation growth.

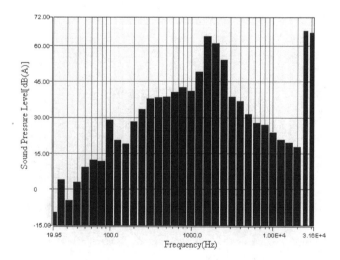

**Fig. 7.** The octave analysis chart of thrush sound

Fig. 8 is the octave analysis chart of a slice of Mozart music (Allegro Molto). Through the octave analysis on Mozart music, it can be found that frequencies around 1500Hz are main frequency components in the Mozart music. This offers us a scientific way in study of music effect on propagation growth.

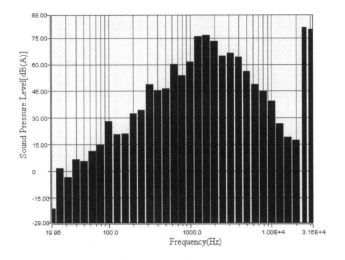

**Fig. 8.** The octave analysis chart of Mozart music (Allegro Molto)

From the test results described above, It can be found that the new-type audio generator system designed in the study not only can produce varies kind of sound wave but also can monitor the sound output and make analysis of the sound wave in the experimental environment. When we make researches on sound wave effects of propagation growth promotion, it is very important to load a specific sound exactly and understand the environment sound characteristic. Therefore, the audio generator designed in the study will be a useful tool to studies in the field of acoustic biology.

# 4    Conclusions

A new-type audio generator system was designed for the study of sound wave effect on propagation growth promotion in the acoustic biology field. The generator system can produce varies kind of sound required in the study of acoustic biology, and it can also do octave analysis of the sound wave in the experiment environments for acoustic biology researchers.

Unlike most of traditional audio generator systems, the generator designed in this study is based on a new embedded development platform with the ARM+DSP+FPGA core and DDFS technology, which enable us to make feedback analysis networks for the output sound and generate arbitrary waveforms.

**Acknowledgments.** Research grant support from the Key Laboratory of Eco-Agricultural Environmental Engineering and Intelligent Equipment of China Agricultural Ministry (Grant Number: 588040*172210214[2]) is acknowledged.

# References

1. Chabris, C.: Prelude or requiem for the "Mozart effect"? Nature 400, 826–827 (1999)
2. Collins, M., Foreman, J.: The effect of sound on the growth of plants. Canadian Acoustics 29, 3–8 (2001)
3. Creath, K., Schwartz, G.E.: Measuring Effects of Music, Noise, and Healing Energy Using a Seed Germination Bioassay. The Journal of Alternative and Complementary Medicine 10(1), 113–122 (2004)
4. Jeong, M.J., Shim, C.K., Lee, J.O.: Plant genes responses to frequency-specific sound signals. Molecular Breeding 21(2), 217–226 (2008)
5. Hou, T., Mooneyham, R.: Applied studies of Plant Meridien System: I. The Effect of Agri-wave Technology on Yield and Quality of Tomato. American Journal of Chinese Medicine 27, 1–10 (1999)
6. Xiao, H.: Vegetables and music. Pictorial Science 6, 36 (1991)
7. Hou, T., Luan, J., Wang, J., Li, M.: Experimental evidence of a plant meridien system III: The Sound Chracteristics of Phylodendron (Alocasia) and the Effects of Acupuncture on those Properties. American Journal of Chinese Medicine 22, 205–214 (1994)
8. Hou, T., Li, B., Guanghui, T., et al.: Application of acoustic frequency technology to protected vegetable production. Transactions of the Chinese Society of Agricultural Engineering 25(2), 156–159 (2009) (in Chinese)
9. Jeng, S., Lin, H., Wu, C.: High-Performance DDFS Design Using the Equi-Section Division Method. IEEE Transaction on Ultrasonics Ferroelectrics and Frequency Control 57(12), 2616–2626 (2010)
10. Chen, Y., Chau, Y.: A Direct Digital Frequency Synthesizer Based on a New Form of Polynomial Approximations. IEEE Transactions on Consumer Electronics 56(2), 436–440 (2010)
11. Shmelev, O.: A two-channel multi-tone computer audio-frequency generator. Measurement Techniques 49(1), 57–58 (2006)
12. Shen, J.: Picosecond fast arbitrary waveform pulse generator. Optical Fiber & Electric Cable and Their Applications 1(2), 11–14 (2010) (in Chinese)
13. Yi, S.: A direct digital frequency synthesizer based on ROM free algorithm. Aeu-International Journal of Electronics and Communications 64(11), 1068–1072 (2010)
14. Texas Instruments Incorporated. OMAP-L137 C6-Integra DSP+ARM Processor (Rev. D) (2010),
   http://focus.ti.com/docs/prod/folders/print/omap-1137.html
15. Xilinx. Spartan-3AN FPGA Family Data Sheet (2007),
   http://www.xilinx.comport/documentation/
   data_sheets/ds529.pdf

# Research and Implementation of Safe Production and Quality Traceability System for Fruit

Juan Pan, Xiaodong Zhu, Li Yang, Shibin Lian, and Na Zhang[*]

Department of Computer and Information Engineering,
Beijing University of Agriculture, Beijing, P.R. China 102206
juan_pan@163.com

**Abstract.** Traceability system is regarded as an effective method to ensure quality safety of agricultural products by countries all over the world. In this study, based on the research of EAN·UCC system, UCC/EAN-128 bar code technology was applied in fruit safety traceability system, coding rule for traceable code was established, and the traceable label for fruit product was designed. By integrating database technology, network technology, bar code technology and GIS technology, a safe production and quality traceability system for fruit was established. The system standardized archival records of fruit production process, proved the level of production management and meet the right to know and right of option of the consumers.

**Keywords:** Traceability System, Fruit Quality, Bar Code, GIS.

## 1 Introduction

Since 1970s, agricultural products security incidents happens frequently both in domestic or abroad, traceability system, as an effective method of controlling the quality of agricultural products, gets growing recognition from countries all over the world. EU, USA and Japan have unveiled laws and regulations requiring manufactured meat, fruits and vegetables sold in the countries said above shall be traceable. China is a large agricultural production country, constructing traceability system not only can provide high quality and safe agricultural products, but also is an important method break down trade barrier placed due to food security traceability by foreign countries, and plays an important role to promote the competitive strength of our agricultural products in international market.

At present, the construction of China's agricultural products traceability system is in the initial stage. The research and experiment of food traceability system was carried out in Beijing, Shanghai, and Shandong etc., for example, "Shanghai Edible Agricultural and Sideline Products Quality Safety Information Query System" was set up in Shanghai, "Beef Product Tracking and Traceability Automatic Identification Technology Application Demonstration System" was built in Beijing, and in Shandong Shouguang, "The Vegetables Traceability Information System" was in

---

[*] Corresponding author.

D. Li and Y. Chen (Eds.): CCTA 2011, Part I, IFIP AICT 368, pp. 133–139, 2012.

application [1]. But most of the existing research focuses on animal product and vegetable, and the traceability information can only be presented in the form of text. In this study, a safe production and quality traceability system was established to implement quality tracing for fruit. The system combines traditional quality safety traceability with GIS to realize the visualization of fruit quality safety information, and provides a new way for the construction of the fruit quality traceability.

## 2    System Framework

The management of fruit quality is concentrated on two aspects. First, in order to strengthen the management of fruit production process and improve the quality of fruit, the product archive is set up and stored in a database, which record the information of field parcel, soil nutrient, planting personnel, production process and etc. Second, According to some coding rules, traceable bar code that with fruit archives information is generated, and fruit quality traceability platform is constructed with the technology of database, network, GIS and .net to solve the fruit quality safety information asymmetry and responsibility.

By inputting the traceable code of fruit at the platform, a consumer can clearly know the varieties of fruit, producing area, soil, water and other environmental situation, and the pesticide, fertilizer, various inputs information in the fruit production management process, thus meet consumers' right to know and option, and their rights and interests are protected. For the producers, they can record and manage all kinds of information in the fruit production process systematically and by standard, establish and perfect the production management archive records, standardize production behavior, continuously improve product quality to ensure product safety.

## 3    System Function Design

According to the above system framework, the fruit quality and safety traceability system mainly consists of producing environmental management, fruit production management, traceability information encoding and traceability information query, to make the producing environmental visualization, production process electronization, and ensure the problems can be traced.

### 3.1    Producing Environmental Management

Ecological environment of producing area is one of basic factors that have influence on fruit quality. Environmental management mainly takes effective management to information such as location, soil, water and air etc., and establishes pre-production, in-production and post-production database for environment of producing area.

### 3.2    Management for Fruit Production

Production management may directly effects quality security of fruit, so it is very important to collect correct and detailed information of production management.

Every field parcel is assigned a scientific and reasonable numbers, the corresponding information such as soil nutrition, soil fertility, weather, varieties of fruit, planting area, planting personnel, and information in production management such as watering, fertilizing, pruning, pesticide delivery and harvesting are recorded. All the information constructs detailed and complete production management database, and provides the basic data for fruit traceability.

### 3.3    Coding for Traceability Information

The key point of making fruit quality traceable is to confirm the "identity " of fruit, based on the research of coding standard and method, this paper makes coding scheme for fruit according to characteristics of fruit, meanwhile realizes traceable label of fruit, and realizes tracking identification.

### 3.4    Query of Traceability Information

Establish traceability platform for quality security of fruit, information such as location and environment of producing area, status of pesticide and fertilizer use, varieties of fruit and harvest, etc. can be easily queried.

# 4    System Realization

In order to ensure the quality and promote the competitive strength of fruit, a safe production and quality traceability system was implemented with the technologies of database, network, bar code and GIS.

### 4.1    Database Construction

Data is the basic that ensures system running correctly. The traceability system consists of two types of data, one is spatial data the other is attribute data. Spatial data shall be mainly obtained by the interpretation of remote sensing image and GPS measurement at site, including information of terrain, administrative division, water system, road and field parcel etc.; Attribute data include information of soil nutrient, soil fertility, diseases and pests, pesticide use, water nutrient management and product inspection etc..Tables designed in the attribute database are as follows: table of environment and climate, table of field parcel, table of fertilizing information, table of irrigation information, table of disease and pest control, table of fruit quality detection and table of user information etc. All the information provided above is saved in the database, and which is the core and base of the fruit traceability system.

   The characteristics of the spatial data and attribute data require respective transactions on the storage and management of data. Spatial data is divided into different layers according to the characteristic of surface features, and is managed in the form of ".shp" files; Attribute data is saved in the SQL Server2005 with information associated by ID code with spatial data, for example, field parcel could be linked with the attribute database when the identification field "fieldid" is put into the layer of the soil nutrient distribution.

## 4.2    Coding Rule for Traceable Code

The traceable code of fruit is the "identity" or "symbol" defined for the tracing and recognition in some way. As the Global Identification System, EAN·UCC has offered a complete set of code system used for marking goods or services in the supply chain, which could be used for the marking of agricultural products.

The traceable code of the system has been designed with UCC/EAN-128 bar code, and the information of fruit production and companies is corresponded with special bar code. When the traceable code on the fruit packing is typed into the tracing service system of the website, corresponding information shall be quickly searched. Fruit with different traceable code shall be with different quality and safety information in the fruit management, and the same kind of fruit produced on the same field parcel and within the same time shall be with same safety information, so the fruit of the same lot is with the same and only traceable code [2]. The traceable code consists of three parts: fruit identification code, production date and source entity reference code [3-5] .

**Fruit Identification Code.** The corresponding code data of AI (01) is a global trade item number (GTIN). GTIN is the only global marking number used for trading products [6]; the coding format is as Fig. 1.

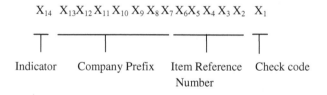

Fig. 1. Coding format of GTIN

Any company tending to realize the tracking and tracing of fruit has to firstly establish and make use of its own GTIN. The company prefix is distributed and managed by GS1 China in order that the code distributed is the only one in the world. The first three digits are the prefix code, and the prefix code distributed to GS1 China by GS1 is from 690 to 695 [7].

Item reference number is distributed by the company obtaining a company prefix, and each different trade item earns the only specific item reference number. The fruit kind code is taken as the item reference number based on the fruit categories in the system, and in order that the system shall be used for the quality tracing of vegetable products, $X_6$ is designed as main categories of goods, such as 1 standing for fruit and 2 standing for vegetable; $X_5X_4$ represents Sub category, such as 01 standing for pear and 02 standing for apple; $X_3X_2$ represents a specific fruit, such as 10 standing for white pear of Beijing. Therefore, the item reference number of this kind of pear is 10110.

The check code is produced by a calculation of its first 13 figures according to certain methods, used for automatically checking the accuracy of the 13 figures when scanning the bar code in order to ensure the code validity.

**Code of Production Date.** The production date could be judged according to the implication of AI (11). The production date means the date of producing, processing or packing. Considering the fruit, the production date is just the date of picking, and the code structure shall be of YYMMDD format.

**Source Entity Reference Code.** The source entity reference code identifier AI (251) represents the primary source of the trade item [8-9]. Field parcel code is used for tracing the primary source of the fruit in the system. The field parcel code which shall be unique is distributed by the production company itself. The field parcel code in the system consists of seven figures, the first two standing for the town with the next two standing for the administrative village and the last three standing for the field parcel position, such as 0105006 representing the No. 006 field parcel of Danli Village of Miaofengshan town.

### 4.3    Design and Realization of the Traceable Label

The traceable label also includes the goods name, producing area and other information consumers concerned in form of the text besides the traceable code.

Fig.2 is an example of the fruit traceable label, the most below is the traceable code meaning the White pear of Beijing was picked on NO. 006 field parcel of Danli Village of Miaofengshan town on Sept. 12, 2010 and the company prefix is 6911326.

**Fig. 2.** Traceable label of fruit

### 4.4    Construction of the Traceable Platform

SuperMap is taken as the GIS software platform, .NET and SQL Server database are used for the system development. B/S architecture is used in the system and a traceable platform is offered to the public in the form of a website. Information about the fruit could be traced after the traceable code has been typed into the platform.

According to the traceable code, the system shall directly illustrate the concrete position of the field parcel of the fruit, and also information such as the corresponding county name, town name and village name could be found. As illustrated in Fig. 3, consumers could learn that the field parcel is in the Danli village, Miaofengshan town of Mentougou District, Beijing. When the user clicks the field parcel on the map, information such as planting personnel, water, air, soil nutrient, fertilizer use, pesticide delivery and product inspection could be queried.

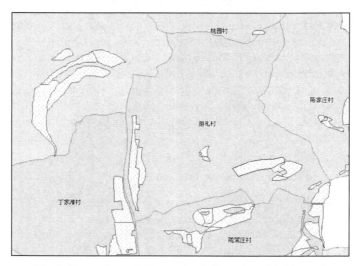

**Fig. 3.** Chart of traceability result—information of field parcel

## 5    Conclusion

The system uses bar code technology, GIS technology, network technology and the database to achieve the "from farm to fork" traceability of fruit. The production process records are standardized to ensure fruit quality and safety, the competitiveness of fruit is improved and the consumer's safety awareness about the food is enhanced. Specifically in the following points:

First, production management database is constructed to standardize production behavior, and which provides basic data for fruit traceability system.

Second, in order to identify fruit, the traceable code for fruit is designed with UCC/EAN-128 bar code, and the traceable label includes the information of production date, goods name, producing area and etc.

Third, a traceable platform is offered to the public, consumers may access the website to trace the related information.

Last, traditional quality traceability is combined with GIS, and that realizes the visualization of fruit quality safety information.

# References

1. An International Standard System—Global Language of Business,
   http://www.ancc.org.cn
2. Yang, X., Qian, J.: Design and Application of Safe Production and Quality Traceability System for Vegetable. Transactions of the Chinese Society of Agricultural Engineering 24(3), 162–166 (2008) (in Chinese)
3. UCC/EAN-128 Bar Code, GB/T 15425-2002
4. Meng, M.: Traceability System of Agricultural Products Quality and Safety Based on B/S Structure. Tropical Agricultural Engineering 34(3), 21–24 (2010) (in Chinese)
5. Ye, C.-L., Zhang, B.: Design and Implement of Traceable Label of Vegetable Produce Applied in Vegetable Quality and Safety Traceability System. Food Science 28(7), 572–574 (2007) (in Chinese)
6. Bar Code for Commodity—Dispatch Commodity Numbering and Bar Code Marking, GB/T 16830-2008
7. Bar Code for Commodity—Retail Commodity Numbering and Bar Code Marking, GB 12904-2008
8. Bar Code for Commodity—Application Identifier, GB/T 16986-2009
9. Zhang, A., Xiao, G.: Development and Application of Quality Safety Traceability System for Vegetables. Agricultural Network Information 4, 17–20 (2010) (in Chinese)

# Determination of Navel Orange Safety Production Traceability Information Based on HACCP

Haiyan Hu[1,2], Huoguo Zheng[1,2], and Shihong Liu[1,2]

[1] Key Laboratory of Digital Agricultural Early-warning Technology of Ministry of Agriculture,
The People's Republic of China, Beijing 100081, Beijing, China
[2] Agricultural Information Institute of Chinese Academy of Agriculture Science,
Beijing 100081, Beijing, China
{huhaiyan,lius}@mail.caas.net.cn, huoguo@caas.net.cn

**Abstract.** The traceability system of navel orange can ensure the quality and safety due to the whole process control from orchard to market. Research on the whole process of navel orange is the foundation and premise of building the traceability system. Based on the analyses of whole food chain of navel orange from origin to market, HACCP is used to evaluate the risk and latent risk of the food chain of navel orange: planting, harvesting, processing, packing, transportation and sale, the critical control point of navel orange were fixed. Further, the traceability information of the navel orange traceability is determinate finally.

**Keywords:** navel orange, critical control point, traceability information, HACCP.

## 1    Introduction

After several food safety related issues, particularly several food sandals, the global food industry and governments in many countries have paid more and more attention to traceability systems for the food chain [1]. There are three meaning to construct traceability systems: one is to give consumers the right to know, the second is to strengthen the responsibility for the enterprises which produce food, and the third is to find the root causes when the food safety issues happened [2].

Navel orange is one of characteristic agricultural products in the middle of china, which is demanding climate for growing. The origin of the navel orange mainly existed in south Jiangxi province, zigui, Hubei province, fengjie, Chongqing province, binzhou, Yunnan province. Gannan is the advantageous product area for navel orange determined by ministry of Agriculture in China. Gannan is the famous base for navel orange, where is known as "town of navel orange in China". Many counties in Gannan have taken navel orange as an important tool for local farmer income. The navel orange produced in Gannan has many unique features, such as large shaped, bright color, crisp flesh and good taste.

However, the incidents occurred in recently years, such as "dyeing navel orange" in Hong Kong in 2004, "bactrocera minax" in guangyuan city, Sichuan province in

D. Li and Y. Chen (Eds.): CCTA 2011, Part I, IFIP AICT 368, pp. 140–146, 2012.

2008, have damaged the orange industry in south of china. For example ,the "dyeing navel orange" incident made 70% order in Hong Kong cancellation, the price of navel orange fell sharply in 2004. In 2008, affected by the "bactrocera minax" incident, all of the consumers don't want to buy navel orange in china. These events cause severe economic losses to fruit growers.

In order to guarantee the quality safety of navel orange, make sure the quality safety information can be tracked and traced, we should monitor the whole process from tree planting to sale [3], which also called "management from orchard to table". As for navel orange, confirm the critical control point based on the analysis of the whole process from tree planting to fruit processing with the HACCP (Hazard Analysis and Critical Control Point)[4] is the foundation of traceability system construction.

## 2    Navel Orange Production Process Analysis

### 2.1    Navel Orange Production Process from Orchard to Market

Generally, there are 11 steps from navel orange tree planting to navel orange fruit sale on market: orchard selection, sapling selection, planting, tree management, soil fertilizer and water management, flower and fruit management, insect control, harvest, washing and packing, storage and transportation [5]. The whole process is shown as Fig. 1.

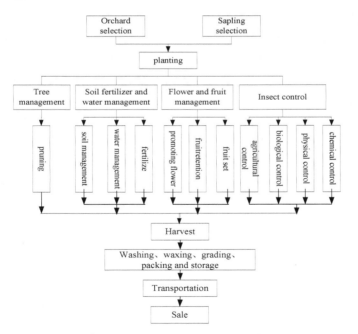

**Fig. 1.** 11 steps of navel orange growing

It needs 2-3 years from tree planting to bear fruit for navel orange tree, and it needs 280-300 days from blooming to outcome for navel orange. There are a lot of links and elements affect the quality safety for navel orange.

## 2.2    Navel Orange Main Hazard Analysis

Generally, there are three kinds of hazard to person in fresh agricultural products: biological hazards, chemical hazards and physical hazards.

The biological hazards of navel orange mainly refer to the biological itself and its metabolites will pollute fruit raw materials, process and products. This pollution will damage consumer's safety. As for fruit, hazard generated creatures are fungi, bacteria, viruses, natural toxins, parasites. Specifically, ulcers are the most occurred bacterial diseases for navel orange, which damage a lot to navel orange.

The chemical hazards of navel orange mainly refer to chemical substances, residues and emissions generated by human activities, which contaminated the fruit. Chemical hazards involves a broader range, including environmental pollution, pesticide residues fertilizer residues, chemical element pollution, packaging materials, such pollution damages the health of consumers. For navel orange, atmospheric pollutants are same with other fruits, including total suspended particulates, sulfur dioxide, nitrogen dioxide, and fluoride. Soil contaminants in navel orange include heavy metals, toxic substances (pesticides, various chemicals) and other pollutants. Soil pollution comes mainly from three aspects: First, the discharge of industrial waste; second pesticide, fertilizer application, etc.; third of sewage irrigation.

Physical hazards of navel orange exist in fruit with potentially harm may cause bodily injury to consumers., which are common glass, wire, nails fragments, stones fragments, metal fragments and so on.

# 3     Analysis of Navel Orange Critical Control Point for Safety Production

## 3.1    Navel Orange Safety Element Analysis

As we known, navel orange can be sold on market after 11 steps. Among all of these process, potential hazard factors include: environmental conditions, water quality, pesticide residues, etc, which we should analyses detailed from biological hazards, chemical hazards and physical hazards three aspects, then identify the significant hazards [6].

Chemical hazards that can impact navel orange safety mainly in the following five areas: first , pesticide residues as well as mercury, cadmium, lead, tin, chromium, arsenic, fluoride and other harmful substances residues in soil; second, fluoride and sulfide in air; third, pesticide residues and mercury, cadmium, lead, tin, chromium, arsenic, fluoride residues in irrigation water, fourth, mercury, cadmium, lead, tin, chromium, arsenic, fluorine, and antibiotics residues in fertilizer; fifth, pesticides and heavy metals exceeded in the fruit during the pest control process.

There is no physical hazard to customers in navel orange basically.

## 3.2    Critical Control Points of Navel Orange

Based on the whole process of navel orange and information of hazard analysis, five critical control points was determined (shown in Table 1):

(1) Surroundings, soil properties, pesticide residues and harmful substances in the orchard.
(2) Pesticides in the pest control.
(3) Disinfectant and wax during the washing, waxing.
(4) Pathogens during transportation
(5) Pathogens in market.

**Table 1.** HACCP based Hazard analysis of navel orange

| Production process | Hazard type | Is significant? | Judgments based on the third column | Precaution | Is CCP? |
|---|---|---|---|---|---|
| Orchard selection | biological hazard | No | | | No |
| | chemical hazard | Yes | harmful substances and heavy metals absorption from the air and water during navel orange growing | test the soil, air and water, make sure all of them line with national standards | Yes |
| | physical hazard | No | | | No |
| Sapling selection | biological hazard | No | | | No |
| | chemical hazard | No | | | No |
| | physical hazard | No | | | No |
| Planting | biological hazard | No | | | No |
| | chemical hazard | No | | | No |
| | physical hazard | No | | | No |
| Navel orange tree management | biological hazard | No | | | No |
| | chemical hazard | Yes | Use growth regulator | limited | No |
| | physical hazard | No | | | No |
| Soil management | biological hazard | No | | | No |
| | chemical hazard | Yes | Use steamed soil fumigant | limited | No |
| | physical hazard | No | | | No |
| Irrigation management | biological hazard | No | | | No |
| | chemical hazard | Yes | Irrigation water contain harmful substances, heavy metals | make sure water line with national standards | No |
| | physical hazard | No | | | No |
| Fertilize management | biological hazard | No | fertilizer storage | separate the fertilizer and fruit | No |
| | chemical hazard | Yes | Fertilizer contain harmful substances, chemical and heavy metals | Handle the organic fertilizer before use | No |
| | physical hazard | No | | | No |

**Table 2.** (*Continued*)

| | | | | | |
|---|---|---|---|---|---|
| Flower management | biological hazard | No | | | No |
| | chemical hazard | Yes | Use fruit growth regulator | limited | No |
| | physical hazard | No | | | No |
| Pest control | biological hazard | Yes | Use biological pesticide | line with national standards | No |
| | chemical hazard | Yes | Use chemical pesticide | line with national standards | Yes |
| | physical hazard | No | | | No |
| Harvest | biological hazard | No | | | No |
| | chemical hazard | Yes | | | No |
| | physical hazard | No | | | No |
| Washing、 waxing、 grading、 packing | biological hazard | No | | | No |
| | chemical hazard | Yes | Use disinfectant and wax | make sure all of them line with national standards | Yes |
| | physical hazard | No | | | No |
| Storage | biological hazard | Yes | Fruit rot during the storage | Control the storage condition | No |
| | chemical hazard | Yes | Use chemical anti-stalling agents | limited | No |
| | physical hazard | No | | | No |
| Transportation | biological hazard | Yes | Generate pathogens during transportation | control transportation condition | No |
| | chemical hazard | No | | | No |
| | physical hazard | No | | | No |
| Sale | biological hazard | Yes | Generate pathogens during sale | temperature control | No |
| | chemical hazard | No | | | No |
| | physical hazard | No | | | No |

# 4    Determination of Navel Orange Traceability Information

In order to track and trace the safety information of navel orange, the traceability information of the whole process from orchard to market should be identified and recorded [7,8]. Generally, there are four main steps information should be acquisitioned and recorded: origin information of the orchard, planting process information, production process information and storage and transportation information.

When an orchard was selected, we should investigate land use history, soil type, soil erosion and ground water quality. Evaluate whether the regional air, soil, irrigation water and other conditions, such as soil heavy metal, suit for navel orange growing. Others information like the place of orchard, the owner of the orchard, the varieties of navel oranges should be known.

In the planting process stage, different measures should be taken to deal with different diseases, pests. So the diseases, pests information and the information about the amount, time of chemical fertilizer, pesticide must be recorded.

During the production process, the information about the enterprise which packing the fruit, the disinfectant and wax during the washing, waxing must be tracked. In the final step before sale, we shall figure out where the navel orange storage, how the condition about the warehouse. The information about the transportation also should be recorded.

The traceability code is the unique identification of navel orange in sales link. All of the quality and safety information of the product can be obtained through this code, combined with the navel orange traceability system.

**Table 3.** Traceability information of navel orange

| Production process | Traceability Information |
|---|---|
| Origin | regional air quality(SO2, fluoride) |
| | irrigation water quality(heavy metal pollution) |
| | navel oranges varieties, place, owner |
| Planting process | diseases, pests information |
| | amount, time of chemical fertilizer use |
| | amount, time of pesticide use |
| | extreme climate, employee information |
| Production process | disinfectant quality safety information |
| | wax quality safety information |
| | Enterprise, employee information |
| Storage and transportation | storage surroundings information(temperature, moisture, sanitary conditions) |
| | transportation information(temperature, moisture, sanitary conditions) |
| | enterprise and employee of transportation |
| Sale | supermarket or terminal market |
| | traceability code of navel orange |

There are many links that make navel orange infected bacteria from orchard to sale, but these hazards can generally be controlled by SSOP (Sanitation Standard Operating Procedure).

# 5    Conclusion

This paper discusses what the traceability system should trace; and which information should be recorded for implementation of the traceability system of navel orange. Three main hazards of navel orange are pointed out in the paper; those may harm consumers' health. Based on analyses the whole process from orchard selection to navel orange sale, as well as safety factor of navel orange, five critical control points of navel orange are determined with HACCP method. These critical control points are the focus of the traceability system; and they should be recorded precisely during the entire process. In the end of this article, the traceability information is determinate basic on the critical control points. This study makes the navel orange traceability system construction possible.

**Acknowledgments.** This study is supported by The National Science and Technology Support Programme (2009BADC4B04).

# References

1. Liu, Y., Chen, L.: Traceability Production System of Beef in EU and USA, food science (8), 182–185 (2003)
2. Pu, Y.: Construction of traceability system for quality safety of apple and apple juice. Transactions of the Chinese Society of Agricultural Engineering 24(2), 289–292 (2008)
3. Fan, H., Feng, Z., Yang, L., Ren, A.: Appliance and Discussion of Traceability System in Food Chain. Ecological Economy 17(4), 30–33 (2007)
4. Bao, D.: Guide to implementation of HACCP. Chemical Industry Press (2007)
5. Xu, J.: Agricultural product supply chain—Guarantee food safety. China Logistics & Purchasing (07) (2005)
6. Yu, H., An, Y.: Theoretical discussion of implementation Traceability System in food supply chain. Agricultural Quality and Standards (03) (2005)
7. Zhang, G., Chen, G.: Food safety and Traceability System. China Logistics & Purchasing (14) (2005)
8. Zhou, Y., Geng, X.: Application of Traceability in Food Safety. Research of Agricultural Modernization (06) (2002)

# Cooling Wet-Pad Fan Control System of Piggery Based on Zigbee

Runtao Wang[1], Fang Yang[1], Ming Li[1], Lei Tian[3], and Yu Zhang[2]

[1] Northeast Agricultural University Engineering Institute, Harbin,
Heilongjiang Province, P.R. China, 150030
[2] Northeast Forestry University Engineering Institute, Harbin,
Heilongjiang Province, P.R. China, 150040
[3] Department of Agricultural and Biological Engineering,
University of Illinois, Champaign-61801, USA

**Abstract.** In view of the traditional faults of wire network that complex wiring and costly wired network, a set of Zigbee wireless network technology based on the temperature and humidity data acquisition and control system is designed in this paper to improve the environmental temperature control in piggery. The Zigbee system which can monitor the real-time information of temperature and humidity in piggery and provide a convenient data supports for the further temperature control synthesizes the advantages of wireless networking and self healing.

**Keywords:** Wet-pad, Fan, Cooling, Control system, Zigbee, Temperature, Relative Humidity.

## 1 Introduction

It is very important to control the ambient temperature in piggery in hot summers. Practice proves that when the temperature is higher than 30 ℃, if we do not take any cooling measures, the health and production of the pig will be badly affected, such as the sows do not heat and decreased appetite; the declining of fattening pigs feed utilization rate and pigs daily gain, thus affecting the pig farm production and economic benefits. Kaiying Wang etc. [1] proves that pigs of 41kg in 29.7 ~ 35.3 ℃ conditions that their daily feed intake decreased by 12% than in 26.3 ~ 30.4 ℃. Xinfu Zeng etc.[2] by researching the period of sows pregnancy (especially in the early periods), the high temperature is not beneficial to the maintenance of pregnancy, performs not only as the increase of the empathema and do not dilivery, but also the decrease of litter size and litter weight at birth. At present, the main use of natural ventilation and Wet-pad fan system to lower the temperature of the pigsty. Since the 1950s , American scholars began to research the Wet-pad fan cooling system, and now it has been used widely all over the world[3,4].

D. Li and Y. Chen (Eds.): CCTA 2011, Part I, IFIP AICT 368, pp. 147–154, 2012.

Wireless sensor network (WSN) as a new development direction in the field of information science, but also the results of cross-field between emerging disciplines and the traditional subjects. Domestic and foreign scholars have applied WSN in the field of agriculture[5-8]. Zigbee technology is a low cost, low power consumption network of close distance and wireless network communication technology. According to the advantages of Zigbee network, this paper designed a set of systems based on Zigbee technology of barn temperature and humidity acquisition and Wet-pad fan controlling, and stored the collecting datum of temperature and humidity in computer.

## 2     System Design

### 2.1     The Operating Principle of Wet-Pad- Ventilator

The Wet-pad cooling system mainly composed by the Wet-pad, fan, water cycle system and auto-matic control device , and the core part is Wet-pad, the principle of the system is: with high temperature the evaporation absorbs the heat in the air and trans-forms the heat into the latent heat vapor to cooling.

Figure 1 is the Wet-pad cooling schemes. A Wet-pad installed at one side of the wall, a fan crates in-stalled at the other side of the wall. The fan exhausts the air leading to negative pressure in piggery, and the outdoor air which exposing with the air in the surface of the Wet-pad is forced into the piggery through the Wet-pad, reling on the evaporation to intake the sensible heat in the air to realize the purpose of cool-ing and humidifying.

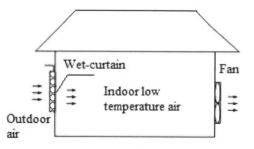

**Fig. 1.** Wet-pad cooling schemes

### 2.2     Zigbee Wireless System Structure

Zigbee is the wireless communication technology of low rate, near field, low power consumption, low complexity, low cost, reliable communications, high network capacity and such characteristics like these. The agreement made by IEEE 802.15.4 task group and Zigbee alliance, and the application layer allows according to the user's application to go on the deve-loppment [9].

As shown in figure 2, Zigbee acquisition and control system composed by the gateway node structure (coordinator), utility node (routers and end device) [10]. Coordinator is responsible for the choice of initial communications channel and the initial network configuration and accepting child nodes to join the network, and also responsible for collecting the temperature and the humidity datum which from the router and the terminal node, and through RS232 universal serial bus transmitted to PC. According to these temperature and humidity datum, the PC judges whether to open the Wet-pad fan.

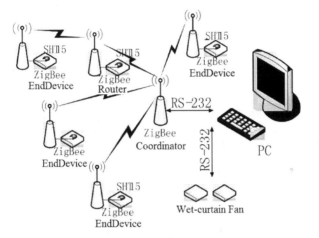

**Fig. 2.** Zigbee wireless system structure

## 2.3    System Hardware

Zigbee wireless temperature and humidity acqui-sition module uses CC2530 processor. CC2530 system function modules integrated RF transceiver, enhanced 8051MCU. Sleep mode current consumption only 0.9μA, can use external interruption or RTC sensei system: standby mode current consumption is less than 0.6μA, and also can use external interruption sensei system: requires a large voltage supply between 2.0V and 3.6V; Integrated with AES safety coprocessor.

Sensor module uses temperature humidity sensor module SHT15. SHT15 integrates temperature humidity sensor, the conditioning and amplifying circuit, A/D converting and $I^2C$ bus in one chip. The serial interface of SHT15 has a definite advantage both on the reading of sensor signor and power consumption. Current consumption is 550uA in measuring, 28uA in average, 3uA during sleep. Figure 3 is the SHT15 temperature and humidity sensor and CC2530 circuit diagram.

The composition of Wet-pad fan controlled by MOC3083M zero optocoupler bilateral triac driver IC, bilateral triac BTA16 and AC contactor. MOC3083M

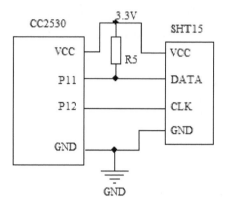

**Fig. 3.** SHT15 temperature and humidity sensor and CC2530 circuit diagram

contains of zero detection circuit, repeating reverse impulse voltage 800 V, LED trigger current Max 5 mA. BTA16 repetitive peak off-state voltage is 600 V, effective output current valu is 16 A. The AC contactor uses Schneider LC1-D09, the contact points are in open state, current is 25 A, compression voltage is 690 V. Figure 4 is the Wet-pad fan control diagram.

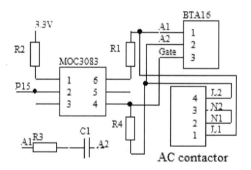

**Fig. 4.** The Wet-pad Fan Control Diagram

### 2.4    Zigbee End Device Software Design

The wireless software is based on the Z-Stack protocol Stack development of TI Company. Z-Stack Protocol Stack has compiled code for the users, the developers just contribute their attentin to the deve-lopment of application layer, eliminating the tedious work of developing the underlying protocal. Z-Stack was be given in the form of operating systerm, all the operations were defined as task or events.

Zigbee End Device collects the temperature and the humidity datum periodically and sending to coordina-tor, therefore, periodic wake-up model can be used, only when collectting datum and sending information are work, other times for sleep mode. Figure 5 is the program flow chart of Zigbee terminal node.

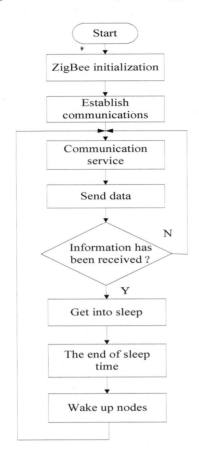

**Fig. 5.** The program flow chart of Zigbee terminal node

## 3    Test

### 3.1    Calculation of the Heat

The main heat produced by pigs is from the basal metabolism and other heat production, estimate the heat production is[11]:

$$Q = 293 * W^{0.75} * 1.2 \tag{1}$$

In the formula:

$Q$—total heat production of the pigs( $kJ / d$ );
W—weight ( $kg$ );

293—the average heat production of metabolic weight a day per kilogram( $kJ$ );
1.2—the other coefficient of heat production;

According to the calculation of formula(1), the heating power of 75 pigs on 100kg is about 9.7 $kW$ , as the solar radiation and high temperatures outside, the heat absorbed by wall is about 5 $kW$ ,the total heat is about 15 $kW$ .

### 3.2      Calculation on Refrigeration Capacity of the Wet-Pad-Ventilator

$$H = \frac{Q * 3600}{(t_1 - t_2) * \rho * c_p} \tag{2}$$

In the formula:

$H$ —after washing the flow of air,( $m^3 / h$ );

$Q$ —sensible heat load power,( $kW$ );

$t_1 - t_2$ —after washing the rise temperatre through the piggery,(°C);

$\rho$ —the air density is 1.165 $kg / m^3$ at 30 ℃;

$c_p$ —the air heat capacity is 1.005 $kJ / (kg \bullet K)$ at 30 ℃;

Good Wet-pad fan cooling system makes the dry-bulb temperature in the outside dropped slightly higher than the outside wet-bulb temperature 1~2°C. When the outdoor temperature is 36°C, the relative humidity is 45%, the wet-bulb temperature is 26°C, the speed of the Wet-pad fan is 1.1 $m/s$ , when the temperature of the exhausted air is falling by 2°C after washing, cooling capacity at 15 $kW$ , according to formula(2)can calculate out the airflow is 23061 $m^3 / h$ , therefore, the usage of four HangYang YWF4D-500 fans, the rated airflow of each fan is 8850 $m^3 / h$ , wind pressure is 190 $Pa$ .

### 3.3      The Actual Temperature and Humidity Data

Zigbee coordinator sends the temperature and humidity datum to the terminal node per minute. Figure 6 is the temperature acquisition figure of the outdoor, Wet-pad and the fan. Figure 7 is the relative humidity acquisition figure of the outdoor, Wet-pad and the fan. The average temperature of outdoor is 36.12°C, the average temperature of the Wet-pad is 28.42°C, of the fan is 30.27°C. The average outdoor relative humidity is 45.32%, the average humidity of the Wet-pad is 86.24%, the average humidity of the fan is 68.85%. The average temperature of the Wet-pad and the fan in piggery is 29.35°C, which is lower than the outdoor of 6.77°C.

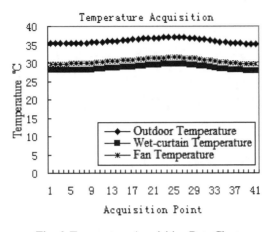

**Fig. 6.** Temperature Acquisition Data Chart

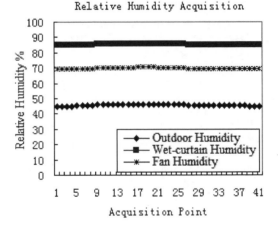

**Fig. 7.** The Relative Humidity Data Acquisition Chart

## 4   Conclusion

A set of controlling system of temperature and humidity acquisition and Wet-pad fan in piggery which combines the advantage of Zigbee's wireless networking and self healing is designed in this paper. The preliminary tests show that the system is stable, timely uploading the data of temperature and humidity. In the condition that the average outdoor temperature of 36.12°C and average relative humidity of 45.32%, the average indoor temperature is lowered to 29.35°C through the controlling of the Wet-pad fan to make the outdoor temperature lowering by 6.77°C. The system effectively reduces the temperature in the piggery and provides convenient data support for the further controlling.

# References

1. Wang, K., Miao, X., Cui, S.: Effects of Ambient Temperature and Relative Humidity on Physiological Parameters and Performance of Growing Pigs. Transactions of The Chinese Society of Agricultural Engineering 18(1), 99–102 (2002)
2. Zeng, X., Chen, A.: Effect of Environmental Temperature on Reproductivity of Sow and Development of Piglet. Ecology of Domestic Animal 22(1), 40–43 (2001)
3. Yu, X., Wu, H., Liuwei: The Usage of Wet-pad Fan in Piggery. Shanghai Journal of Animal Husbandry and Veterinary Medicine (5), 56–57 (2005)
4. Turner Larry, W., Monegue, H.J., Gates Richard, S., et al.: Fan, sprinkler, and sprinkler plus fan systems for cooling growing—finishing swine. In: Proceedings of the 1997 ASAE Annual Iternational Meeting. Part 3(of 3), Minneapo-lis, MN, USA, August 10-14 (1997)
5. Morais, R., Fernandes, M.A., Matos, S.G.: A ZigBee multi-powered wireless acquisition device for remote sensing applications in precision viticulture. Computersand Electronics in Agriculture 62(2), 94–106 (2008)
6. Kim, Y., Evans, R.G., Iversen, W.M.: Evaluation of closed- loopsite-specific irrigation with wireless sensor network. Journal of Irrigation and Drainage Engineering 135(1), 25–31 (2009)
7. Kim, Y., Evans, R.G., Iversen, W.M.: Remote sensing andcontrol of an irrigation system using a distributed wireless sensor network. IEEE Transactions on Instrumentation and Measurement 57(7), 1379–1387 (2008)
8. Liuhui, Maohua, W., Yuexuan, W., et al.: Development of farmland soil moisture and temperature monitoring system based on wireless sensor network. Journal of Jilin University (Engineering and Technology Edition) 38(3), 604–608 (2008)
9. IEEE. Std 802. 15. 4- 2003 Part 15. 4: Wire less Medium Access Control(MAC) and Physical Layer( PHY) Specifications for Low-Rate Wireless Personal Area Networks( LR-WPANs). Institute of Electrical and Electronic Engineers Inc., New York (2003)
10. ZigBee Technical Overview. ZigBee Alliance (May 2007)
11. He, C., Niu, Z., Liao, N.: Numerical Simulation in the Piggery under Vertical Ventilation. Journal of Agricultural Mechanization Research 8, 29–32 (2009)

# Agriculture Wireless Temperature and Humidity Sensor Network Based on ZigBee Technology

Xi Wang[1] and Hui Gao[2]

[1] Heilongjiang Bayi Agricultural Reclamation University, Daqing 163319, China
[2] Lanzhou Jiaotong University, Lanzhou 730070

**Abstract.** Combining with agricultural production practice, we propose the agriculture wireless and humidity sensor network design, which is based on ZigBee technology. And we use the chip based on the CC2530 ZigBee protocol as the sensor nodes and coordinator nodes for data collection, transmission and display, aiming to realize the agricultural production automation and precision agriculture.

**Keywords:** agricultural production, temperature and humidity, wireless network, sensor.

## 1  Introduction

At present, many aspects of production and life need extracting and processing temperature and humidity information of the surrounding environment. In the past, technology was to collect temperature and humidity information by the temperature and humidity sensors, and to transmit the data to the monitoring center by the RS-485 bus or field bus again, so you need to lay a lot of cables to collect and process temperature and humidity information. Traditional agriculture mainly uses isolated, no communication ability of mechanical equipment, and mainly relies on the person to monitor crop growth status. However, if ZigBee wireless sensor network technology is used, the agriculture will gradually shift to information and software-centric mode of production, and use more automation, networking, intelligent, and remote control equipment to farming. Sensors may collect the information such as soil moisture, nitrogen concentration, pH, precipitation, temperature, air humidity, air pressure and so on. The above-mentioned information and the locations of the collected information are passed to the central control equipment for decision-making and reference through the ZigBee network, so we can identify problems early and accurately for helping to maintain and increase crop yield. In many data-oriented wireless network transmissions, low cost and complexity wireless network are widely used.

## 2  ZigBee Technical Features

ZigBee technology is a short distance, low complexity, low power, low data rate, and low-cost, two-way wireless communication technology, employed mainly in the field

D. Li and Y. Chen (Eds.): CCTA 2011, Part I, IFIP AICT 368, pp. 155–160, 2012.

of automatic control and remote control, can be embedded in a variety of devices to achieve their automation [1]. For the various existing wireless communication technology, ZigBee technology will be the lowest power consumption and cost technology.

Transfer rate of ZigBee data is low, ranging from 10KB/s to 250KB/s and focusing on low-transmission applications. Under low power standby mode, the two ordinary No.5 batteries can last 6 to 24 months. ZigBee data transfer rate is low, and its protocol is simple, so it greatly reduces the cost. Network capacity is large to accommodate 65,000 devices. Delay time is short, usually in the 15ms ~ 30ms. ZigBee provides data integrity checking and authentication capabilities, using AES-128 encryption algorithm. Flexible working band, the use of frequency band 2.4GHz, and frequency bands are unlicensed. Such good points as the reliable transmission and the use of collision avoidance strategies are included while the business that requires a fixed bandwidth is reserved specific time slots.

## 3    Overall System Design Concept

Based on ZigBee wireless technology, the temperature and humidity sensor network is composed of three parts: the transmitter, receiver and display system. Transmitter is constituted by a number of terminal nodes; each node consists of a temperature and humidity sensor and a ZigBee wireless RF module. Greenhouse temperature and humidity sensors collect information on temperature and humidity, then temperature and humidity data is transmitted to the ZigBee wireless RF modules. Correction of the temperature and humidity data is processed via a chip embedded in ZigBee wireless RF (radio frequency) module, and the data revised will be sent to the receiver through ZigBee wireless network. Receiver consists of a ZigBee RF module and an RS232 serial port module. Receiver module that is a network coordinator establishes a star structure of the network. The data of each node is received through ZigBee network and transmitted to the display system via RS232. This is the temperature and humidity collection and delivery process of a sending node of the system.

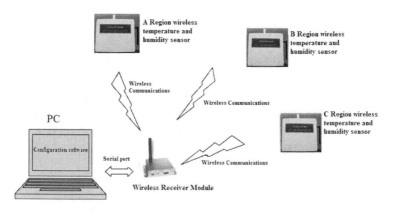

**Fig. 1.** Overall system simulating scheme

# 4    System Hardware Design

CC2530 meets low-cost and low power requirements of the 2.4GHz ISM band based on ZigBee. It includes a high-performance 2.4GHz DSSS (direct sequence spread spectrum) RF transceiver core and a 8051 controller. ZigBee RF front end, memory and microcontroller are integrated on a single chip. It has 128kB programmable flash memory and 8kB RAM, including ADC, timers, 32kHz crystal sleep mode timer, power-on reset circuit, power-down monitor circuit and 20 programmable I/O pins, enabling the node miniaturization [2]. CC2530 wireless single chip is characterized by very low power, standby current consumption of only 0.2μA. Under the run of 32 kHz crystal clock, the current consumption is less than 1μA.

The temperature and humidity sensor SHT11 integrates several circuits into a single chip, such as temperature and humidity detection, signal amplification conditioning, A/D conversion and digital communications interface. Humidity measuring range is 0 ~ 100% RH, temperature measurement range is -40°C ~ +123.8°C, humidity measuring accuracy is ± 3.0% RH, temperature measuring accuracy is ± 0.4°C, and the response time is less than 4s. For digital interfaces, SHT11 provides two-wire digital serial interface SCK and DATA; SCK is the serial clock line for communication between the microprocessors to achieve synchronization. DATA serve as the serial data line, and makes the data transmission between the microprocessors. The chip interface is simple, good at high transmission reliability, and measurement precision can be adjusted by programming. After the measurement and communication, low-power mode is automatically transferred.

## 4.1    The Hardware Design of the Transmitting Node

Transmitting node is the basic unit of the network composed of digital temperature and humidity sensor SHT11 module, CC2530 processor module, antenna module, power supply module. It is responsible for acquiring temperature and humidity data and data preprocessing, and they will be transmitted to ZigBee receiving end. Temperature and humidity sensor module is responsible for collecting and detecting temperature and humidity data of region. Processor module makes analog-digital conversion for the collected data signal, and then processes. The processed data is issued by the antenna [3]. The power module mainly supplies power for the processor. Transmitting hardware framework is shown in Fig. 2.

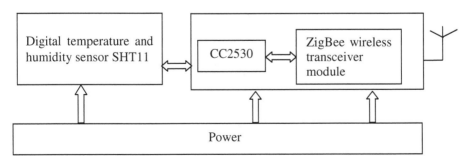

**Fig. 2.** Transmitting hardware framework

## 4.2    The Hardware Design of the Receiving Node

Receiver node is composed of a power supply module, a key module, a serial module, a LCD module, LED lights, a CC2530 processor module and an antenna module. The wireless temperature and humidity sensor network is not an independent communication network, which needs transmitting the monitoring temperature and humidity data to the host computer and displaying them. LED indicator lights are used to display the receiving node network state information (e.g. whether the network is built successfully); LCD module is an interface of the user and sensor network to display the function menu, and the user selects them by pressing buttons. CC2530 is a data-receiving mode. When data is received, RF receiving signals are amplified by the low noise amplifier before they are overturned into the frequency mixer. By mixing frequency, IF (intermediate frequency) signal is produced. In IF processing stage, before the signal into the demodulator is amplified and filtered, the data of demodulation is put into the shift register, and then into RFBUF. After the temperature and humidity data in RFBUF are removed by MCU, they will be put into the data buffer register SBUF of UART, and be transmitted to the host computer through RS232 serial module

# 5    System Software Design

The system using development environment is IAR7.51A while the using protocol stack is Z-STACK of TI. The system connecting the receiving end to PC via the serial

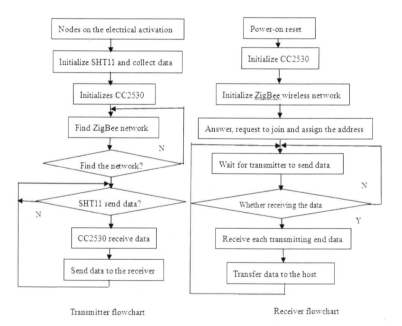

Transmitter flowchart                              Receiver flowchart

**Fig. 3.** Transmitter and receiver software flowchart

port RS232 must know the network address of each sensor node, requiring that the network address is sent to the receiver after each sensor device joins the network. The receiver receiving the network address of the sensor establishes address table to store so that the user collects data of each sensor according to address table when collecting data [4]. Transmitter and receiver software flowchart is shown in Fig. 3.

# 6     Construction of Wireless Sensor Networks Based on ZigBee

The FFD (full functional device) must lead as the network coordinator to establish a network, then the other FFD or RFD join the network, but the RFD (reduce functional device)can only link to FFD. According to the device function in the network, programs are designed beforehand for the device. The coordinator function is to search by scanning and scanning 16 channels set the applicable optimum channel to start a network. The device can form a network (coordinator) in the free channel, or connect to an existed network. Router function is to search by scanning to find an active channel and connect it, then allow connecting other installations. The function of terminal devices is always trying to connect to an existed network. Those terminal devices search other devices that can provide complete search service in the network allowing any network device to initialize the service search [5], and can bind other devices that will provide full service, offering commands and control features for the specified set of conforming devices.

Central control center is connected to a number of the sending end through the network connection. Wireless information transmission between the receiver and transmitter is achieved via Zig Bee technology. The sender is responsible for detecting and processing data and sends it to the receiver. The control center gets the collected relevant information through the network. Multiple senders are distributed in the sensor network, so polling scan is put to the upload data from different ID sink nodes and data of sink nodes can be orderly, completely transmitted after being treated through MCU.

# 7     Conclusions

This paper proposes a wireless temperature and humidity sensor network system based on ZigBee technology, and networking ways are of flexibility, adaptability. Through the practical application in the laboratories and its surrounding offices, this system is proved to be very practical. In practical applications, terminal device number is determined by achieving goal demands. The system can be applied to agricultural production, as well as in more areas of production and life, solving monitor environmental temperature and humidity problems in the areas of high cost and inconvenience arrival of wired network cabling, abominable environment. ZigBee networking ways typical of simple and low power consumption make the temperature and humidity information in real-time delivery reduce system costs, save energy, and conserve resources, and its low cost for the promotion in industry provides convenience. With ZigBee chips at lower prices, the new temperature and humidity monitoring system will also have a broad application prospect.

# References

1. Zhai, L., Liu, S., Hu, Y.: ZigBee Technology and Application, pp. 313–347. Beijing Aeronautics and Astronautics Press (2007)
2. Chipcon semiconductor. CC2530 Data Sheet 1.02, http://www.chipcon.com
3. Liu, Y., Wang, C., Yu, C.: Research on ZigBee wireless Sensors Network Based on ModBus Protocol. Information Technology and Applications, 487–491 (May 2009)
4. Chipcon semiconductor. Chipcon IAR User Manual, http://www.chipcon.com
5. Song, J.: Wireless sensor network node design and implementation. Jilin University School of Instrument Science and Electrical Engineering

# The Development of Decision Support System
# for Production of Layer

Jianhua Xiao, Hongbin Wang, Luyi Shi, Mingzhe Lv, and Haikun Ma

College of Veterinary Medicine, Northeast Agricultural University,
Harbin 150030, China

**Abstract.** The Decision Support System for Production of Commercial Layer was developed based on the demand analysis. VB .NET 2005 and SQL SERVER 2000 was used as main methods for system development. With this system, the data of alternation, growth, breeding, environment, immune for layer production can be recorded, edited, analyzed and be given by a report forms. With this system, the production efficiency can be raised.

**Keywords:** layer, DSS.

## 1 Introduction

For a large-scale layer enterprise, there must be many batches of chickens kept at the same time. And there must be many differences for observed indicators among those batches. Therefore, it was very difficult to ensure that each chicken goes according to plan production. This problem can be solved by developing one decision support system for production of commercial layer. In terms of computer software for layer production, one computer software for breeding was developed by Cai Juandeng, breeding data can be treated and various kinds of genetic parameters can be obtained by this soft [1]. One management system for chicken breeding data was developed by Xiao Fan, which has the pedigree matching, hatching management, determination of egg, report query etc[2]. One system of data acquisition and input for egg production was developed in 1993 by Yang Ning using bar code technology and handheld computer technology [3]. One digital breeding platform for breeding pig was developed by Zhao ruixue [4]. One management information system for layer farm was developed by Wu Xiaohong [5]. In addition, the computer software is also used in retrospective [6], disease diagnosis [7] and so on. The Decision Support System for Production of Commercial Layer was developed in this study aimed at recording and analyzing the data of growth, feeding, egg production, environment, immunization, and disease, changes during brood period, Incubation period, and laying period and out. By management and statistical analysis of production data, the overall situation and problems can be controlled by managers with this system, and the objective, scientific decision can be made by managers.

D. Li and Y. Chen (Eds.): CCTA 2011, Part I, IFIP AICT 368, pp. 161–168, 2012.

## 2     Principle and Methods

### 2.1     The Production Flow-Sheet of Layer

There are four stages during a production cycle of goods layers. They can be listed as follows: birth, incubation, egg, and out. The brood period is from its birth to six weeks. The incubation period is from the seventh to twentieth weeks. The egg period is from twenty to seventy-two weeks; then layer is out, different indicators need to be obtained in each period.

### 2.2     The Development Methods and System Framework

In general, one chicken farm is composed of several branches. moreover easy of use is required, and therefore the C/S framework was used in this system. One computer was set as server and the computer in every branch was installed client soft; to access the data in server by set the only IP address. The operating system for developed this soft was selected as windows XP, and Microsoft VB.NET 2005 was selected as development language[9], the excel component of Microsoft office was used to import and export data, the third party component Dotnet Charting was used to generate figure. Microsoft SQL Server 2000 was used as database.

## 3     Result

The system was divided into 6 modules based on the production processes of layer: the management of farm and house, data input, statistics and report forms, curve diagram, system management and help. The initial data of one batch of chickens was

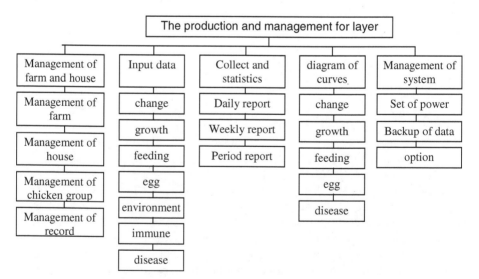

**Fig. 1.** The function and structure of production and management system for layer

recorded after being introduced; the data generating in every production processes was record synchronously. All of data were done statistics in a statistics and report forms module, and also produced daily, weekly, periodic report. The function and structure of system can be found in figure 1.

## 3.1 The Introduction of One Batch of Chicken

The basic data of one batch of chicken include information generated when they were introduced and information generated in every production stages. Those data mainly included serial number, species, source, approach date, born weight, quantity, stocking rate and survival rate after 24 weeks, date when increase light, egg date etc. because different species of chicken have different breeding standard, and those procedures such as increasing light and egg, mix chicken groups must be completed within the limited periods, therefore the standard of production was compiled in software, and the program will compute everyday according to this standard, the current status of chickens can be get, and the attention for change house, increase light, mix groups, etc. was gave to user automatically(fig. 2).

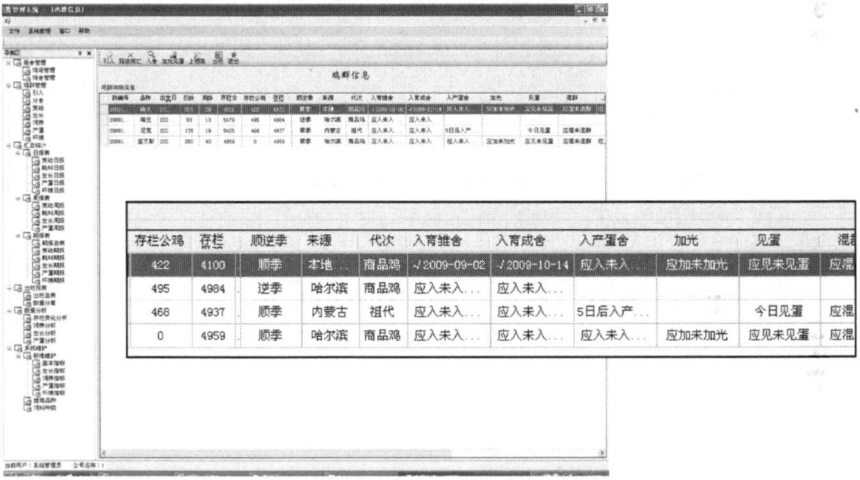

Fig. 2. The introduction of chickens and attentions in key production processes

The data can be modified at any time and export into excel table. The production data need to be backed up and separated when production cycle of one batch of chicken has closed, then the data of this batch of chicken can be deleted from database.

## 3.2 The Management of Change Data for One Batch of Chicken

Death, eliminate, marketing, output and input of chickens are main changes of one batch of chicken in production. These data and data of herbs must be recorded in to computer every day. In order to facilitate data recording, few data (such as death and eliminate etc.) need to be input and closing stock will be computed by numbers of yesterday automatically. By this ways, the efficiency would be improved significantly. The changes of data can be statistics, daily, weekly, and period report and figure of one phase can be generated in system. By these results, more scientific measure can be made by managers. By contrasted to standard, the conclusion of production can be got(fig. 3).

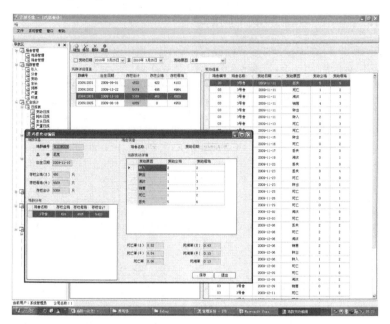

**Fig. 3.** The changes data of one batch of chicken

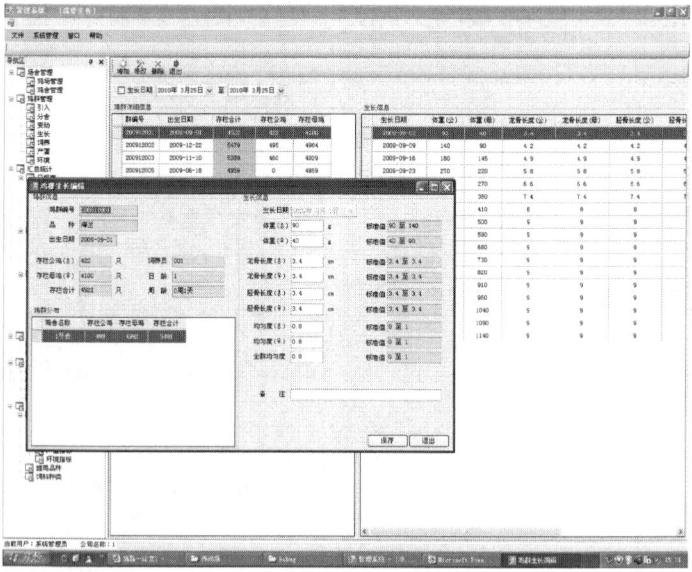

**Fig. 4.** The management of growth data for one batch of chicken

### 3.3    The Management of Growth Data for One Batch of Chicken

The growth was the main observation for management during brood and incubation period. Sound skeletal structure is necessary for egg production. It is very important to monitor redords and analyzation of the chickens growth informotion. Only the weight of chicken at Pre-laying (from 21 to 28 week) need to be record weekly. Based on the general requirement of layer farm, body weight, uniformity, average uniformity, change of feather, length of keel, length of tibia need to be managed in this system. The growth data can be statistics, daily report, weekly report, report of one phase can be generated in system (fig.4).

### 3.4    The Management of Feeding Data for One Batch of Chicken

The feeding is associated with each period of production. The difference among those periods is the feed. Therefore feeding methods, the number of feed, feed consumption, water consumption, feeding time, difference between planning and the actual feed consumption, protein and metabolic energy intake and other related information need to be recorded in database. By comparing, the information whether the actual feed consumption has met the standards will be reminder to user. In addition, the feeding data can be statistics, daily report, weekly report, report of one phase and figure of changing can be generated in system. Thus managers can investigate the reason for insufficiency or excessive, and take effective measures timely (fig.5).

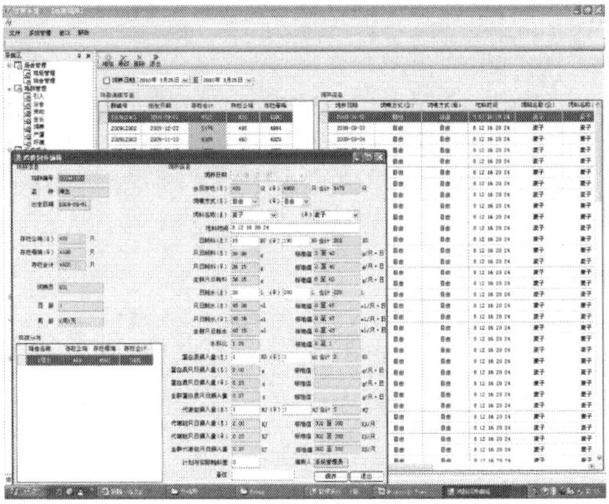

**Fig. 5.** The management of feeding data for one batch of chicken

### 3.5    The Management of Production Data for One Batch of Chicken

Egg number, number of unqualified eggs, fertilized eggs, ratio of feed to egg need to managed. Those data can be input from three routes: ①input by manager directly, ② generated from system by computed, ③obtain from computer directly or generate from system daily. The number of hatching egg, number of goods egg, number of double-yolked egg, number of soft egg need to be recorded by manager daily. And laying rate, pass rate of hatching egg, ratio of commodity egg to total egg, double yellow egg ratio, ratio of soft eggs, broken egg rate, fertilization rate, hatching rate, etc generated from system by computed. Every data can be count(fig.6), and statistical graph can be generated(fig.7).

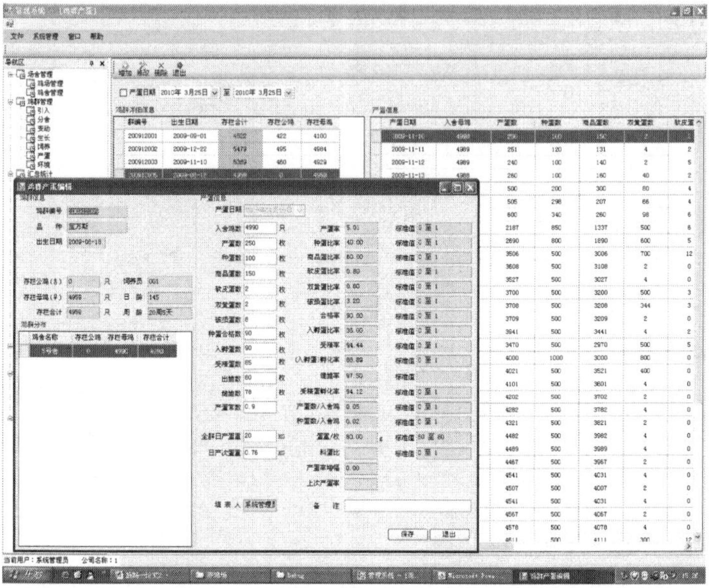

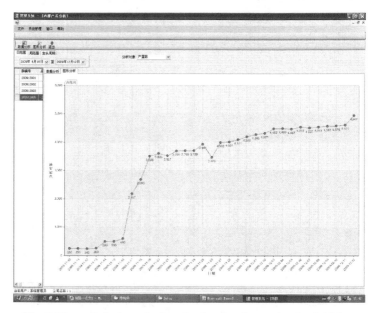

**Fig. 6.** The management of production data for one batch of chicken

**Fig. 7.** The statistical graph of production data for one batch of chicken

# 4    Discussion

## 4.1    Data Inputting of Management System

Too many items and large amounts of data are main factors that restrict the application of software in practices. Although some data can be recorded by auto technology, however, some data still be input manually. It is so important that reduce the input by hand and improve the efficiency. The reducing of input was considered in any parts of this system, besides the keying order of textbox was adjusted, many data can be computed by system automatically. Moreover, the association of items among different modules was enhanced in system, and user can find the data that he wanted in place where he wanted.

## 4.2    The Intelligence of Management System

Generally, many batches of chicken will be feed simultaneously in one large-scale farm, and different batches of chicken will be produced at different stages. Different items need to be managed for each batch of chicken. In order to improve the intelligence of system, the production information will be retrieved and computed by production standard every day, and the works need to be completed can be displayed in a form. The software can be used to look over new task.. By this way, the fault in will be reduced significantly.

## 4.3    Decision Support for Production of Management System

The main purpose that a manager using the software is to do statistics and analyzes production data, thereby finding out the problem during the production, so that making the work plans on the basis of current data.    This quest was considered thoroughly when this system being designed and developed. The production data in every procedure can be statistics by day, week and period, and the statistical graph can be generated directly.

# References

1. Cai, J., Tong, H.B.: The Application of Computer in Breed for Chicken. Shandong Poultry 5, 14–16 (1997)
2. Fan, X.: The Design and Application of Data Management System for High Quality Fowl Breeding. China Poultry 31, 4–7 (2009)
3. Yang, N., Shan, C., Li, J.: Research on Record System Without Paper for Fowl Egg Number. Journal of Chinese Animal Husbandry 29, 3–5 (1993)
4. Zhao, R., Zhao, P., Gong, C.: Research on Digital Cultivation Technique Platform for Goods Layer. Heilongjiang Animal Husbandry and Veterinary 12, 47–48 (2006)

5. Wu, X., Bin, S.: The Computer Network Management for Modern Fowl Fram. Journal of Zhongkai Agrotechnical College 6, 53–59 (1993)
6. Zhao, J.: The Analysis for Application Current Situation of Trace System for Chicken Quality in China. Chinese Journal of Animal Science 47, 45–48 (2011)
7. Xu, J.: The Diagnosis Expert System for Common Disease of Fowl. Chinese Journal of Veterinary Medicine 18, 40–41 (1992)
8. Yin, H.: Useful Course of Studies for Visual Basic.NET. China Railway Publishing House, Beijing (2003)

# Development and Application of a Farmland Test Data Processing System Designed for Wireless Sensor Network Applications

Jinqiu Zou[1,2], Qingbo Zhou[1,2], Peng Yang[1,2], and Wenbin Wu[1,2,*]

[1] Key Laboratory of Resources Remote Sensing and Digital Agriculture,
Beijing 100081, China
[2] Institute of agricultural resources and regional planning,
Chinese Academy of Agricultural Sciences, Beijing 100081, China
{zoujq,zhouqb,yangp,wwb}@mail.caas.net.cn

**Abstract.** Data collected by measuring farmland environmental indicators are vital sources of agricultural information. Wireless sensor networks (WSNs) have been employed to acquire stable and real time farmland environment data. WSNs, recognized as one of the latest development trends, recently attracted widespread attention and application due to their relative economy, stability, and sophistication. In this study, based upon a large amount of WSNs-obtained data, Microsoft Visual Studio 2005 and ESRI ArcGIS Engine 9.3, amongst others, were utilized to develop a farmland test data processing system, resolve information storage and utilization problems and conduct system applications. The data processing software consisted of four modules: data receiving conversion, database maintenance management, data browsing analysis and the generation and application of data spatialization outputs. Specifically, the data receiving conversion module was mainly responsible for converting raw data acquired by WSNs into standard database outputs, including the automatic reception of measured value, error correction and alerting the observer to abnormal data. The Database maintenance management module's primary functions were the generation and maintenance of metadata generated from stored data, authentic data enquiry, display and analysis. The generation and application of data spatialization products module was principally for the spatial expansion application of measured data, including space-time interpolation and conversion. The system underwent pilot scale testing and improvement at the same time as undertaking the processing of real data collected by WSNs deployed throughout the Hebi test zone. The observed results revealed that the system was able to complete real-time conversion and management of field measured data. In addition, it has several advantages, such as, excellent stability, perfect functionality and a convenient human - machine interface.

**Keywords:** Wireless sensor networks (WSNs), Measured value, Monitoring.

---

* Corresponding author.

D. Li and Y. Chen (Eds.): CCTA 2011, Part I, IFIP AICT 368, pp. 169–179, 2012.

# 1     Introduction

Crop farmland ecological environment indicators mainly consist of soil temperature and humidity, air temperature and humidity, photosynthetically active radiation and leaf area index, all of which are indispensable data when assessing an area's suitability for agriculture[1]. In addition, these parameters are strongly linked to crop growth, which is closely correlated with final crop yield and agricultural production efficiency. How best to acquire accurate farmland environmental and soil data and map any space-time dynamic changes that may occur has caught the attention of agriculture departments and scientists both at home and abroad. Some studies looking at information acquisition tools and precision evaluation have been undertaken[2]. Farmland information acquisition tools in particular have undergone constant innovation and change, evolving from artificial spot observations towards assistant observation by remote sensing technology or short-distance wireless collection based upon a PDA and the mobile phone. To date, this tool has developed into a field information collection system integrating accurate positioning and farmland WSNs incorporating the analysis and visualization of field data[3].

New generation WSNs[4] are an integrated technology using computer science techniques, MEMS sensing techniques, network communication techniques and embedded systems. They represent the main trends in the post-PC era for information science technology and also exist at the leading edge of current information science technology. WSNs serve as an important technology that automatically records a range of different data from the physical world. WSNs have become one of the most appealing and vibrant research fields and are regarded as a great opportunity for information technology and application due to their low deployment and maintenance costs, convenient upgrades, and greatly improved mobility that requires no cable connections[5-8]. By installing humidity sensors, temperature sensors, photosensors etc, beneath the observational zone, various farmland data can be directly acquired or inverted and then the data can be automatically transmitted to a laboratory that can process and analyze the observational data automatically collected by the WSNs. This effectively overcomes the drawbacks in traditional farmland environmental monitoring and investigation, and satisfies the application information requirements of modern agriculture[9-11].

WSNs technology has made substantial progress and it now plays a vital role in farmland information data gathering. Present research is mainly inclined to a few front end studies, such as, farmland information collection and information transmission. However, little emphasis has been placed upon back end studies including processing and analysis of the data collected. This study is designed to explore possible application methods for the storage, enquiry, browsing and analysis of measured data based upon the WSN platform. Microsoft Visual Studio 2005 and ESRI ArcGIS Engine 9.3 were utilized to develop a farmland observation data system, integrate the data flow process and the data analysis module to ensure effective application of any data collected. Data obtained by the WSNs was sourced from the sensing network deployed at Hebi city in Henan province which covers a 150 km$^2$ area of the Institute of Natural Resources and Regional Planning, Chinese

Academy of Agricultural Sciences. Thirty-five nodes were placed and a frame of data was collected every 10 min which was then transmitted back to the laboratory via GPRS.

## 2    Structure and Function Module of the Processing System

This system aimed to resolve the problems involved in storage and application of WSNs acquired data. To achieve this goal, information processing technologies need to be analyzed to resolve the problems that are associated with, for example: WSNs-based data transmission, current background organization and data application modes. The system must be established under the principles of openness, high-efficiency, and safety[12-13].The system structure is shown in Fig.1.

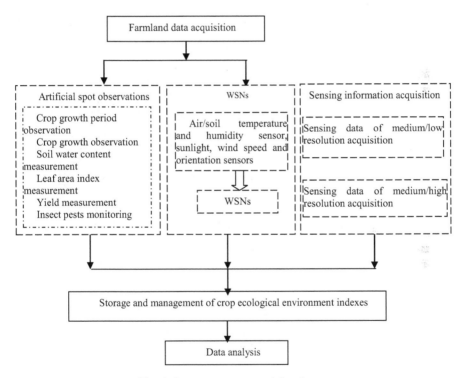

**Fig. 1.** System structure module scheme

Through requirement analysis and data flow abstraction, the system was divided into 4 modules: data receiving conversion, database maintenance management, data browsing analysis and generation and application of data spatialization outputs. Each module was connected via data utilization flow and each served a specific function forming an integrated data processing system which transformed raw data into various outputs. The system function module scheme is shown below in Fig.2:

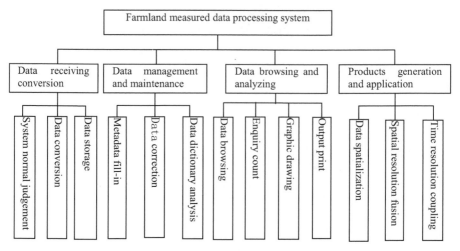

**Fig. 2.** System function module scheme

## 2.1    Data Receiving Conversion Module

This module received the WSNs data, and served as the data entry portal for the whole system. The main functions included: automatically converting WSN-obtained binary file data into tables in a standard database, embracing automatic operational control of the storage module, acquisition synchronization of the WSNs and the automatic capture and highlighting of abnormal conditions. The WSNs performed long-term operations with no interruption and thereafter the module exhibited stable operation. Considering the flaws existing in machine servers and the network environment, unexpected abnormal errors may arise, such as server breakdown and the system halting and the computer restarting. These results suggest that this module

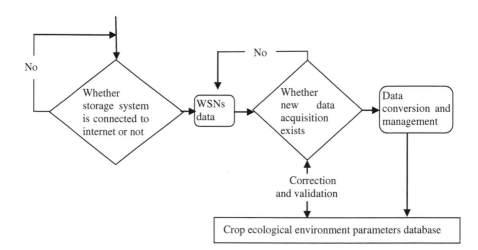

**Fig. 3.** Data reception conversion module scheme

should be able to automatically detect these abnormal conditions and ensure a synchronized link between the local system and WSNs by identifying the underlying cause, auto operation, and network registration. In addition, data remains and losses may be caused by these abnormal conditions. Therefore, this module should evaluate data consistency to avert repeated data storage and data loss. The function module is illustrated as follows Fig.3 .

## 2.2    Functionality of the Database Management and Maintenance Module

This module was mainly designed to record and generate metadata for each indicator measured to complete the fusion between this data set and other data sets including addition and registration of time-space related information. Furthermore, this module was also responsible for revising abnormal values to guarantee that all the observational data stored in the database were consistent with conventional thresholds. When undertaking the database design, metadata technology and a double-backup mechanism were taken into account in order to define an open, standard and integrated series of metadata information for data sets. Metadata was produced while performing data storage and provided a basis for subsequent data enquiry and analysis. Double backups were carried out in the database, one backup served for storing data directly originating from the data receiving conversion module and the second backup was set for qualified standard data after undergoing correction processing.

## 2.3    Functionality of the Data Browsing and Analysis Module

This module performed enquiry, browsing, statistical counts and graphics drawing to stored collected data including some fundamental functions such as, storage, enquiry, printing, data analysis and statistics. It also embraced multiple statistical schemes according to time, node, and location. Statistical methods included maximum, minimum and mean values together with frequency figures. Graphics drawing included various diagrams according to time, node, and index type, etc and drawing methods included line graphs, bar graphs, and pie charts.

## 2.4    Functionality of the Generation and Application of the Data Spatialization Products Module

It was specifically designed for multiple applications to observational data. Due to the dot characteristics of observational data, these data had relatively high precision and good representation. Nevertheless, data assimilation and coupling should be performed to monitor the process of crop growth on a large scale and include all the growth features of farmland crops. To realize data coupling, space-time information registration needs to be performed. Therefore, this module was established. It conducted data spatialization according to node and sensor type. The spatialization interpolation module that was designed provided, amongst other features, Inverse Distance to a Power, Kriging, and polynomial fitting.

# 3    Key Technologies Involved in System Integration

After comprehensive analysis and testing of this system, the system concentrated on farmland observational data flow processing and continuously handled received data by converting original binary files into visual and usable advanced outputs. Several key technologies should be comprehensively employed including database technology, data correction technology and data assimilation and interpolation technology.

## 3.1    Database Technology

This database involved a relatively large data set originating from a wide range of sources and had discord between time and space resolution. To better organize and utilize the data collected, this system utilized Oracle 10g as a database platform and employed metadata technology to establish a database structure, proper handling of a substantial amount of abnormal data and effectively resolving data organization and storage-related problems.

In the current system, each node acquired a frame of observational data every 10 min(including photo and video clips). At the same time, basic geographical information, statistical data, and partial remote sensing data were also collected. Therefore, data abnormalities and the expansion principle should be taken into account when designing a system module. A plausible module should be created to minimize data storage redundancy, enhance data compatibility, realize data sharing, guarantee data security and browse and handle data efficiently.

The database performed data browsing using standard metadata and put in a high-capacity binary file that was written into the metadata field to enhance browsing speed. Additionally, it could undertake data addition, revision, deletion and browsing based upon metadata technology which accelerated data browsing and digging. During the process of metadata field programming and designing, international standard principles were followed and the procedure aimed to comply with current industrial, state, and international standards. This design procedure also considered the specific requirements of the data characteristics and utilization in this database[14]. A total of 12 fields were designed for metadata. Under the prerequisite of satisfying data enquiry and complete data description, a minimum number of data fields were designed to ease the complexity of metadata fill-in and avert data redundancy.

All storage data were upgraded to perform enquiry, statistical and comprehensive analysis. For real-time acquired farmland indicators and data, correction data were also retained as well as original current values. Both original graphics and inversion outputs were saved for graphics data. Regarding graded outputs from obtained data, relevant regulations were enforced about file names and the evolutionary process of pertinent data were described by using data dictionary technology[15]. In addition, dictionary information was used to establish data indices and increase the efficiency of data utilization.

## 3.2    Data Correction Technology

In this system, data correction had two correction stages. The first step was data conversion, which corrected the WSNs' deprived, raw and binary data by converting a photoelectricity signal into standard data showing temperature, humidity, and photosynthesis. The second step was to delete abnormal values and mark them as special data for the purpose of averting the negative influence that using these abnormal data can have on overall data quality.

Data correction flow: 1). Data value conversion: The front-end data sensor used in this study was purchased from the open market. These sensors were corrected under a constant temperature/humidity environment before delivery and the correction coefficient was kept in a standard register. The correction coefficient automatically corrected the signals emitted from sensors and simultaneously exported the measured value of digital quantity via a data bus. These initial measured values were mere 'relative values', which required linear and temperature offset correction. These relative data were in binary data format when sent back from the wireless sensor (bit stream). Prior to data browsing and storage, these data should be converted into another format[9]. Microsoft office Excel 2003 format file was commonly employed. The daily data obtained were saved, according to file acquisition date, as one single file with an extension name of .xls. The data correction procedure was located in the data automatic storage system. A preliminary version of the observational data was created following data storage into the database. 2). Abnormal data handling: Certain large errors or significantly abnormal data may occur that can be caused by impaired sensors and weak photoelectric signals. For example, among the data measured in Hebi city test region, some data showed that soil temperature was below minus 20 °C or above 30°C, which were obviously wrong. Those sorts of abnormal temperature/humidity values should be deleted even after data conversion. Otherwise, obvious calculation errors may occur in subsequent analysis (statistical analysis and spatial interpolation value analysis), leading to misleading and inaccurate monitoring outcomes. Therefore, the second step was indispensable. The procedure was undertaken in the database management and maintenance module. The corrected data were the revised version of the original observational data, which could be regarded as reliable raw observational values.

## 3.3    Data Assimilation and Interpolation Technology

To make coordinate use of background data from other test zones and real-time farmland field indicators, obtained data were subjected to further processing enabling different data to have comparable space-time nodes. The first step was to spatialize obtained data using data assimilation and interpolation technology. The modules used during interpolation included weighing interpolation, Kriging, and polynomial fitting methods.

This project innovatively improved the interpolation procedure the system used in this project, performing orientation interpolation assisted by remote sensing graphics and basic geographical data about the test zone. The basic principle and steps were described as follows. Firstly, the plantation graph was extracted depending upon the land-use map and remote sensing graphics of the current period. Through observing GPS information at each observation point, interpolation modules were selected for formal interpolation in the region where there was uniform planting. The interpolation technology is detailed in Fig.4.

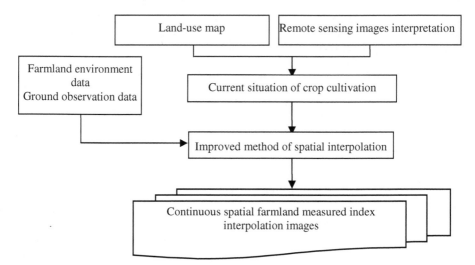

**Fig. 4.** Farmland observational data interpolation flow

# 4    Realization and Application of the System

After reviewing the system's targets and requirements, a detailed design was undertaken. All the potential data in the system were cleaned and analyzed and a corresponding database module was established. An Oracle 10g software platform, designed for business, was employed to set up the database. Microsoft Visual Studio 2005 language was used for system modeling and arithmetic packaging and a human-machine interface was designed. Partial function dynamic databases of ESRI ArcGIS Engine 9.3, amongst others, were used in module integration.

During the process of system integration, an object-oriented method was adopted. The integration system first separated the database from the software system, ensuring universality among various software packages. At the same time, under an object-oriented human-machine operation environment, an instrument panel-like data input interface was designed, providing convenience to customers and allowing visual data browsing. A visually friendly interface was designed in the human-machine dialog box. To enhance utilization efficiency of the system, complex and simple operations were automated, allowing unmanned automatic operation. The system products that have been designed have attractive interfaces and are easy to operate and maintain, e.g. the data input interface was designed as the dialog box shown in Figure.5.

All the data obtained in the Hebi test zone, Henan province, were properly managed using this system. Approximately 5040 real-time monitoring data points were acquired daily and then stored in the database automatically. Since the system was deployed in July 2010, it has operated stably and reliably. WSN-acquired data and farmland information from other test zones were utilized to produce multiple forms of data output, that help monitor agricultural conditions. The system particularly played a vital role during the monitoring process of drought damage caused to winter wheat in December, 2010.

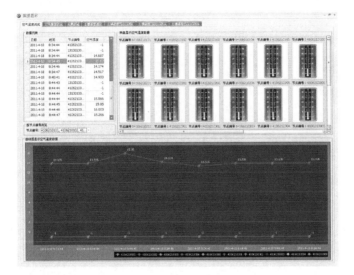

**Fig. 5.** Database storage module

# 5    Conclusion

This study focuses on the processing procedure of WSNs-acquired farmland data. It systematically analyses the information flow during the reception, storage, and analysis processes from farmland data collection. Additionally, this study designed a relevant database module that organized and managed a large amount of collected data. Pertinent software exploration platforms were employed to develop a desirable system for farmland observational data processes.

Application results reveal that software data flow and the integrated module design concept are good. The system has excellent stability and an attractive and simple human-machine interface. It also preliminarily achieves the task of monitoring data flow throughout the whole procedure from acquisition to utilization of the farmland information. Metadata and data dictionary dual techniques were employed in data organization, which improves data browsing and analysis efficiency. At the same time, a commonly used spatial interpolation module had improvements made to its monitoring data spatialization so that there was an increase in the precision of spatial interpolation values. To conclude, the system designed in this study preliminarily achieved the management and utilization functions of WSN-acquired farmland information, supplying an information service for agricultural field monitoring.

**Acknowledgments.** Funding project: National development and planning project for high-tech research of China entitled Remote sensing farmland information based on satellite and land in coordination with inversion technology (grant No. 2009AA12Z143). Surface project of National Natural Science Foundation of China entitled Simulation research on crop yield per unit based on space-time coupling and data assimilation (grant No. 40971218). And foundation of central institutes(iarrp-2011- 15).

# References

1. Cao, W., Yang, B., Pei, Z., et al.: Investigation and analysis of agricultural condition information demand in China. Transactions of the CSAE 20(1), 147–151 (2004)
2. Li, J., Zhang, J., Guan, H.: The technology development of agricultural condition information Both Abroad and Home. Science and Technology of Tianjin Agriculture and Forestry 4(2), 36–39 (2000)
3. Mu, L., Liu, G., Huang, J.: Design of farm field data collection and transmission system based on Java phone. Transactions of the CSAE 22(11), 165–169 (2006)
4. Gong, P.: Wireless sensor network as a new ground remote sensing technology for environmental monitoring. Journal of Remote Sensing 11(4), 545–551 (2007)
5. Song, L., Li, J., Chen, Y., et al.: Wireless Sensor Networks. Tsinghua University Press, Beijing (2005)
6. Mao, X., Yang, M., Mao, D.: Survey on wireless sensor network applications. Computer Applications and Software 25(3), 179–181 (2008)
7. Yang, Y., Zhao, J., Yi, W.: Iterative Joint Source Channel Decoding For Multimedia Wireless Sensor Networks. CWSN, 12–15 (2008)
8. Liu, C., Zhao, J., Yi, W.: Design of wireless image sensor node based on nRF24L01. Electronic Measurement Technology 31(6), 136–139 (2008)
9. Gao, F., Yu, L., Wang, Y., et al.: Development of host computer software for crop water status monitoring system based on wireless sensor networks. Transactions of the CSAE 26(5), 175–181 (2010)
10. Feng, G., Li, Y., Zhang, W., et al.: Research and design of crop water status monitoring system based on wireless sensor networks. Transactions of the CSAE 25(2), 107–112 (2009)
11. Cai, Y., Liu, G., Li, L., et al.: Design and test of nodes for farmland data acquisition based on wireless sensor network. Transactions of the CSAE 25(4), 176–178 (2009)
12. Li, X., Sun, Z., Xiao, C., et al.: Development of remote monitoring system based on $\mu$C/OS-II embedded technology for agricultural environment. Transactions of the CSAE 23(10), 156–161 (2007)

13. Li, X., Sun, Z., Huang, T.: Study on application of embedded system for the agricultural information acquisition based on WEB. Agriculture Network Information (12), 33–37 (2005)

14. Xiong, J., Li, Z., Chen, P., et al.: Design and implementation of metadata-based technology platform for data sharing. Microcomputer & It's Applications (9), 13–16 (2010)

15. Fu, Y., Tian, Z., Zhao, X., et al.: Two applications of oracle DD basing on VBA and ASP. Computer Engineering and Applications (6), 178–181 (2005)

# Study on Query System Based on Pomology Domain Ontology

Qian Sun, Qiulan Wu, and Yong Liang

School of Information Science and Engineering,
Shandong Agricultural University,
Taian, China, 271018
applesq@163.com

**Abstract.** This paper studied the construction of Pomology Domain Ontology (PDO), and the realization of PDO-based query system. First, an approach to build PDO based on Agriculture Science Thesaurus (AST) was proposed, which consists of confirming core concepts, adding the properties of concepts, confirming the relationships between concepts, adding the instances of concepts, and representing domain ontology. Then the PDO-based query system model and implementation algorithm were given. The query system realized class query, instance query, and property query by Jena. Query results indicate that the algorithm is practical and the search time is shortened. Through the query system pomology knowledge can be obtained from PDO according to user needs.

**Keywords:** Protégé, Jena, query, owl, Pomology, ontology.

## 1    Introduction

With the development of owl ontology language, more and more knowledge systems based on domain ontology are developed. The development of knowledge system includes knowledge representation, storage, reasoning, query and so on, in which query technique is one of the key technologies, through it knowledge can be obtained from ontology [1]. In order to realize pomology knowledge query from PDO according to several conditions demanded by users, the query system based on PDO is studied in this paper.

## 2    Tools on Ontology

In recent years, a variety of tools have been developed by different research institutes, including ontology editing tools, ontology parsing tools and so on. Protégé and Jena are used to model and parse PDO in this study.

### 2.1    Protégé

Protégé is a free, open source ontology editor, which allows developers to model ontology. The Protégé platform supports two main ways of modeling ontology via the

D. Li and Y. Chen (Eds.): CCTA 2011, Part I, IFIP AICT 368, pp. 180–187, 2012.

protégé-frames and protégé-owl editors. Protégé ontology can be exported into a variety of formats including RDF(S) [2], OWL [3], and XML Schema. Protégé can be customized to provide domain-friendly support for creating knowledge models. Further more, Protégé can be extended by way of a plug-in architecture and a Java-based Application Programming Interface (API) for building knowledge-based tools [4].

## 2.2    Jena

Jena is a Java framework for building Semantic Web applications. It provides a programmatic environment for RDF, RDFS and OWL, SPARQL and includes a rule-based inference engine [5]. Jena is open source and grown out of work with the HP Labs Semantic Web Programme.

# 3    Construction of Pomology Domain Ontology

At present, ontology construction methodologies have not been standardized, there are numerous frequently quoted approaches. In this paper, thesaurus-based approach for building domain ontology [6] is improved, an approach to build PDO based on Agriculture Science Thesaurus (AST) is proposed. The process of it consists of the following phases:

## 3.1    Confirming Core Concepts

Thesaurus is made up of terms and the relationships between terms of certain domain, so the terms of domain ontology can be selected from it. In this case, core concepts of pomology domain are collected according to Agriculture Science Thesaurus (AST). Firstly, "Fruiter Crop" is selected as the first concept, and then "Fruiter Crop" is classified into eight genres: such as "Kernel Fruits", "Berry" and so on. These terms are all the sub-concepts of "Fruiter Crop". Secondly, the concepts relating to "Fruiter Crop" are selected. Table 1 gives the names and explanations of these concepts.

## 3.2    Adding the Properties of Concepts

Every confirmed core concept has many different properties to be added. For example, "name", "address", "telephone" and so on are added as the properties of "Academic Institution". In addition, properties of concepts can be inherited by their sub-concepts.

## 3.3    Confirming the Relationships between Concepts

By semantic analysis, the relationships between concepts can be classified into two genres:

## 1) Hierarchical relationships

According to part/whole relationship from AST, hierarchical relationships of concepts including broader/ narrower and instances relationships are confirmed.

## 2) Nonhierarchical relationships

For example, Table 2 gives the nonhierarchical relationships between "Expert-Scholar" and other concepts.

**Table 1.** The general concepts of pomology domain

| Name | Explanation |
|------|-------------|
| Fruiter Crop | Refers to the concepts of fruiter species |
| Expert - Scholar | Reflects the personal and academic information of researchers who study pomology in china. |
| Academic_ Institution | Reflects information about academic institutes, research institutes, and associations related to pomology. |
| Establishment | Instances :sprinkler, equipment, greenhouse and so on. |
| Environment | Soil, landform , sunlight .etc |
| Research project | Reflects the projects that are worked by Expert-Scholars |
| Fruit Breeding | Reflects skills of fruit breeding |
| Fruit Planting | Reflects means and conditions of planting |

**Table 2.** The nonhierarchical relationships between "Expert -Scholar" and other concepts

| Name | Explanation | Opposite |
|------|-------------|----------|
| Department | Reflects relationship between "Expert-Scholar" and "Academic Institution" | Researcher |
| Implement | Reflects relationship between "Expert-Scholar" and "Fruit Breeding" | Executant |
| Research Direction | Reflects relationship of "Expert-Scholar" studying on "Planting" ," Breeding" and "Fruiter Crop" | Be studied |
| Using | Reflects relationship between "Expert-Scholar" and "Establishment" | Be used |
| Choosing | Reflects relationship between "Expert-Scholar" and "Environment" | Be chosen |

## 3.4    Adding the Instances of Concepts

It is necessary for building domain ontology to supply the instances of concepts. For example: in this case, "Shandong Agriculture University", "Fruiter Association" are added as the instances of "Academic Institution". Further, the values of all properties of instances are supplied.

## 3.5    Representing Pomology Domain Ontology

In this case, protégé is selected as the developing tool, so the PDO can be represented by OWL. Further illustrate below:

Firstly, according to the confirmed core concepts, corresponding classes of PDO are created by using protégé. Classes hierarchy structure of PDO can be shown by OWLVizTab in protégé. Secondly, data properties and object properties of classes are added. Nonhierarchical relationships between concepts can be represented by means of adding object properties. For example: Fig.1 represents the relationships between "Expert –Scholar" and other classes by JambalayaTab. Finally, instances of classes are added. Since relationships can be inherited, instances have the same relationships (see Fig.2). After that, an owl file (Pomology.owl) is created by protégé.

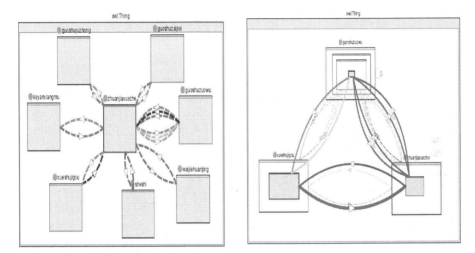

**Fig. 1.** Non-hierarchical relationships between Expert-Scholar and other classes

**Fig. 2.** Non-hierarchical relationships between three instances

# 4   Design and Realization of Query System Based on Pomology Domain Ontology

## 4.1   Architecture of Query Model

In order to design query system, the model of it is built at first .The model consists of five modules, which are shown in the Fig.3. Further illustrate below.

By using interactive query interface, users can customize query conditions, which are sent into query processor. The functions of the query processor are executing corresponding algorithm and calling Jena methods according to the given query conditions, further, this processor supports three kinds of query, which are class query, property query, and instance query. Parsing ontology file, it is a way to access and draw information from ontology file. After reading ontology file, the information of ontology classes, properties, and instances can be obtained and saved into storage structure by calling the Jena methods. Finally, the query results can be outputted in the visual interface.

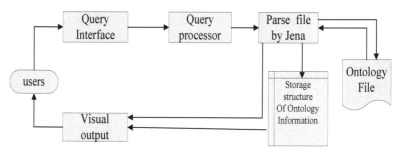

**Fig. 3.** Flow-process diagram of query model

## 4.2     Parsing the Pomology Domain Ontology

Jena is used to parse the PDO in this study. The phases are as follows: firstly, an ontology model is created through the Jena ModelFactory.createOntologyModel(); secondly, using the read () method, an ontology document ( Pomology.owl ) is loaded into the created ontology model; finally, the owl file is parsed by using Jena API.

The methods of Jena that are used in this study are listed below:

All direct subclasses of ontology class can be found by calling listSubClasses (). In order to represent PDO hierarchy as tree structure, an algorithm is designed. The details of it are as below: "owl-thing" is set as root-node of the tree, and then set direct subclasses as child nodes of the root-node, in the end, all subclasses of PDO are obtained through using recursive algorithm. In addition, by using listIndividuals() method, all instances of the PDO can be returned; and all properties can be returned by the method listAllOntProperties().

## 4.3     Realization of Query System

This query system realizes three kinds of query, which are class query, instance query, and property query. Further illustrate below:

### 1) Class query

Firstly, class query realizes functions of class hierarchy queries. Methods of query are as follows: given an ontology class object, a list subclasses of this class are obtained by calling listSubClasses(); the direct superclass of this class is obtained by calling getSuperClass(); and a list instances of this class are obtained by calling listInstances(). In addition, class query lists properties of certain class by using listDeclaredProperties().

Secondly, class query supports interactive query [7], which can execute query on classes according to several conditions demanded by users. Further illustrate below: given the name of property, a list of classes related to this property are saved as to a arraylist by calling listDomain(); then a subclasses collection of the given superclass are saved as to another arraylist by calling listSubClasses(); Finally, the intersection of two arraylists is obtained, which are classes that have given superclass and property together.

The class hierarchy tree is on the left side of visual query interface, and the interactive interface is on the right side. While user clicks a random treenode of this tree, subclasses, superclass, properties and instances of this class are displayed on the right side (see Fig.4). Further more, by clicking "query" button, users can make use of interactive interface, in which several query conditions can be selected from JComboBoxs, and results of query are displayed.

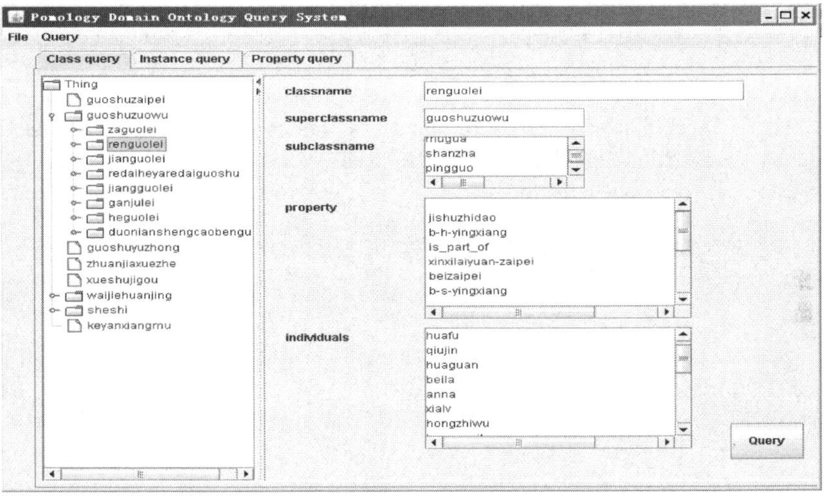

**Fig. 4.** Class query interface

## 2) Instance query

Firstly, the function of finding out all properties of the given instance is realized, details of the method are as follows: given instance, the listProperties() method can return a set of statements (triples), the predicate of a statement (property) can be got by using statement getPredicate() method , the Object of a statement can be obtained by calling getObject()[8],the algorithm is as follows:

```
NS=omx.getNsPrefixURI("");//omx is ontology model
note1=(DefaultMutableTreeNode)
jTree2.getLastSelectedPathComponent();
Individual in=omx.getIndividual(NS+note1);
for(StmtIterator ip=in.listProperties();ip.hasNext();)
{ Statement out=(Statement) ip.next();
  String p=out.getPredicate().getLocalName().toString();
  OntProperty a1=omx.getOntProperty(NS+p);
  s=s+p;//String s
  RDFNode tt= out.getObject();}
```

Since the Object of a statement can be either a resource or literal, the method returns an object typed as RDFNode, the algorithm of processing RDFNode is as follows:

```
if (tt instanceof Resource) //judge RDFNode tt is
Resource
{ s=s+"  value "+(((Resource)
tt).getLocalName().toString()); }
else { s=s+" Value \"" + tt.toString() + "\""; // tt is a
literal}
```

Secondly, interactive instance query supports query on instance according to several conditions demanded by users. Given ontology class, several names and values of properties, all instances of given class can be found and saved to a arraylist, and then instances that have given certain properties and values can be queried too, the query results of different properties are saved to different arraylists, finally, the intersection of all arraylists is obtained.

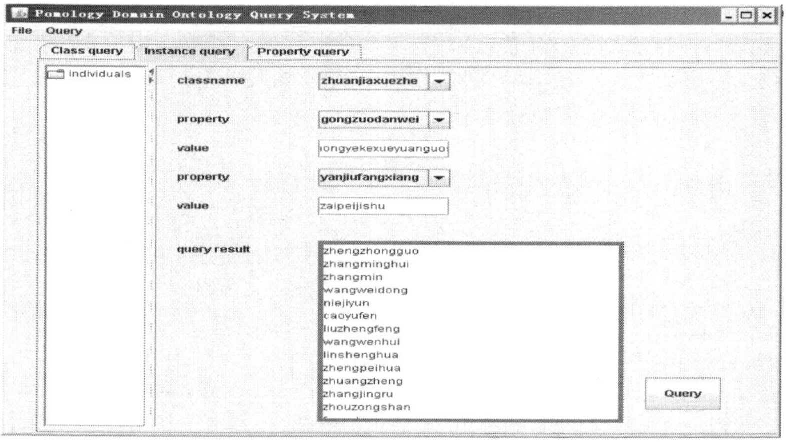

**Fig. 5.** Instance query interface

The list instances of the PDO are displayed on the left side of query interface, while user select one from the list, all properties of the certain instance are displayed. By using the interactive interface, users can accomplish interactive query. For example, while user input "zhuanjiaxuezhe", "gongzuodanwei" 'zhongguonongyekexueyuanguoshusuo", "yanjiufangxiang", "zaipeijishu" in turn, the query results are expert-scholars who research  on  fruit planting and work in Pomology Institute of Chinese Academy of Agricultural Sciences (see Fig.5).

**3) Property query**
The property query realizes returning domain of the given property by calling getdomain(), and the range of the property by calling getrange(). Further, this query supports query on property according to given domain, range, type and so on.

The list Properties of the PDO are displayed on the left side of query interface, while user select one from the list, the domain and the range of the certain property are displayed.

## 5     Conclusion

In this paper, the modeling of PDO is studied, design and realization techniques of the query system based on PDO are proposed. This query system realizes class query, property query, and instance query by using Jena, further more, it supports interactive query. Through it pomology knowledge can be obtained from PDO according to user needs. Query results show that the query system based on PDO is practical for users to query information from PDO.

**Acknowledgements.** I would like to express my gratitude to all those who have helped me during the writing of this thesis. I acknowledge the help of Professor Liang Yong. I do appreciate his professional instructions. I would like to thank Wu Qiulan, who kindly gave me a hand when I was meeting difficulties.

Last but not the least, my gratitude also extends to my family who have been assisting, supporting and caring for me all of my life.

## References

1. Li, H.Q.: Ontology Storage and Querying Technology. Beijing University of Posts and Telecommunications (2007)
2. Resource Description Framework, http://www.w3.org/RDF/
3. Bechhofer, S., Harmelen, F.V., Hendler, J., et al.: OWL Web Ontology Language Reference. W3C Recommendation February 10 (2004), http://www.w3.org/TR/owl-ref/
4. Protégé, http://protege.stanford.edu/
5. Jena A Semantic Web Framework for Java, http://jena.sourceforge.net/
6. Tang, A.M., Zhen, Q.: The Study on Thesaurus-based Construction of Domain Ontology. New Technology of Library and Information Service, 41–45 (2005)
7. Wu, J.L.: Research and Implementation of Semantic Retrieval System based on Domain Ontology. Taiyuan University of Technology (2010)
8. Sheng, Q.Y., Yin, G.S.: Jena-based Dynamic Semantic Retrieval Method. Computer Engineering 35(16), 62–64 (2009)

# Research on Control System of Variable Rate Fertilizer Applicator in Precision Farming Based on Combined Positioning of GPS, Electronic Compass and Gyroscope[*]

Guobing Pan[1,2] and Xiao Feng[2]

[1] Structure Engineering Lab, Chongqing Jiaotong University,
No.66 Xuefu Road Nan'an District Chongqing China, China, 400074
[2] School of Civil Engineering & Archtecture, Chongqing Jiaotong University,
No.66 Xuefu Road Nan'an District Chongqing China, China, 400074

**Abstract.** On the Background of precision farming and the precision positioning of variable rate fertilization, the precision farming was achieved and the per unit yield was raised by the integrated positioning method using GPS, electronic compass, and gyroscope.

**Keywords:** Precision farming, combined positioning, variable rate fertilization.

## 1 Introduction

China is a great agricultural country, but in a situation of large population with relatively little land. Arable land resources limited, however, China feeds 22% of the world's population with less than 10% of the land in the world. With the rapid development of science and technology, the introduction and experiment of the concept of precision farming, and the new challenges of the traditional fertilization systems, exploration has been made domestically and abroad[1,2]. Precision fertilization is only part of precision farming, but with a undefined concept and immature theory and technical system.This paper mainly discussed about the theory and technical system of combined positioning method based on GPS, electronic compass and gyroscope.

## 2 Outline of Precision Farming and the Main Technological Ideas

### 2.1 Meaning of Precision Farming

Precision farming is a modern and meticulous agriculture technology, which based on modern information high-tech and equipment engineering technology. It basically

---

[*] The fund of structure engineering of chongqing jiaotong university (CQSLBF-Y011-4). The fund of experiment teaching and reform of chongqing jiaotong university(SY1201003).

D. Li and Y. Chen (Eds.): CCTA 2011, Part I, IFIP AICT 368, pp. 188–192, 2012.

means to adjust the crop input according to soil properties of the crop. In another words, on one hand it finds out the soil properties insides the plot soils and the space mutation of the productivity. On the other hand, it makes certain of the production target and conducts system diagnostic, optimizing formula,  technical assembly, and scientific management firmly, so that it can mobilize the soil productivity to get equel or higher output with the least or the most economical input, and improve the environment to make the economic benefits and environmental benefits with all kinds of agricultural resources efficiently[3,4].

### 2.2    Main Technological Ideas of Precision Farming

Precision farming includes aspects such as precision seeding, precision fertilization, precision irrigation and precision harvest. However, the development of precision agriculture makes a new requirement for theory and technical of rational fertilization. From the use of fertilizer, the contribution rate on food production is 40%; but the utilization rate of nitrogen is only 50%, phosphorus 30% and potassium 60% even in countries which owns a high fertilizer utilization rate. Low utilization rate of fertilizer makes a higher producing cost, and leads to environmental issues, such as the pollution of underground and surface water, and excessive content of nitrate in fruits and vegetables. In a word, fertilization is closely relevent to agricultural production, product quality, and food and environmental pollution. And the theory and technology of precision fertilization is the key solution[5].

## 3    Necessity of Precise Fertilization

The relationship of soil, crop and nutrient is very complicated. Although the necessary major elements and micro-elements during the growth of crop have been fixed, the degree of nutrient which crops need varies from different plants. The difference in nutrient demands can be great in different growing seasons even for the same crop. Seedling stage is a temporary nutrition period for crop. In this period, there is less requirement for the quantity of nutrient, but the demand of nutrient must be complete, effective and adequate. Many crops need a certain kind of most and best nutrient in the most efficient period of nutrient. The most efficient period of different nutrients for the same crop can be different, and it is also the same with different crops. Different nutrients are irreplaceable, namely, the crop production is limited by the least nutrient which can not be replaced by other nutrients. What is more, the overuse of fertilizer to eliminate  restrictions of minimum nutrient rate brings a series of environment problems. Therefor, in order to adapt to different regions, different crops, different soil and different environment for various crops, and to achieve good economic benefit and environmental benefits, variable rate fertilizing is absolutely the key development direction of fertilization in the future[6,7].

# 4    Integrated Positioning Method Based on GPS, Electronic Compass and Gyroscope

## 4.1    Combined Positioning

It is required for precision fertilization that the agricultural machinery should work on the prearranged route in the field, reach its destination accurately and than complete the work. Precision guiding is one of the key technologies to automate the agricultural machinery, and the positioning accuracy of it directly affects the path tracking of the agricultural machinery. Thus the adoption of efficient and reliable navigation and positioning accuracy should be put to the priority to ensure the path following of agricultural machinery and realize the precision of automatic fertilization. The positioning of agricultural machinery includes heading information and location information. In the respect of navigation technology which mainly based on GPS, RTK-GPS and FOG are taken for existing researches to realize the positioning of the agricultural machinery, but it is of high cost. This paper used GPS of low cost and precision, combined with electronic compass and high accuracy inertial navigation system, to achieve the Precise positioning of agricultural machinery by Kalman filtering, as shown in Fig.1.

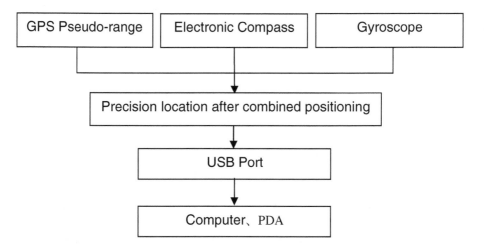

**Fig. 1.** The figure of combined positioning

## 4.2    Idea of Realizing Combined Positioning

1) Firstly, use pseudo-range difference GPS method to locate the primary location of agricultural machinery.

GPS receiver calculates the WGS-84 coordinates by pseudo-range difference. However, the fertilizer application machine uses Gauss plane coordinates, so Gauss projection should be made to convert the coordinates of  pseudo-range positioning to Gauss plane coordinates.

2) Use electronic compass and micromachined gyroscope to measure the heading angle of fertilizer application machine, and to predict the best heading angle.

① The heading angle of electronic compass and gyroscope can be set as $x_d$ and $x_t$ ; the corresponding error are $v_d$、 $v_t$ ; covariances of $x_d$ and $x_t$ are $r_{dd}$ and $r_{tt}$ ; the  covariance is $r_{dt}$ ; the time evaluation of rth sampling is $r_{dd}(r)$; the time evaluation of $r_{tt}$ is $r_{tt}(r)$; and the time evaluation of $r_{dt}(r)$ is $r_{td}(r)$. Time evaluation of $r_{dd}$、 $r_{tt}$ and $r_{td}$ of pre-sampling can be calculated by equations below.

When r<N

$$R_{dd}(r) = \frac{k-1}{k}R_{tt}(r-1) + \frac{1}{k}(x_d - u)(x_t - u) \tag{1}$$

$$R_{tt}(r) = \frac{N-1}{N}R_{dd}(r-1) + \frac{1}{N}(x_t - u)(x_d - u) \tag{2}$$

$$R_{td}(r) = R_{dt}(k) = \frac{k-1}{k}R_{td}(r-1) + \frac{1}{k}(x_d - u)(x_t - u) \tag{3}$$

When r>N

$$R_{dd}(r) = \frac{N-1}{N}R_{tt}(r-1) + \frac{1}{N}(x_d - u)(x_t - u) \tag{4}$$

$$R_{tt}(r) = \frac{N-1}{N}R_{dd}(r-1) + \frac{1}{N}(x_t - u)(x_d - u) \tag{5}$$

$$R_{td}(r) = R_{dt}(k) = \frac{N-1}{N}R_{td}(r-1) + \frac{1}{N}(x_d - u)(x_t - u) \tag{6}$$

In the equation above, $\mu$ is average sample data, and "N" is displacement distance of window.

② Measurement variance $\delta_d^2$、 $\delta_t^2$ of electronic compass and gyroscope can be calculated by equations below.

$$\delta_d^2 = R_{dd} - R_{dt} \tag{7}$$

$$\delta_t^2 = R_{tt} - R_{dt} \tag{8}$$

③ Heading angle "X" can be calculated by equation below.

$$X = \frac{x_d}{\delta_d^2 (\frac{1}{\delta_d^2 + \delta_t^2})} + \frac{x_t}{\delta_t^2 (\frac{1}{\delta_d^2 + \delta_t^2})} = \frac{\delta_d^2 x_t + \delta_t^2 x_d}{\delta_t^2 + \delta_d^2} \tag{9}$$

3) Use adaptive Kalman filter to recombine and amend the multi-source information including the primary location and the heading angle, locate agricultural machinery and precisely evaluate the heading angle information.

## 5    Conclusion

This research realized the precision positioning of agricultural machinery, ensured the principal issue of path tracking quality, and finally achieved the accuracy of automatic fertilization. The precise position after integrated positioning was sent to computer or PDA through USB port. Combined with the data of fertilizing and the field position information from the database, the goal of variable rate fertilization was finally reached, precision farming was realized, and the per unit yield was raised.

## References

1. Blackmore, B.S.: Precision farming:An introduction. Outlook on Agriculture 23, 275–280 (1994) CABI
2. Blackmore, B.S.: An information system for precision farming. Presented at the Brighton Conference Pests and Diseases. British crop Protection Council, pp. 18–21 (November 1996)
3. Lal, R.: Soil management in the developing contries. Soil Science 165(1), 57–72 (2000)
4. Pan, J., Fang, S., Sun, W., Chen, L.: A preliminary study on rice nitrogen application decision-making by soil information system — A case study of Dafeng City,Jiangsu Province. Journal of Nanjing Agricultural University 23(3), 53–56 (2000)
5. Meng, Z., Zhao, C., Liu, H., Huang, W., Fu, W., Wang, X.: Development and performance assessment of map-based variable rate granule application system. Journal of Jiangsu University(Natural Science Edition) 30(4), 338–342 (2009)
6. Sun, Z.-G., Yu, F., Zheng, C.-T., Ren, H.: Design of CPLD Control Module of GPS Variable Fertilization System. Journal of Agricultural Mechanization Research (3), 83–86 (2008)
7. Li, A., Wang, X., Wang, Z., Gao, F.: Research about Variable Rate Fertilization Closed-loop Control System of Electro-hydraulic Speed. Chinese Agricultural Science Bulletin 25(07), 272–275 (2009)

# The Architecture Analysis of Internet of Things

Nihong Wang and Wenjing Wu*

Information and Computer Engineering College of Northeast Forestry University,
Heilongjiang Harbin 150040, China
hlg05wj@126.com, wangnh989@163.com

**Abstract.** The Internet of Things, as an emerging global Internet-based technical architecture, facilitates the exchange of goods and services in global supply chain networks. The phrase Internet of Things (IoT) heralds a vision of the future Internet where connecting physical things, from banknotes to bicycles, through a network will let them take an active part in the Internet, exchanging information about themselves and their surroundings. The IoT industry is still in an early stage of development, whose technologies, standards, product and the market still need to be improved, and whose related areas also need to be studied and discussed. This paper presents detailed analysis and comparison about a misunderstanding of the current awareness: IoT = Internet + WSN, which enable people to understand IoT more thoroughly. The IoT is a network of connecting objects, whose architecture is different from that of the traditional network, which can not simply described by the use of layered network architecture. In this paper, based on the IoT itself, the three dimensions architecture is researched and found, which is the most suitable architecture of IoT.

**Keywords:** the Internet of Things, architecture analysis, wireless sensor network, the three dimensions architecture.

## 1    Introduction

In 1991, Mark Weiser described the vision of a future world under the name of Ubiquitous Computing. Since then, many details of the described vision have become reality: Our mobile phones are powerful multimedia systems, our cars computer systems on wheels, and our homes are turning into smart living environments. All these advances must be turned into products for very cost-sensitive world markets in shorter cycles than ever before [1].

The Internet of Things (IoT) is a network that combines all kinds of information sensing equipments with the internet. Its purpose is that all the items can be perceived and controlled remotely, and combined with the internet to form a more wisdom production and living systems. IoT describes a world where humans are surrounded by machines that communicate with each other and can allow people to interact with

---

* This work was supported by the foundation of the forestry nonprofit industry scientific research special project of the State Forestry Administration, namely "The monitoring technology based on the IoT and its application research in forestry."

D. Li and Y. Chen (Eds.): CCTA 2011, Part I, IFIP AICT 368, pp. 193–198, 2011.

the digital world. To succeed in this vision, it is not only the people who need an understanding of this multi-device environment, but also the network needs a representation of "who" the user is [2]. Vividly speaking, with the help of IoT, the car will automatically alarm when a misuse occurs in driving; the briefcase will put the owner in mind of something that he forgets; the clothes will tell the color and temperature of their requirement to washing machine; the outfall will send out a warning when the pollution exceeds the normal level; the traffic lights will dynamically control according to the crossing situation of pedestrian...

The concept of IoT break the traditional ideas and start a new technology field. Physical infrastructure and IT infrastructure has been separated in tradition. There are the infrastructure construction, such as airports, buildings, etc. on the one hand, and the data center, such as personal computers, broadband, etc. on the other hand. These two aspects exist relatively independently. However, they are integrated into a unified infrastructure in the era of IoT. The Internet of Things as an emerging global Internet-based information architecture facilitating the exchange of goods and services is gradually developing [3]. It will bring a new revolution of world information industry after the computer, internet and mobile communication network.

## 2    IoT = Internet + WSN (Wireless Sensor Network)?

In the research communities, IoT has been defined from various different perspectives. The reason of today apparent fuzziness around this term is a consequence of the name "Internet of Things" itself, which syntactically is composed of two terms. The first one pushes towards a network oriented vision of IoT, while the second one moves the focus on generic "objects" to be integrated into a common framework [4].The Internet of Things is an extension and expansion network based on the internet, whose users extend and expand to the information exchange and communications between any goods. It leads to the emerging saying: IoT = Internet + WSN. To analyze the correctness of this statement, the differences between IoT, internet and WSN are compared below (in Table.1).

From the analysis and comparison of characteristics in table 1, IoT ≠ Internet + WSN is obvious. There are two clear points here. Firstly, IoT may not necessarily use IP network. At least, the IP network that can only provide "best effort" transmission capacity is not inappropriate. The IoT has much higher requirement to its bearer network than the current internet. Secondly, especially small intelligent objects network, IoT requires the best use of lightweight communication protocol. So, complex protocol like TCP/IP can not be used in the smart little things network. By starting from the considerations above, IoT will be a different environment from the internet, but can not be a simple extension of current Internet.

Since the IoT is not only a mere extension of today's Internet, but rather a complex netting of independent but interoperable systems, implemented in a symbiosis with new services and different modes of communication, the traditional Internet Governance concepts are not anymore suitable to identically be applied [5]. We should speed up the process of information social, which lays a good foundation for the development of IoT.

**Table 1.** Differences Between Internet, WSN and IoT

| Feature items | Internet | WSN | IoT |
|---|---|---|---|
| Identify goods | Can not | Can | Must |
| Perceive goods | Can not | Can | Must |
| Nodes types | Active | Active | Active and passive |
| Network coverage | Wide area | Local area | Wide area |
| The number of network nodes | Unlimited | Limited | Unlimited |
| Networking approaches | Determine the backbone, flexible access | Self-organization | Determine the backbone, Independent access |
| Networking time | Unlimited | Unlimited | Timing synchronization |
| Networking data processing | End nodes | End nodes, aggregation nodes | All nodes |
| Information relevance | Unrelated | Related | Related |
| Application relevance | Unrelated | Unrelated | Related |
| Items semantic recognition | No | End nodes | End nodes, aggregation nodes |
| Items semantic processing | No | End nodes optional | End nods, aggregation nodes |
| self feedback control | No | End nodes optional | Multi-stage self-feedback |

## 3     The Three Dimensions Architecture of IoT

The IoT has the potential to add a new dimension to this process by enabling communications with and among smart objects, thus leading to the vision of "anytime, anywhere, anymedia, anything" communications. To this purpose, we observe that the IoT should be considered as part of the overall Internet of the future, which is likely to be dramatically different from the Internet we use today [4]. The IoT is a network in which everything can communicate with each other. Its architecture that is different from the traditional network's, should not be simply described through layered network architecture.

The system of IoT itself is composed of three dimensions which contain information items, independent networks and intelligent applications. In Fig. 1, the main concepts, technologies and features are highlighted and classified with reference to the three dimensions of IoT. The diagram clearly depicts that IoT paradigm will lead to the convergence of the three main dimensions addressed of IoT [6]. Information items are those that can identify and perceive their own message; independent networks have the capabilities of self-configuration, self-healing, self-optimizing, self-protection; intelligent applications mean the application with the capabilities of intelligent control and processing. The three dimensions of IoT (including the independent network) are that the traditional network system does not have, but that the network connected items must have. Otherwise, IoT will not be able to meet the application requirements.

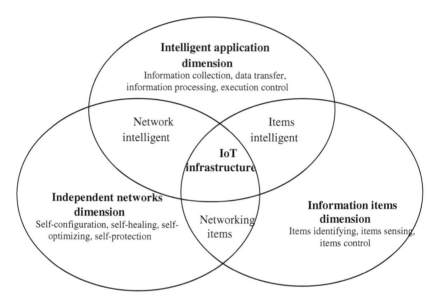

**Fig. 1.** Three dimensions architecture of IoT

The overlapping part of information items, independent networks and intelligent applications is the system of IoT with all the characteristics of IoT, which can be called the IoT infrastructure. Currently, the IoT system is not perfect but a total of general network system to connect items such as Intelligent Transportation System, Intelligent Electric Grid System, Smart City. The infrastructure of IoT here means that the support systems to serve the specific things, which can provide various services including the goods identification, location identification of space objects, features authentication of items' data and privacy protection in different application areas. It is the core of public Internet of Things.

The IoT needs to include items feature dimension, which is that the traditional networks don't have. Items connected to the IoT can be called information items, which have the basic features: with electronic identification, can transmit information. The networks constituting IoT need to connect a variety of items, which have the features of self-configuration and self-protection at least, and belong to a kind of independent network; the application of IoT generally related items which have the automatic collection, transmission and data processing, routine control automatically, and belongs to a kind of intelligent application.

Independent networks are an advanced form of today's networks, which will be simplified to a general network once treat with self-configuring, self-healing, self-optimizing and self-protection, the network can be describe using the hierarchical model; if intelligence applications are entirely   processed through a man-machine interactive interface, it will be reduced to an ordinary network application; if IoT no longer connect items directly but input the item information through the man-machine interactive interface, it will no longer need to identify the items and automatically transfer items information. In this way, the IoT will be simplified into a general network system, which can be described by the layered architecture of modern network. So, existing Internet architecture can be considered as a special case of the three dimensions architecture of IoT.

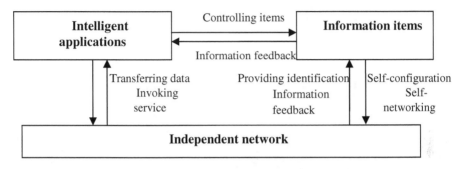

**Fig. 2.** The relationships of three Dimensions of IoT

The relationships between three dimensions of IoT are vividly showed in Fig.2, which make us understand the meaning of IoT intensively. The characteristic of IoT can be analyzed and evaluated, and network system can be determined that whether it is the IoT system by three visions architecture model of IoT. For example, if a network can only connect and perceive the goods but do not have the intelligent application, which does not belong to a complete IoT. Therefore, the sensor network does not belong to a complete IoT, which just has the features of independent network and information items.[7]

## 4     Conclusion

The IoT can be applied extensively in all walks of life such as automation and industrial manufacturing, logistics, business / process management, intelligent transportation, intelligent home, etc., which can be used widely in the agricultural fields. In terms of the different stages in agricultural production, the IoT can be used to improve its efficiency from the planting stage to harvesting stage. For example, in the preparation stage of cultivation, a lot of sensors are arranged in the greenhouse, which can analyze real-time soil information to choose the right crops. In the stages of planting and nurturing, the IoT can be used to collect temperature and humidity information, which provides high-efficient management to respond to environmental changes. Then in the harvest stage of crops, the IoT can be also used to gather the information of various properties in its transmission stage and use stage, back to the front, which can estimate accurately in the stage of harvest. The communication between objects is required, and will create notion value, thus will provide impetus and opportunities for the development of communication, which is the value of IoT.

The vision of the Internet of Things is in an embryonary state. Most of the elements of our world, our things do not have the digital intelligence that enables them to be aware of the existence of a virtual cyberworld, where they could be able to collaborate with literally billions of entities: other things, humans, computational processes, our own physical environment, and so on [8]. NIC foresees that "by 2025 Internet nodes may reside in everyday things – food packages, furniture, paper documents, and more". It highlights future opportunities that will arise, starting from the idea that "popular demand combined with technology advances could drive widespread diffusion of an Internet of Things (IoT) that could, like the present Internet, contribute invaluably to economic development". The possible threats deriving from a widespread adoption of such a technology are also stressed. Indeed, it is emphasized that "to the extent that everyday objects become information security risks, the IoT could distribute those risks far more widely than the Internet has to date".

We should provide effective legal guarantee, supporting policy for IoT by legal, administrative and economic means, so that IoT really become an open, secure, trustable network. Then, we can realize the integration of human social and physical system, and manage the production and life more meticulously and dynamically, and improve the utilization rate of resources and productivity, consequently, improve the relationship between man and nature.

# References

1. Zuehlke, D.: SmartFactory-Towards a factory-of-things. Annual Reviews in Control 34, 129–138 (2010)
2. Sarma, A.C., Girão, J.: Identifies in the Future Internet of Things. Wireless Pers. Commun. 49, 353–363 (2009)
3. Weber, R.H.: Accountability in the Internet of Things. Computer Law & Security Review 27, 133–138 (2011)
4. Atzori, L., Iera, A., Morabito, G.: The Internet of Things: A survey. Computer Networks, 1–19 (2010)
5. Weber, R.H.: Internet of things– Need for a new legal environment? Computer Law & Security Review 25, 522–527 (2009)
6. Bandyopadhyay, D., Sen, J.: Internet of Things: Applications and Challenges in Technology and Standardization. Wireless Pers. Commun. 58, 49–69 (2011)
7. Shen, S.-B., Mao, Y.-Q., Fan, Q.-L., et al.: Conception Model and architecture of the Internet of Things. Journal of Nanjing University of Posts and Telecommunications (Natural Science) 30(4), 1–8 (2010)
8. Roman, R., Alcaraz, C., Lopez, J., et al.: Key management systems for sensor networks in the context of the Internet of Things. Computers and Electrical Engineering 37, 147–159 (2011)

# Design on Cucumber Traceability System Based on the Internet of Things

Bai Qu[1], Xinchao Jing[2], Xiaojun Wang[2], Ying Li[3], and Yong Liang[2,*]

[1] School of Information Science & Engineering,
Shandong Agricultural University, Tai'an 271018
[2] School of Food Science & Engineering, Shandong Agricultural University,
Tai'an 271018
[3] School of Economics & Management, Shandong Agricultural University,
Tai'an 271018, P.R. China
yongl@sdau.edu.cn

**Abstract.** With the development of science and technology, the problem about the quality safety traceability of agricultural products has already become the hot topic of researchers in various fields. Cucumber is one of the main vegetable crops in China. It is convenient for eating and contains various beneficial minerals. With the constant expansion of the planting areas, it plays a more and more important role in the development of agricultural economy. However, the cucumbers sold on the market at present have residues of pesticides and growth hormone and many other problems. In this article, firstly, the author analyses the feasibility of the application of internet of things and electronic label technology in cucumber traceability system. And then, the author puts forward basic requirements of design on cucumber traceability system according to domestic and overseas research situation; Based on this, the author makes the whole design on cucumber traceability system, together with the specific design on three-layer structure and function of the internet of things and the research and development of the enterprise management system and the internet service system of cucumber traceability system. Finally, the author integrates cucumber traceability system based on the internet of things and realizes the traceability management of the whole process of cucumber planting, sales and monitoring, and provides effective technical support for production and sales management.

**Keywords:** Food safety, The internet of things, Cucumber, Traceability system.

## 1 Introduction

Cucumber, originated in the equatorial rain forest area of South Himalayas, belongs to the gourd family of cucumber. It is one-year rampant herb and has a cultivation history of more than 2000 years in China. Cucumber is convenient for eating, rich in

---

* Corresponding author.

D. Li and Y. Chen (Eds.): CCTA 2011, Part I, IFIP AICT 368, pp. 199–208, 2012.

vitamins A and C, and contains a variety of useful minerals. It is one of the main vegetable crops in China. In recent years, with the rapid development of China's economy and the agricultural and industrial structure adjustment, cucumber cultivation in China also experiences great changes. These changes include that planting areas expanded rapidly; variety gets richer; the division of cultivation of crop rotation is more detailed; and annual production was realized. Cucumber is a common kind of vegetables but the distribution of cucumber cultivation areas in China is very uneven in the past, mainly concentrated in the provinces where there are good climatic conditions and natural environment, such as Shandong, Henan and Hainan province. In recent years, the distribution of cucumber cultivation areas in China spreads gradually. Almost every province has some great cucumber production bases around every big city. Regional production is getting increasingly prominent. By the end of 2002, cucumber cultivation area reached 1.253 million hectares in China, which is nearly 3 times of that in 1980. It accounted for about 10% of the national vegetable area. 58% of the cucumber was planted in the outdoors.

At present, the main problem of cucumber sold in the markets is the residues of pesticides and growth hormone. In 2008-2009, the Green Peace Organization of the World conducted sampling tests on 17 kinds of vegetables and fruits in many supermarkets in Beijing, Shanghai and Guangzhou, which showed that pesticide residues of the cucumber ranked the first, containing 4-13 different kinds of pesticide residues. Losses often happened due to heavy pest and disease infestations in the cultivation process of the cucumber. Farmers still use chemical pesticides to control pests, but this often causes serious excessive pesticide residues in cucumber although pests and plant diseases are wiped out. In production, pesticide residues are often caused by unreasonable and improper selection of pesticide and fertilization, such as nitrate toxic residues in fruits, which can cause food poisoning after eating.

Now an important cause of frequent food safety issues is that the consumers, and even managers do not know the food sources of their own consumption, either can they trace back when a problem occurs. This puts illegal businessmen who are manufacturing and trading fake goods and drugs and the consumers in totally unequal positions. How we shall control the food quality and production process effectively has become a problem to be solved urgently. Food traceability system as a means of information communication can collect food quality-related information from field to fork, and realize the delivery and sharing of information between related subjects to overcome information asymmetries. It is convenient for managers to monitor, and the consumer can query at anytime. The producers can keep a record of the relative information during the production, transport and processing of cucumbers, which ensures that the quality control and quality security of the products can be traced back from production to the final of the entire sales process. This is also helpful to the quality control and the management of products in library [1].

At present, the key technology of food traceability is the quick and accurate capture, transmission and data processing of all kinds of information. The internet of things can solve these problems. Therefore, internet technology's application in food traceability will achieve better supervision results, providing effective means for food safety responsibilities. This article is to structure a cucumber traceability system based on the internet of things to address food safety problems of cucumber.

## 2     Application Analyses on Technology of the Internet of Things

The internet of things means to implant embedded chips and software that have perception, calculation ability and executive ability into the physical world entity and make it an intelligent object. It can realize information transmission, collaboration and processing through network facilities, and then realize the association between things and things, or between things and people. It can realize the links at any time, in any place and between any objects, making people to manage production and life in a more delicate and dynamic way to achieve "wisdom" state and improve resource utilization and productivity level. It can improve the relationship between human and nature and enhance the whole social informatization ability. Thus, the technology of the internet of things provides technical support for food safety problems.

The internet of things contains perception layer, transport layer and application layer. Electronic label technology, also named Radio Frequency Identification, is applied in perception layer. The Chinese Items Coding Center of China Standardization Institute has been trying to apply the bar code technology to domestic food traceability for years, and promotes the application of the bar code technology in our country's food traceability though "China Bar Code Push" project. It realizes the internet of things in the entire process of agricultural logistics, and creates RFID tag for the agricultural products, establishing the tracking and monitoring of the whole progress of agricultural products' planting, production, processing, transportation and sales. It realizes the quality traceability system of the entire process from the fields to the table.

In general, the technology of the internet of things can realize the quality control of the entire process of vegetable production from planting and harvesting to transportation and sales, as well as realizing quality tracking, production file management, conversion between FID labels and bar code information, Bar code label printing and the tracing and inquiring functions of vegetable quality safety based on web site, telephone and mobile phone text messages [2].

## 3     Demand Analysis and System Design of Cucumber Traceability System

Tracing system relies on modern database management technology, network technology and bar code technology. It records, collects and inquires the entire link information of the whole food chain from production, processing, packaging, storage and transportation, distribution to sales. It can trace back to the food source and the flow of it. When food has problems, it can inquire back to each link and provide effective supervision for food safety.

### 3.1    Demand Analysis of Traceability System

Tracing system reefers to the tools and hardware facilities applied to carry out trace target, and it combines material flow with information flow through the automatic identification technology and records the production information throughout the whole supply chain. It completes information transmission and release in each link of the supply chain by using the network technology and achieves the purpose of real things' traceability. Tracing system should also meet the following requirements:

① It features low cost, convenient operation and easy to promote. In the food safety field, if we implant a RFID into every piece of vegetable or fish, its cost will be so high that consumers would not pay for the extra spending.

② The structure of the internet of things is reasonable and the function is powerful. It not only involves sensor, processor and other hardware, but the software and agreement. Most of these are far from being perfect and even in a state of blank. Domestic device, the domestic agreement and domestic related software products are highly needed [3].

③ It requires to set up the whole process monitoring and management information system. At present, although there is relevant domestic tracing system, its application scope is limited, most in meat and poultry products. Nowadays, how we shall use the information technology services and application system to improve vegetable quality tracking system and establish the whole process monitoring and management information system "from field to table" is still the common goal for researchers in agricultural information technology and products safety fields [4][5].

④ It also demands information visualized expression. In order to change traditional origin information management mode simply by text statistics, it is urgently needed to realize visual expression of spatial information of origin planting block using GIS technology and return to the specific space position and attributes information of the origin of agricultural products in a graphical way [6].

⑤ Traceability information is standard enough to reach the purpose of the resources sharing. Because the development goals and principle of the existing tracing system are different, traceability information is not standard, while the information flow is not consistent and system software is not compatible, which causes it impossible to share and exchange traceability information [7].

### 3.2    The Overall Design of the System

The system will realize the traceability management of the whole production process of cucumber, including planting, sales and monitoring through the technology of the internet of things, and will realize visual search function through the help of GIS technology and further enrich the query information of cucumber traceability by using three-dimensional encoding technology. Through scanning the traceability code on vegetables product packaging, market terminal inquire system will accurately show the whole information of the cucumber. The system structure and working principle are shown in figure 1.

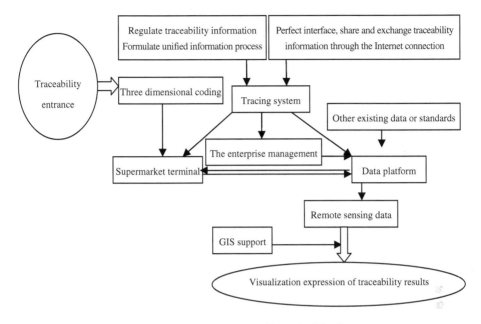

**Fig. 1.** System structure and working principle diagram

This system mainly includes the enterprise management information system, food safety and quality data platform and terminal inquire system.

(1) The enterprise management information system uses a certain information technology and bar code technology for cucumber production enterprises, and enter area server online. As to the information during the production process with multiplied entries, inconvenient online entry, and a small amount of data, automatic acquisition of the three-dimensional code information stored on the RFID attached to the product packaging is conducted through handheld wireless devices. And then the wireless terminal determine geographical locations automatically through the GPS location positioning technologies and send information like three-dimensional information, the name of the company that collects the information, acquisition time, place and responsible person, etc. to the regional server remotely via GPRS. The system controls the process of production and conducts a computer management from cultivation and sales to processing and packaging.

(2) Food safety and quality data platform mainly receives various information from enterprises, inspection bodies and certification bodies. The application of this platform can ensure that end-market (supermarkets) receive the latest information every day.

(3) In the supermarket terminal, by scanning the traceability code on vegetable product packaging, terminal inquiry system will accurately display the basic situation of the company, farmers, vegetable cultivation, drug use fertilizer, acquisition time, processing workers and processing dates, testing information and other data[8-9].

### 3.3    Designs on the System of the Internet of Things

Tracing system is designed to make effective logo of all links of the cucumber production processing and complete the automatic acquisition and storage of information. After the collection of information, the system will make full use of modern database technology to complete automatic management and preservation of mass information and automatically generate file management files. For the convenience of information collection, sharing and effective management, the traceability system is also required to make full use of modern computer network management technology.

The real-time monitoring and real-time decision of cucumber tracing system from "nerve" to the entire operation must be supported by the internet of things. When any nerve end of the system receives an entry information, this system can respond in a very short time and quickly call data and make related information feedback.

Through the use of RFID technology and EPC standards in information collection, transmission and processing, the system can provide agricultural product safety information for each step of cucumber traceability, realize non-contact interaction and processing make fast and efficient convert, processing and feedback and constituent the internet of things. The function design of the three layers of the internet of things is shown in figure 2, and the internet of things throughout the whole process of traceability system is shown in figure 3.

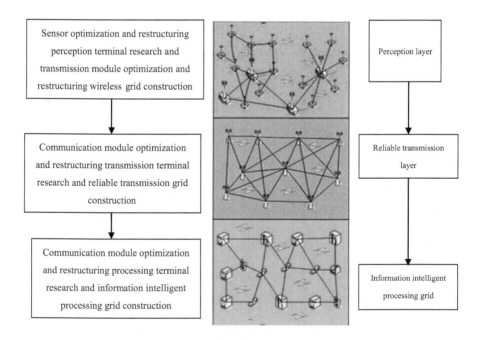

**Fig. 2.** The function design of the three layers of the internet of things

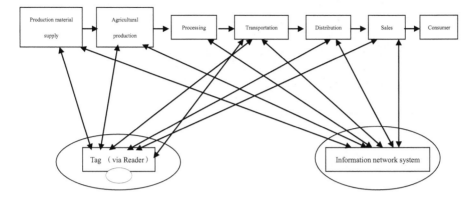

**Fig. 3.** Tracing system that runs through the whole network

## 3.4    Designs on the Enterprise Management Systems

The core part of the system is the enterprise management system, which is shown in figure 4. As the current information provided by the tracing system is too superficial and the value of the information provided by  traceability code is too small, the system collects cucumber-related data including foundational geographic data, origin environmental data, data of added things during production process, data of main harmful materials, technology data of processing/circulation process, quality analysis, testing results data and so on, and then puts them into corresponding database and uses three dimensional coding technology with rich information to sign on the label for abundant traceability information.

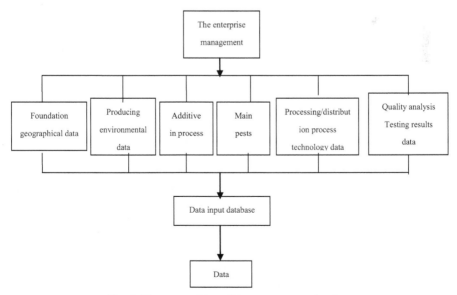

**Fig. 4.** The composition of the target enterprise data

Single server in performance can not effectively support real-time asynchronous information collection and traceability, as the number of the enterprises and products involved in the cucumber supply chain is very big and food traceability information needed for collection in time and space is scattered. As for the information collection of large space scope, the system introduced in this thesis set respective area server connected with the central server according to the division of the geographical location, which is shown in figure 5. As for large quantity of stable information such as enterprise information, products information and structural information, related enterprises will input them into areas server online. As for the product process information with many entries, the online entry is inconvenient and data quantity is small. The system uses a handheld wireless terminal to settle that based on related technology of the internet of things.

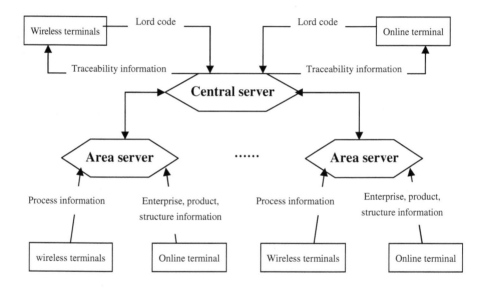

**Fig. 5.** System information collection and way back

## 4    Conclusions

This system uses the internet of things and three dimensional code technology to realize traceability management for the whole "from field to fork" production process of cucumber including cultivation, sales and detection. The features are as follows:

① Three dimensional code technology makes the label has more information. Three dimensional coding is based on EAN · UCC global coding system. Code system is used world wide, both for domestic use and international exchange. It can be used in international tracing in food industry, and can get rid of potential barriers in trade. In terms of the content, as the primary code not only contains the GTIN codes that identify the manufacturer and product items, but also includes the batch number telling the batch information, which can meet the requirements that take the batch number as the unique identification of products when actual dates back happens [10].

② The system can record security information of cucumber's production and sales process. From key control points of the supply chain to the ultimate consumer, the farm enterprises, acquisition, processing and sales of transport enterprises involved in this processes, can form a complete set of agricultural product supply chain network. The production archive of the cucumber purchased will be seen as long as the security bar codes be scanned when consumers put it before the multimedia queries machine. The archive will include the provenance, origin, producer, production environment, the drugs used in the production process, materials processing and certification information, quarantine and other related information.

③ Based on GIS technology, the system realizes visual query. In order to change traditional management mode which shows origin information by simple text figures, the system realizes the visualization of the spatial information in planting blocks through the use of GIS technology, and returns a specific spatial location and attribute information of origin of agricultural products in a graphical manner to meet the urgent need for safe production and date back.

④ The system develops data standards, ensures the stability of the system and improves the sharing and exchange of information. As the development targets and principles of the existing traceability systems are different, traceability information content is not standard, the information flow is not consistent, and the system software is not compatible, causing the difficulty of trace information resources' sharing and exchange. In order to solve this problem, this system gets improved during the design phase. It achieves better sharing of information and exchange function through the interface standards design and information process of unity and traceability information standard. The data in the huge central database of this system can be collected and stored rapidly, and data collection does not affect producers and processors' production technology. It strives to achieve the target that all users are able to use the data in a central database efficiently with no impact on commercially confidential data.

## References

[1] Peng, S., Chen, Y., Wu, Z.: Tracing System in Food Safety Information Management Application and Development. Agriculture Science and Technology Communication 58, 28–30 (2009)
[2] Xing, Z., Fu, X., Fang, J.: Internet of Things Network Technology in the Application of Modern Agricultural Production. Agricultural Technology and Equipment 4, 16–20 (2010)
[3] Wang, C., Zhang, D.: Application of Internet of Things in Agriculture Production and Food Safety. Agriculture Network Information 12, 8–9 (2010)
[4] Yang, T., Chu, B.: Study on Control System of Food Safety from Farm to Table. Food Science 26, 264–268 (2005)
[5] Yang, X., Qian, J., Sun, C.: Design and Application of Safe Production and Quality Traceability System for Vegetable. Transactions of the CSAE 24, 162–166 (2008)

[6] Zhang, A., Xiao, G., Jin, M., Zhou, Y.: Development and Application of Quality Safety Traceability System for Vegetables. Agriculture Network Information 4, 17–20 (2010)

[7] Jin, H., Liu, J.: Produce Quality Quick Tracing System of the Present Situation, Problems and Countermeasures,
http://club.topsage.com/thread-1296051-1-1.html
2010-4-26/2011-5-18

[8] Zhao, M., Liu, X.: Vegetables Quality and Safety of Construction and the Traceability System Practice. China Vegetables 7, 3 (2007)

[9] Zhao, R., Qiao, J.: Development, Evaluation and Prospect of Vegetable Traceability System in ShouGuang. Evaluation and Prospect of Agricultural Outlook 9, 49–52 (2010)

[10] Liang, Z., Ji, Z., Lin, J., Liu, Y., Mou, K.: A Whole Course Food Tracing System Based on Three Dimensional Code. Journal of Shenzhen University Science and Engineering 27, 312–316 (2010)

# Research on Orchard Field Data Service System

Lin Hu, Yun Qiu, and Guomin Zhou

Institute of Agricultural Information of the Chinese Academy of Agricultural Sciences
hulin@mail.caas.net.cn

**Abstract.** The precise management of orchards cannot do without the support of various orchard field data, and the orchard field data server is an effective solution thereto. The orchard field data server consists of data acquisition unit, data communication unit, data analysis unit and such diversified server sockets of user terminal as supportive personal computer (PC), notebook computer, mobile phone and telephone. The orchard workers can set data acquisition cycle according to the requirements, and the processed data can serve the orchard workers in many respects. After its promotion and application in many orchards in such regions as Liaoning and Beijing, the said system has been proved to be of easy use and reliable effect, so that the project has achieved good social, ecological and economic benefits.

**Keywords:** orchard, field data service, diversified terminals, service for orchard workers, precise management.

## 1 Introduction

China's fruit output ranks No. 1 in the world [1], but its output value is low. The main reason is the low level of production and business operation, which has caused the poor quality of fruits [2, 3]. Consequently, it is difficult for us to compete with such countries as the United States, Italy and Japan in the international market. To improve the level of our fruits, we must enhance the level of business operation. It is the international practice to improve and transform the traditional fruit industry by means of standardization and informatization [4] in the industrial production. The basis of the standardization and informatization is the precise control of the basic data in production and management. Orchard is the basic area division in fruit industrial production and the basic organization of production and business operation. Therefore, to acquire, sort out, process and analyze the data in the orchard as a unit, and to use them in serving the orchard before production, during production and after production would constitute the aim of this research. The purpose of the orchard field data server is to acquire the orchard field meteorology and field video. After the data are sent back to the network server, the authorized orchard workers and/or other users are able to refer, in real time, to the orchard field data. After these field data are processed by means of the professional software, they can be used to provide service and guidance for the orchard workers in respect of the production and business operation.

D. Li and Y. Chen (Eds.): CCTA 2011, Part I, IFIP AICT 368, pp. 209–215, 2012.
© IFIP International Federation for Information Processing 2012

# 2    System Design

## 2.1    Aim of the System

Orchard is the basic unit in the production and business operation of fruit industry. So it is in the orchard as a unit that the orchard field data acquisition system designed to provide service for the production and business operation would serve the orchard workers before production, during production and after production. The purpose of this product is designed to improve the orchard workers' level of production and business operation and to strengthen the competitiveness of the products.

## 2.2    Framework of the System

The system consists of field data acquisition unit, data transmission unit, data processing unit and service unit.

The field data acquisition unit is used to acquire the orchard meteorology and video data, and the data transmission unit is designed to transmit them into the server through the communication network. After the data are processed and analyzed on the server, they are used to provide service for the orchard workers and/or other clients.

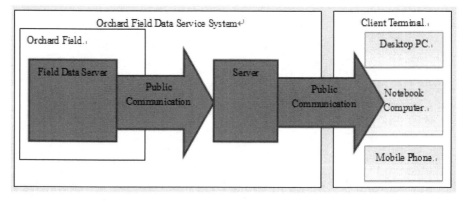

**Fig. 1.** System Frame Diagram of Orchard Field Data Acquisition Server

The field data server consists of such four parts as meteorological data acquisition unit, video image data acquisition unit, data transmission platform and power supply unit. Each of these acquisition units is assembled by such modules as are in conformity with the industrial standards.

The meteorological data acquisition unit can be connected with 20 digital meteorological sensors, which would mainly include such sensors as for air temperature and humidity, soil temperature and humidity, photo-synthetically active radiation and carbon dioxide concentration, but could be increased or decreased according to the actual needs.

The video image acquisition unit is composed by a group of video cameras, including cable video cameras and wireless video cameras.

The data transmission platform is of such functions as video compression and format conversion, voice transmission and data transmission. Two R232 interfaces, two R485 interfaces, one voice input-output interface and one video input interface are used to respectively accomplish the transmission of data, voice and video. Their connections are shown in Figure 2.

The device adopts solar power supply, including solar-cell panel, storage battery and programmable digital switch. The programmable power supply timer is connected with the data transmission platform to receive control instructions.

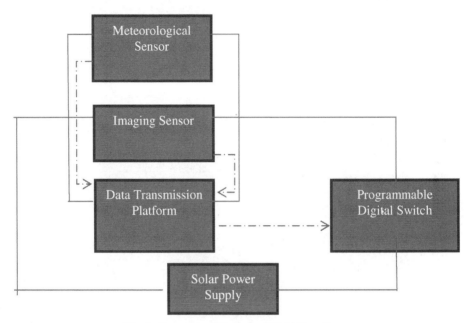

**Fig. 2.** Connection Diagram of Field Data Server

In Figure 2, the solid line indicates the circuit diagram, but the dotted line indicates the signal transmission diagram.

The data transmission platform is the core of the orchard field data server, including four video channels, one audio channel, two R232 channels and two R485 channels, and also including the built-in audio and video compression and format conversion functions, GPRS and WCDMA communication modules, and GPS positioning module.

The meteorological data acquisition unit and video image acquisition unit are used to transmit the signal to the data transmission unit. After various built-in processing, the signal is sent to the public network through the GPRS or WCDMA module. In the built-in communication module, there is a communication signal strength monitoring module, which would automatically use the GPRS module for transmission if the 3G signal becomes very weak.

After the data are transmitted back to the server, they are to be stored in the database. It is not necessary to give more details in respect to the design of the database.

## 2.3    Framework of the System Functions

The application of the system can be designed and developed according to the requirements of the clients. Its core functions are designed to cover the meteorological data service and video image service, but a lot of extended applications can be developed according to the requirements of the clients. The frame diagram of the systemic functions is shown in Figure 3.

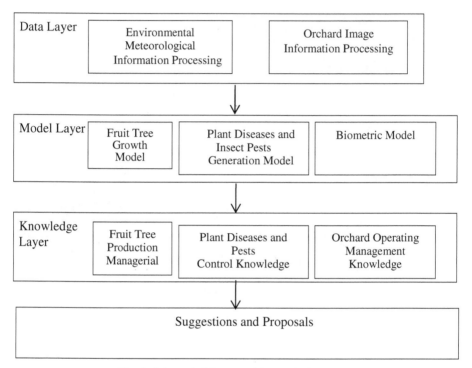

**Fig. 3.** Schematic Diagram of Systemic Functions

# 3    Application Cases

It is with the support of the MOST's State High-tech Program (863) and the Program of Commercialization of Agricultural Research Findings that this system has been gradually developed and matured. In recent years, this system has been applied to many aspects, which has achieved very good social and economic benefits. In the following, the "Hot Line of Orchard Workers" is taken as the case of application to analyze and demonstrate the application and functions of the orchard field data service system.

The "Hot Line of Orchard Workers (http://www.cart.net.cn/)" is an agricultural information service platform in the comprehensive network jointly developed by the Institute of Agricultural Information and the Institute of Pomology of the Chinese Academy of Agricultural Sciences. By use of the "four-in-one" approach of website, telephone, mobile phone and TV, the "Hot Line of Orchard Workers" is designed to provide all-sided and public beneficial agricultural information service for the orchard workers throughout the country, which is related to the latest information on fruit trees and nursery stock, market price quotations, practical cultivation technique, fruiter disease control technique, and so forth. It is the good helper and friend for the orchard workers to acquire wealth.

The system has been developed on the basis of the orchard field data service system. And the system application has been extended and developed on the basis of the functions of the orchard field data service system. The system interface of the "Hot Line of Orchard Workers" is shown in Figure 4.

The system functions include home page, nursery stock recommendations, online consultation, technical service, production and marketing service, market information, expert system and training classroom on-line.

The system data are supported by 20 orchard field data servers, which are located in 20 orchards in China's Liaoning Province and Beijing. The orchard field meteorological data are acquired once every 20 minutes, and the image data are collected once every four hours. If necessary, it is possible to make recording of the video or real-time monitoring of the orchard field. Figure 5 is the schematic diagram of the orchard field data server, which is located in a certain orchard located in Shunyi District of Beijing.

**Fig. 4.** Interface of "Hot Line of Orchard Workers"

**Fig. 5.** Orchard Field Data Server

## 4    Discussion

The orchard field data server is a set of intelligent maintenance-free system, which is all integrated by such modules as are of independent functions. It is so safe and easy to use with stable performance that it has achieved satisfactory results after trial use in some provinces and cities in northern China. It is particularly suitable for the orchard data acquisition service in such districts that are unattended and/or inconvenient in power supply.

At present, the existing problems are focused on the following aspects:

The first is the determination of the battery capacity. In northern China where most of the days are sunny, this system can satisfy the use in most regions, since it can supply power for 20 consecutive hours, in which it can satisfy the power utilization of the system for one week if the system works two hours per day. On such special occasions as necessary to make consecutive video monitoring, consideration may be made to use the electric supply. But in southern China, in some extreme weathers in the rainy season, it may be difficult to satisfy the power supply. In such cases, it is recommended to change even higher capacity of storage batteries and even larger size of solar panels.

The second is the acquisition of video images. In the system's automatic video recording, it may be influenced by the light intensity. In such cases, consideration should be made to add a light intensity detecting unit to the system to automatically adjust the lens angle, so as to ensure the quality of the video and images.

**Acknowledgments.** It is with the support of the Project of "Remote Intelligent Diagnosis System of Field Crop Diseases and Insect Pests (2007AA10Z237)" of the State High-tech Program (863) and the Project of "Remote Intelligent Diagnosis System of Orchard Diseases and Insect Pests and Pilot Plant Test (2009GB23260457)" of the Commercialization of Agricultural Research Findings that the orchard field data service system has been accomplished, for which we would like to extend our heartfelt thanks.

# References

1. China Agriculture Press. China Agricultural Yearbook (2010)
2. Cheng, C., Liu, F., Kang, G.: Technological demands and development countermeasures in China's apple industry. China Fruiter. 9, 58–59 (2007)
3. Li, X., Dai, Y.: International competitiveness evaluation and promotion countermeasures in respect of China's apple industry. Journal of Guangdong College of Finance and Economics 2, 76–80 (2008)
4. Yi, G.: Exploration and practice of the development and export of the apple industry. Fruit Growers' Friend 9, 3–5 (2010)

# A Monitoring and Management System for Farmland Environmental Base on Flex and Web Services[*]

Yanmin Wang[1,2], Yuchun Pan[2,**], Bingbo Gao[2], Zhenyu Zhang[1,3], and Bingjun Li[1]

[1] College of Information and Management Science, Henan Agricultural University,
450002, Henan, P.R. China
[2] Beijing Research Center for Information Technology in Agriculture,
100097, Beijing, P.R. China
[3] Department of Industry and Information Technology of Henan Province,
450008, Henan, P.R. China
wy_min@sina.cn,
panyc@nercita.org.cn

**Abstract.** Farmland environmental deterioration is the main reason which results in the agricultural product quality problems, so it is necessary to build a geospatial information system for farmland environmental monitoring and management. The rapid development of portable farmland environmental surveying or sampling devices and sensor network have made this possible. In this paper, we describe the design and implement of the geospatial system based on Flex and Web Services. This system provides data management, geoprocessing, visualization, as well as analysis functions to mine potential valuable information to support decision making based on the sampling data and other collected environmental data of farmland. Geoprocessing is implemented by directly invoking Geo-processing Web Services or calling Server APIs. To enhance the usability, the system also provides a flex client for users and web service interfaces for client program. Tertiary user structure with strict privileges management is designed to protect the users' data copyright.

**Keywords:** Geospatial Information System, Farmland Environmental Management and Monitoring, Geospatial Web Services, Flex.

## 1 Introduction

The security of agricultural food has been one of the most concerned issues in most countries in the world. The agricultural product quality problem has mainly come from farmland environmental deterioration. The overuse of fertilizers, abuse of pesticides and the heavy metal pollution are the main causes of the environmental deterioration of farmlands. In China, 1.6 million hectares of farmland has been polluted by pesticides, 4.8 million tons of fertilizers are being applied to the farmland

---
[*] Beijing Municipal Natural Science Foundation (4102022)& key Projects for Constructing Scientific and Technological Innovation Ability of Beijing Academy of Agriculture and Forestry Sciences.
[**] Corresponding author.

D. Li and Y. Chen (Eds.): CCTA 2011, Part I, IFIP AICT 368, pp. 216–228, 2012.

every year[1], and more than 20 million hectares of farmland (that's more the one fifth of the total) have been contaminated by heavy metal [2-4]. The Chinese government is paying more and more attentions on the farm land environmental quality and has initiated a series of projects to control the contamination and repair the contaminated soil. To achieve these goals, the primary thing needed to perform is to fig out the pollution status of farmland. The development of sensor network makes it possible to monitor and the emergence of portable sampling equipments with acceptable prices such as TXRF7 and X-MET5000 makes it possible to build farmland environmental information base [5-6]. However, the management and utilizing ability of the collected farmland environment data is very limited in China.

As an effective technology to manage, display, process and analyze the spatial related data, GIS (Geographical Information System) has been applied into many fields. By using WebGIS technology the spatial information and GIS application can be shared over the Internet easily. The ESRI ArcGIS Server provides a flexible framework to create and configure GIS services and applications [7-8], while Adobe Flex which has distinct advantage over traditional web technologies in giving an expressive interface and more effective communication mechanism becomes the most popular RIA (Rich Internet Application) technology. Therefore, in this paper, Web Services, ArcGIS Server, Flex as well as J2EE technology are employed to build the MMSFEFW(abbreviation of A Management and Monitoring System for Farmland Environmental base on Flex and Web Services) to effectively manage, display and analyze the collected farmland environmental data. The design, key technologies and implementation of MMSFEFW are discussed in section 2, section 3 and section 4, respectively.

## 2      System Design

### 2.1      System Structure

The MMSFEFW is composed of data layer, service layer and view layer, shown in fig 1.The data layer contains base data, sampling data, information of system users which can be spatial or non-spatial data. The spatial data is managed by relational DBMS (database management system) and the spatial data engine (in this paper the ArcSDE of ESRI is adopted). The non-spatial data are stored in the relational database and managed by relational RDBMS (Relational Database Management System).

The service layer is composed of spatial service layer, application logic layer and the interaction layer. The ArcGIS Server is paced in the spatial service layer to provide spatial information and functions through spatial services and Server API. The application logic layer acts as the Model of MVC (Model-View-Controller) architecture. It contains the basic function module which encapsulates the common supporting functions into Classes of appropriate granularity and the logic module carrying out the system functions by calling the basic function module. The interaction layer, working between clients and the application logic layer, contains web module for web browsers and web service for client program. The former plays as the controller of MVC architecture and the latter provides standard interface for client program to access system functions.

The view layer is designed to possess two kinds of interface, they are flex interface for users and Web Services interface such as WSDL (Web Service Description Language) for client program. The flex client, written using action script and Adobe tags would finally be compiled to a swf (shock wave flash, a binary file of Adobe Company) files and downloaded to users' web browsers to provide a vivid interface which communicates with the server to get data, write data and call functions according to users' operations. The Web Services interface provides service invoking information such as address, operations, input and output parameters and accepts users' request in SOAP (Simple Object Access Protocol) Envelope.

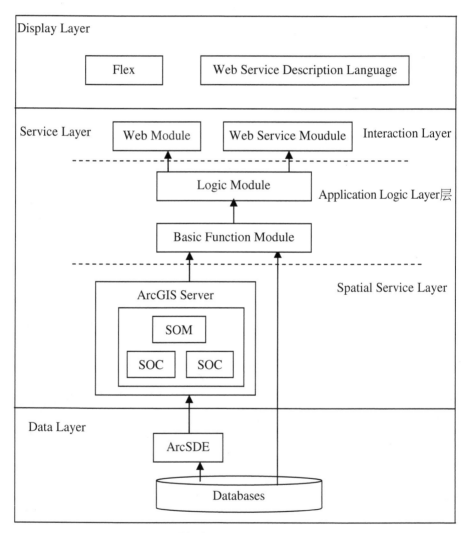

**Fig. 1.** System structure

## 2.2    System Functions

Aimed at managing, visualizing and analyzing the detection data of environment sampling data of farmland, mining the potential value of the collected data, serving data collector, data manager, experts and researchers, related government officials and the public, the MMSFEFW is designed to contain three function groups, namely data management group, query and analysis group, and system management group, shown in fig 2.

(1) Data management group: This group contains functions that support the upload, query and editing of the farmland plot data and the sampling data collected by fixed monitoring sites or survey activity. For the plots data many common GIS data formats are supported, such as Shape file of ESRI, GML and so on. The sampling data can be uploaded in Microsoft Excel file, plain text file or XML file.

(2) Query and analysis group: this group includes functions to query data using attributes restrictions and spatial location or relationship restrictions, apply spatial analysis on the sampling data, evaluate the quality farmland plots, display the results of analysis and evaluations on thematic maps and support users to set levels and rendering colors the results.

(3) System management group: the system configuration function and user management function are in this group. System configuration function supports system administrators to set system parameters and user management function provides medium to manager users, user groups and their privileges.

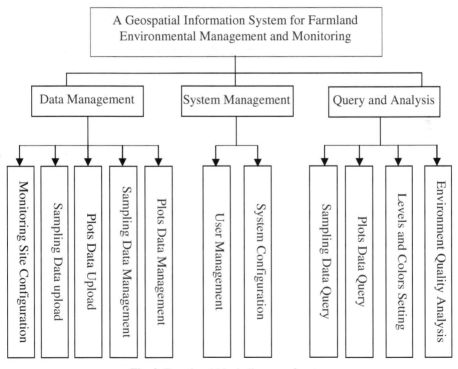

**Fig. 2.** Functional block diagram of system

### 2.3     Data Organization

The data of MMSFEFW include basic data, sampling data of farmland environment and user information. Basic data are composed of different kinds of data, including remote sensing images, terrain data, administrative map, and land use data and so on. The sampling data include observation data of soil, atmosphere environment and water environment of farmland and the metadata describing the observation data. User information includes basic user information and the role and privileges assigned to the user.

Google map is employed to provide background map so images and terrain maps were not built into the database. Other basic data like administrative map, land use map, were publish into ArcGIS Server to provide web map service after being organized into different map documents and given proper styles and visible ranges. Because those background data are stable and do not change frequently, map tiles are created beforehand at 20 scale levels same as Google map. After that, when the server received a web map request, it only needs to return the tiles within the extent at proper scale level. Thus the responsive time is shorted sharply for there is no need to render the map in-time.

The sampling data were represented by point feature type with a point geometry attribute and other non-spatial sampling attributes. The farmland plots data were represented by polygon feature types with a point geometry attribute and other non-spatial attributes. Because the number of non-spatial attributes of sampling data and farmland plots can be accustomed and thus is not fixed, the spatial attributes and the non-spatial attributes are stored in different tables. For example the sampling data, the points was stored in a spatial data table and other attributes are stored in normal table and they are connected with the object id. The metadata of the non-spatial attributes are stored in the meta-table table and the M_Sample_Fields table. Every sampling point and farmland plots has an attributes named "owner" attribute showing which user it belongs to. Besides the spatial index built on the geometry attributes, index must be created on the "owner" attribute because the data access control which is very frequent in MMSFEFW is base on it.

Three tier user structure (induced in 4.3) is adopted in MMSFEFW, so user information, user group information, roles and privileges need to be stored. User table, group table, roles table and privileges table were created to store this information.

## 3     Key Technologies

### 3.1     ArcGIS Server

ArcGIS Server provides the framework to create and configure GIS services and applications. It is a GIS web server software supporting users to configure and publish spatial resources (data, map, functions) as REST style Web Services or SOAP style Web Services, for example mapping service, image service, spatial data service, geocoding service and spatial processing service. Two steps are required to publish a spatial resource as web service: first create a spatial resource use the ArcGIS Desktop, then publish the resource into ArcGIS Server through ArcCatalog or the ArcGIS Server Manager.

ArcGIS Server provides developers with Server APIs which are actually coarse-grained ArcObjects to connect and get objects from the server. Developers can invoke fine-grained ArcObjects through the Server APIs to fully employ the powerful spatial data process and analysis ability of ArcGIS. The architecture of calling ArcObjects of ArcGIS Server in Web Application is shown in Fig 3. The web application server acts as a bridge that connects web clients to the spatial operation and analyzing functions of ArcGIS Server. The web application server and GIS server can reside in different computers. The web application written in java or .net uses ArcObjects proxies which then communicate with the SOM (Server Object Manager) using XML format messages and HTTP protocol to revoke the ArcObjects in the SOC (Server Object Containers). What need to note is that it's the ArcObjects residing in the SOC that actually implement the spatial operation or analysis functions.

ArcGIS Server also offers developers ADF (Application Developer Framework), a robust, standards-based set of components for building and deploying geospatial applications and services. For Java platform, there are the Web ADF for building and deploying Web applications and services base on JSF (Java Server Faces) and Enterprise ADF components for deploying business-tier EJB (Enterprise JavaBeans) applications [9-12].

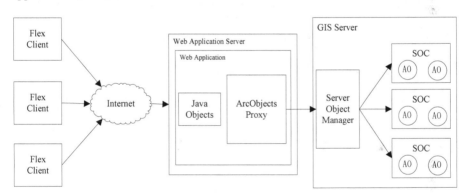

**Fig. 3.** Architecture of calling ArcObjects of ArcGIS Server in Web Application

## 3.2   Flex and BlazeDS

Adobe Flex is a software development kit (SDK) released for developers to develop and deploy cross-platform RIA (Rich Internet Applications). Developers can use the MXML (an XML-based markup language) to lay out graphic user interfaces and use ActionScript to achieve interactivity. The codes would finally be compiled to Flash files which has got wide support and has affluent expressive force. By using the computing ability of client computer to solve multi-step processing, client-side validation, data management and display, the communication times between clients and server can be reduced and web application will become responsive [13-15].

BlazeDS is an open licensed java remoting and web messaging products of Adobe to simply developers' work to access back-end distributed data or push data to the RIA client. A BlazeDS application consists of two parts: a client-side application and a server-side J2EE web application. The client-side can be realized by Flex or Ajax libraries. Flex provide components such as HTTP Service, Web Services, Remote Object, Producer and Consumer to communicate with the BlazeDS server. The BlazeDS server running in J2EE Server container can provide proxy service, RPC service, messaging service and service adapter. Channels which encapsulate message formats, network protocols, and network behaviors are used by client to communicate with endpoints on sever. BlazeDS provides several types of channels, including standard and secure Action Message Format (AMF) channels and HTTP (AMFX) channels. AMF and HTTP channels support non-polling request-response patterns and client polling patterns to simulate real-time messaging [16-17].

# 4     System Realization

## 4.1     Realization Scheme

The MMSFEFW is of B/S (Browser/Server) structure and realized with J2EE technology. The client interface was built using Flex Builder and BlazeDS is employed to finish the communication between clients and server. The web module in the application logic layer was realized using Struts2 and the Axis2 was used to implement Web Service in this layer. ArcGIS Server 9.3 is adopted to act as the GIS Server to provide spatial services and spatial functions. ArcSDE and Oracle is used to manage the data.

## 4.2     Realization of Geoprocessing

ArGIS Server allow users to publish model or script tools created in ArcTool Box, or map document container tool layers to server to provide different kinds of geoprocessing service(GP Service). In addition more flexible geoprocessing can be realized by invoking the server APIs in program. In MMSFEFW both methods were used to process and analyze the sampling data.

**Geoprocessing Using GP Service of ArcGIS.** A GP service in ArcGIS Server is created in two steps. First, build geoprocessing tools on ArcGIS Desktop using model or script tools or creating a map with the built tools as tool layer. In these step much attention need to be paid to following three points: (1) the data types of input parameters and output parameters because unlike the desktop environment only some certain data types are supported on web application clients. (2) the place where middle data and the result data will be stored. (3) how the result will be displayed to the clients. The second step is to publish created tools or map with tool layer. The parameter defining the way in which the service will run and interact with the clients can be set in this step. The analysis of distribution of farmland pollution is realized in this method.

Fig 4 shows the model to using IDW as the spatial interpolation method to analyzing the spatial distribution of harmful substance. The flow of this model have three steps: firstly filter the samples data so that only the data to which the current user at least has read privilege will be used; secondly apply IDW method to the selected sample points within a certain spatial extent; Thirdly classify the results of IDW method according to the thematic classes set by users and set the color scheme of the output.

The Inputs of the model include userids, Extent, Z_value, Cell_size, Reclass_Idw and symbol. Userids are numeric identifies of users whose sampling and plots data can be read by the current user, Extent represent the spatial extent to apply the spatial interpolation, the z_value represents the attribute sample points to be analyzed. The Cell_size assign the actual size each pixel represents. The Reclass_Idw and symbol respectively contains the classes division and symbology set with functions described in 2.2 section. The two outputs of this geoprocessing tool are named Idw_sp_650001 and Recess_Idw which are all of Raster type. Idw_sp_650001 is the result of IDW spatial interpolation method. Reclassfication is the result of reclassifying of Idw_sp_650001 according the input parameter Reclass_Idw.

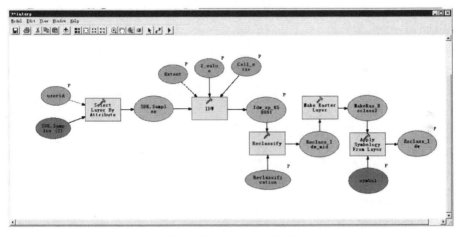

**Fig. 4.** Geoprocessing Tool

The accomplished model can then be published to the ArcGIS Server to provide geoprocessing service. The geoprocessing services can be directly called in flex. Following is the codes snippets calling the spatial interpolation service in asynchronous mode. The interpolation function calls the spatial interpolation service and the jobCompleteHandler function retrieve the result after the task completed. The following is the code snippet of clients to call the service.

```
var params:Object = {
    "Extent":interpolateExtent.xmin+" "+interpolateExtent.ymin+" "
            +interpolateExtent.xmax+" "+interpolateExtent.ymax,
      "Reclassification":reclassification,
      "userid":userids,
            "Z_value":cbItemnew.selectedItem.data,
            "Cell_size":map.scale*0.32*0.001,
            "symbol ": symbol
      };
gp.submitJob(params);
```

**Geoprocessing Based on Server APIS.** The quality evaluation of the farmland plots is realized by calling ArcObjects of ArcGIS Server. It's finished in the following 2 steps:(1) user selects the farmland plots to be evaluated using the select tool and the parameters describing the selection are sent to the Web Server, then the Web Server communicate with the ArcGIS Server to get the geometries of the selected plots and return the geometries fetched to the client to highlight the selected plots;(2) user fires the evaluate function through the client interface, and in answer to the evaluation request the Web Server first fetches samples points data in each selected plots from the ArcGIS Server, then uses the fetched data to evaluate the quality of each selected farmland plots by calling spatial analysis functions of the ArcObjects, and finally returns the evaluation to the Flex client to display to the user.

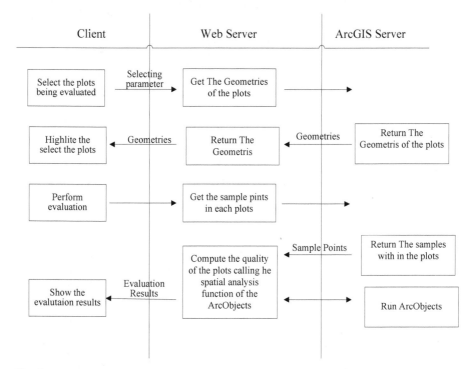

**Fig. 5.** The interaction among client, web application and ArcGIS Server during the operation evaluating the quality farmland plots

### 4.3    User Structure and the Privileges Managements

The tertiary user structure was designed realized MMSFEFW, shown in Fig 6. Users are grouped into different user groups, and each group has group administrators who are responsible for management of the users and data belonging to their group. The users and the user groups forms the lower two layers of the structure. At the top of the structure are the system administrators who have the highest controlling authority, responsible for configuration of the system and management of the user groups.

In order to protect the rights of system users, strict privileges management scheme are adopted. Each user is assigned one or more roles which define the operations that can be performed and the data can read or written. A user with the reader role can only view, query or perform some spatial analysis on the environmental sampling data or farmland plots data belonging to users in the same group. He cannot input, update or remove the data. A user with the writer role can input environmental sampling data or farmland plots data, update, remove and group the data belonging to him besides what a user only with a reader role can perform. A user with the group administrator role can update, remove and group all the data belonging to the users of the group besides what user with a writer role can do. Users with the system administrator role have the highest controlling authority, that's to say they can use all functions the system provided and manage all the data the system have.

Every user in the system has the privilege to alter his own information except which group he belongs to. A group administrator can add, delete, and alter users in his group. The system administrator can add, delete and alter user groups and group administrators.

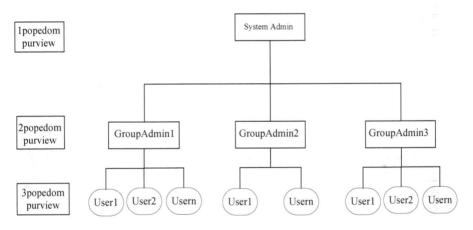

**Fig. 6.** Tertiary User Structure

## 4.4    Results

The interface of MMSFEFW uses the national map of China as background, and provide map control panel, menu bar, toolbox and information window. The menu contents differs after logging in according to the user's roles and privileges and the map will scale automatically to the extents of sampling data to which he has at least read privilege. Fig 7, Fig 8 and Fig 9 are the screenshots of MMSFEFW. Fig 7 shows the thematic map of Cu contents in each sampling points. Fig 8 shows the environmental quality evaluation results of the selected farmland plots. Fig 9 shows the spatial interpolation results of Cu contents in the specified area.

**Fig. 7.** Thematic map of copper contents in each sampling points

**Fig. 8.** Environmental quality evaluation results of the selected farmland plots

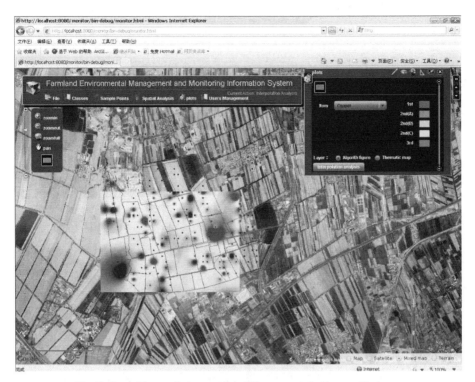

**Fig. 9.** Spatial interpolation results of Cu contents in the specified area

# 5    Conclusions and Future Work

In order to manage, visualize and analyze the sampling data of farmland environment, to mine the potential useful information from the collected data, and to guide the agricultural environmental management and decision making, the design and implementation of MMSFEFW and the key technologies used are introduced in this paper.

The MMSFEFW built using Flex, Web Services, ArcGIS Server and J2EE includes data layer, services layer and presentation layer. The flex was employed to realize the user interface. The spatial visualization and analysis were realized by directly calling configured rest services in flex clients or invoking ArcObjects of ArcGIS Server. To protect user's copyrights on sampling data, tertiary user structure was design and strict privileges management was implemented.

Further works include: 1) additional kinds of environmental data; 2) new environmental analysis models to provide better results for decision-making.

**Acknowledgments.** This research was supported by Beijing Municipal Natural Science Foundation (4102022) and key Projects for Constructing Scientific and Technological Innovation Ability of Beijing Academy of Agriculture and Forestry Sciences. The authors would also like to thank any reviewers for their constructive comments and suggestions.

# References

1. Shi, Z., Wang, F.: Effects of Pesticide Contamination on Microbial Diversity. Journal of Anhui Agricultural Sciences 35(19), 5840–5841, 591 (2007) (in Chinese)
2. Chen, Y.X., Lin, Q., He, Y.F., Tian, G.M.: Behavior of Cu and Zn under combined pollution of 2,4-dichlorophenol in the planted soil. Plant and Soil 261, 127–134 (2004)
3. Li, D., Wu, Z., Liang, C.: Soil Environmental Pollution and Agricultural Product Quality. Bulletin of Soil and Water Conservation 04 (2008) (in Chinese)
4. Wang, L., Gu, G., Zhang, M.: Present situation and problems in studies on environmental qualities of agricultural products producing sites in China. Anhui Agricultural Science Bulletin 12(12), 49–51 (2006) (in Chinese)
5. Huang, W., Cai, Q., Huang, M., et al.: Portable Unit for Rapid Determination of Pesticides Residues in Vegetables and Fruits. Journal of Instrumental Analysis 19(6), 87–89 (2000) (in Chinese)
6. Serpil, Y.K.: Validation and uncertainty assessment of rapid extraction and clean- up methods for the determination of 16 organochlorine pesticide residues in vegetables. Analytica Chemica Acta 571(5), 298 (2006)
7. Liang, T.G., Chen, Q.G., Ren, J.Z., et al.: A GIS-based expert system for pastoral agricultural development in Gansu province, PR China. New Zealand Journal of Agricultural Research 47(3), 313–325 (2004)
8. McCarthy, J.D., Graniero, P.A., Rozic, S.M.: An integrated gis-expert system framework for live hazard monitoring and detection. Sensors 8, 830–846 (2008)
9. ESRI China(Beijing).: The Best of REST Using REST in ArcGIS Server 9.3 (2009)
10. ESRI. Overveiw of ArcGIS for Server (EB/OL),
    http://www.esri.com/software/arcgis/arcgisserver/index.html
11. ESRI. ArcGIS API for Flex online Help (EB/OL),
    http://resources.esri.com/arcgisserver/apis/flex
12. ESRI. The ArcGIs Server and image server architecture (January 2009)
13. Jiang, T.: Design and Realization of Enterprise Web Application System Based on Flex3. China Machine Press, Beijing (2008) (in Chinese)
14. Longley, P., Batty, M.: Advanced Spatial Analysis. ESRI Press, Redlands (2003)
15. Webster, S., McLeod, A.: Developing Rich Clients with Macromedia Flex. Peachp it Press (2004)
16. Cardell-Oliver, R., Smettem, K., Kranz, M., et al.: Field Testing a Wireless Sensor Network for Reactive Environmental Monitoring. In: Proceedings of the International Conference on Intelligent Sensors. Sensor Networks and Information Processing, pp. 7–12 (2004)
17. Fukatsu, T., Hirafuji, M.: Field Monitoring Using Sensor - Nodes with a Web Server. Journal of Robotics and Mechatronics 17(2), 164–172 (2005)

# GPC: An Expert System Based on Multi-branch Structure for Grass Pest Control Information

Zhigang Wu[1], Zehua Zhang[2], Wenxin Li[1], Guangjun Wang[2], and Zhihong Li[1,*]

[1] China Agricultural University, Beijing, 100193, China
lizh@cau.edu.cn
[2] Institute of Plant Protection, Chinese Academy of Agricultural Sciences, China

**Abstract.** Since 1997, 13 provinces and regions in China have experienced grass pest disasters. The average annual hazard area comprised more than 3 million mu and the annual economic losses totaled more than 20 billion Yuan. Because grassland encompasses very large areas, grass pest disasters occur suddenly and frequently; thus, they are very difficult to predict and subsequently monitor. In order to provide technical support for grassland plant protection, we need to develop effective early warning systems and effective control measures. Herein, we develop and evaluate GPC (Grass Pest Control information system), a web-based expert system for identification of grass pests, which included more than 50 species of grass pests. It has been developed by China Agricultural University and Institute of Plant Protection, Chinese Academy of Agricultural Sciences. Based on user needs, GPC was developed with ASP.NET, C# and Microsoft SQL server 2008 database. In its development we used 8 databases including a user information database, basic information database, and identification knowledge database. This tool and information database was developed both for grassland plant protection technicians and farmers.

**Keywords:** grass pest, expert system, pest diagnosis, grassland.

## 1 Introduction

Since 1997, 13 provinces and regions in China have experienced grass pest disasters. The average annual hazard area comprised more than 3 million mu and the annual economic losses totaled more than 20 billion Yuan. Because of the continuous occurrence of grass pest disasters, the grassland environment has been degrading. The local agricultural production has experienced serious losses due to grass pests. Because grassland encompasses very large areas, grass pest disasters occur suddenly and frequently; thus, they are very difficult to predict and subsequently monitor. Meanwhile, as climate and ecological environment change, the types and outbreak areas of grass pests are changing yearly. In order to provide technical support for

---

* Corresponding author, Address: Department of Entomology, College of Agronomy and Biotechnology, China Agricultural University, Beijing 100193, P.R. China.

D. Li and Y. Chen (Eds.): CCTA 2011, Part I, IFIP AICT 368, pp. 229–235, 2012.

grassland plant protection, we need to develop effective early warning systems and effective control measures. Herein, we develop and evaluate GPC (Grass Pest Control information system), a web-based expert system for identification of grass pests, which included more than 50 species of grass pests.

Liao surveyed and classified Expert systems (ES) methodologies using 11 categories: rule-based systems, knowledge-based systems, neural networks, fuzzy Expert systems, object-oriented methodology, case-based reasoning (CBR), system architecture development, intelligent agent (IA) systems, modeling, ontology, and database methodology together with their applications for different research and problem domains [1]. Expert systems have been applied in agriculture from 1980s [2-12]. Most of them are developed for crop production and pest management, animal husbandry, and aquaculture [13-25]. Others also began to integrate mobile communication systems, GIS technology, etc [26-28]. Some scholars also control by expert attempted to apply Expert systems to grassland resources, plantation management, and disease control [29-33].

This paper discusses the development and evaluation of a web-based expert system for identification of grass pests, named as GPC (Grass Pest Control information system). The system included more than 50 species of grass pests. It has been developed by China Agricultural University and Institute of Plant Protection, and Chinese Academy of Agricultural Sciences.

# 2     Users' Needs and Knowledge Acquisition

## 2.1     Users' Needs

Although it is widely accepted among scientists that efficient identification work is vital to formulate viable decisions about pest control measures. It is essential, however to convince technicians and farmers that the correct identification of pests is the first step in implementing control measures. Thus, one must investigate and evaluate technicians' and farmers' attitudes and perceptions relative to any expert system. Essentially, understanding their perceptions and willingness to use the tool is crucial to enhance grassland plant protection.

The system proposed can be accessed anonymously. System users are divided into regional administrators, super administrators and system administrators. They can use and mange the system with different authorities. Regional administrators need to input and maintain local monitoring information of grass pests, and they could answer questions of farmers. Super administrators could input and maintain basic information of grass pests, notice, users' question, law information and user account. Only system administrator have authority of adjust the system parameters and data dictionary.

## 2.2     Knowledge Acquisition and Information Collection

Knowledge acquisition (KA) is the process of transferring knowledge from the sources to the engineers. The translation of the knowledge possessed by the expert into a knowledge base is the bottleneck in the process of knowledge acquisition [33-34]. To acquire the required knowledge, we followed the KA procedure discussed in Morpurgo and Wada [35-36]. We acquired textual information (e.g. species' morphological characteristics, biology, geographic distribution, etc.) from literature reference such as extension booklets, primary and secondary literature, , etc. We obtained symptom descriptions and the identification rules from some entomologists by Expert interviews. We discussed in depth to clarify questions and process identification. Through this method, we provided a trustworthy procedure for knowledge acquisition, which helped us build a multi-branch structural key for grass pest remote identification. We also collected a large number of pictures by photographing.

# 3    System Design and Development

## 3.1    Software and Database

GPC was designed to run on the internet. Its development was based on the use of internet techniques and SQL programming languages. It was developed with ASP.NET and C#. The server database played a very important role in developing GPC. It was used to sort all the information and knowledge which was needed to actualize every function of the expert system. In GPC, there are 8 databases including a user information database, basic information database, and identification knowledge database. They were all designed using MS SQL Server 2008 Database.

## 3.2    Inference Process

Most of traditional expert systems for assistant diagnosis of green plant pests are based on dichotomous structure, which is rule-based. In order to be more flexible, GPC adapted multi-branch structure. In this structure, knowledge is organized in a decision tree, with nodes at different levels. It is another form of hierarchical structure has more advantages for accurate and rapid diagnosis (Fig. 1).

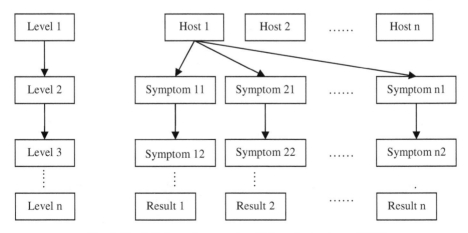

**Fig. 1.** The Inference diagram of multi-branch structure of GPC

### 3.3    Users Interface

To best meet the different users' need, the design must be user-friendly. With the system, users could browse, access, and query any grass pest information easily. Meanwhile, they also can identify a grass pest by the remote pest diagnosis. Regional and super administrators can publish monitoring data and obtain statistics as needed. User interface is the direct media between users and computers, we should consider all users' knowledge level and ensure the interface complete, compact, and easy (Fig.2).

**Fig. 2.** Index page of GPC

## 4    Discussion

Because grass pest species are numerous and widely distributed, their prevention and control are very difficult. In order to reduce pest damage, the government needs to increase investment in the control of grass pests and improve levels and conditions of pest monitoring and forecasting; such efforts would reduce large agricultural losses. GPC can be used to remotely diagnose grass pests  and provide monitoring information for farmers and technicians.   All of these benefits would be enhanced if we strengthen and publicize the system, thereby permittin more people to use the system.

The system was evaluated in two steps: verification and validation [37]. We determined the system code error and perfected it with the white-box testing method. The key which is used for pest diagnosis was also further improved by pest experts. In the second step, we had students and teachers test the system with black-box testing method. All the students selected were majors in plant protection, but without experience in grass pest identification. Although, students using the expert system were able to identify most of cases correctly, some pests with similar taxonomic characters were not easy to be identified. Presumably, it would be easier for the more experienced students or technicians.

**Acknowledgements.** The authors thank Prof. Stauffer at Pennsylvania State University for his valuable suggestions and modifying the draft. We are also grateful to other members of Plant Quarantine and Invasion Biology Laboratory of China Agricultural University (CAUPQL). This study received financial support from the earmarked fund for China Agriculture Research System (201003079), Special Fund for Agro-scientific Research in the Public Interest (CARS-35), Innovation Fund for Graduate Student of China Agricultural University (KYCX2010017).

# References

1. Liao, S.H.: Expert system methodologies and applications—a decade reviews from 1995 to 2004. Expert Systems with Applications 28, 93–103 (2005)
2. Coulson, R.N., Saunders, M.C.: Computer-assisted decision-making as applied to entomology. Annual Review of Entomology 32, 415–437 (1987)
3. Jones, P.: Agricultural applications of expert systems concepts. Agricultural Systems 31, 3–18 (1989)
4. Travis, J.W., Latin, R.X.: Development, implementation, and adoption of expert systems in plant pathology. Annual Review Phytopathology 29, 343–360 (1991)
5. Edwards Jones, G.: Knowledge-based systems for pest management: an application-based review. Pesticide Sciences 36, 143–153 (1992)
6. Edwards Jones, G.: Knowledge-based systems for crop protection: theory and practice. Crop Protection 12, 565–575 (1993)
7. Ramon, M.C.U., Roland, F.: An expert advisory system for wheat disease management. Plant Disease 78, 209–215 (1994)
8. Yialouris, C.P., Sideridis, A.B.: An expert system for tomato diseases. Computers and Electronics in Agriculture 14, 61–76 (1996)
9. Kramers, M.A., Conijn, C.G.M., Bastiaansen, C.: EXSYS, an Expert System for Diagnosing Flower bulb Diseases, Pests and Non-parasitic Disorders. Agricultural System 58, 57–85 (1998)
10. Ellison, P., Ash, G., McDonald, C.: An expert system for the management of botrytris cinerea in Australian vineyards. Development, Agricultural Systems 56, 185–207 (1998)
11. Clarke, N.D., Leslie Shipp, J., Papadopoulos, A.P.: Development of the Harrow Greenhouse Manager: a decision-support system for greenhouse cucumber and tomato. Computers and Electronics in Agriculture 24, 195–204 (1999)
12. El-Azhary, E., Hassan, H.A., Rafea, A.: Pest control expert system for tomato (PCEST). Knowledge and Information Systems 2, 242–257 (2000)

13. Mahaman, B.D., Harizanis, P., Filis, I.: A diagnostic expert system for honeybee pests. Computers and Electronics in Agriculture 36, 17–31 (2002)
14. Mahaman, B.D., Passam, H.C., Sideridis, A.B.: DIARES-IPM: a diagnostic advisory rule-based expert system for integrated pest management in Solanaceous crop systems. Agricultural Systems 76, 1119–1135 (2003)
15. Gonzalez Andújar, J.L., Fernandez-Quintanilla, C., Izquierdo, J.: SIMCE: An expert system for seedling weed identification in cereals. Computers and Electronics in Agriculture 54, 115–123 (2006)
16. Prasad, R., Kumar Rajeev, R., Sinha, A.K.: AMRAPALIKA: An expert system for the diagnosis of pests, diseases, and disorders in Indian mango. Knowledge-Based Systems 19, 9–21 (2006)
17. Mansingh, G., Reichgelt, H., Osei Bryson, K.: CPEST: An expert system for the management of pests and diseases in the Jamaican coffee industry. Expert Systems with Applications 32, 184–192 (2007)
18. López-Morales, V., López-Ortega, O., Ramos-Fernańdez, J.: JAPIEST: An integral intelligent system for the diagnosis and control of tomatoes diseases and pests in hydroponic greenhouses. Expert Systems with Applications 35, 1506–1512 (2008)
19. Li, D., Fu, Z., Duan, Y.: Fish-Expert: a web-based expert system for fish disease diagnosis. Expert Systems with Applications 23, 311–320 (2002)
20. Fu, Z., Xu, F., Zhou, Y.: Pig-vet: a web-based expert system for pig disease diagnosis. Expert Systems with Applications 29, 93–103 (2005)
21. Xiao, J., Wang, H., Gao, L.: Design and Implementation of Expert System for Cow Disease Diagnose Based on. NET Framework. Application Research of Computers 12, 247–248 (2006) (in Chinese)
22. Liu, S., Xu, L., Shen, Y.: Design and implementation of expert system for prawn disease diagnose and prevention based on. NET platform. Computer Engineering and Design 13, 3444–3447 (2008) (in Chinese)
23. Li, Z., Zhang, B., Shen, Z.: The development of Quarantine Pests Information and Identification System in China. Plant Quarantine 17, 273–276 (2003) (in Chinese)
24. Shao, G., Li, Z., Wang, W.: Study on vegetable pests remote diagnosis expert system (VPRDES). Plant Protection 1, 51–54 (2006) (in Chinese)
25. Han, H., Rajotte, E.G., Li, Z.: Qpais: A Web-Based Expert System for Assistedidentification of Quarantine Stored Insect Pests. In: Computer and Computing Technologies in Agriculture II, vol. I, pp. 701–714. Springer, Boston (2009)
26. Yu, S., Zhu, W.: Research on Mobile Expert System of Tomato Pest Diagnose Based on Microsoft. Net and Web Service. Journal of Agricultural Mechanization Research 1, 206–210 (2006) (in Chinese)
27. Wang, A., Miao, T., Cao, J.: Study of Web - Based Expert System for Control of Diseases and Insects in Forest. Computer Technology and Development 4, 228–231, 235 (2008)
28. Xiao, L., Wang, Z., Peng, X.: Remote Diagnosis and Control Expert System for Citrus Agricultural Diseases and Insect Pests Based on BP Neural Network and WebGIS. In: Second International Conference on Intelligent Computation Technology and Automation, pp. 88–93 (2009)
29. Liu, S.: Approach of Grass Resources Classification Expert System (GES). Journal of Wuhan Technical University of Surveying and Mapping 19(1), 45–51 (1994)
30. Shi, W., Nie, S., Ma, Y.: National Database and Information Service System for Forage Germplasm Resources. Grassland of China 2, 20–22, 32 (1996)
31. Wang, Y., Yang, Y.: Analysis and design of GIS based expert system for pasture growing management. Pratacultural Science 20(1), 61–64 (2004)

32. Ma, Z., Ren, Q.: Preliminary study on the system management model of forage grass diseases in Ningxia. Journal of Ningxia Agricultural College 15(3), 23–28 (1994)
33. Edward Jones, G.: Knowledge-based systems for pest management: an application-based review. Pestic 36, 143–153 (1992)
34. Plant, R.E., Stone, N.D.: Knowledge-based Systems in Agriculture. McGraw-Hill, New York (1991)
35. Morpurgo, R., Mussi, S.: I-DSS: an Intelligent Diagnostic Support System. Expert Systems 18, 43–58 (2001)
36. Wada, T., Motoda, H., Washio, T.: Knowledge Acquisition from Both Human Expert and Data. In: Cheung, D., Williams, G.J., Li, Q. (eds.) PAKDD 2001. LNCS (LNAI), vol. 2035, pp. 550–561. Springer, Heidelberg (2001)
37. Harrison, S.R.: Validation of agricultural expert systems. Agric. Syst. 35, 265–285 (1991)

# The Current and Future Potential Geographical Distribution of the Solanum Fruit Fly, *Bactrocera latifrons* (Diptera: Tephritidae) in China

Xingli Ma[1], Zhihong Li[1,*], Wenlong Ni[1], Weiwei Qu[1], Jiajiao Wu[2],
Fanghao Wan[3], and Xuenan Hu[2]

[1] Department of Entomology, China Agricultural University, Beijing, P.R. China
[2] Guangdong Entry-Exit Inspection and Quarantine Bureau, Guangzhou, P.R. China
[3] Institute of Plant Protection, Chinese Academy of Agricultural Sciences, Beijing, P.R. China
lizh@cau.edu.cn

**Abstract.** The solanum fruit fly, *Bactrocera latifrons* (Hendel), is a major pest throughout South and South East Asia, including very few parts of southern China, and has invaded Hawaii and recently the continent of Africa (Tanzania and Kenya). With the development of international trade in fruits and vegetables, *B. latifrons* has become a potential threat to Chinese agriculture. In this study, CLIMEX 3.0 and ArcGIS 9.3 were used to predict the current and future potential geographical distribution of *B. latifrons* in China. Under current climatic conditions, its projected potential distribution includes most parts of southern China (about 32.2% of all 748 meteorological stations), from 16.544°N to 32.442°N. Optimal climate conditions occur in most areas of Yunnan, Guizhou, Sichuan, Chongqing, Hunan, Hubei, Jiangxi, Zhejiang, Fujian, Guangdong, Guangxi, Hainan, Taiwan, Hong Kong and Macao. The factors limiting the boundary of its suitability range are mainly the cold and dry stress. Climate change scenario for the 2020s indicates that the future potential geographical distribution will be increased by 5% of the total land areas of China, and the northern distribution boundary will move from 32.442°N to 33.408°N. There are 34 non-suitable climate sites change into suitable, mainly in Jiangsu, Anhui, Henan, Shanxi, Gansu, Sichuan and Tibet, because of China is likely to become hotter and wetter in the 2020s. In order to prevent the introduction and spread of *B. latifrons*, the present plant quarantine and monitor measures should be enhanced more where are projected to be suitable areas under current as well as future climatic conditions. At the same time, we should strengthen education for the public's awareness of plant protection.

**Keywords:** ArcGIS, *Bactrocera latifrons* (Hendel), climate change, CLIMEX, potential geographical distribution.

## 1 Introduction

The solanum fruit fly, *Bactrocera latifrons* (Hendel) ( Diptera:Tephritidae), native to South and South East Asia [1], is known as a pest of solanaceae crops, and some

---

* Corresponding author. Department of Entomology, College of Agronomy and Biotechnology, China Agricultural University, Beijing 100193, P.R. China.

D. Li and Y. Chen (Eds.): CCTA 2011, Part I, IFIP AICT 368, pp. 236–246, 2012.

cucurbitaceae plants were also reported as host fruits in Hawaii [2]. Now, it is widespread in South and South-East Asia, such as Brunei Darussalam, China (Guangdong, Guangxi, Hainan, Hong Kong, Yunnan, Taiwan), India (Karnataka, Tamil Nadu and West Bengal), Indonesia, Japan (Ryukyu Archipelago), Laos, Malaysia (Peninsular Malaysia and Sabah), Pakistan, Singapore, Sri Lanka, Thailand, Vietnam [3]. It is a very damaging pest wherever it occurs [4], for example, 60–80% of red pepper was lost in Malaysia due to *B. latifrons* [5]. As well as being a serious pest in South and South-East Asia, *B. latifrons* has established in a number of other regions. In Hawaii, *B. latifrons* was first discovered on Oahu in 1983 [6] and became sequentially distributed throughout the major islands [2]. Recently, it has invaded Africa, being detected in Tanzania in 2006 [7] and in Kenya in 2007. Surveys were conducted in different parts of Tanzania during 2006~2007, the species was widespread throughout the country but most abundant in the north-eastern region close to the border with Kenya [8]. They also indicated that the population of *B. latifrons* based on infestation rates and incidence in host fruits, seems to be relatively high during the wet seasons, probably because of availability of many hosts; the surveys further indicated that *B. latifrons* is more abundant in low to medium altitude areas compared to high altitude areas [8].

*B. latifrons* has been intercepted in China from 1994 [9], and the frequency of interception of *B. latifrons* in China in recent years increased annually. For example, from 2003 to 2008, according to the intercepted fruit flies information provided by Chinese Academy of Inspection and Quarantine, China had intercepted *B. latifrons* a total 2156 times, most of which came from the fruit carried by incoming travelers. Ministry of Agriculture of the People's Republic of China (PRC) had listed *B. latifrons* and all other *Bactrocera spp.* on the entry plant quarantine pest list of the PRC in 2007. Predictably, with the increase of Chinese-foreign trade in agricultural products and the further opening of China's agricultural market, the risk of introduction of these fruit flies from abroad as well as further spread in our country will continue to increase. In addition, pest ranges are likely to shift in response to changes in temperature, soil moisture and humidity patterns. Therefore, the effects of climate change should also be taken into account when we are assessing the likely climatic suitability of *B. latifrons*.

CLIMEX is professional biological software that is widely accepted worldwide and used to estimate the potential geographical distribution and seasonal abundance of a species in relation to climate. It was first described by Sutherst and Maywald [10], and has been used successfully to describe the potential distribution of other Tephritid fruit fly species, such as *Ceratitis capitata* (Wiedemann) [11-12], *B. tryoni* (Froggatt) [13-14], *Carpomya vesuviana* Costa [15], *B. tsuneonis* (Miyake) [16]. This model also has previously been used to predict the effects of climate change on species' potential distributions using both global climate model (GCM) [17] and synthetic climates [18-19]. Examples of studied subject species are *B. dorsalis* (Hendel) [20], *Melaleuca quinquenervia* [21] and *Nassella neesiana* [22]. In this study, the CLIMEX 3.0 model was used to infer the response of *B. latifrons* to climate and to predict its potential distribution in China under current climate and future climate scenario out to the 2020s.

The Geographic Information System (GIS) is a space information system, a way of collecting, storing, managing, analyzing, describing the data of the Earth surface and geographical distribution. From the 60's of 20<sup>th</sup> century up to now, the development of the world GIS experienced four stages: Expanding period consolidating period, development period and the consumers' period. It is widely used in almost all areas nowadays. In this article, the CLIMEX outputs were processed and visualized by using ArcGIS 9.3.

# 2    Materials and Methods

## 2.1    Overview of The CLIMEX Model and ArcGIS

CLIMEX is a dynamic model [23] that integrates the weekly responses of a population to climate using a series of annual indices, which is based on the assumption that if you know where a species lives, you can infer what climatic conditions it can tolerate [24]. The model combines the growth index (GI) and the stress indices (SI) into an overall ecoclimatic index (EI) which is scaled from 0 for locations where the species is unable to persist to 100 for environments that provide perfect habitat all year round. In this study, EI is classified into four classes of climatic suitability for *B. latifrons*: unsuitable (EI = 0), marginal ($0 < EI \leq 10$), suitable ($10 < EI \leq 20$) and optimal ($EI > 20$).

ArcGIS provides the integrated environment of mapping, display, edit and output maps, has powerful graphics editing features. Preparation of maps using ArcGIS, we must first get the map data in digital form. Then, symbolic the data and place map annotation. Finally, follow the application needs to produce a complete map, which includes the paper size settings, mapping scope and scale identification, map name, legend, grid reference, a compass and a series of elements placed. We made the maps of special subject display that the current and future potential geographical distribution of *B. latifrons* in China, and carried out the space distribution and analysis that comparing the different suitable degrees of areas projected under current and future climatic conditions by processing the CLIMEX outputs using ArcGIS 9.3.

## 2.2    Meteorological Databases and Climate Change

Two climate databases were used in this modeling exercise. Firstly, the CLIMEX standard meteorological dataset was used to create an initial fit. This dataset that comes with CLIMEX 3.0 consists of 30-year averages from 1961 to 1990 for an irregularly spaced set of 2500 climate stations. Subsequently, the relevant climate data for 748 weather stations from China as used in previous studies [15, 16, 25-27] were appended to the CLIMEX 3.0, which were acquired from the National Weather Bureau of China and include minimum temperature, maximum temperature, relative humidity, and rainfall for each month for each station (average values of 30 years from 1971 to 2000).

Due to the impact of human activities, the significant warming in China might continue. Comparing with the 30 years mean over 1961 to 1990, according to the projections [28], the nationwide annual mean temperature might increase by a range of 1.3~2.1℃ and the annual mean precipitation might increase by 2%~3% in 2020.

The electronic map of national boundary, province boundary and the distribution of national forest land used in this study were downloaded from http://nfgis.nsdi.gov.cn/ with the scale 1:4,000,000.

## 2.3     Fitting CLIMEX Parameters

To fit the CLIMEX model of *B. latifrons*, the parameters were manually and iteratively adjusted until the simulated geographical distribution as estimated by the EI values coincided with the species known native distribution and the reported description of its range. The parameters were then validated using data from regions where *B. latifrons* has invaded or established. Parameters used in the CLIMEX model are presented in Table 1.

**Table 1.** Parameters used in the CLIMEX model for the solanum fruit fly, *B. latifrons*

| Parameter | Mnemonic | Value |
|---|---|---|
| Lower threshold temperature | DV0 | 15.70 |
| Lower optimum temperature | DV1 | 18.00 |
| Upper optimum temperature | DV2 | 33.00 |
| Upper threshold temperature | DV3 | 36.00 |
| Degree-days to complete one generation | PDD | 415.40 |
| Lower threshold of soil moisture | SM0 | 0.10 |
| Lower limit of optimum soil moisture | SM1 | 0.50 |
| Upper limit of optimum soil moisture | SM2 | 1.00 |
| Upper threshold of soil moisture | SM3 | 1.80 |
| Cold stress temperature threshold | TTCS | 2.00 |
| Cold stress accumulation rate | THCS | -0.10 |
| Heat stress temperature threshold | TTHS | 36.00 |
| Heat stress accumulation rate | THHS | 0.005 |
| Dry stress soilmoisture threshold | SMDS | 0.10 |
| Dry stress accumulation rate | HDS | -0.005 |
| Wet stress soil moisture threshold | SMWS | 1.80 |
| Wet stress accumulation rate | HWS | 0.002 |

### *Degree-Days Per Generation (PDD)*

PDD is degree days required for a generation. The Parameter PDD for *B. latifrons* was reported 415.397 degree days [29]; we adjusted it to 415.4 degree days used for the CLIMEX model.

### Temperature Index

The lowest overwintering temperature, the highest over summering temperature and lower threshold temperature of *B. latifrons* were reported as -3.7, 36 and 15.68℃, respectively [29]. At 16°C, reproduction was completely suppressed and the survival rate of larvae was only 2.6% in *B. latifrons* [30-31]. So the minimum temperature and upper threshold temperature for development (DV0 and DV3) was set at 15.7 and 36℃, respectively. *B. latifrons* (Hendel) is native to South and South-East Asia, so the lower and upper temperature optima (DV1 and DV2) were set at 18 and 33℃, respectively.

### Moisture Index

The moisture requirements of *B. latifrons* are mediated through their host plants. The lower soil moisture limit for development (SM0) was set to 0.1 to indicate the permanent wilting point, which is normally about 10% of soil moisture. The lower and upper limits for optimal growth (SM1 and SM2) were set to biologically reasonable levels for many host plants; and *B. latifrons* like moist environment, so SM1 and SM2 were adjusted to be slightly higher, but also ensures distribution of *B. latifrons* in North Asia to Pakistan border. The selected value for SM3 was a compromise determined from fitting the threshold soil moisture wet stress threshold (SMWS). A lower value of SMWS would have made it more difficult to achieve a satisfactory fit to the known distribution in southern Asia.

### Cold Stress

TTCS was set to 2.0℃. The northern Asian boundary of *B. latifrons* is indistinct. Pakistan are suitable; in China, *B. latifrons* was detected in Tianlin and Baise in Guangxi [32], Wanting and Ruili in Yunnan province [33]. Accordingly, parameters were adjusted to allow suitable in some areas of Pakistan, persistence in Yunnan and Guangxi provinces of China and at higher altitudes in Hawaii.

### Heat Stress

According to the highest over summering temperature *B. latifrons* is 36℃ [29] and the upper tolerable temperatures for egg development and hatching of *B. latifrons* was 46 to 48℃ [34], TTHS was set to 36℃ to account for the averaging effect of climate, whereby several days where temperatures exceed 40℃ may be expected in a long-term climate record where the monthly average of daily maximum temperature is 36℃.

### Dry Stress

To be consistent with SM0, SMDS was set to 0.1 to indicate the permanent wilting point, which is normally about 10% of soil moisture.

### Wet Stress

Wet stress was adjusted to limit the southerly distribution in Asia. According to CABI [3] records, in the south, the critical fitting considerations were the reported presence of the fly in Malaysia (Peninsular Malaysia and Sabah), Singapore and Indonesia. SMWS and HWS were adjusted to ensure that the distribution has been reported in Asia in the southern border.

# 3    Results

## 3.1    Potential Geographical Distribution under Current Climate

Under current climate, considering the parameters in Table 1, the potential geographical distribution of *B. latifrons* in China was predicted and mapped. The predictive distribution map (Fig 1) suggested that, from 16.544°N to 32.442°N, about 241 meteorological stations (about 32.2% of all stations) in most parts of southern China are projected to be suitable for *B. latifrons*. Optimal climate conditions occur in most areas of Yunnan, Guizhou, Sichuan, Chongqing, Hunan, Hubei, Jiangxi, Zhejiang, Fujian, Guangdong, Guangxi, Hainan, Taiwan, Hong Kong and Macao. Climatic conditions are projected to be marginal in parts of Jiangsu, Anhui, Henan, Shaanxi, Gansu, Sichuan and Tibet, where the principle range-limiting factor is likely to be cold stress and reduction in rainfall. The remaining 507 meteorological stations in northwest, northeast and central China were unsuitable for the establishment of *B. latifrons*.

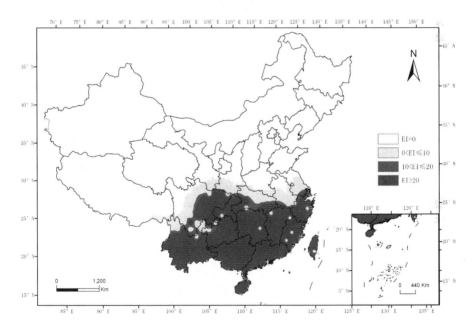

**Fig. 1.** The climate suitability (EI) for the solanum fruit fly under the current climate (1961–1990 averages) projected using CLIMEX3.0 (□, unsuitable (EI=0); , marginal (0 < EI≤10); , suitable (10 < EI≤20); ■, optimal (EI > 20))

## 3.2    Potential Geographical Distribution under Future Climate

Climate change scenario indicates that China is likely to become hotter and wetter in the 2020s. As a result of these changes, the potential range for *B. latifrons* is projected

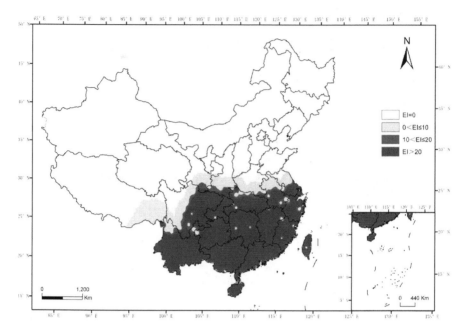

**Fig. 2.** The climate suitability (EI) for the solanum fruit fly in the 2020s projected using CLIMEX3.0 (□, unsuitable (EI=0); , marginal (0＜EI≤10); ▦, suitable (10＜EI≤20); ■, optimal (EI＞20))

to include most areas of southern China and extends into parts of central China (Fig 2). It will be increased by 5% of the total land areas of China compared with the current potential geographical distribution, and the northern distribution boundary will move from 32.442°N to 33.408°N. High suitable areas for *B. latifrons* will increase from 232 meteorological stations to 265, and the expansion is mostly in Guizhou, Sichuan, Hubei, Anhui, Jiangsu. There are 34 non-suitable climate sites change into suitable, mainly in Jiangsu, Anhui, Henan, Shanxi, Gansu, Sichuan and Tibet.

In order to visually see the difference in the potential geographical distribution for *B. latifrons* under current and future climatic conditions, the suitable areas of different degrees projected under current and future climate scenarios were calculated by ArcGIS 9.3 software, respectively. Then, these suitable areas' different proportions of the total land areas of China were displayed in the line graph (Fig. 3). To the 2020s, it was shown that unsuitable areas' proportion of the total land areas of China will fall 5% from 76% to 71%, marginal areas' proportion will increase 2% from 5% to 7%, suitable areas' proportion will maintain at 2% and optimal areas' proportion will rise 3% from 17% to 20%. Therefore, all suitable areas will be increased by 5% when it comes to 2020s.

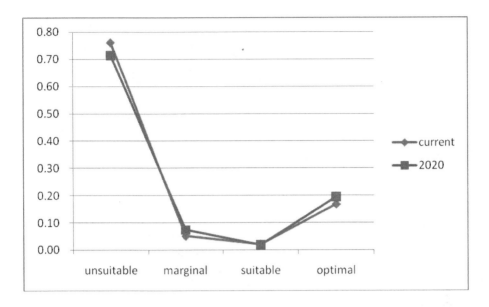

**Fig. 3.** The proportions of the suitable areas of different degrees of the total land areas of China under the current and future climate conditions

# 4    Discussion

## *Analysis of Limiting Factors for Distribution of Pests*

Ecoclimatic factors, such as temperature, humidity and light, are the most direct factors in limiting the potential geographical distribution of pest, in addition, other factors, especially soil types, geographical features, natural barriers, vegetation types should also be considered. Due to the CLIMEX model only taking these ecoclimatic factors into account, there is no doubt that the predicted results have practical restrictions. Therefore, in order to get more scientific predictions, we should take all of the above factors into consideration.

The most important thing is that the relationships between species and human activities will greatly affect the actual distribution of pest in their potential geographical distributions. For example, the development of international trade in fruits and vegetables and the increasing incoming travelers carried fruit will remarkably raise the risk of introduction of pest into a new area. Consequently, these are the starting point and foothold, and then, all of the above factors should be considered when we are framing prevention and control measures.

## *Development of Prevention and Control Measures*

The significant increases in the potential distribution of *B. latifrons* is projected under the climate change scenario in the 2020s suggest that the biosecurity authorities should consider the effects of climate change when undertaking pest risk analysis. Of course, establishing invasive alien species risk assessment system, improving early warning and rapid response mechanisms, strengthen international exchanges and cooperation, and the establishment of data sharing are very important in preventing the invasion of alien species is important.

In order to prevent the introduction and further spread of *B. latifrons*, the airline passengers must be strictly prohibited from bringing fruits or vegetables into China; Quarantine licensing system for imported fruits should be strictly implemented; we must step up port inspection and surveillance work. Last but not least, strengthen the public education is the most basic and most effective measures in limiting the introduction and spread of this fruit fly.

**Acknowledgement.** The authors would like to thank Mr. Ke Chen for his kindly guidance of information collection. We also acknowledge Jing Yu and other members of Plant Quarantine Laboratory of China Agricultural University for their help. This study received financial supports from the 973 project (2009CB119200), the 11th Five-Year Support Project of China (2006BAD08A15), the public service sectors (agriculture) special research project (200903034) and the International Science & Technology Cooperation Program of China (2011DFB30040).

# References

1. White, I.M., Elson-Harris, M.M.: Fruit flies of economic significance: their identification and bionomics (reprint with addendum). CAB International, Wallingford (1994)
2. Liquido, N.J., Harris, E.J., Dekker, L.A.: Ecology of *Bactrocera latifrons* (Diptera: Tephritidae) populations: host plants, natural enemies, distribution, and abundance. Ann. Entomol. Soc. Am. 87, 71–84 (1994)
3. http://www.cabi.org/cpc/
   ?compid=1&dsid=8719&loadmodule=datasheet&page=868&site=161
4. Yuko, S., Tsuguo, K., Takumi, U., Takashi, M., Masaaki, Y.: Invasion of solanum fruit fly *Bactrocera latifrons* (Diptera: Tephritidae) to Yonaguni Island, Okinawa Prefecture, Japan. Appl. Entomol. Zool. 42(2), 269–275 (2007)
5. Vijaysegaran, S., Osman, M.S.: Fruit flies in Peninsular Malaysia: their economic importance and control strategies. In: Kawasaki, K., Iwahashi, O., Kaneshiro, K. (eds.) Proceeding of the International Symposium on the Biology and Control of Fruit Flies, Okinawa Prefectural Government, Naha, pp. 105–115 (1991)
6. Vargas, R.I., Nishida, T.: Life history and demographic parameters of *Dacus latifrons* (Diptera: Tephritidae). J. Econ. Entomol. 78, 1242–1244 (1985)
7. Mwatawala, M., Meyer, M.D., White, I.M., Maerere, A., Makundi, R.H.: Detection of the solanum fruit fly, *Bactrocera latifrons* (Hendel) in Tanzania (Dipt., Tephritidae). J. Appl. Entomol. 131(7), 501–503 (2007)
8. Mziray, H.A., Makundi, R.H., Mwatawala, M., Maerere, A., Meyer, M.D.: Spatial and temporal abundance of the solanum fruit fly, *Bactrocera latifrons* (Hendel), in Morogoro, Tanzania. Crop Protection 29(5), 454–461 (2010)
9. Liang, J.B., Qin, S.J., Zhao, J.W.: *Bactrocera latifrons* (Hendel) was intercepted in the imported chili from Thailand. Entry & Exit Animal &Plant Quarantine of China 1, 12 (1995) (in Chinese)

10. Sutherst, R.W., Maywald, G.F.: A computerised system for matching climates in ecology. Agriculture Ecosystems and Environment 13, 281–299 (1985)
11. Worner, S.P.: Ecoclimatic assessment of potential establishment of exotic pests. J. Econ. Entomol. 81, 973–983 (1988)
12. Vera, M.T., Rodriguez, R., Segura, D.F., Cladera, J.L., Sutherst, R.W.: Potential geographical distribution of the Mediterranean fruit fly, *Ceratitis capitata* (Diptera: Tephritidae), with emphasis on Argentina and Australia. Environmental Entomology 31, 1009–1022 (2002)
13. Yonow, T., Sutherst, R.W.: The geographical distribution of the Queensland fruit fly, *Bactrocera (Dacus) tryoni*, in relation to climate. Australian Journal of Agricultural Research 49, 935–953 (1998)
14. Sutherst, R.W., Collyer, B.S., Yonow, T.: The vulnerability of Australian horticulture to the Queensland fruit fly, *Bactrocera (Dacus) tryoni*, under climate change. Australian Journal of Agricultural Research 51, 467–480 (2000)
15. Lv, W.G., Lin, W., Li, Z.H., Geng, J., Wan, F.H., Wang, Z.L.: Potential geographic distribution of Ber fruit fly, *Carpomya vesuviana* Costa, in China. Plant Quarantine 6, 343–347 (2008) (in Chinese)
16. Wang, J.W., Li, Z.H., Chen, H.J., Geng, J., Wang, Z.L., Wan, F.H.: The potential geographic distribution of *Bactrocera tsuneonis* ( Diptera: Tephritidae). Plant Quarantine 1, 1–4 (2009) (in Chinese)
17. Kriticos, D.J.: The role of modelling in weed management. In: Shepherd, R.C.H. (ed.) Proceedings of the Eleventh Australian Weeds Conference, Weed Science Society of Victoria, Melbourne, Australia, pp. 560–569 (1996)
18. Kriticos, D.J., Sutherst, R.W., Brown, J.R., Adkins, S.A., Maywald, G.F.: Climate change and biotic invasions: a case history of a tropical woody vine. Biological Invasions 5, 145–165 (2003)
19. Kriticos, D.J., Sutherst, R.W., Brown, J.R., Adkins, S.A., Maywald, G.F.: Climate change and the potential distribution of an invasive alien plant: *Acacia nilotica* ssp. *indica* in Australia. Journal of Applied Ecology 40, 111–124 (2003)
20. Stephens, A.E.A., Kriticos, D.J., Leriche, A.: The current and future potential geographical distribution of the oriental fruit fly, *Bactrocera dorsalis* (Diptera:Tephritidae). Bulletin of Entomological Research 97, 369–378 (2007)
21. Watt, M.S., Kriticos, D.J., Manning, L.K.: The current and future potential distribution of *Melaleuca quinquenervia*. European Weed Research Society Weed Research 49, 381–390 (2009)
22. Bourdôt, G.W., Lamoureaux, S.L., Watt, M.S. Manning, L.K., Kriticos, D.J.: The potential global distribution of the invasive weed *Nassella neesiana* under current and future climates. Biol Invasions, November 21 (2010)
23. Sutherst, R.W., Maywald, G.F., Kriticos, D.J.: CLIMEX version 3 user's guide, p. 131. CSIRO, Melbourne (2007)
24. Sutherst, R.W., Maywald, G.F., Bottomley, W., Bourne, A.: CLIMEX v2 CD and User's Guide. Hearne Scientific Software Pty. Ltd., Melbourne (2004)
25. Geng, J., Li, Z.H., Wan, F.H., Wang, Z.L.: Analysis of the suitability of Mexican fruit fly, *Anastrepha ludens* in China. Plant Protection 34, 93–98 (2008) (in Chinese)
26. Kong, L.B., Lin, W., Li, Z.H., Wan, F.H., Wang, Z.L., Huang, G.S.: A Predication of potential geographic distribution of melon fruit fly based on CLIMEX and DIVA-GIS. Journal of Plant Protection 35, 148–154 (2008) (in Chinese)

27. Rao, Y.Y., Huang, G.S., Li, Z.H., Wan, F.H., Wang, Z.L., Lin, W.: A predication of potential geographic distribution analysis of Queensland fruit fly based on DYMEX and DIVA-GIS. Acta Phytophylacica Sinica 36(1), 1–5 (2009) (in Chinese)
28. Qin, D.H.: Climate and Environmental Changes in China, p. 9. Science Press, Beijing (2005) (in Chinese)
29. Huang, Z.: Morphological identification, artificial diet, suitability analysis and Prediction, qualitative and quantitative risk analysis of important *Bactrocera* species. Graduate thesis of Hainan University (2010) (in Chinese).
30. Vargas, R.I., Walsh, A.W., Jang, E.B., Armstrong, J.W., Kanehisa, D.: Survival and development of immature stages of four Hawaiian fruit flies (Diptera: Tephritidae) reared at five constant temperatures. Ann. Entomol. Soc. Am. 89, 64–69 (1996)
31. Vargas, R.I., Walsh, A.W., Kanehisa, D., Jang, E.B., Armstrong, J.W.: Demography of four Hawaiian fruit flies (Diptera: Tephritidae) reared at five constant temperatures. Ann. Entomol. Soc. Am. 90, 162–168 (1997)
32. Deng, Y.P., Qiu, Q.: Investigation and monitoring of fruit flies in Guangxi province. Guangxi Horticulture 19(1), 22–24 (2008) (in Chinese)
33. Liang, G.Q., Zhang, S.M., Xu, W.: The note of fruit flies in south parts of China, and two newly recorded species. Acta Agriculturae Universitatis Jiangxiensis 11(3), 14–20 (1989) (in Chinese)
34. Armstrong, J.W., Tang, J.M., Wang, S.J.: Thermal Death Kinetics of Mediterranean, Malaysian, Melon, and Oriental Fruit Fly (Diptera: Tephritidae) Eggs and Third Instars. J. Econ. Entomol. 102(2), 522–532 (2009)

# Spatial Variability and Lateral Location of Soil Moisture Monitoring Points on Cotton Mulched Drip Irrigation Field[*]

Xiaoyun Lei[1], Fangsong Li[2,**], Shijun Zhou[3], Yan Li[1],
Dachun Chen[1], Huanxian Liu[4], Yu Pan[2], and Xiangmin Shen[2]

[1] College of Civil and Hydraulic Engineering, Xinjiang Agriculture University, Urumqi, 830052
[2] Xinjiang Institute of water Resources and Hydropower Research, Urumqi, 830049
[3] Suining Water Service Bureau, Sichuan Province, 629000
[4] College of Grass and Environmental Science,
Xinjiang Agriculture University, Urumqi, 830052
lxyyx88888@sohu.com, lfsws132@sina.com

**Abstract.** This experiment was conducted from April to September in 2009 in Baotou-lake Farm of Korla city, Xinjiang region, China. Two experiment schemes were designed for analyzing the spatial variability and lateral orientation of monitoring points for soil moisture. In scheme 1, 44 monitoring points were positioned with sampling depth of $0 \sim 60cm$. In scheme 2, 20 monitoring points were placed with sampling depth of $0 \sim 80cm$. Samples were taken in the whole cotton growing period before and after irrigation in both schemes. Statistical analyses including Q-Q test, descriptive statistics, t-test and geo-statistical analysis were performed to the soil moisture data. The results indicate that the increase of soil moisture can enhance their spatial variability. In drip-irrigated cotton cultivation, spatial variability of soil moisture resulted from the combination of several random variables and the structural factors such as climate, topography, soil form. Semi-variogram models belong to spherical model and the range of spherical model for soil moisture is about $9.40m \sim 35.35m$. The accuracy of the fitted model decreases as the soil moisture content increases. The monitoring points should be placed at the range of $0 \sim 0.475m$ from the drip tape and it is not suitable to place them at a farther place. It can be concluded that it is best to position the monitoring points at outward cotton row in consideration of management and soil moisture monitoring. The outcome of this study can be used for the proper design and placement of monitoring points for soil moisture.

**Keywords:** Cotton, Mulched drip irrigation, Soil moisture, Spatial variability, Monitoring point, Geo-statistics.

---

[*] **This Research is sponsored by following projects:** The National Natural Fund Project on the Spatial Variability Mechanism of Soil Moisture and the Sensors' Layout Plan on Cotton Mulched Drip Irrigation (51060002) ; High Technology Research and Development Program in Xinjiang Autonomous Region (200712111); the National Technology Support Program for the 11th five-year Plan (2007BAD38B05); the Key Discipline Construction Fund of Hydrology and Water Resources in Xinjiang.

[**] Corresponding author.

D. Li and Y. Chen (Eds.): CCTA 2011, Part I, IFIP AICT 368, pp. 247–257, 2012.

# 1    Introduction

Xinjiang is not only one of the important cotton production bases but also it has the largest acreage of drip irrigated cotton area in China. In the last decades, Xinjiang has created a miracle of micro-irrigation development in the world. Until the year of 2009, drip irrigated cotton cultivation acreage in Xinjiang has reached about $9 \times 10^5 hm^2$ and the region has become the main area for research & development and application of drip irrigation advanced technology in China. With the promotion of drip irrigation, the technology development, automation and information management have become increasingly important. However, the implementation of irrigation decision-making on cotton still depends on the farmers' experience at present and it's still difficult to achieve accurate irrigation by the real-time monitoring information of soil moisture in field. In recent years, research of accurate drip irrigation on cotton has carried out in Xinjiang region to solve the key scientific problems such as the drip irrigation design theory and the methods for soil moisture monitoring system. However, these issues are extremely difficult to solve due to the unknown spatial variability of soil moisture. For the time being, drip irrigation system designers reduce the layout density of sensor randomly in order to reduce input costs. As a result, these practices affect the reliability of soil moisture information collection and accuracy. Thus the collection system of soil moisture has not yet really worked in decision-making on cotton drip irrigation.

Under drip irrigation, only soils near the root zone is moisturized, which is different to traditional surface irrigation. In addition to the influence of soil factor itself, there are many other factors that have significant impacts on the spatial variability of soil moisture, such as emitter flow, emitter spacing, drip tape uniformity and layout in field. after three years of experiment research, a database management system was established including soil moisture of cotton field, crop growth, irrigation water and social economy. The data measured by soil moisture sensors were transferred to Central Control Computer via the Remote Telemetry Control Unit (RTU) and the automatic evaluation of gathered data was processed through Central Control Computer by experts' system on cotton production and management. Practically, the solenoid valves will be opened or closed through RTU based on the orders issued by central control computer system. For details, see Fig.1.

There are many articles on the researches of spatial variability of soil moisture using statistical methods in literatures [2-10]. However, fewer scholars have done systematic study about method of setting soil moisture sensor in automatic monitoring system for growing cotton. In this study, we focused on this issue. The research results of this study could provide theoretical basis for the scientific design of soil moisture monitoring system and its high-level application in field to conduct study on the characteristics of spatial variability of soil moisture and reasonable layout method of soil moisture sensor. The outcomes from this study could also offer technical support for soil moisture automatic acquisition and processing information, accurate forecasting of soil moisture content, soil moisture intelligent diagnosis and real-time irrigation decision-making. It has important practical significance to realize precise irrigation and efficient use of water in agriculture in Xinjiang.

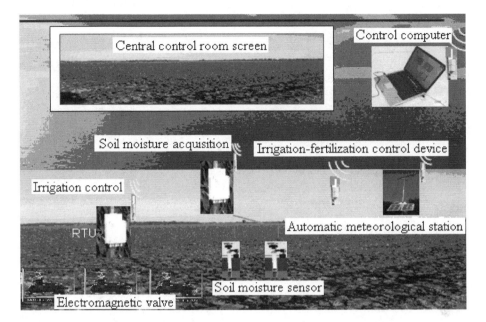

**Fig. 1.** Automatic control system in drip irrigation demonstration

## 2 Materials and Methods

### 2.1 Experimental Site

The study site is located in Baotou-lake Farm in China, East longitude 86°08′~86°26′, north latitude 41°45′~41°56′, which is some 30km away from Korla city. The irrigation condition is very good with Yongfeng Channel on the east and Kongque River on the west. The climate is dry and warm, the annual average temperature is 10.7°C, the annual average sunshine hours is 2886.8h, the annual average accumulated temperature is 4192.1°C, the average annual frost-free period is 132~181 days, the temperature difference between day and night is 12°C~17°C, the annual rainfall is about 103mm. It is abundant in sunshine with a long growing season, less rainfall in summer and less snow in winter.

The study was conducted on a 68-ha cotton field (Automatic Irrigation Demonstration Area on Cotton Mulched Drip Irrigation and the details of the control system are shown in Fig.1). The sources of irrigation network are well. Experimental site selected is at a spacing of 45m×54m and average drip tape space is 1.25m and emitter space is 0.30 m. Soil texture is sandy loam and soil bulk density is 1.45g/cm$^3$. The cultivation mode of cotton is four lines under a film with one drip tape placed in the center. The cotton growing direction is from east to west and cultivation mode is : 25cm+45cm+ 25cm+40cm. The details are shown in Fig. 2.

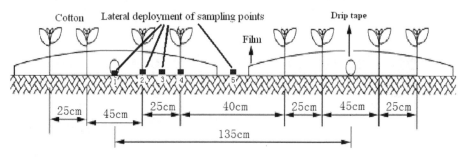

**Fig. 2.** Cotton cultivated pattern and layout of sampling points

## 2.2    Experimental Schemes

### Scheme 1: Analysis of Spatial Variability of Soil Moisture

As indicated in Fig. 3, the grid method was adopted in the layout of sampling points. Five rows of sampling points were designed along drip tape direction and row interval was 10 meters, space between consecutive points was 5 meters along submain direction. The experiment is divided into two stages. The first stage was from April 22nd to June 13th without any precipitation（winter irrigation was occurred at December 15th, 2008）and belonged to water shortage period ; detailed experiment times are shown in Table 1、Table 2 and Table 3. The soil moisture was measured by drying and weighing method in three layers (0～20cm, 20～40cm and 40～60cm).

### Scheme 2: Analysis of Lateral Orientation of Soil Moisture Monitoring Points

In 2009, a control area in one typical drip tape was selected. Four rows of sampling points were placed along vertical direction to drip tape. Row interval was 2 meters, each row has five sampling points and their locations were 0m,0.225m, 0.350m,

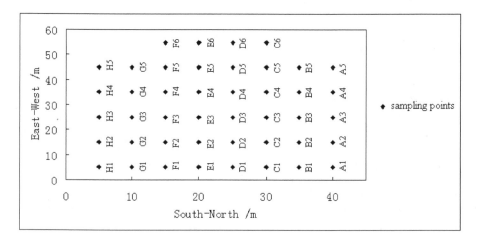

**Fig. 3.** Distribution of sampling points for soil moisture

0.475m and 0.675m from drip tape respectively (namely located in drip tape, inward cotton row, in the center of two cotton rows, outward cotton row and at ditch between two neighboring membranes). The details are shown in Fig.3. Detailed sampling times are shown in Table 6. Soil moisture was measured by drying and weighing method in four layers (0~20cm, 20~40cm, 40~60cm and 60~80cm).

**Table 1.** Descriptive statistics of soil moisture content in Stage One

| Sampling Time | Sample Number | Minimum | Maximum | Mean | Standard deviation | Variation coefficient | Skewness | Kurtosis |
|---|---|---|---|---|---|---|---|---|
| Apr 22 | 44 | 0.184 | 0.258 | 0.217 | 0.021 | 0.097 | 0.311 | -0.961 |
| May 15 | 44 | 0.174 | 0.256 | 0.209 | 0.021 | 0.100 | 0.583 | -0.620 |
| May 24 | 44 | 0.166 | 0.238 | 0.198 | 0.021 | 0.106 | 0.405 | -0.915 |
| Jun 4 | 44 | 0.156 | 0.233 | 0.198 | 0.021 | 0.106 | -0.005 | -0.990 |
| Jun 11 | 44 | 0.141 | 0.235 | 0.187 | 0.020 | 0.107 | -0.003 | -0.029 |

**Table 2.** Descriptive statistics of soil moisture before irrigation in Stage Two

| Sampling Time | Sample Number | Minimum | Maximum | Mean | Standard deviation | Variation coefficient | Skewness | Kurtosis |
|---|---|---|---|---|---|---|---|---|
| Jun 29 | 44 | 0.101 | 0.225 | 0.168 | 0.029 | 0.173 | 0.017 | -0.692 |
| Jul 13 | 44 | 0.169 | 0.242 | 0.197 | 0.022 | 0.112 | 0.625 | -0.835 |
| Jul 24 | 44 | 0.140 | 0.256 | 0.183 | 0.025 | 0.137 | 1.039 | 0.923 |
| Aug 5 | 44 | 0.138 | 0.257 | 0.189 | 0.026 | 0.138 | 0.518 | -0.059 |
| Aug 17 | 44 | 0.124 | 0.242 | 0.183 | 0.026 | 0.142 | 0.360 | -0.128 |
| Aug 27 | 44 | 0.185 | 0.291 | 0.222 | 0.023 | 0.104 | 0.626 | 0.216 |

**Table 3.** Descriptive statistics of soil moisture after irrigation in Stage Two

| Sampling Time | Sample Number | Minimum | Maximum | Mean | Standard deviation | Variation coefficient | Skewness | Kurtosis |
|---|---|---|---|---|---|---|---|---|
| Jun 17 | 44 | 0.185 | 0.287 | 0.237 | 0.025 | 0.105 | 0.434 | -0.270 |
| Jul 4 | 44 | 0.181 | 0.287 | 0.232 | 0.027 | 0.116 | 0.328 | -0.514 |
| Jul 15 | 44 | 0.190 | 0.319 | 0.258 | 0.029 | 0.112 | 0.300 | -0.316 |
| Jul 31 | 44 | 0.185 | 0.288 | 0.234 | 0.028 | 0.120 | 0.236 | -0.919 |
| Aug 10 | 44 | 0.158 | 0.289 | 0.223 | 0.031 | 0.139 | -0.097 | -0.535 |
| Aug 20 | 44 | 0.177 | 0.287 | 0.229 | 0.027 | 0.118 | -0.047 | -0.397 |
| Sep 3 | 44 | 0.197 | 0.299 | 0.236 | 0.026 | 0.110 | 0.826 | -0.022 |

**Table 4.** Corresponding parameters of Semivariogram models and test parameters of regression models for soil moisture

| | Depth | Theory | Nugget | Sill | Range | Nugget/ Sill | Decision | Fractal Dimension |
|---|---|---|---|---|---|---|---|---|
| | cm | Model | $10^4$ | $10^4$ | $A_0$ | $C_0/(C_0+C)$ | $R^2$ | $D_0$ |
| Stage one | 0~20 | spherical | 1.75 | 3.14 | 16.45 | 0.56 | 0.80 | 1.91 |
| | 20~40 | spherical | 1.80 | 3.14 | 19.27 | 0.57 | 0.49 | 1.95 |
| | 40~60 | spherical | 2.77 | 4.88 | 15.04 | 0.57 | 0.82 | 1.83 |
| Before Irrigation in Stage two | 0~20 | spherical | 1.05 | 3.59 | 9.40 | 0.29 | 0.73 | 1.91 |
| | 20~40 | spherical | 6.00 | 6.00 | 18.80 | 1.00 | 0.64 | 1.90 |
| | 40~60 | spherical | 5.40 | 11.59 | 11.75 | 0.47 | 0.38 | 1.92 |
| After Irrigation in Stage two | 0~20 | spherical | 5.50 | 9.33 | 21.92 | 0.59 | 0.70 | 1.82 |
| | 20~40 | spherical | 6.60 | 11.59 | 19.27 | 0.57 | 0.59 | 1.84 |
| | 40~60 | spherical | 4.00 | 12.99 | 35.35 | 0.31 | 0.30 | 1.98 |

**Table 5.** Significance test for soil moisture between soil monitoring points before irrigation

| Scheme | 0-20cm | | 20-40cm | | 40-60cm | | 60-80cm | |
|---|---|---|---|---|---|---|---|---|
| | t | $t_{\alpha/2}^{(n-1)}$ | t | $t_{\alpha/2}^{(n-1)}$ | t | $t_{\alpha/2}^{(n-1)}$ | t | $t_{\alpha/2}^{(n-1)}$ |
| No.1~No.2 | 0.625 | 0.576 | -0.340 | 0.756 | -0.132 | 0.903 | -0.307 | 0.779 |
| No.1~No.3 | -0.131 | 0.904 | 0.121 | 0.911 | 0.395 | 0.719 | -0.692 | 0.539 |
| No.1~No.4 | 0.264 | 0.809 | -0.333 | 0.761 | -0.441 | 0.689 | 2.810 | 0.067 |
| No.1~No.5 | 0.918 | 0.426 | -0.612 | 0.584 | -1.614 | 0.205 | 0.609 | 0.586 |

**Table 6.** Irrigation time and Irrigation requirement at different periods

| Period of growth | Irrigation requirement ($m^3/hm^2$) | Time | |
|---|---|---|---|
| | | Before irrigation | After irrigation |
| Seedling stage | 300 | Jun 11 | Jun 13 |
| Budding period | 300 | Jun 29 | Jul 1 |
| Flowering stage | 300 | Aug 5 | Aug 7 |
| Boll opening stage | 300 | Sep 3 | Sep 4 |

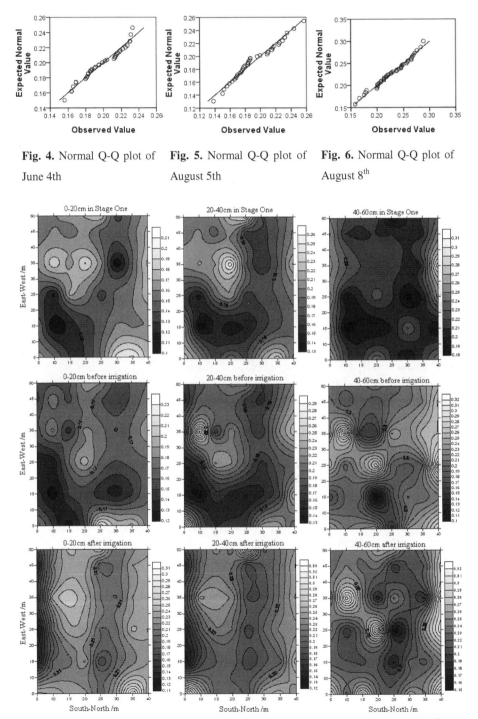

**Fig. 4.** Normal Q-Q plot of June 4th

**Fig. 5.** Normal Q-Q plot of August 5th

**Fig. 6.** Normal Q-Q plot of August 8th

**Fig. 7.** Isogram of soil moisture at three depths in June 4th、 August 5th and July 31st

# 3      Methodology

The traditional and geo-statistical methods were utilized to analyze data in this study. Both methods have been used extensively in the literatures[1-10], readers are referred to above literatures for detailed description of the methods. In this study, a normal Q-Q test was performed and descriptive statistics were computed to the soil moisture data in scheme 1 using SPSS17.0 (Table 1, Table 2 and Table 3). Take the data of Jun 4, Aug 5, and Aug 10 for example, normal Q-Q tests were shown in Fig.4, Fig.5 and Fig 6; T test was performed to the soil moisture data in scheme 2 and the results are shown in Table 5. Geo-statistics analysis was performed to the soil moisture data in scheme 1 by GS+ software and results are shown in Table 4. The isogram of soil moisture for each depth was drawn by Kriging interpolation through Surfer 8.0 software. The details are shown in Fig.7.

# 4      Results and Discussion

## 4.1      Traditional Statistical Analysis of Spatial Variability for Soil Moisture on Cotton Mulched Drip Irrigation

Traditional statistical analysis[11-12] to the sample data of soil moisture in field were analyzed by SPSS 17.0 (only discuss it in two-dimensional plane), and the results are shown in Table 1, Table 2 and Table 3. As indicated from the Tables, in stage one, mean value, minimum value and maximum value of soil moisture in the whole experimental site decrease as time goes except some unusual value (the maximum of June 11th) which maybe attributed to the measurement error. However, the tendency of coefficient of variation Cv is opposite. Coefficient of variation Cv can express the dispersion degree of random variable. Generally speaking, when $Cv \leq 0.1$, it indicates weak variation ；  when $0.1 < Cv < 1.0$, it indicates moderate variation ；  when $Cv \geq 1.0$, it indicates strong variation [13-14]. In stage one, Cv value vary in the range of 0.097 $\sim$0.107, an approximate value is 0.1, thus it should belongs to weak variation ；  in stage two (including after irrigation and before irrigation), Cv value vary in the range of 0.104$\sim$0.173 and should belongs to moderate variation. This showed that the increase of soil moisture can enhance the spatial variability, namely, the spatial variability vary directly with soil moisture.

## 4.2      Geo-statistical Analysis of Spatial Variability of Soil Moisture on Cotton Mulched Drip Irrigation

Wang et al. (2001) [15] suggested that the ratio of nugget variance to sill variance expressed as a percentage is an indication of the spatial dependence of the variable concerned. Cline et al. (1989) [16] and   Cambardella et al.(1994) [17] stated that ratios between 25% and 75% represent moderate spatial dependence, those below 25% strong spatial dependence, and all others weak dependence (Qi Feng et al,2004)[18] when it was not suitable to do spatial forecast by interpolation.

According to Table 4, both in stage one and stage two, Nugget/ Sill variance of soil moisture in all three depths are between 25% and 75%,which represents moderate spatial dependence or autocorrelation. Thus this case of soil moisture spatial variability is resulted from the combination of several random variables and structural factors including climate, topography, and soil form and so on. From the coefficient of determination in Table 4, we can obtain that the best theory model is spherical model [18] for each stage. However, with the increment of soil moisture content, the accuracy of regression model has a tendency of decreasing. From Table 4, we can easily found that the range of spherical model is about 9.40m~35.35m, about the same value for placing monitoring points for soil moisture. However, fractal dimension did not show significant changing rule.

From the results of Geo-statistical analysis above, we obtained that it was suitable to do spatial interpolation in consideration of the moderate spatial dependence of soil moisture. So, the isogram [19-22] of soil moisture for each depth was obtained by Surfer 8.0, the details are shown in Fig.7. As indicated in Fig.7, lines of the isogram are not too dense in all the three depth layers which indicate that the spatial correlation of soil moisture is strong while its variability is weak.

### 4.3    Lateral Location Research on Monitoring Points of Soil Moisture

The purpose of performing lateral location research of monitoring points on soil moisture is to obtain the best location of monitoring points by seeking the best vertical distance from monitoring points to the drip tape. This can improve the layout efficiency of monitoring points on soil moisture and their monitoring accuracy. The vertical profile of soils was divided into four layers, 0~20cm、 20~40cm、 40~60cm and 60 ~80cm. In order to perform t-test, the soil moisture data was divided into two Groups.Group 1 is composed from data of No.2~No.5 monitoring points observed from Jun 11, Jun 29, Aug 5 and Sep 3, and Group 2 is including the data of No.1 observed from Jun 11, Jun 29, Aug 5 and Sep 3 (monitoring points of No.1 are used to locate points in drip tape). A t-test to the data between Group 1 and Group 2 was performed to estimate its significance of soil moisture difference in vertical profile distribution and to determine the relative position between monitoring points and drip tape. The results are shown in Tab.5.

When $|t| \geq t_{\alpha/2}(n-1)$, the difference from the two data observed is significant; when $|t| < t_{\alpha/2}(n-1)$, there is no significant difference. As indicated in Tab.5, compared to No.1 point, there are significant differences in vertical profile 0~20cm soil moisture from No.2 point but 20~80cm ; At 0~60cm vertical profile, there is no significant differences between No.3 and No.4 points. Compared to No.1 point, there is significant difference in No.5 point at 0~80cm. This research showed that: At top 0~60cm layer, there are no significant differences about soil moisture distribution among the points which are at 0.225m, 0.350m and 0.475m from the drip tape, respectively. However, there are significant differences between drip tape and at points 0.675m away from it. So, it is better to place the monitoring points at the range of 0~0.475m from drip tape while farther points from the drip tape is not suitable for placing monitoring points.

## 5    Conclusions

Through the analysis of spatial variability of soil moisture and lateral orientation of soil moisture monitoring points, following conclusions can be made: (1) The increase of soil moisture can enhance their spatial variability. (2) In the drip irrigation system and cotton cultivation mode, spatial variability of soil moisture is resulted from the combination of several random variables and the structural factors including climate, topography, and soil form and so on. (3) Semi-variogram models belong to spherical model and the range of spherical model for soil moisture is about 9.40m~35.35m (4) With the increment of soil moisture content, the accuracy of regression models have a tendency of decreasing. (5) The monitoring points should be placed at the range of 0~ 0.475m from drip tape and it is not suitable to place them at a farther place. It is best to place them at outward cotton row in consideration of management and monitoring of soil moisture.

In this research, the range of spatial variability, field size and monitoring accuracy of soil moisture are considered in analysis of monitoring point lateral layout for soil moisture. The results from this research are helpful to guide the monitoring points' layout of soil moisture. As for how to place vertical direction monitoring points, it still needs a further study.

## References

[1] Hillel, D.: Fundaments of Soil Physics. Academic Press, New York (1980)
[2] Burgess, T.M., Webster, R.: Optimal interpolation and isarithmic and isarithmic mapping of soli properties. Soil Sci. 31, 315–341 (1980)
[3] Nielsen, D.R., Biggar, J.W.: Monitoring soil water properties utilizing geostatistical techniques. ISRSS China 21, 211–223 (1985)
[4] Bárdossy, A., Lehmann, W.: Spatial distribution of soil moisture in a small catchment. Part 1: geostatistical analysis. Hydrology 206, 1–15 (1998)
[5] Anctil, F., Mathieu, R., Parent, L.-E., Viau, A.A., Sbih, M., Hessami, M.: Geostatistics of near-surface moisture in bare cultivated organic soils. Hydrology 260, 30–37 (2002)
[6] Wilson, D.J., Western, A.W., Grayson, R.B.: Spatial distribution of soil moisture over 6 and 30 cm depth, Mahurangi river catchment. Hydrology 276, 254–274 (2003)
[7] Western, A.W.: Spatial correlation of soil moisture in small catchments and its relationship to dominant spatial hydrological processes. Hydrology 286, 113–134 (2004)
[8] Veronese Jr., V., Carvalho, M.P., Dafonte, J., Freddi, O.S., Vidal Vazquez, E., Ingaramo, O.E.: Spatial variability of soil water content and mechanical resistance of BraZilian ferralsol. Soil & Tillage Research 85, 166–177 (2006)
[9] Huang, J., Du, Z.-D., Zhu, X.-G., Liu, L., Wu, W.-H., Liu, B.: Spatial Variability Research of Soil Moisture. Water Saving Irrigation 10, 20–21, 25 (2010)
[10] Bi, H., Li, X., Liu, X., Guo, M., Li, J.: A case study of spatial heterogeneity of soil moisture in the Loess Plateau, western China: A geostatistical approach. International Journal of Sediment Research 24(1), 63–73 (2009)
[11] Brocca, L., Morbidelli, R., Melone, F., Moramarco, T.: Soil moisture spatial variability in experimental areas of central Italy. Hydrology 333, 356–373 (2007)

[12] Famiglietti, J.S., Devereaux, J.A., Laymon, C.A., Tsegaye, T., Houser, P.R., Jackson, T.J., Graham, S.T., Rodell, M., van Oevelen, P.J.: Ground-based investigation of soil moisture variability within remote sensing footprints during the Southern Great Plains 1997 (SGP 1997) Hydrology Experiment (1997)

[13] Yao, F., Xu, Y., Lin, E., Yokozawa, M., Zhang, J.: Assessing the impacts of climate change on rice yields in the main rice areas of China. Climatic Change 80, 395–409 (2007), doi:10.1007/s10584-006-9122-6

[14] Lin, H., Wheeler, D., Bell, J., Wilding, L.: Assessment of soil spatial variability at multiple scales. Ecological Modelling 182, 271–290 (2005)

[15] Wang, J., Fu, B.J., Qiu, Y., Chen, L.D., Wang, Z.: Geostatistical analysis of soil moisture variability on Da Nangou catchments of the loess plateau. China Environmental Geology 41(1), 113–116 (2001)

[16] Cline, T.J., Molinas, A., Julien, P.Y.: An auto-CAD-based watershed information system for the Hydrologic Model HEC-1. Water Resources Bulletin 25(3), 641–652 (1989)

[17] Cambardella, C.A., Moorman, T.B., Parkin, T.B., Karlen, D.L., Turco, R.F., Konopka, A.E.: Field scale variability of soil properties in Central Iowa soils. Soil Sci. Soc. Am. J. 58, 1501–1511 (1994)

[18] Feng, Q., Liu, Y., Masao, M.: Geostatistical analysis of soil moisture variability in grassland. Journal of Arid Environments 58, 357–372 (2004)

[19] Taschetto, A.S., England, M.H.: An analysis of late twentieth century trends in Australian rainfall. International Journal of Climatology (2008), http://www.interscience.wiley.com, doi:10.1002/joc.1736

[20] De Silva, C.S., Weatherhead, E.K., Knox, J.W., Rodriguez-Diaz, J.A.: Predicting the impacts of climate change—A case study of paddy irrigation water requirements in Sri Lanka. Agricultural Water Management 93, 19–29 (2007)

[21] Lin, H., Zhou, X.: Evidence of subsurface preferential flow using soil hydrologic monitoring in the Shale Hills catchment. European Journal of Soil Science 59, 34–49 (2008)

[22] Petrone, R.M., Price, J.S., Carey, S.K., Waddington, J.M.: Statistical characterization of the spatial variability of soil moisture in a cutover peatland. Hydrol. Process 18, 41–52 (2004)

# A Separating Method of Adjacent Apples
# Based on Machine Vision and Chain Code Information[*]

Juan Feng[1,2], Shengwei Wang[1,3], Gang Liu[1,**], and Lihua Zeng[2]

[1] Key Laboratory of Modern Precision Agriculture System Integration Research,
Ministry of Education, China Agricultural University, Beijing, 100083, China
[2] College of Information Science & Technology,
Agricultural University of Hebei, Baoding, 071001, China
[3] College of mathematics and information science,
Northwest Normal University of Gansu, Lanzhou, 730070, China
pac@cau.edu.cn

**Abstract.** Fruit location is an important parameter for apple harvesting robot to conduct picking task. However, it is difficult to obtain coordinates of each apple under natural conditions. One of the major challenges is detecting adjacent fruits accurately. Previous studies for adjacent detection have shortcomings such as vast computation, difficulty in implementation and over-segmentation. In this paper, we propose a novel and effective separating method for adjacent apples recognition based on chain code information and obtain the centroid coordinates of each fruit. Firstly, those valid regions of fruit are extracted by pre-processing the initial image. Secondly, chain code information is obtained by following the contour of extracted regions. Thirdly, through observing the changing law of chain code difference and adopting local optimum principle, concave points are found. Finally, the best point pairs are determined with different matching principles, and those adjacent apples are separated exactly. The experimental results show that the average rate of successful separation is greater than 91.2% with the proposed method, which can meet the requirements of applications in harvesting robots.

**Keywords:** Separating method, Chain code difference, Concave point, Match principle, Local optimum.

## 1    Introduction

Apple harvesting robot is one of important research and application fields in agriculture, the accurate and automatic recognition of fruit is part of its primary task [1] [2] [3]. In the process, multi-fruit adjacent recognition is more difficult than the others, because the adjacent region is apt to be considered as a whole, and centroid coordinates acquired are not the ones of single fruit. In this case, Not only is recognition rate

[*] The research was financially supported by National Natural Science Foundation(31071333).
[**] Corresponding author.

D. Li and Y. Chen (Eds.): CCTA 2011, Part I, IFIP AICT 368, pp. 258–267, 2012.
© IFIP International Federation for Information Processing 2012

affected, but also fruit may be damaged by hard manipulator and its quality can be affected. How to recognize centroid coordinates of each apple is a problem not satisfactorily resolved yet, due to the complexity of environment.

In the research of adjacent objects separation, many scholars have put forward different methods, Such as mathematics morphological operation [4] [5] [6], improved watershed algorithm [7], and active contour model tracking algorithm [8], etc. However, there are some obvious shortcomings in these algorithms, including a need to track the process of calculation every time, computation is vast, the demand of computer software and hardware is higher, and results often appear over-segmentation. Other scholars have studied unique brightness information within adjacent region to separate the fruit [9], but the brightness difference on the surface of fruit is an indispensable factor. Edge concave points split touching objects are widely used in the field of cell segmentation [10]. Its main advantage is in a faster processing speed. Extracting and matching those concave points are two important aspects. Using the method for separating adjacent fruit has never been reported before. Under natural conditions, noises, branches and leaves make fruit boundary uneven, and the adjacent fruit recognition in real time also need to be taken into account, in this way, conventional method is not applicable.

This paper presents a new separating method of adjacent apples based on machine vision and chain code information. It consists of six main steps: extraction of valid region, acquirement of chain code information, computation of chain code difference between discrete points, selection of concave points referring to given thresholds, match of those points according to different principles, determination of the separating point pairs and realization of fruit separation. The experimental results show that method is simple, effective, accurate and ideal for separating adjacent apples.

## 2     Materials and Methods

### 2.1     Materials

In this study, the cultivar of apple was Fuji. A digital camera (DH-HV3130UC, CMOS color camera) was selected and shooting distance was 1.5m. A laptop was used to program and drive the camera to acquire the RGB images. Image frames were 512×512 pixels in the BMP format. The software for image processing was MATLAB7.0.

### 2.2     Valid Region Extraction

Observing those apple pictures taken from natural environment, the color of ripe fruit is red while most of background is green. Both ends of a component of Lab color space are just the two colors. Therefore, the model was used for segmentation. The component can be matched by a non-linear combination of tricolor (Red, Green and Blue) [11]. The transformational relationship is known as Eq. (1).

$$a=500[1.006(0.607R+0.174G+0.201B)^{1/3}-(0.299R+0.587G+0.114B)^{1/3}] \qquad (1)$$

**Fig. 1.** Filtering the apple image (a) Original image, (b) Blurring image

Due to the influence of natural luminance, some objective colors aren't red, which results in losing some pixels after image segmentation. In order to reduce the effect, a Gaussian lowpass filter was used to blur the initial image [12]. An example is displayed in Fig.1.Then a component was used to separate fruits from background. OTSU is regarded as an optimal means for auto threshold selection, it was used here to convert filtered image to binary form [13]. Medium value filter and area threshold were employed to remove noises.

The size of each ripe fruit is approximate and its shape is close to circle. When shooting distance is fixed, the size of fruits located the same distance on the image is similar. Calculating the sum of pix in many single-fruit regions, average area of fruit is obtained; Rotating single fruit region to find maximal width of all external rectangles and treating the width as average diameter of apple. By means of these methods, $S_{threshold}$ and $D_{threshold}$ were calculated, which are both a vital requirement of region extraction and constrain separating. It has been validated using data, finding that best value was obtained when $S_{threshold}$ was set at 5800 and $D_{threshold}$ was set at 97. Every area in the binary image was calculated. There was a multi-fruit adjacent region if its area value was greater than $S_{threshold}$ and the region was kept. On the contrary, there was a single apple and the region should be deleted by way of turning its gray value into zero [14].

From the above process, adjacent region on the apple image was extracted, which was called valid region. Speeds of separation and centroid coordinates determination would be accelerated.

## 2.3    Separating Method

Fig.2a shows that ideal cut-points always locate the position of concave points for realizing apples separation. Therefore, it is significant that concave points are extracted accurately. There are a lot of methods used for detecting concave points. This paper exploits an idea based on boundary curvature to detect, because curvature usually indicates the curving degree of border well. However, discrete curve is discontinuous and non- differentiable, it is difficult to calculate the curvature directly. Using the slope-difference of adjacent boundary line to describe curvature of line segment intersection proves to be reasonably effective [15].

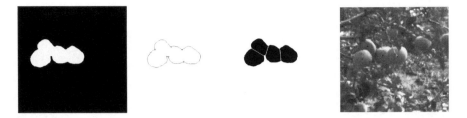

**Fig. 2.** Procedure of separation (a) Valid region image (b) Concave points image (c) Separated image (d) Centroid coordinates image

This Freeman chain code represents a chain as a sequence of direction codes from one pixel to the adjacent one. This code is highly effective for compression of line images. According to the contour information of valid region from the boundary trace, chain code is obtained [16]. The common eight-direction chain code for the representation of line-drawing data has low precision , because one difference equals to 45°[17]. The concept of average chain code is introduced, which describes the direction of line approximately, and can be replaced by chain code sum if the number of points involved is fixed. $Sum(i)$ denotes chain code sum and is given as Eq.2.

$$Sum(i)=A(i)+A(i-1)+\cdots A(i-n+1)   (i=1,2,\cdots n) \tag{2}$$

Where $A(i)$ denotes absolute chain code of current point, specific procedure can be found in [18]. A local boundary is similar to straight line, so its tangent direction(slope) can be figured by the absolute chain code sum of $n$ sequential points. Selecting $n=3$ means the whole circle being divided into 24, one difference equals to 15°, therefore, the accuracy of direction judgment improves greatly.$Diff(i)$ denotes the difference of chain codes sum between the $n$ sequential points ingoing and outgong, and is shown as Eq.(3). The value is proportional to curvature, which indicates the direction of boundary exactly and its positive and negative describes the convexo-concave of concerns. If the boundary is clockwise, those positive chain code difference shows concave points, while those negative shows convex points. The graph of $Sum(i)$ and $Diff(i)$ is shown as Fig.3.

$$Diff(i)= Sum(i+n)-Sum(i)   (i=1,2,\cdots n) \tag{3}$$

In order to calculate an arc length of boundary, a concept of accumulated length is introduced, which indicates a length between starting and current point. Therefore, arc length between any two points is equal to difference of each accumulated length. For briefness, a step of level and vertical direction was set at 1,while other steps were set at 1.5. The corresponding rate of arc and chord was obtained by calculating distance and accumulated length between two points.

The boundary of the digital image is not absolutely smooth, and corners are mainly points ,whose chain code differences do not belong to the interval [-1,2]. For the sake of finding concave points of adjacent fruit boundary, those points corresponding to big curvature are extracted, where $Diff(i)>M(i=1,2,\cdots n)$ is a requirement. After repeated test, $M=2.5$ was proved to be the best threshold. Chain code information of points extracted was stored into a two-dimensional array.

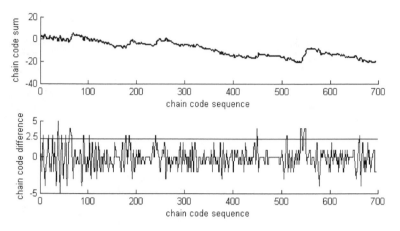

**Fig. 3.** Graph of chain code sum and chain code difference

Because the accuracy of chain code difference is limited in the process of extraction, several neighbouring concave points may be selected at the same time. For this condition, the point of local maximal curvature should be selected from points meeting the expression as $d_{mn}<K$, where $d_{mn}$ is the distance between two concave points, where $K$ denotes a theshold of selecting candidate points. After experimental comparison, this paper was set at $K=9$. Result of extracting concave points is shown as Fig.2b.

According to different matching principles, point pairs matched could be located. Then, these point pairs were connected to form a separating line, which could realize the separation of adjacent apple. It is shown as Fig.2c.

If there is a region of two adjacent fruit, namely, expression is exhibited as $S_{threshold}<S_l\leq2S_{threshold}$, where $S_l$ is the area of No.$l$ valid region, only is a pair of concave points obtained at last , so there is no need to match, but to connect points directly.

If there is a region of many adjacent fruits, several pairs of concave points are obtained, which is shown in Fig.2b. It is obvious that there is a problem of concave pointe's combination and match. On the basis of test and analysis, the matching procedure includes two following steps:

(1) Start from the first element in the two-dimensional array of concave points, and calculate the chord length between current and other point. The Equations can be expressed as Eq.(4):

$$C(i,j)= ((x_i-x_j)^2+(y_i-y_j)^2)^{1/2}   (i,j=1,2, \cdots n) \qquad (4)$$

Where $C(i,j)$ is chord length between $i$ point and $j$ point. In order to advoid the over-segmenting, those point pairs satisfy the predefined distance limits $C(i,j)<D_{threshold}$, Which are saved as matching point candidate.

(2) Let $AC=Arc(i,j)/C(i,j)$ denotes the rate of arc and chord. Objective boundary satisfied the major arc limitation, $AC>\pi/2$ can form arc.As far as optimum separating position is concerned, not only is its curvature relatively big but $AC$ is local maximum. By comparision $AC$ of point pairs obtained from step 1 , the maximum and mark the corresponding points position can be found. As soon as a pair of matching points is

determined, the gray value of separating line is changed into 0, then the region is divided into two parts.To judge from $S_{threshold}$, whether and which part has still adjacent fruits, and repeat the above process until all adjacent regions are separated completely. The separating flow is described as Fig.4.

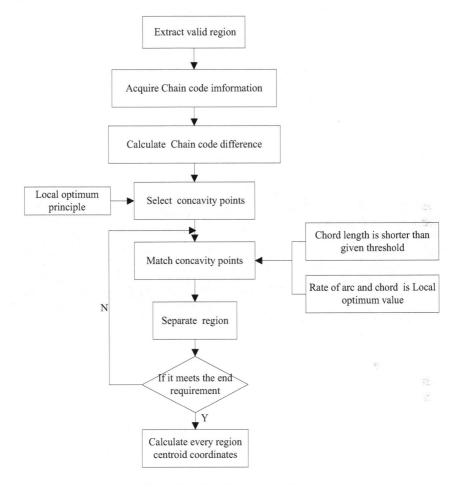

**Fig. 4.** The flow chart of separation

## 2.4  Centroid Coordinates Computation

After the separation of adjacent fruit region, each centroid coordinates calculated was regarded as approximate central position corresponding to a apple. Result is shown in Fig.2d. Their values are often not an integer. Considering a fruit region's size is far greater than a pixel'one, and the rounding coordinates will not cause an obvious effect on accuracy for post process.

## 3    Results and Discussion

With the purpose of evaluating the accuracy of centriod coordinates acquired after using the separating method, 100 apple images were tested in this study. 3 images were randomly selected to show the validate process. Each image was different from shooting and adjacent conditions. Fig.5a with a back light included two adjacent fruits occluded by leaves partly; Fig.5b with a back light included many adjacent fruits occluded by leaves and branches partly; Fig.5c with a front light included three adjacent regions, one was multi-fruit, two other were double-fruit. The aim of recognition is to separate adjacent apples each other and acquiring every centroid coordinates. The results acquired between by artificial and the newly presented methods have been compared. The distance between the two centroid coordinates weighs the disparity, the expression is followed as Eq.(5):

**Fig. 5.** Images for experiment (a)The back lighted apple images including a two adjacent apples region (b)The back lighted apple images including a multi-apple adjacent region (c)The front lighted apple images including three adjacent regions

$$d_{mc}= ((x_m-x_s)^2+(y_m-y_s)^2)^{1/2} \qquad (5)$$

Where $(x_m,y_m)$ denotes centroid coordinates acquired by artificial method, $(x_s,y_s)$ denotes centroid coordinates acquired by the separating method. Table.1 exhibits the comparison.

When $d_{mc}<10$, it means successful in separation, Table.1 showed the most of results meeting the above requirement, only two was largely different.No.5 fruit was overlapped by front fruits on the Fig.5b, most parts occluded were separated during the image processing, which resulted in notable coordinates migration; No.7 fruit was occluded by the leaves and branches, which made its area smaller after the separation of a component and its coordinates migrate. The rate of successful separation is defined as Eq.(6).

$$R_S=(N_S/N_T) \times 100\% \qquad (6)$$

**Table 1.** Comparison of experimental results between artificial calculation and separating methods

| Figure Number | Apple number | Centric coordinate of artificial calculation $(x_m, y_m)$ | Centric coordinate of separating method $(x_s, y_s)$ | centroid distance $d_{ms}$ |
|---|---|---|---|---|
| a | 1 | (161,253) | (162,253) | 1.00 |
|   | 2 | (198,214) | (201,213) | 3.16 |
| b | 3 | (334,170) | (337,172) | 3.61 |
|   | 4 | (395,202) | (395.198) | 4.00 |
|   | 5 | (440,172) | (426,165) | 15.65 |
|   | 6 | (456,197) | (460,196) | 4.12 |
| c | 7 | (226,172) | (232,181) | 10.81 |
|   | 8 | (279,210) | (282,213) | 4.24 |
|   | 9 | (315,280) | (314,277) | 3.16 |
|   | 10 | (200,377) | (198,376) | 2.24 |
|   | 11 | (272,375) | (273,382) | 7.07 |
|   | 12 | (358,458) | (354,453) | 6.40 |
|   | 13 | (412,418) | (412,417) | 1.00 |

Where $N_S$ is the number of apple meeting the expression, $d_{ms}<10$, $N_T$ is the total number of adjacent apples. Through testing with 100 apple images, we draw a conclusion that the average rate of successful separation is greater than 91.2%, which meets the requirements of application in harvesting robots. Furthermore, variable light has not obvious impact on the separation.

## 4    Conclusion

In this study, a novel and effective method for separating adjacent apples is developed in spite of various natural lighting conditions. Characteristics are as follows:

(1) In order to reduce the effect of natural luminance, a Gaussian lowpass filter is used to blur the inital image. Considering the feature of apple image itself, the a component of Lab color space is employed to separate fruits from background, then medium value filter and area threshold are made use of removing image noises. Following the above steps, ideal binary images of apple are acquired for post processing.

(2) Valid regions of adjacent apples are extracted by area threshold method, which can improve the speed of total image processing. Following the contour of extracted

regions, chain code information is obtained. Observing the changing law of chain code difference and adopting local optimum, concave points are found. Through the different matching principle, best point pairs are determined and adjacent apple can be separated accurately. The rate of arc and chord and the length of segment chord are key parameters of matching principle. Experimental results shows that average rate of successful separation is greater than 91.2% by this method, and meet the practical need of harvesting robot.

(3) However, there are some limitations for this method: Need of obvious concave-convex change of adjacent boundary; chain code information can be taken full advantage for separating fruits; Fruits are occluded by leaves and branches and its boundary is brought about some marked concave points, which will influence extraction and match of concave points.

# References

1. Bulanon, D.M., Kataoka, T., Ota, Y., Hiroma, T.: A Color Model for Recognition of Apples by a Robotic Harvesting System. Journal of the JSAM 64(5), 123–133 (2002)
2. Stajnko, D., Cmelik, Z.: Modelling of Apple Fruit Growth by Application of Image Anlaysis. Agricultura Conspectus Scientificus 70(2), 59–64 (2005)
3. Zhao, J., Tow, J., Katupitiya, J.: On-tree Fruit Recognition Using Texture Properties and Color Data. In: 2005 IEEE/RSJ International Conference on Intelligent Robots and Systems, pp. 3993–3998. IEEE Press, New York (2005)
4. Zhou, T.J., Zhang, T.Z., Yang, L.: Comparison of Two Algorithms Based on Mathematical Morphology for Segmentation of Touching Strawberry Fruits. Transactions of the CSAE 23(9), 164–168 (2007) (in Chinese)
5. Luengo-Oroz, M.A., Faure, E., Angulo, J.: Robust iris Segmentation on Uncalibrated Noisy Images Using Mathematical Morphology. Image and Vision Computing 28, 278–284 (2009)
6. Chinchuluun, R., Lee, W.S.: Citrus Yield Mapping System in Natural Outdoor Scenes Using the Watershed Transform. ASABE Paper No. 063010, St. Joseph, MI USA (2006)
7. Lee, W.S., Slaughter, D.C.: Recognition of Partially Occluded Plant Leaves Using a Modified Watershed Algorithm. Transactions of the ASAE 47(4), 1269–1280 (2004)
8. Wang, Y.C., Chou, J.J.: Automatic Segmentation of Touching Rice Kernels with an Active Contour model. Transactions of the ASABE 47(5), 1803–1811 (2005)
9. Zhang, Y.J., Li, M.Z., Liu, G.: Separating Adjoined Apples Based on Machine Vision and Information Fusion. Transactions of the Chinese Society for Agricultural Machinery 40(11), 180–183 (2009) (in Chinese)
10. Liu, W.H., Sui, Q.M.: Automatic Segmentation of Overlapping Powder Particle Based on Searching Concavity Points. Journal of electronic measurement and instrument 24(12), 1095–1100 (2010) (in Chinese)
11. Annerel, E., Taerwe, L.: Methods to Quantify the Colour Development of Concrete Exposed to Fire. Construction and Building Materials 25(10), 3989–3997 (2011)
12. Lak, M.B., Minaer, S., Amiriparian, J., Beheshti, B.: Apple Fruits Recognition Under Natural Luminance Using Machine Vision. Advance Journal of Food Science and Technology 2(6), 325–327 (2010)
13. Otsu, N.: A Threshold Selection Method from Gray-level Histograms. IEEE Transactions on System Man and Cybernetics 9(1), 62–69 (1979)

14. Bulanon, D.M., Kataoka, T.: A Fruit Detection System and an End Effector for Robotic for Robotic Harvesting of Fuji Apples. Agricultural Engineering International: the CIGR Ejournal 12(1), 1285–1298 (2010)
15. Gonzalez, R.C.: Digital Image Processing Using MATLAB. Publishing House of Electronics Industry (2005)
16. Liu, K., Fei, S.M., Wang, M.L.: Cotton Recognition Based on Randomized Hough Transform. Transactions of the Chinese Society for Agricultural Machinery 41(8), 160–165 (2010) (in Chinese)
17. Freeman, H.: Computer Processing of Line-drawing Date. Computer Surveys 6(1), 57–96 (1974)
18. Zhu, Y., Jiang, L.J., Xiao, Y.L.: Concave Spots Localization and Region Segmentation in Fibrous Material Image Based on Chain Codes. Journal of Nanjing University of Science and Technology (Natural Science) 32(1), 110–113 (2008) (in Chinese)

# Design of Precision Fertilization Management Information System on GPS and GIS Technologies[*]

Zhimin Liu[1,2], Weidong Xiong[3], and Xuewei Cao[1]

[1] Geomatics College, Shandong University of Science and Technology,
Qingdao, China
[2] Key Laboratory of Surveying and Mapping,
Technology Shandong Prince, China, 266590
[3] Survey mapping and planning office,
Qingdao Development Zone, Qingdao,China, 266555
liuzhimin010@163.com

**Abstract.** Aimed on the efficiency, energy-saving, yield and pro-environment, the precision agriculture is needed to develop. Presently, the field information quick-acquisition technology has become the important topics in the international precision agriculture research fields, because that still far behind the development of other precision agriculture technologies. The technological innovations focus on the new surveying technology, such as the fast real-time operation, which are helpful for improving sampling densities and accuracy. The author firstly summarized the three aspects development of data acquisition, data processing and management information system based on GPS and GIS of Precision Fertilization Management Information System (PFMIS), then we designed the framework of PFMIS which included the data-acquisition technique on the continuously operating reference stations (CORS), the data-processing methods on intelligence algorithms and Management Information System (MIS) on ArcGIS Engine, in order to satisfy the needs of network publication and query to precision fertilization.

**Keywords:** Precision Fertilization, PFMIS, GPS, GIS, CORS.

## 1 Introduction

In the information society, precision agriculture has become the focus on the frontier forces to how to use rationally the agricultural resources, enhance the quality and quantity of the agricultural production, reduce the production costs, and improve the ecological environment and sustainable agricultural development in the international developed country in the 21st century [1]. Based on the information and knowledge to the agricultural production management systems, the practice to this new concept would have the revolutionary significance, that promote the transformation of the information technology application, and enhance the civil traditional agriculture level

---

[*] Sponsored by the National Natural Science Foundation of China (40704001, 40876051).

D. Li and Y. Chen (Eds.): CCTA 2011, Part I, IFIP AICT 368, pp. 268–277, 2012.
© IFIP International Federation for Information Processing 2012

and agricultural equipment technology, develop the research and application of agricultural production-oriented of information technology, and achieve sustainable agricultural development [2,3]. Food shortage and fertilizer price-rising is a global issue. And with the multifaceted problems on national economy of the impact on food security, environmental pollution, lack of resources, increased costs, the precision fertilizer management information systems (PFMIS) would be established, that included the spatial data collection, soil nutrient data test, data standardization, management information system platform, the expert systems of the fertilizer recipes and fertilization model, and network queries, in order to achieve "increased food production and fertilizer efficiency". Therein the soil nutrient tester [4] had been put into the full production. Moreover the foundation on the expert systems would not research in this paper including the fertilizer recipes and fertilization model with the different crops, geographical location and climate varies [5-9].

Presently, the research of field information rapid acquisition technology is still far behind the other technologies in support of precision agriculture, and it had become an important issue on the international related research field. The keys on technological innovation are the fast real-time survey method in order to increase the sampling density, and find new sensor technology to meet the actual production requirements or even further improvements [2]. Author firstly overviewed three areas development of PFMIS on data collection, data processing and information management systems based on GPS (Global Positioning System) and GIS (Geographic Information System) technologies, secondly designed the PFMIS framework with the new technical methods, thirdly its advantages and feasibility were analyzed.

## 2    The Development of Precision Fertilization Based on GPS and GIS

Precision fertilization agriculture technologies are generally the agriculture management information system [10], which can capture quickly and efficiently and describe the spatial information of the variable environment impacted on crop growth, and are important to carry out the precision agriculture practice. The spatial coordinates and their varieties attribute information of soil resources were obtained after collecting data. Then data-processing technology and information management systems of attribute information based on spatial coordinates are keys.

### 2.1    The Spatial Data Surveying Technique of PFMIS

RS (Remote Sensing) and GPS single point positioning were the popular surveying modes on the spatial data acquisition [11, 12]. RS technology was one of main field-data sources to precision agriculture, which collect the ground spectral reflectance features used relative high-resolution-rate sensors, to monitor comprehensively in different crop growing period, in order to provide a large number of the space-time change information in farming field. Then the analyses of spatial characterization and location were finished based on the spectral information [13]. The time-series images, obtained by RS, were widely applied on the large-scale agricultural yield estimation. Because of some shortages such as the low-resolution rate spatial information, data post-processing, related support needs and lack of infrastructure, and so on, now GPS was used to make up the soil samples collected and fertilizer operations in positioning and navigation. GPS single point positioning can collect spatial information on kinematic real-time, all-weather, and convenient mode. Only one GPS receiver was used to arrive to the positioning accuracy in the 10m level.   But the accuracy level can not meet the requirements of the precise agriculture, while time, some shortages of high cost, low efficiency and poor real-time on the updating database; Otherwise DGPS (differential GPS) requires less than 2 receivers, one for the base-station, others for the mobile-stations, which must keep distance to base-station within 20km, and the code observations can be achieved [14-16], which is a large farm operations is limited.

With the development of CORS established more and more in the region, and in different fields, the RTK positioning and navigation realized conveniently in the centimeter-level precision used the network RTK technology on at least one receiver [15-19]. This paper designed the spatial data - soil resources information and data acquisition subsystem by GPS CORS technology, and improved the positioning accuracy and stability by accordingly data processing and software development.

## 2.2     Data Processing Method of the Soil Resource Information

After data collection, a variety of attribute information on spatial coordinates data were accessed: The physical and chemical properties of soil include soil types, soil texture, organic matter and soil pH, and other data. Soil nutrient data include soil nitrogen, phosphorus, potassium and other large number of nutrients and available nutrient data, calcium, magnesium, sulfur, chlorine, zinc, manganese, copper, iron, molybdenum and boron and other micronutrients data are included [6]. The key issue is how to process the data transformation from point-to-surface of the soil resource attribute data. The spatial interpolation methods were adopted on data-processing, mainly the Kriging geo-statistical interpolation and inversely proportional to distance interpolation method. On the condition of the same sampling density, in descending order of interpolation precision is plains, post area, hills, mountains, that is, with the complexity increased of the terrain interpolated, the accuracy was reduced. While time the sampling density increased more on the hills, mountains, etc., and the accuracy of the results were improved more [20]. Compare with the neural network methods (NN), as the sampling density is high, the same accuracy of the results of Kriging and inversely proportional to distance interpolation methods was obtained; but the case of low sampling density, the results of neural networks were the better accuracy.

Mueller T.G. and so on [21] experimented on the impact of soil fertility distribution to the different grid sampling density and interpolation methods. They selected the three fields, the different sampling plan were made according to the different sampling instance points and the different interpolation of Kriging and inversely proportional to distance methods. They drew the different attribute the spatial distribution of the soil available P, K and PH value, and calculated the standard deviation values of the above interpolation results. The results showed that Kriging interpolation accuracy is different for the soil available P, K and PH in the different plots of the same kind of soil properties. And in the same plot, the available P of different sampling interval of Kriging results indicated that the higher sampling density, the higher the interpolation accuracy.

In summary, the spatial variability laws of the agricultural soil information have their own characteristics. And the qualitative and quantitative relationship between crop production and soil properties on the spatial distribution was reported rarely. So the spatial heterogeneity of the soil information under certain conditions still needs further study. The artificial neural network (ANN) is a self-adaptive method of mapping, and do not make any assumptions in data processing. ANN is reasonable in theory, and be able to avoid the unknown factors, to reduce the model error. So ANN's results are high accuracy. The spatial interpolation accuracy based ANN are higher and more stable than the usual variety of data interpolation methods, and the fewer number of sample points are required, the results can be directly obtained, the loss of accuracy are reduced in the middle link. Therefore, the rational design of NN can be efficient to solve the fertilization test zone on the condition of the less known points.

## 2.3    Management Information Platform on GIS

GIS are computer software platforms used for input, storage, retrieval, analysis, processing and presentation of geospatial data. And it associated with each other coordinates on the same location values based the geo-spatial database of the geographic characteristics. GIS is the brain of precision agriculture. And GIS firstly deposited the advance decision-making system, such as expert systems, and the data processing module, then received the collected information from the real-time sensor on variable rate fertilizer and the monitoring systems (GPS, RS, etc.), thirdly showed and mapped electronic pictures on unified coordinate system for these data through organization, processing, statistical analysis, finally made intelligent decisions through the expert system and achieve adjust the amount of inputs or operations used automatic controller-executer equipment [13]. Domain is the computer jargon of the functional domain covered with group systems on the similar needs or software applications. Domain engineering is the procedure that certain a system of domain application was analyzed, the common and variability of demands was refined, the domain models were made, and the architectures were designed, then the reusable components of domain were developed and organized. Domain engineering includes several parts of domain analysis, design, implementation and spread out. Domain engineering provides a strong support to software reuse, which helps to produce components with high reusability, and its product is the domain analysis model and domain-specific software architecture [22, 23]. In this part, authors make a guide use the knowledge and theory of the domain engineering, software components, design patterns and others, and utilize the ESRI's ArcGIS Engine as the platform for the needs of GIS application functional modules were met in of GIS application development component, and the developers only focused on the specific business development of the module, to avoid duplication of functions of development on based GIS applications, so as to improve the development efficiency, reduce the development costs. After the function of operational modules has been refined and standardized, they can be added to the component library used component management tools, for use the other similar GIS application system development in future [24-26].

In the practice of precision agriculture, GIS is mainly used for the establishment of agricultural land management, the development trend of soil data, natural conditions, production conditions, the seedlings crop growth and insect pest, and the geographic statistical processing, graphics conversion and expression of crop yields and other spatial information, in order to offer prescription scheme of the analysis of spatial differences and implementation of control [27, 28]. The multi-layer maps of farmland yield and spatial information were firstly generated on GIS. Then the decision-makers analyzed the causes, make a diagnosis, and provide scientific prescription based on yield-spatial differences with crop production management decision support systems and expert intelligent management systems. Thirdly the field crop management prescription maps were produced on GIS, and zoning regulation implemented to guide the scientific operations. When the agricultural geography spatial information map were produced, how to define the sampling density, sampling costs and data-processing methods, satisfied to more accurately reflect the spatial distribution of parameters, is still next-step study [2].

## 3    Design of PFMIS Based on CORS and GIS

As known, two and above GPS receivers are used on DGPS to collect the spatial information on fields. However, with the regional CORS (Continuously Operational Reference System) widely development in the domestic, only one GPS receiver can be finished the spatial data of large-scale, all-weather, high-precision, kinematic real-time observation on CORS, which make up for the shortages of RS, such as low-precision of spatial information, time-delay of collection. The accuracy, reliability and real-time characters of spatial data were improved on CORS technology.

3-dimensional spatial coordinate information on GPS and soil resources attribute information on soil nutrient testing device were obtained to found the fields database, and the thematic maps of crop growth environment and yield spatial distribution were generated in real time or near real-time, in order to update the achievement on current trend. Then these maps overlay with other soil elements maps based spatial-consistency to analysis. Finally the corresponding mathematical models were founded to provide the basis of the soil fine fertilization.

Based GIS platform, the spatial data grid maps of soil resource were re-developed on ArcGIS Engine, including of some management information functions, such as analysis, queries, additions and deletions, updates, and contrast of the collected soil resource data. Then the basis on decision making was provided to variable-rate fertilization with the expert systems. WebGIS system were built with ArcGIS Server to complete the web publishing or query information of precision fertilization, and the efficient fertilization programs and crop fertilizer criteria were recommended for users in order to achieve the modern agricultural production patterns and the technology system of the higher yield, quality and level, and arrive to high efficiency, saving-energy, high production, environmental protection.

## 3.1    Technique of PFMIS on CORS and GIS

According to the Shandong Province's actual situation of agriculture, soil and climate, the research of application of technology of data collection, data processing and management information system queries were carried out on the soil resource information of PFMIS. And PFMIS were designed aimed to reducing the investment on crop early growth, low waste in the growth-medium, increasing the profits the later, and reducing the environmental pollution in the long term. When PFMIS were established based on GPS and GIS technology. The farmland spatial information were collected using GPS, and the accuracy, reliability and real-time of the spatial data were improved with CORS technology. The keys on data standardization technology were researched, and the spatial grid distribution maps of soil nutrients and crop yield were produced by GIS re-development on soil topics, some functions of web publishing and query were realized to provide the basis on decision making, above as shown in Fig. 1, including:

(1) To argue the scheme design of CORS of the geographic information acquisition subsystem of PFMIS;

(2) To model on the from-point-to-surface data processing of soil resources information and contour of soil resources property information, such as geostatistical Kriging, surface fitting, ANN and each other algorithms comparison;

(3) To realize the standardization of data processing methods on the soil resource information, including the undulating terrain classification, sampling interval grading, sample units install, etc., and achieve the layover and analysis on multi-character-layers of a variety of space-based information.

(4) To determine the communication and query tool on the Web-platform of PFMIS, to interactive services, including synchronous communication: IRC, ICQ, MSN, Skype; and asynchronous communication: E-mail, Mailing list and so on.

## 3.2    Design of PFMIS on CORS and GIS

Research procedures and data-process flow shown in Fig. 2, including:

(1) Design the collection subsystem of PFMIS on CORS technology. As a large areas of farmland, a long time measurement, mobile frequently, basically covered by CORS of Shandong Province, to prove the scheme of network distribution and the feasibility of cm-level accuracy. A GPS receiver was used to observe and receive real-time differential signal, and cm-level positioning was obtained by data processing. The

agricultural nutrient tester, temperature-hygrometer and others were used to collect the soil resources information samplings. To ensure the accuracy of those, the sorts data were input GIS platform to manage, the kinematic real-time acquisition subsystem of the spatial and soil attribute information of PFMIS was completed. And this subsystem provided these real-time or near real-time various soil-attribute layer to analysis on the follow-up GIS applications.

(2) Re-development of the scheme GIS based on ArcGIS Engine. To research the key technologies of data standardization, mainly attribute data standardization and a variety of data analysis and processing, including geostatistics, neural networks, genetic algorithms, to generate DEM, soil resources, nutrients (N, P, K, Ca, etc.), temperature, humidity and yield, etc. Attribute distribution maps, then various types of thematic maps were produced by the spatial analysis and mapping capabilities of GIS, through spatial overlay analysis of land resources. Next-step the variable fertilizer distribution maps were generated together with expert knowledge. It is keys to develop GIS analysis component library on this stage of system design.

(3) To renew collecting data and update the variable fertilizer maps with the growth of crops in different time periods. The network applications of PFMIS were achieved by Web GIS, including the dissemination of information, interactive inquiry service, and so on.

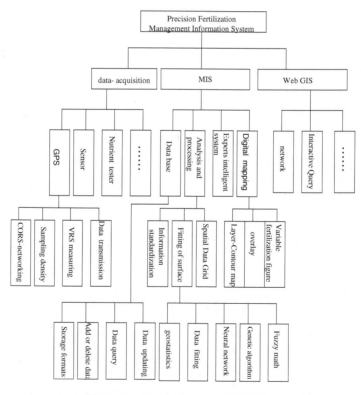

**Fig. 1.** The Design Structure of PFMIS

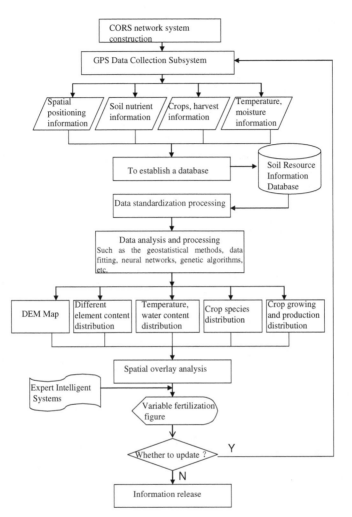

**Fig. 2.** The processing flow of PFMIS

## 4    Conclusions

Precision agriculture is an inevitable trend on the agriculture development from the coarse type to the fine. The research on the high-precise spatial data real-time collection, data processing and management information system technology is presently one of focuses on precision agriculture. On the topics the key technologies include: firstly the achievements of real-time data collection and processing were obtained used CORS technology, and whose accuracy levels would be better than 10cm; secondly the models of data processing and analysis of soil attribute and crop yield on spatial data were founded based on multi-intelligence computing algorithms; thirdly the re-developments of the soil-thematic GIS on ArcGIS Engine were run. While, how to define the sampling density, sampling costs and data-processing methods, to more accurately reflect the spatial distribution of parameters, is worth of deeply study.

**Acknowledgments.** This work is supported by National natural science foundation of China (No. 40704001, 40876051).

# References

1. Edan, Y., Han, S., Kondo, N.: Automation in Agriculture. Springer Handbook of Automation, Part G, pp. 1095–1128 (2009)
2. Wang, M.: Development of precise agriculture and innovation of engineering technology. Transaction of Agriculture Engineering 15(1), 1–8 (1999) (in Chinese)
3. Wang, M.: Thinking Through the Experiment, Demonstration and Development Research on Precision Agriculture. Review of China Agricultural Science and Technology 5(1), 7–12 (2003) (in Chinese)
4. http://china.toocle.com
5. Chen, Z., Wei, L., Lin, Q.: Design and implementation of precision rubber fertilization information system based on Web GIS. Chinese Agricultural Science Bulletin 24(7), 473–477 (2008) (in Chinese)
6. Chen, W., Hua, Y., Zhang, S.: Tobacco Precision Fertilization Formula Information System Based on GIS. Journal of Geomatics Science and Technology 25(6), 455–458 (2008) (in Chinese)
7. Sun, Z., Zhang, X., Jiang, W., et al.: Design and realization of vegetable precise fertilization expert system. Agriculture Network Information (8), 15–17 (2005) (in Chinese)
8. Wang, Q., Ma, Y., Hu, H., et al.: The Research on the Method of Precision Fertilization Based on GIS and GPS in China. Chinese Agricultural Science Bulletin (7) (2006) (in Chinese)
9. Xu, Y., Ni, M., Liu, G., et al.: The Pre-Investigation of Precision Fertilization and Expert Consultation System. Tibet Journal of Agricultural Sciences (3), 31–36 (2009) (in Chinese)
10. Blackmore, B.S.: Precision Agriculture: an introduction. Outlook Agric. 23(4) (1994)
11. Lu, J., Guo, J.: Application of GPS in Precision Agriculture. Geotichnical Investigation and Surveying (1), 50–51 (2002) (in Chinese)
12. Zhang, S.: The Study of the Collection and Process of Field Information of Precision Agriculture Based on the GPS and GIS. University of Zhejiang PhD (2003) (in Chinese)
13. Wang, C., Niu, Z., Tang, H.: The earth observation technology and precision agriculture. Science Press, Beijing (2001) (in Chinese)
14. Zhou, Z., Yi, J., Zhou, Q.: Theory and application of GPS satellite surveying (Revision). Surveying and Mapping Press, Beijing (1997) (in Chinese)
15. Hofmann-Wellenhof, B., Lichtenegger, H., Collins, J.: GPS Theory and practice, 5th revised edn. Springer, Wien (2001)
16. Xu, G.: GPS Theory, Algorithms and Applications. Springer, Berlin (2003)
17. Dang, Y., Bei, J., Cheng, Y.: Principles and applications of global navigation satellite system. Surveying and Mapping Press, Beijing (2007) (in Chinese)
18. Huang, D., Xiong, Y., Yuan, L.: Theory and Practice of Global Positioning System. Southwest Jiaotong University Press, Chendu (2006) (in Chinese)

19. Tang, W., Sun, H., Liu, J.: Ambiguity resolution of single epoch single frequency data with baseline length constraint using LAMBDA algorithm. Geomatics and information science of Wuhan University 30(5), 444–446 (2005) (in Chinese)

20. Lei, N., Wang, X., Jiang, J., et al.: Comparison of Kriging interpolation precisions in different topographical units and number of samples:a case study of spatial distribution of soil total nitrogen in the Shucheng County. Hydrogeology & Engineering Geology (5), 86–91 (2008) (in Chinese)

21. Mueller, T.G., Wells, K.L., Thomas, G.W., et al.: Soil fertility map quality: case studies in Kentucky. In: Proceedings of Fifth International Conference on Proceedings Agriculture (CD), USA (2000)

22. Ren, J., Lv, G., Wang, Q.: Research on the Integration of Geography Information System and Model in Multiple Tier System. Acta Geodaetica Et Cartographic Sinica 32(2), 178–182 (2003) (in Chinese)

23. Wang, J., Bao, S., Yu, Y., et al.: Realization of geological section map model based GIS template. Science of Surveying and Mapping 33(5), 184–186 (2008) (in Chinese)

24. Liu, Z., Meng, Y., Yin, A.: Design and Realization of ArcGIS Engine Component. Geospatial Information (1), 43–47 (2008) (in Chinese)

25. Xiong, W., Liu, Z., Wang, S.: Design and Realization of the Cartography Template Management System. Geospatial Information (2), 90–92 (2010) (in Chinese)

26. Zhang, Z., Yang, J.: Transport planning information system based on Arc GIS. Science of Surveying and Mapping 30(1), 86–89 (2005) (in Chinese)

27. Runquist, S., Zhang, N., Taylor, R.: Development a field-level geographic information system. Computers and Electronics in Agriculture 31, 201–209 (2001)

28. Zhang, N., Taylor, R.: Applications of a field-level geographic information system(FIS) in precession agriculture. In: Proceedings of Fifth International Conference on Precision Agriculture (CD), USA (2000)

# Models of Dry Matter Production and Yield Formation for the Protected Tomato[*]

Yuli Chen[1,2], Zhiyou Zhang[1,2], Yan Liu[2],
Yan Zhu[1,**], and Hongxin Cao[2,**]

[1] College of Agronomy, Nanjing Agricultural University, Nanjing 210095,
Jiangsu province, P.R. China
{2009101038,2008101050,yanzhu}@njau.edu.cn
[2] Institute of Agricultural Economy and Information/Engineering Research
Center for Digital Agriculture, Jiangsu Academy of Agricultural Sciences,
Nanjing 210014, Jiangsu province, P.R. China
liuyan0203@yahoo.com.cn, caohongxin@hotmail.com

**Abstract.** 【Objective】 In order to quantify the yield formation of protected tomato, 【Method】 the field experiments on varieties and fertilizer were conducted in 2009 and 2010, and cultivars: (B1) American mole 1 (early maturing), (B2) Chaoshijifanqiedawang (late maturing), and (B3) American 903 (medium maturing) were adopted; The models of dry matter production and yield formation for protected tomato were built by analyzing the relationships between yield and the number of fruit letting and the mean fruit weight, between yield and biomass and the economic coefficient at harvest, and between the mean fruit weight and economic coefficient and biomass of different varieties and fertilizer levels in accordance with the theory of yield formation. Independent experiments data was used to validate the models. 【Result】 The results showed that root mean squared error (RMSE), mean absolute error ($X_{de}$), and the determined coefficient ($R^2$) between the simulated and measured values of dry matter production was 363.135kg/ha (n=63), 79.016kg/ha, and 0.900, respectively, and RMSE, $X_{de}$, and $R^2$ between the simulated and measured values of yield based on yield components was 186.842g per plant (n=36), -1.069g per plant, and 0.854, respectively, and RMSE, $X_{de}$, and $R^2$ between the simulated and measured values of yield based on economic coefficient was 137.302g per plant (n=27), 21.170g per plant, and 0.785, respectively. 【Conclusion】 It indicated that the dry matter production and yield formation under different varieties and fertilizer levels for protected tomato could be well simulated by these models.

**Keywords:** protected tomato, dry matter production, yield formation, biomass, economic coefficient, models.

[*]  **Foundation Information:** Sub-topic for Science & Technology Pillar Program of Jiangsu Province of China (BE2008397-1); Agricultural Science & Technology Independent Innovation Foundation of Jiangsu Province of China (CX(10)221).

[**] Corresponding author.

D. Li and Y. Chen (Eds.): CCTA 2011, Part I, IFIP AICT 368, pp. 278–292, 2012.
© IFIP International Federation for Information Processing 2012

# 1    Introduction

Crop growth models are one of the powerful tools to support the optimum regulation for production environment and cultivation management of the protected crops, and tomato is one of the main protected crops [1]. So, it has an important role in the digital regulation management of protected tomato production to build yield formation models. Nowadays, there have been many reports on the yield formation models of field crops, however, the research of protected crops is not more [2-4], and the most reports about tomato yield were research on the relationships between yield formation and environmental factors in cultivation physiology and cultivation practice. For example, Song et al. [5] researched the tomato yield formation rules and its correlation to the environmental factors in modern greenhouse, Liu et al. [6] studied effects of soil moisture stress on greenhouse tomato yield and its formation under drip irrigation, Chen [7] built the simulation models of relationship between individual plant yield and physiological development time. However, the models were with more empirical, less mechanistic. Ni et al. [8] established the models of greenhouse tomato dry matter partition and yield prediction based on relationships between partitioning coefficient and harvest index and product of radiation by quantity of heat, and tested by various varieties, substratum, and sites, which had high precision and less parameters. Yang [9] studied the influence of growth environments on tomato fruits yield using the functional structural plant models, GreenLab, based on source-sink relationship with greenhouse environment factors such as temperature, humidity, light intensity, and so on. These models were more suitable for protected greenhouse, but less suitable for the environments of plastic shed. The objective of this research was to simulate protected tomato yield formation under various varieties and fertilization levels based on yield components factors and economic index, build protected tomato dry matter production and yield formation simulation models in accordance with the principle of yield formation, and provide a theoretical basis for growth and yield prediction as well as cultivation management and environment regulation of protected tomato.

# 2    Materials and Methods

## 2.1    Materials

This study used 3 tomato cultivars representing wide variation in maturing characteristics, and they are: (B1) American mole 1 (early maturing, determinate growth type, good disease resistance, growth period 100 ∼ 110days), (B2) Chaoshijifanqiedawang (late maturing, sub-determinate growth type, super large fruit type, growth period 109∼119days), and (B3) American 903 (medium maturing, determinate growth type, strong growth, growth period 106∼116days).

## 2.2    Methods

The experiments were conducted in plastic shed with 80m long, 9.8m width, and horse liver soil (the total nitrogen, 0.239 g/Kg; total phosphorus, 1.297 g/Kg; available phosphorus, 202 mg/Kg; and pH, 6.344 in pre-planting in soils) at Suoshi village in Nanjing from July to October of 2009 and from March to June of 2010. The experiments was a split plot design with three whole-plot treatments arranged in a randomized complete block design with three blocks and three sub-plot treatments. The whole-plot factors were the fertilizer levels: A1 (CK: 1/2 $F_N$), A2 (Normal: $F_N$), and A3 (High fertilizer: 3/2 $F_N$), and the sub-plot factors were varieties (B1, B2, and B3), with 3 replications and 27 plots (2.96×4.6m$^2$). $F_N$ was the normal fertilizer level: compound fertilizer (N:P:K=16%:16%:17%) 750 kg·ha$^{-1}$, in that 40 percent of this fertilizers was basal, 60 percent was top dressing applied in early fruit stage and maximum fruit number stage. The planting density was 3-4 plants/m$^2$, and the other cultivation practices were the same as the conventional high yield field.

### 2.2.1    Data Acquisition

After planting, the representative samples were taken every 7d from seedling to flowering and every 14d during fruit period. Three representative plants selected in each treatment were separated into organs after determining fruits number, dried in 30 min. at 105°C, then at 80°C until reaching a constant weight, measured using a 0.001 g electro-level, and leaf area was determined by method of dry weight.

HOBO-H8 was placed in three different positions in the plastic shed to collect environment elements automatically every 10 s, including air temperature, relative humidity and dew point, the absolute humidity, and light intensity, etc. In that average values every 15 minutes were recorded.

At the main growth period of tomato, ECA-PB0402 was used in measuring photosynthetic rate (including $CO_2$ concentrations, relative humidity (RH), canopy temperature (TC), leaf temperature (TL), net photosynthetic rate (Pn), and photosynthetically available radiation (PAR), etc.) of the top three leaves on plants tagged in each treatment around midday. According to the data, light response curve was made, and the max photosynthetic rate value (Pmax) was confirmed.

### 2.2.2    Data Treatments

In this study, Excel.2007and SigmaPlot V 10.0 were used to analysis experimental data. The experiment data in 2009 were applied to model establishment and parameter determination, and the experiment data in 2010 were applied to model verification.

### 2.2.3    Model Verification

Simulation values were calculated using Visual C++6.0, and model precision was verified using root mean squared error (RMSE), mean absolute error ($X_{de}$), the determined coefficient ($R^2$), and 1:1 plotting between measured values and simulated values. If $X_{de}$ and RMSE were smaller and $R^2$ was larger, the simulated values were better agree with measured values, i.e. the deviation between simulated values and measured values was smaller, and simulation results of model were more accurate and reliable. The calculation formula of RMSE and $X_{de}$ can be expressed as follows:

$$RMSE = \sqrt{\frac{\sum_{i=1}^{n}(OBS_i - SIM_i)^2}{n}}$$

$$de = |OBS_i - SIM_i|$$

$$X_{de} = \frac{\sum de}{n}$$

where $OBS_i$ is measured values, $SIM_i$ is simulated values, de is absolute error, and n is sample numbers.

# 3    Results

## 3.1    Model Description

### 3.1.1    Dry Matter Production Simulation of Protected Tomato

#### 3.1.1.1    The Calculation of Leaf Photosynthetic Rate
The leaf photosynthetic rate was expressed by negative exponential model [10-13]:

$$Pg = P_{max} \times \left[1 - e^{\left(\frac{-\varepsilon \times PAR}{P_{max}}\right)}\right] \qquad (1)$$

where Pg is leaf photosynthetic rate in kg $CO_2 \cdot ha^{-1} \cdot h^{-1}$, Pmax is single leaf maximum photosynthetic rate in kg $CO_2 \cdot ha^{-1} \cdot h^{-1}$, with the ranges from 20 to 50 kg $CO_2 \cdot ha^{-1} \cdot h^{-1}$ at the weak light and usual carbon dioxide concentration in greenhouse, and it was 37 kg $CO_2 \cdot ha^{-1} \cdot h^{-1}$ in accordance with the observation data. $\xi$ is the initial slope of photosynthesis-light responsive curve, called initial light utilized efficiency in kg $CO_2 \cdot ha^{-1} \cdot h^{-1}/J \cdot m^{-2} \cdot s^{-1}$, in other words, at the early stage of leaf received light, the quantity of carbon dioxide fixed by unit area leaf in ha when it absorbed $1 J \cdot m^{-2} \cdot s^{-1}$ PAR at unit time in h, and it was always regarded as a constant under the weak light of greenhouse [10, 14, 15]. $\xi$ equals to 0.40 kg $CO_2 \cdot ha^{-1} \cdot h^{-1}/J \cdot m^{-2} \cdot s^{-1}$ [16], and PAR is photosynthetically active radiation in this paper in $J \cdot m^{-2} \cdot s^{-1}$.

#### 3.1.1.2    The Calculation of Canopy Photosynthesis
Canopy photosynthesis is the total photosynthesis of all plant leaves on unit area. According to the research of Goudriaan [13, 17], Gauss Integral was applied to compute the canopy photosynthesis rate in this paper, and it can be calculated as follows:

$$LGUSS_i = DIS_i \times LAI \ (i = 1,2,3) \qquad (2)$$

$$L_i = PAR \times k \times e^{(-k \times LGUSS_i)} \qquad (3)$$

$$Pg_i = P_{max} \times \left[1 - e^{\left(\frac{-\varepsilon \times L_i}{P_{max}}\right)}\right] \qquad \qquad 4)$$

$$Pg_t = \sum(Pg_i \times WT_i) \times LAI \qquad \qquad (5)$$

$$DTGA = Pg_t \times DL \qquad \qquad (6)$$

where $LGUSS_i$ is canopy depth of gauss layer, $DIS_i$ is distance coefficient of gauss integral (table 1), LAI is leaf area index, i is layer number of canopy layers, $L_i$ is the quantity of PAR of arriving the $i^{th}$ layer, k is the extinction coefficient of canopy (it equals to 0.8[16] in this paper), $Pg_i$ is the instantaneous photosynthesis rate of the $i^{th}$ layer in kg $CO_2 \cdot ha^{-1} \cdot h^{-1}$, $Pg_t$ is the instantaneous photosynthesis rate of all canopy at the time of t in kg $CO_2 \cdot ha^{-1} \cdot h^{-1}$, $WT_i$ is weight of gauss integral (table 1), DTGA is the total photosynthetic amount of one day in $kgCO_2 \cdot ha^{-1} \cdot d^{-1}$, and DL is day length in h.

**Table 1.** The Gaussian weight and distances for the method of 3 points [16]

| i | 1 | 2 | 3 |
|---|---|---|---|
| $DIS_i$ | 0.1127 | 0.5000 | 0.8873 |
| $WT_i$ | 0.2778 | 0.4444 | 0.2778 |

### 3.1.1.3    The Simulation of Protected Tomato Leaf Area Index (LAI)

The protected tomato LAI continuously increased with the adding of biomass in accordance with the data in 2009, and it's changes like as power function (Fig.1).

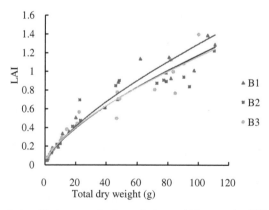

**Fig. 1.** The relationship between leaf area index and biomass for different varieties

The figure 1 showed: LAI of B1, B2 and B3 continuously increased as a power function with the raising of per plant biomass, and during growth and development of B2 (late maturing) and B3 (medium maturing), the changes in LAI were almost the same, B2 was appreciably higher than B3, and the two obviously lower than B1(early maturing). With the further raising of biomass, LAI of three protected tomato varieties also tended to stable.

According to the relationship between LAI and per plant biomass of protected tomato, the changes in LAI with the per plant biomass of different protected tomato varieties can be expressed as follow:

$$LAI = a_1 \times DW^{b_1} \tag{7}$$

where $a_1$ and $b_1$ are parameters, and DW is total dry matter weight of per plant. All parameters and its statistical test are showed in table 2.

**Table 2.** Analysis of variance for LAI models and its coefficient test

| Varieties | Correlation coefficient | F | a1 | b1 |
|---|---|---|---|---|
| B1 | 0.984** | 439.226** | 0.067** | 0.630** |
| B2 | 0.971** | 262.439** | 0.083** | 0.554** |
| B3 | 0.971** | 234.101** | 0.058** | 0.650** |

Note: *P<0.05 and **P<0.01, the follows were as the same.

### 3.1.1.4    The Calculation of Respiration

Respiration includes maintenance respiration and growth respiration generally. The former is the energy needed by living organism maintaining its normal biochemical and physiological process, and it can be computed by formula (8) in accordance with the research of Spitters et al. [17]. The later is the energy needed by organic matter synthesis, plant growth as well as metabolism consumption in plant, in other words, it is partial photosynthesis consumed in the process of carbon dioxide translating into $CH_2O$, and it is considered at the formula (9) for calculating dry matter increment.

$$Rm = Rm(T_{25}) \times W \times 2^{\frac{T-25}{10}} \tag{8}$$

where Rm is consumption of plants maintenance respiration in kg $CH_2O \cdot ha^{-1} \cdot d^{-1}$, Rm $(T_{25})$ is the maintenance respiration coefficient at 25°C (it equals to 0.015 kg $CH_2O \cdot kg^{-1} DM \cdot d^{-1}$ [17] in this paper), W is the total dry matter weight in kg $DM \cdot ha^{-1}$, and T is daily average temperature in °C.

### 3.1.1.5    The Calculation of Dry Matter Production

Dry matter increment can be expressed as follow:

$$\Delta W = \frac{30/44 \times DTGA - R_m}{ASRQ} \times F(N) \tag{9}$$

where $\Delta W$ is dry matter increment in kg $DM \cdot ha^{-1} \cdot d^{-1}$, ASRQ is the conversion coefficient which is from $CH_2O$ to dry matter (it equals to 1.43 kg $CH_2O \cdot kg^{-1} DM$ [17]

in this paper), 30/44 is the molecular weight conversion coefficient which is from $CO_2$ to $CH_2O$, DTGA is daily total photosynthate in kg $CO_2 \cdot ha^{-1} \cdot d^{-1}$, F(N) is nitrogen influencing factor, and it can be computed as follows [18-19]:

$$F(N) = (SN + CKN + RFN \times CURN)/TNP \tag{10}$$

$$SN = Nc \times \gamma \times H \times \left(\frac{1-\delta_{2mm}}{100}\right) \times 10^{-1} \tag{11}$$

$$CURN = (NBY - NCK)/RFN \tag{12}$$

where SN and Nc are the 0-30cm topsoil total nitrogen storage in $g \cdot m^{-2}$ and content in $g \cdot kg^{-1}$, respectively; CKN is the nitrogen rate of CK in $kg \cdot ha^{-1}$ (it equals to 60 $kg \cdot hm^{-2}$ in this paper), RFN is nitrogen rate in $kg \cdot ha^{-1}$ (it includes high nitrogen level and normal nitrogen level), the compound fertilizer amount of high fertilizer, CK, and the normal levels is 1125 $kg \cdot ha^{-1}$, 375 $kg \cdot ha^{-1}$, and 750 $kg \cdot ha^{-1}$, respectively (nitrogen rate is 180 $kg \cdot ha^{-1}$, 60 $kg \cdot ha^{-1}$, and 120 $kg \cdot ha^{-1}$, respectively), TNP is nitrogen requirement of high yield level (it equals to 189.321 $kg \cdot ha^{-1}$ in this paper). $\gamma$ is the bulk density (1.3 $g \cdot cm^{-3}$), H is the thickness (30 cm), and $\delta_{2mm}$ is the <2mm fraction (%) of soil. CURN is nitrogen use efficiency (%). NBY and NCK is the nitrogen absorbed by tomato plant at the RFN and CK levels in $kg \cdot ha^{-1}$, respectively.

The total biomass on any day can be computed by initial dry matter and daily dry matter increment, $\Delta W$, and the formula was follow:

$$Biomass_{i+1} = Biomass_i + \Delta W \tag{13}$$

where $Biomass_{i+1}$ is the total dry matter of the $(i+1)^{th}$ day in kg $DM \cdot ha^{-1}$, $Biomass_i$ is the total dry matter of the $i^{th}$ day in kg $DM \cdot ha^{-1}$.

### 3.1.2   Yield Formation Models for Protected Tomato

#### 3.1.2.1   *The Model of Yield Formation for Protected Tomato Based on the Method of Yield Component*

The yield formation of protected tomato can be determined by per plant fruit number and mean fruit weight. Therefore, the model of yield formation for protected tomato can be expressed as follow:

$$Y = FN \times MFW \tag{14}$$

where Y is per plant yield, FN is per plant fruit number, and MFW is mean fruit weight.

(1)  The model of per plant fruit number for protected tomato
Individual plant fruit number (FN) is the result of balance between per plant potential fruit number (PFN) and per plant fruit abscission number (DFN). Therefore, it can be computed as follow:

$$FN = PFN - DFN \tag{15}$$

where PFN can be estimated by per plant flower number (FLN) and the ratio of FN to total flower number per plant (PFLN), and the formula is as follow:

$$PFN = FLN \times P6FLN \qquad (16)$$

where FLN can be estimated by per plant bud number (BN) and the ratio of PFLN to total bud number per plant (PBN), PFLN can be computed by FN and per plant maximum flower number (FLNMAX), and FLNMAX is a variety parameter. Therefore, FLN and PFLN can be computed respectively as follows:

$$FLN = BN \times PBN \qquad (17)$$

$$PFLN = FN/FLNMAX \qquad (18)$$

where BN can be decided by varieties and environment factors, and PBN can be computed as follow:

$$PBN = FLN/BNMAX \qquad (19)$$

where BNMAX is per plant maximum buds number, can be regarded as a variety parameter.

It has been analyzed in the other paper because of its complexity.

(2)  The model of mean fruit weight for protected tomato

The protected tomato mean fruit weight continuously increased with the raising of biomass in accordance with the data in 2009, and it's increasing was the same as a power function (Fig.2).

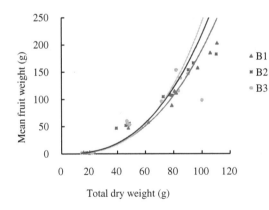

**Fig. 2.** The relationship between mean fruit weight and biomass for different varieties

The figure 2 showed: when per plant biomass of B1, B2, and B3 all achieved about 14g, it started to set fruit, and changes in mean fruit weight of three varieties with per plant biomass were basically similar, and the same as a power function. However, the growth rate and extreme value were different obviously, all in all, medium maturing B3>late maturing B2>early maturing B1, the maximum mean fruit weight of B1 and B2 were similar (about 200g), and all higher than B3 (about 160g).

According to the relationship between mean fruit weight and per plant biomass of protected tomato, the changes in mean fruit weight with the per plant biomass of different protected tomato varieties can be expressed as follow:

$$MFW = a_2 \times DW^{b_2} \tag{20}$$

where DW is dry weight in per plant, it is computed section 3.1.2.2, $a_2$ and $b_2$ are all parameters. All parameters and its statisticoal test are showed in table 3.

**Table 3.** Analysis of variance for the mean fruit weight models and its coefficient test

| Varieties | Correlation coefficient | F | $a_2$ | $b_2$ |
|-----------|------------------------|---|-------|-------|
| B1 | $0.952^{**}$ | $378.588^{**}$ | $1.321 \times 10^{-3*}$ | $2.579^{**}$ |
| B2 | $0.908^{**}$ | $779.857^{**}$ | $3.785 \times 10^{-4*}$ | $2.903^{**}$ |
| B3 | $0.923^{**}$ | $53.586^{**}$ | $1.102 \times 10^{-3*}$ | $2.649^{**}$ |

### 3.1.2.2  The Model of Yield Formation for Protected Tomato Based on Economic Coefficient Method

Economic coefficient was a vital standard to measure crop yield, and tomato yield simulation model based on economic coefficient method was expressed as follow:

$$Y = DW \times EC \tag{21}$$

where Y is yield per plant, DW is biomass per plant and EC represents economic coefficient per plant at harvest.

(1)  The per plant biomass model for protected tomato
The formation of biomass per plant was the joint action of photosynthesis and respiration of protected tomato. And its model could be expressed as follow:

$$DB_{i+1} = DB_i + \Delta DW \tag{22}$$

where $DB_{i+1}$ and $DB_i$ were total dry weight per plant in the $(i+1)^{th}$ day and the $i^{th}$ day, respectively, $\Delta DW$ is increment of dry weight per plant. In that the harvest date of protected tomato in 2010 field trials was from 2 to 6 July.

(2)  The calculation of per plant economic coefficient for protected tomato
Economic coefficient per plant is an important index for crop production. It can be calculated as follow:

$$EC = Y/DW \tag{23}$$

where EC is economic coefficient per plant, Y is mean yield per plant and DW is biomass per plant at harvest. Economic coefficient per plant of treatments showed in table 4. According to table 4, B3 had a higher economic coefficient per plant than B1 and B2 under different fertilizer levels. As the raising of fertilizer rate, the highest economic coefficients of B1 and B2 can be gained at medium fertilizer levels, while B3 was at high fertilizer level.

**Table 4.** The economic coefficient of different treatments in 2009

| Treatments | A1B1 | A1B2 | A1B3 | A2B1 | A2B2 | A2B3 | A3B1 | A3B2 | A3B3 |
|---|---|---|---|---|---|---|---|---|---|
| Economic coefficient | 12.840 | 11.576 | 18.424 | 15.710 | 12.366 | 16.879 | 12.992 | 10.780 | 19.671 |

## 3.2   Model Verification

### 3.2.1   The Model Verification of Population Dry Matter Production for Protected Tomato

#### 3.2.1.1   *The Model Verification of Population Dry Matter Production for Protected Tomato*

The population dry matter production model was verified by independent data in 2010 (Fig.3). The figure 3 showed: RMSE, $X_{de}$, and $R^2$ of between the measured and simulated values for protected tomato population dry matter were 363.135kg/ha (n=63), 79.016kg/ha, and 0.900, respectively. The correlation coefficients (r) was 0.949 ($r_{0.01\,(61)}$ =0.322) with 0.01 significant level. Therefore, the measured values agree well with the simulated values.

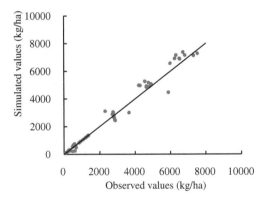

**Fig. 3.** The 1:1 plotting comparison between observed and simulated total dry weight for protected tomato population

#### 3.2.1.2   *The Model Verification of LAI for Protected Tomato*

The leaf area index model was verified by independent data in 2010 (Fig.4). The figure 4 showed: RMSE, $X_{de}$, and $R^2$ of between the measured and simulated values for LAI of different protected tomato B1, B2, and B3 were 0.144 (n=24), 0.051, and 0.868; 0.109 (n=24), 0.048, and 0.912; 0.137 (n=24), 0.051, and 0.894, respectively. The correlation coefficients (r) were 0.932 ($r_{0.01\,(22)}$ =0.517), 0.955 ($r_{0.01\,(22)}$ =0.517), and 0.946 ($r_{0.01\,(22)}$ =0.517) with 0.01 significant level, respectively. Therefore, the measured values agree well with the simulated values.

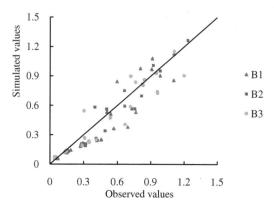

**Fig. 4.** The 1:1 plotting comparison between observed and simulated LAI values

## 3.2.2 The Model Verification of Yield Formation for Protected Tomato

*3.2.2.1   The Model Verification of Yield Formation for Protected Tomato Based on the
Method of Yield Component*

(1) The model verification of yield formation for protected tomato based on the method
of yield formation

The yield formation model was verified by independent data in 2010 (Fig.5). The
figure 5 showed: RMSE, $X_{de}$, and $R^2$ of between the measured and simulated values for
protected tomato yield formation were 186.842g per plant (n=36), 1.069g per plant, and
0.854, respectively. The correlation coefficients (r) was 0.924 ($r_{0.01\ (34)}$ =0.424) with
0.01 significant level. Therefore, it had better consistency between the measured and
the simulated values.

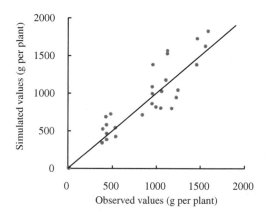

**Fig. 5.** The 1:1 plotting comparison between observed and simulated Y values

(2) The model verification of mean fruit weight for protected tomato

The mean fruit weight model was verified by independent data in 2010 (Fig.6). The figure 6 showed: RMSE, $X_{de}$, and $R^2$ of between the measured and simulated values for mean fruit weight of different protected tomato B1, B2, and B3 were 10.308g (n=12), 3.806g, and 0.768; 9.434g (n=12), 0.625g, and 0.932; 8.402g (n=12), 0.524, and 0.819, respectively. The correlation coefficients (r) were 0.877 ($r_{0.01\ (10)}$ =0.517), 0.965 ($r_{0.01\ (10)}$ =0.517), and 0.905 ($r_{0.01\ (10)}$ =0.517) with 0.01 significant level, respectively. Therefore, it had better consistency between the measured and the simulated values.

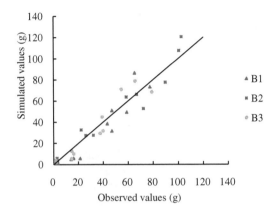

**Fig. 6.** The 1:1 plotting comparison between observed and simulated MFW values

### 3.2.2.2   The Model Verification of Yield Formation for Protected Tomato Based on the Method of Economic Coefficient

The yield formation model based on the method of economic coefficient was verified by independent data in 2010 (Fig.7). The figure 7 showed: RMSE, $X_{de}$, and $R^2$ of

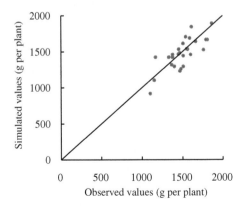

**Fig. 7.** The 1:1 plotting comparison between observed and simulated Y values

between the measured and simulated values for protected tomato yield formation were 137.302g per plant (n=27), 21.170g per plant, and 0.785, respectively. The correlation coefficients (r) was 0.924 ($r_{0.01\ (25)}$ =0.487) with 0.01 significant level. Therefore, it had better consistency between the measured and the simulated values.

# 4    Discussion

The yield of two kind of yield formation models were all theoretical yield in this paper, however, actual yield and theoretical yield had a certain difference because of the effects of environments factors such as light, temperature as well as water, and so on and the quality factors such as malformed fruit, disease fruit, pest fruit, cracked fruit as well as minimal fruit, and so on, and the actual yield was the sixty percent of theoretical yield. In addition, the actual LAI of protected tomato was smaller than simulated LAI because of the influence of planting density and artificial pruning, but the results of simulation were good. The yield formation models based on yield component factors and economic coefficient were built by analyzed the influence of varieties and fertilizer on yield formation of protected tomato. Compared with the results reported, it had a better mechanism, and simulated results. Moreover, the structure of plastic shed, genetic effect factors of tomato as well as environmental factors all affected the yield formation certainly. Lian et al. [20] researched the dynamic relationship between tomato yield formation and meteorological element in plastic shed, Fadhl [21] studied the heterosis of related traits and genetic effect of tomato yield, Han et al. [22] built the harvest date and yield prediction models of Brassica L.in planted in plastic shed covered with insect-proof screens. In addition, Diao et al. [23] simulated the yield formation of greenhouse sweet pepper using harvest index (it is a ratio of harvested fruit dry matter weight to total fruit dry matter weight). Further research should comprehensively considerate these factors, specially introduce temperature, light, soil water and so on in population dry matter production, establish the quantitative relationship between them and yield component factors, increase the feasibility and precision of models, and supply theoretical basis and technical support for cultivation management of protected tomato. In this paper, the phosphorus and potassium influencing factors were not studied because of the restricted of experiment conditions. Besides, the models established in this paper dealt with three varieties, and had a suitable environment, the results of these models was good, but the corresponding conditions would be used to verify and revise it if these models were applied to any other conditions.

# 5    Conclusions

The yield formation models based on yield component factors and economic coefficient were built respectively by analyzing the relationships among yield formation factors, varieties, and biomass as well as among yield and per plant biomass at harvest and per plant economic coefficient in accordance with rules of yield formation, and using the field experiment data of protected tomato in 2009 and 2010, and it included mean fruit weight model, per plant economic coefficient model, LAI model, dry matter production model, and so on. These models were verified using independent experiment data, the statistical analysis (RMSE, $X_{de}$ and $R^2$) and 1:1 diagram all showed: the models could simulate the yield formation of different varieties and fertilizer levels well, and the $X_{de}$ of yield formation based on economic coefficient larger than that of based on yield formation factors, while the RMSE and $R^2$ were all smaller than the later. Conclusively, the simulation results of yield formation model based on yield component factors was better than that of based on economic coefficient.

# References

1. Ni, J.H., Luo, W.H., Li, Y.X., Dai, J.F., Jin, L., Xu, B., et al.: Simulation of leaf area and dry matter production in greenhouse tomato. Scientia Agricultura Sinica 38(8), 1629–1635 (2005) (in Chinese)
2. Zhang, L.Z., Cao, W.X., Zhang, S.P.: Dynamic simulation on dry matter partitioning and yield formation in cotton. Scientia Agricultura Sinica 37(11), 1621–1627 (2004) (in Chinese)
3. Zheng, G.Q., Zhang, S.G., Duan, S.F., Gao, L.Z.: Simulation models of the photosynthetic production and yield formation in maize. System Sciences and Comprehensive Studies In Agriculture 20(3), 193–197, 201 (2004) (in Chinese)
4. Wang, X.D.: Study on the simulation model of the yield and grain quality formation of wheat. Agriculture University of Heibei, Heibei (2003) (in Chinese)
5. Song, Y.Z., Zhang, J.P., Song, H.T., He, W.G., Liu, Y.H.: Tomato production laws and its correlation to the environmental factors in modern greenhouse. Journal of Gansu Agricultural University 41(6), 38–42 (2006) (in Chinese)
6. Liu, H., Duan, A.W., Sun, J.S., Liang, Y.Y.: Effects of soil moisture regime on greenhouse tomato yield and its formation under drip irrigation. Chinese Journal of Applied Ecology 20(11), 2699–2704 (2009) (in Chinese)
7. Chen, X.J.: Research on tomato fruit development and yield formation model under facility condition, pp. 36–37. Northwest A & F University, Yangling (2010) (in Chinese)
8. Ni, J.H., Luo, W.H., Li, Y.X.: Simulation of greenhouse tomato dry matter partitioning and yield prediction. Chinese Journal of Applied Ecology 17(5), 811–816 (2006) (in Chinese)
9. Yang, L.L., Wang, Y.M., Kang, M.Z., Dong, Q.X.: Simulation of tomato fruit individual growth rule based on revised logistic model. Transactions of the Chinese Society for Agriculture Machinery 39(11), 81–84 (2008) (in Chinese)
10. Cao, W.X., Luo, W.H.: Crop system simulation and intelligent management. Higher Education press, Beijing (2003) (in Chinese)
11. Spitters, C.J.T., van Keulen, H., van Kraalingen, D.W.G.: A simple and universal crop growth simulator: SUCROS87. In: Rabbinge, R., Ward, S.W., van Laar, H.H. (eds.) Simulation and Systerms Management in Crop Protection, Simulation Monograghs 32, Pudoc, Wageningen, pp. 147–181 (1989)
12. Nederhoff, E.M., Gijzer, H., Vegter, J.: A dynamic simulation model for greenhouse cucumber (Cucumis sativus L.): validation of the submodel for crop photosynthesis. Acta Horticulturae 248, 255–263 (1989)

13. Goudriaan, J., Van Laar, H.: Modelling protential crop growth processes: textbook with excercises. Current issues in production ecology. Kuwer Academic Publishers, Dordrecht (1994)

14. Schapendonk, A.H.C.M., Brouwer, P.: Fruit growth of cucumber in relation to assimilate supply and sink activity. Scientia Horticulturae 23, 21–33 (1984)

15. Hugo, C., Ep, H.: Photosynthesis driven crop growth models for greenhouse cultivation: advances and bottle-necks. Acta Horticulturae 417, 9–22 (1996)

16. Goudriaan, J.: A simple and fast numerical method for the computation of daily totals of crop photosynthesis. Agricultural and Forest Meteorology 38, 249–254 (1986)

17. Spitters, C.J.T.: Separating the diffuse and direct component of global radiation and its implications for modeling canopy photosynthesis. Part II: Calculation of canopy photosynthesis. Agricultural and Forest Meteorology 38, 231–242 (1986)

18. Gao, L.Z.: Foundation of agricultural modeling science. Tianma Book Limited Company, Hong Kong (2004) (in Chinese)

19. Lian, H., Ma, G.S.: The research of dynamic relationship between tomato yield formation and meteorological element in plastic shed. Journal of Jilin Agricultural Sciences 30(1), 52–56 (2005) (in Chinese)

20. Fadhl, A.: Heterosis and inheritance of productive characters in tomato. Yangzhou University, Yangzhou (2006)

21. Han, X.B., Dai, J.F., Xu, R.: Prediction model for harvest date and yield of Brassica chinensis L.in plastic tunnels. Transactions of the CSAE 24(12), 155–159 (2008) (in Chinese)

22. Diao, M., Dai, J.F., Luo, W.H.: Model for simulation of growth and yield of greenhouse sweet pepper. Transactions of the CSAE 25(10), 241–246 (2009) (in Chinese)

# The Technology System Framework of the Internet of Things and Its Application Research in Agriculture

Hong Zhou[*], BingWu Liu, and PingPing Dong

School of Information Science & Technology, Beijing Wuzi University, Beijing, China

**Abstract.** Directing at the current development condition of the internet of things and based on the available technology analysis of the internet of things, the paper makes analysis and research on the internet of things in terms of technological levels and systems. Started from three aspects, respectively, data collection, network service, date fusion and computation, the paper analyzed the technologies like RFID, ZigBee, sensors, Cloud Computing and so on, based on which the paper further brought forth the technological system framework of the internet of things. By combining the technology system framework, the paper carried out the application research in aspect of intelligent agriculture and raised the system construction of production monitoring system of agriculture standardization which is based on the internet of things. Moreover, the paper carried analysis and research works on the sensor nodes of the system, made analysis and discussion on the various technologies involved.

**Keywords:** the internet of things, intelligent agriculture, information collection, ZigBee, Sensor.

## 1 Introduction

Internet of Things refers to a network allows a series of intelligent activities like identification, positioning, tracking, monitoring and management by linking devices like RFID, Smart Sense, GPS (Global Positioning System) and 2-D Code, etc. in objects to wireless network via interfaces to endow objects with intelligence, therefore realize the communication and dialogue between human and objects as well as objects and objects.

IOT and relevant technologies have already been highly values by enterprises and in academic circles both inside and outside the country. Moreover, series of research and exploring works have been launched. However, both inside and outside the country, IOT's research and development works still remain in a preliminary condition and their architecture and system model haven't been developed. There are certain blindness in the research and development of the IOT technology. In terms of the proper definition, the fundamental principles, the architecture and the system

---

[*] Supported by Funding Project for Academic Human Resources Development in Institutions of Higher Learning Under the Jurisdiction of Beijing Municipality (PHR200906210), Beijing Social Science Project(09BAJG258), Beijing-funded project to develop talents (PYZZ090420001451).

D. Li and Y. Chen (Eds.): CCTA 2011, Part I, IFIP AICT 368, pp. 293–300, 2012.

model of IOT, there are plenty of questions to be considered and discussed. Based on the current IOT technology analysis, by analyzing and discussing the technological levels and systems of IOT, the paper is going to start the research on the architecture and the framework of IOT.

Started from the intelligent transportation, logistic scheduling and tracing and base station monitoring, IOT extends its application domain to public oriented personal medical treatment, intelligent home furnishing and so on, and its applications can be found in all walks of life. However, being in the preliminary stage and asking for innovations, IOT hasn't been popularized in large scales. The IOT industry covers sensors, transmission tunnels, computation and process, industrial application and so on, which involves technologies like RFID, sensors, wireless network transmission, computation with high-performance, intelligent control and so on. The paper is going to unfold the introduction by combing the application of IOT in the monitoring system for the agricultural standardized production.

## 2     Key Technologies of IOT

Internet of Things is an open architecture with a variety of technical supports, including radio frequency identification technology, middleware technology, logistics management, e-commerce technology and so on. It involves three key technologies: (1) sensing technology--obtain the object information simultaneously and accurately through the use of RFID, sensor, two-dimensional product code and other equipments and technologies; (2) information transfer technology-- deliver real-time and accurate object information by using the deep integration between a variety of telecommunications networks and the Internet; (3) intelligent processing technology--analyze and sort out large amounts of information and data as well as implement intelligent control of the goods through cloud computing and fuzzy intelligent recognition technology. Considering the content of IOT, in the following part, we are mainly focused on analyzing and researching the information collection technology (ID identification, location information), network service technology (wireless sensor networks, core network element and so on), data merger and computation technology (Cloud computing, mass data merger) and so on.

### 2.1     Technology of Information Collection

The gathering technology of IOT is sensing technology which is the foundation of IOT. Currently, information collection mainly depends on electronic tags and sensors, etc. In sensing technology, the electronic tag is used to standardize the identification of the collected information; and the data acquisition and device control are realized through radio frequency identification and two-dimensional code readers, etc. In data collection and processing stages, it mainly uses various types of sensor technologies, RFID, two-dimensional code and other information gathering techniques to collect data and then receive the control signals from upper receiver, respond, and complete the corresponding actions to process information.

RFID is a non-contact automatic identification technology and it identifies targets automatically and collects relevant data by radio-frequency signal. By affixing electronic labels to the objects, RFID realizes high efficient and flexible management and it becomes the most critical technology for IOT. Typical RFID system is comprised by electronic labels, readers and information process system. Without the manual involvement, the identification process is capable of all kinds of severe environment. RFID is able to identify high-speed traveling object and multiple labels at the same time, with great convenience and efficiency in operation. By absorbing technologies like internet, communication and so on, RFID realizes the object tracing and the information sharing all around the world.

Currently, in the field of RFID, most of researches are based on label cost, uniform technology standard, key technology and so on. Besides RFID, the sensor technology is another frequently applied technology in the ITO. Sensor refers to devices and equipment which are able to perceive the determined test object and the transform it into useful signals in accordance with certain rules. In most cases, the sensor is comprised by sensitive element and conversion element, which are able to detect, perceive external signals, physical and chemical and physical conditions. Meanwhile, the sensor technology is the premise of the sensor node technology.

## 2.2    Technology of Network Communication

In communication technologies of IOT, there are a variety of technologies to choose. They are mainly divided into two types, wired technology (e.g. DSL, PON, etc.) and wireless technology (e.g. CDMA, GPRS, IEEE 802.11a/b/g and WLAN, etc.), which are relatively mature. Referring to the implementation of IOT, the wireless sensor network technology is particularly important.

WSN is a network system which integrates distributed data collection, transmission and process technology and it is widely concerned for its network method and installation method with low cost microminiaturization, feasibility, reliability and flexibility and its capacity for moving object. By sensor node and networks spread in different place, IOT is able to perceive the world. The network construction of WSN can be classified into physical layer, data link layer, internet layer, transmission layer and application layer. The basic composition of sensor's network node includes sense unit, process unit, communication unit and energy unit.

In the technologies of IOT's network and communication, ZigBee is not only a technology between wireless labeling technology and Bluetooth, but also a bidirectional wireless communication technology with close range, low complexity, low power consumption, low cost. ZigBee is applicable in the domain of automatic control and long-range control. ZigBee, as a transmission standard, can be applied in multiple frequencies and working segments and is widely applied for its low power consumption and low cost. In domains of safety system, sensor network, industrial monitoring and other IOT areas, ZigBee has great development space. Moreover, by integrating IPv6 technology into the IOT, we can realize the end to end communication with the current network equipment and improve the retransmission efficiency, which further enhance the safety of information transmission.

## 2.3    Technology of Data Fusion and Computing

IOT is comprised by numerous nodes in the sensor network. In the process of information perception, it is not feasible to adopt the method of single nodes transmitting the date to the sink independently. Because there is enormous redundant information, they would waste much communication width and precious energy resource. Besides, they would lower the efficiency of information collection and affect the timeliness of information collection. For this reason, we need to adopt data merger and intelligent technology to deal with the problem, during which distributed data merger and cloud computing are involved.

Cloud computing is one of distributed computing. By automatically dissembling the huge computing and processing processors into countless subprograms, it handled these subprograms to the huge system composed by multiple servers for searching, computing and analysis, after which it transfers the procession result to the user. Via this technology, web service providers is able to process millions and millions, even billions and millions of information, and thus be capable of net service as powerful as "super computer". By taking advantage of the low cost, super powerful procession ability and storage ability of Cloud Computing Center, and the everywhere information collection of IOT, we combined them together, and enable all kinds of objects to exchange and communicate, thus realizing the intelligent identification. By means of visualization technologies, single server can support multiple virtual machines in running multiple operating systems, and therefore improving the use ratio of servers. Cloud Computing is a service which provides those dynamic, scalable and visualized computing resources by internet.

Visualization, elastic range extension, distributed storage, distributed computing and multiple lessees are critical technologies of Cloud Computing. Distributed storage aims at the target of satisfying the storage requirement which can't be satisfied by single server by utilizing the storage resources of multiple servers inside the cloud environment, and its characteristic is that storage resource is able to be expressed abstractly and be managed in uniform. Moreover, it is capable of ensuring the security and reliability and other requirements generated in the data read-write and operation.

# 3    Processor Architecture of IOT System

Based on the research and analysis on IOT's critical technologies, in the general technological system architecture of IOT, we shall ensure the size of IOT (only with certain size can we enable the object intelligence to play their role), mobility (we need to ensure the object can realize instant communication under moving condition even with high speed ) and security (as for those which involve national security, trade secret and personal privacy, core technology with proprietary intellectual property rights are necessary) The application of IOT is still relatively fragmented in China, and there is no large-scale, systematic development trend, so a scalable and open architecture of IOT should be established in the industrial chain technology as well as application and formation system in ideal aspects in order to break through the barriers of application in large-scale and promote the IOT industry's transition from the start-up period to the growth period. The overall technical architecture of IOT includes data acquisition layer, information exchange layer and application layer. The overall technical architecture of IOT is shown in Figure 1.

Data collection layer consists of two-dimensional code tags and readers, RFID tags and readers, cameras, sensors, GPS, sensor gateways, sensor networks and other equipment and technologies. In this layer, it mainly solves the issues like data collection and object identification, etc. It is composed by the various types of acquisition and control modules, and the main function is to complete IOT's information perception, data collection and the control of facilities. It is an important foundation of IOT.

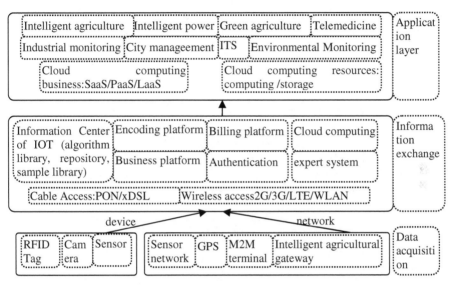

**Fig. 1.** The technical architecture of IOT

The layer of information exchange is based on the network of IOT and communication technologies, such as mobile communication network and the Internet, which is a converged network formed by a variety of communication networks and the Internet. It includes information center, management center of IOT, expert systems and cloud computing platform, which are responsible for the massive part of Intelligent Information Processing. Therefore, the network layer not only requires the ability to operate the network, but also the ability to enhance operational efficiency of information. It is the infrastructure to make the IOT become a universal service.

Application layer refers to solutions of integrating IOT technologies with industrial technical expertise to achieve a wide range of application with intelligent technologies. Through the application layer, IOT ultimately realizes deep integration with information technology and industrial professional technologies. The application layer lies on the top which is the ultimate goal of IOT applications. It consists of a variety of servers and its main functions include the collection, transformation and analysis of the gathered data as well as the adaptation and triggers of things for users. The key issue in this layer is socialization of information's sharing and information security.

## 4    Monitoring System for Agricultural Standardized Production Based on IOT

In the process of agricultural production, the most critical part is the true time data collection in terms of temperature, moisture, carbon dioxide content, and soil temperature and soil moisture content. By making use of the IOT platform and GPRS/TD, by means of SMS, WEB, WAP and other methods, we can make the users dealing with agricultural production acquire these real-time information. Monitoring System for Agricultural Standardized Production based on IOT aims at the target of making information collection towards several indexes in crop growing and carrying out systemic monitoring towards the plantation area, crop pattern, crop growing, the breaking out and development of agricultural damages, crop output and so on.

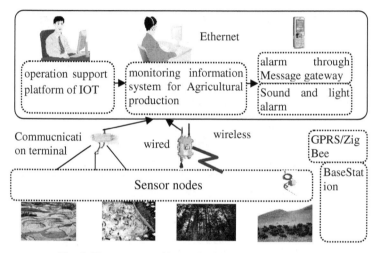

**Fig. 2.** The system architecture of Monitoring system

The monitoring system is composed by the wireless sensor monitoring network and distant monitoring information system. ZigBee sensor nodes set in the plastics tents or greenhouse collect the critical index in crop growing like air temperature, moisture, soil temperature, moisture, illumination intensity, CO2 concentration and so on. Moreover, by means of ZigBee short range wireless communication technologies, we can realize the date transmission and transmit all the node date to the base state where we can carry out TCP/IP packaging on the data we've received, after which we can send them to the remote control center by means of GORS. The control center receives data, analyze and express them. Moreover, they can make parameter setting. Once environmental parameters go beyond the set values, it is possible to make acousto-optic alarming or message alarming. By making use of cell phone or remote computer, researchers can make real-time control on the environmental conditions and information in the crop growing spot. The architecture of monitoring system is shown by the Picture 2.

Monitoring system is composed by three parts: (1) sensor node, sending the information like atmosphere collected by the senor in periodicity to the monitoring and management center of agricultural environment by means of multiple hop transmission. (2)gate way. Located in the edge of sensor network. Realizing the interconnection and communication between the sensor network and internet. In the gateway, we can realize the conversion from the sensor network protocol to the internet protocol. (3) Monitoring and management center of agriculture environment (user), being responsible for the information storage, procession, evaluation and so on. One management center usually is capable of managing multiple monitoring areas. Remote control and PDA users are able to visit the data of the environmental monitoring center by means of internet and they can make real-time inquiry via the center.

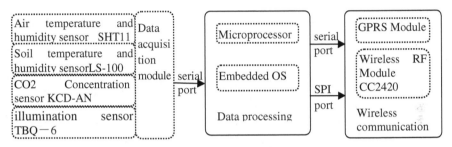

**Fig. 3.** Structural framework figure of the sensor nodes

Sensor network is basically comprised by sensor board which is set with sensors of air temperature and moisture, soil moisture and temperature, soil PH value, light intensity and $CO_2$ concentration. These sensors can be selected and set in the sensor board. The sensor board makes adjustment on the input signals of sensors which is collected by the terminal node of wireless sensor network. The general architecture of sensor node is shown by picture 3. Temperature and moisture sensors are more and more widely applied in the areas of industrial and agricultural production, whether, environment protection and so on. We've selected the SHT11, a digital moisture and temperature sensor with high-accuracy, which is produced by Sensirion in Switzerland. The sensor is a new typed and digital relative moisture and temperature sensor with two passes of serial interface. The sensor has monolithic calibration and can be used to measure relative moisture, temperature, dew point and other parameter, with characteristics of digital output, adjustment free, standardization free, peripheral circuit free, good exchanges. As for the air moisture and temperature sensor, we've adopted SHT11, digital moisture and temperature sensor with high accuracy, which is produced by SENSIRION in Switzerland. As for the soil temperature moisture sensor, we've adopted the LS-100, soil moisture sensor, which is produced by domestic companies. As for the $CO_2$ concentration sensor, we've adopted KCD-AN, produced by Korean companies.

Data procession module is comprised by micro processor, data storage circuit and embedded operation system and it is the core component of sensor node. Moreover, it is responsible for data's storage and procession, scheduling system tasks, carrying out the communication protocols and so on. Wireless communication module is responsible for the communication among the sensor nodes and between the nodes and the station, information exchange and control among sensor nodes and the data collected by the receiving and sending station. When design the system, we adopted CC2420 ship which supports ZigBee protocols, with a frequency band of 2.4 GH z. we've adopted DSSS (Direct Sequence Spread Spectrum) under the specification of IEEE 802.25.4.

# 5     Conclusion

The paper has analyzed the current situation of IOT and made analytical research on the major technologies of IOT. Directing at the practical requirement of national agricultural environment, we've design a agricultural standardized production monitoring system based on the IOT. The system can realize the automatic configuration and self organized transmission of information collected node, realized the real-time collection, transmission, expression and storage of agricultural environmental information. By applying it to the construction agriculture, we can better solve the defect in the traditional monitoring system of green house and plastic tents and make people acquire agricultural environment information at any time. Moreover, we can realize the remote, real-time and accurate monitoring on the agricultural environment. In many aspects, IOT has displayed its promising research and application values. What is more, its application in agriculture has become one of hotspots because it constructed a precious technological platform for the precision agriculture in turning from demonstration to the practices. IOT enables traditional agricultural pattern to evolve into a information network centered production mode and brings automation, networking and intelligentializing to the agricultural production.

# References

1. Cai, B., Bi, Q.-S., Li, F.-C., Wang, D., Yang, Y., Yuan, C.: Research and Design of Agricultural Environment Monitoring System Based on ZigBee Wireless Sensor Network. Acta Agriculturae Jiangxi (11) (2010)
2. Xu, X.-R., Gao, Q.-W., Li, Z.-Y.: Design of wireless sensor networks applied to survey of agriculture environment communication. Transducer and Microsystem Technologies (07) (2009)
3. Zhang, W., Yu, J., Yu, F., Luan, R.: Study on Agricultural Distance Monitoring and Diagnosing Integration Platform Based on XMPP. Chinese Agricultural Science Bulletin (11) (2011)
4. Liu, Z.-S., Wei, F., Chai, Y.-T., Shen, X.-S.: Study on the Construction of the Internet of Things in China. Logistics Technology (07) (2010)
5. Li, G.-G., Li, X.-W., Wen, X.-C.: Influence of Internet of Things Technology on the Development of Automatic Environmental Monitoring System. Environmental Monitoring in China (01) (2011)
6. Liu, H.-J.: Research on Key Technology for Internet of Things. Computer Era (07) (2010)
7. Shen, S.-B., Fan, Q.-L., Zong, P., Mao, Y.-Q., Huang, W.: Study on the Architecture and Associated Technologies for Internet of Things. Journal of Nanjing University of Posts and Telecommunications (Natural Science) (6) (2009)
8. He, K.: The Key Technologies of IOT with Development & Applications. Radio Frequency Ubiquitous Journal (1) (2010)

# Water-Saving Irrigation Management and Decision Support System Based on WEBGIS

Zhifang Chen[1,2], Jinglei Wang[1,2], Jingsheng Sun[1,2], Aiwang Duan[1,2],
Zugui Liu[1,2], Ni Song[1,2], and Xiaofei Liu[1,2]

[1] Key Lab for Crop Water Requirement and Regulation of Ministry of Agriculture,
Xinxiang 453003, China
[2] Farmland Irrigation Research Institute, Chinese Academy of Agricultural Sciences,
Xinxiang 453003, China

**Abstract.** To improve the management of irrigation district is a key to develop water-saving agriculture. Based on the basic principles of water-saving irrigation, and using the method of Modified Penman Monteith and water balance equation, The system of irrigation management and decision support based on WEBGIS was developed, which is according to the soil moisture, crop growth status, meteorology change and the physiological and ecological index of crop that is monitored, and the situation of water supply and crop water-saving irrigation system were also combined with the system. With the help of the GIS, the system under discussion can predict the water requirement of the irrigation district so as to optimize the allocation of the water resources, to provide a decision support for irrigation managers, and to finally realize desirable irrigation practice. Besides, it will promote the automation, informationization, and intelligent of the irrigation district management.

**Keywords:** WEBGIS, SuperMap IS.net, Irrigation management, Spatial analysis.

## 1 Introduction

As the basic resource, water is indispensable to social development. However, more and more problems in relation to water arise with the increase of population and the rapid economic development in China. Among other things, the conflict between water supply and demand becomes more and more serious. Accordingly, how to improve the management of the irrigation area, how to use the water resource in an effective and safe way, and how to yield the greatest returns on the regional water resource are becoming a new task[1]. Fortunately, modern technological development, in particular, Computer, Database, Networks, and Geographic Information System, makes possible the precision management of water resources for the agricultural irrigation[2].

As a new computer-based technology, GIS is a technological system for the management and study of the spacial database. With the support of both the software

D. Li and Y. Chen (Eds.): CCTA 2011, Part I, IFIP AICT 368, pp. 301–312, 2012.

and hardware, GIS could effectively manage the spacial database in accordance with the geographical coordinates or the spacial location and obtain needed information based on an analysis of all the related factors and finally show the result of processing in the form of data, graph or map. When applied to the management and decision support of the irrigation area, it could predict more precisely the water demand of the irrigation area and also play an important role in improving management, optimizing allocation of the water resource, and realizing a desirable irrigation. Besides, a combination of GIS, the Networks and the expert system of irrigation management could promote the informationization and intelligent of the irrigation district management [3].

The GIS has been widely applied to the city traffic control, electric energy and cadastre management in foreign countries. Rather, it has been mainly used in the river basin management, flood control and disaster alleviation, as well as soil and water conservation in China. Anyway, it is scarcely used in the management and decision support of irrigation. With the help of SuperMap Deskpro 2008, Super Map IS .NET 2008, Microsoft Visual Studio 2010 and Microsoft SQL Server 2008, the system under discussion could be used to improve the management and decision support system of irrigation when the management mode of irrigation is combined with GIS, in particular, its mass data input and pre-processing, spacial analysis and visual expression.

## 2     System Architecture

Centering on service, three architectures –the presentation layer,  the business logic layer and the data layer, are established as follows[4-6]:

The client browser is HTML and could receive ordinary HTML webpage. Its task is to read the contents in WEBGIS related to ASP.NET webpage and to require the map data. Then the server transmits all the requirements to the client through the HTTP protocol and all this will be shown on the browser.

The business logic layer is made up of two parts: the Web server software, such as IIS (Microsoft Internet Information Server) and MTS (Microsoft Transaction Server), and the server components based on GIS. When the WEBGIS receives the requirements from the browser, it could process, analyze and compute with the help of GIS Server components. If the data of GIS data server is needed, it could require the GIS data server.

The data layer could complete the definition, storage and retrieval, integrity constraint of data, and realize the functions of inquiry, modification, update of the database. It sends the processing results to the WEBGIS server after it has received the data requirement from the WEBGIS server.

The system architecture is shown in figure 1.

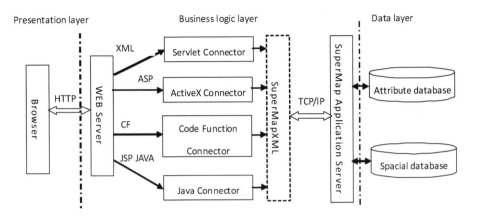

**Fig. 1.** System architecture

# 3    System Development Environment

The system is developed with the help of SuperMap IS.NET 2008 provided by Beijing SuperMap Software Company,Ltd. It makes use of WebControls or AjaxControls, and API- AjaxScripts to design by adopting B/S structure relying on .net 3.5 technical framework and SuperMap Objects 6.0. The server adopts the Asp.net technology, the client uses Http and Tcp/Ip protocol and the backend database employs Microsoft SQL Server 2008[7]. By using the spacial database engine of SuperMap SDE+, it makes possible visit to the spacial data. The programming environment is Microsoft Visual Studio 2010[8,9] , and the background uses C# for programming. Taking the SuperMap[10,11] as the main developing tool, The system makes possible the management of agricultural water information and the visual expression of irrigation decision support.

# 4    Design of Database

Data is the most important part of GIS system and database is the center of all the data. Database includes basic database, spacial database and attribute database[12-14].

The basic database includes data related to soil type, crop type, crop coefficient, crop growth stage, irrigation and drainage, field monitoring and so on.

Attribute database is an important part of the system. It is the core tool to realize data processing, analysis, assessment, and storage of the decision functions.

Spacial database is the basis of the GIS system. The spacial geographical data are obtained by processing the scanned graph which is stored in the form of grid data structure. In order to improve the image quality of the grid data, we use other image processing software for further treatment, such as graphic joining together, noise reduction, refined, etc. Finally the grid data is transformed to the vector data for need. Spacial data and attribute data are processed in SuperMap deskpro 2008 in which modifying or editing data could also be conducted if the SDB is used. If the spacial vector data of the system is voluminous, the spacial data and the attribute data could be easily managed in the basic database. When the vector data is not so voluminous, the spacial vector data would be managed in the form of documents. In this case, the attribute data could be linked to the basic database to realize the remote dynamic linkage in order to enhance the efficiency of the system.

Take the meteorological data as an example. The data structure designed in this paper is shown in Table 1 and part of the data diagram in Figure 2.

**Table 1.** Data structure of meteorological data sheet

| Field Name | Data Type | Note |
|---|---|---|
| Guid | Int | Serial number |
| StadiaCode | Varchar | Station code |
| Date | Datetime | Date |
| Rainfall | Float | Rainfall |
| AvgWind | Float | Average wind velocity |
| TemMax | Float | Maximum temperature |
| TemMin | Float | Minimum temperature |
| AvgTem | Float | Average temperature |
| Suntime | Float | Sunshine duration |
| Moisture | Float | Relative humidity |

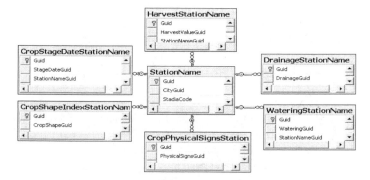

**Fig. 2.** The data relations of some tables

## 5     Design and Realization of the System

Based on the collection materials and survey, the system makes use of many technologies and the functions of GIS provided by SuperMap IS.NET to establish a

GIS-based supporting system for the visual water resources management and decision support of irrigation district according to the management of the irrigation information and the requirement of the irrigation decision support. By the system, the manager could grasp the general situation of the irrigation area and could integrate, analyze, and show the scattered materials. It could increase the quantity and quality of the information that the manager obtains, and quickly and easily realize the visual expression and web publishing of the irrigation decision so as to provide the technological support for scientific irrigation [15-20].

## 5.1    Map Display

Create a webpage with the name of map.aspx as the main window of the map. Switch this webpage to the design page and add Mapcontrol. Click the right key of the mouse and choose'Load Map'in the menu. Input the IP address of GIS server and the port of the map service in the editor of MapControl. Click'Validate'to verify. If the connectivity is succeeded, there will be a notice about it in the below and all the names of the maps which will be issued have been released. Choose the map needing to be released. Click 'Preview' and the image of the map will appear. Click 'OK' and the function of map display will be okay. See Figure 3 as following.

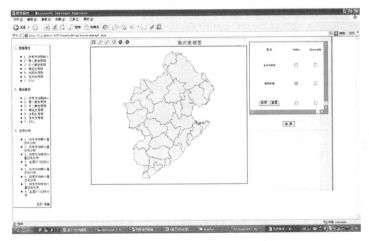

**Fig. 3.** Map Display—the diagram of Haihe river basin

## 5.2    Map View

Map view could be used to zoom in or zoom out the map, to do the map random,and to show the whole map. These functions are developed by using the SuperMap controls.

### 5.2.1    Zoom In or Zoom Out the Map

When the usres browse the maps, they will do the different operation on the different ratio graphics. When one user selects the tools of zoom in or zoom out the map, click the mouse on the map, the map will be magnified or minified correspondingly.

### 5.2.2    Map Random

When the map is shown on the client, due to the limit of the display window size, the whole map often fails to display on the window, if the users want to browse the entire map, they need move the mouse on the map, when randomming on the map, the client need again get the data from the server, but, the new data which are obtainde from the server need wait for a certain amount of time.

### 5.2.3    View Changes

When the map is be magnified, minified or random, the view of the map will change. If the users want to return to the front view or the back view, they only need click the button of the previous view or the back view.

The function of map view could be performed by adding any of the controls mentioned above to the design page(Figure 4).

**Fig. 4.** Map View

## 5.3    Query and Retrieval of Information

To inquire and locate the spacial information is one of the basic functions of GIS. There are mainly two modes of query and retrieval based on the GIS. One is to search through the attribute information and to locate the result; the other is to search for the attribute information related to the target through the map. The former is called 'Property Map Search', and the latter is called 'Map Property Search'. Property Map Search is a kind of fuzzy query. Namely, all the information with the keywords will be shown in the layers of the map when one or more keywords are inputted. The inquiry results will be displayed in the result show box and the target information will be shown in a highlighted way in the map.

### 5.3.1    Property Map Search

The following controls should be added in the main window in the system: 'DropDownList1, DropDownList2 and DropDownList3' for inputting the keywords, 'Button' whose ID name is 'Search' for submitting, and 'Gridview' for showing the result list. The key codes are as follows.

```
protected void Search_ServerClick(object sender, EventArgs e)
    {
        string querysql;
        string Promary =
this.DropDownList2.SelectedItem.Text.ToString();
        string Stadia =this.DropDownList1.SelectedValue.ToString();
        string StadiaCode =
this.DropDownList3.SelectedValue.ToString();
        querysql = "Province_ Name like  '*" + Promary + "*'  and
        Stadia_Name like '" + Stadia + "' and Stadia_Code like '"+
```

```
StadiaCode + "' ";//and Year_ Frequency > " + min + " and Year_
Frequency < " + max + " ";
QueryParam param = new QueryParam();
QueryLayer querylayer = new QueryLayer();
querylayer.ReturnFields = new string[8];
querylayer.ReturnFields[0] = " Province_ Name ";
querylayer.ReturnFields[1] = " Stadia_Name";
querylayer.ReturnFields[2] = " Sowing ";
querylayer.ReturnFields[3] = " Overwintering ";
querylayer.ReturnFields[4] = " Turning_green ";
querylayer.ReturnFields[5] = " Jointing ";
querylayer.ReturnFields[6] = "Heading";
querylayer.ReturnFields[7] = "Maturity";
querylayer.Name = "Growth stage of winter wheat @5";
querylayer.WhereClause = querysql;
param.Layers = new QueryLayer[1];
param.Layers[0] = querylayer;
param.Highlight.HighlightResult = true;
ResultSet Rs = MapControl1.QueryBySQL(param);
ds = Rs.ToDataSet();
gvStadia.DataSource = ds;
gvStadia.DataBind();
}
```

The interface of growth stage of winter wheat through the Property Map Search is shown in Figure 5.

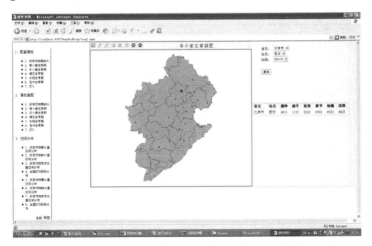

**Fig. 5.** Property Map Search—the diagram of growth stage of winter wheat

### 5.3.2    Map Property Search

Another way of spacial information query is to search the target-related attribute information through map, which is called 'Map Property Search'. SuperMap IS.NET provides several ways of map query including query by clicking the target map, query by rectangular box selecting sphere, query by circle selecting sphere, query by polygon selecting sphere, and query by selecting buffer sphere.

Map Property Search released by the system requires that the Button is added to the main window of the map. The Value of the button is set as 'select'. Click 'select' to make the map in the state of selection and make a rectangle by pushing the left key of the mouse on the map. The results will be shown in Gridview in the bottom right of the map window and the eligible targets will be shown at the time in the window map in the highlighted way. The key codes are as follows.

```
protected void MapControl1_Querying
(object sender,
SuperMap.IS.WebControls.EventArguments.QueryingEventArgs e)
    {
        e.Params.Highlight.HighlightResult = true;
        e.Params.Layers = new QueryLayer[1];
        e.Params.Layers[0] = new QueryLayer();
        e.Params.Layers[0].Name = "ET₀@5";
        e.Params.Layers[0].ReturnFields = new string[4];
        e.Params.Layers[0].ReturnFields[0] = "Stadia Name";
        e.Params.Layers[0].ReturnFields[1] = "Stadia Code";
        e.Params.Layers[0].ReturnFields[2] = "Year_ Frequency";
        e.Params.Layers[0].ReturnFields[3] = "ET₀";
    }
```

The interface of inquiring the reference crop water requirement($ET_0$) through the Map Property Search is shown in Figure 6.

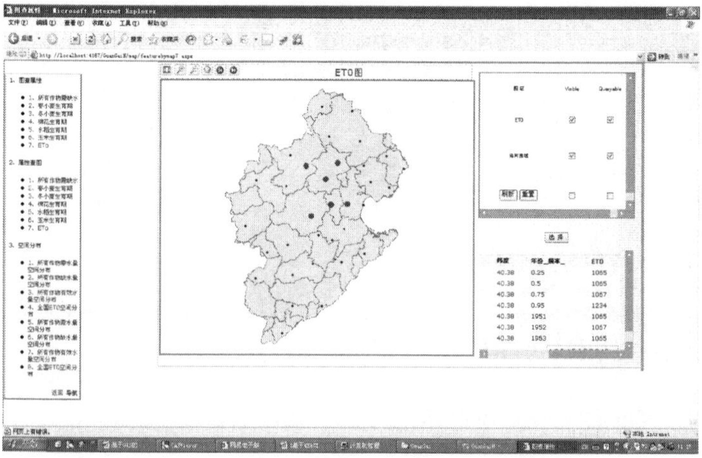

**Fig. 6.** Map Property Search —the diagram of $ET_0$

## 5.4    Spacial Analysis

Spacial variability of the soil moisture is common and complex. To get a full understanding of the spacial distribution of the crop water requirement and the soil moisture is of great significance for irrigation decision support.

Spacial analysis could extract and transmit the spacial information. As the basis of comprehensive geosciences analysis mode, the spacial analysis provides a basic tool for establishing a complicated mode. Spacial analysis mode is a kind of mathematics mode used in GIS spacial analysis. This study adopts the method of point kriging, which is also named general kriging method, to interpolate the soil moisture data. Taking the regionalized variables theory as the basis and the variograms as the main tool, the kriging method is a science which can be used to study the natural phenomena that is random, structural, and spacially correlation and dependence. It is a fast developing field in modern measurement geography. Kriging interpolation could describe the spacial distribution of the soil moisture in a directly perceived way.

Based on the data computed by adopting the irrigation management and decision support system, combination the experiment results of field and modern technology, and using GIS for the technical support means, the system could analyze the spatial distribution characteristics of soil moisture. First,the point data of soil moisture are visualized through the SuperMap deskpro 2008, and the data are integrated to the Chinese map which has been adjusted in the same projection coordinate system. Then using grid as the basic unit, the data such as crop water requirement and soil moisture being quantified are transformed into the grid distribution. Through adopting the WebControls and AjaxControls of SuperMap IS.NET 2008 to establish spacial geographical mode and to integrate the complicated spacial analyzing process, the work efficiency is improved and more attention from those concerned is attracted to the procedure and methods of solving problems.

Figure 7 is the spacial distribution chart of the soil moisture for winter wheat in Guangli Irrigation District.

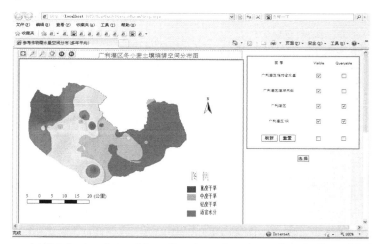

**Fig. 7.** The spacial distribution chart of the soil moisture for winter wheat in Guangli Irrigation District

## 5.5    Visualization of Irrigation Results

Irrigation prediction is the main contents of field water management, which predicting the irrigation date and irrigation quota of crops in certain condition. Based on the basic principles of water-saving irrigation, and using the method of Modified Penman Monteith and water balance equation, The system of irrigation management and decision support based on WEBGIS is developed, which is according to the soil moisture, crop growth status, meteorology change and the physiological and ecological index of crop that is monitored, and the situation of water supply and crop water-saving irrigation system are also combined with the system. Using GIS, the information of irrigation area and the result of the decision support are visualized. Figure 8 is the spacial distribution chart of the forecast results of soil moisture for winter wheat in Guangli Irrigation District of Henan Province.

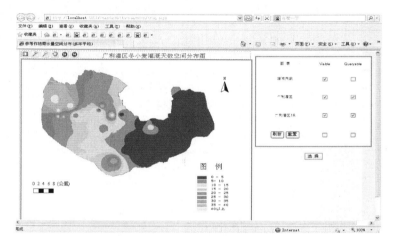

**Fig. 8.** The spacial distribution chart of the forecast results of soil moisture for winter wheat in Guangli Irrigation District

## 6    Conclusion

The paper combines the management and decision support mode of irrigation area with such functions of GIS as inputting and pre-processing of mass data, spacial analysis, and visual expression. It greatly helps users to improve the management of the irrigation area, use the water resources more effectively, predict the water requirement of the irrigation area more precisely, optimize allocation of the water resources, make better decision related to irrigation, and realize the automatic management of the irrigation area.

What to be noted is that there are some problems to which more attention should be directed. They include: (1) the relation between the attribute data of databases and the structure of the data table should be further optimized so as to reduce undesirable data and enhance the efficiency of query and retrieval of the system; (2) the application of

GIS to decision support of irrigation is shown by two-dimensional graphics. Therefore, three-dimensional presentation should be developed so that decision related to irrigation could be more directly perceived and users could conduct the spacial analysis more favorably.

**Acknowledgements.** We acknowledge the financial supports by the Key Lab for Crop Water Requirement and Regulation of Ministry of Agriculture Foundation (CWRR201006), the National Natural Science Foundation of China (51079154), the earmarked fund for China Agriculture Research System (CARS-3-1-30).

# References

1. Li, S.: The present situation and countermeasures of water resources in China– The shortage of water resources restricts the economic and social development of our country. Journal of Yan'an Vocational&Technical Institute 23(6), 101–103 (2009)
2. Wang, Y.-B., He, W.-Q., Shang, H.-J.: Application of GIS technique to the management in irrigation districts. Northwest Water Resources & Water Engineering 14(3), 39–42 (2003)
3. Chen, X., Cheng, J.-L., Jiang, X.-H.: Study of decision support system (DSS) in irrigation districts based on GIS. Journal of Yangzhou university (Natural Science Edition) 9(2), 43–47 (2006)
4. Hu, H., Li, Q.: Research on Informationization Construction in Village and Township Based on WebGIS. Agriculture Network Information (2), 35–37, 54 (2010)
5. Liu, R., Hu, S., Pan, Y.-C.: A System for Forestry Resources Management and Decision-Support Based on WebGIS and Portal. Computer Technology and Development 20(4), 203–206, 210 (2010)
6. Chen, Y.-Y., Xu, Y.-Z., Dong, J.-L.: Design and implementation of property management information systembased on WebGIS. Computer Engineering and Design 30(15), 3676–3679 (2009)
7. Zhou, W., Wang, L.: The tutorial of database application and development. The press of China railway, Beijing (2009)
8. Li, B., Chen, J.: The development practice of web application system (Visual C# 2008). The press of China railway, Beijing (2010)
9. Luo, F., Bai, Z., Yang, J.: The programming tutorial of Visual C#.net. The press of People's post and telegraph, Beijing (2009)
10. The User's Manual of SuperMap Deskpro.: SuperMap Software Co., Ltd, Beijing (2008)
11. The User's Manual of SuperMap IS.NET.: SuperMap Software Co., Ltd, Beijing (2008)
12. Xu, D., Yuan, X., Xu, C.: The design and implementation of agricultural information system based on WebGIS. The Agricultural Science of Guangdong (9), 220–223 (2010)
13. Li, Y., Yan, A., Jiang, P.-A.: Design of Information System of Korla Fragrant Pear Based on WebGIS. Xinjiang Agricultural Sciences 47(10), 2068–2073 (2010)
14. Pang, Y.-Q., Yang, L.-N., Zhang, L.-L.: Design and Realization of Farmland Soil Information Management Platform Based on WebGIS. Journal of Anhni Agriculture Science 37(5), 2302–2303 (2009)
15. Zhou, Y.-W., Shi, S.-L., Wei, F.: Design and Implementation of Administrative System for Ocean Map Services Based on ArcGIS Server. Geomatics& Spatial Information Technology 32(1), 51–53 (2009)
16. Chen, Z., Song, N., Wang, J.: Study On Water-saving Irrigation Management and Decision Support System. Transactions of the CSAE 25(suppl. 2), 1–6 (2009)

17. Teng, D.-Q., Zheng, J.-G., Zhang, M.-H., Li, C., Huang, P.: Design and Realization of Xían Urban Geographic Information Query System Based on SuperMap IS.NET. Geomatics& Spatial Information Technology 33(3), 108–110 (2010)
18. Yang, J., Guo, J., Chu, G.: Disaster Situation Map Issue System of the Wenchuan Earthquake Based on SuperMap IS.NET. Geomatics& Spatial Information Technology 32(2), 179–180, 186 (2009)
19. Liu, B., He, X., Pu, S., Zhang, W.: Developed of irrigation decision support system based on WebGIS. Yellow River 30(1), 53–54 (2008)
20. Liao, Y.: Design and Implementation of Map Website Based on SuperMap IS.NET. Geospatial Information 5(3), 38–40 (2007)

# Key Technology Study of Agriculture Information Cloud-Services

Yunpeng Cui and Shihong Liu

Key Laboratory of Digital Agricultural Early-warning Technology, Ministry of Agriculture,
Beijing, The People's Republic of China 100081
cyunpeng@163.com, lius@mail.caas.net.cn

**Abstract.** The rural information service in the rural area in China developed rapidly these years. But the agriculture information resources need to be further development and utilization, the key of agriculture information service at the present stage is to summarize the real demand of the rural users, choose suitable technology, find the right solution, solve the information sharing and fusion problems fundamentally. AISC(Agriculture Information Cloud-Services) is a cloud service platform, which tried to import different datasets in different data sources that constructed by different organizations, and combine all these datasets into one big dataset logically. Based on the "big dataset", many applications such as semantic information retrieve, intelligent information push, self-organized knowledge base construction etc. were developed, so the service efficiency is improved.

**Keywords:** Agriculture Information, Cloud-Services.

## 1    Introduction

Along with the information technology revolution influence continues to expand, the infomationization course in China progress steadily, Meanwhile informationization in China started to gradually penetrate from city to rural area. As the rural information infrastructure project ("CunCunTong Project") completed successfully, the rural area oriented information service in China become possible.

However, at present, in China, Rural information service development is not balanced, especially in the west regions of China, farmers' information literacy and information consciousness still need to be improved; The agriculture information resources need further development and utilization, the way that rural users obtaining and receiving information should be enriched too; The standard system of agriculture information should be established to regulate and promote the sharing, exchange and integration of agricultural information resources, and ensure the quality of information resources; the personalization of agriculture service also need to strengthen so that service can meet the requirements of different rural users.

So, the key of agriculture information service at the present stage is not database and system construction, but is to summarize the real demand of the rural users, choose suitable technology, find the right solution, solve the information sharing and fusion problems fundamentally, explore the effective mechanism and model of information

D. Li and Y. Chen (Eds.): CCTA 2011, Part I, IFIP AICT 368, pp. 313–317, 2012.

service, develop available information products, provide quality and efficient information services, help them solve the problems in their production and living.

The goal of the study is to establish a comprehensive agriculture information service cloud through global catalogue exchange technology, universal data element and data item presentation and mapping technology, implement the fusion of distributed agriculture data sources, develop a personalized, easy-to-use comprehensive agriculture information service cloud(AISC) and its portal, provide precise information service to rural users.

## 2    The Technical Architecture of Agriculture Information Service Cloud(AISC)

As shown in figure 1, AISC has four layers, from bottom to top are data resource layer, management layer, service layer, application layer and respectively.

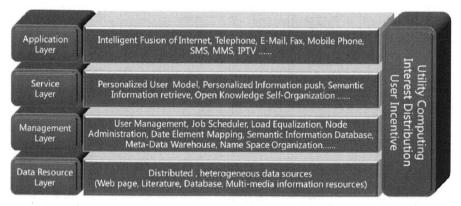

**Fig. 1.** Technical Architecture of AISC

The data resource layer include all the distributed, heterogeneous data sources which join the cloud, include web pages, literatures, databases and multi-media information resources etc., the data sources will be integrated into a transparent logic "big single data source", which can provide data to upper layers/

The management layer is consist of different functional components such as global user management, job scheduler, load equalization, node administration etc., these components can manage the cloud effectively,

## 3    Core Technology of Agriculture Information Service Cloud(AISC)

To construct the AISC, the following problems must be solved:
(1) The mapping technology between universal agriculture information data elements and data items in databases

Because the AISC is constructed based on the distributed information datasets, so it's very important to make the datasets connect logically and interoperable. The solution is to construct a warehouse that contains all the mapping relationship between the universal standard agriculture information data elements and the data items of all the distributed database.

So we must first construct the universal standard agriculture information data elements, we can construct them by brain storm, and also we can develop a tool to extract related concepts from articles. As the basis of the future intelligent retrieve, we establish the semantic relationship between data items, and save the relationships in the data warehouse.

(2) Study of agriculture information dataset metadata and service metadata standards

To implement the universal information fusion, we must have a set of standard metadata to describe the datasets consistently, so a core metadata standard is required. We compiled agriculture information datasets core metadata standard[1], which include 75 metadata elements, for every element there are 9 attributes(see Table 1) to describe and restrict it.

On the other hand, the agriculture information core metadata can only implement the universal datasets description, if we want to import all the datasets into AISC and make them to be accessed as a logical single data source, we must have service metadata support. The service metadata provide the universal, standard description for different services, such as HTTP Service, FTP Service, Data Connection Service, Data Access middleware etc., with these service metadata, computer can read the values of service metadata, locate and access the dataset, so retrieve data from different data sources. figure 2 shows an example of service metadata, which is dataset connection service metadata, through it computer can get the information like IP address of database host, access port number, database name etc., and then computer can locate the host and connect to the database.

**Table 1.** The attributes of the elements of agriculture information resources dataset core metadata

| Name of attribute | Description |
|---|---|
| Chinese name | Chinese name of the element |
| English name | English name of the element |
| Identification | The unique identification of the element, string. |
| Definition | The specifications description of the meaning of the element. |
| Type | The type of the element, the available types include: composite(the element contains sub elements),integer, float, text, date, time, datetime etc. |
| Range | The allowed range of the value of the element |
| Optional | The element is required or optional |
| Maximun appearance | The maximum appearance of the element, such as 1(only once)、 N(unlimited times)etc. |
| Note | Supplementary specifications of the element |

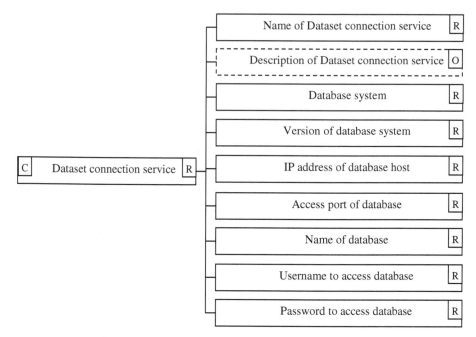

**Fig. 2.** The example of dataset connection service metadata

So the agriculture information datasets core metadata can map different data items in different datasets and connect all the datasets into one single big dataset logically, through service metadata, computer find where the dataset is and access the dataset directly, so all the datasets are "imported " into the cloud and can be managed in the cloud.

(3) Construction of ASIC platform and portal

We have logically bunched different information resources together in last step, so the problem now is how to use the resources, and how to let the information reach the user effectively.

So first of all, we should make agriculture information service individualized. We established user information requirement model to describe the users' information requirements dynamically through data mining from users' information behavior[2], and use the model in the user information retrieve process[3], and also push the subscribed information to users actively.

On the other hand, not all the farmers own a computer, or can connect to internet, so we must import different technology and create different models, so all the farmers can access the platform and service portal through the applicable way. We tried to import universal information technology into agriculture information service, so farmers can access the platform and get information with telephone, fax, email, SMS, IPTV and special information terminal equipment.

To improve information retrieve efficiency, we studied semantic information retrieve technology based on the semantic relationship establish in step (1), analyze the information resource in the cloud, aggregate the related information together automatically, and also use the technology in information retrieve and push process.

Though there is plenty of information in the cloud, it's not enough for farmers to solve all their problems, so we let them fill the knowledge base themselves. We studied the open knowledge self-organized technology, everyone can raise their question and everyone can answer any question raise by anybody, the people who raise the question can then evaluate the answer and score the answers, the best answer will be adopted by the platform as the final answer of the question and be saved in the knowledge base. When a user raise a question, he/she must choose tags to identify the question, the tags is in fact the keywords of the question which are provided by the platform, the tags in the platform are organized by a set of ontologies, so the questions and their answers is organized.

(4)Study of stimulate mechanism of information sharing

To stimulate the dataset providers contributing more resources to the clouds, there must be a set of mechanism to encourage them[4]. The principle is "more contributions, more rights". Not all the information are free in the platform, the provider can also ask the users pay for special information, so attract the dataset providers and users participate in the service and communication.

## 4     Conclusion

The AISC is an attempt to promote agriculture information service. It tried to import different datasets in different data sources that constructed by different organizations, and combine all these datasets into one big dataset logically. Based on this "big dataset", we can develop many applications such as semantic information retrieve, intelligent information push, self-organized knowledge base construction etc., so improve the service efficiency.

**Acknowledgement.** The research was supported by the special project from ministry of agriculture of the people's republic of China, named study of agriculture informatization standards system and special fund of basic commonweal research institute project of information institute of CAAS, and National 11th five-year technology based plan topic named study of Agricultural product quantity Safety Data obtained standards (2009BADA9B02).

## References

[1] Cui, Y., Liu, S., Sun, S., Zhang, J., Zheng, H.: A Metadata Based Agricultural Universal Scientific and Technical Information Fusion and Service Framework. In: Li, D., Liu, Y., Chen, Y. (eds.) CCTA 2010, Part I. IFIP AICT, vol. 344, pp. 56–61. Springer, Heidelberg (2011)

[2] Xun, G.: Research on web structure mining algorithm based On cloud computing. Master's degree thesis

[3] He, J.-J., Ye, C.-M.: Cloud computing-oriented data mining system architecture. Application Research of Computers 28(4), 1372–1374 (2011)

[4] Yin, X.: Research on business model of cloud computing based on value net, Master's degree thesis

# A SVM-Based Text Classification System for Knowledge Organization Method of Crop Cultivation

Laiqing Ji[1], Xinrong Cheng[1], Li Kang[1], Daoliang Li[1], Daiyi Li[1], Kaiyi Wang[2], and Yingyi Chen[1,*]

[1] College of Information and Electrical Engineering,
China Agricultural University, Beijing 100083
[2] Beijing Research Center for Information Technology in Agricultural,
Beijing 10097
chyingyi@126.com

**Abstract.** The organization of crop cultivation practices is still far from completion, and Web Resources are not used adequately. This paper proposed a method, based on SVM, to organize the knowledge of crop cultivation practices efficiently from Web Resources. The knowledge organization method of crop cultivation was proposed with Good Agricultural Practices (GAP) in the application of the crop cultivation practices. It is that how to organize the existing crop cultivation knowledge, according to the requirements of crop cultivation practices. It mainly includes a text classification method and a search strategy on the knowledge of crop cultivation. For the text classification method, it used a text classification method based on SVM Decision Tree; for the search strategy, it used a strategy, organized by Ontology and custom knowledge bases. The experiment shows that performance of the proposed text classification method and the knowledge organization method with wheat, is workable and feasible.

**Keywords:** Support Vector Machine (SVM), Text Classification, organization method, crop.

## 1    Introduction

The amount of information about the knowledge of crop cultivation in Web pages is huge and the information is disorganized, so that it is a big workload to organize the related knowledge and not sufficient to use it, resulting in a number of waste of the useful resources. So it is a meaningful thing to organize the related knowledge [1].

To solve these problems, a lot of methods were proposed both at home and abroad. However, these methods [2] only collect the content from the Web Resource, not

---

* Corresponding author.

D. Li and Y. Chen (Eds.): CCTA 2011, Part I, IFIP AICT 368, pp. 318–324, 2012.
© IFIP International Federation for Information Processing 2012

classifying the collected content and getting what we truly need. The search engine is a retrieval tool for the network information, but the performance of traditional search engine is unsatisfactory[3]. By analyzing Web documents to get the related knowledge, Text mining, as an important branch of data mining, can help have a better use of Web knowledge, based on information retrieval, data mining and knowledge management and so on.

This paper proposed a method on how to organize the knowledge for more effectively organizing and analyzing the documents about the related knowledge. This method involved in how to classify the documents and set the search strategies on the knowledge of crop cultivation.

## 2    The Knowledge Organization Method

### 2.1    Knowledge Characteristics Analysis

The complexity of crop cultivation brings about the complexity of the related knowledge organization, and there is not a very clear knowledge or practice to guide the process of crop cultivation. However, the current research for crop cultivation practices, mainly combined with Good Agricultural Practices (GAP), has also had some progress. In this paper, it mainly referred the document "Combinable crops control points and compliance criteria" in GAP as required.

With the analysis of GAP as a prerequisite, it divided the process of crop cultivation into three phases: pre-production, in-production and post-production. The pre-production mainly consisted of land selection and seed selection. The land selection mainly referred the land type, the time of sowing and so on, and the seed selection mainly referred varietal characteristics, suitable areas for planting, output, resistance, price and so on. The in-production mainly referred sowing and seedling raising, fertilization, irrigation, pest and disease control and so on. For different crops in different areas, the detailed operating of crop cultivation may be different. For example, some crops just need seedling raising, not sowing; the crop cultivation in outdoor and greenhouse is different. The post-production mainly consisted of agricultural harvest, storage and so on.

### 2.2    The Knowledge Organization Model

Although the knowledge of crop cultivation is numerous and messy with the above analysis, it has certain law so that we can organize it with the knowledge of GAP. The following graphic shows this method.

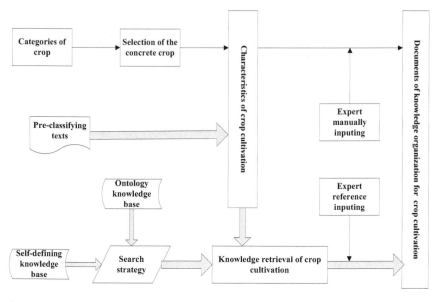

**Fig. 1.** Knowledge organization model of crop cultivation

As shown in Fig.1,  the kernel of this model is the text classification method and a search strategy on the related knowledge of crop cultivation. For the strategy in this model, it mainly includes the retrieve key provided by Ontology knowledge database and self-defining knowledge database. For the search strategy for Ontology knowledge database, it is domain Ontology built in accordance with the request of GAP; for the search strategy for self-defining knowledge database, its setting rule is that the key in the self-defining knowledge database can stand for the most common characteristics in some category.

Taking the wheat as an example, the key in the search strategy of pest and disease control stands for the following: the symptom and their solutions. These solutions mainly refer the irrigation time, the irrigation methods and so on. Because the setting of the search strategy directly affects the accuracy rate of the related knowledge retrieve, we should analyze a lot of related texts, and summarize the most common characteristics of these texts, then make the related search strategy, using the key which can best represent the characteristics.

# 3    Text Classification Method of Crop Cultivation

This paper proposed the text classification method with actual demand and text classification algorithm, based on the knowledge characteristics of crop cultivation. Firstly, collect the sample texts on the knowledge on crop cultivation; then get the training model of the text classification through training the samples; Finally classify the related texts and get the categories of the related knowledge. The following graphic shows the knowledge classification model of crop cultivation.

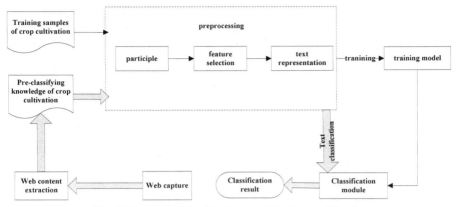

**Fig. 2.** Knowledge classification model of crop cultivation

## 3.1    Support Vector Machine (SVM)

Based on the minimization principle to structure risk, SVM is a non-linear method. It maps the limited training data(Input Vector) to high dimension feature space, resulting

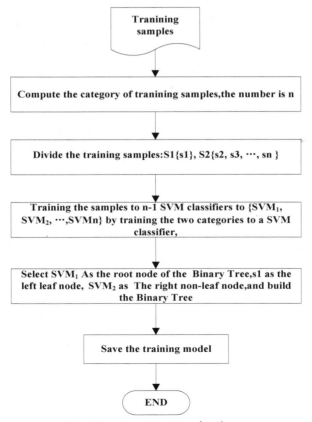

**Fig. 3.** Training Algorithm（n>2）

in transforming the problem of the non-linear separability in the sample spaces into the problem of linear separability in the characteristic spaces. In other words, it is how to search the best linear classification Hyperplane. For the finding this Hyperplane, SVM is realized by the Support Vector (SV) and the decision boundary.

## 3.2    The Text Classification Ideology and Algorithm

Through analyzing the related knowledge characteristic of crop cultivation, we know that the knowledge classification is the multi-class issue. As we know, SVM can only solve the two-class classification, so that we need graft many SVMS onto one to realize the knowledge classification of crop cultivation.

Through analyzing the flaws of algorithm and the related knowledge characteristics, this paper proposed a method, combined binary decision tree with SVM, to realize the related knowledge classification of crop cultivation. Every non-leaf node refers to a SVM classifier and every leaf node refers to the final classified category. The text classification algorithm of crop cultivation, and the algorithm were described as Fig.3 and Fig.4 [11-12]:

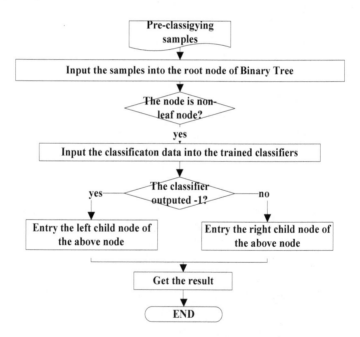

**Fig. 4.** Classification Algorithm

## 4    Results and Discussions

The text classification of crop cultivation is the kernel of the related knowledge organization. According to the actual requirement of the related document arrangement, this paper divided the crop cultivation into six critical control points: land selection, seed selection(seedling raising),fertilization, irrigation, pest and disease control ,harvest. It extracted the related content, using the knowledge of Web crawling and Web analysis, finally classified the content, and made these documents be the training samples in experiment.

It mainly adopt the recall ratio(r) and the precision ratio(p) to evaluate the quality of text classification, and it also refers to the comprehensive evaluation indexes of the recall ratio and precision ratio[10]: F1,its mathematical formula is:  $F1 = \dfrac{r * p * 2}{r + p}$  [10]

Taking the pest and disease control of wheat as an example. For the search strategy of the pest and disease control, it mainly includes the symptoms of pest and disease control, the name of the medicines, the usage and dosage of the medicines and so on. Let the number of the related texts about the pest and disease control be *num2*; Let the number of the related texts about the pest and disease control of wheat be *num2*; Let the number of the texts including all of the search strategies on the pest and disease control of wheat be *num3*.

Let M be the reference values of the specialists, and the specific definition of M is that it is the ratio of the number of the text, including all of the search strategy in a category, and the number of the related texts in a category. It is shown by the definition of M , M =*num3* / *num1*.It shows the result of the experiment about the text classification method of crop cultivation and the knowledge organization method of the pest and disease control to wheat in the following table1.

**Table 1.** Result of the text classification and the knowledge organization method of the pest and disease control to wheat

| categories | Training samples | p | r | F1 | num1 | num2 | num3 | M |
|---|---|---|---|---|---|---|---|---|
| Land selection and preparation | 205 | 87.3% | 86.5% | 86.9% | × | × | × | × |
| Seed selection and seedling raising | 170 | 93.2% | 93.0% | 93.1% | × | × | × | × |
| Fertilization | 205 | 95.8% | 96.1% | 95.9% | | × | × | × |
| Irrigation | 160 | 90.6% | 89.7% | 90.1% | × | × | × | × |
| Pest and disease control | 263 | 91.5% | 89.5% | 90.5% | 113 | 40 | 12 | 0.107 |
| Harvest | 200 | 94.1% | 95.4% | 94.7% | × | × | × | × |

# 5    Conclusions

On the premise of the related knowledge characteristics analysis of crop cultivation, this paper proposed the knowledge organization model of the crop cultivation. In this model, it mainly described the principle how to set the search strategy and the SVM-Based text classification ideology and algorithm.   This paper had the related test. The experiment result shows that the organization method is workable and feasible, and it can effectively provide the data for the document arrangement of crop cultivation practices. The experiment result also shows that it needs a lot of data to achieve the effectiveness, or the effectiveness is not apparent.

**Acknowledgements.** Funding for this research was provided by National Key Technology R&D Program. The project name is Study on the comprehensive evaluation system of crop cultivation practices. The project number is 2009BADB6B02-01.

# References

1. Usama, M.F.: Data Mining and knowledge discovery: making sense out of data. IEEE Expert 11(5), 20–25 (1996)
2. Hand, D.J.: Intelligent Data Analysis: Issues and Opportunities. In: Liu, X., Cohen, P.R., R. Berthold, M. (eds.) IDA 1997. LNCS, vol. 1280, pp. 1–14. Springer, Heidelberg (1997)
3. Jiang, G., Cheng, X., Kang, L., et al.: Building Knowledge base for Consulting System on Agricultural Practical Techniques. In: IEEE Proceedings of the 2009 International Conference on Computer and Computing Technology Applications in Agriculture (2009)
4. Mangasarian, O.L., Musicant, D.R.: Active set support vector machine classification. In: Advances in Neural Information Processing Systems, pp. 577–583 (2000)
5. Joachim's, T.: Making large-scale support vector machine learning practical. In: Advances in Kernel Methods: Support Vector Machines (1999)
6. Niu, Q., Wang, Z., Chen, D., et al.: The method of the Web text classification based on Support Vector Machine. Microelectronics and Computer 23(9), 102–104 (2006)
7. Zou, H.: Application of Support Vector Machine in the text classification (2006)
8. Hsu, C.W., Lin, C.J.: A comparison on methods for multi-class Support Vector Machine. Technical report, Department of Computer Science and Information Engineering (2001)
9. Knerr, S., et al.: Single-layer learning revisited:A stepwise procedure for building and training a neural network. In: Fogclman-Soulie, et al. (eds.) Neuro-Computing: Algorithms,Architectures and Applications, NATO ASI. Springer, Heidelberg (1990)
10. Rao, W., Ke, H.: Research and implementation of Web Text Classification. The Computer Technology and Development 16(3), 116–118 (2006)
11. Osuna, E., Freund, R., Girosi, F.: Training support vector machines: An application to face detection. In: Proceedings CVPR 1997 (1997b)
12. Osuna, E., Freund, R., Girosi, F.: Training support vector machines: An application to face detection. In: Proceedings of CVPR 1997 (1997)

# Near-Infrared Spectroscopy Technology for Soil Nutrients Detection Based on LS-SVM

Yandan Qiao[1] and Shujuan Zhang[2,*]

[1] Center for Popularization of Agricultural Machinery Technology of Shanxi Province
[2] College of Engineering, Shanxi Agricultural University, Taigu, Shanxi,
030801, China
zsujuan@263.net

**Abstract.** The detection method of the soil nutrients (organic matter and available N, P, K) were analyzed based on the near infrared spectroscopy technology in order to decision-making for precision fertilization. 54 samples with 7m×7m was collected using DGPS receiver positioning in a soybean field. The soil organic matter, available nitrogen (N), available phosphorus (P), available potassium (K) content was determined, the near-infrared diffuse reflectance spectrum of the soil samples were obtained by FieldSpec3 spectrometer. 54 samples were randomly divided into 40 prediction sets and 14 validation sets. After smoothing, the eight principal components of original spectra were extracted by principal component analysis (PCA). Prediction model of soil organic matter, available nitrogen (N), available phosphorus (P), potassium (K) were respectively established with the eight principal component as input and soil nutrients by measured as the output, and the 14 validation samples were predicted. The results showed that the soil organic matter, available nitrogen (N), available phosphorus (P), potassium (K) prediction model were set up with principal component analysis and LS-SVM, which the correlation coefficients between the prediction value and measurement value were 0.8708, 0.7206, 0.8421 and 0.6858, the relative errors of the LS-SVM prediction was smaller and those mean values were 1.09%, 1.06%, 4.08% and 0.69%. The method of soil organic matter content prediction is feasible.

**Keywords:** Near infrared spectroscopy, Soil nutrient, Detection, PCA, LS-SVM.

## 1 Introduction

Soil nutrients are fast nondestructive measurement for agriculture information collection (LUO et al.,2006). Recently, with widely applications of near-infrared spectroscopy, it has become a focus of many domestic scholars that soil nutrient information were gained by near infrared spectroscopy(Ben-Dor E et al.,1995).The spectral characteristics of the soil was analyzed of mechanism(Wu Yun Zhao et al.,2003). The nitrogen, calcium and magnesium of dry, after sifting the soil was studied using near infrared spectroscopy(Lee et al.,2003); soil constituents were studied by near infrared spectroscopy(Chang et al.,2001). Yu Fei Jian found that

D. Li and Y. Chen (Eds.): CCTA 2011, Part I, IFIP AICT 368, pp. 325–335, 2012.
© IFIP International Federation for Information Processing 2012

NIRS and total nitrogen, organic matter, nitrogen of after sifting the soil has a good correlation. The Near-infrared spectral characteristics of the soil after sifting treatment were studied by He Yong et al. The exchange capacity of Soil organic matter, cation and soil moisture were studied using a portable NIRS spectrometer in the laboratory and field (Sudduth et al.,1993).

Near infrared reflectance(NIR) spectroscopy(NIRS) is a physical non-destructive, rapid, reproducible and low-cost approach that characterizes materials according to their reflectance in the wavelength range between 800 and 2500 nm. The analysis of NIR spectra relies on calibration, which in general is a multivariate regression procedure that that expresses a given property, determined using a conventional method, as a function of absorbance at all or selected wavelengths of the NIR region. The calibration equation can then be used to predict that property on new samples from their NIR spectra only, the acquisition of which is time- and cost-effective (<1 min per sample, no consumables required). The application of NIRS to soil has been mentioned from the 1960sand it has been used extensively to determine soil content in carbon and nitrogen(Bernard et al.,2011).

Accurate NIRS determination of C and N have been extensively reported, especially for rather homogeneous textural sets (Dalal and Henry,1986;Morra et al.,1991;Brunet et a.,2007).Several studied have also reported NIRS determination of C/N(Chang and Larid,2002;Ludwig et al.,2002)The main objective of this study was to investigate the potential of NIR reflectance spectroscopy as a rapid tool for the measurement of soil nutrients.

## 2    Materials and Methods

### 2.1    Soil Samples

The soil was sampled to 7m ×7m grid using DGPS navigation system in a soybean field of Shanxi Agricultural University campus on November 9, 2009. Depth of samples was 20cm and the number of samples was 54. The soil type and texture is cinnamon and sandy loam.

### 2.2    Measurement of Spectral Characteristics of the Soil

The test device was composed of computer, spectrometer, halogen light, white board and other components correct in the spectral measurements of soil. Spectrum was obtained using FieldSpec3 spectrometer (Analytical Spectral Device company, USA), with sampling collection interval of 1nm, spectrum range of 350 ~ 2500nm, and the resolution of 3.5nm. 54 soil samples were air-dried, hand ground, and samples of particles of 2mm were got. The glass Petri dishes that diameter was 90mm and thickness was 15mm were selected to place the soil.Spectrometer was placed in soil samples and the distance between spectrometer and soil surface was 100nm and test angle was 45 °, field view probe was 10°. Sample spectrum was collected with diffuse reflection mode. Each soil sample was six repeated and each sample was scanned 10 times. The spectrum was processed for average processing by ASD View Spec pro software, and the absorbance was converted according to log [1/R]. The spectral data was exported in ASCII format, and processed was use of ASD View Spec Pro, Unscramble V9.8 and MATLAB2009.

## 2.3   Measurement of Soil Nutrients

The soil nutrients of soil organic matter, nitrogen, available phosphorus and potassium were determined by routine laboratory analysis. The measured were divided into two steps: firstly, the elements of analysis were extracted from the isolated from the soil; then those elements were quantitative tested. The soil was dried, sieved, extraction, those element were obtained using the following chemical analysis methods:

1) Soil organic matter content was determined by potassium dichromate volumetric method - external heating method.
2) Soil nitrogen content was determined using 1mol / L NaOH diffusion.
3) Soil available phosphorus content was measured using 0.5mol / L NaHCO$_3$ extraction - molybdenum blue method.
4) Soil potassium was measured using 1mol/L NH$_4$OA$_C$ extraction - flame photometry.

The statistical parameters of chemical measurement results of soil organic matter (SOM), available nitrogen (N), phosphorus (P), available potassium (K) were shown in Table 1.

**Table 1.** Soil chemical constituents statistical parameters

| Nutrients | Sample number | Minimum | Maximum | Mean | Standard Deviation | Coefficient of variation(%) |
|-----------|--------|---------|---------|------|----------|-----------|
| N(mg/kg) | 54 | 30.63 | 40.86 | 35.77 | 1.89 | 5.28 |
| P(mg/kg) | 54 | 3.23 | 16.34 | 8.04 | 2.69 | 33.40 |
| K(mg/kg) | 54 | 209.45 | 287.55 | 235.56 | 15.30 | 6.50 |
| SOM(g/kg) | 54 | 19.00 | 29.47 | 24.53 | 1.61 | 6.55 |

# 3   Soil Available N, P, K and Organic Matter Spectrum

## 3.1   Data Preprocessing

In order to remove the effects from the high-frequency random noise, baseline drift, uneven samples and light scattering, spectra was processed using average smoothing, and smoothing window size was 9. The soil near infrared spectra of pretreatment was shown in Figure 1.

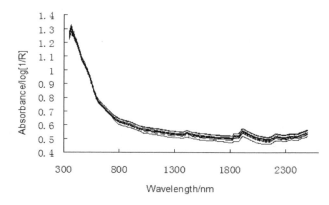

**Fig. 1.** Absorbance graph of soil near-infrared spectroscopy

## 3.2    Principal Component Analysis of Soil Nutrients and the Least Squares Support Vector Machine Modeling

### 3.2.1  Principal Components Are Extracted Based on Principal Component Analysis

The 54 samples were randomly divided into test set of 40 and validation set of 14. The spectral bands of samples had total 2151 points from 350 ~ 2500nm, those computationally intensive and the spectral information of samples in some regions was very weak. The correlation lack between nature and the spectral bands. Principal component analysis(PCA) takes a dimension reduction method, The original number of indicators transform into a few new indicators using linear algebra and related knowledge, both of these new indicators unrelated to each other to avoid overlap and duplication of information, but also a comprehensive reflection of the original number of indicators. The sets of validation and prediction were analyzed by PCA, the credibility of its main components was shown in Table 2.

**Table 2.** Accumulative reliabilities of the first 6 PCs

| PC | PC01 | PC02 | PC03 | PC04 | PC05 | PC06 |
|---|---|---|---|---|---|---|
| Cumulative reliability prediction set (%) | 96.829 | 99.180 | 99.624 | 99.823 | 99.882 | 99.919 |
| Accumulated credibility validation set (%) | 96.087 | 98.865 | 99.551 | 99.780 | 99.859 | 99.906 |

The explanation of original variables was collected through the accumulated credibility. The accumulated credibility of the first six principal components was to 99.9% in prediction set from Table 2, and 99.9% of the original variable wavelength was interpreted; The accumulated credibility of the first six principal components was to 99.906% in validation set, and 99.9% of the original variable wavelength was interpreted, Least squares vector machine model was established that the six principal components were selected as input.

### 3.2.2    The Predictive Models of Soil Organic Matter Based on Least Squares Vector Machines (LS-SVM)

The LS-SVM model was established with 6 principal components as an input layer and measured values of soil organic matter as output layer. Hyper-parameters gam and the RBF kernel parameter sig2 were obtained by grid search method with cross-validation, The optimal combination of two parameters were obtained that gam was 1251.8, and sig2 was 174.6. The set of 14 forecasts was predicted and correlation analysis between predicted and measured values was shown in Figure 2. The error analysis results was shown in Table 3.

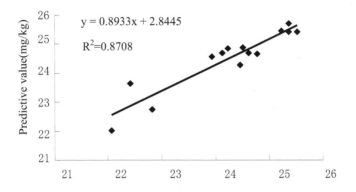

Measured values(mg/kg)

**Fig. 2.** Relationship between chemical analysis values and prediction values of SOM

**Table 3.** Prediction results for SOM by LS-SVM model

| Sample No. | Measured values | Predictive value | Absolute error | Relative error |
|---|---|---|---|---|
| 1 | 22.07 | 22.02 | -0.05 | -0.25 |
| 2 | 23.93 | 24.56 | 0.63 | 2.63 |
| 3 | 25.53 | 25.42 | -0.11 | -0.43 |
| 4 | 25.22 | 25.47 | 0.25 | 0.99 |
| 5 | 25.37 | 25.70 | 0.33 | 1.29 |
| 6 | 24.24 | 24.84 | 0.60 | 2.50 |
| 7 | 25.37 | 25.44 | 0.07 | 0.27 |
| 8 | 24.62 | 24.69 | 0.08 | 0.31 |
| 9 | 24.46 | 24.29 | -0.17 | -0.72 |
| 10 | 22.42 | 23.64 | 1.22 | 5.48 |
| 11 | 22.83 | 22.75 | -0.08 | -0.38 |
| 12 | 24.77 | 24.67 | -0.10 | -0.41 |
| 13 | 24.50 | 24.90 | 0.40 | 1.62 |
| 14 | 24.12 | 24.69 | 0.57 | 2.33 |

The coefficient of determination of prediction set between the predicted value and the measured values was 0.8708. The maximum absolute error of soil organic matter was 1.23mg/kg, and the average absolute of relative error was1.09%.

### 3.2.3    The Predictive Models of Soil Available N Based on Least Squares Vector Machines (LS-SVM)

The LS-SVM model was established with 6 principal components as an input layer and measured values of soil organic matter as output layer. Hyper-parameters gam and the RBF kernel parameter sig2 were obtained by grid search method with cross-validation, The optimal combination of two parameters were obtained that gam was 13.5, and sig2 was 17.0. The set of 14 forecasts was predicted and correlation analysis between predicted and measured values was shown in Figure 3. The error analysis results was shown in Table 4.

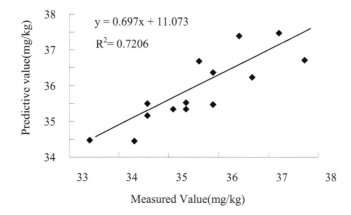

**Fig. 3.** Relationship between chemical analysis values and prediction values of available N

The coefficient of determination of prediction set between the predicted value and the measured values was 0.7206. The maximum absolute error of soil organic matter was 1.92mg/kg, and the average absolute of relative error was 1.06%.

### 3.2.4    The Predictive Models of Soil Available P Based on Least Squares Vector Machines (LS-SVM)

The LS-SVM model was established that 6 principal components as an input layer and measured values of soil organic matter as output layer. Hyper-parameters gam and the RBF kernel parameter sig2 were obtained by grid search method with cross-validation, The optimal combination of two parameters were obtained that gam was 47.7, and sig2 was 153.3. The set of 14 forecasts was predicted and correlation analysis between predicted and measured values was shown in Figure 4. The error analysis results was shown in Table 5.

**Table 4.** Prediction results for available N by LS-SVM model

| Sample No. | Measured values | Predictive value | Absolute error | Relative error |
|---|---|---|---|---|
| 1 | 33.40 | 34.47 | 1.07 | 3.20 |
| 2 | 34.57 | 35.16 | 0.59 | 1.70 |
| 3 | 34.57 | 35.49 | 1.92 | 5.55 |
| 4 | 36.67 | 36.24 | -0.43 | -1.17 |
| 5 | 35.36 | 35.35 | -0.01 | -0.02 |
| 6 | 35.36 | 35.54 | -0.82 | -2.32 |
| 7 | 35.62 | 36.68 | 1.06 | 2.97 |
| 8 | 35.10 | 35.34 | 0.24 | 0.68 |
| 9 | 35.88 | 35.47 | -0.41 | -1.16 |
| 10 | 34.31 | 34.45 | 0.14 | 0.42 |
| 11 | 35.88 | 36.38 | 1.50 | 4.17 |
| 12 | 37.72 | 36.71 | -1.01 | -2.67 |
| 13 | 37.20 | 37.48 | 0.28 | 0.75 |
| 14 | 36.41 | 37.40 | 0.99 | 2.73 |

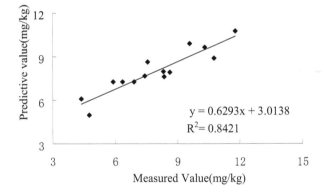

$$y = 0.6293x + 3.0138$$
$$R^2 = 0.8421$$

**Fig. 4.** Relationship between chemical analysis values and prediction values of available P

The coefficient of determination of prediction set between the predicted value and the measured values was 0.8421. The maximum absolute error of soil organic matter was 1.71mg/kg, and the average absolute of relative error was 4.08%.

**Table 5.** Prediction results for available P by LS-SVM model

| Sample No. | Measured values | Predictive value | Absolute error | Relative error |
|---|---|---|---|---|
| 1 | 8.36 | 7.62 | -0.74 | -8.85 |
| 2 | 5.89 | 7.29 | 1.40 | 23.73 |
| 3 | 4.37 | 6.08 | 2.71 | 62.10 |
| 4 | 4.75 | 5.00 | 0.25 | 5.31 |
| 5 | 7.41 | 7.68 | -1.73 | -23.34 |
| 6 | 8.61 | 8.93 | -0.68 | -7.85 |
| 7 | 8.30 | 8.00 | -0.30 | -3.56 |
| 8 | 6.33 | 7.25 | 0.92 | 14.60 |
| 9 | 7.54 | 8.66 | 1.12 | 14.82 |
| 10 | 11.78 | 10.76 | -2.02 | -17.19 |
| 11 | 9.59 | 9.90 | 1.31 | 13.61 |
| 12 | 6.90 | 7.27 | 0.37 | 5.30 |
| 13 | 10.32 | 9.66 | -0.66 | -6.37 |
| 14 | 10.77 | 8.90 | -1.87 | -17.41 |

### 3.2.5    The Predictive Models of Soil Available K Based on Least Squares Vector Machines (LS-SVM)

The LS-SVM model was established with 6 principal components as an input layer and measured values of soil organic matter as output layer. Hyper-parameters gam and the RBF kernel parameter sig2 were obtained by grid search method with cross-validation, The optimal combination of two parameters were obtained that gam was 615.9, and sig2 was 153.3. The set of 14 forecasts was predicted and correlation analysis between predicted and measured values was shown in Figure 5. The error analysis results was shown in Table 6.

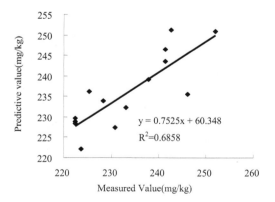

**Fig. 5.** Relationship between chemical analysis values and prediction values of available K

**Table 6.** Prediction results for available K by LS-SVM model

| Sample No. | Measured values | Predictive value | Absolute error | Relative error |
|---|---|---|---|---|
| 1 | 225.43 | 236.15 | 10.72 | 4.75 |
| 2 | 223.65 | 222.17 | -1.48 | -0.66 |
| 3 | 222.47 | 228.34 | 5.87 | 2.64 |
| 4 | 233.12 | 232.23 | -0.89 | -0.38 |
| 5 | 230.75 | 227.41 | -3.34 | -1.45 |
| 6 | 242.58 | 251.20 | -14.36 | -5.92 |
| 7 | 228.38 | 233.93 | 5.55 | 2.43 |
| 8 | 222.47 | 229.64 | 7.17 | 3.22 |
| 9 | 222.47 | 228.81 | 6.34 | 2.85 |
| 10 | 241.40 | 243.60 | 10.20 | 4.23 |
| 11 | 246.13 | 235.61 | -10.52 | -4.27 |
| 12 | 237.85 | 239.10 | 1.25 | 0.52 |
| 13 | 252.05 | 250.98 | -1.07 | -0.43 |
| 14 | 241.4 | 246.43 | 5.03 | 2.08 |

The coefficient of determination of prediction set between the predicted value and the measured values is 0.6858. The maximum absolute error of soil organic matter was 10.72mg/kg, and the average absolute of relative error was 0.69%.

There are been a few attempts to predict variables related to the soil by NIR reflectance spectroscopy. Good predictions($0.81<R2<0.90$) were obtained for exchangeable calcium and magnesium, water soluble carbon, water holding capacity and urease activity (ZORNOZA,et al,.2008). The prediction of K, P and Na was classified as good(R2pre=0.68-0.74 and RPD=1.77–1.94), where quantitative predictions were considered possible. It is recommended to adopt BPNN-LVs modeling technique for higher accuracy measurement of the selected soil properties with vis–NIR spectroscopy, in comparison with PCR, PLS and BPNN-PCs modeling techniques(A.M.Mouazen,et al,.2010).

# 4    Results and Discussion

(1) The least squares support vector machine model of soil organic matter, available nitrogen, phosphorus, available potassium were established using principal component analysis, and predicted results are verified that the coefficient of determination of soil organic matter was 0.8708 and the average absolute of relative error was 1.09%. It's proved that the method is feasible to predict the soil organic matter content.

(2) The coefficient of determination of prediction model of soil available nitrogen and available potassium were 0.7206 and 0.6858 by Near-infrared spectroscopy, and the

average of relative error were 1.06% and 0.69%. The predicted error of those models was small, but the coefficient of determination was not high. The coefficient of determination of soil phosphorus was 0.8421 and the average of relative error was 4.08%, the correlation between measured and predicted was high and the relative error was large.The prediction for the content of soil available nitrogen, phosphorus and potassium by Near-infrared spectroscopy is feasible and practical.

**Acknowledgements.** This study was supported by Research Fund for the Doctoral Program of Higher Education (20101403110003) and Science & technology project of Shanxi (2007031109-2).

# References

Ben-Dor, E., Banin, A.: Near-infrared analysis as a rapid method to simultaneously evaluate several soil properties. Soil Science of American Journal 59, 364–372 (1995)

Bernard, G., Barthe, D., Brunet, B.R., et al.: Near infrared reflectance spectroscopy (NIRS) could be used for characterization of soil nematode community. Soil Biology & Biochemistry 43, 1649–1659 (2011)

Brunet, D., Barthes, B.G., Chotte, J.L., Feller, C.: Determination of carbon and nitrogen contents in Alfisols, Oxisols and Ultisols from Africa and Brazil using NIRS analysis: Effects of sample grinding and set heterogeneity. Geoderma 139, 106–117 (2007)

Chang, C., Laird, D.A., Mausbach, M.J., et al.: Near-infrared reflectance spectroscopy-principal components regression analyses of soil properties. Soil Science of American Journal 65, 480–490 (2001)

Chang, C.W., Laird, D.A.: Near-infrared reflectance spectroscopic analysis of soil C and N. Soil Science 167, 110–116 (2002)

Dalal, R.C., Henry, R.J., et al.: Simultaneous determination of moisture,organic carbon and total nitrogen by near infrared reflectance spectrophotometry. Soil Science Society of America Journal 50, 120–123 (1986)

He, Y., Song, H., Pereira, A.G., Gómez, A.H.: A New Approach to Predict N, P, K and OM Content in a Loamy Mixed Soil by Using Near Infrared Reflectance Spectroscopy. In: Huang, D.-S., Zhang, X.-P., Huang, G.-B. (eds.) ICIC 2005. LNCS, vol. 3644, pp. 859–867. Springer, Heidelberg (2005)

Lee, W.S., Sanchez, J.F., Mylavarapu, R.S., et al.: Estimating chemical properties of Florida soil using spectral reflectance. Transactions of the ASAE 46(5), 1443–1453 (2003)

Li, W., Zhang, S.H., Zhang, Q., et al.: Rapid prediction of available N,P and K content in soil using near-infrared reflectance spectroscopy. Transactions of the Chinese Society of Agricultural Engineering 23(1), 55–59 (2007)

Ludwig, B., Khanna, P.K., Bauhus, J., Hopmans, P.: Near infrared spectroscopy of forest soils to determine chemical and biological properties related to soil sustainability. Forest Ecology and Management 171, 121–132 (2002)

Luo, X., Zang, Y., Zhou, Z.: Research progress in farming information acquisition technique for precision agriculture. Transactions of the Chinese Society of Agricultural Engineering 22(1), 167–173 (2006)

Morra, M.J., Hall, M.H., Freeborn, L.L.: Carbon and nitrogen analysis of soil fractions using near-infrared reflectance spectroscopy. Soil Science Society of America Journal 55, 288–291 (1991)

Mouaze, A.M., Kuang, B., Baerdemaeker, J.D., et al.: Comparison among principal component, partial least squares and back propagation neural network analyses for accuracy of measurement of selected soil properties with visible and near infrared spectroscopy. Geoderma 158, 23–31 (2010)

Sha, J.M., Chen, P.C., Chen, S.L.: Characteristics Analysis of Soil Spectrum Response Resulted From Organic Material. Research of Soil and Water Conservation 10(2), 21–24 (2003)

Sudduth, K.A., Hummel, J.: Soil organic matter, CEC and moisture sensing with a portable NIR spectrophotometer. Transactions of the ASAE 36(6), 1571–1582 (1993)

Zornoza, R., Guerrero, C., Mataix-Solera, J., et al.: Near infrared spectroscopy for determination of various physical, chemical and biochemical properties in Mediterranean soils. Soil Biology & Biochemistry 40, 1923–1930 (2008)

Wu, Y.Z., Tian, Q.J., Ji, J.F., et al.: Soil Remote Sensing Research Theory Method and Application. Remote Sensing Information (1), 40–47 (2003)

Yu, F.J., Min, S.G., Ju, X.T., et al.: Determination the content of nitrogen and organic substance in dry soil by using near infrared diffusion reflectance spectroscopy. Chinese Journal of Analysis Laboratory 21(3), 49–51 (2002)

Zhu, D., Wu, D., Song, H., et al.: Determination of organic matter contents and pH values of soil using near infrared spectroscopy. Transactions of the Chinese Society of Agricultural Engineering 24(6), 196–199 (2008)

# Large System Multi-objective Model of Optimal Allocation for Water Resources in Jiansanjiang Branch Bureau[*]

Ping Lv and Dong Liu[**]

School of Water Conservancy & Civil Engineering, Northeast Agricultural University,
Harbin Heilongjiang 150030, China
pingping.85@163.com, liu72dong@126.com

**Abstract.** According to the imbalance development and utilization of water resources, water shortages and other issues in Sanjiang Plain, taking Jiansanjiang branch bureau as an example, the multi-objective optimal allocation model of water resources is established with goal of maximum economic and social benefits. Only surface water, groundwater and transit water are considered overall and different water demands in industry, life and agriculture are satisfied can we realize the rational allocation of regional water resources. The large system decomposition-coordination theory and multi-objective genetic algorithm are applied to solve the model. The optimization results showed that, the water shortage situation in Jiansanjiang branch bureau is improved in planning years and surface water supply capacity can be increased gradually and groundwater resources can be effectively protected. The optimal allocation model and solution method are effective and feasible, and the optimal allocation results are reasonable. The research can provide scientific basis for rational development and utilization of water resources in Jiansanjiang branch bureau and Sanjiang Plain.

**Keywords:** Jiansanjiang branch bureau, optimal allocation of water resources, multi-objective genetic algorithm, large system decomposition-coordination.

## 1 Introduction

Optimal allocation of water resources refers to the scientific and rational allocation of limited and different forms water resources, with both engineering and non-engineering measures in a particular watershed or region. The purpose is to achieve the sustainable utilization of water resources, to coordinate the benefit conflict between each region and water use department, to improve the regional overall water consumption efficiency as much as possible[1] , to ensure the harmonious development of social economy, resources and ecological environment to get the biggest integrative benefit which including economic, environmental and social benefits and other goals.

---

[*] Main research direction is agriculture and water resources system analysis and optimal using.
[**] Corresponding author.

D. Li and Y. Chen (Eds.): CCTA 2011, Part I, IFIP AICT 368, pp. 336–345, 2012.
© IFIP International Federation for Information Processing 2012

Jiansanjiang branch bureau locates in northeast of Heilongjiang Province and belongs to Sanjiang Plain, which is an important grain production area in China. The total area is 12300km$^2$[2], with cultivated acreage of 682000hm$^2$[3], and the main grain crop is paddy. In recent years, the paddy is planted in mostly field as the economic benefits, then the demand of water resources for irrigation is increasing rapidly. The issues such as over-exploitation of groundwater and imbalance utilization of groundwater-surface water are serious in several areas[4]. It is necessary to optimize the water resources scientifically and reasonably, in order to utilize the limited water resources legitimately and develop sustainable agricultural and improve utilization efficiency of water resources.

As the complexity of water resources system and multi-objective optimization problem, the traditional planning methods are difficult to solve such problems. The genetic algorithm has been considered to be the most suitable method for multi-objective optimization[5], so large system decomposition coordination theory and multi-objective genetic algorithm are introduced into the solution of water resources optimal allocation model in this article.

# 2    The Establishing of Multi-objective Model of Optimal Allocation

## 2.1    Description of the Decision Variables

The regional water source which based on the water delivery range can be classifying into public and independent water sources two types. Public water source simultaneously supplies water to two or more subareas, such as mainstream transit water. Independent water source only supplies water to its own subareas, such as local interval runoff and groundwater[6].

Assuming that there are $K$ subareas and $M$ public water sources in the regional water resources system, and $C(k)$ independent water sources in $k$ subarea[7, 8]. So $k$ subarea has $I(k)=C(k)+M$ water supply sources. Define $R^k = \left( r_{ij}^k \right)_{m \times n}$, the supply and demand relationship matrix between water sources and users in $k$ subarea; $r_{ij}^k$, the supply-demand relation coefficient between water sources and users in the subarea, $i=1$ to $m$, different water supply sources; $j=1$ to $n$, different water use departments. $r_{ij}^k =1$ when there is the supply-demand relationship between the water source $i$ and the user $j$, otherwise $r_{ij}^k =0$.

Referring the water supply quantity $x_{ij}$ from water source $i$ to user $j$ as the decision variable, then the decision variable in $k$ subarea is described as follow:

$$X^k = \begin{bmatrix} x_{11}^k & x_{12}^k & \cdots & x_{1,J(k)}^k \\ x_{21}^k & x_{22}^k & \cdots & x_{2,J(k)}^k \\ \vdots & \vdots & \ddots & \vdots \\ x_{I(k),1}^k & x_{I(k),2}^k & \cdots & x_{I(k),J(k)}^k \end{bmatrix} \qquad (1)$$

Where, $I(k)$,  the number of water supply sources in $k$ subarea; $J(k)$, the number of water use departments(including domestic, industrial, agricultural and other departments)in $k$ subarea.

$x_{ij}^k$ is corresponding to the coefficient $r_{ij}^k$. $r_{ij}^k$ =0, water source $i$ does not supply water to department $j$ in $k$ subarea, so $x_{ij}^k$ =0; $r_{ij}^k$ =1, water source $i$ supplies water to department $j$ in $k$ subarea, then $x_{ij}^k \geq 0$.

## 2.2     Objective Function

The article follows the regional sustainable development ideology, taking the regional economic and social benefits as goals to establish the optimal allocation model[9-11].

(1) Economic goal. The economic net benefits produced by different water use departments of region are maximum in the target year.

$$\max f_1(x) = \max \sum_{k=1}^{K} \sum_{j=1}^{J(k)} \sum_{i=1}^{I(k)} (b_{ij}^k - c_{ij}^k) x_{ij}^k \alpha_i^k \beta_j^k \tag{2}$$

Where,  $x_{ij}^k$, the water supply quantity from water source $i$ to user $j$ in $k$ subarea $(10^4 \text{m}^3)$; $b_{ij}^k$, the benefit coefficient of water supply from water source $i$ to user $j$ in $k$ subarea $(10^4 \text{Yuan/ m}^3)$; $c_{ij}^k$,  the cost coefficient of water supply from water source $i$ to user $j$ in $k$ subarea $(10^4 \text{Yuan/ m}^3)$; $\alpha_i^k$,  the water supply order coefficient of water source $i$ in $k$ subarea; $\beta_j^k$,  the water use fair coefficient of user $j$ in $k$ subarea.

(2) Social goal. The total water shortage quantity of region is minimum in the target year.

$$\max f_2(x) = -\min \sum_{k=1}^{K} \sum_{j=1}^{J(k)} \left( D_j^k - \sum_i^{I(k)} x_{ij}^k \right) \tag{3}$$

Where,  $D_j^k$, the water demand quantity of user $j$ in $k$ subarea $(10^4 \text{m}^3)$.

## 2.3     Constraints

The constraints of water resources optimal allocation model is mainly considering the water supply capacity constraints of water supply system and water demand capacity constraints of water use system of region.

(1)     Water supply constraints

Public water source: 
$$\begin{cases} \sum_{j=1}^{J(k)} x_{mj}^k \leq W_m^k \\ \sum_{k=1}^{K} W_m^k \leq W_m \end{cases} \tag{4}$$

Independent water source: $\sum_{j=1}^{J(k)} x_{cj}^k \leq W_c^k$ \hfill (5)

Where, $x_{mj}^k$ and $x_{cj}^k$, the water supply quantity form public water source $m$ and independent water source $c$ to user $j$ in $k$ subarea ($10^4 m^3$); $W_m^k$ and $W_c^k$, the water supply capacity of public water source $m$ and independent water source $c$ in $k$ subarea ($10^4 m^3$); $W_m$, the water supply capacity of public water source $m$ ($10^4 m^3$).

(2)    Water demand constraints

$$L_j^k \leq \sum_{i=1}^{I(k)} x_{ij}^k \leq H_j^k \tag{6}$$

Where, $L_j^k$ and $H_j^k$, the lower and the upper limit of water demand department $j$ in $k$ subarea ($10^4 m^3$).

(3)    Nonnegative variable constraints

$$x_{ij}^k \geq 0 \tag{7}$$

# 3    Mode Solution

## 3.1    The Process of Large System Decomposition-Coordination

Large system decomposition-coordination theory can be applied to establish the large system multi-object optimal allocation model for above large-scale water resources system with multi-source and multi-user[12]. According to the theory of large system decomposition-coordination and the actual condition of water resources supply and demand, two-stage hierarchical multi-objective optimization model is established[13]. The related constraint variables also are the regional public water resources are allocated in advance which make the system divided into $K$ independent subsystems by the model coordination method. Then the distribution amount is coordinated repeatedly until the best integrated goal of system is achieved (Figure.1).

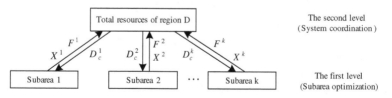

**Fig. 1.** The level transfer decomposition-coordination structure of water resources optimal allocation

Figure.1 shows that the model after large system decomposition-coordination is actually going to achieve two-level optimizations, which are the allocation of water sources between different users in each subarea and water quantity between subareas[14].

(1) The optimization of first level subsystem

The region is divided into $K$ subareas based on the natural geographical or administrative conditions in the first level. Each subarea optimize inside independently, under the premise of a given water resources amount from the second level (coordination level), which satisfied $\sum_{k=1}^{K} D_c^k = W_c$. The optimization of subarea is still a multi-objective optimal allocation model which solved by accelerated multi-object genetic algorithm. The internal optimal solution in each subarea and the corresponding fitness value are not necessarily the best balanced solution of region. Therefore, we need to feed back the optimal solution $X^k(D_c^k)$ and the target value $F^k(X^k, D_c^k)$ in each subarea that got from the first level to the second level, and do the second level system coordination.

(2) The coordination of second level system

The task of the second level coordination is to get the optimal allocation of public resources in subareas, to coordinate the partial optimal solution of each subarea to find the best balanced solution of the entire region. The solution of the second level coordination is still solved by accelerated multi-object genetic algorithm. The main steps are as follows:

① Producing the pre-allocated resources $D_c^k$, and transferring them to each subarea in the first level.

② Optimizing the first level subsystem, and getting the feedback value of the first level.

③ Doing the genetic operation based on the feedback information, and getting the new pre-allocated project.

④ Cycle calculation until the solution satisfied the termination requirement or the number of evolution generation, and getting the optimal allocation of water resources.

## 3.2    Multi-objective Genetic Algorithm

The genetic algorithm does not require the problem with the requirements of linearity, continuation, convexity and others, and it has high computation efficiency, global search ability and strong robustness[15,16] compared with other traditional algorithms. The population in genetic algorithm is made up of individuals, in which each individual corresponds to a basic water supply allocation program in the water resources system. The size of population is determined by the number of individuals. The greater the population or the more individuals, the more pre-allocated programs.

According to the features of water resources multi-objective optimization, the calculation method of fitness that based on the sort in the paper only depends on the multi-objective itself. Therefore, we can rank all individuals in the population separately by their responds to different objective functions, and calculate the total fitness. Thus, an individual in the genetic algorithm population is a allocation program of water resources, and each program reflects multi-objective function values[17].

$f(i)$ ($i=1$ to $n$) stands for the objective function, $n$ is the number of target, $N$ is the total number of individual. For each goal $i$, every individual will generate a sorting sequence $\vec{X}_i$ of feasible solution based on the quality of function value. The overall performance of individuals to all objective functions can be got after sorting each goal. According to the sorting of the individual calculated the fitness:

$$F_i(X_j) = \begin{cases} (N - Y_i(X_j))^2 & Y_i(X_j) > 1; \\ kN^2 & Y_i(X_j) = 1; \end{cases} \quad i = 1,2,\cdots,n \tag{8}$$

$$F(X_j) = \sum_{i=1}^{n} F_i(X_j) \quad j = 1,2,\cdots,n \tag{9}$$

Where, $n$, the total number of objective function; $N$, the total individual number; $X_j$, the individual $j$ of the population; $Y_i(X_j)$, the serial number of $X_j$ to the target $i$ in the population; $F_i(X_j)$, the fitness of $X_j$ to target $I$; $F(X_j)$, the comprehensive fitness of $X_j$ to all targets; $K$, a constant between 1 and 2, which is used to increase the fitness when the function value of individual is optimal.

The above formula shows that, the better the individual represent the greater fitness it will get, and acquire more opportunities of involving in the evolution[18]. The individual that has the optimal overall performance is the best program for the multi-objective function in all solutions.

# 4    Case Study

## 4.1    Model Parameters

Jiansanjiang branch bureau is divided into 15 subareas according to its administrative division of farms, they are Farm Bawujiu, Shengli, Qixing, Qindeli, Daxing, Qinglongshan, Qianjin, Chuangye, Hongwei, Qianshao, Qianfeng, Honghe, Yalvhe, Erdaohe and Nongjiang. Each subarea has groundwater, surface water and transit water three forms of water sources. Groundwater and surface water are independent water sources, and transit water is public water sources. In this plan, we only consider domestic, agricultural and industrial water use departments. The planning years are 2010, 2015 and 2020.

In this plan, in order to protect local limited groundwater resources, to improve ecological environment, we should gradually control the exploitation of groundwater and improve the utilization of surface water resources. Therefore conforming the groundwater exploitation extent of each farm are 50%(moderate intensity), 40%(moderate intensity) and 30%(moderate intensity), and the supply of surface water are 10%, 15% and 20% of the multi-year average surface water resources. Heilong River and Ussuri River are the main transit water resources in the region, in the future, Heilong River can supply water $11.98\times10^8 m^3$, $12.41\times10^8 m^3$ and $12.84\times10^8 m^3$, and Ussuri River can supply $5.15\times10^8 m^3$, $5.27\times10^8 m^3$ and $5.39\times10^8 m^3$.

The industrial and domestic water demand are calculated according to the development goals of production value, industrial water use quota, the development scale of population and the per capita water use quota. The agricultural water demand is calculated based on the irrigation quota, the area of crops and the utilization coefficients of irrigation water.

## 4.2     Results and Analysis

The calculation parameters of genetic algorithm are as follows: the population size $N=200$, the crossover probability $P_c=0.8$, mutation probability $P_m=0.2$, the random number of mutation direction required $M=10$ and the acceleration times $C_i=10$.

Due to the length limitations, the water resources optimal allocation results of Farm Qixing in the future years are listed only in this article (Table 1).

**Table 1.** The water resources optimal allocation results of Farm Qixing (Unit: $10^4 m^3$)

| Year | Water consumption department | Ground water | Surface water | Transit water | Water supply | Water demand | Water shortage |
|---|---|---|---|---|---|---|---|
| 2010 | Domestic water | 191.47 | 53.92 | 1.73 | 247.13 | 247.36 | 0.23 |
| | Agricultural water | 7192.10 | 699.23 | 20790.00 | 28681.33 | 29012.04 | 330.71 |
| | Industrial water | 46.42 | 47.00 | 64.47 | 157.89 | 159.19 | 1.30 |
| | Total | 7429.99 | 800.15 | 20856.20 | 29086.34 | 29418.60 | 332.26 |
| 2015 | Domestic water | 239.18 | 16.36 | 16.52 | 272.07 | 272.18 | 0.11 |
| | Agricultural water | 5684.50 | 1067.35 | 21363.00 | 28114.85 | 28345.23 | 230.38 |
| | Industrial water | 22.87 | 121.41 | 55.06 | 199.34 | 199.72 | 0.38 |
| | Total | 5946.55 | 1205.12 | 21434.59 | 28586.26 | 28817.13 | 230.87 |
| 2020 | Domestic water | 278.47 | 24.43 | 4.91 | 307.81 | 307.82 | 0.01 |
| | Agricultural water | 4055.10 | 1497.90 | 22045.00 | 27598.00 | 27667.85 | 69.85 |
| | Industrial water | 124.76 | 79.81 | 33.07 | 237.64 | 237.91 | 0.27 |
| | Total | 4458.33 | 1602.15 | 22082.97 | 28143.45 | 28213.57 | 70.12 |

Table 1 shows that, along with the population growth and socio-economic development, domestic and industrial water supply both represent the trend of steady increase, agricultural water supply decreased each year in Farm Qixing. The variation trend is same as the water demand prediction.

The water sources supply structure of each water use department shows that, domestic water is mainly supplied by groundwater, agricultural and industrial water supply are shared by groundwater, surface water and transit water. In this allocation, transit water resources gradually assume the most water demand, which remits the shortage situation of groundwater supply and protect the local groundwater resources effectively.

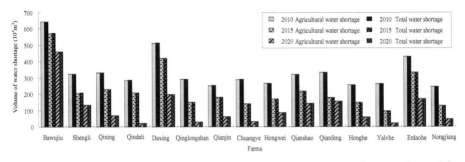

**Fig. 2.** The comparison between agricultural water shortage and total water shortage in Jiansanjiang branch bureau in future years

Under the condition of total water supply can not satisfied the demand, agricultural water shortage is the main representation (Figure.2). The reasons on the one hand, the paddy area is increasing massively to meet the food production demand, but the water supply cannot quickly satisfy the irrigation water requirements. On the other hand, the quantity and quality of irrigation and water conservancy facilities cannot follow the increment speed of irrigation water demand.

From the comparison results of water shortages we can see that, along with the gradually constructing of water conservancy project, the condition of water shortage improving gradually, and the volume of water shortage decreasing yearly.

## 5     Conclusions

This paper considering the multi-object character in the optimization of water resources system, established the water resources system multi-objective optimization model in Jiansanjiang branch bureau, taking the economic and social maximum benefits as the objective function, the water supply capacity, water demand capacity of water use system and variable non-negative as the constraints. The large system decomposition-coordination theory is applied and the model is solved by the real coding based accelerating genetic algorithm, the water resources optimal allocation results of each water use department in 2010, 2015 and 2020 are obtained.

The optimization results show that, the condition of water shortage improving gradually, the utilization efficiency of surface water resources is increasing and the local groundwater resources are effectively protected in planning years. Thus the optimal allocation model and solution method are effective and feasible, and the optimal allocation results are reasonable. The results can support scientific evidence for water resources optimization in Jiansanjiang branch bureau in the future.

On the other hand, the shortage of agriculture water is still severe. In order to solve this problem, we should control the growth rate of paddy planting, increase the utilization efficiency of irrigation water and reduce the irrigation quota.

**Acknowledgments.** Thanks to the support of the National Natural Science Foundation of China (No.41071053), Postdoctoral Science Foundation of China (No.20080440832), Postdoctoral Science Foundation Special Funds of China (No.201003410), Specialized Research Foundation of Colleges and Universities Doctoral Program (No.20102325120009), National Natural Science Foundation of Heilongjiang Province (No.C201026), Science and Technology Research Project of the Education Bureau in Heilongjiang Province (No.11541024) and Doctoral Start-up Foundation of Northeast Agricultural University (No.2009RC37).

# References

1. Xu, X., Wang, H., Gan, H., et al.: Macro-economic water resources planning theory and method in North China. Yellow River Water Conservancy Press, Zhengzhou (1997)
2. Guo, L., Ma, K., Zhang, Y.: Landscape assessment on wetland degradation during thirty years in Jiansanjiang region of Sanjiang Plain, Northeast China. Acta Ecologica Sinica 29(6), 3126–3135 (2009)
3. Zhao, Q.: Research on the trend of underground water change in Jiansanjiang area based on gray prediction. Journal of Water Resources and Water Engineering 20(5), 128–130, 134 (2009)
4. Li, H., An, R., Wei, Y.: Applying of the GM(1,1) model to forecast the groundwater movement in Jiansanjiang land reclamation area. Journal of Agricultural Mechanization Research (3), 42–44 (2007)
5. Lu, X., Tan, Y.: Study on multi-objective genetic algorithm. Journal of Nanyang Teachers' College 3(9), 62–64 (2004)
6. Deng, C.: Study on model and it's application of regional water resources optimal allocation. Wuhan University, Wuhan (2005)
7. Smith, T.F., Waterman, M.S.: Identification of Common Molecular Subsequences. J. Mol. Biol. 147, 195–197 (1981)
8. Tang, D.: A model of multiobjective optimal allocation of water resources in Yellow River Basin. Journal of Hohai University (Natural Sciences) (1), 46–52 (1994)
9. Hei, B.: An optimum model of large scale system for optimum allocation of regional water resources. Journal of Wuhan University of Hydraulic and Electric Engineering (5), 110–118 (1988)
10. Hipel Keith, W.: Multiple Objective Decision Making in Water Resource. Water Resource Bulletin 28(1), 187–203 (1992)
11. Buras, N.: Operation of a Complex Water Resource Utilization System. In: Intern. Conf. Water for Peace, Washington D.C (1967)
12. Feng, S.: Multi-objective decision theory and application. Huazhong University of Science and Technology Press, Wuhan (1990)
13. Feng, S.: Water resources system engineering. Hubei Science and Technology Press, Wuhan (1991)

14. Hei, B., Zhou, L., Ma, X., et al.: Optimal allocation model of regional water resources based on genetic algorithm. Hydroelectric Energy 20(3), 10–12 (2002)
15. Chen, N., Li, Y., Xu, C.: Optimal deployment of water resources based on multi-objective genetic algorithm. Journal of Hydraulic Engineering 37(3), 308–313 (2006)
16. Yang, K., Zhang, J., Hu, T.: Application of genetic algorithms in identification of water production parameters. China Rural Water and Hydropower (8), 10–13 (2002)
17. Liu, X., Fu, Q., Cui, H., et al.: A large system decomposition coordination model of optimal operation on water resoures in Chahayang Irrigation District. China Rural Water and Hydropower (11), 15–18 (2008)
18. Chen, N.: Theory and practice of complex system water resources reasonable disposition. Xi'an University of Technology, Xi'an (2006)
19. You, J., Ji, C., Fu, X.: New method for solving multi-objective problem based on genetic algorithm. Journal of Hydraulic Engineering (3), 64–69 (2003)

# Research on Digital Agricultural Information Resources Sharing Plan Based on Cloud Computing[*]

Guifen Chen[1,**], Xu Wang[2], Hang Chen[1], Chunan Li[1],
Guangwei Zeng[1], Yan Wang[1], and Peixun Liu[1]

[1] College of Information and Technology Scince,
Jilin Agricultural University Chang Chun, 130118
[2] College of Computer Science and Technology,
Jilin University Chang Chun, 130012
guifchen@163.com

**Abstract.** In order to provide the agricultural works with customized, visual, multi-perspective and multi-level active service, we conduct a research of digital agricultural information resources sharing plan based on cloud computing to integrate and publish the digital agricultural information resources efficiently and timely. Based on cloud computing and virtualization technology, we establish a cloud computing server storage architecture, design deployment of server virtualization service, and present information resource sharing plan, so the users on different network environment could access to digital agricultural information resources at any time. Application examples demonstrate the use of cloud computing technology can provide heterogeneous resource sharing services for all agriculture-related facilities.

**Keywords:** cloud computing, digital agricultural, information sharing, virtualization.

## 1    Introduction

With the development of agricultural information, agricultural information websites have sprung up. But because of uneven geographical distribution, imperfect management system and other reasons, many sites did not play a real role[1].Digital agriculture as the representative of precision agriculture is an emerging discipline, the domestic service-oriented sites focusing on digital agricultural information and technology are very few and did not use advanced technologies, such as cloud computing, grids and others. They cannot become a professional, efficient, real-information services sites.

Cloud computing is presented in a commercial implementation of grid computing[2]. It is a low cost for providing vast amounts of data processing for many customers, and has important scientific value and commercial value in agricultural

---

[*] Foundation project: National"863"High-tech Project(2006AA10A309), National Spark Project(2008GA661003) and Changchun Technology Correspondent Project(2009245).
[**] Research direction: Expert Systems, Data Mining, Precision Agriculture.

D. Li and Y. Chen (Eds.): CCTA 2011, Part I, IFIP AICT 368, pp. 346–354, 2012.

information network construction. According to the current problems in construction of agricultural information website, this paper apply the storage structure of cloud computing server to digital agricultural information resources sharing, and analyze the Open Grid Services Architecture. On this basis, by using virtual machine way, we virtualize the cloud computing server, plan overall structure of grid and resource sharing model, and focus on the applications of virtualization technology in information sharing services. Through the existing server virtualization, only one or a few servers can be realized that requires multiple servers running the service, it significantly reduced the overall cost including hardware acquisition, maintenance investment, management investment and energy consumption. Virtualization technology allows hardware resources will be well allocated[3]. Virtualization technology automatically deploy the hardware resources for the service so that improving the effective of utilization. It also improve the stability and security, provide the service independently in the operating system and operating environment, and reduce management complexity. At the same time, the security and reliability are guaranteed. Even if a service fails, just for processing this virtual machine, and do not affect other services.

Based on the complexity of agricultural information, ever-changing environment and the status and features of cloud computing, with the applications of cloud computing, we proposed digital agricultural information resource sharing plan. It makes the further sharing of agricultural information resources and will play a more active and effective role for agricultural production decisions, agricultural extension, agricultural product sales and other information services.

## 2    Basic Theory

Cloud computing is first presented in 2006 Amazon's Elastic Compute Cloud, which uses virtual machine technology to provide low-cost network but better quality of service for users[4]. While cloud computing was not first proposed as efficient computational model, but it greatly promote the popularization of the Infrastructure-as-a-Service (IaaS).

### 2.1    Concepts

Cloud Computing is the fusion of Grid Computing, Distributed Computing, Parallel Computing, Utility Computing, Network Storage Technology, Virtualization, Load Balance and other traditional computer and network technology[5,6]. Narrow Cloud Computing is the delivery of IT infrastructure and usage patterns, refers to the network on-demand and scalable way to obtain the necessary resources (hardware, platform, software). Generalized Cloud computing refers to the broad service delivery and usage patterns, that is, by on-demand and scalable way, through the network to obtain the necessary services. Such services can be IT and software, related internet, you can also make any other services.

### 2.2    Features

The important idea of cloud computing is to connect a large number of computing resources with a unified network management and scheduling, to form a pool of computing resources on-demand services for users[7].The network providing resources is called "cloud". The resources in cloud are infinitely expanded in the user location, and can be obtained at any time, on-demand used, at any time extended and paid per use. This feature is often referred to as water and electricity as the use of IT infrastructure. Cloud computing break the traditional Internet sharing restrictions on the network and achieve a unified management of heterogeneous resources. According to the user's demand, the users do not perceive their own location and other details of the application, can obtain the corresponding services through the connected network.

### 2.3    Composition

Cloud computing model mainly consists of three parts: the client, the transmission network and the server [8]. The front-end user show is PC and other devices, which is known as a client and may not load the application. The middle transmission network includes a variety of wired and wireless network transmission facilities to implement the data transfer between the client and the server, while the users do not realize that the network exists. The server in cloud computing model is very important for cloud computing, operating system, application and services, the data users need are stored on the server, it can provide better service.

## 3    Research on Digital Agricultural Information Resources Sharing Plan

Combining the demand for agricultural information resource sharing with the features of cloud computing model, we designed a platform for digital agricultural information resources sharing plan, the overall platform framework are shown in Figure 1.

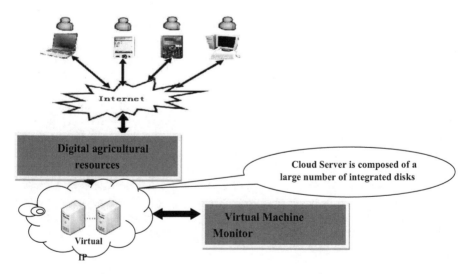

**Fig. 1.** The general framework for the platform of cloud computing

The server is built using the integrated hard disks, pre-stored a variety of operating platforms including operating system environment, applications and the corresponding digital information. The open source software XEN[9] implement the server virtualization, and build storage cloud of digital agricultural information resources. The platform has a good dynamic, scalability and flexibility. The server can timely publish information resources, the users can choose their own interest information resources, so that each user obtain and build the operating environment from the server to meet the demand for different information resources, to achieve the purpose of heterogeneous platforms.

## 3.1 Cloud Computing Server Storage Structure

In the process of building a cloud computing servers, we can use the large servers. Applying this approach, although the storage capacity meet the requirements of the users, the expense is relatively too much. With the expansion of hard disks capacity and the falling of hard disks prices on the market, we can integrate a lot of hard disks together and build a large capacity and low-cost server.

As the requests between users are isolated from each other, so the server can select the independent user to store relatively, the whole system can be extended to large scale. On the server side, we can distribute the digital agricultural information to multiple hard disks of multiple nodes, and allow users to read and write in multiple hard disks. We can handle redundant error information on the server in order to ensure user to access the safe and effective information.

## 3.2 Cloud Computing Server Virtualization

Through open source software XEN, we can implement the server virtualization and build storage cloud of digital agricultural information resources, the virtual configuration shown in Figure 2.

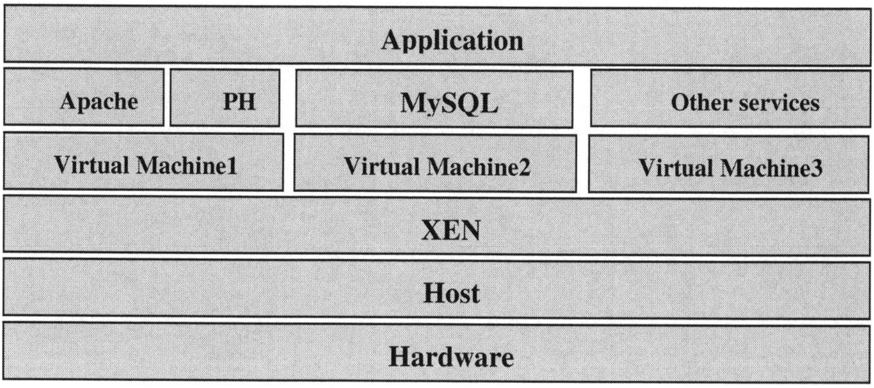

**Fig. 2.** The configuration diagram of virtualization

This structure need to configure three virtual machines running different services. Their functions are:

Virtual Machine1 is responsible for Http service, running Apache and PHP.
Virtual Machine2 is responsible for database services, using MySQL.
Virtual machine3 is responsible for other services, such as email servers, etc.

PHP is a script interpreter which run in the manner of Apache module, so Apache and PHP will be deployed in the same virtual machine at the same time.

### 3.3    Information Resource Sharing Plan

On the basis of these researches, we take retrieval module of digital agricultural information resources for example, and design digital agricultural information resources sharing services plan. Through virtualization technology the users can manage interface to search agricultural information. Although the information services from cloud in different locations[10], the user do not need to know the specific location of the distribution of the information. The information is completely transparent for users, which feel as easy as accessing the database on the local computer and publish the retrieved results in time. The process of resources retrieval and publication is shown in Figure 3.

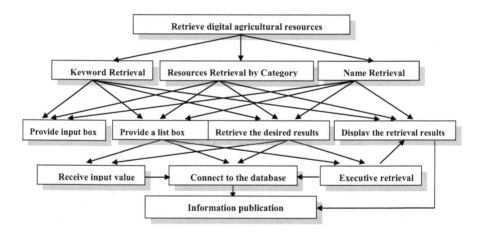

**Fig. 3.** The retrieval and publish of the resources

## 4    Application Examples

This paper apply digital agricultural information resources sharing plan based on cloud computing in Jilin digital agricultural information website construction. Jilin digital agricultural information website mainly consist of digital agricultural information vertical portal module, CA certificate management module, digital agricultural resources retrieval module, digital agricultural data analysis module, expert answers service module, personalized service module and agricultural BBS forum module.

The site uses the Linux operating system, cloud computing, virtualization technology and Mysql, Arcgis server database. It realizes communication of digital agricultural information resources and provides users with a unified and transparent services to achieve maximum resource sharing. System's main interface shown in Figure 4.

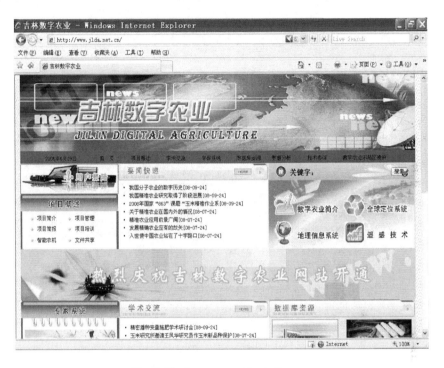

**Fig. 4.** The home page of website

Taking agricultural resources retrieval module and data analysis module for example, we illustrate the main functions of this site.

### 4.1    Agricultural Resources Retrieval Module

This module provides retrieval services of the resources, through the use of keyword retrieval, resource retrieval by category and name retrieval, the users can obtain the corresponding information. After the users submit a search condition, the system will implement retrieval process based on submitted information, and output the required information in a timely manner. The retrieval interface shown in Figure 5.

农业资源检索

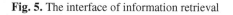

**Fig. 5.** The interface of information retrieval

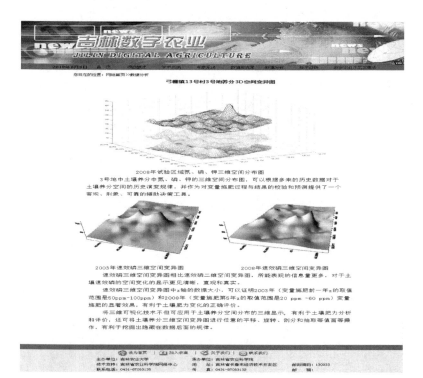

**Fig. 6.** The interface of data analysis

## 4.2     Data Analysis Module

This module can analyze the soil historical nutrient data such as nitrogen, phosphorus, potassium, organic matter, moisture and ph value, and generate two-dimensional and three-dimensional nutrient maps for many years. These maps can clearly, intuitively, really represent soil nutrients historical evolution, and provide objective and reliable decision support for the validation and prediction of variable rate fertilization process and results. Data analysis interface shown in Figure 6.

# 5     Conclusion

Through research on cloud computing and virtualization services, this paper present digital agricultural information resources sharing plan based on cloud computing. For the emerging field of digital agriculture, we establish a professional information resource sharing platform among agricultural enterprises, units, research staff and users. We also build a powerful polymeric platform of information resources retrieval, communication and sharing. The platform has a good dynamic, scalability and flexibility, the server can timely publish information resources, and the users can choose their own interest information resources. This paper has done the following work:

1.Using the integrated hard disks to build cloud computing servers, pre-stored a variety of different operating platforms, including operating system environment, applications and the corresponding digital agricultural information.

2.Utilizing a virtual machine, the open source software XEN implement the server virtualization, we build the efficient and low- cost virtual structure and storage cloud of digital agricultural information resources.

3.With the storage structure of cloud computing and virtual deployment, we design a cost-effective, high efficiency and easy to manage solution, achieve the sharing of agricultural information resources, and provide a personalized, visual, multi-prospective and multi-level active service model.

Our agriculture is focusing on the construction of agricultural information website. As the rapid development of agricultural sites in our country today, focusing on digital agricultural information resources sharing plan, establishing the authority of the agricultural information and providing services for agricultural employees, will be bound to do its due contribution for our agricultural development.

# References

1.  He, Y.-J., Zhang, J.-H.: Research on Operation Situation Development Strategy of Chinese Agricultural Information Website. Journal of Huazhong Agricultural University (Social Science Edition) 3(49), 12–14 (2003)
2.  Feng, D.-G., Zhang, M., Zhang, Y., Xu, Z.: Study on Cloud Computing Security. Journal of Software 22(1), 71–83 (2011)

3. Rosenthal, A., Mork, P., Li, M.H., Stanford, J., Koester, D., Reynolds, P.: Cloud computing: A new business paradigm for biomedical information sharing. Journal of Biomedical Informatics (43), 342–353 (2010)
4. Mateescua, G., Gentzsch, W., Ribbens, C.J.: Hybrid Computing—Where HPC meets grid and Cloud Computing. Future Generation Computer Systems 27, 440–453 (2011)
5. Zissis, D., Lekkas, D.: Addressing cloud computing security issues. Future Generation Computer Systems, 1–10 (2010)
6. Murphy, M.A., Goasguen, S.: Virtual Organization Clusters: Self-provisioned clouds on the grid. Future Generation Computer Systems (26), 1271–1281 (2010)
7. Vázquez, C., Huedo, E., Montero, R.S., Llorente, I.M.: On the use of clouds for grid resource provisioning. Future Generation Computer Systems (27), 600–605 (2011)
8. Chen, K., Zheng, W.-M.: Cloud Computing: System Instances and Current Research. Journal of Software 20(5), 1337–1348 (2009)
9. Li, Y.-Q., Song, Y., Huang, Y.-B.: A Memory Global Optimization Approach in Virtualized Cloud Computing Environments. Chinese Journal of Computers 34(4), 684–693 (2011)
10. Tian, G.-H., Meng, D., Zhan, J.-F.: Reliable Resource Provision Policy for Cloud Computing. Chinese Journal of Computers 33(10), 1859–1872 (2010)

# Mechanisms of Soil Aggregates Stability in Purple Paddy Soil under Conservation Tillage of Sichuan Basin, China

Xiaohong Tang[1,*], Youjin Luo[2], Jiake Lv[2], and Chaofu Wei[2]

[1] College of Urban and Rural Development, Sichuan Agricultural University,
611830 Sichuan, China
jianglj_2003@163.com

[2] College of Resource and Environment, Southwest University, 400716 Chongqing, China

**Abstract.** Ridge culture is a special conservation tillage method, but the long-term influence of this tillage system on soil aggregate-size stability in paddy fields is largely unknown in southwest of china. The objectives of this paper are to evaluate soil aggregates stability and to determine the relationship between SOC and soil aggregate stability. Soil samples at 0-20 cm layer were adopted from a long-term (16 yr) field experiment including conventional tillage: plain culture, summer rice crop and winter upland crop under drained conditions (PUR-r), and conservation tillage: ridge culture without tillage, summer rice and winter fallow with floodwater layer annually (NTR-f), and winter upland crop under drained conditions (NTR-r), and wide ridge culture without tillage, summer rice crop and winter upland crop under conditions (NTRw-r), respectively. The determination of aggregate-size stability distribution involves the assumptions that soil aggregates can be categorized in terms of their size and water stability (slaking resistance). Experimentally this procedure involves the slaked and capillary-wetted pretreatments; and a subsequent slaking treatment of aggregates >0.250 mm in size. WSMA and NMWD were applied to simulate the breakdown mechanisms of aggregates for studying soil stability based on aggregate resistance to slaking in paddy soil. The results showed that the amount of aggregates-size was greatly observed in the fraction of 2~6.72 mm under ridge culture in paddy soil (more than 50%) under slaking and capillary-wetting pretreatment. The proportion of soil macro-aggregates ($>0.25$ mm) in conservation tillage was greatly higher than that in conventional tillage under subsequent slaking treatment. Minimal differences of aggregate stability between slaking and wetting were observed, while significant differences were found between ridge culture and plain culture. The aggregates stability under slaking treatment ranked in the order of NTR-r $>$ NTRw-r $>$ NTR-f $>$ PUR-r, while under wetting was NTRw-r $>$ NTR-r $>$ NTR-f $>$ PUR-r, respectively. There was a positive correlation between the aggregates stability and SOC concentrations under wetting, and low correlation was observed under slaking pretreatment. Soil exposure with tillage and lack of rice/rape-seed stubble inputs caused declines in aggregation and organic carbon, both of which make soil susceptible to water erosion. Adoption of ridge culture with no-tillage

---

* Corresponding author.

D. Li and Y. Chen (Eds.): CCTA 2011, Part I, IFIP AICT 368, pp. 355–370, 2012.
© IFIP International Federation for Information Processing 2012

integrated with crop rotation and stubble mulch significantly alter soil organic concentration, suggesting it was a valuable conservation practice for soil aggregation and soil organic carbon sequestration on paddy soil.

**Keywords:** ridge culture, rotation, aggregate stability, organic carbon, paddy soil.

# 1    Introduction

Soil organic carbon (SOC) plays a crucial role in sustaining crop production and environmental soil services. A loss of SOC due to inappropriate land use or soil management practices can affect soil properties and lead to $CO_2$ emissions into atmosphere. On the other hand, appropriate land use and soil management can lead to an increase in SOC, improve soil properties and partially mitigate the rise in atmosphere $CO_2$ (Christensen, 1996; Lal and Kimble, 1997; Bernoux et al., 2006). Among the numerous strategies that permit sequestering atmospheric carbon in agroecosystems, ridge culture practices have been well documented (Halvorson et al., 2002; Franzluebbers, 2005). But the impacts of no-tillage practices on soil aggregates composition and its stability can vary drastically with soil properties and no-tillage practices (Puget et al., 1999; Bernoux et al., 2006). Conventional tillage systems enhance SOC mineralization; soil aeration and water fluctuation (Balesdent et al., 2000). Conventional tillage also can disrupt soil aggregates and expose physically protected SOC to microbial decomposition, decreasing SOC content and soil aggregate stability. Conversely, conservation tillage accumulate residues on the soil surface as much and reduce soil mixing and disturbance and promotes soil aggregation through enhanced binding of soil particle as a result of greater SOM content and. Soil aggregation can increase SOC storage by reducing loss by erosion and from mineralization (Paustian et al., 2000; Six et al., 2002a, 2002b). Soil organic matter (SOM) can be physically protected from microbial mineralization through sorption to clay minerals (Hassink et al., 1993; Beare et al., 1994a; 1994b) and enclosure within soil aggregates (Tisdall and Oades, 1980; 1982). Soil structure and soil organic matter (SOM) are two of the most dynamic properties that are extremely sensitive to crop and soil management. Soil aggregates are used for structural unit, which is a group of primary soil particles that cohere to each other more strongly than other surrounding particles. SOM is a major resource that links the chemical, physical and biological properties of soils, and is considered a major binding agent that stabilizes soil aggregates. Soil structure moderates soil and plant functions and is the framework for water, air, and nutrient flow to plants. Plants, in turn, furnish the soil with fresh residues and roots for aggregate structure development. The nature and properties of aggregates are thus determined by the quantity and quality of coarse residues and humus material and by the degree of their interaction with soil particles (Jastrow et al., 1996; Haynes and Francis, 1993; Elliott, 1986). Plant roots, Fungal hyphae, mycorrhizal hyphae, bacterial cells, and algae develop simultaneously with the growth of plant roots and build up a visible organic skeleton to enmesh the mineral particles by adsorption to form young macro-aggregates, and they are greatly affected by tillage operations (Tisdall and Oades, 1982). Polysaccharides or mineral colloid form bonds of micro-aggregates through cementation of carboxylic or hydroxide groups with polyvalent bridges (Puget et al., 2000; Kemper and Rosenau, 1984; Caron et al., 1992; Cambardella and Elliott, 1992.).

Soil aggregate stability is the result of complex interactions among biological, chemical, and physical processes in the soil (Tisdall and Oades, 1982). A close relationship between SOC and aggregate stability has been established for temperate and tropical soil (Six et al., 1998; 2002a, 2002b). Water-stable breakdown mechanisms of soil aggregates involve the slaked and capillary-wetted pretreatments, and slowly wetting pretreatments. The slaked pretreatment causes considerable disruption. When air-dried soil is submerged in water, the air that is trapped inside the soil pores is rapidly displaced with water. Weak aggregates are disrupted as a consequence of the sudden release of this large buildup of internal air pressure. In contrast, the wetting pretreatment before wet sieving produces minimal disruption, because misted aggregates do not buildup air pressure in the pores and the air escapes with minimal aggregate disruption (Cambardella and Elliott 1993a; 1993a; Chen, 1998; Gale et al., 2000; Li et al., 2006). Subsequent slaking can differentiate stable and unstable macro-aggregates (Marquez et al., 2004; Beare and Bruce, 1993).

Chongqing is mountainous, where most of rice fields are located at the foot of mountains. About half of rice fields are flooded permanently (Xie, 2002). The crop system of permanently flooded rice fields is, commonly, a single middle rice crop and in fallow with floodwater layer after rice harvesting. Ridge culture is an innovative approach to present permanently flooded rice fields from over reduced in redox potential due to permanently flooded. Fixed ridges are constructed about 30 cm wide, and rice plants and winter wheat plants (or oil-seed rape) were cultivated on both sides of the ridge without tillage instead of a single rice crop a year (Xie, 2002). All the changes involved in the innovative approach, such as changes from plain to ridge, from single middle rice crop to single middle rice crop and winter upland crop, and from permanently flooded to drainage in the winter crop season would improve soil conditions that influenced soil aggregates formation and transformation. Literature is replete with information on the effects of maturing, nutrient management, vegetative restoration, and tillage practices on the soil aggregates stability, and the combined effects of conservation tillage on the formation and stabilization of aggregates in purple paddy soil in related to SOC reservoir are limited (Diego et al., 2006; Li et al., 2004; Peng et al., 2004; Grandy et al., 2002). Therefore, a long-term field experiment was conducted to understand the mechanisms of soil aggregate stability under conservation tillage in a permanently flooded rice field with various treatments.

# 2    Materials and Methods

## 2.1    Site and Soil

Soil aggregates-size stability distribution measurement was conducted in a field experiment site (30°26′N, 106°26′E) set up in 1990 for comparison of nutrient cycling among convention (plain) culture and ridge culture with different crop systems of in the permanently flooded rice fields at the Experimental Farm of South-west China University, Chongqing (223 m elevation) (Gao et al., 2008). Annual average rainfall and temperature were 1105 mm with 70 % in May to September and 18.3 ℃, respectively. the annual sunshine time is 1,276 h; and the frost-free period is about 334 d. The soil is Hydragric Anthrosol developed from the parent material of Jurassic purple shale and sandstone weathering product. Soil particles and aggregates-size distribution were determined in the treatments with plain culture and ridge culture, which were described in detail as follows: (1) plain culture: one treatment of PUR-r was prepared. In PUR-r, the field was ploughed 3-5 days before rice transplanting and a floodwater layer was maintained during the rice crop season, but was drained in the winter crop season for winter crop growth. (2) Ridge culture: three treatments of NTR-f, NTR-r and NTRw-r were prepared. In NTR-f, a fixed ridge was conducted at about 30 cm wide, and rice plants were planted on both sides of the ridge with no tillage. Before rice transplanting, weeds grew in the winter crop season and rice stubbles remained from the previous rice plants were covered with mud in ditches nearby (table 1). Through this practice, the ridges could be maintained for a long time. Ditches between two ridges were filled with water to the level of 0-3 mm below the top of ridge during the rice-growing period. After rice harvesting, the field was in fallow and water level in ditches dropped to 5-10 cm below the ridge top in the winter crop season. In NTR-R, management for rice culture was the same as that for NTR-f. Winter crops were planted in both sides of ridge in the same way as for rice crop. Water in ditches was drained in the winter crop season. In NTRw-r, management for rice culture and winter crop was the same as that of NTR-r. The width of ridge was three times more than that of NTR-r (figure 1). Winter crop planted in the treatments of PUR-r, NTR-r and NTRw-r was winter wheat from 1990 to 1997 and oil-seed rape from 1998 to 2000 (Cai et al., 2003).

**Table 1.** Annual amount of rice crop residues and weeds to field under different tillage system kg hm$^{-2}$ y$^{-1}$

| Treatment | Straw (kg ha$^{-1}$ y$^{-1}$) | Rape residues (kg ha$^{-1}$ y$^{-1}$) | Weed (kg ha$^{-1}$ y$^{-1}$) |
|---|---|---|---|
| PUP-r | 3900 | 2880 | 1970 |
| NTR-f | 3250 | - | 2500 |
| NTR-r | 4775 | 1575 | 1725 |
| NTRw-r | 2750 | 2125 | 1900 |

The paddy soil of the experiment field was Eutric Cambisol derived from purple rock. Before the experiment started in 1990, soil organic carbon content was 13.0 ± 1.2 g kg$^{-1}$, soil pH was 6.91 ± 0.24, and clay (0.001 mm) content was 144.2 g kg$^{-1}$.

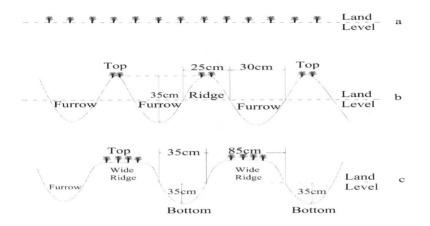

**Fig. 1.** The type of the bulletin for experimental culture (a: plain culture, b: ridge culture, c: wide ridge culture)

Chemical fertilizers were applied to all the plots at an equal rate in every rice-growing season, i.e. 273 kg urea ha-1, 500 kg superphosphate ha$^{-1}$, and 150 kg KCl ha$^{-1}$. Superphosphate was applied as basal fertilization, urea and KCl were applied as basal fertilization and topdressing. No exogenous organic manure was applied to each plot at a rate of about 20 t ha$^{-1}$, before rice transplanting. After rice harvesting, rice stubbles about 50~60 cm above ground stood in the field until incorporation into soil before the following period of rice transplanting. The treatment plots, with 4 m×5 m each, were arranged in a complete randomized block experimental design with four replications. Under ridge culture, obvious changes of primary properties in paddy soil were found after 16 years (Table 2). Clay contents significantly increased by 34%, 79% and 51% under NTR-f, NTR-r and NTRw-r compared to that under PUR-r, respectively. SOC content decreased under NTR-f (10.11%), while increased under NTR-r and NTRw-r (18.00% and 9.66%, respectively). Changes of soil porosity indicated that soil structure had been improved under long-term conservation tillage.

**Table 2.** Primary properties of paddy soil under long-term conservation tillage systems

| Treatment | Sand (%) | Silt (%) | Clay (%) | Organic C (g kg$^{-1}$) | Porosity (%) |
|---|---|---|---|---|---|
| PUP-r | 36.12 | 52.75 | 11.13 | 22.05 | 71 |
| NTR-f | 31.78 | 48.88 | 19.33 | 19.82 | 65 |
| NTR-r | 29.10 | 45.07 | 25.83 | 26.02 | 65 |
| NTRw-r | 31.72 | 46.55 | 21.73 | 24.18 | 59 |

## 2.2    Water-Stable Aggregates Separation

Soil samples were collected to assess SOC and aggregates stability in October 2006 (one and a half months after rice harvesting). Soil was sampled at 0-20 cm for aggregates stability and SOC. Six samples were collected from each subplot and mixed to produce a composite sample from each treatment and replicate. In the laboratory, Subsamples for SOC determination were air-dried and sieved through a 0.25 mm mesh. Subsamples for aggregates-size separation were air-dried and sieved through a nest of two sieves to collect all the aggregates with a diameter between 2 and 6.72 mm mesh sizes.

Wet sieving using air-dried 2-6.72 mm sieved soil isolated aggregate-size fraction. Two 100-g subsamples of air-dried soil were used to analyze the aggregate stability distribution. Two pretreatments are applied before wet sieving: air drying followed by rapid immersion in deionized water (slaked) and air drying plus capillary rewetting to field capacity plus 5% (capillary-wetted) in two 250 ml beaker (Six et al., 1998). Both subsamples were stored overnight in a refrigerator at 4°C before wet sieving. Aggregates were physically separated in four aggregate-size fractions: (1) large macro-aggregates 2-6.72 mm in diameter, (2) small macro-aggregates between 0.25 and 2 mm in diameter, (3) micro-aggregates between 0.053 and 0.25 mm in diameter, and (4) the mineral fraction <0.053 mm in diameter. All the subsamples in 250 ml beakers were transferred on the top of a 3-nested sieve set (2 mm, 0.25 mm, and 0.053 mm) and submerged in deionized water for 5 minutes to allow slaking. A gentle vertical movement (strokes 2-3cm in amplitude and 5 min) within a column of water was done for 10 min using a wet sieving apparatus. After wet sieving, all the fractions were oven-dried at 70°C, except the large and small macro-aggregates obtained by the capillary-wetted pretreatment. These macro-aggregates were air dried and later used for the separation of larger and smaller stable macro-aggregates (Pojasok et al., 1990; Elliott and Cambardella, 1991; Six, 1998; Marquez et al., 2004).

## 2.3    Organic Carbon Concentration

SOC was determined from samples collected in aggregates separations using sulfuric acid oxidation with external heating (Anderson and Ingram, 1993).

## 2.4    Calculations and Statistical Analyses

### 2.4.1    Calculations
The mean size of aggregates is represented by the mean weight diameter (MWD) and natural mean weight diameter (NMWD). MWD and NMWD were obtained as indicated in Eqs. (1) and (2) (Six, 1998; Marquez et al., 2004; van Steenbergen, et al., 1991).

$$MWD = \sum_{1}^{n+1} \frac{r_{i-1} + r_i}{2} \times m_i \qquad (1)$$

Where $r_i$ is the mean equivalent diameter for each particle size interval (mm), $r_0 = r_1$, $r_n = r_{n+1}$, $m_i$ is the weight of particles in the interval.

$$NMWD = \frac{MWD}{r_{max} - r_{min}} \qquad (2)$$

Where $r_{max}$ is the biggest initial diameter and $r_{min}$ is the smallest initial diameter.

### 2.4.2   Statistical Analysis

Statistical differences were determined with $t$ Student test using statistica software (Statsoft, 2004).

## 3   Results

### 3.1   Soil Aggregates Composition

Distribution of soil aggregates under different breakdown mechanisms pretreatments was shown in table 3 and table 4. Although the multitude of disruption of aggregates was different, soil aggregates contents was mainly discovered in the fraction of 2~6.72 mm in particle size in each treatment under different pretreatments. After slaking treatments, the percentage of 2~6.72 mm size was lowest in PUR-r and highest in NTR-r, which suggested that multitude of disruption of aggregates in PUR-r was more severe than that in NTR-r. There were strongly differences between conservation tillage and CT of 2~6.72 mm size contents. 2~6.72 mm size aggregates in NTR-r and NTRw-r were significantly higher compared to its value in PUR-r, about 130.18% and 144.33%, respectively. And 2~6.72 mm class also increased in NTR-f by 1.113 times over that in PUR-r. Significant differences between NTR-r and other treatments were discovered of the aggregates contents in the size of 0.25~2 mm, and its content under NTR-r was the lowest.

**Table 3.** Composition of aggregates in purple paddy soil under slaking pretreatment %

| Treatment | <0.053 mm | 0.053~0.25 mm | 0.25~2 mm | 2~6.72 mm | Recovery |
|-----------|-----------|---------------|-----------|-----------|----------|
| PUP-r | 13.21±1.48a | 10.20±0.81ab | 20.60±3.05a | 52.92±0.75c | 96.93 |
| NTR-f | 9.40±0.53b | 13.12±1.88a | 16.61±4.62ab | 58.90±5.44bc | 98.02 |
| NTR-r | 5.27±0.42c | 5.66±0.86c | 11.50±3.25c | 76.41±4.56a | 98.83 |
| NTRw-r | 4.77±0.99c | 7.88±3.76bc | 15.11±4.13ab | 68.89±8.65ab | 96.65 |

**Table 4.** Composition of aggregates in purple paddy soil under slowly wetting pretreatment %

| Treatment | <0.053 mm | 0.053~0.25 mm | 0.25~2 mm | 2~6.72 mm | Recovery |
|---|---|---|---|---|---|
| PUP-r | 14.48±0.56a | 13.23±0.71a | 18.30±1.08a | 51.84±2.53b | 97.85 |
| NTR-f | 10.06±1.42b | 11.11±0.53b | 14.09±4.06a | 63.26±5.90ab | 98.52 |
| NTR-r | 2.65±0.49c | 8.95±1.26c | 15.61±8.48a | 68.47±10.32a | 95.68 |
| NTRw-r | 6.72±4.10bc | 6.50±1.16d | 14.74±0.59a | 70.42±3.68a | 98.38 |

Aggregates contents in all treatments under wetting treatment ranked in the order of PUR-r<NTR-f<NTR-r<NTRw-r, which was different from that under slaking treatment. The amount of 2~6.72 mm in NTR-f, NTR-r and NTRw-r increased by 22.02%, 32.07% and 35.84% to comparison with the control, respectively. There were no significant differences of 0.25~2 mm aggregates-size contents between conservation and conventional tillage. The contents of 0.25~2 mm aggregates-size under slaking treatment were higher than that under wetting treatment in each treatment except that in NTR-r. Aggregates contents decreased with the decrease of aggregates-size, which indicated that conservation tillage might increase water-stable macro-aggregates proportion at cultivated layers in purple paddy soil.

## 3.2    Soil Aggregates Stability

According to wet sieving as above, the contents of 2~6.72 mm and 0.25~2 mm aggregates-size macro-aggregates under subsequent slaking treatment, which were collected from the fractions of 2~6.72 mm and 0.25~2 mm under wetting treatment and then air-dried, were determined (Table 5). 0.25~2 mm stable aggregates in all

**Table 5.** Effects of subsequent slaking treatment on the percentage of macroaggregates in paddy soil

| Treat-ments | 0.25~2 mm | | | 2~6.72 mm | | |
|---|---|---|---|---|---|---|
| | Stable aggregate (g kg$^{-1}$) | Total aggregates (g kg$^{-1}$) | Stable Aggregate percentage % | Stable aggregate (g kg$^{-1}$) | Total aggregates (g kg$^{-1}$) | Stable aggregate percentage % |
| PUP-r | 11.35 | 18.30 | 62.02 | 33.72 | 51.84 | 65.04 |
| NTR-f | 9.51 | 14.09 | 67.49 | 47.80 | 63.26 | 75.56 |
| NTR-r | 11.83 | 15.61 | 75.78 | 50.88 | 68.47 | 74.31 |
| NTRw-r | 10.37 | 14.74 | 70.35 | 50.55 | 70.42 | 71.78 |

treatments were increased in the order of PUR-r (0), NTR-f (5.47%), NTRw-r (8.33%) and NTR-r (13.76%). The proportion of stable aggregates 2~6.72 mm in NTR-f, NTRw-r and NTR-r was increased by 10.51%, 9.27% and 6.74% compared to the control, respectively. The percentage of stable macro-aggregates contents in all treatments (PUR-r, NTR-f, NTRw-r and NTR-r) after subsequent slaking treatment was 64.26%, 74.09%, 93.31% and 94.31%, respectively. Consequently, conservation tillage could enhance the resistance of aggregates to slaking stresses in paddy soil, and reduce the multitude of the disruption of aggregates.

The aggregate-size stability distribution is the quantity of stable and unstable soil aggregates categorized by their size and stability to disruption. Water-stable aggregates can improve soil stability, and enhance physical protective ability for soil organic carbon. The aim of agricultural management is to create the stable soil structure. The percentage of water-stable macro-aggregates decreased in the order of NTR-r, NTRw-r, NTR-f and PUR-r under fast slaking treatment and NTRw-r, NTR-r, NTR-f and PUR-r under wetting treatment, respectively. Similar distribution trends of water-stable macro-aggregates were observed under slaking treatment and wetting treatment when the stability of aggregates was represented as MWD and NMWD (table 6).

**Table 6.** Percentage and mean weight diameter of the water stable macroaggregates (>0.25 mm)

| Treatments | WSMA (%) | | MWD (mm) | | NMWD (mm) | |
|---|---|---|---|---|---|---|
| | Slaking Pretreatment | Wetting Pretreatment | Slaking Pretreatment | Wetting Pretreatment | Slaking Pretreatment | Wetting Pretreatment |
| PUP-r | 75.84 | 71.68 | 2.56 | 2.49 | 1.31 | 1.28 |
| NTR-f | 77.04 | 78.51 | 2.78 | 2.94 | 1.43 | 1.51 |
| NTR-r | 88.86 | 87.88 | 3.47 | 3.18 | 1.78 | 1.63 |
| NTRw-r | 86.91 | 88.11 | 3.19 | 3.25 | 1.64 | 1.67 |

## 3.3   Organic Carbon in Aggregates

Organic carbon (OC) contents were mainly found in the fraction of 0.25~2 mm and 2~6.72 mm, and then in <0.053 mm size aggregates and least in 0.053~0.25 mm under fast slaking treatment in all treatments (Figure 2). There was a pronounced difference of SOC contents in the fraction of 2-6.72 mm between conservation and conventional tillage. SOC contents under NTR-r, NTRw-r and NTR-f were 42.24%, 43.03% and 33.31% higher than that in PUR-r, respectively. Significant difference was observed among treatments of organic carbon in 0.25~2 mm size class, ranked in the order of NTRw-r > NTR-r> NTR-f> PUR-r. SOC contents in 0.053~0.25 mm under NTRw-r and NTR-r were significantly higher 1.11 and 0.59 times over that in

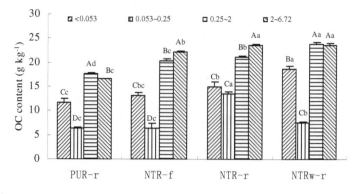

**Fig. 2.** Organic carbon contents in broken aggregates under slaking pretreatment

the control, while in the fraction of <0.053 mm were higher about 16.43% and 58.98%, respectively.

Distribution trends of SOC contents in aggregates under wetting pretreatment in all treatments were similarly to that under fast slaking pretreatment. Significant differences of SOC contents were found in aggregates of the tillage treatment and size fraction in each treatment and also found in micro-aggregates among treatments under wetting pretreatment. OC content in 0.053~0.25 mm after wetting treatments was higher than that under fast slaking pretreatment (Figure 3). Compared with the control, OC contents in the fraction of 2~6.72 mm and 0.25~2 mm under NTR-r were increased by 10.91% and 19.93%, while 0.7% and 28.47% under NTRw-r, respectively. It was worth paying attention to that OC content in each aggregates-size in the control under wetting pretreatment was higher than that under fast slaking pretreatment. There may be something wrong with the soil porosity when it was high in control, which could cause majority of particulate organic matter with internal or external aggregates to float upward during fast slaking pretreatment. Particle organic carbon was about more than 27% of total organic carbon in cultivated layer of purple paddy soil (Huang et al., 2005; Tufekcioglu et al., 1999) and was significant positive correlated with aggregates stability (Li et al., 2004).

OC contents in stable and unstable macro-aggregates under subsequent slaking pretreatment were measured (Figure 4). OC contents in stable aggregates were always higher than that in unstable aggregates, and the OC contents in 0.25~2 mm stable aggregates were higher than that in 2~6.72 mm stable aggregates. Under subsequent slaking pretreatment, significant differences were observed between conservation tillage and the control. OC contents in 0.25~2 mm stable aggregate under NTR-r, NTRw-r and NTR-f were significantly increased by 38.64%, 24.26% and 24.52% compared to the control, respectively. OC contents in 2~6.72 mm stable aggregates under NTR-r and NTRw-r were 9.94% and 20.57% higher than that in the control, respectively. It may be sure that most of OC contents were enriched in stable macroaggregates under long-term ridge or wide ridge culture integrated with no-tillage, crop rotation and rice stubble.

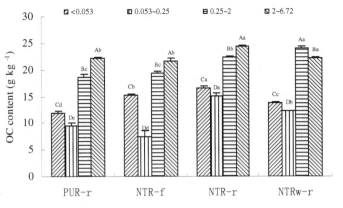

**Fig. 3.** Organic carbon contents in slaked aggregates under slowly wetting pretreatment

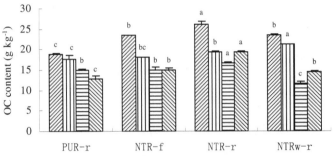

**Fig. 4.** Organic carbon contents in broken aggregates under subsequent slaking pretreatment

# 4    Discussion

## 4.1    Effects of Ridge Culture on the Aggregates-Size Stability Distribution

SOC contents increased under long-term ridge culture and aggregates stability was significantly enhanced. The disruption of aggregates during the slaking and wetting treatment produces smaller constituent aggregates. Aggregates contents decreased with the decrease in aggregates size, and the proportion of 2~6.72 mm aggregates-size was more than 50%. The magnitude of stable macro-aggregates under conservation tillage was also significantly higher than that under conventional tillage after subsequent slaking treatment. Excellent soil structure was determined not only by macro-aggregates but also by the quality and quantity of micro-aggregates, which may indicate the potential ability to format soil structure. Under wet-shaking treatment, bulk soil was mainly separated into the fraction of 0.02~0.25 mm aggregates-size (45~54%), and then 0.002~0.02 mm aggregates-size, macro-aggregates and its organic carbon increased at surface layers (0~10 cm) in paddy soil

(Tang et al., 2007). In conclusion, fast slaking and wetting processes under natural condition may be the major breakdown mechanisms of macro-aggregates in purple paddy soil.

Aggregates stability is a quality indicator that directly related to soil organic matter, which can be redistributed within soil by tillage. Water stable aggregates in cultivated layers mainly caused by strike and extrusion of crop roots and cementation of secretion. The quantity of straw mulch returning into purple paddy soil ranked in the order of PUR-r > NTR-r > NTRw-r > NTR-f (Table 6). OC contents and aggregates stability in plain culture were lower than those in ridge culture. Macro-aggregates, which are C-rich substances under conventional tillage, were disrupted, and increased smaller aggregates contents, which are lack of organic carbon, resulting in low soil organic matter content. Moreover, long-term tillage practices diminish the quality and length of fine roots and microbial population in the upper horizons, and reduced the amount of macro-aggregates. Crop residues were enriched in soil surface layer by making ridge and plot in NTR-r and NTRw-r and increased unstable carbon inputs (soil biomass carbon and particulate organic matter), which are the main binding (cementing) agent to form macro-aggregates. From conversion, conventional submersion or drying to ridge/plot capillary-wetted cultivation, gravity water has been eliminated, and water erosion has been mitigated under conservation tillage (NTR-r and NTRw-r), thus soil maintains capillary wetting. Because water, gas, and heat regime exchanges frequently, these enable soil under ridge to contract itself and consequently form stable soil structure. Pore character of soil aggregates is the main factor influencing wetting speed, such as pore size and camber. Caron reported that pore camber indexes in NT is three times more compared to in CT, water immerse rate decreased by 70% and increased aggregates stability (Mazurak et al., 1950; Caron et al., 1996). It is suitable to form soil structure for soil pore type and quantity and soil density which was lower in NTR-r and NTRw-r compared to PUR-r that was caused by stable heat capability, relative stable electrical field, continuous immersing and strong water retention ability of labile organic matters which were rotted from root straw internal or external soil pore (Xie et al., 2002; Wei et al., 2006).

## 4.2    Relationship between Soil Organic Carbon and Aggregates-Size Stability

Organic matter is one of the key factors influencing soil stability. OC magnitude has close connection with aggregates stability, but the multitude of correlation was site-specific. There was low correlation between organic carbon and aggregates stability under fast slaking pretreatment, however, significant positive correlation was observed under wetting pretreatment (Li et al., 2006; Hernanz et al., 2002). Soils organic compounds not only buildup the cohesion and tensile strength among aggregates, and heighten soil aggregates stability, but also mitigate the wetting velocity because water capability of soil compounds was greatly higher than that in soil mineral. Moreover soil organic compounds hydrophobicity affects the wetting velocity. The addition of straw can promote microbe activity, and reinforce cohesion and hydrophobicity of aggregates. The impact of addition of straw multchon aggregates was greater than wet-dry cycles. Enhancement of soil hydrophobicity would hinder or delay infiltration velocity of soil water (Hallett et al., 1999), and make air in soil pore release slowly, thus reduce slaking resistance and enhance soil aggregates stability (Capriel et al., 1990). Soil hydrophobicity may illuminate the relationship between soil organic carbon and soil structure stability. Soil texture also has great impact on Soil hydrophobicity. When soil texture is different, Soil hydrophobicity has significant difference. Clay contents were 3.32 and 2.95 times in NTR-r and NTRw-r over that in PUR-r, respectively. Ridge culture could protect soil from erosion because crop residues remain relatively undisturbed on the soil surface in contrast to plain culture, and the precipitation infiltrated soil in the form of capillary water. For the reduction of water erosion, the proportion of clay in soils under ridge culture increased. Hallett (1999) reported that when clay content was more than 25% or even more 40%, soil hydrophobicity was all the same great, and even the soil hydrophobicity in high soil clay content was greater than in low soil clay content. This may be because that hydorphobic organic particulate itself was rather small or organic matter content was greatly high, which can enwrap large and small particulate and lead to more greatness of specific surface of soil hydrophobic organic compounds.

## 5   Conclusion

Under slaking and wetting pretreatment, the amount of aggregates-size was mainly found in the diameter of 2~6.72 mm under ridge culture in paddy soil (more than 50%). The proportion of macro-aggregates under ridge culture treatment was greatly higher than that in conventional tillage soils under subsequent slaking pretreatment. The proportion of macro-aggregates and its OC content increased under long-term ridge culture in paddy field, which straightened soil aggregates stability. No significant difference of aggregates stability was found between slaking and wetting pretreatment. Organic carbon contents were obviously enriched in macro-aggregates, and SOC in aggregates were highly correlated with aggregates stability under wetting treatment. It is important to seek management practices that sustained soil resource. Keeping the soil in place is the best defense against soil degradation. Ridge culture without tillage could protect soil from erosion because crop residues remain undisturbed on the soil surface in contrast to plain culture where residue was incorporated. These evidences suggested that Long-term ridge culture may lead to changes of straw mulch inputs and soil microenvironment and enhancement of aggregates water stability.

**Acknowledgements.** This work is supported by the Key Projects in the National Science & Technology Pillar Program (No.2006BAD05B0-02) and the foundation of Sichuan Educational Committee for Youths (No.09ZB049), and the Natural Science Foundation of Chongqing, China (No. CSTC, 2009BB1115).

# References

Anderson, J.M., Ingram, J.S.I.: Tropical soil biology and Fertility: A Handbook of Methods. In: CAB International, Wallingford, pp. 235–274 (1993)

Balesdent, J., Chenu, C., Balabance, M.: Relationship of soil organic matter dynamics to physical protection and tillage. Soil Till. Res. 53, 215–230 (2000)

Beare, M.H., Bruce, R.R.: A comparison of methods for measuring water-stable aggregates: Implications for determining environmental effects on soil structure. Geoderma 56, 87–104 (1993)

Beare, M.H., Hendrix, P.F., Colemn, D.C.: Water-stable aggregates and organic matter fractions in conventional and no-tillage soils. Soil Sci. Soc. Am. J. 58, 777–786 (1994a)

Beare, M.H., Cabrera, M.L., Hendrix, P.F., Coleman, D.C.: Aggregate-protected and unprotected organic matter pools in conventional- and no-tillage soils. Soil Sci. Soc. Am. J. 58, 787–795 (1994b)

Bernoux, M., Cerri, C.C., Cerri, C.E.P., Siqueira Neto, M., Metay, A., Perrin, A.-S., Scopel, E., Razafimbelo, T., Blavet, D., Piccolo, M.D.C., Pavei, M., Miline, E.: Cropping systems, carbon sequestration and erosion in Brazil, a review. Agron. Sustain. Dev. 26, 1–8 (2006)

Cai, Z.C., Haruo, T., Gao, M.: Option for mitigation methane emission from permanently flooded rice field. Global Change Biology 9, 37–45 (2003)

Cambardella, C.A., Elliott, E.T.: Particulate soil organic matter changes across a grassland cultivation sequence. Soil Sci. Soc. Am. J. 56, 777–783 (1992)

Cambardella, C.A., Elliott, E.T.: Methods for physical separation and characterization of soil organic matter fractions. Geoderma 56, 449–457 (1993a)

Cambardella, C.A., Elliott, E.T.: Carbon and nitrogen distribution in aggregates from cultivated and native grassland soils. Soil Sci. Soc. Am. J. 57, 1071–1076 (1993b)

Capriel, P., Beck, T., Halter, P.: Relationship between soil aliphatic fractions extracted with supercritical hexane, soil microbial biomass and soil aggregate stability. Soil Sci. Soc. Am. J. 54, 415–420 (1990)

Caron, J., Kay, B.D., Stone, J.A.: Improvement of structural stability of a clay loam with drying. Soil Sci. Soc. Am. J. 56, 1583–1590 (1992)

Caron, J., Espindola, C.R., Angers, D.A.: Soil structural stability during rapid wetting: Influence of land use on some aggregate properties. Soil Sci. Soc. Am. J. 60, 901–908 (1996)

Chen, Z., Pawluk, J.N.G.: Impact of variations in granular structures on carbon sequestration in two Alberta Mollisols. In: Lal, R., et al. (eds.) Soil Processes and the Carbon Cycle. Adv. Soil Sei., pp. 225–243. CRC Press, Boca Raton (1998)

Christensen, B.T.: Carbon in primary and secondary organomineral complex. In: Carter, M.R., Stewart, B.A. (eds.) Structure and Organic Matter Storage in Agricultural Soils, pp. 97–165. CRC Press, Boca Raton (1996)

Diego, C., Claire, C., Yves, L.B.: Aggregate stability and microbial community dynamics under drying-wetting cycles in a silt loam soil. Soil Biol. Biochem. 38, 2053–2062 (2006)

Elliott, E.T.: Aggregate structure and carbon, nitrogen, and phosphorus in native and cultivated soils. Soil Sci. Soc. Am. J. 50, 627–633 (1986)

Elliott, E.T., Cambardella, C.A.: Physical separation of soil organic matter. Agric. Ecosyst. Environ. 34, 407–419 (1991)

Franzluebbers, A.J.: Soil organic carbon sequestration and agricultural greenhouse gas emissions in the southeastern USA. Soil Till. Res. 83, 120–147 (2005)

Gale, W.J., Cambardella, C.A., Bailey, T.B.: Root-derived carbon and the formation and stabilization of aggregates. Soil Sci. Soc. Am. J. 64, 201–207 (2000)

Gale, W.J., Cambardella, C.A.: Carbon dynamics of surface residue-and root-derived organic matter under simulated no-till. Soil Sci. Soc. Am. J. 64, 190–195 (2000)

Gao, M., Luo, Y.J., Wang, Z.F., Tang, X.H., Wei, C.F.: Effects of tillage systems on distribution of soil aggregates and organic carbon in purple paddy soil of Chongqing, China. Pedosphere 18, 574–581 (2008)

Grandy, A.S., Porter, G.A., Erich, M.S.: Organic amendment and rotation crop effects on the recovery of soil organic matter and aggregation in potato cropping system. Soil Sci. Soc. Am. J. 66, 1311–1319 (2002)

Hallett, P.D., Young, I.M.: Changes to water repellence of soil aggregates caused by substrate-induced microbial activity. Eur. J. Soil Sci. 50, 35–40 (1999)

Haynes, R.J., Francis, C.S.: Changes in microbiological biomass C, soil carbohydrate composition and aggregate stability induced by growth of selected crop and forage species under field conditions. J. Soil Sci. 44, 665–675 (1993)

Halvorson, A.D., Wienhold, B.J., Black, A.L.: Tillage, nitrogen and cropping system effects on soil carbon sequestration. Soil Sci. Soc. Am. J. 66, 906–912 (2002)

Hernanz, J.L., Lopez, R., Navarrete, L., Sanchez, G.V.: Long-term effects of tillage systems and rotations on soil structural stability and organic carbon stratification in semiarid central Spain. Soil Till. Res. 66, 129–141 (2002)

Huang, X.X., Gao, M., Wei, C.F.: Tillage effect on organic carbon in a purple paddy soil. Pedosphere 16, 660–667 (2006)

Jastrow, J.D.: Soil aggregate formation and the accrual of particulate and mineral-associated organic matter. Soil Biol. Biochem. 28, 656–676 (1996)

Kemper, W.D., Rosenau, R.: Soil cohesion as affected by time and water content. Soil Sci. Soc. Am. J. 48, 1001–1006 (1984)

Li, X.G., Li, F.M., Zed, R.: Cultivation effects on temporal changes of organic carbon and aggregate stability in desert soil of Hexi Corridor region in China. Soil Till. Res. 91, 22–29 (2006)

Li, J.T., Zhang, B., Peng, X.H.: Effects of fertilization on particulate organic carbon matter formation and aggregate stability in paddy soil. Acta Pedologica Sinica 41, 912–917 (2004)

Mazurak, A.P.: Effect of gaseous phase on water-stable synthetic aggregates. Soil Sci. 69, 135–148 (1950)

Marquez, C.O., Garcia, V.J., Cambardella, C.A.: Aggregate-size Stability Distribution and soil stability. Soil Sci. Soc. Am. J. 68, 725–736 (2004)

Paustian, K., Six, J., Elliott, E.T., Hunt, H.W.: Management options for reducing $CO_2$ emissions from agricultural soils. Biogeochemistry 48, 147–163 (2000)

Peng, X.H., Zhang, B., Zhao, Q.G.: A review on relationship between soil organic carbon pools and soil structure stability. Acta Pedologica Sinica 41, 618–623 (2004)

Pojasok, T., Kay, B.D.: Assessment of a combination of wet sieving and turbidimetry to characterize the structural stability of moist aggregates. Can. J. Soil Sci. 70, 33–42 (1990)

Puget, P., Angers, D.A., Chenu, C.: Nature of carbohydrates associated with water-stable aggregates of two cultivated soils. Soil Biol. Biochem. 31, 55–63 (1999)

Puget, P., Chenu, C., Balesdent, J.: Dynamics of soil organic matter associated with particle-size fractions of water-stable aggregates. Eur. J. Soil Sci. 51, 595–605 (2000)

Six, J., Elliott, E.T., Paustian, K., Doran, J.: Aggregation and soil organic matter accumulation in cultivated and native grassland soils. Soil Sci. Soc. Am. J. 62, 1367–1377 (1998)

Six, J., Elliott, E.T., Paustian, K.: Soil structure and soil organic matter: II. A normalized stability index and the effect of mineralogy. Soil Sci. Soc. Am. J. 64, 1042–1049 (2000b)

Six, J., Paustian, K., Elliott, E.T.: Soil structure and organic matter. I. Distribution of aggregate-size classes and aggregate associated carbon. Soil Sci. Soc. Am. J. 64, 681–689 (2000a)

Tang, X.H., Shao, J.A., Gao, M.: Effects of conservation tillage systems on aggregates composition and organic carbon storage in purple paddy soil. Journal of Applied Ecology 18, 1027–1032 (2007)

Tisdall, J.M., Oades, J.M.: Organic matter and water-stable aggregates. Journal of soil science 33, 141–163 (1982)

Tisdall, J.M., Oades, J.M.: The effect of crop rotation on aggregation in a red-brown earth. Aust. J. Soil Res. 18, 423–433 (1980)

Tisdall, J.M., Oades, J.M.: Organic matter and water stable aggregates in soils. J. Soil Sci. 33, 141–163 (1982)

Tufekcioglu, A.W., Raich, J.W., Isenharl, T.M., Schultz, R.C.: Fine root dynamics, coarse root biomass, root distribution, and soil respiration in a multispecics riparian buffer in central Iowa. Agrofor. Syst. 44, 163–174 (1999)

Wei, C.F., Gao, M., Shao, J.A.: Soil aggregate and its response to land management practices. Particuology 4, 211–219 (2006)

Xie, D.T., Chen, S.L.: Theory and Technique of Paddy Field under Soil Virginization, pp. 65–168. Chongqing Press, Chongqing (2002)

van Steenbergen, M., Cambardella, C.A., Elliott, E.T., Merckx, R.: Two simple indices for distributions of soil components among size classes. Agric. Ecosyst. Environ. 34, 335–340 (1991)

# Design and Application of Quality Traceability System Based on RFID Technology for Red Jujubes

Fenghua Huang[1], Shujuan Zhang[2,*], and Huaming Zhao[2]

[1] College of Information Science and Engineering of Shanxi agricultural University
[2] Engineering College of Shanxi agricultural University, Taigu, Shanxi, 030801, China
zsujuan@263.net

**Abstract.** The traceability system is regarded as an effective method to ensure safety quality for farm products by many countries all over the world. Although this system is common for a range of farm products, few reports for red jujube are available nowadays. Our study focuses on constructing a traceability system in terms of information technology in order to implement quality tracing for red jujube products for the first time. Based on the RFID technology, QR (Quick Response) codes and EAN/UCC-128 barcode technology, this system was established in detail by analyzing the whole sector data such as land management, planting and picking, processing and packaging, transporting, selling of products and so on, which formed the traceability information. It was also put into SQL2005 database system and C# was used to develop the quality traceability system based on C/S for red jujubes. From this research, we can see it is beneficial and easy to thoroughly master the quality and safety information of red jujubes from production to circulation for manufacturers and customers by this system.

**Keywords:** Traceability system, RFID, EAN/UCC-128, QR code, Red jujubes.

## 1   Introduction

During recent years, poor food quality has occurred frequently such as milk powder containing Melamine in 2008, Changli counterfeit wine in Hebei province in 2010, Shuanghui lean meat adding "Lean meat power", and dyed mantou. In addition, some diseases, mad cow disease, foot-and-mouth disease, bird flu, which affect food safety, also broke out now and then. Poor food quality not only does harm to Chinese's health, but also affects the export of agricultural product and food in China. According to international rules, some developed countries, America, EU, etc, set regulations that some imported food to their countries must be traced back. Consequently, trade barriers to Chinese food and agricultural products are formed. Hence, it is urgent to set food traceability system for breaking trade barrier for food and enlarging international export.

Red jujube in Taigu County, Shanxi province, especially Huping Jujube is very popular in local areas because of its largeness, thin skin, and nice chewy texture. But

---

* Corresponding author.

D. Li and Y. Chen (Eds.): CCTA 2011, Part I, IFIP AICT 368, pp. 371–380, 2012.
© IFIP International Federation for Information Processing 2012

it also faces questions of planting, untraceability of processing, and food safety. Hence, traceability system should be set to improve the transparency of food safety and to improve its competitive ability.

The study of traceability system, a response to mad cow disease, was first set by EU in 1997. At the end of 2000, EAN International established new "beef label law" which was first carried out by Meet Export Group in EU, and applied EAN.UCC system to the producing and supplying chain of beef [1,2]. In July, 2002 EU issued a decree that all food sold in EU should be able to be traced from 2004, and *Regulations of Food and Fodder Safety in EU* should be carried out in the early of 2006, which emphasizes the control management of food from farm to table and its traceability[3]. Over 40 years ago, America set laws for chemistry remains in food [4]. The Congress heightened food safety to country safety level, so the government made compulsory administration to food safety and enterprises were asked to set the production traceability system [5]. The modernization of food safety was realized from tracing and checking production to prevent the pollution of meat and bird food [6]. The traceability system of agricultural product in Japan was the most advanced, which focused on product information, attracting consumers' most attention, such as the information of applying fertilizer in fruit plant and the information of spraying fruit with insecticide etc. [7]. With the driving of government, other food traceability system except beef was set in Japan from December, 2004[8].

At abroad, the constructive goal that traceability system of vegetable safety in Beijing will be primitively set and tracing mark of vegetable safety should be applied to 20 enterprises which process and distribute vegetables was put forward by Beijing city government [9]. The control and traceability system of Olympic Games food safety was first used on $8_{th}$, August, 2007, which effectively guaranteed food safety during Olympic Games. On $5_{th}$, March, 2009, Prime Minister Wen Jiabao gave a report in the second conference of $11_{th}$ NPC, and he claimed that one of the main tasks in 2009 was to strictly implement the system of market access, traceability system of product quality, and the system of recalling poor quality product[10]  so as to heighten the constructing traceability system in our country to a new level. At present, food traceability system has been or is being established in many areas and provinces. In 2004, vegetable traceability system was tried in the vegetable base in Shouguang, based on the cooperation of State Bureau of Quality Testing and Shandong Bureau of Quality and Technical Supervision etc [11]. In 2003 Jufang Xie etc. studied pork traceability system [12]. Based on Web cultivating quality of Tilapia, Xi Ren in Chinese Agricultural University studied traceability system [13]. Besides, some universities such as Chinese Academy of Agricultural Sciences, South China Agricultural University, Shanghai Ocean University, Nanjing Agricultural University also studied traceability system for pork, beef, and mutton [14-19].

All the studies focused on livestock product, and these systems can only trace back to production enterprises. So according to red jujube producing in Taigu county, this paper aims at establishing a set of database which consists of production base, product, and certification and supervision information to supervise jujubes, identify the production base of jujubes, and to evaluate production environment. This research also focuses on developing traceability system for government and enterprises to realize the government's certification and anti-counterfeiting administration for red jujubes in Taigu county.

## 2   The Design of System

### 2.1   The Design of System Structure

As is shown in figure 1, the system is divided into seven subsystems according to the supply chain of produce together with planting, processing, inspection and quarantine, sales information, process of tracing of red jujubes in Taigu. It used C/S structure and the central database was maintained by relevant government departments.

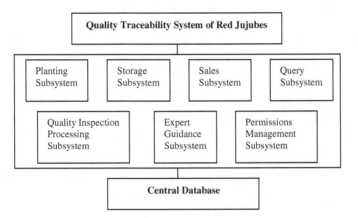

**Fig. 1.** The structure of traceability system

When the system is registered by the users, the administrator can fully control it. Other users can only upload and access to their own subsystem data and public data. Query subsystem doesn't need to register.

### 2.1.1   Planting Subsystem

Planting subsystem includes information of planting base, farmer's information, environment monitoring information of planting base, plant drugging information, fertilizing information etc.

The special information administrators are responsible for the input of planting information of each village's cooperatives. Each information administrator has RFID CARDS. They can input information and manage the module by registering with the card.

Information administrators record information of red jujube tree species, tree-age, fertilization type, fertilization date, fertilizer quantity, drug types, drug date, drug quantity and so on and put them in the system. They also have the responsibility to guide planting of red jujube and management and the purchase, storage and safe usage information of fertilizers. Through understanding the information of expert guidance subsystem, information administrators convey guidance of experts in time to each village and provide guidance to applying of fertilizers and pesticides. The system's database provides certain limits to the amount of fertilizers. If there is excessive drug uses after the information recording, the system will give some hints in order to be corrected immediately.

Unified numbers are given to each piece of red jujube planting cooperatives and each field has its own RFID tag used to store information of the plot and varieties of red jujubes. When red jujubes are picked, the RFID tags should be fixed on the storage bag in order to trace the information.

### 2.1.2     Storage Subsystem

Storage subsystem includes the time of warehousing, outbound time, deliver destination, warehouse numbers, temperature, humidity, health monitoring and other information of each batch of red jujubes. It services the red jujube processing enterprises and it's the responsibility of the enterprises to maintain the information in the database.

Storage subsystem includes processing of red jujubes before and after storage. After the red jujubes are picked, they are transported to the local constant temperature warehouse for processing. The gates of the warehouse are equipped with electronic label RFID readers. Before warehousing, the reader will read the information of origin in the electronic label and automatically generate storage time, which is stored in the database. Red jujubes are drawn according to processing needs. Passing the gate, RFID tags are reread and the outbound time is generated automatically. After processing, the finished products are transported to the finished-product warehouse, with a RFID tag attached to each batch. By reading the tag, the database automatically adds the additional information to the information stored last time and forms complete information of database for this group of red jujubes.

### 2.1.3     Quality Inspection, Processing Subsystem

Since each batch of red jujube has to be screened and divided into various grades, it uses two-dimensional code for information traceability in order to reduce production costs and add information easily. When the red jujubes are transported to the processing plant from the warehouse, the RFID reader will firstly read the corresponding tag and then generate the corresponding two-dimensional QR code according to the database information. Then the red jujubes are classified by its size, cleaned and disinfected. After that, the new processing information will be added to the two-dimensional code. Processed red jujubes will be sent into fruit inspection and quarantine center for pesticide residue inspection, and sampled according to the national standard indicators of fruit sampling. If they don't meet the needs, they will be sent directly to waste-processing sector. The inspection information will be added to the two-dimensional bar code of the qualified red jujubes and generate corresponding inspection information. These red jujubes are stored in the finished-product warehouse waiting to be sold.

### 2.1.4     Sales Subsystem

Sales subsystem serves local sales agents or supermarkets, which have a unique radio frequency identity card. Authenticated by the RF card, they can read the two-dimensional code on the packaging of the red jujubes distributed to their stores after registering and bound the information of red jujubes with the sales information. When the final trace information is completed, the one-dimensional trace code will be printed and affixed to the packaging of the product for sales.

### 2.1.5    Query Subsystem

Query subsystem serves the vast numbers of consumers. After purchasing red jujubes, consumers can query and trace product information through various means. By inputting the one-dimensional code, consumers can access WAP network via internet or mobile phones. Consumers can also trace the product by reading the two-dimensional code on the package through phone camera with two-dimensional code decoding software. They can also call 800 tracing phone. A complete product traceability information can be got through any of the ways mentioned above.

### 2.1.6    Expert Guidance Subsystem

This system can not only trace product information, but also provide expert guidance system for planting red jujubes. Expert guidance subsystem offers a variety of technical guidance and video files for majority of red jujube growers and co-workers as to how to plant red jujubes. The system also provides fertilizing, spraying, pruning information in different stages of planting red jujubes. The administrators are responsible for conveying the information to each village.

### 2.2    Design of System Database and Interface

The amount of data collected by this system is approximately from 5000 to 50000 every day. In order to achieve higher stability and easy maintenance, Microsoft SQL Server 2005 database is the most appropriate choice. Windows 2000 / XP/windows7 is chosen as operating system of the client Software, whereas Windows 2003 is used as operating system of Server. The technology of reliable Hot Standby should be used to ensure data security by duplicating data regularly.

After the system clients are installed, user can login the system by entering user name and passwords, selecting the corresponding user types, and then clicking the submit button. If all the items are correct, system will change into the corresponding subsystem or Query Interface, as shown in figure 2.

**Fig. 2.** Trace back system information query interface

The system provides a variety of ways to search the terminal. Firstly, user can use touch-screen terminal provided by supermarket to query, once the traceability code of one-dimension labeled on the goods is inputted into the system you can view the information to be traced. The results on touch-screen terminal are shown in Figure 3. Secondly, two-dimensional code on the packaging of goods can be taken by mobile phone and sent to China Mobile service platform 700066 to query. Thirdly, user can login trace website provided on the package to query, just entering the traceability code of 28-digit number one-dimensional, query information can be generated. Fourthly, user can query via mobile phone by inputting WAP site labeled on the packaging, which has the same effect as www sites. No matter what query modes, the system will provide detailed traceability information.

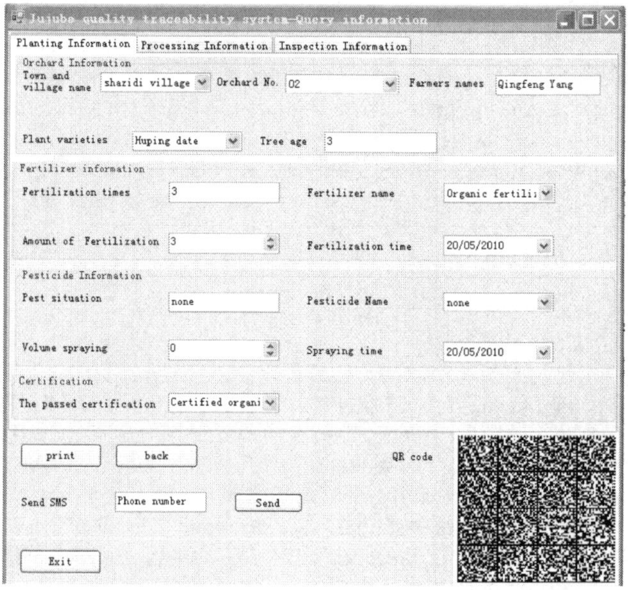

**Fig. 3.** The red jujube cultivation information queried by tracing system

## 3   Design of System Barcode

RFID tags are used in the trace chain. Generally there are two ways: one is that the information stored on the RFID tag. Information is extracted from RFID tag when it is traced. This method is easy to extract information, but the label's storage capacity is limited, not covering all the information of the whole logistics process; another way is that agricultural information is stored in the online database, so using RFID tags as the index to access information has the better scalability. If a two-dimensional code is used as an information carrier after processing, it has more cost-effect [20]. Based on RFID tag traceability system for agricultural products, it constitutes three aspects, agricultural production, processing, and circulation. The system of agricultural production during producing uses RFID tags to store information, and combines processing with circulation to produce two-dimensional code to the record information.

The system uses the most common EPC-96 as the Electronic Product Code, to record agricultural information in producing. EPC-96 has 96-bit memory storage capacity. To facilitate the expansion of the system in the future, it sets aside out of 36 bits as an extension bit. The remaining 60 bits are used to record red jujube about village information, cultivated land information, batch information, picking date information and so on. The information of original place accounted for 36 bits, and date information accounted for 24 bits. As land-related information is already stored in the database, system can inquiry variety planting information of the batch red jujube, if the label stores into the origin and processing connects with the database.

## 3.1   Original Place Code

According to the Ministry of Agriculture promulgated the *Rules of Farm Produce Original Place Code* (standard number: NY / T 1430-2007), farm producing origin code are composed of county and above-county administration and constituted of 20 decimal digits [21]. If the 20 decimal numbers are directly transferred into binary bits, which need 63 bits, RFID tags can not directly store original place code. The system needs choice and coding, as the use of the system is now concentrated on Taigu County, and all red jujube are produced in various towns in Taigu, so classification code of county and above the county is directly cancelled, which means encoding from the town.

According to GB/T10114-2003 *the Establishment Rules of Code Divisions in the Following County-Level Administrative*, the code of county-level administrative consists of nine-digit number, separating into two parts. The top six of first paragraph is six-digit of the GB/T2260 code, representing the county administration. The second paragraph is constituted by three digital [22], representing below-county administration. The last three digits in the rules are used as the top three digits in the new coding, which represents town code of origin planting red jujube. Behind the township code is village and block coding, and the system codes number of villages according to Taigu County township: 01-99, meanwhile the same number code of each block is also: 01-99. For example: Taoyuanbu village, Houcheng town, Taigu county, the number of original planting place is: 1044901, (Taoyuanbu village No. 49 in the system), so the binary code is: 0001 0000 0,100,010,010,010,000 0001.

## 3.2   Picking Date Code

The code of picking time selects six bits as the date code, such as the September 1, 2010, is replaced 100 901 code. But it should be 24 bits in the tag, that is 0001 0,000,000,010,010,000 0001 after encoding.

## 3.3   The Design of Two-Dimensional QR Code

The system selects QR Code as two-dimensional barcodes based on the actual situation in China and selects M-class as correction level based on the requirements of traceability design and information. Two-dimensional QR code should show much detail information during the whole traceability process, which includes planting, testing, processing, selling information and so on. They are stored within the two-dimensional code, and the resulting two-dimensional code is as Figure 4.

**Fig. 4.** QR bar code generated by traceability system

### 3.4    One-Dimensional Traceability Code

The system traces information with EAN/UCC-128 as the last bar code, which is required to link with a database when using it, so the bar code information includes original place of red jujube, batch picking, picking date. The three kinds of information can determine the other information of red jujube. For example, the third batches jujubes are picked on September 16, 2010, in 02 orchard in Shazidi village, Xiaobai town. The code of Taigu county Xiaobai town is 140 726 112, 01 for number of Shazidi village, 100916 for picking date code, 03 for batch coding, so the corresponding one-dimensional trace code is: (10) 03 (11) 100 916 (251) 1407261120102, generating one-dimensional back yards in Figure 5.

**Fig. 5.** The resulting one-dimensional bar code created by traceability System

## 4    Conclusion

The research and application of red jujbes product quality and traceability systems will improve the traceability system of agricultural information, and play an increasingly important role in agricultural products trade and consumption market, it is a important measure to ensure agricultural products quality and safety.

This paper selects traceability system of agricultural products as the research object. Based on the successful experience of domestic agricultural products about traceability system and a lot of red jujube datas about quality and safety standards and detailed information at various stages, producing stage, processing stage, and selling stage, this paper deeply explored traceability system for the quality of Taigu's red jujube. It filled the gap of product quality and traceability system, and provided the base of the rules and technical guidance for enterprises and governments for the quality and safety of agricultural products. The main conclusions are summarized as follows:

(1) After analyzing the domestic agricultural supply chain, every link of red jujubes in Taigu, planting, storing, processing, and selling is digitized and standardized, and proper information data for management system is established to provide more perfect and possible data collection system for domestic red jujube market.

(2) The overall framework of a red jujube supply chain system is built, and the traceability method of red jujube products are investigated, eventually the spatial structure and the overall functional structure of red jujube quality traceability system are proposed.

(3) A technology based on RFID and the concept of traceability, which combined one-dimensional bar codes with two-dimensional bar codes, is proposed. Traceability information can not only achieve the purpose of tracing information, but also overcome the high cost only when using RFID technology, and overcome shortcomings of easily defacing only when using bar code technology. And this article built various traceability methods including WAP network to facilitate consumers' inquiring.

**Acknowledgement.** This research was supported by Research Fund for the Doctoral Program of Higher Education (201014031100003).

# References

1. Diekinson, D.L., Dee Dee Von, B.: Meat traceability:Are U.S.consumers willing to pay for it. Journal of Agricultural and Resource Economies 27(2), 348–364 (2002)
2. Massimo, B., Maurizio, B., Boberto, M., et al.: FMECA approach to product traceability in the food industry. Food Control 17(9), 1–9 (2004)
3. Food Traceability.Health & Consumer Protection Directorate General (July 2007)
4. Souza-Monteiro, D.M., Caswell, J.A.: Implamenting Traceability in Beer Supply Chains. Deperment of Resource Economics of University of Massachusetts Amherst Working Paper 2004-6 (June 2004)
5. Yang, X., Qian, J., Fan, B., et al.: Establishment of Intelligent Distribution System Applying in Logistics Process Traceability for Agricultural Product. Transactions of the Chinese Society for Agricultural Machinery (5), 125–130 (2011)
6. Zhou, X.: Design and Implementation of Iformation Safety Certification System of Agricultural Products, pp. 10–11. Huazhong Agricultural University, Master's Degree Paper, Wuhan (2008)
7. Li, M.: Research of Traceability System of Agricultural Products of Safety. Tongji University, Master's degree Paper, Beijing (2007)
8. Yang, X., Qian, J., Sun, C., et al.: Design and Implementation of Traceability system of vegetable safety production. Journal of Agricultural Engineering 24(3), 162–164 (2008)

9. Wang, L., Lu, C., Xie, J., et al.: Research of Livestock and Livestock product Traceability System. Journal of Agricultural Engineering 21(7), 168–174 (2005)
10. Wen, J.: The Government Work Report of the Second Meeting 11th National People's Congress (March 2009)
11. Zhou, Y., Geng, X.: Application of Traceability Systems in Food Quality and Information Security. Agricultural Modernization 23(6), 451–454 (2002)
12. Xie, J., Liu, J.: Research of Traceability System of Agricultural Product Quality Status, Problems and Countermeasures. Business Times (25), 66–68 (2009)
13. Ren, X., Fu, Z., Mu, W., et al.: Design of Traceability System of Based Web Information on quality and safety of Farmed Tilapia. Journal of Agricultural Engineering 25(4), 163–166 (2009)
14. Zhang, S.: Research of Chilled Pork Supply Chain Tracking and Tracing System. Chinese Academy of Agricultural Sciences, Master Paper, Beijing (2008)
15. Jiang, L.: Research of Pork Quality Safe Traceability System. Shanghai Ocean University, Master Degree Paper, Shanghai (2008)
16. Ren, S., Xu, H., Li, A., et al.: Design and Implementation of Meat Traceability System Based on RFID / GIS. Journal of Agricultural Engineering 26(10), 229–233 (2010)
17. Standards Press of China. Assembly of National Standards Barcodes, pp. 73–74. China Standard Press, Beijing (2004)
18. Wang, X., An, Y.: Research on the Logistics Information Tracing System of Vegetable Agricultural Products. China Business and Market 25(3), 34–37, 128 (2011)
19. Wang, L., Wang, F.: Analysis on the Barriers for Implementation Traceability System into Agricultural Product—a Framework Based oft SCP Form. Lanzhou Academic Journal (8), 40–42, 77 (2010)
20. Zhou, X., Wang, X.: Radio Frequency Identification (RFID) Technology Principle and Application Examples. People's Posts and Telecommunications Press, Beijing (2006)
21. Wang, H.: Research of Strategy of China Mobile Phone in Two-Dimensional Coding, pp. 23–24. Beijing University of Posts and Telecommunications, Master Paper, Beijing (2010)
22. Zhu, S., Zhang, S., Peng, W.: Design and Implementation of Pork Traceability Certificate Management System. Research of Agricultural Modernization (11), 99–104 (2010)

# The Knowledge Representation and Semantic Reasoning Realization of Productivity Grade Based on Ontology and SWRL

Li Ma, Helong Yu, Yue Wang, and Guifen Chen[*]

College of Information and Technology Science,
Jilin Agricultural University, Chang Chun, Jilin, China
mary19801976@sohu.com

**Abstract.** Semantic not consistency, and knowledge base is difficult to reuse and sharing are the key problems affecting the system development and application. This paper studies how to express the soil fertility level information using of the ontology and generate OWL (Ontology Web Language) document, and how to make use of SWRL (Semantic Web Rule Language) to express inference rules. On this basis, this paper integrates SWRL rules editor and JESS (java expert shell system) rules engine, establishes the reasoning framework based on JESS reasoning engine, and realizes the productivity grade evaluation based on ontology and SWRL.

**Keywords:** productivity grade, ontology, SWRL, reasoning, JESS.

## 1    Introduction

Knowledge and the rules are descriptions of traditional method mostly in productivity grade evaluation. Due to lack of unity Semantic description of knowledge resources, the user is difficult to find the related knowledge and hard to realize the related resources of semantic fusion [1]. In addition, how to realize the knowledge reuse and sharing is also met in the knowledge engineering development. These questions also make expert system of intelligent reasoning problems have been not effectively solved. The ontology and semantic reasoning and other technologies research provides a complete concept of the definition and concept organization relationship, It not only support underlying data content queries, but also reflect a declarative description of the correlation between data through to the semantic information, and can realize the intelligent reasoning knowledge in semantic level [2].

The paper constructs soil productivity grade ontology，integrates rules editor based on SWRL [3] and JESS rules engine [4], through the JESS rules into manipulate OWL knowledge base, develops the semantic rules system to realize soil productivity grade intelligence assessment based on semantic.

---

[*] Corresponding author.

D. Li and Y. Chen (Eds.): CCTA 2011, Part I, IFIP AICT 368, pp. 381–389, 2012.

## 2     Construct the Soil Productivity Grade Ontology

This paper used protégé tools, building the soil productivity grade ontology. Protégé is an open source ontology editor tool developing by Stanford Medical Informatics [5]. The basic Modeling primitives of ontology include classes, relations, functions, axioms, and instances, a total of five [6]. The realization in Protégé is shown in table 1.

**Table 1.** Protégé of modeling primitives in implementation

| Basic Modeling primitives | The elements of Protégé |
|---|---|
| Classes or Concepts | Through the type, natural language definition, attribute and other aspects as description |
| Relations | Relationships between classes |
| Functions | Reasoning rules |
| Axioms | A special kind of reasoning |
| Instances | instances of a class |

### 2.1     Data Sources

The data this paper used is from the cultivated land fertility survey data, the NongAnXian(2006), offers by agricultural technology extension center of NongAnXian. The data includes 25 attributes, such as soil humidity, groundwater depth, light radiation intensity, soil irrigation capacity, annual rainfall, soil drought resistance and soil erosion degree, soil texture, crop rotation suitability, topography, soil parent material, part into layer thickness, salt concentration, humus soil pH value, effective copper, iron, effective slowly available k, effective k, effective fierce, total nitrogen, phosphorus, organic matter and cationic content, effective zinc and productivity grade. Part of the data is as shown in table 2.

**Table 2.** Some fertility data

| ground water depth | soil irrigation capacity | annual rainfall | soil drought resistance | soil texture | soil parent materia | part into layer thickness | salt concentration | pH value | effective copper | effective iron |
|---|---|---|---|---|---|---|---|---|---|---|
| 3-5m | no | 400-450mm | strong | Light clay | alluvial | 10-20cm | <0.1 | 6.6 | 1.25 | 8.72 |
| <3m | strong | 400-450mm | strong | Light clay | alluvial | 10-20cm | >0.1 | 6.7 | 1.26 | 8.47 |
| 3-5m | strong | >450mm | strong | loam | alluvial | 10-20cm | <0.1 | 6.7 | 1.39 | 4.70 |
| 3-5m | strong | 400-450mm | strong | sandy loam | alluvial | 10-20cm | <0.1 | 6.5 | 1.21 | 9.45 |
| <3m | strong | 400-450mm | strong | sandy loam | alluvial | 10-20cm | >0.1 | 6.7 | 1.27 | 9.71 |
| 5-8m | no | 400-450mm | weak | sandy loam | loess | 0-10cm | <0.1 | 6.6 | 1.20 | 8.30 |
| 3-5m | no | 400-450mm | weak | sandy loam | diluvial | 20-30cm | <0.1 | 6.6 | 1.30 | 8.50 |
| <3m | strong | 400-450mm | strong | sandy loam | alluvial | 10-20cm | >0.1 | 6.7 | 1.28 | 8.48 |
| <3m | strong | 400-450mm | strong | sandy loam | alluvial | 10-20cm | >0.1 | 6.7 | 1.30 | 0.10 |
| 3-5m | no | 400-450mm | strong | sandy loam | alluvial | 10-20cm | <0.1 | 6.6 | 1.27 | 8.28 |

The parts of the reasoning rules are:

Rule1: if effective phosphorus<=21.8 and Salt content =2 and topography =21 effective phosphorus >16.8 and cationic content >21.15 and （soil parent material =2 or soil parent material =3 or soil parent material =5）then productivity grade =4;

Rule2: if effective phosphorus <=21.8 and Salt content =2 and topography =21 effective phosphorus >16.8 and cationic content >21.15 and soil parent material =1 and pH >7.4 then productivity grade =4;

Rule3: if effective phosphorus <=21.8 and Salt content =2 and topography =21 effective phosphorus >16.8 and cationic content >21.15 and soil parent material =1 and pH <=7.4 and effective iron <=8.15 then productivity grade =3;

## 2.2     Construct the Ontology

The steps of ontology construction used protégé are:
  (1) Collect all kinds of fields term, concept, and determine the relationship between the concepts.
  (2) Start protégé, choose engineering format.
  (3) Select OWL Classes Tab, add various concepts and child concept.
  (4) Select Properties Tab, add various characteristics and child characteristics.
  (5) Select Individual Tab, add the Individuals.
  (6) Again and again modification, complete ontology editor.

The specific Constructing process:
    Define classes and class rating system: establish the profile and physical and chemical properties class named physical, including attributes of pH value, soil moisture, salt concentration, humus layer thickness, soil texture, cationic content and groundwater depth. Establish the class site conditions named site, including attribute of site topography, soil erosion degree and parts into soil organic. establish meteorological conditions class named weather, contain rainfall and light radiation intensity. Establish the nutrient content named nutrient, contain effective iron, slowly available k, effective k, total nitrogen, phosphorus, effective organic matte. Establish the soil management class named management, including attributes soil drought resistance, irrigation and crop rotation suitability. Set up class soil named soil, soil is as the father all kinds. Establish class named class, including productivity grade attribute.

    Define a relationship class_is, used to determine a specific example belonging to which productivity grade, its domain of definition is soil, its range is the class.

    The exact make up of soil ontology is:

Class soilclass {
        Class physical （ph，moisture，salinity，humus，textrue，cation，groundwater）
    Class site （position，erosion，material）
    Class weather （rainfall，light）
    Class nutrient （fe，slow k，k，n，p，om）

Class management（irrigation，drought，crop）
    }
Class class（attribute is soil_class）
Class relations attribute: class_is

The domain of definition of these attributes is soil, these attributes including pH, fe, slow k, k, n, p, om, cation, and the range is int. The domain of definition of these attributes those including moisture, groundwater, light, irrigation, rainfall, drought, erosion, texture, crop, position, material, humus, salinity, is soil, and the range is float. The domain of definition of soil_class is class，and the range is int.

    Ontology construction results are as shown in figure 1.

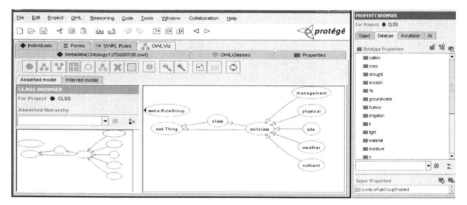

**Fig. 1.** Ontology building results

The part of the OWL document of this ontology is as follows:

> xmlns:xsp="http://www.owl-ontologies.com/2005/08/07/xsp.owl#"
> xmlns:swrlb="http://www.w3.org/2003/11/swrlb#"
> xmlns:swrla="http://swrl.stanford.edu/ontologies/3.3/swrla.owl#"
> xmlns="http://www.owl-ontologies.com/Ontology1270600106.owl#"
> xmlns:swrl="http://www.w3.org/2003/11/swrl#"
> xmlns:protege="http://protege.stanford.edu/plugins/owl/protege#"
> xmlns:rdf="http://www.w3.org/1999/02/22-rdf-syntax-ns#"
> xmlns:xsd="http://www.w3.org/2001/XMLSchema#"
> xmlns:rdfs="http://www.w3.org/2000/01/rdf-schema#"
> xmlns:owl="http://www.w3.org/2002/07/owl#"
> xmlns:sqwrl="http://sqwrl.stanford.edu/ontologies/built-ins/3.4/sqwrl.owl#"

# 3    Produce SWRL Reasoning Rules

## 3.1    SWRL Reasoning Rules

Although ontology support inference，but it dose not provide the reasoning rules, its ability is very limited, it will not be able to express these rules such as "If... Then...".

It needs to add user defined rules of OWL ontology. SWRL (Semantic Web sex) is established to solve this problem [7].

SWRL is a language that shows rules in the semantic way. It is a rules description language based on OWL DL Language, OWL Lite and Unary/Binary Datalog RuleML, its purpose is to make the first-order predicate logic horn-like rules(don't allow function to appear in Horn clauses) combining with OWL knowledge base.

A rule of SWRL is implies, and is made of the premise and conclusion. When the premise is tenable, the conclusion is tenable. The form is:

$$rule :: = \text{Implies(antecedent, consequent).}$$

SWRL in a class instance situation, storage rules, is comprised of the Imp, Atom, Variable and built-in total four parts. Every rule is divided into conclusion part (head part) and condition part (body part) total two compositions.

In the framework of SWRL, constraints of conditional judgment is built on Atom, rules are established in imp. The head and body are contained in Imp, and the source of the constraints of the both is provided by the Atom, these constraints can be used again by different rules.

## 3.2    Produce SWRL Rules

This article will use the two constraints in productivity grade evaluation rules:

C (x): C is OWL description
P (x, y): P is the OWL attribute, in which x, y can is variable, OWL individuals or OWL data value [8].

Table 3 is the atom list of SWRL rules:

**Table 3.** SWRL rules atom table

| Atom | description |
| --- | --- |
| soilclass(?x) | Y is a soil examples |
| greaterThan(x, y) | x is more than y |
| class_is(?x, y) | The grade of Examples x is y |
| lessThanOrEqual(x, y) | X is not more than y |

According to the decision rules, building Imp using the Atom defined, parts of the SWRL rules setting up as follows:

soilclassrule1:
soilclass(?x)∧swrlb:greaterThan(p,21.8)∧swrlb:greaterThan(salinity,1)∧swrlb:greater Than(rainfall,5)∧swrlb:greaterThan(position,21)→class_is(?x,class2)

soilclassrule2:
soilclass(?x)∧swrlb:greaterThan(p,21.8)∧swrlb:greaterThan(salinity,1)∧swrlb:greater Than(rainfall,5)∧swrlb:lessThanOrEqual(position,21)→class_is(?x,class3)

With SWRL describe rules, the realization in ontology are shown in figure 2:

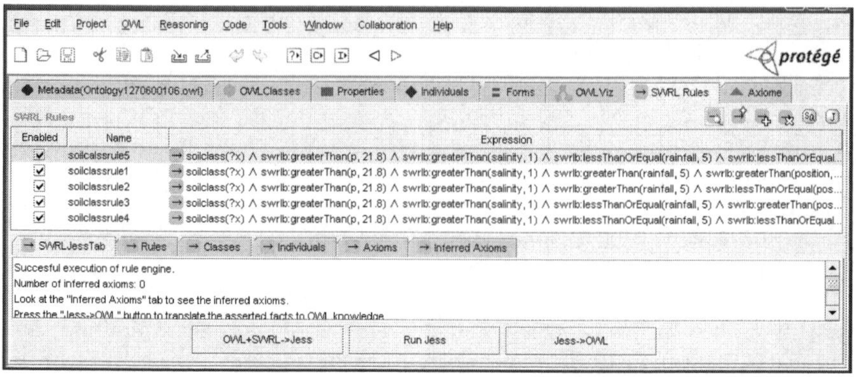

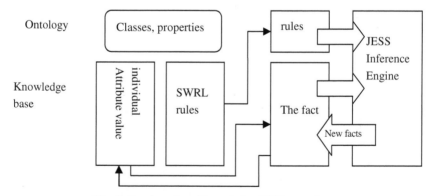

**Fig. 2.** SWRL described in protege

# 4    The Reasoning Based on JESS Inference Engine

When in ontology reasoning, can maps to JESS (Java expert shells system) reasoning inference engine. JESS is CLISP inference engine based on the Java language, its advantages are: inference engine is open, can undertake in different areas of reasoning work when users provide different rules system, it can also expand the reasoning ability of the inference engine.

Its working process is as shown in figure 3.

**Fig. 3.** Ontology-based knowledge JESS reasoning

Converting SWRL rules into JESS rules, parts of the conversion of the rules are shown as follows:

Rule soilclassrule :

    IF      "x" IS A soilclass
    AND IF      "position" IS LESS THAN OR EQUAL TO 31
    AND IF      "rainfall" IS LESS THAN OR EQUAL TO 5
    AND IF      "p" IS GREATER THAN 21.8
    AND IF      "salinity" IS GREATER THAN 1

AND IF        "light" IS LESS THAN OR EQUAL TO 4
THEN          "x" class is "class3"

Converting results is shown in figure 4:

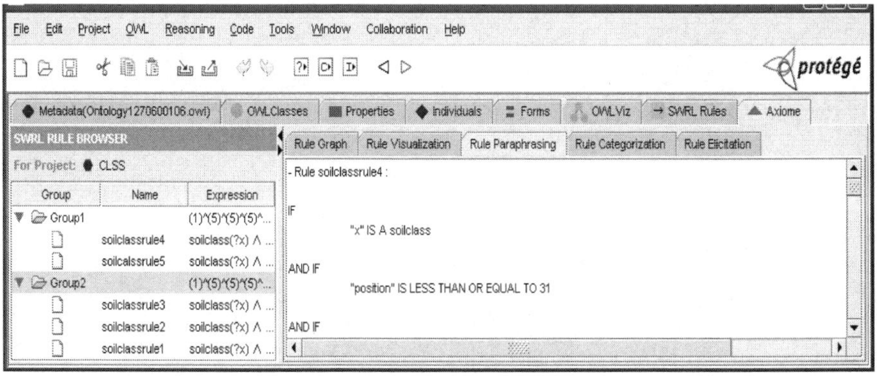

**Fig. 4.** Converting results

By JESS ontology to the rules of the conversion, JESS rules convert into ontology, and stored in the ontology. When inquiry by ontology reasoning, it can get productivity grade. The rules storage in ontology is shown as bellow:

```
<swrl:Imp rdf:about="soilcalssrule5">
    <swrl:body>
        <swrl:AtomList>
            <rdf:first>
                <swrl:ClassAtom>
                    <swrl:argument1 rdf:resource="#x"/>
                    <swrl:classPredicate rdf:resource="#soilclass"/>
                </swrl:ClassAtom>
            </rdf:first>
            <rdf:rest>
                <swrl:AtomList>
                    <rdf:first>
                        <swrl:BuiltinAtom>
                            <swrl:arguments>
                                <rdf:List>
                                    <rdf:first rdf:resource="#p"/>
                                    <rdf:rest>
                                        <rdf:List>
                                            <rdf:rest
```

## 5    Realize the Productivity Grade Evaluation System

System is designed by Java language. Protégé is use to edit ontology, SWRL is used to edit ontology rules, and deposit to ontology, the treat decision data uses JESS reasoning to get productivity grade. The system includes data layer, model layer and reasoning layer, total three layers, and the overall framework as shown in figure 5:

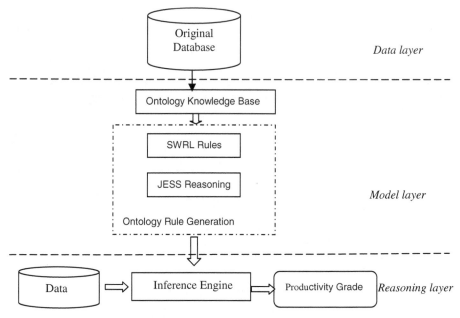

**Fig. 5.** Overall system framework

User input awaiting decision making data through the user interface of the system, the system calls inference engine to do the decision, and then get the productivity grade.

## 6    Conclusion

This paper uses protégé 3.4 the ontology development environment to create the ontology classes, properties, and individuals, in SWRL Tab environment edit SWRL reasoning rules, based on this,  establishes the reasoning frame system on the basis of JESS inference engine. This paper realizes knowledge base reasoning component by the OWL and SWRL, and provides rule-based reasoning mechanism for semantic Web. The reasoning method based on ontology and SWRL is a supplement for reasoning, and provides a new way for intelligent reasoning.

**Acknowledgments.** Funding for this research was provided by youth fund of Jilin agricultural university (NO.201133) and the development of science and technology plan projects of Jilin province (NO. 201101114), the national science and technology support projects(NO. 2009BADA5B03), the spark plan project (NO. 2008GA661003).

# References

1. Zhu, L., Tao, L., Huang, C.: Semantic Web: Concept, Approach and Application. Computer Engineering and Applications (03) (2004)
2. Liu, C.: The Research of Corn Disease and Pest Prevention and Cure Semantic Searching System Based on Ontology. JiLin University (2007)
3. CIM Engineering, Inc. ProtegeWiki: SWRLTab(EB/OL) (March 05, 2009), http://protege.cim3.net/cgi-bin/wiki.pl?SWRLTab (June 21, 2009)
4. Sandia National Laboratories. JESS, the Rule Engine for the Java Platform(EB/OL) (November 11, 2008), http://Herzberg.ca.sandia.govJESS (July 12, 2009)
5. Guo, J.: Domain ontology construction and its application in information retrieval. Beijing University of post and telecommunications (2007)
6. Li, J., Su, X.-L., Qian, P.: The methodology of developing domain ontology. Computer and Agriculture 7, 7–10 (2003)
7. Dai, W.: The semantic web information organization technology and method, pp. 238–254. Harvard University press, Shanghai (2008)
8. Ji, Z.-H., Li, C.-H.: Constructing and Strategy Analyzing of Rule System for the Semantic Web Based on SWRL and Jess. Journal of Huaihai Institute of Technology (Natural Sciences Edition) (04), 26–29 (2009)

# Research on the $k$-Coverage Local Wireless Network and Its Communication Coordination Mechanism Design

Rongchang Yuan[1,2], Haigan Yuan[3], Si Chen[4], Longqing Sun[2,*], Feng Qin[2],
Han Zhang[5],Yukun Zhu[2], and Daokun Ma[2]

[1] Power Automation Department, China Electric Power Research Institute,
Beijing100192, P.R. China
[2] College of Information and Electrical Engineering, China Agricultural University,
Beijing 100083, P.R. China
[3] School of sciences, South China University of Technology, GuangZhou510640, P.R. China
[4] Department of Electrical Engineering,
State University of New York (SUNY) at Buffalo, New York 14260, U.S.
[5] School of management, Tianjin University, Tianjin300072, P.R. China
sunlq@cau.edu.cn

**Abstract.** Based on the analysis of the present situation and features of local wireless network, combined the networking technologies, we constructing the wireless network layout algorithm and sensor nodes model. Through delaminating iterative optimization algorithm, optimal layout of sensor data collection and satisfy recognition, quasi-geoids orientation, signal coverage optimization have been realized. Compared the triangular, square and hexagon scheme, and get a general scheme of multiple complete coverage by calculate the length of sides on the polygon. Monte Carlo algorithm is used in choosing the optimum proposal comparing among the regular triangle, square and the hexagon in different conditions. For locating network, analyze the advantages and disadvantages of triangle, square and hexagon schemes in deferent positioning accuracy of double coverage, we set different layout schemes to different situations. Application manual is provided for the constructor to refer to these table lookup to attain the right numerical value.

**Keywords:** $k$-coverage, local wireless network, communication coordination, Monte Carlo.

## 1    Introduction

In the subject of internet of things, different kinds of information are transferred by sensor nodes. In order to improve the efficiency and stability of the transmission through networks, the layout of the nodes must be optimized. (Zhang Honghai and Hou Jennifer,2005; Yu Hongyi,2008).

Zigbee is one of the hardware equipment used in the wireless communication technology. It has many advantages, for example, the connection distance is shorter

---

* Corresponding author.

D. Li and Y. Chen (Eds.): CCTA 2011, Part I, IFIP AICT 368, pp. 390–401, 2012.
© IFIP International Federation for Information Processing 2012

and the complexity is smaller, the power consumption is lower and so on. In the automatic control and remote control field, it is widespread. Many communicators are inset with Zigbee. It consists of three models: the response model; the data manipulation model; the communication model. The response model is to receive the information. The information is transferred through the communication model. With such information, we can attain the location of the moving nodes. (Duc A. Tran, Usman Khan,  2006)

## 2    Methods and Algorithms

### 2.1    The Network Evaluation Function

When to evaluate a network, we often consider the following two factors: the network performance and the cost. The network performance includes the stability in transfer information and the accuracy in location. It depends on the overlapping area. The cost depends on the number of nodes. The more nodes there are the higher cost and power consumption.

When the target area is  $k$ -coverage, the size of area covered is:

$$S_{be\,covered} = ab \tag{1}$$

If the number of nodes in this area is  $n$ , the coverage area is:

$$S_{all} = n\pi R^2 \tag{2}$$

Where:  $a$  is the length of the target area,

  $b$  is the width of the target area

  $R$  is the effective communication radius.

At the same time, every point in the target area has the very same information collection accuracy.

**Definition 1.** The coverage rate of sensor  $\eta$ 

This passage comes up with the concept of coverage rate. It means the ratio between the size of target area and the sum of all the coverage area provided by the nodes.

$$\eta = \frac{\bigcup_{i=1}^{n} S_i}{\sum_{i=1}^{n} S_i} \tag{3}$$

It can reflect on the utilization of the coverage area. The larger  $\eta$ , the better the net performance is. At the same time, it can reflect the number of nodes. The fewer the nodes are, the lower the cost is. In another words, the lower the coverage rate, the better the layout of the network.

In a 1-coverage network, the calculation function is defined:

$$g_1 = (S_{cover} - S_{be\,covered})/S_{be\,covered} = \frac{1}{\eta} - 1 \qquad (4)$$

Through the discussion, the coverage rate is solved. In the 1-coverage network, it is 82.7%. In fact, it can't reach the perfect value 1.

In a $k$-coverage network, the covered area can be considered as:

$$kS_{be\,covered} = kab \qquad (5)$$

All in all, in a $k$-coverage network, the calculation function is defined:

$$g_k = (S_{cover} - S_{be\,covered})/S_{be\,covered} = \frac{k}{\eta} - 1 \qquad (6)$$

## 2.2    The Layout of Nodes in 1-Coverage Network

To design the nodes layout, for a target area, the main problem is how to make the area is covered without blind spot, which means that the point can't be covered. According to the simplification of the covered area—the circle, we can turn the problem into geometric. For a $ab$ rectangle region, how to be fitted together can use the least circles and how many circles are needed. As no matter small the radius of the circle is, it impossible to cover the area without blind point, so we take the second best solution that the circle is replaced with its inscribed polygon and the node is located on the center of the polygon.

If there are $x$ polygons put on the same vertex, and every $n$ gon's interior angle is:

$$(n-2)*180° / n \qquad (7)$$

Then:

$$x\frac{(n-2)*180°}{n} = 360° \qquad (8)$$

The solution is:

$$x = 2 + \frac{4}{n-2} \qquad (9)$$

Because $x$ is positive integer, then:

$$n = 3, x_3 = 6;$$
$$n = 4, x_4 = 4; \qquad (10)$$
$$n = 6, x_6 = 3;$$

From that we can see the polygon can be regular triangle, square and the hexagon like the following Figure 1 shows.

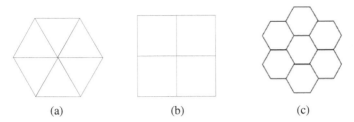

| (a) | (b) | (c) |

**Fig. 1.** Three different kinds of repetitive units

Locate the nodes according to the above way, then we can get the covered area without blind points.

$$A_C = A_S - A_L = \pi R^2 - \frac{nR^2}{2}\sin\frac{2\pi}{n} \tag{11}$$

Where:

$A_C$ means the size of overlapping area.

$A_L$ means the size of the circle with the effective communication radius.

$A_S$ means the size of inscribed polygon. $n$ is the number of the sides on the polygon.

When $n \to \infty$, $A_C \to 0$. So in order to make sure, there is no blind node. When $n = 6$, the overlapping area is minimum:

$$A_{C\min} = (\pi - \frac{3\sqrt{2}}{2})R^2 \tag{12}$$

Using the hexagon to locate the nodes is the best layout(Zhang Chaohui,2010).

Using the Definition 1 in the model one, we can calculate the coverage rate $\eta_S$:

$$\eta_S = \frac{A_S}{A_L} = \frac{3\sqrt{3}R^2 / 2}{\pi R^2} = 82.7\% \tag{13}$$

Then the calculation function is:

$$g_1 = \frac{1}{\eta_S} - 1 = 0.2092 \tag{14}$$

## 2.3    The Layout of Nodes in $k$-Coverage Network

During the research on $k$-coverage network, the two puzzles challenge us. One is that if the geometric shapes in $k$-coverage network is the same to the $1$-coverage network. Another one is that how to calculate the distance between the two nodes.

We regard the second question as the breakthrough point to compute the distance between two nodes in $k$-coverage network. we have proven that there are three possibilities: regular triangle, square and the hexagon. And the node is located on the vertex.

We can see the vertex is the most difficult point to be covered. So if the vertex is covered by $k$ times, the area is covered by $k$ times.

We select one of the vertex $M$, to solve $(x_M, y_M)$ using the equation of the straight lines: $L_1$, $L_2$. In order to make sure $M$ is covered $k$ times, which is that there are k nodes lie in the effective communication circle of $M$:

$$\sqrt{(x_M - x_N)^2 + (y_M - y_N)^2} \le R^2 \tag{15}$$

$(x_N, y_N)$ is one of nodes $N$ surrounded the node $M$.

Define a distance function:

$$G = R^2 - \sqrt{(x_M - x_N)^2 + (y_M - y_N)^2} \tag{16}$$

Only if G>0,the target area is $k$-coverage.

Assume that: N is the point of intersection between $L_1{}', L_2{}'$.

Then we can get the $L_1{}', L_2{}'$ through translating $L_1$, $L_2$ passing $k_1$ and $k_2$ units.

Then $N(x_N, y_N)$ can be expressed by $M(x_M, y_M)$.

$$x_N = x_M(k_1);$$
$$y_N = y_M(k_2); \tag{17}$$

Then the distance $G$ can be expressed by $k_1$ $k_2$.

$$G(k_1, k_2) = R^2 - \sqrt{(x_M - x_N)^2 + (y_M - y_N)^2} \tag{18}$$

We must find out the $k_1$ $k_2$, then we can get the distance between $M$ and $N$.

## (1) Solution

Taking the 2-coverage for example, introduce above model in detail.

We have proved there are three shapes; regular triangle, square and the hexagon showed in the following Figure 2:

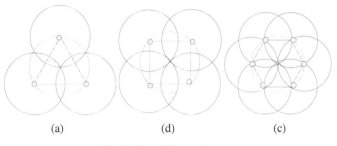

|     (a)     |     (d)     |     (c)     |

**Fig. 2.** The different shapes

From above Figure 2(a), we can see: when it is regular triangle, it has the least nodes

So we take the 2-coverage using regular triangle for example.

$L_1$、 $L_2$ showed in the Figure 3:

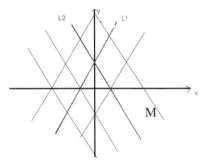

**Fig. 3.** 2-coverage using regular triangle

The equation of $L_1$、 $L_2$ :

$$y_2 = \sqrt{3}x - \frac{\sqrt{3}}{2}m \tag{19}$$

$$y_2 = -\sqrt{3}x - \frac{\sqrt{3}}{2}m \tag{20}$$

We select one of the vertexes $M\ (0, \sqrt{3}m/2)$.

Then we can get the $L_1'$, $L_2'$ through translating $L_1$, $L_2$ passing $k_1$ and $k_2$ units

$$y_1 = \sqrt{3}(x + k_1 m) - m\sqrt{3}/2 \tag{21}$$

$$y_2 = -\sqrt{3}(x + k_2 m) - m\sqrt{3}/2 \tag{22}$$

Then coordinates of $N$:

$$x_N = -(k_1 + k_2)m/2 \tag{23}$$

$$y_N = (k_1 - k_2 - 1)\sqrt{3}m/2 \tag{24}$$

Then the distances function:

$$\begin{aligned} G &= R_2 - (x_M - x_N)^2 + (y_M - y_N)^2 \\ &= R_2 - m_2/4*(k_1 + k_2)^2 + 3/4m^2*(k1 - k2)^2 \end{aligned} \tag{25}$$

For $k$–coverage, we can express $k$ using the multiply of $k_1$ and $k_2$.

It means the number of points of intersection.

$$k = ab \tag{26}$$

Where:

$$k_1 = a, k_2 = b. \tag{27}$$

From that, we can get the numerical value. Then we can get the function: $G(k_1, k_2)$

$$\begin{aligned} G &= R^2 - (x_M - x_N)^2 + (y_M - y_N)^2 \\ &= R^2 - m^2/4*(k_1 + k_2)^2 + 3/4m^2*(k_1 - k_2)^2 \\ &= R^2 - m^2/4*(k_1^2 - k_1 k_2 + k_2^2) \end{aligned} \tag{28}$$

To simply the distance $G(k_1, k_2)$ into the $D(k_1, k_2)$:

$$D = k_1^2 - k_1 k_2 + k_2^2 \tag{29}$$

Because $k_1$ and $k_2$ are all integer, we can get the value of them through gradual enlargement from (0,0), for example: (0,1) , (0,-1) , (-1,0) ...... After getting the value of $D$, put the value in order of from small to bigger. The value order is the order to pick up $k_1, k_2$.

We can get the value of the function $D$ showed in Table 1:

**Table 1.** The value of the function $D$ when $k_1, k_2$ change from -10 to 10

| | -10 | -9 | -8 | -7 | -6 | -5 | -4 | -3 | -2 | -1 | 0 | 1 | 2 | 3 | 4 | 5 | 6 | 7 | 8 | 9 | 10 |
|---|---|---|---|---|---|---|---|---|---|---|---|---|---|---|---|---|---|---|---|---|---|
| -10 | 100 | 91 | 84 | 79 | 76 | 75 | 76 | 79 | 84 | 91 | 100 | 111 | 124 | 139 | 156 | 175 | 196 | 219 | 244 | 271 | 300 |
| -9 | 91 | 81 | 73 | 67 | 63 | 61 | 61 | 63 | 67 | 73 | 81 | 91 | 103 | 117 | 133 | 151 | 171 | 193 | 217 | 243 | 271 |
| -8 | 84 | 73 | 64 | 57 | 52 | 49 | 48 | 49 | 52 | 57 | 64 | 73 | 84 | 97 | 112 | 129 | 148 | 169 | 192 | 217 | 244 |
| -7 | 79 | 67 | 57 | 49 | 43 | 39 | 37 | 37 | 39 | 43 | 49 | 57 | 67 | 79 | 93 | 109 | 127 | 147 | 169 | 193 | 219 |
| -6 | 76 | 63 | 52 | 43 | 36 | 31 | 28 | 27 | 28 | 31 | 36 | 43 | 52 | 63 | 76 | 91 | 108 | 127 | 148 | 171 | 196 |
| -5 | 75 | 61 | 49 | 39 | 31 | 25 | 21 | 19 | 19 | 21 | 25 | 31 | 39 | 49 | 61 | 75 | 91 | 109 | 129 | 151 | 175 |
| -4 | 76 | 61 | 48 | 37 | 28 | 21 | 16 | 13 | 12 | 13 | 16 | 21 | 28 | 37 | 48 | 61 | 76 | 93 | 112 | 133 | 156 |
| -3 | 79 | 63 | 49 | 37 | 27 | 19 | 13 | 9 | 7 | 7 | 9 | 13 | 19 | 27 | 37 | 49 | 63 | 79 | 97 | 117 | 139 |
| -2 | 84 | 67 | 52 | 39 | 28 | 19 | 12 | 7 | 4 | 3 | 4 | 7 | 12 | 19 | 28 | 39 | 52 | 67 | 84 | 103 | 124 |
| -1 | 91 | 73 | 57 | 43 | 31 | 21 | 13 | 7 | 3 | 1 | 1 | 3 | 7 | 13 | 21 | 31 | 43 | 57 | 73 | 91 | 111 |
| 0 | 100 | 81 | 64 | 49 | 36 | 25 | 16 | 9 | 4 | 1 | 0 | 1 | 4 | 9 | 16 | 25 | 36 | 49 | 64 | 81 | 100 |
| 1 | 111 | 91 | 73 | 57 | 43 | 31 | 21 | 13 | 7 | 3 | 1 | 1 | 3 | 7 | 13 | 21 | 31 | 43 | 57 | 73 | 91 |
| 2 | 124 | 103 | 84 | 67 | 52 | 39 | 28 | 19 | 12 | 7 | 4 | 3 | 4 | 7 | 12 | 19 | 28 | 39 | 52 | 67 | 84 |
| 3 | 139 | 117 | 97 | 79 | 63 | 49 | 37 | 27 | 19 | 13 | 9 | 7 | 7 | 9 | 13 | 19 | 27 | 37 | 49 | 63 | 79 |
| 4 | 156 | 133 | 112 | 93 | 76 | 61 | 48 | 37 | 28 | 21 | 16 | 13 | 12 | 13 | 16 | 21 | 28 | 37 | 48 | 61 | 76 |
| 5 | 175 | 151 | 129 | 109 | 91 | 75 | 61 | 49 | 39 | 31 | 25 | 21 | 19 | 19 | 21 | 25 | 31 | 39 | 49 | 61 | 75 |
| 6 | 196 | 171 | 148 | 127 | 108 | 91 | 76 | 63 | 52 | 43 | 36 | 31 | 28 | 27 | 28 | 31 | 36 | 43 | 52 | 63 | 76 |
| 7 | 219 | 193 | 169 | 147 | 127 | 109 | 93 | 79 | 67 | 57 | 49 | 43 | 39 | 37 | 37 | 39 | 43 | 49 | 57 | 67 | 79 |
| 8 | 244 | 217 | 192 | 169 | 148 | 129 | 112 | 97 | 84 | 73 | 64 | 57 | 52 | 49 | 48 | 49 | 52 | 57 | 64 | 73 | 84 |
| 9 | 271 | 243 | 217 | 193 | 171 | 151 | 133 | 117 | 103 | 91 | 81 | 73 | 67 | 63 | 61 | 61 | 63 | 67 | 73 | 81 | 91 |
| 10 | 300 | 271 | 244 | 219 | 196 | 175 | 156 | 139 | 124 | 111 | 100 | 91 | 84 | 79 | 76 | 75 | 76 | 79 | 84 | 91 | 100 |

The constructor can refer to this application manual table lookup to attain the numerical value of $k_1$ and $k_2$, then they can get the best layout. Using the same solutions, we can get the results of square and the hexagon.

## (2) Algorithm

The flow chart in $k$-coverage network, See Figure 4:

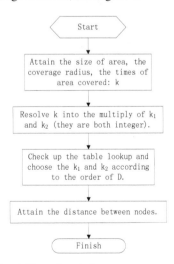

**Fig. 4.** Flow chart in k-coverage network

## (3) Cost of Network

**Definition 1.** Minimum repeat unit: the minimum unit while attaching the nodes, namely, triangular, square and hexagonal.

**Definition 2.** Node densities: the ratio of minimum repeat units and the number of the nodes in it. Symbol by $n$.

Because the cost of network only related to the numbers of nodes, the cost of a network can be expressed by $S/n$, where $S$ represent the area of minimum repeat unit.

**Table 2.** The value of $n$

| scheme | $n$ |
|---|---|
| triangular | 1/2 |
| square | 3/4 |
| hexagonal | 2 |

From the three discussing above Table 2 , the evaluation function is

$$g = q*k*\frac{S}{n} \tag{30}$$

## 2.4    Communication Coordination

When the effective radius of repeater is larger than or equals to the area radius (some repeater radius can reach more than 100 meters), only a repeater can cover the whole area. In order to mitigate interference, besides the geographical separation, the "continuous tone-coded squelch system" (CTCSS), sometimes nicknamed "private line" (PL), Since a repeater has a special frequency pair and a particular PL, and there are different demand of network serves (different frequencies used for different purposes) and the number of user, the spectrum range need to be divided into multiple channels.

So our task is optimizing frequency channel coordinate and the use of PL according to the users' quantities and purposes on the basis of complete coverage.

## 3    Results and Analysis

We already know that the layout scheme of triangular, square and hexagon by model two. The graphics respectively shown as figure…

Hypothesis environmental conditions and sensor performance is the same. Then analyze their advantages and disadvantages below Figure 5.

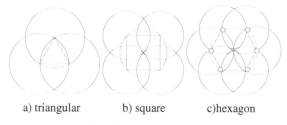

a) triangular          b) square          c)hexagon

**Fig. 5.** Layout scheme

Use Monte Carlo Simulation to calculate the three area ratio of double covered area with the whole area. The result shows in table 3 and table 4.

**Table 3.** The area ratio in square

| Simulation times | The number of nodes | The area ratio |
|---|---|---|
| 50000 | 268 | 0.00536 |
| 80000 | 441 | 0.005513 |
| 100000 | 554 | 0.00554 |
| 500000 | 2709 | 0.005418 |
| 900000 | 4989 | 0.005543 |

**Table 4.** The area ratio in hexagon

| Simulation times | The number of nodes | The area ratio |
|---|---|---|
| 50000 | 14678 | 0.29356 |
| 80000 | 23475 | 0.293438 |
| 100000 | 29393 | 0.29393 |
| 500000 | 146564 | 0.293128 |
| 900000 | 263982 | 0.293313 |

We have known that the double covered network in triangular scheme is actually covered triple by model two. So the ratio of double covered area with the whole area is 0 that is the positioning accuracy is 1.

As for square and hexagon, we take the area ratio by most times of simulation to calculate positioning accuracy and function values. The results show in table5:

**Table 5.** The positioning accuracy and function values

| scheme | triangular | square | hexagon |
|---|---|---|---|
| Area ratio | 0 | 0.005543 | 0.293313 |
| positioning accuracy | 1 | 1 | 0.71 |
| function value | 0.866 $q * R^2$ | 1.333 $q * R^2$ | 0.922 $q * R^2$ |

The higher value of function is, the better scheme of layout is. In order to select better layout scheme, we give a weight to each scheme based on the environment as table 6 shows.

**Table 6.** The weights based on environment

| environment | Good | Medium | bad |
|---|---|---|---|
| triangular | 0--0.3 | 0.3-0.7 | 0.7--1 |
| square | 0.7--1 | 0.3-0.7 | 0--0.3 |
| hexagon | 0--0.3 | 0.7--1 | 0.3-0.7 |

In conclusion, the layout scheme is as follows.

(1) If the environment condition is good, choose the square scheme.
(2) If the environment condition is medium, choose the hexagon scheme.
(3) If the environment condition is bad, choose the triangular scheme.

From table 3-4, The positioning accuracy of triangular and square scheme can reach to 1, but is too low in hexagon scheme. So we take the method of reducing the distance of nodes to increase the positioning accuracy.

Use Monte Carlo Simulation; we get the relation of nodes distance and the positioning accuracy. It's show in table7:

**Table 7.** The relation of nodes distance and the positioning accuracy

| Nodes distance | positioning accuracy |
|---|---|
| $m = R$ | 71% |
| $m = 0.9R$ | 81% |
| $m = 0.8R$ | 89.30% |
| $m = 0.7R$ | 95.90% |
| $m = 0.6R$ | 99.70% |
| $m = 0.5R$ | 100% |

So the procedure of layout is to choose the scheme based on the environment. And if the hexagon scheme is chosen, choose the nodes distance based on positioning accuracy.

## 4    Discussions

(1) To once complete coverage network, choose the hexagon scheme, and the node lies in the center, the length of sides is the effective radius.
(2) To more than once complete coverage, compared the triangular, square and hexagon scheme, and get a general scheme of multiple complete coverage by calculate the length of sides on the polygon.
(3) To locating network, compared the advantages and disadvantages of triangular, square and hexagon scheme based on positioning accuracy of double complete coverage.

**Acknowledgement.** This work was supported by 863 programs (2009BADB0B05).

## References

Yuan, R.: Wireless Network Organize Algorithm and the Application in Cotton Warehouse Management, China Agricultural University, Master Dissertation, Beijing (2011)

Yu, H., Li, O., Zhang, X.: Wireless sensor network theory, technology and implementation, Beijing, pp. 100–300 (2008)

Tran, D.A., Nguyen, T.: Localizatio in Wireless Sensor Networks based on Support Vector Machines

Usman, K.: Localization in Sensor Networks using Message Passing Algorithm

Zhang, H., Hou Jennifer, C.: Maintaining Sensing coverage and connectivity in large sensor networks. Jounral of Ad Hoc and Sensor Wireless Networks 1(1-2), 89–124 (2005)

Yang, B., Yu, H., Li, L., Li, H.: An Energy Efficient Coopenrative Density Control Algorithm in Large Wireless Sensor Networks. In: WCNC 2007 Proceedings (2007)

Klaus, F.: RFID Handbook, 2nd edn. John Wiley & Sons Ltd, England (2003)

Wang, R.: Treatment of sensor network covering localization method research (2009)

Qi, W.: Wireless sensor network node localization and covering technology research (2008)

Fan, Z.: Wireless sensor network covered with nodes deployment issues research (2008)

Zhang, C.: Hexagon node coverage model research (2010)

Gao, X.: The regional telecommunication covers node localization launch algorithm (2010)

Yang, Z.: Wireless sensor networks positioning problem solving linear programming algorithm (2008)

Yang, C.: Buildings fire monitoring wireless sensor node cover algorithms (2009)

# Design and Development of Variable Rate Spraying System Based on Canopy Volume Measurement

Kaiqun Hu[1], Zetian Fu[2], Ronghua Ji[3], Jun Wang[4], and Lijun Qi[2,*]

[1] College of Mechanical Engineering, Chongqing Technology and Business University,
Chongqing, 400067, P.R. China
[2] College of Engineering, China Agriculture University, Beijing, 100083, P.R. China
qilijun@cau.edu.cn
[3] College of electric and information engineering, China Agriculture University,
Beijing, 100083, P.R. China
[4] Chinese Academy of Agricultural Mechanization Sciences, Beijing, 100083, P.R. China

**Abstract.** Variable rate spraying technology can improve the pesticide utilization ratio, reduce the waste of pesticide, and canopy volume was a very important variable rate reference in orchard spraying, so a variable rate spraying system based on canopy volume measurement was presented and developed. The system was mainly made up of PC, ultrasonic sensor, single chip, flow control mechanism and nozzles. Ultrasonic sensors were used to measure the distances between sensors and canopy foliage. Data detected by sensors were sent to computer by single chip for further processing. Flow control mechanisms were used to adjust the flow rates of nozzles real-timely. Hardware and software design were introduced. Hardware design included hardware choice, connections and installation positions designs, and software design included flow chart design and system operation interfaces designs which were used to display the measurement results real-timely and vividly, and some spraying controls of the system could be completed in the system operation interfaces.

**Keywords:** Variable rate spraying system, Canopy Volume measurement, Ultrasonic sensor, Single chip.

## 1  Introduction

Variable rate spraying technology could be divided into map-based and sensor-based variable rate technology by the information source of variable rate decision. Crop protection workers did many studies on variable rate spraying technology of map-based. American MICRO-TRAK company developed the MT series automatic variables control system, the monitoring member surveyed the insect situation by the GPS antenna equipments mounted in the field. When insect situation was monitored, position of the disease insect area, type and density of the disease insects could be

---

* Corresponding author.

D. Li and Y. Chen (Eds.): CCTA 2011, Part I, IFIP AICT 368, pp. 402–413, 2012.
© IFIP International Federation for Information Processing 2012

recorded and sent to the PC by the GPS , and the prescription map was built and imported to the corresponding GIS[1]. Baijing Qiu et al. developed a variables application control equipment of Automatic target detection based on GIS, whose work principle was as follow: information about the application prescription map was gained by GPS, the analysis and processing of real-time data and history data were completed by GIS, during application, the application instruction was built by the computer console based on GPS equipment orientation, speed information transmitted by radar sensors, circuit pressure and decision information[2,3]. Wanping Shi et al. analyzed the makeup and control technology of variable rate control system based on GPS and GIS[4]. Many studies were also done on the variable rate application technology based on sensor. Schumann et al. developed a measurement system of canopy volume, the Durand-Wayland ultrasonic ranging system[5] was used in their study[6]. Ritchie et al. measured the canopy height using an airborne laser altimeter[7]. Nilsson developed a system to measure tree height and canopy volume, which included an airborne lidar system[8]. Lei Tian et al. developed an "automatic weed control system in tomato field based on machine vision" and a "application system based on difference GPS"[9,10,11]. The variable rate application system could be divided into chemical injection control system and coordinate injection control system of chemical and water. Ess et al. of Purdue University presented the chemical injection control system. Rehfeld designed a constant-ratio and coaxial direct injection equipment[12]. Womac et al. designed a coordinate control system of chemical and water[13]. Yubo Guo et al. applied the static mixer into the direct injection variable rate spraying system[14]. Haiyan Zhou et al. presented a new variable ratio and rate injection spraying system[15].

A variable rate spraying system based on canopy volume measurement was developed, which used ultrasonic sensors to measure the tree canopy volume.

## 2    Overall Design of Variable Rate Spraying System

The orchard air-assisted sprayer Hardi LB-255 was fitted with ten ultrasonic sensors which were mounted on the mast fixed on the sprayer (five on each side of the mast) and two flow control mechanisms(one on each side of the machine) to modify the flow rate of the nozzles in real time. The ultrasonic sensors were used to detect the distances from the sensors to the foliage at the corresponding height. The canopy diameters of different heights would be computed by the distances detected by sensors, and then the canopy volumes could be calculated by the measurement method introduced by Kaiqun Hu[16]. The single chips were used to send data from sensors to portable computer and transfer instructions from computer to flow control mechanisms in real time. Canopy volumes and canopy diameters measured by sensors were stored in the portable computer. The system was mainly made up of portable computer, single chips, ultrasonic sensors, flow control mechanisms and nozzle sets, and its schematic view is shown in Figure 1.

Where ultrasonic sensors L1-L5 and R1-R5 were mounted on the left and right side of the mast respectively, nozzles L1-L5 and R1-R5 were fixed on the left and right side of the sprayer respectively, flow control mechanism L and R were used to control the flow rates of Nozzles L1-L5 and Nozzles R1-R5 respectively.

Sensors mounted on left and right side were numbered from L1 to L5 and R1 to R5 respectively, and were used to detect the trees on the left and right side of the sprayer respectively. In order to reduce the signal interferences between adjacent sensors, the sensors on each side of the mast were divided into two groups respectively: sensor 1, 3, 5 and sensor 2, 4, which worked by turns. Sensors on the left side were taken as an example to introduce the work detail of sensors and single chip, whose work schematic view is shown in Figure 2. The temperature wouldn't affect the measurement precision of the system obviously, so temperature compensation circuits of ultrasonic sensors were not designed in this system.

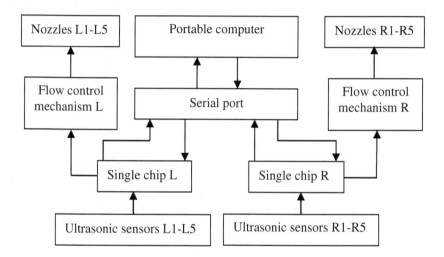

**Fig. 1.** Schematic view of variable rate spraying system based on canopy volume measurement

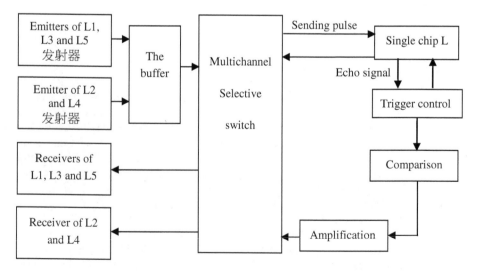

**Fig. 2.** Work schematic view of ultrasonic sensors and single chip

# 3     Hardware Design

## 3.1     Choice of Ultrasonic Sensor and Single Chip

Ultrasonic distance measurement module DYP-ME007 produced by JieYue Science and Technology Ltd in Shen Zhen was used in this research, whose photograph is shown in Figure 3. Five pins were set in the sensor, which were VCC, Trig, Echo, Out and GND.

**Fig. 3.** Photograph of ultrasonic sensor

STC12C5A60S2 series single chip produced by Hong Jing Science and Technology Ltd was used in this research, which was a single clock/machine period single chip, and had characteristics of high speed, low power consumption and strong anti-interference. MAX810 special replacement circuit was integrated in the single chip. The photograph of single chip is shown in Figure 4.

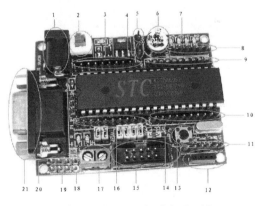

**Fig. 4.** The photograph of single chip

1 power plug  2 power switch  3 P0 port  4 power contact pin  5 5V power contact pin  6 buzzer  7 running light  8 AD interface 1-4  9 P2 port  10 P3 port  11 AD import interface 5-8  12 wireless module interface  13 replacement key-press  14 selection jumper of motor power  15 motor drive interface  16 P1 port  17 heavy current terminal  18 power supply contact pin of motor power  19 COM2 interface  20 TTL power level of COM2  21 serial port head

## 3.2     Connection of Ultrasonic Sensor and Single Chip

Four interfaces were needed by a ultrasonic sensor, VCC and GND were connected with VCC and GND of single chip, Trig and Echo were connected with the P port. Taking the left column sensors as an example, the connection of ultrasonic sensors and single chip is shown in Figure 5.

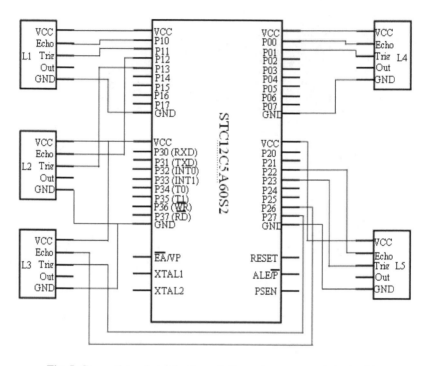

**Fig. 5.** Connection schematic view of ultrasonic sensors and single chip

## 3.3     Installation Positions of Ultrasonic Sensors and Single Chips

A mast was fixed on the center of tractor tail, whose length, width (which was parallel with crop row) and height were 5m, 0.08m and 0.05m respectively. Sensors and single chips were mounted on the mast, whose installation schematic view is shown in Figure 6. Where $H_T$ is the tree height above the ground, $H_S$ is the height from ground to canopy skirt, $D_R$ is the crop row spacing, $D_C$ is the distance between sensors and center line of crop row, $D_i$ is the distance between sensor i and the canopy foliage, $D_S$ is the sensor spacing. The height above the ground of sensors and the sensor spacing could be adjusted by the actual experimental objects.

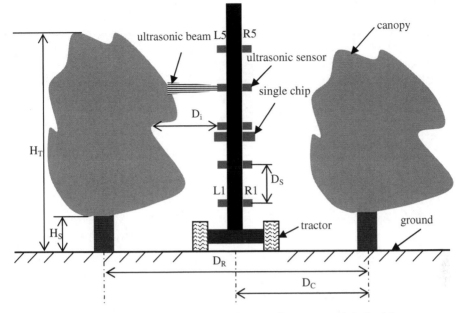

**Fig. 6.** Installation schematic view of ultrasonic sensors and single chips

### 3.4 Design of Flow Control Mechanism

Nozzle flows were changed with the change of canopy diameter values measured by sensors, so electro proportion control valve (EPCV) and electromagnetism valve (EV) were used to adjust the nozzle flows. Schematic view of flow control mechanism is shown in Figure 7. Electro proportion control valves and electromagnetism valves were controlled by single chip based on the canopy diameters detected by ultrasonic sensors. Pressure of pump outlet was reduced by proportional decompressing valve, and was maintained between 0 and 0.6MPa to ensure the normal application pressure needed by application equipment. The flow and pressure were measured by flow meter and pressure meter respectively.

## 4 Software Design

### 4.1 System Interface Design

Start interface of the whole system designed by VC software is shown in Figure 8. Three systems could be accessed from the start interface, which were laboratory measurement system of canopy volume, orchard measurement system of canopy volume and variable rate spraying system based on canopy volume measurement.

The working screen capture of orchard measurement system of canopy volume is shown in Figure 9, where "parameters setup" area is used to set system working parameters, such as the distance between sensors and center line of crop row, sensor spacing and heights above ground of sensors. "Canopy diameter display" is used to display the canopy diameters detected by sensors, the crop number is also displayed in this area. "Tree shape display" area is used to display the tree shape vividly. The buttons on the bottom of the interface are used to start or stop the work of sensors and quit the system. "Start left series sensors" and "start right series sensors" in Figure 9 are grayer, which indicates that the left and right series sensors are working. The experiment details were introduced by Kaiqun Hu[17].

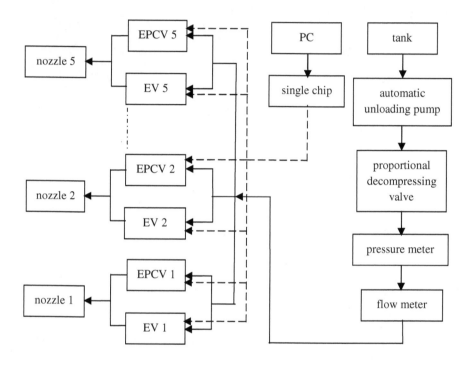

**Fig. 7.** Schematic view of flow control mechanism

The working screen capture of variable rate spraying system based on canopy volume measurement is shown in Figure 10, where "parameters setup" area is used to set system parameters, "crop parameter display" area is used to display the crop number, canopy volume of a single crop and canopy diameters detected by sensors. "Nozzle flow display" area is used to display the current nozzle flows. Buttons on the bottom left of the interface are used to start or stop spraying and quit the system. "Start left spraying" button in Figure 9 is grayer, which indicates that only the left spraying unit is started, so only the crop parameters and nozzle flows of left spraying unit are displayed in Figure 10.

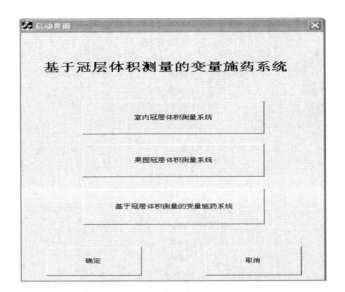

**Fig. 8.** Start interface of the whole system

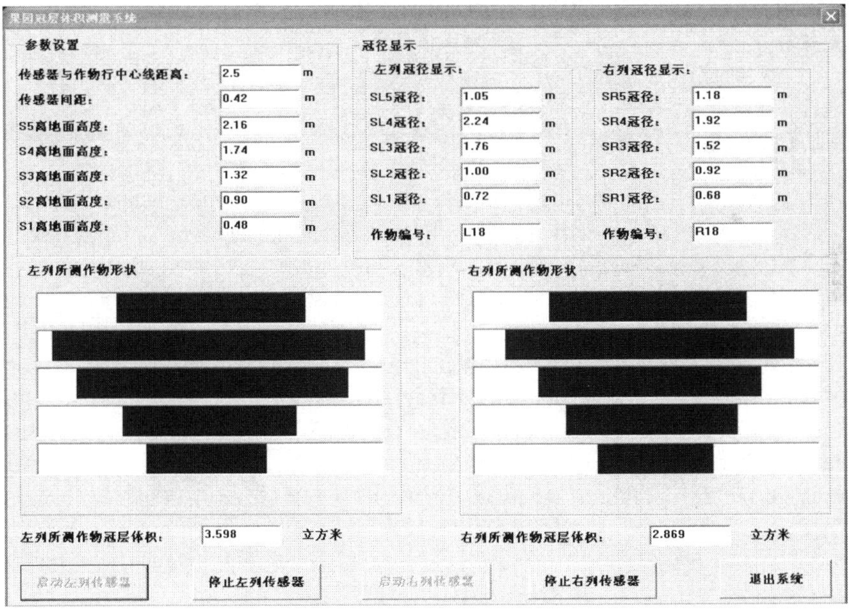

**Fig. 9.** The working screen capture of orchard measurement system of canopy volume

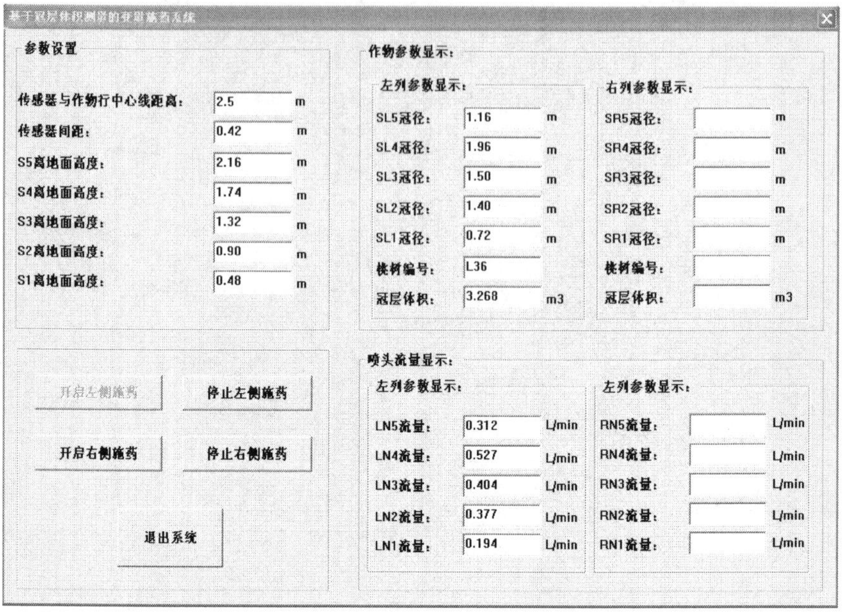

**Fig. 10.** The working screen capture of variable rate spraying system based on canopy volume measurement

## 4.2    Flow Chart Design

The control flow chart of single chip to ultrasonic sensors is shown in Figure 11. Where the single chip is started and initialized first, and then waits for instructions from host computer. The single chip controls ultrasonic sensors by instructions of host computer, and also sends the measured data to computer by RS232 serial port for further data processing.

Taking one ultrasonic sensor as an example, the work flow chart of sensor is shown in Figure 12. Where t is the calculagraph reading after completing sampling, the subscript represents sampling times, buffer T is used to store the lesser calculagraph reading of two adjacent samplings. At last, the minimum value was gained, and the minimum distance between sensors and canopy foliage was calculated.

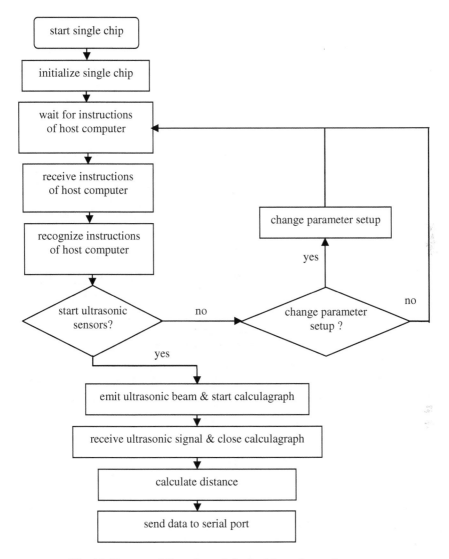

**Fig. 11.** The control flow chart of single chip to ultrasonic sensors

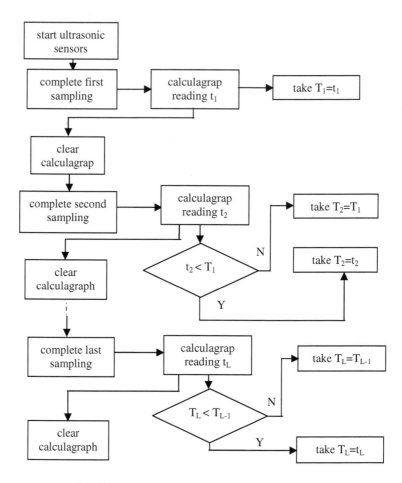

**Fig. 12.** The work flow chart of ultrasonic sensor

# 5    Conclusion and Discussion

A variable rate spraying system based on canopy volume measurement was presented and developed, which included PC, single chip, ultrasonic sensors, flow control mechanism and nozzles. Hardware and soft ware designs were introduced in this research. Hardware design mainly included choice of hardware, connections of hardware and installation of hardware. Software design mainly included system interface design and flow chart design. Canopy volumes could be measured by this system, the measurement results could be displayed in system interface vividly, and the system control could be implemented from the system interface.

The system realized the automatic measurement of canopy volumes, but more experiments should be done to determine the accuracy and applicability of the system, affection of weather conditions such as wind velocity, wind direction on the system, and the canopy volume measurement time of the system should be analyzed to confirm whether the time delay is allowed in the whole variable rate spraying system.

**Acknowledgements.** We wish to thank Zhang Jianhua for their technical assistance. The work was funded by the National Key Technology R&D Program of China (2007BAD89B04) and the National High-tech R&D Program of China (2008AA100905).

# References

1. The MT-9000 Automatic Rate Control. GPS and PC Compatible for Variable Rate Application, http://www.micro-trak.com/2004Catalog/
2. Qiu, B.J., Li, H.F., Wu, C.D., et al.: One variable-rate spraying equipment and its key technology. Jiangsu University: Natural Science Edition 25(2), 97–100 (2004)
3. Li, H.F., Qiu, B.J., Liu, B.L., et al.: Study on the control of variable-rate spraying in precision agriculture. Chinese Agricultural Mechanization 3, 25–27 (2004)
4. Shi, W.P., Wang, X., Wang, X.Z., et al.: Variable rate spraying technology on the basis of GPS and GIS. Journal of Agricultural Mechanization Research 2, 19–21 (2007)
5. Durand-Wayland Inc., Smart spray operator's manual. LaGrange, GA (1998)
6. Schumann, A.W., Zaman, Q.U.: Computers and Electronics in Agriculture 47, 25 (2005)
7. Ritchie, J.C., Evans, D.L., Jacobs, D., Everitt, J.H., Weltz, M.: Transactions of ASAE 36, 1235 (1993)
8. Nilsson, M.: Remote Sensing and Environment 56, 1 (1996)
9. Tian, L.: Sensor-based precision chemical application systems. World Congress of Computers in Agriculture and Nature Resources, 279–289 (2002)
10. Tian, L.: Development of a sensor-based precision herbicide application system. Computers and Electronics in Agriculture 36, 133–149 (2002)
11. Tian, L., Reid, J.R., Hummel, J.W.: Development of precision sprayer for site-specific weed management. Transaction of ASAE 42(4), 893–900 (1999)
12. Rehfeld, F. L.: Fluid motor metering device:USA, 4832071[P] (December 28, 1987)
13. Womac, A.R., Valcore, D.L., Maynard, R.: Variable-concentration direct injection from fixed-ratio diluent-driven pumps. Transactions of the ASAE 45(6), 1721–1728 (2002)
14. Guo, Y.B., He, X.K., Song, J.L., et al.: Application of static state blender in auto mix pesticide equipment. Journal of Agricultural Mechanization Research 2, 147–149 (2008)
15. Zhou, H.Y., Yang, X.J., Yan, H.R., et al.: Variable ratio spraying pesticide injection system. In: China Agricultural Machinery Association 2008 Annual Conference Proceedings (2008)
16. Hu, K.Q., Qi, L.J., Fu, Z.T.: Research on the Influence Factors of Ultrasonic Measurement System of Tree Canopy Volume. Sensor Letters 9, 1220–1224 (2011)
17. Hu, K.Q.: Design and Research of Variable-rate Spraying System Based on Canopy Volume Measurement, doctoral dissertation of China Agriculture University (2011)

# A Wireless Sink Node Using Information Fusion for Water Quality Information Collection in Factory Aquaculture

Yuting Yang, Haijiang Tai, Daoliang Li[*], and Yaoguang Wei

College of Information and Electrical Engineering, China Agricultural University,
Beijing 100083, P.R. China
dliang1@cau.edu.cn

**Abstract.** Water quality information collection is an important part of factory aquaculture. This paper proposes a kind of wireless sink nodes using information fusion for water quality information collection in factory aquaculture. In the sink nodes, Support Vector Regression and fuzzy algorithmic approach are used for information fusion. Making decisions according to information fusion, it converts the collected water quality information into a simple parameter that signified the current state of water quality. The sink nodes can eliminate redundant information, reduce information transmission, thus save energy effectively and prolong the network life.

**Keywords:** the wireless sink node, information fusion, Support Vector Regression, Fuzzy Algorithmic Approach.

## 1 Introduction

In china, the traditional aquaculture is usually in the consumption of natural resources and at the cost of environmental pollution. Recently, the factory aquaculture has occupied an important position in china, and been the representative of the advanced agriculture and the trend of agricultural modernization. So the development of factory aquaculture is the inevitable requirement to realize the fishery breeding sustainable development. As we know, infrastructure equipment modernization is the basic condition to develop factory farming. Similarly, as the important component of factory aquaculture, water quality monitoring is the key link to promote factory aquaculture toward automation, large-scale, high yield and high quality. In monitoring area, sensor nodes usually gather all kinds of water quality information, such as temperature, light, dissolved oxygen, Ph, etc, which codetermine to the current water quality conditions[1-2].

Presently, the great majority water quality monitoring systems adopt the same method that data which was collected by each node will be transferred to the monitoring center directly, besides the monitoring center process data and send the

---

[*] Corresponding author.

D. Li and Y. Chen (Eds.): CCTA 2011, Part I, IFIP AICT 368, pp. 414–426, 2012.

control instruction. But this method brings so big burden that transmission speed is slow. Moreover, many of the data transmission are redundant information for the monitoring center. Actually, the monitoring center just pays attention to the abnormal water quality conditions, and it will take control measures about water environment in abnormal conditions [3-5].

This paper, we refer to add the wireless sink node gather into the water quality monitoring system. Through information fusion at the sink node, all kinds of complicated water quality information will be converted into a simple parameter, and only send the abnormal water environmental data, which can extremely eliminate redundant information, effectively reduce the input data, thus save energy, prolong the network life, and improve the reaction of the whole monitoring system validly and accurately.

## 2     Hardware Structure Design

Figure 1 is the structure diagram of the wireless sink node, the device works as follows: As the CPU of the wireless sink node, the chip S3C2410 that was made by Samsung Company integrated the ARM920T core processor with 32-bits micro controller. The microprocessor contains 16KB instructions, 16KB data cache, LCD controller, RAM controller, NAND flash controller, a 12C bus controller, a 12S bus controller, four PWM timer and an internal timer, touch screen interface, two USB interface controller, four DMA channel, three UART, two SPI, parallel I/O interface, and maximum   basic frequency is 203MHz.   Depending on the rich peripherals and interface, it can accomplish some full-featured application under the condition of low cost and low power consumption. SPI serial port makes it possible to connect S3C2410 with XBEE chips, which realizes the data transmission between the embedded platform and the sensor nodes via ZigBee network; Two-way UART serial port connect respectively with MC35I chip and MAXI490 chip, so as to realize cable connection between the sink node and the monitoring centers, then accomplish data and control instructions transmission and related data storage via the GPRS network [6].

This equipment introduces dual mode communication. On the one hand, data which are collected by each sensor node that is deployed in the factory aquaculture area will be transferred to the wireless sink node through ZigBee communication module based on the RF chip XBEE. Furthermore, the on-site environment parameters and control instructions are sent via the ZigBee wireless network, which obtains reliable, accurate data transmission and data analysis. Its characteristics are at short range, low complexity, low power consumption, low cost, communication distance from standard of 75 meters to hundreds of meters or a few kilometers, and supporting for unlimited expansion. According to the demand of factory aquaculture, and considering the difference between the factory breeding and the standardization pond farming, the structure of wireless sensor network is based on the ZigBee protocol.

In addition, ZigBee network has different network topology of tree, star, etc. The paper is designed with the tree network structure, namely a cluster is constituted with a wireless

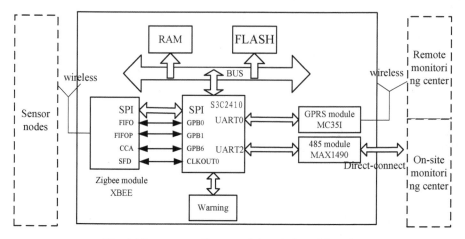

**Fig. 1.** The structure diagram of the wireless sink node

sink node (primary device), lots of wireless sensor nodes and some wireless control nodes (slave unit), and relay node; then a network is constituted with many clusters [7-8].

On the other hand, the connection of sink node with monitoring centers is in two ways of wired and wireless. Via GPRS network, the sink node could connect with the remote monitoring center. The MC35I GPRS module was designed into the equipment, and its output pins connect directly with the ARM processor's serial port 0(UART0). With stable performance and large working temperature range, low power consumption ARM serve as master controller, it can deal with protocol at high speed and a large number of data transmission. Moreover, convenient configuration, long communication distance, wide coverage area, real-time online terminal are all achieved. Based on TCP/IP protocol, it's convenient to manage network with high transmission rate, large data volume, low cost. Based on GPRS technologies, it improves the real-time and reliability of system.

On-site monitoring center can directly connect to sink nodes through cable connection. RS485 communication interface adopt the MAXI490 chip which is a kind of complete photoelectric coupling isolation RS485 data interface chip, simplex work way, maximum transmission baud rate can reach 2.5 Mb/s. Connecting directly with the ARM processor's serial port 2(UART 2), the relevant data of time, coordinate, etc, are read by the ARM processor as broadcasting information. It fully satisfies the needs of different monitoring centers with low cost, strong practical applicability.

## 3    Information Fusion

Because what the monitoring center just pays attention to is the abnormal water quality condition. Only when the environmental conditions are in the abnormal situation may take control measures. If doing Information Fusion at sink node to find abnormal water environment and only sending abnormal water quality data, which can eliminate the redundant information, reduce the amount of data transmission, save energy, prolong the network life effectively, improve the rapidity and correctness of the whole monitoring system's response[9-10]. After each collection node power up, do the port and memory initialization first and apply for the ZigBee network. After getting the response of the network, scan each node by the network and then assign the network address that is not used within the given time to the node. Detection of whether the response of sensor is normal. If not, storage the alarm information for preparation to exchange information with the sink node, and at the same time set to 1 at the alarm bite. If it's normal, it can transmit data to sink node at short distance by the ZigBee. Then information fusion can be done at the sink node. The whole process of information fusion is shown in figure 2.

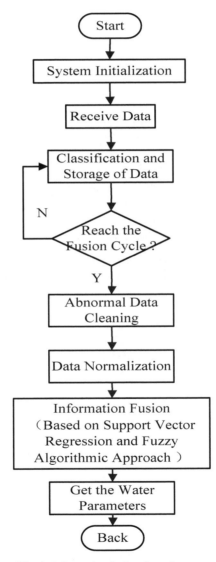

**Fig. 2.** Information fusion flow chart

This part of the information fusion is divided into two components, the first part is data fusion pretreatment.

## 3.1    Data Fusion Pretreatment

Data fusion pretreatment includes both abnormal data cleaning and data transformation.

### 3.1.1    Abnormal Data Cleaning

In this section, the main responsibility are abnormal data identification, eliminating noise, correcting the inconsistent data , deleting data redundancy and the completion of detection with sample data that are significant difference with other data in the collected data set. For abnormal data and noise, the principles of management is cleaning and not to participate in the fusion processing. Here we adopt the $3\delta$ standards based on statistic analysis. Firstly, it's assumption that a set of test data only contain the random error, and carry on calculation processing to get standard deviation, determine a range according to certain probability. It's supposed that exceeding the error range is rather the random error than the gross error, and contains the gross error of data should be rejected. With $3\delta$ criterion for judging calculation, firstly it's to get the average $x$ of the value $x_i$ to replace true value, then residual obtained $v_i = x_i - x$, getting standard deviation calculated by Bessel formula to replace $\delta$ , comparing the value of 3S with each residual $v_i$ , if the residual $v_i$ of some suspicious data $x_i$ meet next type, the data $x_i$ should be gross error and be eliminated.

$$| v_i |=| x_i - \overline{x} |> 3S \tag{1}$$

After every obliterating gross error, the rest of data will be recounted S. According to the new numerical that had become smaller S, further determining are measured again to judge whether there is gross error until without gross error. Bessel formula is as follow:

$$S(x_ik) = \sqrt{\frac{1}{n_i - 1} \sum_k (x_ik - x_i)^2} \tag{2}$$

### 3.1.2    Data Normalization

In order to eliminate error that is caused by differences in the dimension within different data source, the data from different data source will be normalized.

$$\widehat{x}_i = \frac{x_i - x_{min}}{x_{max} - x_{min}} \tag{3}$$

## 3.2    Data Fusion

Completing data pretreatment, the second part of information fusion is data fusion based on Support Vector Regression (SVR) and fuzzy algorithmic approach.

### 3.2.1    Support Vector Regression

In the factory aquaculture, because of indoor cultivation we can rule out the interference of natural environment, such as wind speed, wind direction, rainfall, etc. What we mainly concern is two factors, the water temperature and dissolved oxygen. Besides, the dissolved oxygen is the most important factor to effect the healthy growth of aquatic products. However, the adjustment of water quality in the breeding relate to what water quality factor are measured accurately and timely. But as circumstances change, there are certain delay itself for dissolve oxygen, and there is also the problem of transmission delay. So, the paper puts forward the information fusion algorithm which gets dissolved oxygen and water temperature as the input parameters of SVR, then the predicted value of dissolved oxygen as the result of information fusion. What the dissolved oxygen of next time is on behalf of water quality conditions make it convenient to control breeding environment timely and accurately [11-12].

The standard SVR algorithm is divided into the linear and nonlinear. The basic idea of the SVR is: it will transform the sample space into another feature space through the nonlinear transformation, and construct regression function in the feature space. The nonlinear transformation could be achieved by defining the appropriate kernel function $K(x_i, x_j)$ . Besides, $K(x_i, x_j) = \varphi(x_i) \cdot \varphi(x_j)$ , $\varphi(x)$ is a kind of nonlinear functions.

Given the training data, $\{(x_i, x_j), i = 1, 2, \cdots, n\}$ , $x_i$ is learning samples, and $y_i$ is the corresponding target. Define linear insensitive loss function is:

$$|y - f(x)|_\varepsilon = \begin{cases} 0 & |y - f(x)| \le \varepsilon \\ |y - f(x)| - \varepsilon & |y - f(x)| > \varepsilon \end{cases} \tag{4}$$

Namely, if the D-value between the target y and after learning of the structure regression estimation function f(x) is less than $\varepsilon$ , the loss is 0.

With the nonlinear circumstances, the regression estimation function is:

$$f(x) = \omega^T \cdot \phi(x) + b \tag{5}$$

Looking for a couple of $\omega$ and $b$ , which minimize $\dfrac{1}{2} \omega^T \omega$ under the same type (1).

Also consider to introduce the relaxation value $\xi_i, \xi_i^*$ when the constraint conditions could not be fulfilled, so the optimization problem is:

$$\begin{cases} Min \dfrac{1}{2} \omega^T \omega + C \sum_{i=1}^{n} (\xi_i + \xi_i^*) \\ s.t. y_i - \omega \cdot \phi(x_i) - b \le \varepsilon + \xi_i \quad \xi_i^* \ge 0, i = 1, 2, \cdots, n \\ \omega \cdot \phi(x_i) + b - y_i \le \varepsilon + \xi_i^* \end{cases} \tag{6}$$

Using Lagrange multiplier to solve the constrained optimization problem, so construct the Lagrange function:

$$L_p = \frac{1}{2}\|\omega\|^2 + C\sum_{i=1}^{n}(\xi_i + \xi_i^*) - \sum_{i=1}^{n}[\varepsilon + \xi_i - y_i + \omega \cdot \phi(x_i) + b] - \sum_{i=1}^{n}\alpha_i^*[\varepsilon + \xi_i^* + y_i + \omega \cdot \phi(x_i) - b] - \sum_{i=1}^{n}(\beta_i\xi_i + \beta_i^*\xi_i^*)$$

(7)

By the optimization theory, make $L_p$ to $\omega, b, \xi_i, \xi_i^*$ respectively for asking partial differentia, and make its 0.

$$\frac{\partial L}{\partial \omega} = 0 \Rightarrow \omega - \sum_{i=0}^{n}(\alpha_i - \alpha_i^*)\phi(x_i) = 0$$

(8)

$$\frac{\partial L}{\partial b} = 0 \Rightarrow \sum_{i=0}^{n}(\alpha_i - \alpha_i^*) = 0$$

(9)

$$\frac{\partial L}{\partial \xi_i} = 0 \Rightarrow C - \alpha_i - \beta_i = 0$$

(10)

$$\frac{\partial L}{\partial \xi_i^*} = 0 \Rightarrow C - \alpha_i^* - \beta_i^* = 0$$

(11)

When applies the type (5) in the type (4), we get the dual optimization problem.

$$\begin{cases} Max\left[ -\frac{1}{2}\sum_{i-1}^{n}\sum_{j=1}^{n}(\alpha_i - \alpha_i^*)(\alpha_j - \alpha_j^*)K(x_i, x_j) - \varepsilon\sum_{i-1}^{n}(\alpha_i + \alpha_i^*) + \sum_{i-1}^{n}y_i(\alpha_i - \alpha_i^*) \right] \\ \\ s.t.\sum_{i-1}^{n}(\alpha_i - \alpha_i^*) = 0 \\ \\ 0 \le \alpha_i \le C, 0 \le \alpha_i^* \le C \end{cases}$$

(12)

Support vector (SV) is part of parameters that make $\alpha_i - \alpha_i^* \neq 0$. Through learning and training, we can get the regression estimation function:

$$f(x) = \sum_{x_i esv}(\alpha_i - \alpha_i^*)K(x_i, x) + b$$

(13)

We also get:

$$b = \frac{1}{N_{NSV}}\left\{\sum_{0<\alpha_j<C}\left[y_i - \sum_{x_i esv}(\alpha_j - \alpha_j^*)K(x_j, x_i) - \varepsilon\right] + \sum_{0<\alpha_j<C}\left[y_i - \sum_{x_i esv}(\alpha_j - \alpha_j^*)K(x_j, x_i) + \varepsilon\right]\right\}$$

(14)

Besides, the function $K(x_i, x)$, which is known as the Kernel Function. Kernel functions enable dot product to be performed in high-dimensional feature space using low dimensional space data input without knowing the actual transform function $\phi$. All kernel functions must satisfy Mercer' condition that corresponds to the inner product of some feature space. The radial basis function (RBF) is commonly used as the kernel for regression:

$$K(\mathrm{x}_i, \mathrm{x}) = \exp^{\left\{-\gamma|x-x_i|^2\right\}}$$ (15)

After training and learning, we will establish the support vector regression model so as to realize the information fusion of acquisition. Then we will convert the results to practical engineering unit through inverse transformation [13-14].

$$\overline{x}_i = \widehat{x}_i * (x_{\max} - x_{\min}) + x_{\min}$$ (16)

Where $x_{\max}, x_{\min}$ is respectively the maximum and minimum value before normalization in Eq. (3).

### 3.2.2 Fuzzy Algorithmic Approach

Through the analysis of real object, Fuzzy algorithm is developed to process data and construct fuzzy mathematical model. With subordinate relations, the data set was changed into the fuzzy set to determine the membership function. Fuzzy statistics is more than the basis of experience a psychological process. It often works through the psychological measurement, and search the fuzziness of the thing itself [15].

In the paper, we adopt fuzzy algorithmic approach with triangle membership functions to make fuzzy computation for dissolved oxygen that had been calculated via the support vector regression algorithm. Then it's divided into the different water quality abnormal conditions as table 1:

**Table 1.** Water quality abnormal state

| The DO value | Numerical water quality state | Water quality state of fuzzy language description |
|:---:|:---:|:---:|
| (0,3] | 0 | The worst   poor |
| (3,4] | 1 | Secondly poor |
| (4,5] | 2 | poor |
| (5,8] | 3 | A bit poor |
| (8,+∞) | 4 | normal |

## 4    Study Site and Implementation

The practical wireless sink nodes had already been integrated in the water quality monitoring system which was implemented in the factory aquaculture farm of Xin Yongfeng aquaculture Co., LTD, located in Tianjin, China, one of Intensive Aquaculture Research Demonstration Centers of China Agriculture University. The system has stable operated more than one year and has obtained many water quality parameters.

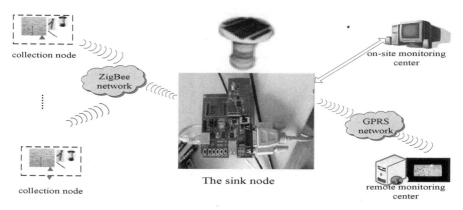

**Fig. 3.** Water quality monitoring system

The water quality monitoring system is shown in Figure 3. According to the actual demand, the collection nodes include DO sensor and temperature sensor which have the ability of self-calibration, self-compensation and self-diagnosis. Besides, the sensors are solar powered and adopt dormancy strategy to save energy. So the whole working process is that collection nodes collects water temperature and dissolved oxygen, and then sends the data to sink nodes through ZigBee wireless protocol; Secondly, in the sink nodes. making decisions according to information fusion, which converts the collected water quality information into a simple parameter that signified the current state of water quality; On-site monitoring center can directly get the regularly updated data from sink nodes through RS485 interface, then provide the function of data show, data storage and data download; At the same time, the sink nodes can transmit the data to remote monitoring center through GPRS channel, and remote monitoring center can also undertake the works of data receiving, data storage and data download. Besides the monitoring center will take control measures with water environment in abnormal condition.

## 5    Results and Conclusion

When being used in the water quality monitoring of factory aquaculture, the water quality monitoring system is stable and can meet the production need. The data which has been adopted in this paper spanned 6 days, from June 8 to June 13, 2011. The sampling interval is 30 minutes, which means 48sets of data has been collected per day, the total samples is 284. Figure 4 shows accurate value of water temperature and dissolved oxygen collected by the system.

In this paper, we put forward the information fusion algorithm which gets dissolved oxygen and water temperature as the input parameters of SVR, then the predicted value of dissolved oxygen as the result of information fusion. So we adopt 230sets of data as the training data to train the SVR modes, the last 54 sets of data as testing data to analysis the prediction performance of SVR. After the regression process, we get the optimal function as shown in Eq. (13) that can be used to take prediction. Because the sampling interval is 30 minutes, so we predict the dissolved oxygen value of 30 minutes later.

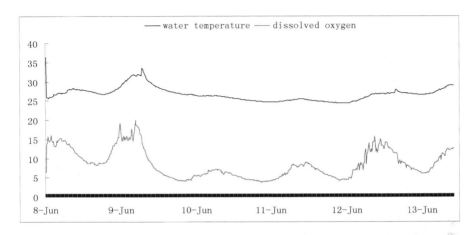

**Fig. 4.** Accurate value of water temperature and dissolved oxygen

In the experiments, the LIBSVM package had been used for SVM pattern recognition and regression. The package was designed by the Taiwan university professor LinChin-Jen. The specific steps as follows: (1) Format data sets according to the requirements of the LIBSVM package. Put the 230 sets of data that will be used to forecast into a file called "train", the rest of the 54 group into another file called "text". Content with the following format: 8.791 1:8.791 2:27.572, "8.791" on the left side is dissolved oxygen concentration, the rest said two variables influencing DO; (2) Choose the proper kernel function. The radial basis function (RBF) was used as the kernel for regression; (3) Select the optimal parameters with the cross validation method. The principle of the cross validation is dividing the training data into n parts (here for 10), selection n-1 parts for training every time, leaving one part as test. With MSE as evaluation standards, taking the punishment coefficient C, ε, kernel function parameter γ which are corresponding to the minimum MSE after the traverse all way. And the results can be seen from Table 2; (4) Adopt the optimal parameters to train the whole training set for the support vector machine model and forecast the dissolved oxygen value of 30 minutes later.

At the same time, we can get the Accuracy = 90.7407% (49/54). It proves the feasibility of the information fusion algorithm which gets dissolved oxygen and water temperature as the input parameters of SVR, then the predicted value of dissolved oxygen as the result of information fusion. Moreover, the prediction precision satisfies our demand, and the sufficient training data guarantee what the test data will forecast results accurately.

**Table 2.** The optimal parameters

| C | ε (MSE) | γ |
|---|---------|---|
| 128 | 0.0625 | 0.0078125 |

## 6    Conclusion

To solve the problems of water quality information collection and satisfy the needs of factory aquaculture farms, this paper designs a sink node using information fusion to integrate into the water quality monitoring system.

The ARM7 architecture of the 32-bit processors was introduced in the sink nodes as the hardware foundation. And depending on the rich peripherals and interface, it can accomplish some full-featured application under the condition of low cost and low power consumption. According to the actual requirements, the multi-mode of communication were adopted as follow: Firstly, the use of GPRS communication module will assist with collection data transmission to the sink nodes; Secondly, the on-site monitoring center could directly get the water quality information that had been processed at the sink nodes through the 485 interface; Furthermore, for the remote monitoring center, the on-site environment parameters and control commands of platform were via the ZigBee wireless network for data transmission. can obtain reliable, accurate data transmission and analytical. It can not only obtain reliable, accurate data transmission and analysis, but also satisfy the different operating requirements of farmers.

What's more, the sink nodes also have the function of information fusion that adopts Support Vector Regression and fuzzy algorithmic approach. According to information fusion, we can make decision to convert the collected water quality information into the simple parameters that could be on behalf of the current state of water quality. The measurement can eliminate redundant information, reduce information transmission, thus save energy effectively and prolong the network life. With information fusion, Water quality abnormal information can be found in real time, so as to improve the reaction validly and accurately of the whole water quality monitoring system.

Besides, the paper puts forward the information fusion algorithm that gets dissolved oxygen and water temperature as the input parameters of SVR, then the predicted value of dissolved oxygen as the result of information fusion. What the dissolved oxygen of next time is on behalf of water quality conditions make it convenient to control breeding environment timely and accurately.

At present, the sink nodes have been applied successfully into the water quality monitoring system, which were implemented at Intensive Aquaculture Research Demonstration Center in Tianjin. So it has a widely application value and market prospect.

**Acknowledgment.** This research is financially supported by the Science and Technology Projects of Tianjin Binhai new area: the Integrated Application and Demonstration of Factory Breeding Technology with High Efficiency and Low Carbon, the Twelfth Five-Year-Plant Outline for National Economic and Social Development of the People's Republic of China (2011BAD21B01) and Beijing Natural Science Foundation (4092024). The authors would like to thank the members of Intensive Aquaculture Research Demonstration Center in Tianjin for their hospitality and assistance.

# References

[1] Chatzigiannakis, I., Kinalis, A., Nikoletseasal, S.: Efficient data propagation strategies in wireless sensor networks using a single mobile sink. Computer Communication 31, 896–914 (2008)

[2] Zhang, Y.C., Qian, X., et al.: Field Measurement and Analysis on Diumal Stratification in Taihu Lake. Environmental Science and Management 6, 117–121 (2008)

[3] Alex, H., Kumar, M., Shirazi, B.: Mid Fusion: An adaptive middleware for information fusion in sensor network applications. Information Fusion 9, 332–343 (2008)

[4] Wang, Z., Leung, K.-S., Wang, J.: A genetic algorithm for determining nonadditive set functions in information fusion. Fuzzy Sets and Systems 102, 463–469 (1999)

[5] Bomberger, N.A., Waxman, A.M., Rhodes, B.J., Sheldon, N.A.: A new approach to higher-level information fusion using associative learning in semantic networks of spiking neurons. Information Fusion 8, 227–251 (2007)

[6] Du, Z.G., Xiao, D.Q., et al.: Design of water quality monitoring wireless sensor network system based Oil wireless sensor. Computer Engineering and Design 17, 4568–4570 (2008)

[7] González-Soriano, G., Ortega-Corral, C., González-Vázquez, S., Maeda-Martínez, A.: Remote Web Monitoring and Activation of an Experimental On-off Dissolved Oxygen Concentration Control Model Applied to Aquaculture Tanks. In: 52nd International Symposium ELMAR-2010, September 15-17, pp. 167–171 (2010)

[8] Cheng, C.R., Mao, X.G., et al.: An Online Monitoring System of Water Quality Based on ZigBee. Chinese Joumal of Electron Devices 5, 942–945 (2009)

[9] Jin, N., Ma, R.Z., Lv, Y.F.: A Novel Design of Water Environment Monitoring System Based on WSN. In: ICCDA 2010, China JiLiang University, pp. V2-593–V2-597 (2010)

[10] Yan, M.X.: Short-Term Predicting Model for Dissolved Oxygen of Hyriopsis Cumingii Ponds Based on Elman Neural Network (2011)

[11] Wang, Z., Hao, X.Q., et al.: Remote Water Quality Monitoring System Based ON WSN and GPRS. Instrument Technique and Sensor 1, 48–52 (2010)

[12] Li, C.N., Tan, C.H.H., Kao, S.J., Wang, T.S.: Improvement of remote monitoring on water quality in a subtropical reservoir by incorporating grammatical evolution with parallel genetic algorithms into satellite imagery. Water Research 42, 296–306 (2008)

[13] Liu, X.Q., Liu, Y., Gong, X.X.: Design of Intelligent Dissolved Oxygen Detecting System Based on CAN Bus and Embedded USB Host. In: 2009 International Conference on Measuring Technology and Mechatronics Automation (2009)

[14] Wei, Y.G.: Prediction of Dissolved Oxygen Content in Aquaculture of Sea Cucumber Using Support Vector Regression. China Agricultural University (2011)

[15] Huang, H.-C.L.L.-T., Lae, L.-F., Chi, Y.-F.: A Remote Automated System for a Case Study of Dissolved Oxygen Monitoring and Control. In: ISIE 2009, pp. 2184–2189. Chienkuo Technology University, Taiwan (2009)

# Experimental Study on the Reasonable Inbuilt-Ring Depth of Soil One-Dimensional Infiltration Experiment in Field

Guisheng Fan, Yonghong Han, and Min Song

College of Water Resources Science and Engineering of Taiyuan University of technology
Taiyuan shangxi province, China 030024
Fanguis5507@263.net

**Abstract.** Based on the field double-ring infiltration experiment under the condition of the same soil and with the different inbuilt-ring depths, the changes of soil cumulative infiltration and infiltration rate with inbuilt-ring depths were analyzed and a reasonable inbuilt-ring depth of the filtration test in field was confirmed. The results indicate that the measured precision of soil infiltration parameters is influenced by the inbuilt-ring depths. Namely, within a certain inbuilt-ring depth range, infiltration rate shows a trend of decreasing with the increasing of inbuilt-ring depth. nevertheless, when the inbuilt-ring depth reaches 19cm to 22cm the Infiltration rate curves are basically coincident. Therefore, the reasonable inbuilt-ring depth of the infiltration experiment in field should be between 19cm and 22cm. Through comprehensive consideration of the measurement accuracy, test instrument cost and test labor intensity, the reasonable inbuilt-ring depth of infiltration experiment in field can be targeted for 19cm if plough depth is less than 20cm; otherwise, the inbuilt-ring depth can be 20cm to 22cm.

**Keywords:** Double-Ring Infiltrometer, Inbuilt-Ring Depth, Infiltration Rate, Lateral Infiltration, Soil Moisture Infiltration.

## 1    Introduction

Double-ring infiltrometer is the most commonly used to measure the infiltration parameters of field soils. Its working principle is that the condition of one-dimensional vertical downward motion of soil moisture is formed in the inner rings with the help of the homocentric outer rings embedded in certain depth below the surface, and through measuring the infiltrating water amount in the inner rings the infiltration process and parameters of soils are obtained. The buried depth of homocentric inner and outer rings below the surface is defined as inbuilt-ring depth. At present, the international standards about double-ring infiltration apparatus is as follows, inner ring is 20cm high and inner diameter is 26.2cm; outer ring is 20cm high and inner diameter is 60cm; both the inbuilt-ring depth are 10cm. several decade field infiltration test datum obtained by writer with the standard double-ring infiltration apparatus showed that the height of the standard ring is not enough for obtaining the accurate test datum, the inbuilt-ring depth is lacking and the soil infiltration capacity

D. Li and Y. Chen (Eds.): CCTA 2011, Part I, IFIP AICT 368, pp. 427–436, 2012.

measured is deflective. Therefore, writer had processed a set of d double-ring infiltration apparatus with different ring heights and had performed a series of soil infiltration experiment with different inbuilt-ring depths in the same soil conditions, in order to attempt to explore the reasonable inbuilt-ring depth of double-ring infiltration experiment under the agricultural soil condition. Based on field experimental datum of soil infiltration, the change of soil accumulation infiltration and infiltration rate along with inbuilt-ring depth and the reasonable inbuilt-ring depth was measured. The results provided will be of important values for enhancing the measurement precision of field soil infiltration parameters.

## 2    Experiment Condition

### 2.1    Soil Condition

The tests measuring the influence of inbuilt-ring depth to soil infiltration ability was conducted in Shanxi Province center irrigation experimental station. The station is located in the middle reach of Taiyuan basin where the terrain is flat. The quality of soil material is mainly constituted of the River alluvial and proluvial deposit, and the soil type is moisture soil. The burial depth of Ground water table is between 1.5 and 3.5 meters. The soil plough layer depth is between 18cm and 22cm. The dry density of the surface soils is $1.05g/cm^3$, the volumetric water content is 15.9%; in the $10\sim20cm$ soil layer, the soil dry density is $1.346g/cm^3$ and the soil volumetric water content is 21.6% ; in the plough bottom layer, the soil dry density is $1.408g/cm^3$, and the volumetric water content is 27.1%; the soil dry density at underside of the plough bottom layer is $1.358g/cm^3$. the texture of 0-20cm surface soil is loam, clay content ( grain size < 0.002mm ) is 22.3%, silt content ( 0.002mm <grain size < 0.05mm ) is 47.5%,sand content ( grain size > 0.05mm ) is 30.2% ; the texture of 20-40cm soil layer is clay loam, clay particle content is 38.2%, silt content is 54.1%,and sand content is7.7% ; the texture of 40-60cm soil layer is sandy loam, clay content is 18.1%, silt content is 45.7%,and sand content is 36.2%.

### 2.2    Experiment Equipment

Three pieces of equipment were used in the tests. One is the international standard double-ring infiltration experiment which was manufactured by Northwest water resources research institute, the height of inside and outside rings is separately 20cm and 26cm, the inbuilt-ring depth into soils is 10cm.It is made of stainless steel. There are two stainless steel slices fixed symmetrically on both sides of the inside ring to control inbuilt-ring depth. Other two infiltration equipments is self-regulating, the inside ring diameter is 26cm,outside ring diameter is 64.4cm,the maximal inbuilt-ring depth of inside and outside rings can respectively reach 20cm and 25cm.

### 2.3    Experiment Program

In the selected test field, a set of soil infiltration tests were proceeded under the same soil condition, the inbuilt-ring depth is singly 10cm, 13cm, 16cm, 19cm and 22cm. The aim of the experiment was to reveal influence of inbuilt-ring depth to soil infiltration rate, and to ascertain the reasonable inbuilt-ring depth of field infiltration experiment. To ensure the consistency of the tested soil conditions, five infiltration tests with different inbuilt-ring depth were arranged within small plot with 3m×3m scale.

The tested time was identified as 90min (At this time, soil moisture infiltration rate of all tests reach relatively stable rate), in the ahead two minutes after infiltration begin, the long of each observed time interval was 30 seconds; within 2-15 minutes was 60-180 seconds; within 15-60 minutes was 300 seconds; after 60 minutes was 600 seconds.

# 3    Experimental Results and Analysis

## 3.1    Influence of Inbuilt-Ring Depth on Infiltration Processes

Fig.1 shows soil cumulative infiltration amount and infiltration rate curves with 10cm and 22cm inbuilt-ring depths in the same soil condition where moisture content, soil structure, content of organic matter, salinity content were the same. From fig.1 it can be aware that the influence of inbuilt-ring depth on soil infiltration processes and capacity was obviously.

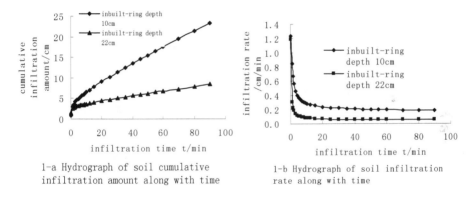

1-a Hydrograph of soil cumulative infiltration amount along with time

1-b Hydrograph of soil infiltration rate along with time

**Fig. 1.** Soil accumulative infiltration amount and infiltration rate curves with different inbuilt-ring depths

In Fig.1-a, it shows that the soil cumulative infiltration curve with 10cm inbuilt-ring depth is all along above the cumulative infiltration curve with 22cm inbuilt-ring depth, the cumulative infiltration amount within 90 minutes of the former is 23.3cm which is more twice than 8.381cm of the latter. Thus it can be seen that infiltration amount of the former was much larger than the latter. In Fig.1-b, the soil infiltration rate with 10cm inbuilt-ring depth is bigger than with 22cm inbuilt-ring depth, the relative steady infiltration rate of the former is 0.1889cm/min which is three times more than 0.0535cm/min with 22cm inbuilt-ring depth. By the above contrast of the infiltration rate and cumulative infiltration amount, it is showed that the measured infiltration capacity with small inbuilt-ring depth is greater than with big inbuilt-ring depth. therefore, inbuilt-ring depth had an distinct affect on the measured value of soil infiltration capacity. The deviation value should be occurred by the different lateral infiltration amount round the infiltration rings with different inbuilt-ring depths.

Fig.2 indicates the lateral infiltration processes generating in double-ring infiltration test.

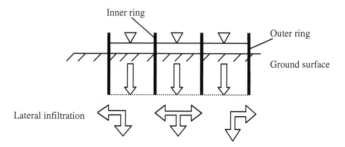

**Fig. 2.** Sketch map of lateral infiltration generating process in union thimbles infiltration experiment

Specific process of the lateral infiltration is as follows. Before moisture infiltration front arrives below interface of ring (such as 10cm), due to the hinder of inner and outer impervious ring wall, moisture infiltration belongs to the strict one-dimensional vertical infiltration, where no lateral infiltration takes place. After moisture infiltration front gets to 10cm depth, lateral infiltration begins to occur firstly in outer ring. The dynamical mechanism is that horizontal water potential gradient which is caused by inner and outer moisture content difference of outer ring boundary wall drove soil moisture migrate from outer ring inside to outer ring outside, namely, the moisture content in outer ring inside boundary overtops the moisture content in outer ring outside boundary, soil matrix potential of outer ring boundary inside is higher than outside.

Along with the happening of lateral infiltration on outer ring boundary, the advancing speed of infiltration stream vertical front in outer ring slows down, while the advancing of infiltration stream vertical front in inner ring keeps normal, which leads to the results that on the same horizontal surface, the soil moisture content in inner ring exceeds that in outer ring, a horizontal matrix potential gap between the inner ring and the outer ring is formed, and then infiltration stream moves from the inner ring to the outer ring. Namely, one-dimensional vertical infiltration condition is broken and lateral moving of infiltration stream in the inner ring occurs.

By above analysis, following conclusion is easily gained. Theoretically, no matter how much inbuilt-ring depth is, as long as infiltration time is enough long, lateral infiltration will emerge in both inner and outer rings. Here the key problem is explaining why the lateral infiltration of shallow inbuilt-ring depth is bigger than deep inbuilt-ring depth. Hereon and Green-Ampt infiltration pattern is introduced to explain the phenomenon. Model sketch map is showed in Fig.3.In Fig.3, $Zf_{22}$ and $Zf_{10}$ respectively are infiltration wetting front position with 22cm and 10cm inbuilt-ring depth, $\triangle x_{22}$ and $\triangle x_{10}$ respectively are sometime lateral infiltration travel length of 22cm and 10cm, i.e. horizontal infiltration distance $\triangle x$ which changes with time.

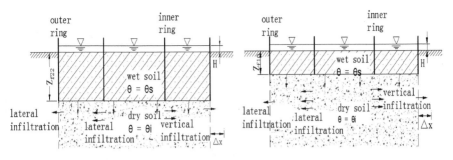

**Fig. 3.** Pattern sketch map with 22cm and 10cm inbuilt-ring depth

Based on the capillary theory, the infiltration problem of initial dry soil with lamina ponding on soil surface was researched with the help of Green-Ampt pattern. The pattern assumes are as follows: a horizontal wetting front exists definitely during soil moisture infiltrating, humid and non- humid region are separated by the horizontal wetting front, soil moisture content distribution is with ladder shape, moisture content in humid region is saturated content $\theta_s$ , soil moisture content underneath the wetting front is initial moisture content $\theta_i$. Surface ponding depth is supposed as $H$ and is not mutative along with time, the position of wetting front is $z_f(t)$ and migrated with infiltration time. Soil water suction underneath the wetting front is $s_f$ and is considered as a fixed value. Z coordinate origin zero is set on the surface, was positive downward. The total water potential on the surface is $H$ ,on the wetting front was $-(s_f + z_f(t))$ , therefore, water potential gradient is $[-(s_f + z_f(t)) - H]/z_f(t)$ .The flux from surface into soil, that in essence is the infiltration rate $i(t)$ of the surface was gotten by Darcy law.

$$i(t) = K_s \frac{z_f(t) + s_f + H}{z_f(t)} = K_s \left[ 1 + \frac{s_f + H}{z_f(t)} \right] \tag{1}$$

Formula (1) shows the relation between infiltration rate $i(t)$ and wetting front $z_f(t)$ .Here: $K_s$ is saturated hydraulic conductivity.

Formula (1) is vertical infiltration rate formula. A formula of horizontal infiltration rate $i'(t)$ representing lateral infiltration can be derived from vertical infiltration rate formula. Because the lateral infiltration is horizontal, the gravity potential gradient in horizontal direction is inexistent. Therefore, formula (1) could be turned into as follow:

$$i'(t) = K_s \left[ \frac{s_f + H + z_f(t)}{\Delta_x(t)} \right] \tag{2}$$

Next, On the basis of formula (2), it is analyzed why lateral infiltration of shallow inbuilt-ring depth is bigger than deep inbuilt-ring depth (taking 10cm and 22cm for instance).As it is seen from formula (2) that the value of $i'(t)$ is depended on the two

items $K_s$ and $\dfrac{S_f + H + z_f(t)}{\Delta_x(t)}$ . The effect of the two items to lateral infiltration

rate are separately analyzed as follow.

（1）Soil saturated hydraulic conductivity is related to soil texture and soil volume weight, the value becomes smaller when soil becomes dense and viscous. When inbuilt-ring depth is 10cm, Lateral infiltration occurs at 10cm depth, where the soil layer is located in plough layer, the soil type is loam, the soil volume weight is 1.05g/cm$^3$, the soil texture was lighter and volume weight was smaller. When inbuilt-ring depth is 22cm, lateral infiltration occurs at 22cm depth, where the soil layer is located in plough pan, the soil type is clay loam, the soil volume weight is 1.408g/cm$^3$, the soil texture was heavier and volume weight was bigger. Therefore, $K_{s22}$ of the latter is less than $K_{s10}$ of the former.

（2）In the item $\dfrac{S_f + H + z_f(t)}{\Delta_x(t)}$ , surface ponding depth H is definite value, soil

water suction $S_f$ in wetting front is related to soil moisture content, the value of $S_f$ becomes smaller along with increasing of moisture content. When inbuilt-ring depth is 10cm, the soil moisture content at 10cm depth where lateral infiltration occurs initially is 15.9%, while the soil moisture content at 22cm depth where lateral infiltration occurs initially is 27.1% .Therefore, $S_f$ of the latter is less than the former, namely, $S_{f22} < S_{f10}$. $z_f(t)$ expresses wetting front position. the value of 22cm and 10cm inbuilt-ring were 0.22 and 0.1.So following formula (3) is got.

$$\frac{S_{f22} + H + 0.22}{\Delta_{x22}(t)} < \frac{S_{f10} + H + 0.1}{\Delta_{x10}(t)} \tag{3}$$

By synthesizing above analyses, it can be achieved that the lateral infiltration rate with 22cm inbuilt-ring depth is smaller than with 10cm, namely, $i'_{22}(t) < i'_{10}(t)$ . Meanwhile, because the starting time of lateral infiltrating with 22cm inbuilt-ring depth is posterior to with 10cm, the sustain time for lateral infiltrating is shorter, and the soil area of the lateral infiltrating with 22cm inbuilt-ring depth is smaller than with 10cm. Therefore, the infiltration rate with 22cm inbuilt-ring depth was smaller than with 10cm, and the lateral infiltration rate with shallow inbuilt-ring depth is bigger than with deep inbuilt-ring depth.

## 3.2    Quantitative Influence of Inbuilt-Ring Depth on Infiltration Capacity

Fig.4 shows five sets of accumulative infiltration curve and infiltration rate curve under the same soil conditions and with different Inbuilt-ring depths.

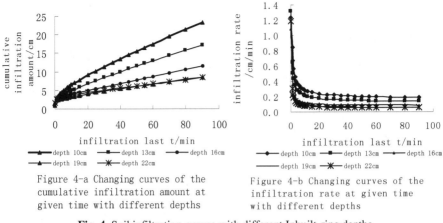

Figure 4-a Changing curves of the cumulative infiltration amount at given time with different depths

Figure 4-b Changing curves of the infiltration rate at given time with different depths

**Fig. 4.** Soil infiltration curves with different Inbuilt-ring depths

From Fig.4, following outcomes can be got.

⑴ The Cumulative infiltration curves with shallow inbuilt-ring depths are always above the curves with deep inbuilt-ring depths. In Fig.4, when inbuilt-ring depth increases from 10cm to 22cm, the cumulative infiltration amount at 90 minutes reduces from 23.302 cm to 9.381cm.

⑵ From Fig.4-a, it can be seen that when the inbuilt-ring depth increases to over 19cm, cumulative infiltration curves overlaps. Namely, the cumulative infiltration curve with 19cm inbuilt-ring depth overlaps basically with the curve with 22cm inbuilt-ring depth.

⑶ Fig.4-b indicated that during the whole process of infiltration, the infiltration rate curves with shallow inbuilt-ring depths are always above the curves with deep depth. When inbuilt-ring depth increases from 10cm to 22cm, the infiltration rate at 90min reduces from 0.1889cm/min to 0.0535cm/min.

⑷ When the inbuilt-ring depth increases to over 19cm, the infiltration rate curves overlaps nearly, namely, the infiltration rate curves of 19cm and 22am overlap basically.

The analysis above indicates adequately that inbuilt-ring depth has obvious influence on determining of soil infiltration capacity, along with the increasing of inbuilt-ring depth, measured cumulative infiltration amount and infiltration rate reduces, after the inbuilt-ring depth increases to 19cm the measured values are inclined to stabilizing instead of decreasing, namely, the curves of 19cm and 22cm overlap basically. Consequently After the inbuilt-ring depth achieves over 19cm infiltration processes is not influenced by inbuilt-ring depth.

Fig.5 and Fig.6 present respectively the changing curve of the cumulative infiltration amount at 90 minutes with inbuilt-ring depths and the changing curve of the steady infiltration rate at 90 minutes with inbuilt-ring depths.

⑴ In Fig.5, the changing curve of the cumulative infiltration amount at 90 minutes presents a reductive trend with the increase of inbuilt-ring depth and tends to stable after inbuilt-ring depth increases to more than 19cm.As showed in Fig.5, $H_{90}$ of 19cm is 8.506cm and $H_{90}$ of 22cm is 8.381cm.

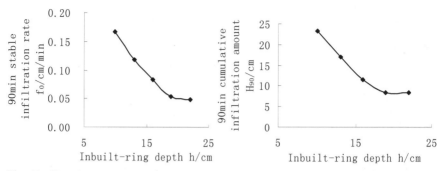

**Fig. 5.** Changing curve of the cumulative infiltration amount at 90 minutes with inbuilt-ring depths

**Fig. 6.** Changing curve of the infiltration rate at 90 minutes with inbuilt-ring depths

⑵  In Fig.6, the steady infiltration rate at 90 minutes presented a decreasing trend with the increasing of inbuilt-ring depth, last, the curve tended to horizontal. As Fig.6 showed, $f_0$ of 19cm is 0.0538cm/min and $f_0$ of 22cmis 0.0489 cm/min.

According to Fig.5 and Fig.6, following outcome can be got. After inbuilt-ring depth reaches more than 19cm, the cumulative infiltration amount and infiltration rate at 90min all tends to basically stable, which shows that when the inbuilt-ring depth reaches more than 19cm, soil moisture infiltration has reached a relatively stable level.

### 3.3    Reasonable Inbuilt-Ring Depth

Factors which should be considered in determining reasonable inbuilt-ring depth should be as follows:

⑴  Certain measurement precision should be guaranteed. The measured value should be close to the true value. Upper segment analysis shows that when the inbuilt-ring depth into soil were 19～22cm ,the measured infiltration rate already have tended to steady, therefore, the measured value with 22cm inbuilt-ring depth could be as approximation to true value.

⑵  Production cost of measuring apparatus should be considered. If inbuilt-ring depth into soil were too shallow, the production cost of measuring apparatus could be reduced, but the required measuring precision could not be achieved; if depths were too deep, though measuring precision could be achieved, production cost of measuring apparatus would increase greatly.

⑶  Difficulty and Labor intensity of driving rings into soil should be considered. If the inbuilt-ring depth was deep, thickness of ring walls should be increased, so the difficulty and labor intensity of driving rings into soil increased.

To determine reasonable inbuilt-ring depth the above three factors must be synthetically considered.

Fig.7 shows cumulative infiltration amount curve at each given time with different inbuilt-ring depths. In Fig.5, $H_{10}$ signified cumulative infiltration amount at 10min after tests begin, and so on. From Fig.5,it could be discovered that at every given moment, the cumulative infiltration amount presents the same variation trend. Namely Along with increasing of the inbuilt-ring depth, the every given moment, the cumulative infiltration amount decreases, and when depth reach 19cm~22cm the curves became parallel to the horizontal coordinates.

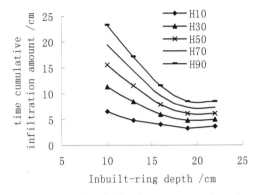

**Fig. 7.** Changing curves of the cumulative infiltration amount at given time with different depths

The measured Value with 22cm inbuilt-ring depth could be considered as standard in order to calculate other depths corresponding relative errors. Table 1 presents the relative error with different inbuilt-ring depth corresponding each given time cumulative infiltration relative to 22cm inbuilt-ring depth. From Table 1, it can be discovered that the relative error of cumulative infiltration amount reduces along with the increase of inbuilt-ring depth; for the same inbuilt-ring depth, the relative error of cumulative infiltration amount reduces along with increase of infiltration time. When the depth achieved above 19cm and infiltration time reached more than 60min,the relative error of cumulative infiltration amount is less than 1.49%.Above analysis makes clear that sideward infiltration aroused by lacking depth has reached negligible level when inbuilt-ring depth reached more than 19cm.Therefore,19~22cm could be defined as reasonable inbuilt-ring depth from the requirements of test precision.

**Table 1.** Relative error of the cumulative infiltration amount at given time under different depths relative to 22cm depth

| Inbuilt-ring depth (cm) | Relative error (%) | | | | | | | | |
|---|---|---|---|---|---|---|---|---|---|
| | the cumulative infiltration amount at given time | | | | | | | | |
| | $H_{10}$ | $H_{20}$ | $H_{30}$ | $H_{40}$ | $H_{50}$ | $H_{60}$ | $H_{70}$ | $H_{80}$ | $H_{90}$ |
| 10 | 78.61 | 107.53 | 126.37 | 140.21 | 150.99 | 159.62 | 166.81 | 172.85 | 178.03 |
| 13 | 32.64 | 54.48 | 68.35 | 78.37 | 86.03 | 92.10 | 97.11 | 101.27 | 104.81 |
| 16 | 7.76 | 14.57 | 19.70 | 23.82 | 27.24 | 30.11 | 32.58 | 34.74 | 36.64 |
| 19 | 11.94 | 7.89 | 5.36 | 3.49 | 2.07 | 0.93 | 0.03 | 0.82 | 1.49 |
| 22 | 0 | 0 | 0 | 0 | 0 | 0 | 0 | 0 | 0 |

Through analysis above, measurement accuracy would also improve slightly through further enlarged depths, but would increase apparatus production cost, difficulty of inbuilt-ring and labor intensity during the experiments greatly. The following suggestions were putted forward combining years of field infiltration experience of author: if the buried plough bottom was less than 20cm,the inbuilt-ring depth could be 19cm;if the buried plough bottom was more than 20cm,the inbuilt-ring depth could be 20~22cm.

## 4     Conclusion

(1) Adopting double-ring infiltration apparatus to measure field soil infiltration parameters, inbuilt-ring depth has obvious effect on measuring accuracy. The inbuilt-ring depth ruled by international is smaller and the measured infiltration rate value is bigger than the truth-value.

(2) Measuring error decreases gradually along with the increase of the inbuilt-ring depth. When the depth reached 19cm~22cm, its relative error could be ignored.

(3)Considering measurement precision, instrument cost and labor intensity, if the buried plough bottom is less than 20cm, the reasonable inbuilt-ring depth should be 19cm; if the buried plough bottom is more than 20cm, the reasonable inbuilt-ring depth should be 20~22cm.

## References

1. Li, X., Fan, G.: Influence of organic matter content on infiltration capacity and parameter in field soils. Transactions of the CSAE 22(3), 188–190 (2006)
2. Li, X., Fan, G.: Experimental study on main factors influencing the infiltration capacity of unsaturated earth canal. Journal of Hydraulic Engineering 40(5), 630–634 (2009)
3. Lai, J., Luo, Y., Ren, L.: Effects of Buffer-Index of the Double-Ring Infiltrometer on Saturated Hydraulic Conductivity Measurements. Acta Pedologica Sinica 47(1), 19–25 (2010)
4. Fan, G., Dang, Z.: Approach on Infiltration Reducing Mechanism of Infiltration under Surge Irrigation. Bulletin of Soil and Water Conservation 13(6), 30–33 (1993)
5. Xie, W., Fan, G.: Influence of moisture content on infiltration characteristics in field soils. Journal of Taiyuan University of Technology 35(3), 273–275 (2004)
6. Wang, Q., Horton, R., Fan, J.: An analytical solution for one-dimensional water infiltration and redistribution in unsaturated soil. Pedosphere 19(1), 104–110 (2009)
7. Moroke, T.S., Dikinya, O., Patrick, C.: Comparative assessment of water infiltration of soils under different tillage systems in eastern Botswana. Physics and Chemistry of the Earth 34, 316–323 (2009)
8. Zhu, J., Mohanty, B.P.: Effective scaling factor for transient infiltration in heterogeneous soils. Journal of Hydrology 319, 96–108 (2006)

# A Bayesian Based Search and Classification System for Product Information of Agricultural Logistics Information Technology

Dandan Li[1], Daoliang Li[1,3], Yingyi Chen[1,3], Li Li[1],
Xiangyang Qin[3], and Yongjun Zheng[1,*]

[1] China Agricultural University, P.O. Box 121, Beijing, 100083, P.R. China
[2] Key Laboratory of Modern Precision Agriculture System Integration, Ministry of Education,
P.O. Box 121, Beijing, 100083, P.R. China
[3] Beijing agricultural information technology research center, Beijing, P.R. China
zyj@cau.edu.cn

**Abstract.** In order to meet the needs of users who search agricultural products logistics information technology, this paper introduces a search and classification system of agricultural products logistics information technology search and classification. Firstly, the dictionary of field concept word was built based on analyzing the characteristics of agricultural products logistics information technology. Secondly, the system used meta-search engine to search related pages on the Internet based on keywords collections, and then used Web mining to analyze and filter the relevant pages. Finally, classify the agricultural products logistics information technology by web text classification according to different users' needs. The results showed that the system could efficiently and accurately search the required information, and classification with good results.

**Keywords:** Agricultural products logistics, Web mining, information technology, classification of web text.

## 1 Introduction

Agricultural products logistics refers to moving material objects and related information from producer to consumer physically for meeting customer's needs and achieve the value of agricultural products [1]. It mainly includes agricultural production, purchase, transport, storage, loading and unloading, handling, packaging, circulation, processing, distribution, information activities and many other aspects. Each aspect will be involved in many information technologies and products, also new technology will come out continually, and relevant information on the network has become increasingly rich. People want to know the existing information technology and products and hope to fully use them, but in the sea of information in the network, it is a great difficulty to find the information needed quickly and accurately.

---

* Corresponding author.

D. Li and Y. Chen (Eds.): CCTA 2011, Part I, IFIP AICT 368, pp. 437–444, 2012.

According to the above requirements, Web mining and Web text classification were used to retrieve and classify agricultural product logistics information technology. Web mining can generally be divided into three types [2], which are Web content mining, Web structure mining and Web usage mining. Web content mining is a process of getting useful knowledge from the summary and the document content of pages, generally, including text files and multimedia documents mining [3-4]. Web text classification is an important technology of text mining, which refers to that each document of documents collection, will be included in a pre-defined category [5-6]. At present, the main classification algorithm includes the decision tree based on inductive learning, the K-nearest neighbor based on vector space model, Bayes classification based on probabilistic models, neural networks, the support vector machines based on statistical learning theory, etc. [7].

The aim of this paper is to design a system of agricultural products logistics information technology search and classification based on the above analysis. Firstly, the dictionary of field concept word was built based on analyzing the characteristics of agricultural products logistics information technology. Secondly, the system used meta-search engine to search related pages on the Internet based on keywords collections, and then used Web mining to analyze and filter the relevant pages. Finally, classify the agricultural products logistics information technology by web text classification according to different users' needs. The classified information can be a good decision support for the future.

# 2    Materials and Methods

## 2.1    Systems Framework Analysis and Design

The agricultural product logistics information technology search and classification system was designed to help users in the field of agricultural logistics to search required information from the Internet and make full use of this information more easily. The system's main functions included the following aspects:

1) According to the user's search request, match the agricultural product logistics concept word dictionary which the system has been built, and get effective keywords collection.
2) Considering the custom search scheme of the system, use meta-search technology to search the page information that meet the search request from the Internet.
3) Use web services method based on semantic vector model to judge match degrees between the information searched from the Internet and demanded by users. Then filter out irrelevant information, and store useful information.
4) The system achieved automatic classification function for searched useful information, and provided decision support for users to select technologies and products.

System work flow is shown in fig.1.

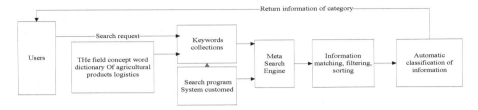

**Fig. 1.** System workflow chart

## 2.2    Analysis of Agricultural Products Logistics Information Technology

Agricultural product logistics technology refers to the machine, equipment, facilities and other hardware and software and a variety of opportunities method which are used in the process of agricultural product from producers to consumers.   Informatization of agricultural products logistics namely agricultural product logistics technology is applied to the logistics field. Agricultural product logistics can be divided into agricultural product production logistics, sales logistics and waste logistics according to supply chain function; and can be divided into food logistics, economic crops logistics, fresh food logistics, livestock product logistics, aquatic product logistics, forest product logistics and other agricultural product logistics according to concrete object; while, can be divided into room temperature chain logistics, cold chain logistics and fresh chain logistics and so on accordance with the logistics storage and transportation conditions. Agricultural product logistics information technology is very different, for that the system provided a diverse and differentiated information services according to the different demand and the needs of different levels to achieve the system's utility and meet the information needs of individual use.

According to the above analysis of agricultural product logistics information technology fields, the field concept word dictionary has been built. The system can obtain a valid set of search keywords by extracting valid search terms from users' input, semantic analyzing and matching with the the concept diction. This will reduce irrelevant information from the returned search results.

## 2.3    Search Method Framework

As the general search engine is limited coverage of the entire web, and search results will return many useless information, so the system selected meta search engine technology. Because the system is aim to search agricultural products logistics information technology, users' needs are logistics technology and product-related information, such as technical characteristics of the products, scope and price information, and so on. Based on the above considerations, the system specifically customized search scheme, defining a term including three words such as warehouse management system, system features and the price. When a keyword is inputted, for example, warehouse management system, the system will search uses the term which the keyword relevant in the Internet and return relevant information to the user. Users send search requests to meta search engine [8], and the meta search engine send the actual search requests to multiple search engine according to the users' requests, and multiple search engines perform search requests from the meta search engine, and sent search results to the meta-search engines by the response form. The meta-search engines send the obtained and search results to the actual users.

The system filters valuable information by judging relevance between the search results and user's queries to. There are many kinds of methods or models to judge relevance between the search results and user's queries, such as vector-based, based on probability, fuzzy set, latent semantic models, and so on. Here draw lessons from the vector model based on semantic Web service matching method for decision making [9].

In the model, data items to be matched compose of the concept a public body, and set the concept of space vector ( $c_1, c_2, \cdots , c_n$ ) finally getting the data items to be matched vector model    is   $d_j = (w_{1,j}, w_{2,j}, \cdots , w_{n,j})$   ,   User   query   is $q_j = (w_{1,q}, w_{2,q}, \cdots , w_{nj})$, The formula of weight is shown as follows.

$$w_{i,j} = \begin{cases} 1 & freq_{i,j} > 0 \\ \max_t S(c_i, c_t) & freq_{i,j} = 0 \cap c_i \, \mathrm{Re} \, lc_t \\ 0 & others \end{cases} \quad (1)$$

$freq_{ij}$ is the frequency of concept in the data item $d_j$ , Re / represent the relationship between the concepts, $S(c_i, c_t)$ is the semantic similarity between $c_i$ and $c_t$,

The formula is as follows.

$$S(c_i, c_t) = e^{-al} \times \frac{e^{\beta h} - e^{-\beta h}}{e^{\beta h} + e^{-\beta h}} \quad (2)$$

In the formula, l is the shortest path length between $c_i$ and $c_t$ , h is the depth of the deepest common ancestor concept of $c_i$ and $c_t$, $\alpha \in (0,1)$, $\beta \in (0,1)$ are the Impact coefficient of the two factors which are the length of the shortest path and the concept depth to the concept of semantic similarity.

Finally, the formula of the matching degree of the data item $d_j$ and $q_j$, being the same with the cosine of two data items vectors, is as follows.

$$Sim(d_j, q) = \frac{d_j \times q}{|d_j| \times |q|} = \frac{\sum_{i=1}^{t} w_{i,j} \times w_{i,q}}{\sqrt{\sum_{i=1}^{t} w_{i,j}^2} \times \sqrt{\sum_{i=1}^{t} w_{i,q}^2}} \quad (3)$$

$|d_j|$ and $|q|$ are the model of data item vector and inquires the vector, $Sim(d_j, q)$ is between 0 and 1, finally, matching result is sorted according to $Sim(d_j, q)$.

Through this method, the system can effectively extract relevant information of agricultural logistics information technology from the results of general search engines.

## 2.4    Automatic Text Classification

After searching agricultural products logistics information technology and related information, the system would automatically classify the obtained information. In the process of Web text classification, including the four key steps as follows, namely the text pretreatment, the text says, characteristic dimension reduction, training methods and classification algorithms. The text pretreatment process take out some HTML or XML tags, a key link of Chinese text classification of is the Chinese automatic segmentation.Web document content is described in natural language, computer difficult to handle its semantic, to facilitate the computer process, so must transform the content of the text features into the computer can process format. After word segmentation and removing stop words and high frequency from the training text and the text to be classified, the dimension of vector space and category vector for said text is very big, so the need for feature dimension reduction. The job of training algorithm is to statistics each text corresponding word table in training set of documents, calculate category vector matrix simultaneously normalization, finally save the table get from the training, namely classification knowledge base. The classification algorithm was designed based on the classification knowledge base.

Now many text classification algorithm has come up and improvement, such as based on group classification method, multiple classifier fusion method, based on RBF network text categorization model, latent semantic classification model , K-neighbor algorithm and support vector machine, etc. This paper adopted the bayes classification algorithm [10].

The bayes classification algorithm as follows,

Step 1,    Take out entry from the entry set $^{T}$, one by one, and match with the word in the feature vocabulary, if $t_{xk}$ and $t_i(c_j)$ match, then give category $c_j$ to $t_{xk}$, recorded as $t_{xk}(c_j)$; if $t_{xk}$ and $t_i(c_j)$ not match, then take out next entry until $T_x$ is null, at last, get the entry set classified is

$$\{t_{xk}(c_j)\} \quad k = (1,2, \cdots, n; j = 1,2, \cdots mx)$$

Step 2, Calculate conditional probability of each entry in the category, the formula as follows.

$$P(t_{xk} \mid c_j) = \frac{n_{kj} + mp}{n_{xj} + m} \tag{4}$$

m is a constant, called the equivalent sample size; P is the priori estimates of the probability to be defined.

Step 3, Calculate conditional probability of text x, the formula as follows.

$$P(t_x \mid c_j) = P(t_{x^1} \mid c_j) \times P(t_{x^2} \mid c_j) \times \cdots \times P(t_{x^n} \mid c_j) = \prod_{k-1}^{n} P(t_{xk} \mid c_j) \quad (5)$$

Step 4, Calculate the probability of text x belong to category $c_j$ , the formula as follows.

$$P(c_j \mid T_x) = \frac{P(c_j)P(T_x \mid c_j)}{P(T_x)} . \quad (6)$$

and

$$P(T_x) = \sum_{j-1}^{m} P(c_j)P(T_x \mid c_j) \quad (7)$$

Step 5, Take text category when

$$\max\{P(c_1 \mid T_x), P(c_2 \mid T_x), \cdots, P(c_{mx} \mid T_x)\} \quad (8)$$

as the category of text x.

This system takes two indexes for classification of evaluation methods, namely the accuracy and recall ratio. Let the correct number of text classification be num1, and let the actual number of text classification be num2, and let the number of should have text be num3.

The definition of accuracy, $accuracy = \dfrac{num1}{num2}$

The definition of recall ratio, $recall\ ratio = \dfrac{num1}{num3}$

## 2.5    Results and Analysis

The test aimed to prove the search and classification effect of the system. The search object of this system was agricultural product logistics information technology and related product, including the transportation, loading and unloading handling, storage, packaging, circulation processing, collection and processing of information and containers unitization in agricultural logistics activities. Here selected three items as search request, and compared the precision ratio with general search engines. Precision ratio is the ratio of effective search page to the total number of pages. The results are shown in table 1.

**Table 1.** The comparison of search results

| Search request | Precision ratio of general search engines | Precision ratio of this system |
|---|---|---|
| Automatically lead machine | 90.3% | 92.5% |
| Automation warehouse | 91.2% | 93.7% |
| Warehousing management system | 90.5% | 93.2% |

Table 1 shows that the precision ratio of the system is improved than the precision ratio of general search engines.

Through detailed analysis of agricultural logistics information technology and the characteristics of the products, the system divided agricultural product logistics information technology into seven parts according to the function, as follows.

(1) Transportation, including rail, road, water transport, air and pipeline transportation.

(2) Material handling, including loading and unloading machinery, transportation machinery and material handling machinery, such as forklifts, automated guided machines, lifts, stackers, etc.

(3) Storage, including storage of materials, storage equipment, such as automated warehouses, shelves, trays, temperature and humidity control equipment.

(4) Packaging, including filling machines, sealing machines, labeling machines, sterilization machine, and multi-functional packaging machinery.

(5) Distribution processing, means the professional machinery and equipment used in the activity such as packaging, split, measurement, sorting, assembling, pay the price stickers, labels pay and so on.

(6) Information collection and processing, including computer and network related hardware and software, information identification devices, communication equipment.

(7) The equipment of container unitization includes containers, trays, slide, FIBC, container network goods bundle, container handling equipment, transport equipment, container, and container identification system.

The system pre-set six categories such as transport, handling, storage, packaging, distribution processing, information collection and processing. and then selected the 600 piece of pages in the above searched page, the 480 of them as a training text, the other 120 as a test text. The test results of the system automatically classified shown as Table 2.

**Table 2.** The test results of the system automatically classified

| Category | Accuracy | Recall ratio |
|---|---|---|
| Transportation | 91.5% | 90.3% |
| Material handling | 95.2% | 94.6% |
| Storage | 90.1% | 89.7% |
| Packaging | 92.6% | 93.2% |
| Distribution processing | 87.9% | 88.6% |
| Information collection and processing | 94.7% | 93.5% |

# 3   Conclusions

A system of agricultural products logistics information technology search and classification was designed in order to meet the needs of users in the field of agricultural products logistics information technology. Firstly, the dictionary of field concept word was built based on analyzing the characteristics of agricultural products logistics information technology. Secondly, the system used meta-search engine to search related pages on the Internet based on keywords collections, and then used Web mining to analyze and filter the relevant pages. Finally, classify the agricultural products logistics information technology by web text classification according to different users' needs. The results showed that the system could search the required information efficiently and accurately, and classification with good results.

**Acknowledgements.** This work was supported by Special Fun for Agro-scientific Research in the Public Interest (200903009). The research was also financially supported by the national science and technology support plan (2009BADC4B01).

# References

1. Liu, D., Zhang, G.: Modern technology and management of agricultural product logistics. China Logistics Publishing House (2009)
2. Velasquez, J.D., Dujovne, L.E., L'Huillier, G.: Extracting significant Website Key Objects: A Semantic Web mining approach. Engineering Applications of Artificial Intelligence 1(2), 1–10 (2011)
3. Mustapasa, O., Karahoca, D., Karahoca, A., Yucel, A., Uzunboylu, H.: Implementation of Semantic Web Mining on E-Learning, Procedia - Social and Behavioral Sciences. Innovation and Creativity in Education, 5820–5823 (2010)
4. Mustapasa, O., Karahoca, D., Karahoca, A., Yucel, A., Uzunboylu, H.: Implementation of Semantic Web Mining on E-Learning, Procedia - Social and Behavioral Sciences. Innovation and Creativity in Education 2(2), 5820–5823 (2010)
5. Chen, J., Huang, H., Tian, S., Qu, Y.: Feature selection for text classification with Naive Bayes. Expert Systems with Applications 3(36), 5432–5435 (2009)
6. Lo, S.: Web service quality control based on text mining using support vector machine. Expert Systems with Applications 34(1), 603–610 (2008)
7. Ozel, S.A.: A Web page classification system based on a genetic algorithm using tagged-terms as features. Expert Systems with Applications 38(4), 3407–3415 (2011)
8. Hamdi, M.S.: SOMSE: A semantic map based meta-search engine for the purpose of web information customization. Applied Soft Computing 11(1), 1310–1321 (2011)
9. Mao, X., Guan, J., Zhu, F.: Web services matchmaking approach based on semantic vector space model. Application Research of Computers 27(10), 3754–3758 (2010)
10. Han, H., Ko, Y., Seo, J.: Using the revised EM algorithm to remove noisy data for improving the one-against-the-rest method in binary text classification. Information Processing & Management 5(43), 1281–1293 (2007)

# Research on Agent-Based Bee Product Traceability Platform and Barcode System

Shengping Liu[1,2], Yeping Zhu[1,2], and Shijuan Li[1]

[1] Agricultural Information Institute, Chinese Academy of Agricultural Sciences,
Beijing, China, P.R. China, 100081
[2] Key Laboratory of Digital Agricultural Early-warning Technology, Ministry of Agriculture,
The People's Republic of China, Beijing, P.R. China, 100081
spliu@caas.net.cn

**Abstract.** Establishing agricultural product quality safety traceability platform and barcode system have become a worldwide trend. Bee product traceability platform that can be used to identify all aspects from farm to table has been laid out based on China law and global standards. An integrated bee product traceability system which involving all of the process along the supply chain can be applied to increase consumer confidence of bee products by making traceability data accessible to the consumer. In this bee product traceability platform, barcode system is of enormous significance and due to its applications in the all tracing stage of platform, standard barcode system architecture and infrastructure become very important.

In this paper, we study safety situation of bee product quality, research status of bee product traceability and barcode system. We construct bee product traceability platform by adopting agent technology, build barcode system by adopting GS1 global traceability standard as well as realize standardization barcoding of bee product data content during four links: materials collection, purchase, processing and sales. Applying barcode system and traceability platform in bee products distribution process can realize bee products tracking and tracing, offer strong guarantee for Chinese bee product quality safety and improve competitiveness of bee products in international market.

**Keywords:** bee product, traceability system, barcode.

## 1 Introduction

### 1.1 Current Situation of Bee Products Quality Safety

The annual capacity of honey is about 293,000 tons at present in China, which including royal 3,000 tons jelly honey bee, 3,000 tons pollen and 350 tons propolis, the total output value of honey is about 8 billion RMB and annual export value is about $133 million [1]. As advantage products in our country, bee products have important function for export, human health. Bee products quality safety problems are not only in relation to the bee industry development, but also in relation to consumer

D. Li and Y. Chen (Eds.): CCTA 2011, Part I, IFIP AICT 368, pp. 445–454, 2012.

safety and the improvement of bees' international competitiveness. Consequently, Study the quality safety problems of bee products has important meaning to promote bee industry development [2].

In recent years the rapid growth of bee products processing industry, and meanwhile an extension of the industrial chain and bees industry itself exists many factors that caused various quality problems of bee products, which directly affect bee products export, and also shock Chinese domestic market. EU and some countries took trade barriers like forbid export and stop selling to Chinese honey in 2002 [3], which made great loss to Chinese beekeeping industry, seriously impacted normal development of beekeeping industry, and also caused Chinese government departments to pay attention to bee products quality problems. The key problem of bee products quality safety is doping fake and drug residue in China, and these kinds of problems have not been able to get fundamental solution [4]. The production and purchase link of Chinese bees industry especially the raw honey are loose management, small scale, and bad degree of organization, but effective supervision need reliable technical means, so the demand for bee products' quality safety traceability system is more pressing.

## 1.2     Current Situation of Bee Products' Traceability System Research

Bee products are particular agricultural products, so all countries in the world pay very attention on the quality safety, and the traceability research of bee products is actively developing at home and abroad.

On the law level, EU Traceability Regulations-Regulation (EC) No 178/2002 article 18 Traceability, trade operator must ensure product's traceability. Our country "Food Safety Law" and "Produce Quality Safety Law" also provide legal protection for the implementation of traceability system on legal level [5].

EU sixth framework program put forward the standard of record information during honey sales chain traceability process, the content of record is to achieve good traceability purpose, and detailed information that should be recorded in honey sales chain. Greece and Hungary proposed joint and implemented "Trace Honey" project, Hungary-Greece food network traceability and transparency research raised pilot research for honey production and processing and sales chain management. Argentina Agriculture Food Sanitation and Quality Bureau(SENASA) put forward honey refining room is the core of the traceability system; Refining room, beekeeping producers and honey barrels are required to pass through SENASA registered commercial Apitrack traceability system has been promoted in many countries [6-9]. Ontario, Canada agricultural food and rural affairs traceability pilot plan, also including bee products.

Due to long industry chain, no specified industry standard and many influencing factors for quality safety, currently research work of Chinese bee products quality safety tracing system is mainly conducted by Bee Research Institution and Agriculture Information Research Institution of Chinese Academy of Agricultural Science [10].

This article, through the analysis of the Chinese bee products quality safety and bar code system research status, proposes to introduce modern information technology into bee industry in order to realize whole process trace of bee products, uses GS1 standard to set up bee products traceability bar code system, and constructs bee products trace platform which is based on Agent according to industry characteristics.

# 2    Research Status of Barcode System

Unified code system is the foundation of launching bee product traceability and the premise of information exchange and process in trace process. Bee product traceability barcode must have some standard principles: uniqueness, stability, versatility, extensibility and applicability. In trace process trace key points mainly include raw honey gathering barcode, honey purchase barcode, process barcode and the products barcode. All these key elements must be bar-code uniformly and standardly so that information of different trace link is unique identification. In this research GS1 system is used for realizing uniform and standard barcode of bee product.

## 2.1    GS1 System

The GS1 System is an integrated system of global standards that provides with accurate identification and communication of information regarding products, assets, services and locations. It is the most widely implemented supply chain standards system in the world. It is the foundation of a wide range of efficiency-building supply chain applications and solutions and is composed of the following two areas: GS1 barcodes and GS1 traceability.

GS1 unified label system performs an important function for physical implementation of agricultural products barcode, especially for agricultural products' standardized management in logistics links. GS1 system has been widely used in the logistics and retai industry of the global supply chain. It reduces system operation cost and avoids causing supply chain's uncertainty. Adopting global unified identification system can realize rapid and accurate seamless links between Information flow and material flow.

**Table 1.** Symbols and abbreviations. Table 1 shows symbol and abbreviation in GS1 system.

| Symbol | Abbreviation |
| --- | --- |
| AI | GS1 system Application Identifier |
| GLN | GS1 system Global Location Number |
| GMP | Good Manufacturing Practice |
| GS1 | Global Solution 1 |
| GS1 system | Unique global identification system |
| GTIN | GS1 system Global Trade Item Number |
| ID | Identification |
| ISO | The international Organization for Standardization |
| n2 or n14,etc | GS1 identifier numbers consisting for 2 or 14, etc digits |
| SSCC | GS1 system Serial Shipping Container Code |

## 2.2    Barcode Research Situation of Agricultural Product Traceability System

At present agricultural product traceability systems are widely developing in at home and abroad. Zheng has analyzed traceability chain of cooking oil products and designed cooking oil product system based on batch management, meanwhile, zheng proposed barcoding rules of core link which included origin, process and final product [11-12]. Liu has encoded Fruit and vegetable products. According to characteristic of lamb industry chain as well as actual information level of lamb manufacturing enterprises, Wang has developed lamb barcode system. Xiong has realized pork quality safety traceability. Deng has studied producing area code of agricultural product, divided tea planting area and uniformly encoded tea. Sheng has developed beef traceability barcode system.

In general most research organizations have carried out traceability barcode system research according to pork, beef, lamb, grain and oil, fruit and vegetable [13]. However, research about bee product traceability barcode system has not been reported. Developing bee product barcode system is a difficult task because that collection source of bee product scattered and honey adulteration are widely spread.

## 3    Agent-Based Bee Products Traceability Platform

Agent theory and technology, as a part of distributed artificial intelligence, has developed rapidly since it arose from 1970s, it is a popular direction of artificial intelligence now [15-16]. The researches on agent have received a great deal of attention because of its characteristics, such as autonomy, collaboration, intelligence, mobility, and the potential to build complex systems [17]. In recent years agent theory and technology research have been rapidly developed, many studies, which including agent-oriented development language, development framework, and method, decision support system and collaboration work model, make good progress. Agent and multi-agent system technology have given us a new way to look at distributed systems and provided a path for more robust intelligent applications [18].

In food processing, the term traceability refers to the recording through means of barcodes & other tracking media, all movement of product and steps within the production process. One of the key reasons is in instances where an issue of contamination arises, and a recall is required. Where traceability has been closely adhered to, it is possible to identify, by precise date & location which goods must be recalled, and which are safe, potentially saving millions of dollars in the recall process. Traceability within the food processing industry is also utilized to identify key high production & quality areas of a business, versus those of low return, and where points in the production process may be improved.

This research has built agent-based bee products traceability platform which based on agent theory and quality tracing method. In figure 1, on account of the characters of independent interaction among the key control points in the bee product traceability platform, a development platform and multiple principal body system of bee product traceability are designed with agent-based method, the platform agent is adopted to perform data acquisition, bar code manufacturing, data inquiry, information surveillance and task management; and task management agent is employed to realize bee farm management, supplier management, processing management and sales management. And data acquisition system developed in this paper is managed by data acquisition agent, the data thus obtained is transmitted via ACL language to the platform management agent to achieve data sharing and surveillance, as well as to fulfill the purpose of bee product information traceability.

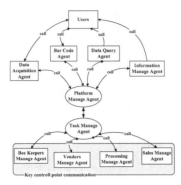

**Fig. 1.** Agent-based Bee products traceability platform

## 4    Barcode System of Bee Product Traceability

Bee product traceability platform mainly consists of the following flows (Figure 2): tracking process (clockwise direction) begins from the origin of honeybee, covering a couple of key control points like place of production, distributor, processing plant and seller, so raw material purchase process, honeybee processing process, product selling process and retail process are traced. Tracing process (counter-clockwise direction) is traced back from customers, including the tracing of selling, production, raw material and place of origin. By means of the bee product traceability platform, tracking and tracing of several key control points like place of origin, distributor, processing plant, seller and customer can be realized, and bee product quality safety can be safeguarded.

**Fig. 2.** Bee product traceability road map

In various links of bee products tracking and tracing, GS1 system was used for barcoding and providing uniform code standards. Standardization bar code can provide accurate, safe and reliable traceability information.

**Table 2.** Barcode system information of bee product supply chain. Table 2 shows information exchange process of bee products traceability links.

| Supply chain | Gathering | Purchase | Process | Sale |
|---|---|---|---|---|
| Diagram | → | → | → | |
| Label type | Apiary label | Purchase label | Process label | Logistics label |
| Code system | EAN-128 | EAN-128 | EAN-128 | EAN-128 |
| Key information | AI(7030) AI(13) AI(10) | AI(7030) AI(13) AI(10) | AI(01) AI(10) | AI(01) SSCC |
| Attribute information | Apiary information Honey kinds Honey origin Production date ...... | Factor Honey kinds Bee pasture Honey origin Date of packaging ...... | Processors Honey kinds Honey origin Processing date Processing country ...... | Processing country country of destination Global trade code ...... |

## 4.1    Honey Gathering Process

When bee farmers finished gathering honey in apiary, they attach different apiary honey traceability label to different honey barrels. Table 3 shows barcode information and label text information in apiary traceability links. And Figure 3 indicates apiary traceability barcode label which including necessary text and barcode. The traceability information can be used in information exchange between apiary and purchase trader or between apiary and processing factory.

**Table 3.** Barcode and information of gathering process

| Data content | Data name | UCC/EAN-128 | Example | Categorisation | |
|---|---|---|---|---|---|
| | | | | Shall | may |
| Gathering process | | | | | |
| Traceability code of gathering honey | PROCESSOR+ PACAK DATE + LOT | AI(7030)+AI(13 )+AI(10) | (7030)156510183010 01(13)080527(10)011 | ✓ | |
| Apiary code | PROCESSOR | AI(7030) | n4+n3+an...27 | | ✓ |
| Production date | PACK DATE | AI(13) | n2+n6 | | ✓ |
| Lot number | LOT | AI(10) | n2+an...20 | | ✓ |
| Global location number of honey | GLN | AI(414) | n3+n13 | | ✓ |
| Honey kinds | REF.TO SOURCE | AI(251) | n3+an...30 | | ✓ |
| Honey weight | NET WEIGHT | AI(3100) | n4+n6 | | ✓ |
| Global location number of supplier | GLN | AI(412) | n3+n13 | | ✓ |
| Apiary name text | Text information | — | Sichuan Wangshun | ✓ | |
| Production date text | Text information | — | 2008-05-27 | ✓ | |
| Lot number text | Text information | — | 025 | ✓ | |
| Honey origin text | Text information | — | Hubei | ✓ | |
| Honey weight text | Text information | — | 100kg | ✓ | |
| Honey kinds text | Text information | — | Eucalyptus honey | ✓ | |

**Fig. 3.** Honey gathering label and Honey purchase label

## 4.2    Purchase Process

When purchase traders buy honey from bee keeper, they need to attach purchase traceability label to their honey barrels. Table 4 displays barcode information and label text information in purchase traceability link. And Figure 3 shows purchase traceability barcode label which consists of necessary text and barcode. The traceability information can be used in information exchange between purchase trader and processing factory.

**Table 4.** Barcode and information of purchase process

| Data content | Data name | UCC/EAN-128 | Example | Categorisation | |
|---|---|---|---|---|---|
| | | | | Shall | may |
| Purchase process | | | | | |
| Traceability code of purchase honey | PROCESSOR+ PACAK DATE + LOT | AI(7030)+AI(13 )+AI(10) | (7030)156420804020 01(13)090621(10)025 | ✓ | |
| Purchase code | PROCESSOR | AI(7030) | n4+n3+an...27 | | ✓ |
| Production date | PACK DATE | AI(13) | n2+n6 | | ✓ |
| Lot number | LOT | AI(10) | n2+an...20 | | ✓ |
| Global location number of honey | GLN | AI(414) | n3+n13 | | ✓ |
| Honey kinds | REF.TO SOURCE | AI(251) | n3+an...30 | | ✓ |
| Honey weight | NET WEIGHT | AI(3100) | n4+n6 | | ✓ |
| Global location number of supplier | GLN | AI(412) | n3+n13 | | ✓ |
| Purchase trader name text | Text information | — | Hubei Heqingbiao | ✓ | |
| Package date text | Text information | — | 2009-09-13 | ✓ | |
| Lot number text | Text information | — | 025 | ✓ | |
| Honey origin text | Text information | — | Hubei | ✓ | |
| Honey weight text | Text information | — | 100kg | ✓ | |
| Honey kinds text | Text information | — | Cole honey | ✓ | |

## 4.3    Processing Process

Processors package honey products according to consuming unit or distribution unit as well as transport products through highway, aviation or sea transportation. Table 5 presents barcode information and label text information in process traceability link. And Figure 4 shows process traceability barcode label which is made of necessary text and barcode. The traceability information can be used in information exchange between processing factory and seller.

**Table 5.** Barcode and information of processing process

| Data content | Data name | UCC/EAN-128 | Example | Categorisation | |
|---|---|---|---|---|---|
| | | | | Shall | may |
| Processing process | | | | | |
| Traceability code of process honey | PROCESSOR+ PACAK DATE + LOT | AI(7030)+AI(13 )+AI(10) | (7030)156510106030 01(13)100310(10)001 | ✓ | |
| Global trade number | GTIN | AI(01) | n2+n14 | | ✓ |
| Lot number | LOT | AI(10) | n2+an...20 | | ✓ |
| Package date | PACK DATE | AI(13) | n2+n6 | | ✓ |
| Production date | PROD DATE | AI(11) | n2+n6 | | ✓ |
| Date of minimum durability | BEST BEFORE | A(15) | n2+n6 | | ✓ |
| Global location number of honey | GLN | AI(414) | n3+n13 | | ✓ |
| Honey kinds | REF.TO SOURCE | AI(251) | n3+an...30 | | ✓ |
| Global location number of supplier | GLN | AI(412) | n3+n13 | | ✓ |
| Processor name text | Text information | — | Hangzhou Changqing | ✓ | |
| Production date text | Text information | — | 2010-10-03 | ✓ | |
| Lot number text | Text information | — | 001 | ✓ | |
| Honey origin text | Text information | — | Sichuan | ✓ | |
| Net weight text | Text information | — | 1.5 kg | | ✓ |
| Honey kinds text | Text information | — | Sophorae honey | ✓ | |

**Fig. 4.** Product process label and Commodity sale label

## 4.4    Sale Process

When dealer affords product to consumer necessary traceability information includes bar code for commodity and traceability code. Table 6 displays barcode information and label text information in sale traceability link. And Figure 4 demonstrates shows sale traceability barcode label which composed by necessary text and barcode. Through querying traceability barcode in website, consumer can get all traceability information of bee product.

**Table 6.** Barcode and information of sale process

| Data content | Data name | EAN/UPC | Example | Categorisation | |
|---|---|---|---|---|---|
| | | | | Shall | may |
| Sale link | | | | | |
| Bar code for commodity | EAN-13 | EAN/UCC-13 | 6901234567892 | ✓ | |
| Commodity traceability barcode | PROCESSOR+PAC AK DATE + LOT | EAN-128 | 51010604001100706105 | ✓ | |
| Processor name text | Text information | — | Hangzhou Changqing | | ✓ |
| Production date text | Text information | — | 2010-07-06 | | ✓ |
| Lot number text | Text information | — | 105 | | ✓ |
| Honey origin text | Text information | — | Sichuan | | ✓ |
| Net weight text | Text information | — | 1.5 kg | | ✓ |
| Honey kinds text | Text information | — | Sophorae honey | | ✓ |

## 5    Conclusions

Agricultural products quality safety becomes the hot topic which the people at home and abroad generally pay attention to in recent years. As ways of guaranteeing quality safety, tracing and tracking technology have been widely used in the developed countries such as America, Canada, Japan, New Zealand and so on. In recent years Chinese government has been paying much more attention to food quality safety and also has done a lot of work for quality safety and traceability. As the largest bee-keeping country in the world, beekeeping is Chinese traditional industry, in addition honey is important traditional product of foreign exchange income. So how to use tracing and tracking technology to further strengthen bee product safety control and management is an urgent affair. On the basis of analyzing the present situation of Chinese bee product quality safety, this paper proposes developing bee product traceability platform and barcode system and finally realizes bee product general quality control.

1) This paper first analyzes bee product quality safety status and research situation of bee product traceability system. We should develop bee product traceability barcode system and quality safety platform which are suitable for Chinese situation.

2) Secondly based on GS1 system we respectively encoded in four links of bee products circulation. Unique and standardization bee product barcode system are used in traceability platform.

3) Finally we developed agent-based bee product quality traceability platform which could realize farm-to-table traceability.

**Acknowledgments.** This research was supported by the National Natural Science Foundation of China (Grant No.60972154).

## References

1. Li, S., et al.: Status quo of quality safety of bee products and construction of whole-process traceability system. Nongye Gongcheng Xuebao/Transactions of the Chinese Society of Agricultural Engineering 24(Suppl. 2), 293–297 (2008)
2. Zhu, Y.P., et al.: Design of bee products quality monitoring information service platform. Computer and Computing Technologies in Agriculture ii 3, 2141–2149 (2009)
3. Liu, S., Zhu, Y., Li, S.: Research on data acquisition system for agent-based bee product traceability platform. In: 2010 World Automation Congress, WAC 2010, pp. 375–381 (2010)
4. Zhu, Y., et al.: Agent-based bee product quality control system. In: 2nd International Conference on Data Mining and Intelligent Information Technology Applications, pp. 346–350 (2010)
5. Zhu, Y., Li, S., Liu, S., Yue, E.: Design of Agent-Based Agricultural Product Quality Control System. In: Li, D., Liu, Y., Chen, Y. (eds.) CCTA 2010, Part I. IFIP AICT, vol. 344, pp. 476–486. Springer, Heidelberg (2011)
6. Borkovcova, I., et al.: Quality and safety of Czech honey. Acta Scientiarum Polonorum - Medicina Veterinaria 7(4) (2008)

7. Casillas, P., Echazarreta, G.: Factors that influence the quality and safety of honey. Revista Chapingo. Serie Ingenieria Agropecuaria 5(1/2) (2002)
8. Mahaman, B.D., et al.: A diagnostic expert system for honeybee pests. Computers and Electronics in Agriculture 36(1), 17–31 (2002)
9. Montet, D., et al.: Future topics of common interest for EU and SEA partners in food quality, safety and traceability. Quality Assurance and Safety of Crops & Foods 2(4), 158–164 (2010)
10. Yue, E., Zhu, Y., Cao, Y.: Multi-agent Quality of Bee Products Traceability Model Based on Roles. In: Li, D., Liu, Y., Chen, Y. (eds.) CCTA 2010, Part II. IFIP AICT, vol. 345, pp. 110–117. Springer, Heidelberg (2011)
11. Zheng, H., et al.: Construction of traceability system for quality safety of cereal and oil products. Scientia Agricultura Sinica 42(9), 3243–3249 (2009)
12. Liu, S., et al.: Study on quality safety traceability systems for cereal and oil products. In: Proceedings of 2009 WRI World Congress on Software Engineering, vol. 1, pp. 163–166 (2009)
13. Pouliot, S., Sumner, D.A.: Traceability, liability, and incentives for food safety and quality. American Journal of Agricultural Economics 90(1), 15–27 (2008)
14. Zhu, Y.P., et al.: Agriculture and forestry economy decision support system based on agent. New Zealand Journal of Agricultural Research 50(5), 1339–1346 (2007)
15. Zhu, Y., Feng, Z., Yue, E.: Application of Agent in agricultural expert system inspection software. Scientia Agricultura Sinica 39(8), 1553–1557 (2006)
16. Zhu, Y., Li, S., Yue, E.: Application of the agent in agricultural expert system inspection software. Agricultural Sciences in China 7(1), 117–122 (2008)
17. Bordini, R.H., Wooldridge, M., Hübner, J.F.: Programming multi-agent systems in agentspeak using Jason. Wiley Series in Agent Technology. John Wiley & Sons (2007)
18. Bordini, R.H., Fisher, M., Visser, W., Wooldridge, M.: Verifying Multi-Agent Programs by Model Checking. J. Autonomous Agents and Multi-Agent Systems 12(2), 239–256 (2006)

# A Collision Detection-Based Wandering Method for Equipment Deploy Scene in Land Reclamation Area of Mining Dump

Juncheng Ma[1], Daoliang Li[1], Yingyi Chen[1], Li Li[1],
Fei Gao[1,2], and Lingxian Zhang[1,*]

[1] College of Information and Electrical Engineering, China Agricultural University,
Beijing 100083, China
[2] College of Information, ShanDong Agricultural University, Tai'an 271018, China
zlx131@163.com

**Abstract.** Aiming at developing a simple and efficient collision detection method to support the wandering in equipment deploy scene in land reclamation area of mining dump. This paper presents an efficient algorithm for collision detection in the waste dump land reclamation equipment deploy scene using a bounding volume nestification which consists of an oriented bounding boxes (OBBs) enhanced with axially aligned bounding boxes (AABBs). This approach combines the compactness of OBBs and the simplicity of AABBs. The majority of distant objects are separated using the simpler AABB tests. The remaining objects are in close proximity, where OBBs test is needed to detect. Implementation results show that our algorithm achieves considerable speedup in most cases.

**Keywords:** Collision Detection, Bounding Volume nestification, OBBs, AABBs.

## 1    Introduction

With the development of virtual techniques, collision detection is widely used in areas such as robotics, computer graphics, animation, computer games, virtual reality, simulation and haptic rendering (Tomas Möller, 2002). The application of collision detection technique can improve the authenticity of 3D scene and avoid the phenomenon of go through a wall or go into the land when come into buildings and slopeland. There are many collision detection algorithms with different characteristics, but they all face the same problem: how to improve the real time and accuracy of detection.

The topographic condition of the waste dump is complicated with several sloping land that emerged in stair distribution and there are many pits and ditches. During the land reclamation monitoring of the waste dump, a large number of monitoring equipment is deployed which is irregularly shaped, of small size and easy neglected. Thus, a

---

* Corresponding author.

D. Li and Y. Chen (Eds.): CCTA 2011, Part I, IFIP AICT 368, pp. 455–460, 2012.

collision detection algorithm that is both real time and accurate is badly need in the wandering of the waste dump land reclamation equipment deploy scene.

Bounding volumes algorithm has proved to be the most widely used in contemporary systems. In this method, a simple bounding volume with slight volume is occupied to bound the complicated object, then the intersect test of the objects is carried only when the bounding volumes overlap. The bounding volumes that are widely used are Spheres, axially aligned bounding boxes (AABBs), oriented bounding boxes (OBBs) and discrete orientation polytopes (k-DOP)(J.A. Corrales,2011).

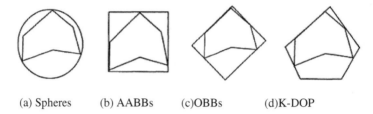

(a) Spheres        (b) AABBs        (c)OBBs        (d)K-DOP

**Fig. 1.** Two-dimensional sketch map of bounding boxes

Spheres and AABBs allow the simplest overlap tests while OBBs and K-DOP fit volumes more tightly(Jung-Woo Chang et al, 2010). In this paper, we propose a bounding volumes nestification based on conventional approach that combines the simplicity of AABBs and the compactness of OBBs to produce an efficient algorithm.

## 2    Related Work

Research about collision detection problems started from the 1970s, after thirty years of research, domestic and foreign scholars in the field of collision detection have done a lot of work, formatting some of mature technology. Space decomposition method and the hierarchical bounding volumes method became the most widely used method in collision detection for two Geometries.

In Space decomposition method, the entire virtual space is divided into a small volume of the cell, only applying intersection test to the same cell or adjacent cells of the geometric object. typical examples of Space decomposition is kd-tree (JLBenile, 1975), octree (H. Nobor et al, 1989), BSP tree (B. Nayl et al, 1990), tetrahedral mesh and the regular grid and so on. Space decomposition method is usually applied to the collision detection for more evenly distributed geometric object between the in sparse environment. In 1976, Clark put up with bounding techniques, characterized by the simplicity and compactness (J.M.Snyder, 1995). The basic idea is to use slightly larger size but geometrically simple bounding box to give an approximate description of complex geometric objects (I.J.Palmer, 1995), Axis-Aligned Bounding Boxes (A. Smith et al, 1995), and oriented Bounding Box (Gottschalk, 1996) and so on. With further studies,   many new algorithm were proposed, such as fixed direction hull(Wei Yingmei, 2000) object-oriented collision detection method(Wang Zhaoqi et al, 1998).

In practice, collision detection was widely used in many areas. Kuan-Chen Lai et al (2009) applied the collision detection techniques to virtual construction stimulation. He proposed VC-COLLIDE method that support real-time rendering and effectively reduced the collision detection computation. Ehsan Arbabi et al (2009) proposed two kinds of collision detection methods for medical diagnosis and surgical planning. Many scholars improved the conventional method to meet the need of all kinds of need. Jung-Woo Chang (2009) proposed triangle-triangle intersection test algorithm based on the OBB bounding box. Jung-Woo Chang (2010) proposed a OBB-sphere bounding volume hierarchy and experiment 5 potential separating axes for OBBs.

# 3    Collision Detection Algorithm Method for Equipment Deploy Scene

Based on the characteristics of AABBs and OBBs, the topographic condition of the waste dump and the character of the equipment, this paper presents a bounding volumes nestification of AABBs and OBBs. The basic idea is: two levels of bounding volumes are set for the object, the outer bounding volume choose the bounding volumes that allow the simplest overlap tests while the inner bounding volumes select the volumes that fit the object more tightly. When the intersect test occurs, the outer bounding volume whose intersect test is simple is used to detect preliminarily so that the majority of distant objects are separated. The remaining objects are in close proximity where the OBBs are used to tested. This approach combines the compactness of OBBs and the simplicity of AABBs so that the overlap calculation is less and the efficiency is improved.

When the nestification on the equipment is constructing, because of the poor compactness of AABBs and the slender shape of the equipment, the nestification of AABBs and OBBs still exist a lot of space at the. Consequently, the algorithm is divided to 3 steps to ensure the accuracy.

(1)AABBs-AABBs overlap test

This test is very simple due to the construction of AABBs, only when the two shadows overlap that the two AABBs cast on the three coordinate axes, the two AABBs are detected intersection.

(2)AABBs-OBBs overlap test

The AABBs can be seen as special OBBs so that the AABBs-OBBs overlap test is the same as the OBBs-OBBs: separating axis theory. If the shadows that two OBBs cast on the same axis(may not the coordinate axis), the axis is called a separating axis. If a separating axis between two OBBs exists, this two OBBs don't overlap. There are only 15 potential axes for OBBs. We take one of them to explain the test process.

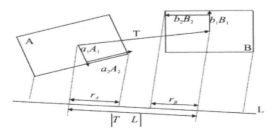

**Fig. 2.** OBB-OBB overlap test

A, B are two OBBs, $a_i$, $b_i$ is half the length of the border of A, B (i =1, 2, 3); $A_i$, $B_i$ is the unit vector along the axis(i =1, 2, 3); T is the distance of the center of A, B; L is the unit vector parallelled to the separating axis. $r_A$ is the sum of the shadows that $a_i$ cast on the direction of L, $r_B$ is the sum of the shadows that $b_i$ cast on the direction of L. We just need to compare |T·L| with ( $r_A$+ $r_B$ ) to detect whether the two OBBs overlap.

$$r_A = \sum_{i=1}^{3} \left| a_i A_i \cdot L \right|, \quad r_B = \sum_{i=1}^{3} \left| b_i B_i \cdot L \right| \tag{1}$$

Consequently, whether the two OBBs overlap is detected by (2), L is one of the 15 separating axes.

$$\left| T \cdot L \right| > rA + rB = \sum_{i=1}^{3} \left| a_i A_i \cdot L \right| + \sum_{i=1}^{3} \left| b_i B_i \cdot L \right| \tag{2}$$

When (2) holds, the two OBBs do not overlap. Otherwise the shadows that A, B cast on the other 14 separating axes should be calculated and compared by (2) till there exists one axis that meets(2). If there is no such a separating axis, the two OBBs overlap.(Fan Xiaoping, 2011).

(3)OBBs-OBBs overlap test

The same method in step(2) is occupied in this step. If the two OBBs overlap, the objects collide. If the two OBBs do not overlap, even though step(2)passed, the object do not collide.

## 4    Results

We have implemented our collision detection algorithm in C++ and Multigen Vega Prime API on an AMD Athlon(tm) 2.4 GHz PC with a 1.0 GB main memory.

Vega Prime is a cross-platform and extensible developing environment, which contains complete C++ API. A typical Vega prime program consist of five parts:

(1)Initialize. Invoke vp::initialize() to initialize Vega prime.
(2)Define. Create the objects that the program needed though code or ACF file.
(3)Configure. The system is configured at this stage according to the parameters set beforehand.
(4)Run loop. All the threads are occupied to render the scene.
(5)Shutdown. Free the memory and stop the threads inprocess.

MFC contains powerful application structure based on windows, and offers a large number of windows and events management function. The document/view structural framing is becoming the mainstream structural framing for developing Windows application. So we use MFC to invoke Vega Prime, which implements the virtual wandering in equipment deploy scene of Mining Dump.

**Fig. 3.** Wandering rendering in Fuxin Haizhou dump

During the wandering in the equipment deploy scene in land reclamation area of mining dump, viewpoint firstly contact with the ground, at the same time, collision detection occurs. When the viewpoint come into the deployed equipment, t collision detection occurs between the viewpoint and the equipment. Consequently the viewpoint can't go on wandering unless its changes its direction.

## 5     Conclusions and Future Work

We have presented a bounding volumes nestification of AABBs and OBBs collision detection algorithm that uses both OBBs and AABBs bounding volumes. We have shown how to combine the compactness of OBBs and the efficient overlap test for AABBs. We have implemented this algorithm C++ and Multigen Vega Prime API. Implementation results show that our nestification makes favorable speed up.

In future work, we plan to introduce a general selection model for separating axes to further reduce the calculation amount in the OBBs-OBBs overlap test. Furthermore, we plan to design a collision detection algorithm intelligent model. Based on different kinds of objects, the collision detection algorithm design beforehand will be chosen.

**Acknowledgement.** This work was supported by Project of National Natural Science Foundation of China (40901279). The research was also financially supported by Chinese Universities Scientific Fund (Project No. 2011JS143).

## References

1. Smith, A., Kitamu-Ra, Y., Takemura, H., Kishino, F.: A simple and Efficient Method for Accurate Collision Detection among Deformable Polyhedral Objects in Arbitrary Motion. The IEEE Virtual Reality Annual International Symposium 2, 136–145 (1995)
2. Naylor, B., Amanatides, J., Thibault, W.: Merging BSP Trees Yelds Polyhedral Set (SIGGRAPH 1990 Proceedings). Operations ACM Computer Graphics 24(2), 115–124 (1990)

3. Chang, J.-W., Kim, M.-S.: Efficient triangle–triangle intersection test for OBB-based collision detection. Computers & Graphics 33, 235–240 (2009)
4. Arbabi, E., Boulic, R., Thalmann, D.: Fast collision detection methods for joint surfaces. Journal of Biomechanics (42), 91–99 (2009)
5. Fan, X., Hou, J., Liao, Z., et al.: Research on Hybrid Hierarchical Bounding Box Algorithm in Virtual Environments. Journal of Chinese Computer Systems 5(5), 994–997 (2011)
6. Noborio, H., Fukuda, S., Arimoto, S.: Fast Interferenee Cheek Method Using Octree Representation. Advanced Robotics 3(3), 193–212 (1989)
7. Palmer, I.J., Grimsdale, R.L.: Collision detection for animation using sphere-trees. Computer Graphics Forum 14(2), 105–116 (1995)
8. Snyder, J.M.: An interactive tool for placing curved surfaces without interperetration. ACM Computer Graphics 29(4), 209–218 (1995)
9. Beniley, J.L.: Multidimensional Binary Seareh Trees Used for Assoeiative Searehing. ACM Communications 18(9), 509–517 (1975)
10. Corrales, J.A., Candelas, F.A., Torres, F.: Safe human–robot interaction based on dynamic sphere-swept line bounding volumes Original Research Article. Robotics and Computer-Integrated Manufacturing 27(1), 177–185 (2011)
11. Lai, K.-C., Kang, S.-C.: Collision detection strategies for virtual construction simulation. Automation in Construction (18), 724–736 (2009)
12. Gottachalk, S., Lin, M.C., Manocha, D.: OBB-Tree: A Hierarchical Structure for Rapid Interference Detection. In: The Proceedings of ACM SIGGRAPH 1996, pp. 171–180 (1996)
13. Akenine-Moller, T., Hains, E.: Real-time rendering. A.K. Peters (2002)
14. Chang, J.-W., Wang, W., Kim, M.-S.: Efficient collision detection using a dual OBB-sphere bounding volume hierarchy. Computer-Aided Design (42), 50–57 (2011)
15. Wei, Y.: Research on Collision Detection in Virtual Evironment. National University of Defense Technology (2000)
16. Wang, Z., Zhao, Q., Wang, C.: An object-oriented collision detection method and its application on distributed virtual environment. Chinese Journal of Computers 21(11), 990–994 (1998)

# A Low-Cost Positioning System for Parallel Tracking Applications of Agricultural Vehicles by Using Kalman Filter[*]

Fangming Zhang[1,2], Ximing Feng[2], Yuan Li[2], Xiuqin Rao[3], and Di Cui[2]

[1] Ningbo Institute of Technology, Zhejiang University
1 Xuefu Road, School of Mechanical and Energy Engineering, Ningbo, Zhejiang, China
fangmingzhang@126.com
[2] Ningbo Yinzhou MicroAgriculture Technology Ltd., Ningbo, Zhejiang, China
feng_63589506@163.com, 330204651@qq.com
[3] Zhejiang University, Hangzhou, Zhejiang, China
xqrao@zju.edu.cn

**Abstract.** A position-velocity (PV) model and a multi-sensor system, consisted of a consumer application GPS, a MEMS gyro, two encoders, and a turning angle sensor, was constructed for the positioning system. The two encoders augmented the positioning accuracy greatly that the fluctuation of vehicle position was greatly smoothed comparing with a GPS-only system. The minimal fluctuation was falling from 2.21 m to 0.52 m (east direction), from 0.68 m to 0.23 m (north direction). The maximum XTE was reduced from 2.5 m to 0.77 m, and the RMS value was improved to 0.22m. The GPS bias error was the major difficulty to produce better performance.

**Keywords:** Positioning system, GPS, Kalman filter, parallel tracking, low-cost.

## 1 Introduction

Parallel tracking is the main operation method of agricultural vehicles. Global Positioning System (GPS) acts as an important role in navigating agricultural vehicles with parallel tracking. Some researches [1-3] have been reported to use high–accuracy GPS receivers, Real Time Kinematic Global Positioning System (RTK-GPS) or Carrier-Phase Differential GPS (CPD-GPS), to develop automated agricultural vehicles. However, both RTK-GPS and CPD-GPS are too expensive for its actually application in agriculture. Low-cost consumer application GPSs are now widely used in automobile industry, i.e., car navigator, path tracking, but their position accuracy, 2-3 meters, could not be satisfied with requirement of agriculture application.

Kalman filter has been extensively used to smooth raw DGPS signals [4-5], which improved the positioning accuracy, and more importantly, it provided reliable positioning information during a short period of time when the GPS signal is lost. For

---

[*] This paper is supported from the Science Foundation of NingBo (Projects No. 2010A610140).

D. Li and Y. Chen (Eds.): CCTA 2011, Part I, IFIP AICT 368, pp. 461–470, 2012.

example, Will [1] constructed a position-attitude (PA) model-based extended Kalman filter. Han et al. [4] set up a position-velocity (PV) model for the Kalman filter. Guo et al.[5] integrated IMU and DGPS data and formed a position-velocity-attitude (PVA) model for fusion algorithms. Fiengo et al.[6] developed a model for vehicle by combinating of a GPS, speed sensor, and a gyro sensor. Guo [7] developed a GPS/IMU/magnetometer integrated system with Kalman filtering for vehicles. The author [8] had integrated a vision sensor and two encoders to construct an extended Kalman filter. Those results showed that fusion system could decrease the cost of sensors while kept the necessary accuracy for agricultural applications.

As sensor technology is developing rapidly, low-cost positioning system shows possible and attractive for agricultural vehicles. Rong Zhu et al.[9] developed an extended Kalman-based fusion algorithm for attitude estimation by using inexpensive micromachined gyroscopes, accelerometers and magnetometers. Akira Mizushima et al.[10] used low-cost sensors, three vibratory gyroscopes and two inclinometers, to estimate tilt angles (roll and pitch) by least-squares method. The drift error of the gyroscopes was estimated using the inclinometers. Ndjeng et al.[11] solved the problem of outdoor vehicle localization with Interacting Multiple Model (IMM) and Extended Kalman Filter (EKF) approaches, which allows the method to be optimized for highly dynamic vehicles with low-cost IMU-odometer-GPS composition. Zhi Shen et al.[12] integrated low-cost sensors, a MEMS-grade gyroscope, a vehicle built-in odometer, and a GPS to provide 2D navigation for land vehicles. Fast Orthogonal Search is suggested for modeling the higher order of reduced inertial sensor system RISS errors.

The objective of this research was developing a positioning system with low-cost guidance sensors for agricultural parallel tracking application.

## 2    Materials and Methods

A multi-sensors system was constructed on a rice transplanter (ZP60, ISEKI, Japan) as shown in figure 1, which consists of a consumer application GPS receiver (U-blox LEA-5S, Zoglab Inc., China), a MEMS gyro as heading angle sensor (GX1, Xunjie Inc.,China),two encoders as speed sensor (E6B2-CWZ6C, Omron Inc., Japan), and a precision potentiometer as turning angle sensor (Copal N35,Japan). The antenna of the U-blox GPS was mounted on a rigid frame in the front the vehicle 2.5 m above ground level. The receiver transmitted data at 1 Hz with Baud rate of 9600 bps. A RTK-GPS (S82E, South surveying & mapping instrument Inc, china) was used to record track of the vehicle with its antenna mounted beside the U-blox one. The gyro, measured angular velocity for yaw direction at maximum ability of ±70°/s, was installed on the body of vehicle. Two encoders, outputted 360 pulses per round, were driven by the left and right rear wheel through a pair of gear transmission with rate of 1:1. The potentiometer, whose resistance is 5KΩ within rotary angle of 345°, was installed under the turning axis. A computer system consists of one embedded central computer (ECC) (ARM S3C2440 Developing board, Tianxiang Inc., China) and five electric circuit units (ECU) (PIC 16F873A Developing board, Microagriculture Inc.,

China), which were connected by a RS-485 net. The 1st ECU acted as transferring data from the GPS receiver to the ECC. The 2nd and 3rd ECUs acted as sampling tracking speed from the left encoder and right encoder at the left and right rear wheel correspondingly. The 4th ECU acted as sampling turning angle from the potentiometer and sampling heading angle from the gyro sensor, and the last one acted as controlling a step motor to steering the rice transplanter. The outputs of these sensors were acquired through a 10-bit analog/digital converter. The total cost of this attitude sensor was approximately \$250, only 1/5 of a DGPS.

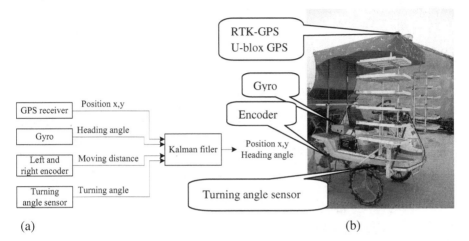

(a)    (b)

**Fig. 1.** (a) configuration of the multi-sensor system; (b) the test platform on the ISEKI ZP60

The GPS signal triggered all ECUs to begin sampling signal from corresponding sensors at the same time. When the ECU1 received the '\$GPGGA' frame, it extracted latitude and longitude and then sent them into the RS-485 net, which could be received by the ECC and all other ECUs, while the latter would sampled signal from corresponding sensors. The ECC processed the latitude and longitude after a button in its monitor, 'START', was pressed, and it got all sensor data by serial communication between one ECU and itself. The ECC transformed those data into significative decimal value, such as turning angle, left wheel speed. All data were then sent to the Kalman Filter for further processing.

A local coordinate system was set up that the 1$^{st}$ point in every test was thought as the origin point, and the x coordinate pointed to east direction and y coordinate pointed to north direction. Coordinate x and y of any position were transformed from the latitude and longitude of GPS according to Chang's method [13]. Furthermore, the rice transplanter was modeled as a three-tyre vehicle as shown in figure 2. Relying on kinematics analysis, a position-velocity (PV) model was set up for the Kalman filter. It shows the angle between the road and y-axis is fixed value, $\alpha$, while the heading angle, $\Psi$, offset, $e$, and speed, $v_1$ and $v_2$, changed when driving the vehicle.

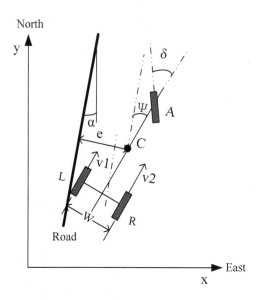

North

**Fig. 2.** The vehicle model, which is transformed into three-tyre vehicle, locates on the local coordinates. Point 'C' represents the estimated position point.

The discrete Kalman filter recursive equations are [4]:

$$X_{k+1} = \Phi_k X_k + w_k \tag{1}$$

$$Z_k = H_k X_k + v_k \tag{2}$$

where

$X_k$ is the (n × 1) process state vector at time $t_k$

$\Phi_k$ is the (n × n) state transition matrix

$w_k$ is the (n × 1) process noise vector with a known covariance $Q_k$

$Z_k$ is the (m × 1) measurement vector at time $t_k$

$H_k$ is the (m × n) measurement connection matrix

$v_k$ is the (m × 1) measurement noise vector with a known covariance $R_k$.

Equation 1 is the process model, and equation 2 is the measurement model. Since the objective of this study was to improve the 2–D positioning accuracy, four state variables were set as following:

$$X_k = [x_k, y_k, \Psi_k, v_k]^T \tag{3}$$

where

$x_k$ and $y_k$ are local coordinates to be estimated.

$\Psi_k$ is heading angle to be estimated.

$v_k$ is velocity to be estimated.

The state transition matrix was:

$$\Phi_k = \begin{bmatrix} 1 & 0 & 0 & T\sin(\psi_k + c \cdot \Delta\delta) \\ 0 & 1 & 0 & T\cos(\psi_k + c \cdot \Delta\delta) \\ 0 & 0 & 1 & T\tan(\Delta\delta)/W \\ 0 & 0 & 0 & 1 \end{bmatrix} \tag{4}$$

The raw receiver outputs, $x_{GPS}$ and $y_{GPS}$ transformed from latitude and longitude by GPS, heading angle from gyro, speed from encoders, and turning angle from potentiometer, are the measurement variables. The measurement vector and the measurement connection matrix are:

$$Z_k = [x_{GPS}, y_{GPS}, \psi_{GYRO}, v_{GPS}, \delta_{Turntyre}]_k^T \tag{5}$$

$$H_k = \begin{bmatrix} 1 & 0 & 0 & 0 \\ 0 & 1 & 0 & 0 \\ 0 & 0 & 1 & 0 \\ 0 & 0 & 0 & 1 \\ 0 & 0 & 0 & 0 \end{bmatrix} \tag{6}$$

The numerical solution to the discrete Kalman filter model is a step–wise procedure [4]:

Step 1: Compute the Kalman gain, $K_k$:

$$K(k) = P(k \mid k-1)H^T[R + H \cdot P(k \mid k-1)H^T]^{-1} \tag{7}$$

where $K_k$ is the Kalman gain, $P_{k,k-1}$ is the initial error covariance matrix, and $R$ is the covariance matrix for the measurement noise vector.

Step 2: Update the estimate, $\hat{X}_{k,k}$, with the measurement, $Z_k$:

$$\hat{X}(k \mid k) = \hat{X}(k \mid k-1) + K(k)[Y(k) - H\hat{X}(k \mid k-1)] \tag{8}$$

where $\hat{X}_{k,k-1}$ is the updated estimate, and is a priori estimate.

Step 3: Compute the error covariance, $P_{k,k}$, for the updated estimate:

$$P(k \mid k) = [I - K(k) \cdot H]P(k \mid k-1) \tag{9}$$

where $P_{k,k-1}$ is a priori error covariance matrix.

Step 4: Project ahead:

$$\hat{X}(k+1 \mid k) = \Phi(k)\hat{X}(k \mid k) \tag{10}$$

$$P(k+1 \mid k) = \Phi(k)P(k \mid k)\Phi(k)^T + Q_k \tag{11}$$

where $\hat{X}_{k+1,k}$ and $P_{k+1,k}$ are the projected estimate and projected error covariance matrix that the next iteration requires.

In the application of the above procedure, three matrices, the process noise covariance matrix $Q_k$, the measurement noise covariance matrix $R_k$, and the initial error covariance matrix $P_{k,k-1}$, need to be defined prior to the start of the iteration. We derived these matrices by trial:

$$Q_k = \begin{bmatrix} 0.033 & 0 & 0 & 0 \\ 0 & 0.033 & 0 & 0 \\ 0 & 0 & 0.003 & 0 \\ 0 & 0 & 0 & 0.0025 \end{bmatrix} \tag{12}$$

$$R_k = \begin{bmatrix} 6.25 & 0 & 0 & 0 & 0 \\ 0 & 6.25 & 0 & 0 & 0 \\ 0 & 0 & 0.25 & 0 & 0 \\ 0 & 0 & 0 & 0.025 & 0 \\ 0 & 0 & 0 & 0 & 0.025 \end{bmatrix} \tag{13}$$

$$P(k \mid k-1) = \begin{bmatrix} 2 & 0 & 0 & 0 \\ 0 & 2 & 0 & 0 \\ 0 & 0 & 0.1 & 0 \\ 0 & 0 & 0 & 0.01 \end{bmatrix} \tag{14}$$

The updated estimate, equation 8, is the best estimate of the current position.

The first experiment was done on a road (50 meter long) located in campus of Ningbo Institute of Technology, Zhejiang University on Jan. 29, 2011, where tracks of right wheel were drew by Chalks, and another one was done on a road (90 meter long) located in Jiangshan, NingBo on July 1, 2011, where tracks of the center of the vehicle were recorded by the RTK-GPS. The vehicle was driven along two parallel rows, transecting approximately 2.2 m in the former experiment, and 4.0 m in the later one. Data were recorded with a 1–s interval in all experiments. Every experiment was repeated 2 times with 3 travel speeds, 0.25m/s, 0.73 m/s, and 1.1 m/s.

One program, including serial communication and Kalman filter module, was written, compiled and run real time in the ECC, and another Matlab program was written for data analysis. The record of chalk or RTK-GPS was used as a baseline (reference) to evaluate the performance of the filters. A cross–track error (XTE) [4] is defined as the distance between the currently measured GPS position and the desired track. Minimal fluctuation was defined as coordinates jumping in east direction or north direction to evaluate performance of the kalman filter when RTK-GPS was not available.

## 3    Results and Discussion

Figure 3 shows one results by drawing line on ground. It shows that the Kalman filter improves the positioning system. The state variables, coordinates $x$, $y$, and heading angle $\Psi$ were smoothed. In these experiments, the minimal fluctuation was falling from 2.21m to 0.52 m (east direction), from 0.68 m to 0.23 m (north direction). However, the absolute bias still could not be evaluated by drawing line on ground.

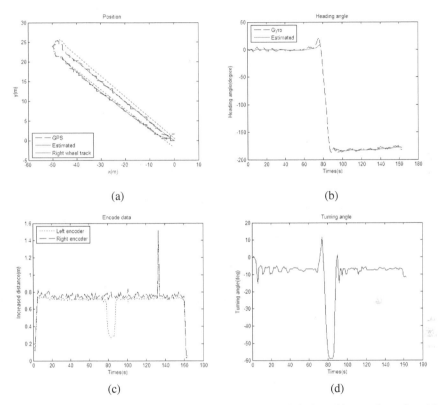

(a)                                        (b)

(c)                                        (d)

**Fig. 3.** Experiment data by drawing line on ground, (a)original GPS position, estimated position and track of right wheel; (b) original gyro data and estimated heading angle; (c) left encoder and right encoder data; (d) turning angle sensor data

The truth was exposed when receiving position data both from the U-blox GPS and the RTK-GPS at the same time. Figure 4 shows one result of this kind of experiments. The first point got by the RTK-GPS was also the original point of the U-blox coordinates system, where the first point got by U-blox deviated to coordinates (2.610747, 2.771199). Though positioning coordinates were smoothed by the Kalman filter, they deviated in most time that the mean bias was 2.32m, and the RMS is 0.72m, and the difference between the maximum and minimum XTE is 5.30m. The two lines formed by the U-blox GPS are not parallel. Compared with the former experiments, bad performance might be caused by close distance of the two antennas.

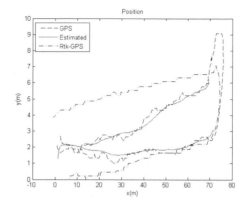

**Fig. 4.** Experiment data by using the two GPSs together. The track go and back are nearly parallel, but whether the U-blox GPS or the estimated coordinates are not parallel.

Results shows high accuracy sensors improve performance of positioning system. A close look at the GPS data we found the least GPS data changing is 1.5 m in x axis, and 0.45 m in y axis, the original GPS output could hardly be used to navigate an agriculture vehicle. After Kalman filter, the average data changing decreases to 0.45 m in x axis, and 0.20 m in y axis. This improvement owes to two encoders as they provide high accuracy tracking distance. The turning angle sensor is another high precision sensor; however, its output was not used as state variable yet, so it hardly contributed to improve positioning system. If it will be added as a state variable in future work, it will then bring more positive effect.

Another way to improve accuracy is speeding up the update of sensors. The maximum ability of this GPS receiver is 4Hz, while the working frequency was 1Hz only in this experiment due to stability of serial communication. Moreover, the gyro could update its output in 10 Hz. So software should be improved in future work to obtain more accuracy positioning data.

This experiment also certified that combine of some low cost guidance sensors could produce high accuracy position. The most expensive sensor in this system is the gyro, $100, and the total sensor cost is less than $250. It is important to use one or two low cost, high precision sensor, such as encoder, to improve the performance.

The experiments showed that Kalman filter does not work when the vehicle is turning around which Han [4] mentioned. In our experiments, estimated position might move to wrong direction when starting turning, and heading angle will lag behind the gyro data greatly. Solution to this difficulty is closing the Kalman filter when turning, and initializing it when it goes into a new row. If using a local coordinate system, we could set the first GPS data in the first row as the origin, and set the initial state variable with changed x and y, as well as adjust the state transition matrix, whose sign of encoder should be reversed.

# 4     Conclusions

A low-cost positioning system, consisted of a consumer application GPS receiver, a MEMS gyro, two encoders and one turning angle sensor, was developed to improve positioning accuracy of the GPS by using Kalman filter. A computer system embedded on vehicles was constructed, which composed of an ECC (ARM embed computer), 5 ECUs (PIC16 microcomputer), and a RS-485 net. Local coordinates, heading angle, and vehicle speed were set as state variables in the Kalman filter. Experiment results show positioning coordinates got by the GPS were improved after filter processing that they were smoothed, but bias of the GPS made the estimated coordinates uncertainty. The minimal fluctuation was falling from 2.21 m to 0.52 m (east direction), from 0.68 m to 0.23 m (north direction). The maximum XTE was reduced from 2.5 m to 0.77 m, and the RMS value was improved to 0.22m. However, the Kalman filter could not remove bias of GPS. In addition, the proposed Kalman filter makes inaccurate position estimates when turning around. Further work should be on reducing the GPS bias error for parallel tracking applications.

**Acknowledgments.** The authors wish to express their sincere thanks for the financial support from the Science Foundation of NingBo (Projects 2010A610140), Agriculture R&D project of Yingzhou (3rd batch, 2010), Machine R&D project of Ningbo Agriculture Machinery Bureau (2010-2011), and Initial Research Foundation of NIT.

# References

1. Will, J.D.: Sensor fusion for field robot localization. Ph.D thesis, University of Illinois at Urbana-Champaign (2001)
2. Noguchi, N., Reid, J.F., Zhang, Q., Will, J.D., Ishii, K.: Development of Robot Tractor Based on RTK-GPS and Gyroscope. In: 2001 ASAE Annual International Meeting, Paper Number: 01-1195, Sacramento, California, USA, July 30-August 1 (2001)
3. Bell, T.: Automatic tractor guidance using carrier-phase differential GPS. Computers and Electronics in Agriculture 25, 53–66 (2000)
4. Han, S.F., Zhang, Q., Noh, H.K.: Kalman filtering of GPS positions for a parallel tracking application. Transactions of the ASAE 45(3), 553–559 (2002)
5. Guo, L., He, Y., Zhang, Q., Han, S.: Real-time tractor position estimation system using a kalman filter. Journal of CSAE 18(5), 96–101 (2002)
6. Fiengo, G., Domenico, D.D., Glielmo, L.: A hybrid procedure strategy for vehicle localization system: Design and prototyping. Control Engineering Practice 17, 14–25 (2009)
7. Guo, H., Yu, M., Zou, C., Huang, W.: Kalman filtering for GPS/magnetometer integrated navigation system. Advances in Space Research 45, 1350–1357 (2010)
8. Zhang, F., Ying, Y., Zhang, Q., Shin, B.: Vision-based Position System for Agricultural Vehicle Using Extended Kalman Filter. In: ASAE Annual International Meeting, Paper No. 061157, Portland, Oregon, July 9-12 (2006)
9. Zhu, R., Sun, D., Zhou, Z., Wang, D.: A linear fusion algorithm for attitude determination using low cost MEMS-based sensors. J. Measurement 40, 322–328 (2007)

10. Mizushima, A., Ishii, K., Noguchi, N., Matsuo, Y., Lu, R.: Development of a low-cost attitude sensor for agricultural vehicles. J. Computers and Electronics in Agriculture. 76, 198–204 (2011)
11. Ndjeng, A., Gruyer, D., Glaser, S., Lambert, A.: Low cost IMU–Odometer–GPS ego localization for unusual maneuvers. J. Information Fusion 12, 264–274 (2011)
12. Shen, Z., Georgy, J., Korenberg, M.J., Noureldin, A.: Low cost two dimension navigation using an augmented Kalman filter/Fast Orthogonal Search module for the integration of reduced inertial sensor system and Global Positioning System. Transportation Research Part C. (Article in press, 2011)
13. Chang, C., Chen, Y., Xiao, T.: Research of GPS used in Farm machines guidance system. In: Annual Meeting of CSAE, pp. 952–957 (2006) (in Chinese)

# A Data Acquisition System Based on Outlier Detection Method for Weighing Lysimeters*

Wenqian Huang[1,2], Chi Zhang[1,2,**], Xuzhang Xue[1,2], and Liping Chen[1,2]

[1] Beijing Research Center of Intelligent Equipment for Agriculture, Beijing Academy of Agriculture and Forestry Sciences, Beijing, 100097, China
[2] National Research Center of Intelligent Equipment for Agriculture, Beijing, 100097, China
zhangchi@nercita.org.cn

**Abstract.** The weighing lysimeters provide scientist the basic information for research related to the evapotranspiration, high quality of the collected data from lysimeters is of great significance. However there are many factors that can affect the measurement accuracy of the weighing lysimeter. In this paper, a data acquisition system was developed to collect the data from 24 weighing lysimeters. The calibration process of the load cell was described. An outlier detection method based on the 3-sigma rule and the median filter was proposed to improve the measurement accuracy of the weighing lysimeters. The performance of the proposed method was compared with the method based on Savitzky-Golay filter. Results show that the standard deviations of the 15-point median filter and the 15-point Savitzky-Golay filter applied to the 283 data points were 0.413Kg and 0.422Kg respectively, which means that the performance of the median filter was better than the Savitzky-Golay filter. Moreover the outliers were successfully eliminated using the median filter and were not removed by the Savitzky-Golay filter.

**Keywords:** Weighing lysimeter, outlier detection, median filter, Savitzky-Golay filter.

## 1 Introduction

Evapotranspiration (ET) is used to describe the sum of evaporation and plant transpiration from the Earth's land surface to atmosphere [1]. Evapotranspiration is an important part of the water cycle. Precision measurement of the evapotranspiration is of great importance for accurate irrigation scheduling due to economic factors and the scarcity of water resources in many parts of the world [2]. It is also very important for the protection of ground water resources by studying soil water movement and nutrient transportation through the lysimeters.

* National Natural Science Foundation of China (Project No. 31071324) and National Key Technologies R&D Program of China (Project No. 2008BAB38B06).
** Corresponding author.

D. Li and Y. Chen (Eds.): CCTA 2011, Part I, IFIP AICT 368, pp. 471–478, 2012.

There are various methods to measure the evapotranspiration, but weighing lysimeters are most accurate and widely applied. The weighing lysimeter was used to measure the evapotranspiration directly by measuring the change in mass of an isolated soil tank. When the drainage and the water input such as irrigation and precipitation are taken into account, the evapotranspiration of the crop and soil can be accurately determined. Many works have been done in the construction and installation of weighing lysimeters and the measuring principle of the weighing lysimeter was described [3-6]. Some advanced data acquisition systems equipped with high-precision load-cell for the weighing lysimeters have been developed [7-9]. Much attention has been paid to the research on the application of the weighing lysimeter. Su Meishuang et al. studied the crop water demands for sprinkler-irrigated winter wheat and sweet corn using a weighing lysimeter and calculated the crop coefficients [10]. Niu Yong et al. employed a large-scale weighing lysimeter to study cucumber transpiration processes in solar greenhouse and established three empirical models for estimation of cucumber transpiration rate [11]. Changming Liu et al. studied the daily evapotranspiration of irrigated winter wheat and maize using a large-scale weighing lysimeter to improve field water utilization efficiency [12].

Because weighing lysimeters provide scientist the basic information for research related to the evapotranspiration, high quality of the collected data from lysimeters is of great significance. However there are many factors that can affect the measurement accuracy of the weighing lysimeter. The error analysis of the collected data from lysimeters indicate that evapotranspiration uncertainty was sensitive to number of rainfall events, the daily percolation quantity, load-cell uncertainty and potentiometer uncertainty [13]. The accuracy of lysimeter was directly proportional to the surface area and the accuracy of the scale and inversely proportional to the lysimeter mass, was also limited by the resolution of the datalogger or data recording system [14]. The systematic measurement error caused by the load-cell and the data acquisition system can be minimized through regular calibration [15-17].

But the error caused by the mechanical vibration and the change of environmental factor such as the wind speed and soil temperature was stochastic, cannot be eliminated through the calibration process. R. W. Malone et al. found that electronic changes can affect the performance of the weighing lysimeters and provide a statistically valid quality control plan using control charts to improve the measurement accuracy of the weighing lysimeters [18]. P.J. Vaughan et al. pointed out that lysimeter and improved the lysimeter data processing to eliminate bad data and minimize variations in the measurements through noise reduction method based on a seven-point Savitsky-Golay filter [19-20]. However, the Savitzky-Golay filter is useful for to eliminate noise with high frequency, but is less successful to detect the high magnitude and low-frequency noise such as sharp pulse noise. In order to improve the measurement accuracy of the weighing lysimeters, it is important to detect the outliers in the measurement data and eliminate them.

In this paper, a data acquisition system based on outlier detection method is developed. The outlier detection method is based on the combination of two digital filters, one is the filter of three sigma rule and another is the median filter. The hardware and software design of the data acquisition system is described, as well as the calibration process of the load-cell sensor. The data processing result is compared with the one based on Savitzky-Golay filter.

# 2    Materials and Methods

## 2.1    Description of the System

The weighing lysimeters system is located in National Precision Agriculture Demonstration Station in Xiaotangshang Town of Beijing. The system is consisted of 24 lysimeters with 1.0m*0.75m*2.3m (L*W*H). The machine structure of the lysimeter was counter-balanced and the schematic diagram of the lysimeter is shown in Fig.1.

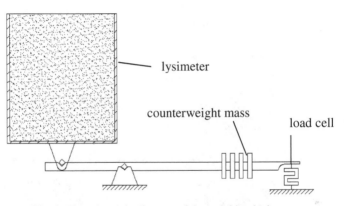

**Fig. 1.** The schematic diagram of the weighing lysimeter

The load cells used in the system are NS1-3M2-100Kg with a sensitivity of 1.9951mV/V for the lysimeters and the NS6-2-50Kg of 1.9969mV/V for percolation. A four-wire bridge configuration is used for load cells in which 2-wire for the input of the excitation voltage and 2-wire for the output of differential voltage. As the change of the mass of the lysimeter can be measured using the load cell. The measurement data of the load cell can be converted to the evapotranspiration (ET), usually calculated by mm, through dividing the change of mass by the surface area of the lysimeter $0.75m^2$.

A station for observing climatic parameters was establish to collected the data of air temperature, precipitation, solar radiation, humidity and wind velocity/direction. Then the ET could be calculated using the following equation:

$$ET = P + I + Q - \Delta R - \Delta S \qquad (1)$$

Where $P$ is the precipitation, mm; $I$ is the irrigation, mm; $Q$ is underground drainage, mm; $\Delta R$ is surface runoff, mm; and $\Delta S$ is the change of the amount of water stored in a certain period, mm.

## 2.2    Design of the Data Acquisition System

In the developed data acquisition system, a master/slave structure is adopted. The measurement system consists of communication modules, data acquisition modules, personal computer, RS485-RS232 converter and software. The schematic of the data acquisition system is shown in Fig.2. The data acquisition module is developed based on a 16bit Analog/Digital Convert (ADC) and a 16bit Digital/Analog Converter (DAC). The ADC is used for differential-input of the load cells, and the input range is configured as -15mv to +15mv. The DAC is used to provide +5V excitation voltage with 40mA maximum driven current for the load cells. Each data acquisition module can connect to 3 load cells. There are 24 load cells for the lysimeters and 24 load cells for percolation and total 16 data acquisition modules. Every 4 data acquisition modules are connected to a communication module and the 4 communication modules are connected to a personal computer via RS485 bus and a RS485 to RS232 converter. Software was developed to collected data from the data acquisition modules and a user-defined communication protocol based on Modbus was adopted.

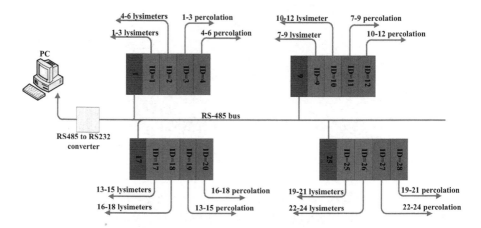

**Fig. 2.** The schematic diagram of the data acquisition system

## 2.3    Calibration of the Load Cells

In order to improve the weighing accuracy, the calibration of the load cells is needed. The calibration can be used to convert the voltage of the load cells into the weight of lysimeters. During calibration procedure, the load cell output was measured every 3 seconds and the average of the 1-min data is calculated. The mass weight is 6.932Kg. Each time a weight was added and the corresponding voltage of the load cell was recorded. Total 6 weights were cumulatively added. The calibration procedure was conducted for all 24 lysimeters and the calibration line is ploted. The data processing was finished using Microsoft Excel 2011.

### 2.4    Outlier Detection of the Measurement Data

The load-cell mass data were recorded every three seconds and the measurement results were saved in txt file for further processing. The data measurement was conducted from 14:42pm of 9th March to 9:39am of 18th March, 2011. For easy analysis, only the data of the No.2 lysimeter collected in 14th March was used for further processing. First, the outlier of the measurement data was detected based on 3-sigma rule. The data out of the range of [mean-3sigma, mean+3sigma] was defined as outlier and eliminated. The data over a 5-min period (100 total values) was used as a group to calculate the mean and the standard deviation. The data from 100 total values after eliminating the outliers were used to calculate the averages. Second, the 5, 7, 11, 15 and 25 points media filters and Savitzky-Golay filters were applied to the averages respectively. The performances of the two-type filters were compared. The mean and standard deviation were used to evaluate the performance. The data processing was finished using Matlab 2011 and Microsoft Excel 2011.

## 3    Results and Discussion

### 3.1    Load Cell Calibration Results

The 24 lysimeters were calibrated respectively. The calibration results of No.1 and No.2 lysimeters were shown in Fig.3. There was a strong linear relationship between the load cell output (mV) and the calibration mass (Kg). The determination coefficients of the No.1 and No.2 lysimeters were 0.9998 and 0.99992 respectively. The calibration equations were established and the calibration coefficients were used for the conversion from the load cell output to the change of mass of the lysimeters.

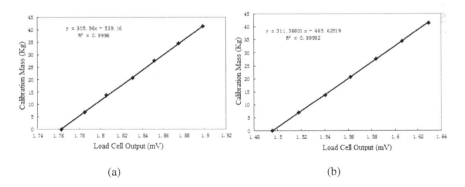

|                |                |
| :------------: | :------------: |
| (a)            | (b)            |

**Fig. 3.** Calibration results of (a) No.1 lysimeter and (b) No.2 lysimeter

### 3.2    The Outlier Detection Results

The 28300 data points collected from No.2 lysimeter were used for outlier detection. The result after the outlier detection using the 3-sigma rule and the averaging of the

100 data points was shown in Fig.4. After the above processing, there were 283 data points used for further processing. It was obvious that there were some outliers in the 283 data points and should be eliminated.

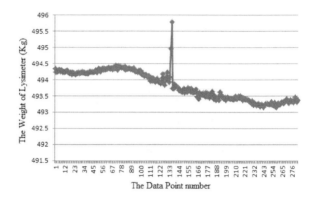

**Fig. 4.** Data processing using 3-sigma rule and averaging

The 5, 7, 11, 15 and 25 points media filters and Savitzky-Golay filters were applied to the 283 data points respectively. The mean and standard deviation of the different filters were listed in Table 1. As shown in Table.1, the standard deviation using the media filter reached a minimum when the data point of the filter was 15-point. And the standard deviation of the media filter was smaller than that of the Savitzky-Golay filters, which means that the performance of the median filter was better than the Savitzky-Golay filters.

**Table 1.** The mean and standard deviation of the 5, 7, 11, 15 and 25 points media filters and Savitzky-Golay filters

|  | 5-point | 7-point | 11-point | 15-point | 25-point |
|---|---|---|---|---|---|
| **Meadian filter** | | | | | |
| Mean | 493.814 | 493.813 | 493.813 | 493.811 | 493.813 |
| Standard Deviation | 0.415 | 0.414 | 0.414 | 0.413 | 0.414 |
| **Savitzky-Golay** | | | | | |
| Mean | 493.823 | 493.824 | 493.824 | 493.824 | 493.824 |
| Standard Deviation | 0.432 | 0.427 | 0.424 | 0.422 | 0.420 |

The processing results using 15-point median filter and 15-point Savitzky-Golay filters were shown in Fig.5. The outliers in the Fig.4 were successfully removed after using the 15-point median filtering as shown in Fig.5a. However, the outliers still existed after using the 15-point Savitzky-Golay filtering.

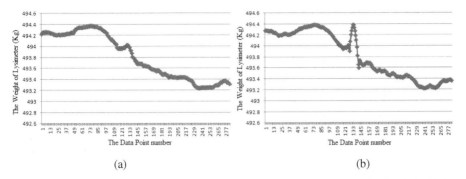

**Fig. 5.** Data processing using (a) 15-point median filtering and (b) 15-point Savitzky-Golay filtering

# 4    Conclusion

In this paper, a data acquisition system was developed to collect the data from 24 weighing lysimeters. The calibration process of the load cell was described. An outlier detection method based on the 3-sigma rule and the median filter was proposed to improve the measurement accuracy of the weighing lysimeters. The performance of the proposed method was compared with the method based on Savitzky-Golay filter. Results show that the standard deviations of the 15-point median filter and the 15-point Savitzky-Golay filter applied to the 283 data points were 0.413Kg and 0.422Kg respectively, which means that the performance of the median filter was better than the Savitzky-Golay filter. Moreover the outliers were successfully eliminated using the median filter and were not removed by the Savitzky-Golay filter.

**Acknowledgments.** Our project is supported by National Natural Science Foundation of China (Project No. 31071324) and National Key Technologies R&D Program of China (Project No. 2008BAB38B06).

# References

1. Davie, T.: Fundamentals of hydrology (Routledge 2003), pg. 35 (2003), http://books.google.com/books?id=XAGt03ANojgC& source=gbs_navlinks_s
2. Molden, D., Oweis, T.Y.: Water for food, water for life: A comprehensive assessment of water management in agriculture, pp. 279–310. Earthscan, International Water Management Institute, London, SriLanka (2007)
3. Wu, Y., Luo, J.-Y., Wang, F.: Development and implementation of the intelligent weighing lysimeter system. Research and exploration in laboratory 25(4), 432–434, 438 (2006)
4. Sun, Q., Zhang, W., Gao, L., Zhang, J.: A new weighing type of measuring and controlling system by lysimeter with high precision. Journal of Xi'an University of Technology 15(1), 56–60 (1999)

5.  Barani, G.-A., Khanjani, M.J.: A large electronic weighing lysimeter system design and installation. Journal of the Amercican Water Resources Association 38(4), 1053–1060 (2002)
6.  Howell, T.A., McCormick, R.L., Phene, C.J.: Design and Installation of Large Weighing Lysimeters. Transactions of the ASAE 28(1), 106–112, 117 (1985)
7.  Sun, Q., Zhang, J., Zhang, W., Gao, L.: Computer measuring and controlling system of high precision balance lysimeter. Journal of Soil Erosion and Soil and Water Conservation 5(5), 80–84 (1999)
8.  Yang, X., Shen, B., Zhang, J., Liang, Y.: Computer measure and control of a large high precision lysimeter. Transactions of the CSAE 12(3), 72–76 (1996)
9.  Johnson, A., Mathews, T.J., Matthews, G.P., Patel, D., Worsfold, P.J., Andrew, K.N.: High-resolution laboratory lysimeter for automated sampling of tracers through a 0.5m soil block. Journal of Automated Methods & Management in Chemistry 25(2), 43–49 (2003)
10. Su, M., Li, J., Rao, M.: Estimation of crop coeffcients for sprinkler- irrigated winter wheat and sweet corn using a weighing lysimeter. Transactions of the CSAE 21(8), 25–29 (2005)
11. Niu, Y., Liu, H., Wu, W., Yang, S.: Cucumber transpiration by large-scale weighing lysimeter in solar greenhouse. Transactions of the CSAE 27(1), 52–56 (2011)
12. Liu, C., Zhang, X., Zhang, Y.: Determination of daily evaporation and evapotranspiration of winter wheat and maize by large-scale weighing lysimeter and micro-lysimeter. Agricultural and Forest Meteorology 111, 109–120 (2002)
13. Malone, R.W., Bonta, J.V., Stewardson, D.J., Nelsen, T.: Error Analysis and quality improvement of the Coshocton weighing lysimeters. Transactions of the ASAE 43(2), 271–280 (2000)
14. Payero, J.O., Irmak, S.: Construction, Installation, and Performance of Two Repacked Weighing Lysimeters. Irrigation Science 26, 191–202 (2008)
15. Yan, J., Li, Y., Deng, Z., Wang, S., Liu, H., Yang, Q., Li, X.: Automatic monitoring system of LG-I weighing lysimeter. Transactions of the CSAE 25(S2), 43–48 (2009)
16. Meshkat, M., Warner, R.C., Walton, L.R.: Lysimeter design, construction and instrumentation for assessing evaporation from a large undisturbed soil monolith. Applied Engineering in Agriculture 15(4), 303–308 (1999)
17. Howell, T.A., Schneider, A.D., Dusek, D.A., Marek, T.H., Steiner, J.L.: Calibration and scale performance of Bushland weighing lysimeters. Transactions of the ASAE 38(4), 1019–1024 (1995)
18. Malone, R.W., Stewardson, D.J., Bonta, J.V., Nelsen, T.: Calibration and quality control of the Coshocton weighing lysimeters. Transactions of the ASAE 42(3), 701–712 (1999)
19. Vaughan, P.J., Trout, T.J., Ayars, J.E.: A processing method for weighing lysimeter data and comparison to micrometeorological ETo predictions. Agricultural Water Management 88, 141–146 (2007)
20. Vaughan, P.J., Ayars, J.E.: Noise Reduction Methods for Weighing Lysimeters. Journal of Irrigation and Drainage Engineering 135(2), 235–240 (2009)

# Key Technology of South Sea Pearl Industry Management Information Service Platform Based on the Internet of Things

Longqin Xu[1,*], Shuangyin Liu[1,2], and Daoliang Li[2]

[1] College of Information; Guangdong Ocean University, Zhanjiang Guangdong 524025, China
[2] College of Information and Electrical Engineering, China Agricultural University, Beijing, P.R. China 100083
{xlqlw,hdlsyxlq}@126.com

**Abstract.** This research constructs the south sea pearl industry management information service platform based on the Internet of Things, analyzing the features and technical advantages of Internet of Things, as well as the current existing problems of the pearl Industrial management. We have investigated the application management model of the Internet of Things in the product flow of pearl industry from production to processing management and explored the application of the key technologies, like radio frequency identification (RFID), wireless sensor network (WSN), physical markup language (PML) and the Electronic Product Code (EPC), to the Internet of Things in the pearl industrial management information services application platform. With the hope to bridge and eliminate the gap caused by differences in technology and standards among various sectors in the South Sea pearl production, processing, marketing and distribution, thus integration and optimization of pearl industrial management will be promoted and developed healthily.

**Keywords:** Internet of things, Pearl industry, WSN, RFID, EPC, PML, Cloud computing platform.

## Introductions

China is one of the countries which is first to culture pearls, and has become the world's major pearl farming country in the late 20th century, accounting for 96% annually pearl production in the world, about 30 tons of them are sea water pearls, of which about 60% is mainly from Zhanjiang, Guangdong[1]. Pearl is not only a traditional Chinese herbal medicine and qualified facial products, but also a major channel to increase coastal pearl farming income. With concentration and support of all levels governments, pearl industry in Zhanjiang has been rapidly developed in recent years. However, in the huge production and consumption of the pearl industry, there are still problems[1-2] as follows: 1) The model of current Sea water pearl

---

* Corresponding author.

D. Li and Y. Chen (Eds.): CCTA 2011, Part I, IFIP AICT 368, pp. 479–490, 2012.

farming descended traditionally, which consumes a lot of resources and extensively cultivated. New products and technologies cannot be fast promoted, which produces low value-added products; 2) Low level of information collection and control in sea water pearl process of production and in short of water management system for the whole process of pearl production, thus resulted in low level of industrialization; 3) With substandard and unreasonable feeding, spraying, fertilizing, resulted in higher cost as well as risks of investment for formers; 4) Over farming with high-density caused environmental pollution and deterioration of sea water as well. The experience is far enough to clearly get to know the pearl growth environment, which is impossibly assisted by current techniques and disease resistant warning mechanism of sea water pearl poorly works; 5) Lacking of information, irrational expansion of the scale, and unsmooth channel in sales and cyclical fluctuations in market conditions, which hurt the enthusiasm of farmers; 6) without a set of pearl industrial management system to cover the whole process of production, the current information systems in this field is only suits for a single enterprise system and a single custom developed, which resulted in diversified description of pear introduction and the waste of resources and the development of modern management is blocked.

In this paper, for the existing problems in the management of the whole process of sea water pearl production in Guangdong areas, we has built the pearl industrial management information services platform based on the Internet of Things which combines pearl cultivation and processing techniques, networking technology and intelligent information processing technologies, to achieve the automatic production process control product traceability and scientific management of sea water pearls. Then high yield, efficient, safe, and healthy farming and sustainable development water pearl could be possible.

The research on morphological characteristics of corn seed had got good identification results while much less study of corn purity identification and much more application about corn side features. This paper proposed that the color features of crown core area had significant function on corn purity after the study on three commonly used maize varieties. The DBSCAN was optimized by farthest first traversal algorithm for the purity identification. The experimental result indicated this method had high classification rate and the higher precision and offered a reference for building accurate purity identification system.

# 1    Internet of Things and Working Principle

## 1.1    The Concept of Internet of Things

Internet of things is a network which combines information sensing devices such as the smart sensors, radio frequency identification (RFID), laser scanners, global positioning system (GPS), in accordance with the agreed protocol, to connect Internet with anything, to exchange information and communication in order to achieve intelligent identification, positioning, tracking, monitoring and management[4-5].

## 1.2     Internet of Things in the Current Development Home and Abroad

Currently, in Japan, the United States, South Korea, EU and other countries corresponding policy has been introduced in support of the development of internet of things, and has made a lot of basic research and application development.

In the United States and Europe, internet of things have greatly developed in intelligent power, intelligent home, intelligent transportation, intelligent logistics, ecological monitoring, e-health and other fields[6]. IBM proposed the concept that "wisdom of the Earth, internet of things and cloud computing" which leads the new round of IT technology revolution in 2009 [7].

The starting and development in internet of things in our country has not lagged behind other countries, and a long-term planning "next-generation broadband mobile wireless communications network" has been made, which specially focuses on the research and development of "sensor and its network."

Premier Wen Jiabao proposed "Feel China" when visiting Wuxi on August 7, 2009. The concept of internet of things in China has attached great importance and become a new wave core areas after the computer, Internet, mobile communications information industry.

Some provinces have a large number of domestic uses of sensor networks to solve the power, agriculture, fisheries and transport in the "M2M" and other information and communication services[6-9]. In the future things will not only penetrate into the smart city, smart transportation, smart homes, public safety, environmental protection and other fields, but also greatly promote the economic development, which is seen as a new emerging industries.

## 1.3     Workflow of Internet of Things

The basic work flow of internet of things is composed by the entity markup language Information Server (Physical Markup Language Information Server, PML-IS), information collection system, the object name server (Object Name Service, ONS) and information management system [6]. The function of each is as follows:

1) Information collection system. The system includes wireless water sensors, weather sensors, RFID tags, wireless sensor network (WSN), readers (reader)\GPRS wireless communication, data exchanging, monitoring and management software, mainly to complete the collection of the water environmental factors, transmission and storage, in order to achieve automatic information collection for farming environment. The information is transferred by wireless sensors and GPRS connection to the central server which handles the processor installed in information processing software, such as the collected data conversion, analysis, comb, integrity checking, data recovery and other operations, the processed data to the appropriate database management software for individual use.

2) The object name server (Object Name Service, ONS)[6]. The ONS server main function is achieving correlation between the various sensor points and PML-IS

server and established the maps with ecological information on pearl breeding, pearl Electronic Product Code EPC tag and the PML description of pearl product.

3) Physical Markup Language Information Server, PML-IS.[6]. The user can first create and maintain data, define the rules, and then the user can product a code in accordance with predetermined rules of pearl, and then use the XML information on the items described in detail in order to facilitate access to other servers.

4) Information management system. The system with the help of hardware and software to obtain environment, processing and production management information in the whole process of pearl production management, products information is provided through the mapping between the object name server information and the PML-IS server retrieving the detailed description about the product in the PML-IS Information Server for pearl farmers and consumers, such as information search, product traceability and other functions in the form of the Web, also users can master all process of pearl production status by phone or wireless PDA.

## 1.4    The Application Model of Internet of Things in the Pearl Industry Management Network Information Service Platform

The application of the internet of things in pearl industrial management information service platform, whose advantage has been taken to reach seamless in monitoring and management containing sea water pearl production, processing and product traceability. The diagram is shown in Figure 1.

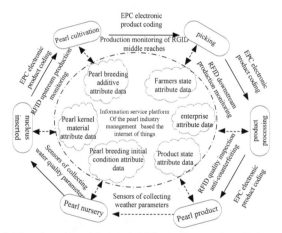

**Fig. 1.** Internet of things based pearl industrial information service platform structure diagram

As shows in Figure 1, Internet of things has achieved environment information collection, pearl product identification and monitoring by smart sensors and RFID and completed the mapping among pearl environmental information, the Electronic Product Code EPC tags and the PML-IS server by The ONS server which has achieved correlation between the various sensor points and PML-IS server in the processing of products such as the nursery, nucleus inserted, rest, picking. All information can be optimized through the pearl industrial information service platform transferred by a wireless or wired network. That can make the existing internal management system to be compatible with the maximum and became integral part of internet of things.

RFID, WSN and electronic product code (EPC) are integral essential factors in the pearl industry. It will effectively monitor and convert data each other in all aspects of the process in sea water pearls farming, product processing and product distribution, to establish a landmark product and quality of traceability; the standardization and unified of data collection, transmission and seamless in sectors of production in the pearl industry will also be achieved.

## 2    Pearl Industrial Management Information Service Platform

### 2.1    System Goals

For the realization of intelligent processing and digitization process in south sea pearl production, the pearl industrial management information service platform has been established with key technology of the Internet of Things, artificial intelligence and expert systems theory and computer-assisted decision-making strategies development. On this account, it will improve the standard of management and production process of water pearl enterprises and farming on the level of pearl, thus the intensive pearl industry development and scientific management is secured.

### 2.2    System Architecture Design

The system is divided into data acquisition layer, transport layer, data servers, business logic (functional layer) and the presentation layer with the use of the N-tier B/S structure mode; Development platform uses NET Framework which effectively reduces the system client requirements, and the distribution of the client applications and version control problems will be avoided. System architecture is shown in Figure 2.

In architecture, the presentation layer has completed the function of interface interaction with the end-user, and the applications layer has .aspx page and related code; Business logic layer is used to encapsulate business rules and business logic, which is packaged as. NET components in the application layer. Data server layer has adopted the layer style persistence (CMP) design pattern with container, in which pattern the business object data does not consider where the original data is from and how to store it, as long as the data access components interact with data server (or servers ), all data is manipulated through stored procedures.

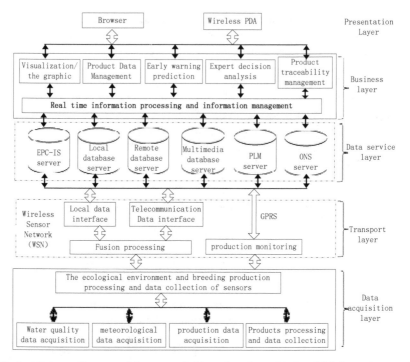

**Fig. 2.** Architecture diagram of Internet of things based pearl industrial information service platform

## 2.3    System Features Module Design

According to actual needs of the majority of pearl farmers and management staff of enterprises and institutions, in addition to problems of existing software systems are badly in need of upgrading, as well as independence of pearl farming industry model and complexity of culturing in the process of breeding, feeding, disease prevention and control management, such as insertion of nuclear, fishery drugs, disinfection, rest, oxygen, microscopic examination, testing, painting, drilling, water quality control and so on, these large number of knowledge is classified through theoretical guidance such as information intelligent perception, artificial intelligence, expert systems and knowledge engineering, to sort out their internal relations, and optimize the combination of knowledge based on expression of a variety of methods. With research of the knowledge of high effective south sea pearl production model to built pearl databases, production and processing information database, disease diagnosis prevention and treatment knowledge database, then shared south sea pearl management information service platform is set up and rebuilt for the pearl industry to provide assisted strategic supplementary decision for south sea pearl enterprises and units.

The functions of this platform includes: environmental data collection and management,  prediction and warning,  water quality control management, production management, quality and traceability management, expert systems, supply and demand information, farming techniques information, processing technology information, technical services, expert consultation, decision analysis, system maintenance. So users can easily use this system in multi-angle multi-channel. The system function structure is shown in Fig.3:

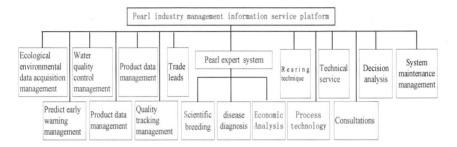

**Fig. 3.** Function structure of management information service platform based on Internet of things

Through the pearl industrial management information services platform, pearl farming information services in prenatal and postnatal and science information, aquaculture management and remote intelligent decision-making services in products are provided; effectively achieve a smooth channel for the transformation of pearl culture technology, significantly enhance the quality of sea water pearls, greatly improve production and promote sea water pearl industry's enthusiasm for aquaculture and create the northern Gulf region "pearl" industry. While the research institutes of the new technology, new achievements and new products in the marine pearl culture in the promotion of the use can increase the stocking density, shorten the breeding cycle, reduce farming risk, reduce production costs and improve the level of aquaculture technology and quality control, reduce labor intensity, expand production scale, advance the automation of production management, putting forward pearl culture toward equipment engineering, digital culture, information-oriented, which has great scientific significance and practical value in the healthy development of pearl industry.

# 3     Analysis of Key Technology and Its Applications in Internet of Things

## 3.1     Wireless Sensor Network (WSN)

WSN is the key information technology in the pearl culture industry, the management environment monitoring and collection, which use wireless sensor node (Node) to collect and perceive farming environment information, and timely send or receive information with aggregation node (Sink).[9] Connected the DNS cloud server, on-site monitoring center with aggregation node (Sink) of wireless sensor network through the RS-232 serial cable or GPRS , forming on-site real-time information collection system(Figure 4)

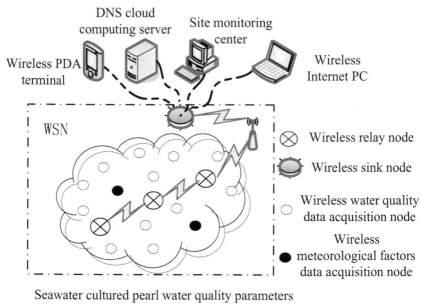

Seawater cultured pearl water quality parameters
of meteorological data collection area

**Fig. 4.** Application of WSN technology in pearl industry management

While monitoring seawater pearl environmental information on-site with the wireless sensor networks, we deploy a certain number randomly sensor information collection nodes in the pearl farming region, each node can form wireless sensor network by self-organizing. The data monitored by sensor nodes can be transmitted and processed through multi-hop route between other sensor node and the sink node (base station) [10], and then transmitted via the GPRS or Internet monitoring center to the scene, server or terminal device.

The pearl industrial management information service platform based on internet of things is in use of the wireless sensor nodes which have integrated solar panels, low-power and the 433MHz communication frequency based on the thought that pearl farms has larger areas for information collection, so nodes is distributed, and cable power supply is not convenient and monitoring and collection for eco-environmental factors and other characteristics is dynamic. Communication distance between nodes is 500m, and communication speed can reach 76.8kbps, thus achieve the real-time dynamic acquisition and transmission for water quality and climate pearl farming environment factors.

## 3.2    RFID

RFID is encoding vector in the process of pearl production, processing and product distribution, which transform environment information collected by the WSN, production, processing chain to the corresponding coding and record in the RFID chip, the application model is shown in Figure 5. RFID tags of pearl products are scanned by the sensor, then the code analysis is transmitted to the local coding system for data processing; ONS is responsible for queries and mapping management with processing Electronic Product Code EPC and the corresponding PML-IS server address; Information through the network will be transferred to DNS cloud computing services platform for the information management with other aspects of pearl culture [11]. RFID has the advantages of automatic sensing, transmission information content, Mass and dynamic storage, and can record with multi-dimensional pearl industry-related information; also coding hidden to prevent malicious copy, safe and reliable without human intervention and so on.

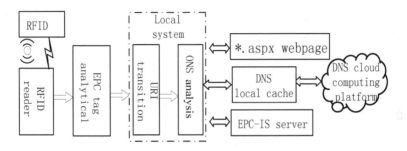

**Fig. 5.** RFID application model

## 3.3    Electronic Product Code （EPC）

EPC code (electronic product code) is the Auto-ID Center which is assigned to each physical target with only sign of the query code, it includes a string information on behalf of pearl and production categories and its ID, the date of the various stages of cultivation, production dates of purchase, production date, manufacturer, expiration date, pearl processing date [12]. Meanwhile, with the whole process of pearl farming in the various aspects of changing, the production management data can be updated in real time. Typically, EPC code can be made of silicon into electronic tag and attached to kernel of pearl to be identified, transferred and checked by information-processing software. When the pearl products through the data collection authorized points,   it is not only correctly read the code of the unique pearl products but also read out of production with other inter-relate through the ONS system and PML system, so as to achieve the seamless of all aspects and improve management efficiency pearl industry.

Pearl industry standard EPC code and coding rules need to be encoded by the national standards and industry research institutions and departments jointly developed, comprehensive, unambiguous, practical, scalable and open, etc., are common pearl culture industry compliance with coding standards and rules, which can effectively eliminate all aspects of pearl production and processing of fault information management, enhance the management efficiency of pearl farming.

### 3.4    PML Entity's Markup Language

PML is a standardized language, which helps user to define rules and maintain the data, can be coded with information about the name of pearl products, categories, attributes of the breeding, production and processing status, production and other aspects of information according to the rules in advance and use XML to descript the product information [13-15]. It solves problem of the limited capacity of electronic tag storage without saving a lot of physical information. Concerning the Internet of Things, PML server is mainly used to provide a common mode of the original information items defined in the rules, to facilitate the access to other servers.

### 3.5    Technology Integration

According to the demand of south sea pearl industry management and technique expansion,  integrated technology services concept is adopted, sensor networks, distributed technology, artificial intelligence, forecasting and decision-making, gray theory, artificial neural networks, hybrid intelligent diagnostic reasoning, fuzzy reasoning, database technology, MIS Technology, Rich Internet, WebGIS technology and disaster monitoring and early warning technology etc. is integrated. This platform with integrated hardware and software, large-grained, loosely coupled, dynamic binding characteristics, overcomes differences in shielding characteristics of a heterogeneous network.

Pearl industry management information service platform that contains pearl and pearl products processing and marketing enterprise business applications, including local, covering pearl breeding, processing, distribution and the whole process, before, during and post-natal and other various links on the River platform, according to a unified transport protocol, EPC encoding, ONS system via a wired or wireless networks, relying on the local computing and cloud computing to support distributed on the basis of the built; pearl cultivation and processing in accordance with the upper, middle and lower reaches various aspects of water quality and meteorological sensors transfer the state property, state property of production, processing, deployment of personnel, operating environment, complete the quantity, quality control and direction of information flow and feedback intelligent deployment, from "farm to the sales counter." The seamless link for the pearl quality control, production information management, creating brand offers reliable protection.

## 4    Conclusions

We explore the technology of on internet of things in the pearl industrial management information services application platform focusing on the current pearl industrial management problems. It combines the Internet with pearl industry, and restricts the Pearl environmental information, various aspects of production factors, product processing and marketing of pearl. It has become a modern information technology to drive the fisheries modernization.

Considering characteristics of cultured pearl industry and culture of enterprise information progress, the application of things is not so easily to realize, it is the integration of multiple technologies and integration of multiple applications in a systematic works, some key technology such as transfer protocol, integrated and embedded technology and information security and so on still need further improvement. In the future, the gradual integration of networking technology into pearl culture industry management will push forward the healthy and sustainable aquaculture industry development.

**Acknowledgements.** This research is financially supported by the China Spark Program Project (2007EA780068), Guangdong Science And Technology Program Project (2010B020315025) and Zhanjiang Science And Technology Program Project (2010C3113011).

# Reference

1. Li, Z.: Economical analysis of dilemma of chinese pearl industry and outlet. Research of Agricultural Modernization 28(4), 443–445 (2010)
2. Yi, L.: Development strategies of "south pearl" industry in Zhanjiang. Chinese Fisheries Economics 27(5), 36–42 (2009)
3. Wang, Z., Zhang, C.: EPC and Internet of thing. China standards press, Beijing (2004)
4. Wen, J.: In 2010 the government work report (EB/OL). (March 15, 2010),
   http://www.gov.cn/2010lh/content-1555767.htm (May 15, 2010)
5. Sun, Q.-B., Liu, J., Li, S.: Internet of things: summarize on concepts, architecture and key technology problem. Journal of Beijing University of Posts and Telecommunications 33(3), 1–9 (2010)
6. Commission of the European communities, COM (2009) 278 final. Internet of things an action plan for Europe, Brussels(EB/OL). (June 18, 2009),
   http://ec.europa.eu/information_society/
   policy/rfid/documents/commiot2009.pdf
7. South Korean Ministry of Information and Communication. South Korea plans to 2012 networking infrastructure building internet of things (December 4, 2009),
   http://www.c114.net/news/17/a450913.html
8. European Research Projects on the Internet of Things (CERP-IoT) Strategic Research Agenda(SRA).Internet of things-strategic research roadmap (September 15, 2009),
   http://ec.europa.eu/information_society/policy/
   rfid/documents/in_cerp.pdf
9. Zhu, W., Qi, W., Xiaoqiang, H.: The Design of the Remote Water Quality Monitoring System based on WSN. In: Proceedings of 5th International Conference on Wireless Communications, Networking and Mobile Computing, WiCOM, pp. 3639–3644 (2009)
10. Cao, Y., Wang, X.: Design of Farmland Weather Monitoring System Based on WSN. Research of Agricultural Modernization (12), 163–165 (2008)

11. Liu, Q., Cui, L.: Key Technologies and Applications of Internet of Things. Computer Science 37(60), 1–5 (2010)
12. Li, L., Zhu, Q.-X.: Research on middleware of EPC system. Computer Engineering and Design 27(18), 3360–3363 (2006)
13. He, K.: The Key Technologies of IOT with Development & Applications. The Key Technologies of IOT with Development & Applications (3), 32–35 (2010)
14. Tim, W., Peter, C., Pavan, S., et al.: Transforming agriculture through pervasive wireless sensor networks. IEEE Pervasive Computing 6(2), 50–57 (2007)

# Design and Implementation of Farmland Prescription Fertilization System Based on WEBGIS and Target Yield Model

Qingfeng Wei, Changshou Luo[*], and Junfeng Zhang

Institute of Information on Science and Technology of Agriculture, Beijing Academy of
Agriculture and Forestry Sciences, Beijing, 10009, China
luochangshou@163.com, {weiqf,zhangjf}@agri.ac.cn

**Abstract.** To meet the need that real-time access to scientific fertilizer suggestions, and make full use of existing digital resources of cultivated land, a solution is proposed based on WebGIS and fertilization model. With Jinshan county of Hubei province as a case, under the support of spatial database of cultivated land resource, the prescription fertilization system is developed based on MapXtreme and target yield model. It provides intuitive and convenient services on scientific fertilization. It is also good to improve the utilization rate of fertilizer and reduce investment to achieve greater economic benefits.

**Keywords:** Prescription fertilization, WebGIS, Target yield model.

## 1 Introduction

Fertilization is an important measure which is closely related to crop yield, product quality soil fertility and non-point pollution. According to the survey of China Agricultural University, fertilizer used in China is 341 kg per hectare. It is much higher than the EU standard of 170 kg per hectare. The heavy use of fertilizers will lead to nitrate content increase, soil sealing and acidification, microbial activity decreased, ultimately, make the lower fertility, fertilizer input-output ratio decline, and water contamination[1]. According to the nutritional status of soil, scientific and rational prescription fertilization is the key to solving the problem. In recent years, the Ministry of Agriculture carries out the soil fertility survey and quality assessment throughout the country. After extensive data collection, processing, analysis of the cultivated land during the work, it has accumulated a wealth of basic data resource for the purpose of prescription fertilization. However, farmers who want to obtain fertilizer suggestion, should go to ask the relevant departments. it not only feedback delay, but also miss the farming season.

With the rapid development of WebGIS, it provides strong support for visual fertilization guidance services in the network with the advantages of easy and efficient development, seamless combination with professional application model[2]. In this study, taking MapInfo's MapXtreme as the core components of GIS, based on the target yield model which is mainly used in scientific fertilization, in support of Ajax, taking Jingshan County in Hubei province for example, a farmland prescription

D. Li and Y. Chen (Eds.): CCTA 2011, Part I, IFIP AICT 368, pp. 491–497, 2012.

fertilization system is developed to provide farmers with more convenient and effective fertilizer consulting services.

# 2     Materials and Methods

## 2.1     Materials

**Study area:** Choose the hinterland of Jingshan County in Hubei province for the study. Jingshan County is located in the east longitude 112 ° 43'-113 ° 29 ',   latitude 30 ° 42'-31 ° 27'. The total area is 3520 square kilometers. The climate is conducive to the growth of various crops. It is also an major rice areas and high-quality cotton production base of the province.

**Soil Nutrient Data:** Sampling the study area, through the laboratory tests, these data were obtained include of the content of organic matter, total nitrogen, available nitrogen, total phosphorus, available phosphorus and potassium were gain, to provide an analytical basis for the amount of fertilizer calculation.

**GIS Maps:** Digitize 1:50,000-scale topographic maps, contour maps, administrative map, present land use maps and soil maps,  to provide the necessary maps for the visual fertilization.

## 2.2     Methods

**Target yield model:** It determines the amount of fertilizer based on a pre-set target yield. The principle is: Crop nutrient is supplied from the soil and fertilizer. The difference between the nutrient requirement to achieve the target yield and the amount of soil fertilizer supply is the amount of fertilizer required for the production. It fully takes into account of crop demand and soil supply, so widely used in scientific fertilization. The calculation formula, as it is in the literature 3.

**MapXtreme:** It is one of the most important ways to realize WebGIS. It can fully integrate with the Visual Studio which is a mainstream development platform. With the advantages of cross-linguistic, creating web services, deployment of distributed applications, it can develop the powerful internet geographic information systems quickly and efficiently. It works in thin-client. Client map images are dynamically generated based on user requests. Specific process are : The client submits HTTP requests to the Web server. Web server receives the request, and then, submits map operation requests to map server. The MapX server was called by map server to response to user operation requests. After spatial analysis and processing, a new map image was generated to return to the web server and was embedded in a HTML page to return to the client's browser. With its support,  the developer can create flexible GIS applications.

**Ajax:** Ajax is composed of multiple technologies including XHTML, CSS, DOM, XSTL and JavaScript etc. It is a development patter which used to create interactive web application [4]. In the WebGIS application system, for the map data is larger than text, longer time required to read and display. Users always need to wait for several seconds to gain the result information after refresh. Ajax can solve the problem. The main feature of it is that the operations on the web don't need to refresh the page. It can significantly shorten the waiting time.

# 3    System Design

## 3.1    System Architecture

It is a three-tier architecture which contains presentation layer, business logic layer and the data layer. The user requests to business logic layer through the MapXtreme control. The request is sent to the ASP.NET engine and MapXtreme components for processing by IIS (Internet Information Server). According to the application model, the data is called from the spatial database by the MapInfo ADO.NET. And eventually, send the result back to the client in a way of Html [5].

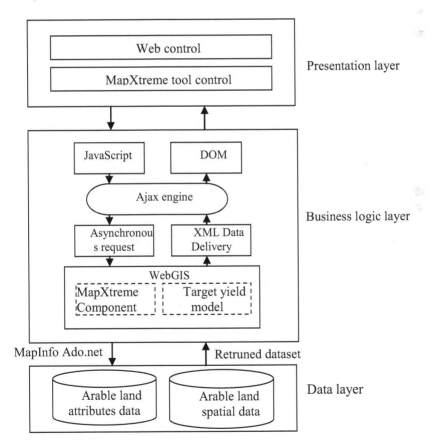

**Fig. 1.** The three-tier architecture of the system

## 3.2     System Function

The system functions are mainly divided into three parts:1）Farmland information query and operation module, to provide land search, and map operations. 2）prescription generation module, it provides fertilizer calculation, and fertilization prescription printing.3) Spatial database management, including the map data and attribute data management.

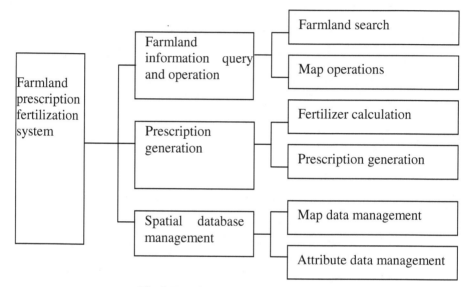

**Fig. 2.** Functional modules of the system

## 3.3     Spatial Database Construction

This study mainly has the following characteristics: Spatial database is composed of spatial data and attribute data. Spatial data is managed by .tab file of MapInfo, it is the data source of visual map in browser. Fertility evaluation unit map was associated with soil nutrient information by ID, so that spatial data and attribute data are connected. The attribute data of soil nutrient, crops type, fertilizer type, fertilizer parameters are managed by the ACCESS.

The system collected the nutrients required per 100kg production of 30 kinds of crops, and nutrient content data of 40 kinds of fertilizer which is commonly used. The nutrient test correction coefficient and utilization rate of fertilizer were calculated by statistical data which is provided by the district.

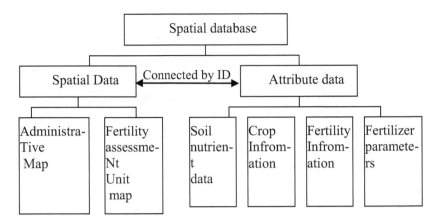

**Fig. 3.** The structure of spatial Database

### 3.4    Prescription Fertilization Process

The prescription generation process is designed as follows:

Step 1: Prescription fertilization block selection. Based on user selection, corresponding nutrient information of the block is recorded by the system.

Step 2: Crops selection. Based on user selection, fertilizer requirement data of the crop is recorded by the system.

Step 3: Input target yield. The value of target yield is entered by the user or provided by system. The system default value is calculated according to the rule that grain crop increases 13%,vegetable increases 25%,fruit increases 18% base on the last three-year average yield.

Step 4: Fertilizer selection. Based on user selection, corresponding nutrient content in the   fertilizer is recorded by the system.

Step 5: Call the target yield model and calculate the amount of fertilizer. Due to legume crops have the capacity of nitrogen fixation, nitrogen absorption from the soil only about one-third, therefore, its nitrogen requirement need multiply the result which the model was calculated by one-third [6].

### 3.5    Function Realization

In the map operation page, select or enter the town and village names where the block is located, then, use the information tool select the target location. The selection result will be marked by the Find Object of MapXtreme. And the block attribute information will be show in the textbox in the bottom of the page, Including fertility level, paddy field or dry land, nutrient status, physical and chemical properties, section properties, site conditions, etc. Click the button of "处方施肥"（Fig 4）， the attribute information of the block is  passed to the prescription page. According to the tip of the page, select the crop, fertilizer, click the "生成施肥处方"（Fig 5）， fertilizer prescription will be generated.

**Fig. 4.** The block information interface

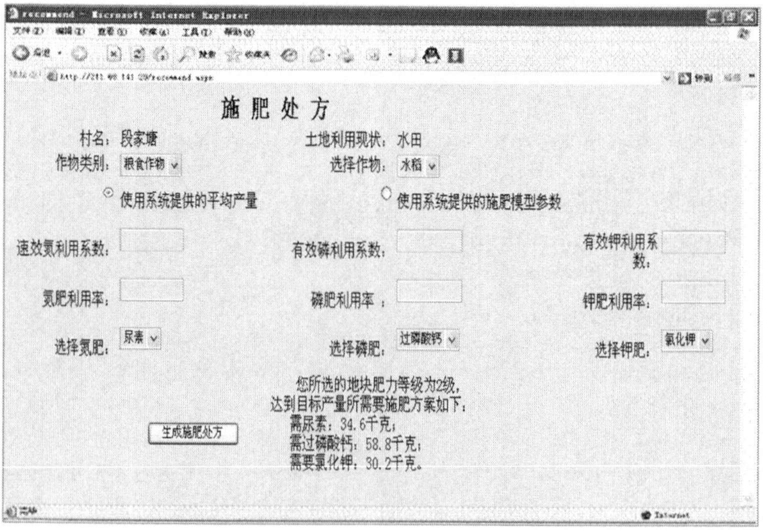

**Fig. 5.** The prescription generation interface

# 4    Discussion and Conclusion

In this study, a farmland fertilization prescription system based on WebGIS and target yield model was applied to provide fertilizer guidance. In the support of Ajax, it has the advantages of real time response to the fertilization consulting. It is intuitive and easy to use, and will provide agricultural related user with a new tool to solve the fertilization problems. It is good to less investment to achieve greater economic benefits.

This study conducts a preliminary exploration of farmland prescription fertilization using WebGIS and target yield model. As the system application, the functions are needed to be improved. In research, •with the increasingly demand of precision fertilization service, model improvements are needed to further explore.

# References

1. Chen, Y.P., Zhao, C.J., Wang, X., Ma, J.F., Tian, Z.K.: Prescription Map Generation Intelligent System of Precision Agriculture Based On Knowledge Model and WebGIS. Scientia Agricultura Sinica 6, 1190–1197 (2007)
2. Li, G.M., Chen, L.S.: Farmland Grade Information Publication System Based on WebGIS. Computer Engineering, 261–262 (2008)
3. Wei, J.Y., Gao, B.D., Suo, Q.Y., Wang, C.Z.: Study on fertilization of flax by using target yield model. Inner Mongolia Agricultural Science and Technology, 4–6 (1998)
4. Wen, H.B., Liu, F.: Design and Implementation of Ajax Based Web Vehicle Monitoring and Control Systems. J. Huazhong Univ. of Sci. & Tech (Nature Science Edition), 77–79 (2007)
5. Lv, Y.H., Qing, S.Y.: Soil testing and fertilizer, pp. 165–233. China Agriculture Press, Beijing (2002)
6. E, Z.G., Zhuang, J.Y., Qian, Q.: Management system for rice molecular breeding information platform based on ASP. NET. Computer Engineering and Design 5, 1299–1300 (2009)

# Design of Distributed Traceability System for Wheat Products Quality

Xingye Zhang[1], Jianqin Wang[1,2,*], Jianye Cui[1], Jie Zheng[2],
Jing Pan[2], and Manlin Chen[2]

[1] College of Information and Electrical Engineering, China Agricultural University,
Beijing, 100083, P.R. China
[2] Great Wall Computer Software & System Inc.
wjqcau@126.com

**Abstract.** The circulation of wheat products involves a number of different types of food-related enterprises, including planting bases, grain trading companies, warehousing enterprises, food processing plants, sales companies and so on. The centralized traceability architecture cannot meet the requirements such as transaction data security. While, the distributed traceability architecture faces the difficulty and complexity of information processing for the traceability data stored and managed by different enterprises. In order to meet the requirements imposed on distributed data management and diversity of deployment requirements, an EPC (Electronic Product Code) coding scheme is proposed, in addition, based on which we design and implement a distributed wheat products quality traceability system in this paper. The test indicates that the distributed quality traceability system can track the wheat products quality information in the whole supply chain of wheat products effectively.

**Keywords:** wheat products traceability system, EPC coding scheme, ONS.

## 1  Introduction

China's wheat production and consumption is huge. Wheat products safety is a serious matter for consumers as well as for companies involved in the food chain. Because of the complexity and diversity of the wheat products circulation chain, it is extremely difficult to track the details of the wheat products information in each circulating step. Hence, it is urgent for business to build a traceability system for wheat products supply chain which is suitable to China's situation.

EPC (Electronic Product Code) is designed to give each product a unique identification number in order to effectively improve supply chain management. It can be used to track the movement of physical products throughout an entire supply network based on RFID (Radio-Frequency Identification) technology and the associated computer networks[1]. RFID is a non-contact and multi-objective automatic identification technology, widely used in traceability from farm to consumer[2]. The EPCIS (EPC Information Service) provides storage and query

---

* Corresponding author.

D. Li and Y. Chen (Eds.): CCTA 2011, Part I, IFIP AICT 368, pp. 498–507, 2012.

services for the EPC-related data of physical products, using EPC as index key[3]. ONS (Object Name Service) is a global query service, using the existing DNS (Domain Name System), used to help to locate the EPCIS when retrieving the EPC-related information from EPCIS which are hosted at each supply chain participant through the traceability system, by converting the EPC to a URL (Universal Resource Locater)[4].

Up to now, many traceability systems have been proposed based on EPC and RFID, such as aquatic product traceability system[5], meat product traceability system[6], agricultural products traceability system[7], cattle breeding traceability system[8]. Bello proposed a general model of traceability system in the field of food manufacturing chain[9]. However, most of the existing traceability systems are owned by one or several enterprises and require a central server to store the trace information in the whole supply chain.

Considering the diversity and complexity of the wheat products supply chain and the granular or powdered property of the wheat products itself, we develop a distributed traceability system for wheat products to meet the requirements imposed on distributed EPC-related data management and diversity of deployment requirements. With the help of ONS, each EPCIS server can exchange data of the products details, so as to track the wheat products quality information in the whole supply chain of wheat products effectively.

## 2    Wheat Products Supply Chain Model

Taking into account the reality in China, the wheat products supply chain is illustrated by Figure 1. The circulation includes wheat production, wheat trade and processing and wheat products sales. The wheat may come from an individual farmer or a planting base. Before sales company, the wheat or wheat products may go pass several grain trading companies, warehousing enterprises and food processing plants. Similarly, the wheat products may go pass several sales companies before a certain consumer. In each transaction, an EPC is generated for a batch of wheat products and the detail information of the products is stored and associated with it as well as in every process inside these enterprises.

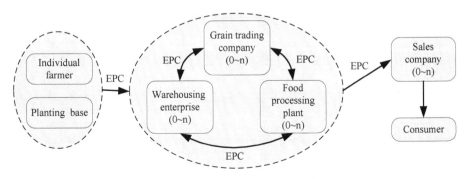

**Fig. 1.** Wheat products supply chain

For a certain batch of wheat products, its raw materials may come from several enterprises. We show a batch of flour chain as an example represented in Figure 2. In this case, food processing plant F which produces the batch of flour, buys the raw materials (wheat) from warehousing enterprise D and warehousing enterprise E. The batch of raw materials from warehousing enterprise D comes from farmer G and planting base B. Besides, the batch of raw materials from warehousing enterprise E comes from grain trading company C and grain trading company C buy it from planting base A. And, the batch of flour is sold to food processing plant H.

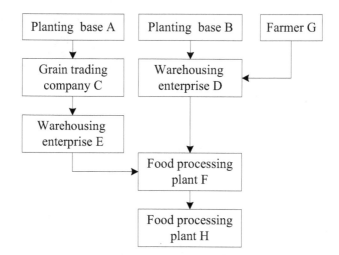

**Fig. 2.** A batch of  flour chain

In order to trace out all the supply chain nodes and the detail information of the wheat products, each business entity in the wheat products supply chain should record the necessary information related to quality and security and so on, which provides the basis for the traceability system.

(1) Each business entity should record the production data for each batch of wheat products. For example, planting base and farmer should record the seed information and the details of the use of chemical fertilizers and pesticides, warehousing enterprise should record the rate of mildew, food processing plant should record the rate of water and so on.

(2) Each business entity should record the information of the flow of products. For a certain batch of wheat products, the information of the correspondence between container or vehicle and itself, the details about where it comes from and where it goes to, the details of the raw materials and so on should be recorded.

(3) Each business entity should generate a unique serial number for each batch of wheat products within it. All the information related to the batch of wheat products should be established links with the unique number. The unique serial number can be an EPC. When a transaction occurs, an EPC should be generated and the EPC is associated with all the related information of the certain batch of wheat products. The EPC will be used to trace the records of all the movements within the supply chain.

# 3    Wheat Products Distributed Traceability System Architecture

The wheat products supply chain in China is complicated and diverse. Not every business entity has ability to maintain a traceability system service. However, in order to trace the whole information of the supply chain, all the business entities in the supply chain should have the ability to use the traceability system.

Taking into consideration the factors such as the diversity and complexity of the wheat products supply chain and the granular or powdered property of the wheat products, we design a distributed traceability system for wheat products to meet the requirements imposed on distributed EPC-related data management and diversity of deployment requirements. The architecture of the distributed traceability system is represented in Figure 3.

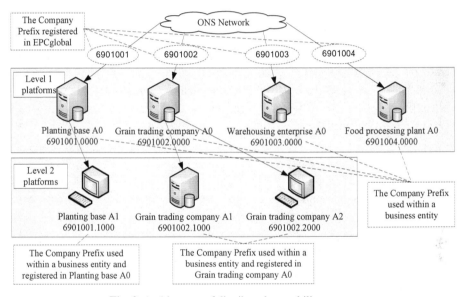

**Fig. 3.** Architecture of distributed traceability system

As is shown in Figure 3, this distributed traceability system is divided into two levels. The platforms in level 1 form the backbone of the system, while the platforms in level 2 are essential parts of the whole system. In this distributed traceability system, each business entity in the wheat products supply chain has its own company prefix in EPC, while not every business entity has its own EPCIS servers. The business entity in level 1 must has an EPCIS server and has got its own company prefix from the registration center. In other words, if a business entity owns an EPCIS server and has got its own company prefix from the registration center, its EPCIS server is a member of platforms in level 1. The business entity in level 2 has to register its own company prefix in the entity which is in level 1 and it can store its EPC-related data in its own EPCIS server as well as in the EPCIS server in level 1 which is owned by the business entity who gives the company prefix to it. On the condition that the EPC-related data is stored in the servers in level 2, the parent server in level 1 serves as a proxy when data query occurs which will transmit the requests from the servers in level 2 to other servers and send back the responses as well.

The EPCIS servers in this system are independent, equal in status with each other and connect with each other through the ONS. Each EPCIS server has complete software system to support the storage and query service, including middleware software, business support system, web services system, the local ONS service system and so on. Each local client needs to equip RFID Reader & Writer, middleware system in order to read data from and write data to RFID tags.

## 4    EPC Coding Scheme for Distributed Traceability System

EPC coding is a coding standard which is compatible with EAN/UCC coding system. EPC is a unique number used to identify a specific item in the supply chain. The general structure of EPC consisting of a fixed length (8-bits) header followed by a series of numeric fields whose overall length, structure, and function are completely determined by the header value[10]. EPC can indicate different type of encoding, such as SGTIN, SSCC, SGLN, GRAI, GIAI, and so on.

Considering the various coding schemes, we choose SGTIN-96 to identify a batch of wheat products. SGTIN (Serialized Global Trade Identification Number) is a kind of new coding schemes, based on GTIN (Global Trade Item Number) which from the general specification EAN/UCC. A single GTIN can only mark a particular object class, not to identify a specific physical object. In order to give a single object a unique symbol, a serial number is appended to GTIN. GTIN and the unique serial

**Table 1.** EPC coding scheme based on SGTIN-96

|  | Header | Filter Value | Partition | Company Prefix | Item Reference |  | Serial Number |
|---|---|---|---|---|---|---|---|
| Coding Segment Bit Count | 8 | 3 | 3 | 24 | 14 | 4 | 38 |
| planting base A0 | 00110000 | 3 | 5 | 6901001 | 0000 | -- | -- |
| planting base A1 | 00110000 | 3 | 5 | 6901001 | 1000 | -- | -- |
| grain trading company A0 | 00110000 | 3 | 5 | 6901002 | 0000 | -- | -- |
| grain trading company A1 | 00110000 | 3 | 5 | 6901002 | 1000 | -- | -- |
| grain trading company A2 | 00110000 | 3 | 5 | 6901002 | 2000 | -- | -- |
| warehousing enterprise A0 | 00110000 | 3 | 5 | 6901003 | 0000 | -- | -- |
| food processing plant A0 | 00110000 | 1 | 5 | 6901004 | 0000 | -- | -- |

number are called serial GTIN (SGTIN)[11]. SGTIN-96 has ninety six bits, and consists of six fields: header, filter value, partition, company prefix, item reference and serial number. Each SGTIN shares the same Header 00110000[12]. The filter value is used to distinguish the business type of the enterprise and the partition number is used to define the count of bits that the item reference and the company prefix can take up. The company prefix is used to distinguish business entities. Each business entity must register its own company prefix in the registration center and it can assign the item reference and serial number by itself. For example, after a planting base gets its company prefix, it can assign four decimal digits (fourteen bits) in the item reference to their subsidiaries to identify them as is shown in Table 1.

According to the EPC coding scheme shown in Table 1, a business entity's company prefix takes up eleven decimal digits. For example, a sequence of 96-bit binary data - 00110000 011 101 110010001101100001110110110100101000 0000 01 00000000000000000000000000001111101001 can be converted to a standard URI: urn:epc:tag:sgtin-96:6901001.0000.1.1001, 6901001, in which, 6901001 is a company prefix got from the register center, 0 is a company prefix from a business entity in level 1, 1 is an item reference and 1001 is a batch number of wheat products.

# 5     Details of Distributed Traceability System Process

## 5.1     Data Flow within a Business Entity

When a bath of wheat products is passing through a RFID reader equipped on one place or a transaction occurs or some information which needs to be recorded of a batch of wheat products is generated, a series of automatic or manual operations will be done to handle and store the information. The general data flow within a business entity is represented in Figure 4.

As is shown in Figure 4, EPCIS is the core node for the data flow within a business entity. Several signals such as an EPC number from a RFID reader, a query message from the business system will trigger a data flow. For example, when a bath of wheat products is passing through a RFID reader equipped on a gateway of a warehouse, the RFID reader will read all the RFID tags adhere to containers and vehicles and all the data from the reader will be transferred to a savant, then a report about the data from the savant will be "pushed" to EPCIS. After that, EPCIS will store the data and invoke the business system to deal with the data, then a set of data from the business system will be returned to EPCIS and EPCIS will store the set of data. Besides, when the business system handles the data, it may call EPCIS to do other things.

## 5.2     Data Flow between EPCIS Servers

To track a supply chain, a series of data will be exchanged between EPCIS servers. The communication between any two EPCIS servers is private and they should agree on communication protocols and data formats before they exchange private data. In general, two EPCIS servers exchange data via the Internet and using HTTP or HTTPS provided by web services.

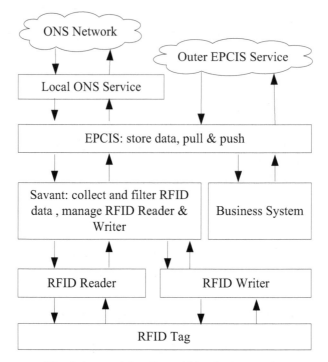

**Fig. 4.** A general data flow within a business entity

Each EPCIS server is listening for requests from other servers almost all the time. When an EPCIS server gets requests from other servers, it will handle these requests and return responses in turn. In order to trace out a supply chain, an EPCIS server needs to send several requests to other servers to query the traceability information. Before an EPCIS server sends a request to another EPCIS server, it needs to get the IP address of that server by ONS network using an EPC. The general ONS query process is represented in Figure 5.

Taking the EPC 00110000 011 101 110010001101100001110110110100101 0000 01 00000000000000000000000001111101001 as an example, first, the URI conversion converts it to a standard URI: urn:epc:tag:sgtin-96:6901001.0000.1.1001, then, the ONS resolver converts the URI form to a domain name: 011001.6901001.sgtin-96.tag.ons.com, finally, the ONS network return the record of the domain name: 202.205.80.215.

For each EPC query, an EPCIS server will answer a series of record related to the EPC, including rate of mildew, rate of water and so on. Sometimes the server also answers a list of EPCs and the EPCs include where it comes from or the source of raw materials or where it goes to. By querying all the EPCs which come from the answer of each query, the detailed information of a supply chain is tracked. Taking the chain shown in Figure 2 as an example, the data flow is represented in Figure 6.

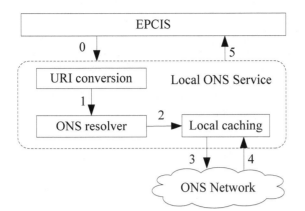

**Fig. 5.** The general ONS query process

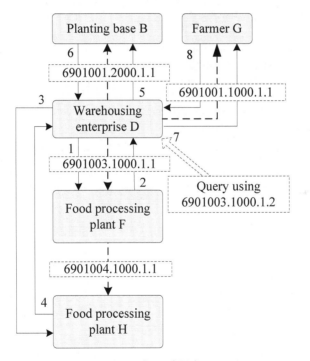

**Fig. 6.** A general data flow of EPC query process

As is shown in Figure 6, a track process of an EPC includes as many times of requests as the number of the nodes involved in the supply chain. In this case, a user queries the EPC 6901003.1000.1.2 from D to track the information of the circulation of the EPC. Firstly, D finds out three EPCs 6901003.1000.1.1, 6901001.2000.1.1 and 6901001.1000.1.1 which are associated with 6901003.1000.1.2 in itself. Then, D sends the first request 1 using EPC 6901003.1000.1.1 to F and gets the reply 2 with the information related to EPC stored in server F and one EPC 6901004.1000.1.1 which is from H. Then D sends one request 3 using EPC 6901004.1000.1.1 to H and gets the reply 4 with the information related to EPC stored in H from H. In this way, D sends one request using EPC 6901001.1000.1.1 to G and one request using EPC 6901001.2000.1.1 to B, and gets one reply with information related to the requested EPC from each server. Finally, the detailed information of the circulation related to EPC 6901001.1000.1.2 is tracked.

# 6     Conclusion

In this paper, we presented a distributed traceability system for wheat products based on EPC and ONS. The system allows a user to track the detailed information of the whole supply chain. The architecture of the system has been described from several points of view and it has shown to have the ability to meet the requirements imposed on distributed EPC-related data management and diversity of deployment requirements.

In the architecture described above, each node of the supply chain involved in retrieving traceability information can be queried for detailed information. Therefore, the system's availability depends on each node's response time and the reliability of each node.

For this reason, our future work will cover the study of dynamic storage query and RQC (Reliability and Quality Control).

**Acknowledgement.** This work is supported by Electronic Development Fund Project "Based On Service-Oriented Architecture (SOA) Traceability System for Food Quality", which is financed by Ministry of Industry and Information Technology of the People's Republic of China.

# References

1. Barchetti, U., Bucciero, A., De Blasi, M., Mainetti, L., Patrono, L.: RFID, EPC and B2B convergence towards an item-level traceability in the pharmaceutical supply chain. In: 2010 IEEE International Conference on RFID-Technology and Applications, RFID-TA (2010)
2. Zangroniz, R., Pastor, J.M., Dios, J.J.D., Garcia-Escribano, J., Morenas, J., Garcia, A.: RFID-based traceability system for architectural concrete. In: 2010 European Workshop on Smart Objects: Systems, Technologies and Applications (RFID Sys. Tech.), pp. 1–8 (2010)
3. Tribowski, C., Goebel, C., Gunther, O.: EPCIS-Based Supply Chain Event Management: A Quantitative Comparison of Candidate System Architectures. In: International Conference on Complex, Intelligent and Software Intensive Systems, CISIS 2009 (2009)
4. Object Naming Service (ONS) Version 1.0.1,
   http://www.gs1.org/sites/default/files/docs/ons/
   ons_1_0-standard-20051004.pdf

5. Zhiqiang, W., Xiaoping, Y., Dongning, J., Gang, W.: An aquatic product traceability system based on RFID technology. In: 2010 IEEE International Conference on Software Engineering and Service Sciences, ICSESS (2010)

6. Ren, S., Xu, H., Lian, Zhou, G.: Research on RFID-based meat product track and traceability system. In: 2010 International Conference on Computer Application and System Modeling, ICCASM (2010)

7. Li, Y., He, D.: Design and implementation of traceability information system for agriculture product quality. In: 2010 2nd International Conference on Advanced Computer Control, ICACC (2010)

8. Zaiqiong, W., Zetian, F., Wei, C., Jinyou, H.: A RFID-based traceability system for cattle breeding in China. In: 2010 International Conference on Computer Application and System Modeling, ICCASM (2010)

9. Bello, L.L., Mirabella, O., Torrisi, N.: A general approach to model traceability systems in food manufacturing chains. In: 10th IEEE Conference on Emerging Technologies and Factory Automation, ETFA 2005 (2005)

10. Chenghai Zhang, D.Z.: Automatic Identify Technology. Wuhan University Press (2010)

11. Study on Traceability Coding of Wheat Quality and Distributed Object Name Service, http://www.ingentaconnect.com/content/asp/senlet/2011/00000009/00000003/art00022

12. EPC Tag Data Standard Version 1.5, http://www.gs1.org/gsmp/kc/epcglobal/tds/tds_1_5-standard-20100818.pdf

# Least-Squares Approach for Harmonic and Interharmonic Analysis in Power System

Hong Luo and Hui Xue

China Agricultural University, Beijing, China, 100083
xue_huicn@yahoo.com.cn

**Abstract.** A new algorithm based on least-squares method for harmonic and interharmonic analysis is proposed. The approach employs least-squares method and is based on a linear prediction relation for multiple sinusoidal signals. It is shown that the method allows for accurate harmonic and interharmonic estimation with high frequency resolution. The approach is compared with that of DFT method and prony method.

**Keywords:** Least square, linear prediction, interharmonic, harmonic.

## 1    Introduction

Harmonic/interharmonic measurement is an important function of a power quality analyzer widely used in monitoring the quality of power. The use of power electronic devices which increases the harmonic pollution in power system on the one hand and the widespread use of sensitive loads such as computers and microprocessor-based industrial controllers on the other hand signify the ever-increasing need for harmonic/interharmonic measurement devices. To monitor and maintain the power quality, there has been an increasing interest in devising harmonic/interharmonic measurement methods and devices over the last decade[1]-[2].

Discrete Fourier transform(DFT) has been widely used for spectral analysis of harmonics, however, DFT suffers from leakage and picket fence effect and suffers from the major problem of resolution because of some invalid assumptions(zero data or repetitive data outside the duration of observations) make in this method[3]-[4]. It is very important to develop better tools of interharmonic and harmonic estimation to avoid possible damages due to its influence.

This paper proposed a least square approach for harmonic and interharmonic analysis in power system. Least square is time-domain approach which has to do with the criterion for selecting a solution to the overdefined equations produced when more measurements than states are represented in the estimation problems[5], and has been widely used in power quality analysis. Tests show that this proposed approach can give an accurate harmonic and interharmonic estimation with high frequency resolution, the test results are compared with DFT and Prony method.

D. Li and Y. Chen (Eds.): CCTA 2011, Part I, IFIP AICT 368, pp. 508–512, 2012.
© IFIP International Federation for Information Processing 2012

## 2     The Proposed Algorithm

Suppose the power signal is represented

$$x_k = \sum_{i=1}^{L} A_i \cos(\omega_i t_k + \phi_i) \tag{1}$$

In [6], It has been shown that $x_k$ can be uniquely expressed as a linear combination of its previous 2L samples as follow.

$$x_k = -\sum_{i=1}^{L} a_i x_{k-i} \tag{2}$$

Where $a_i = a_{2L-i}$ (i=1, 2..L);
   Then (2) can be expressed as follows

$$x_k = -\sum_{i=1}^{L} a_i [x_{k-i} + x_{k+i}] \tag{3}$$

Since

$$x_{k+1} + x_{k-1} = \sum_{i=1}^{L} 2\cos \omega_i \Delta t A_i \cos(\omega_i t_k + \phi_i)$$

$$\vdots \tag{4}$$

$$x_{k+L} + x_{k-L} = \sum_{i=1}^{L} 2\cos \omega_i L \Delta t A_i \cos(\omega_i t_k + \phi_i)$$

From (1), (3) and (4) we obtain

$$\sum_{i=1}^{L} a_i 2\cos i\omega_i \Delta t = -1 \tag{5}$$

Equation (5) can be expressed as follows

$$\sum_{i=1}^{L} a_i (e^{-j\omega_i i \Delta t} + e^{j\omega_i i \Delta t}) = -1 \tag{6}$$

Equation (6) can be expressed as follows

$$\sum_{i=0}^{2L} b_i e^{i\omega \Delta t} = 0 \tag{7}$$

Where $b_i = b_{2L-i} = a_{L-i}$, (i=0,1,..L-1) and $b_L = 1$. Then the positive phase angles of the roots of (7) are the frequencies of the sinusoidal. The parameter of $a_i$ can be obtained as follows. Since (3) can be expressed as following

$$X_{k0} = X_{k1} S \tag{8}$$

Where $X_{k0} = \begin{bmatrix} x_k \\ \vdots \\ x_{k+M} \end{bmatrix}$, $S = [a_1, \ldots a_L]^T$ and

$$X_{k1} = \begin{bmatrix} x_{k-1} + x_{k+L} & x_{k-L} + x_{k+L} \\ & \vdots \\ x_{k+M-1} + x_{k+M+1} & x_{k+M-L} + x_{k+M+L} \end{bmatrix},$$

where the value of M is bigger than L, Then S can be solved using the least mean square method, that is

$$S = \bar{X}_{k1} X_{k0}, \tag{9}$$

where $\bar{X}_{k1} = (X_{k1}^T X_{k1})^{-1} X_{k1}^T$

After the parameter $a_i$ obtained, the frequencies can be obtained using (7), and we can construct a matrix, denoted as E.

$$E = \begin{bmatrix} e^{j\omega_1} & e^{j\omega_2} & \cdots & e^{j\omega_L} \\ e^{j2\omega_1} & e^{j2\omega_2} & \cdots & e^{j2\omega_L} \\ \vdots & & & \\ e^{jN\omega_1} & e^{jN\omega_2} & \cdots & e^{jN\omega_L} \end{bmatrix} \tag{10}$$

Notice

$$EA = Y \tag{11}$$

Where $A = [A_1 e^{j\phi_1} \quad A_2 e^{j\phi_2} \quad \cdots \quad A_L e^{j\phi_L}]^T$, $Y = [x_1 \quad x_2 \quad \cdots \quad x_N]^T$.

Then the amplitude and phase angle can be calculated again using the least mean square method again as

$$A = (E'E)^{-1} E'Y \tag{12}$$

## 3    Simulation Resuls

We investigate the performance of the proposed approach. Matlab is used to perform the simulations. The sample frequency is 3840Hz. And the data window length is 64 points, which is (1/60) second. The DFT, Prony and proposed method are compared for two cases.

Case 1:   Suppose the test signal is as : \

$$x(t) = \cos(2\pi f_1 t) + 0.2\cos(2\pi f_2 t) + 0.2\cos(2\pi f_3 t)$$

Where $f_1 = 60.2\,\text{Hz}$, $f_2 = 90.3\,\text{Hz}$, $f_3 = 180.6\,\text{Hz}$.

There is a 0.2Hz frequency deviation of fundamental components, and the signal contains an 20% interharmonic with a frequency of 72Hz and a 20% 3rd harmonic component with a frequency of 180.6Hz. The measurement results using DFT, Prony and LMS are given in Fig.1. Fig.1 shows that DFT cannot separate the three components, Prony can separate the different frequency components but the amplitude estimation is mistaken, LMS can not only separate the different components, but also can give an accurate estimation of the amplitude as shown in Fig.1. In fact the frequency resolution of LMS can be very high, another experiment is given as follows.

Case 2: The test signal is $x(t) = \cos(2\pi f_1 t) + 0.5\cos(2\pi f_2 t)$

Where $f_1 = 60.2 \, \text{Hz}$, $f_2 = 64 \, \text{Hz}$ .

There is a 0.2Hz frequency deviation in the fundamental frequency, and a 50% 64Hz interharmonic exists in the signal. The frequencies of the fundamental component and interharmonic frequency are near to each other which make it hard to separate them. The measurement results are given in Fig.2. Fig.2 shows that DFT and Prony cannot separate the two components because their frequencies are so near to each other, while the proposed LMS method can give an accurate estimation of these two components.

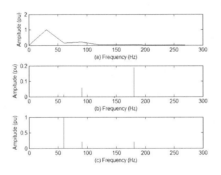

**Fig. 1.** Spectra obtained. (a) DFT (b) Prony (c) LMS

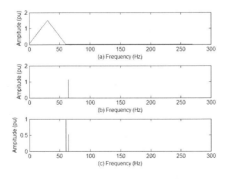

**Fig. 2.** Spectra obtained. (a) DFT (b) Prony (c) LMS

# 4   Conclusion

A new algorithm based on Least-squares method for harmonic and interharmonic analysis in power system was proposed in this paper. The algorithm uses the linear prediction model of the sinusoidal. Theoretical analysis and simulation experiments validate the proposed algorithm have high frequency resolution in harmonic and interharmonic analysis.

# References

1. Joorabian, M., Mortazavi, S.S., Khayyami, A.A.: Harmonic estimation in a power system using a novel hybrid least squares-adaline method. Electric Power Systems Research 79(1), 107–116 (2009)
2. Lu, Z., Ji, T.Y., Tang, W.H., Wu, H.: Optimal harmonic estimation using a particle swarm optimizer. IEEE Transactions on Power Delivery 23(2), 1166–1174 (2008)
3. Girgis, A.A., Ham, F.M.: A Quantitative Study of Pitfalls in the FFT. IEEE Transactions on Aerospace and Electronic Systems AES-16(4), 434–439 (1980)
4. Kay, S.M.: Modern Spectral Estimation: Theory and Application, pp. 224–225. Prentice-Hall, Englewood Cliffs (1988)
5. Phadke, A.G., Thorp, J.S.: Synchronized phasor measurements and their applications. Springer, New York (2008)
6. Chan, Y.T., Lavoie, J.M.M., Plant, J.B.: Aparameter estimation approach to estimation of frequencies of sinusoidals. IEEE Trans. Acoust. Speech, Signal Process. ASSP 29(2), 214–219 (1981)

# A Research of Agricultural Informationalization Evaluation and Decision Support System

Lifeng Shen, Xiaoqing Yuan, and Daoliang Li

College of Information and Electrical Engineering, China Agricultural University,
P.O. Box 121, 17 Tsinghua East Road, Beijing, 100083, P.R. China

**Abstract.** This research aims to develop a comprehensive evaluation method to help the establishment of agricultural informationalization evaluation and decision support system. The research has made considerable progress in the realization of the evaluation index systematic establishment, the index data acquisition, statistic analysis, the presentation of the evaluation result, etc. It provides a tool with great effectiveness and practical values. With these findings, both horizontal and vertical comparison of the agricultural informationalization evaluation work by different provinces can be made easily.

**Keywords:** Agricultural Informationalization, Evaluation, Decision Support System.

## 1 Introduction

14 indexes. Liu Shihong(2007) argued that there need to be 6 factors and a total of 25 indexes included in the rural i In recent years, both the Party Central Committee and the State Council have paid considerable attention to agricultural informationalization of China, developed a series of documents and policies, and implemented a number of informationalization projects. As a result, the construction of basic facilities in China's agricultural informationalization, the ability to develop and use information resources, and the system of information services are continuously improved, so that the information technology has been better adopted during agricultural affairs. The environment for informationalization development has been gradually enhanced, and the agricultural informationalization progress of China has been obviously accelerated.

Despite those achievements that China has made, some problems have been emerged during the agricultural informationalization development. For example, from the country level to the local level, the agricultural informationalization development lacks of a scientific and appropriate agricultural informationalization evaluation index system. Under this circumstance, a practical agricultural informationalization evaluation index system has been established for the urgent need of guiding the development of agricultural informationalization in various regions. This should be the guidelines of the agricultural informationalization in different regions, and the basis for the examination of the agricultural informationalization progress. Therefore, the establishment of a

D. Li and Y. Chen (Eds.): CCTA 2011, Part I, IFIP AICT 368, pp. 513–523, 2012.

scientific agricultural informationalization evaluation index system means the motivation for guiding the agricultural informationalization work nationwide.

Taking the above analysis into consideration, the establishment of a scientific agricultural informationalization evaluation index system for the promotion of agricultural informationalization evaluation work is of particular necessary. Using a survey, Bai Wanping(2008)has succeeded in the establishment of a rural informationalization construction effect evaluation index system in western regions. Huang Zhiwen(2009), for the evaluation of rural informationalization level in various regions throughout China, has designed 5 index numbers and nformationalization evaluation index system. Zhang Xicai, Qin Xiangyang, Zhang Xingxiao (2008)applied the industry chain theory of agricultural informationalization, and developed a series of Beijing rural informationalization evaluation index system including 6 first-class indexes and a total of 23 second-class indexes. Gao Ya and Gan Guohui(2009) have selected 24 indexes from 6 perspectives for the establishment of agricultural informationalization evaluation index system.

There seems no attempt to develop the agricultural informationalization evaluation and decision support system so far. Based on the technology of Geographical Information System, an evaluation and decision support system developed by Zhao Yongpeng(2007), combining data storage, managing, analysis, and decision support, used to evaluate the effect of the vegetation recovery on dumps, has been a decision support system related to evaluation. Xia Yuanyong, Yan Dongmei, Shen Hong and Zhou Qiangxin (2006)contributed a evaluation and decision support system based on Web to the stability of side slopes around the Three Gorges reservoir areas, and took the actual situation of side slopes around the Three Gorges reservoir areas into consideration during the analysis of the demand, function, and operation process of the system, so that the operation modules are divided, and the frame graph of the entire system is finally figured out. Based on the characteristics of systematicness, diversity, spatiality, dynamicness during the urban sustainable development, Wang Guixin and Chen Ping(2006) have established a evaluation and decision support system for the future sustainability of urban development from the perspectives including architecture, functional module, integration methods, etc. In order to solve the problem of the fuzzy comprehensive evaluation of the eco-cities, Hu Jianyuan and Huang Kun(2006) set up an evaluation and decision support system for eco-cities, and presented the eco-city multilevel fuzzy comprehensive evaluation model and an evaluation support system.

Based on the need of the establishment of agricultural informationalization evaluation index system, this paper presents a study on the design of a an agricultural informationalization evaluation and decision support system. The system incorporates the analytic hierarchy process and aggregative index number in supporting the evaluation processes.

## 2    System Analysis

### 2.1    Analysis of System Users

There are mainly three groups of users of this system, including system administrators, provincial administrators, and experts. System administrators use the system, mainly for the purpose of division and management of system users and their limits of authority, and for the maintenance of the stable operation of the evaluation and decision support system, who, at the same time, have to be equipped with considerable system maintaining knowledge to re-adjust relative parameters of the evaluation index system in accordance with the evaluation requirements in necessity. What provincial administrators mainly do is to collect and update the data of local agricultural informationalization; therefore, a certain amount of system maintaining knowledge is needed. As for experts, some web application skills are required to be grasped, so that they are able to grade on the website and submit the grading result.

## 2.2   Analysis of Functional Requirements

According to surveys, it is concluded that there are mainly five perspectives of functional requirements of the system as follows:

(1) User information management. This system, with three groups of users involved, is in a prerequisite need of settings of the user management function.
(2) Setting of the index system. The evaluation index put forward in this article is in need of the criterion of practices, and it has to be modified appropriately according to the actual situation during the application period. Accordingly, the setting function of the index system has to be reserved.
(3) Setting of index weights. Experts have to grade via the analytic hierarchy process, and the system will process the grading result and finally figure out the weight values of all indexes.
(4) The collection and process of index data. The stability of this system and the regularity of the efficient functioning have to depend on the reliability of the data, which is the basis of the entire evaluation process. Due to the fact that most of the index data collected in the research are quantified, the collection of data is one of the major function of the system.
(5) The calculation of agricultural informationalization indexes and the display of the evaluation result. The core of the system is the scientific and reasonable evaluation for agricultural informationalization levels in various provinces. Therefore, on the basis of the confirmation of index weights and index database, the code design is wanted for the realization of the calculation of agricultural informationalization indexes, whose result has to be displayed in tables or histograms via an efficient MSMMI.

## 3   System Design

### 3.1   System Structural Design

The agricultural informationalization evaluation and decision support system adopts layered structure, involving data layer, application layer, and presentation layer, shown in Figure 1.

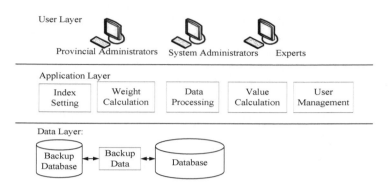

**Fig. 1.** System Structure

## (1) Data layer

The database of this system has to save the data information as follows: 1) user information; 2) information of index system setting; 3) index weight information; 4) index normalized value; 5) the data input by provincial administrators and the database after data integration. For the reliability of the system, the backup database was kept on this layer, and all data will be saved as backups all the time.

## (2) Application layer

The application layer, which has been regarded as the core of the system, calls relative data in the database for the realization of agricultural informationalization evaluation and analysis, and adopts the needs during the evaluation to achieve further system management, including the setting of indexes and the modification of index weights.

## (3) User layer

The client for human machine interface is various commonly used internet explorers, where users are allowed to enter the interface of the agricultural informationalization evaluation and decision support system, e.g. experts are able to grade, system administrators are capable of system maintenance, and the provincial administrators can have a visualized understanding of the evaluation results.

## 3.2    Design of System Function

According to the demand analysis of system function, the function of agricultural informationalization evaluation and decision support system can be figured out as what Figure 2 demonstrates, including following functional module:

## (1) Index setting module

According to the agricultural informationalization evaluation system established in this article, three first-class indexes including agricultural informationalization fundamental facilities, agricultural production and management informationalization, agricultural management and service informationalization, involving a total of 12 second-class indexes. At the same time, the system has been successful in reserving flexible customization, which provides the system with more applicability and expansibility with the ability to add and delete indexes.

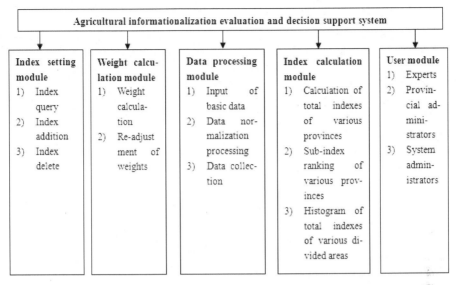

**Fig. 2.** The figure of system function

### (2) Weight calculation module
With this module, experts are able to grade via the analytic hierarchy process based on the index weights, during when judgment matrix establishment, single-level sort with its consistency check, and multilevel sort with its consistency check are needed to figure out the index weight. At the same time, system administrators are able to have the system weight further adjusted.

### (3) Data processing module
Provincial administrators are able to input original data of indexes through this module, which leads to the realization of storage management of collected data. At the same time, this module is used to normalize all data, when system administrators can get all input data automatically for further calculation of agricultural informationalization indexes.

### (4) Index calculation module
This module can be applied for the calculation of the total indexes of agricultural informationalization of various provinces, and the calculation of the sub-indexes of different indexes of agricultural informationalization of various provinces, which can be displayed in tabular forms. When the agricultural informationalization levels of various provinces are evaluated, the evaluation results of various provinces can be ranked and displayed intuitively in histograms.

### (5) User module
The module contributes to the appropriate distribution and management of the authority limits of three groups of users including system administrators, provincial administrators, and experts.

### 3.3    Design of System Workflow

The agricultural informationalization evaluation and decision support system has integrated functions including index setting, information collection, analysis display, etc. After the indexes are set, index information will be collected. Then, the system, based on the setting of indexes and the collected data, will select an applicable evaluation method for the realization of evaluation, whose results will later be displayed on the stage page for reading and reference. The workflow of the system is shown in Figure 3.

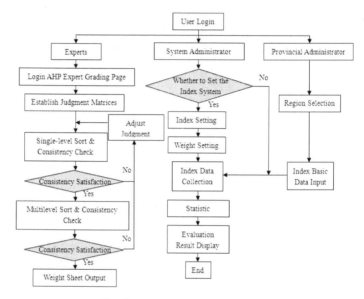

**Fig. 3.** The workflow of the system

### 3.4    Database Design

The database of the agricultural informationalization evaluation and decision support system embodies a considerable number of data sheet, including the data sheet of administration regions, a relative sheet of index system structural information, relative sheet of index data collection information, and a relative sheet of index data summarization. On account of the limited length of the article, merely some representative sheets will be listed as examples.

**Sheet 1.** Administration Regions Information

| Field Name | Name | Data Type | Size | Non-null | Explanation |
|---|---|---|---|---|---|
| regID | region ID | varchar | 11 | Yes | Six-figure administrative codes united by the country are used |
| regName | region name | varchar | 30 | Yes | Names of provincial administrative units |
| regNameforshort | region name for short | varchar | 30 | Yes | Names of provincial administrative units for short |

**Sheet 2.** Index System

| Field Name | Name | Data Type | Size | Non-null | Explanation |
|---|---|---|---|---|---|
| IndextID | Index number | int | 8 | Yes | |
| IndexName | Index name in Chinese | varchar | 40 | Yes | |
| IndexCode | Index name in English | varchar | 40 | Yes | |
| IndexDimension | Index dimension | varchar | 30 | Yes | |
| IndexDescartes | Index description | varchar | 1000 | Yes | |
| ClassOneIndexSum | First-class index sum | int | 11 | Yes | |
| ClassTwoIndexSum | Second-class index sum | int | 11 | Yes | |

**Sheet 3.** Index Weight

| Field Name | Name | Data Type | Size | Non-null | Explanation |
|---|---|---|---|---|---|
| IndextID | Index number | int | 8 | Yes | |
| IndexName | Index name in Chinese | varchar | 40 | Yes | |
| IndexCode | Index name in English | varchar | 40 | Yes | |
| IndexWeight | Index Weight | decimal | 8 | Yes | |

**Sheet 4.** Index Standard Value

| Field Name | Name | Data Type | Size | Non-null | Explanation |
|---|---|---|---|---|---|
| IndextID | Index number | int | 11 | Yes | |
| IndexName | Index name in Chinese | varchar | 40 | Yes | |
| IndexCode | Index name in English | varchar | 40 | Yes | |
| IndexStandardValue | Index standard value | Int | 8 | Yes | |

**Sheet 5.** Originality Data

| Field Name | Name | Data Type | Size | Non-null | Explanation |
|---|---|---|---|---|---|
| ID | Record number | int | 8 | Yes | |
| regID | Region code | varchar | 11 | Yes | |
| IndextID | Index number | int | 8 | Yes | |
| IndexValue | Index data | Int | 8 | Yes | |
| IndexDimension | Index dimension | varchar | 30 | Yes | |
| GatherDate | Collection data | date | 40 | Yes | |

# 4    Key Technology

Eclipse, the development tool of the agricultural informationalization evaluation and decision support system, has been developed, compiled and debugged in the environment of Windows XP+ JDK 1.5.0+Tomcat 5.0+SQL Server 200, seen in the figure as follows. The development mode of MVC, based on Struts, was adopted for the establishment of the agricultural informationalization evaluation and decision support system, in the B/S systematic structure based on WEB. Struts is the framework of considerable popularity based on MVC in nowadays, which has led to the general realization of the separation between the business logic layer, the presentation layer, and the control layer, and at the same time contributes to the promotion of extendability and circulativity of the application software.

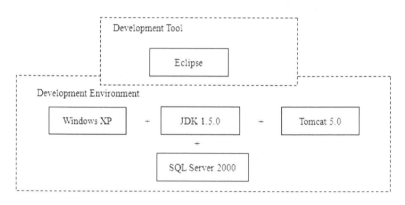

**Fig. 4.** The Software Environment of System Development

## 4.1    The Realization of MVC Design Mode

The MVC mode embodies 3 categories of components: 1) the model object is the core of the entire application software, in charge of packaging the structure of software data and the operation as well as the work flow of processing services; 2) the view object is the connector between the application software and the outside, by forwarding the input of its user to the controller, consulting the business situation, and synchronizing the relative date to the user via visualization; 3) the controller object is the link between models and the view. On the one hand, it provides the user input with analysis into the order for model implementation; on the other hand, it, in accordance with the user input, calls relevant models and the view to satisfy the demand data visualization for the user.

With the application of MVC mode, the data processing, the control of system input and output are both separated with data presentation, making the system structure clear and flexible, so that it leads to the avoidance of entanglement and confusion of the data processing, program function, and show code when early developers are using the method starting from the interface and then code. The design of Struts MVC mode is demonstrated as follows.

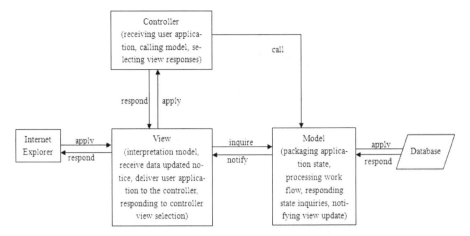

**Fig. 5.** The Design of Struts MVC Mode

This system uses Struts framework for realization. The Struts framework is a frame realized based on the application of JSP Model2. The mode of MVC contributes the advantages as follows to this system: 1) data model, the control of input and output, and the user view are of mutual independence, making the system design progress more clear, and strengthening the system maintainability; 2) With the MVC mode, each model can be counted as an independent category, and the controller is used to link different models and provide the structure with greater clearness; 3) the function that each model is able to offer several views data has improved the flexibility of data presentation and the reusability of codes.

### 4.2    HTML

HTML, short for Hypertext Markup Language, as a common language in the internet and a simple and universal explanatory markup language, is a descriptive text consists of HTML orders. The HTML order is able to explain languages, images, movies, sounds, figures and interlinkages. The structure of HTML can be divided into the head part and the body part, in which, the former one is used for the description of the information demanded by the explorer, and the latter one is the detailed and specific content of the page.

### 4.3    Javascript

Javascript is a scripting language developed from LiveScript by Netscape. As a script, it is able to write Javascript code into HTML files, and it can be compiled and executed while the internet explorer reads it. Javascript can effectively save the download time on the client page by increase the interactivity of webpage and simplify some regularly repeating HTML files. Furthermore, Javascript is capable of transferring some operations such as user authentification on the client side and reduce the burden of servers.

## 4.4    JSP

JSP, similar to the ASP technology, is a technology realizing mixed code of regular static HTML and dynamic HTML. It inserts Java program segment and JSP label into traditional webpage HTML files. The JSP is of the ability to realize the separation between web logics, design and presentation, for the design based on the reusable components, resulting in rapidity and simplicity of the application software development based on Web.

## 4.5    Servlet

Servlet, namely the server applet, is Java application software independent from both the system operation platform and the network and transport protocols server, for the extension of server functions and the generation of dynamic Web pages. It is the Java application software at the server side inside the Web server, which differs from the Java application software that is started from the traditional order line. Servlet is loaded by Web server, which has to embody the Java virtual machine for Servlet support. Servlet, in the MVC mode, is capable of the matching of models and views and the accomplishment of the user request.

## 4.6    Struts

Struts is an open source project organized by Apache organization, based on the Web application in MVC mode, which provides the MVC system development with bottom support. It, adopting Servlet as the main technology, is able to reduce the time to develop Web application with the application of MVC design model. Struts frameworks such as JSP, user custom tags or so are helpful for the improvement of developing efficiency and for development of system maintainability and extendibility.

# 5    Conclusion

Addressing the need of the agricultural informationalization evaluation and decision support system,a agricultural informationalization evaluation and decision support system is developed based on MVC development mode in the environment of Windows XP+Tomcat 5.0+SQL Server2000. This article provided information on the system design, functions, database and work flows. The research has achieved its objectives by developing a tool which can support the agricultural informationalization evaluation effectively and efficiently.

**Acknowledgements.** This research has been substantially supported by the program of National Agricultural Informationalization Evaluation Index System Research carried out by Market and Economic Department in the Ministry of Agricultural.

# References

1. Bai, W.P.: A Research of New Rural Informationalization Construction Effect Evaluation Index System. Journal of Anhui Agricultural Sciences (31), 13910–13912 (2008)
2. Huang, Z.W.: A Research of Rural Informationalization Level Evaluation in China. Science and Technology Progress and Policy (23), 158–162 (2009)
3. Liu, S.H.: A Research of Rural Informationalization Measuring Index System in China. Library and Information Service (9), 33–36 (2007)
4. Zhang, X.C., Qin, X.Y., Zhang, X.X.: A Research of Beijing Agricultural Informationalization Evaluation Index System. Beijing Agricultural Professional College Journals (1), 42–46 (2008)
5. Gao, Y., Gan, G.H.: A Preparatory Research of Agricultural Informationalization Evaluation Index System. Agriculture Network Information (8), 9–13, +17 (2009)
6. Zhao, Y.P., Li, D.L.: The Design and Realization of the Evaluation and Decision Support System for Environmental Effect Brought by Vegetation Recovery on Dumps Based on the Technology of GIS. Open Mining Technology (3), 65–67 (2007)
7. Xia, Y.Y., et al.: The Preparation and Development of Side Slopes around the Three Gorges Reservoir Stability Evaluation and Decision Support System Based on Web. Microcomputer Information (30), 65–67 (2006)
8. Wang, G.X., Chen, P.: The Design and Development of Cities' Future Development Sustainability Evaluation and Decision Support System, China's Population. Resources and Environment (5), 41–46 (2006)
9. Hu, J.Y., Huang, K.: Eco-City Multilevel Fuzzy Comprehensive Evaluation and Evaluation Support System. Modern Management Science (2), 69–72 (2006)

# Design of Expert System for Fault Diagnosis of Water Quality Monitoring Devices

Qiucheng Li, Daoliang Li[*], and Zhenbo Li

College of Information and Electrical Engineering,
China Agricultural University, Beijing, 100083, P.R.China
dliang1@qq.com

**Abstract.** A new system for automatic detect fault of water quality monitoring devices used in aquaculture is proposed in this paper. The proposed system can detect the whole system which includes platform gateway WSN sensor actuator. China is the world's largest freshwater culture nation which provides 80% of the freshwater culture fish. The water quality is essential to freshwater culture, and the environment is controllable. In this paper, water quality sensors are used to detect the water quality of culture ponds. By the use of wireless sensor networks, the data can be sent to remote server. So farmers can check the state of the culture ponds where the internet is available. This paper is proposed to detect the state of the monitoring system, if the monitoring system falls, the system will alarm to the user.

**Keywords:** Automatic, On-line, Fault diagnosis, Aquaculture, Water quality monitoring.

## 1    Introduction

China is the world's largest freshwater culture nation which provides 80% of the freshwater culture fish. The water quality is essential to freshwater culture, and the environment is controllable. In this paper, water quality sensors are used to detect the water quality of culture ponds. By the use of wireless sensor networks, the data can be sent to remote server. So farmers can check the state of the culture ponds where internet is available. Water quality is very important in aquaculture. We use WSN technology to monitoring the water quality to ensure the circumstance is suitable for the fish to grow. In this way, human has been released from hard working. The water quality monitoring system is essential for the aquaculture. If the monitoring system fails, and the water quality become bad, a lot of fish will die, farmer will lost a lot. So a new system for automatic detect fault of water quality monitoring devices used in aquaculture is proposed in this paper [1].

## 2    Water Quality Monitoring Model

The water quality monitoring system proposed in this paper is used in outdoor aquaculture. The most important attributes of the water quality are dissolved oxygen

---

[*] Corresponding author.

D. Li and Y. Chen (Eds.): CCTA 2011, Part I, IFIP AICT 368, pp. 524–529, 2012.

and water temperature. If the dissolved oxygen is lower than 3mg/l, the growing of fish will be constrained. If the dissolved oxygen is lower than 1mg/l, the fish will die. Both the water temperature is too high or too low will constrain the growing of fish. The water quality monitoring model is illustrated by Figure 1. The first part is sensor which can detect both dissolved oxygen and water temperature. The second part is a transformer which is powered by solar battery and sends out the data collected by sensors wirelessly according to H 15.4 communication protocol. The third part is gateway which receives the data send from transformer and sends them out to the remote server.

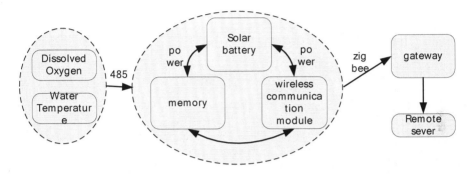

**Fig. 1.** Water quality monitoring model

In this system, the sensor has three channels, includes dissolved oxygen, water temperature, and dissolved oxygen engineering value. The transformer has three channels, include device information, device voltage, and signal strength[2]. The gateway has seven channels, includes city power supply, current one, current two, switch signal, analog signal one, analog signal two, and device voltage. That information is the source of the fault diagnosis system [3].

## 3     Design of Fault Information Database Table

After three months observation of the current water quality monitoring system, fault object can be divided into five categories: software platform, gateway, transformer, sensor, and actuator. Fault grade can be divided into three categories: mild, moderate, serious[4]. Mild means that operation and maintenance staffs should know that. Moderate means that if operation and maintenance staffs have time, they should deal with the problem. Serious means that the fault is fatal, operation and maintenance staffs should deal with the problem as soon as possible. The fault information database table is illustrated by Figure 2. The fault diagnosis system stores the fault occurring time, and records fault reason and deal method which is added by operation and maintenance staffs. In this way, if the same kind of fault occurs again, we can check the database to check the previous records [5].

| Field meaning | Field name | Data type |
|---|---|---|
| ID | def_id | varchar |
| Smart device ID | dev_id | varchar |
| Fault type | def_type | int |
| Fault grade | def_grade | int |
| Fault occur reason | def_occurReason | Varchar |
| Fault occur time | def_occurTime | Datetime |
| Fault solved time | def_dealTime | Datetime |
| Deal method | def_dealMethod | Varchar |
| Channel ID | ch_id | Varchar |
| Fault description | def_desc | Varchar |

**Fig. 2.** Fault information table(smart device)

# 4    Design of Fault Diagnosis Rule Database

The fault diagnosis rule database is illustrated by Figure 3.Rules is made on the base of careful observation of the water quality monitoring system. Each fault object has the expert to give the suggestion of the rule-making. Each fault object has four attributes, communication state, device state, data continuation state, data rationality[6]. Fault level has been divided into three levels. Serious means that the fault is fatal to the operation of the water quality system. Moderate means that the fault is not fatal to the operation of the water quality monitoring system, but the fault will be fatal to the operation of the water quality monitoring system. Mild means that the fault is not fatal to the operation of the water quality monitoring system, but the fault has the possibility to be fatal to the operation of the water quality monitoring system[7].

| Fault object | Fault level | Rule |
|---|---|---|
| Software platform | serious | Receive no data in 10 minutes; |
| Software platform | serious | Illegal register; |
| Software platform | serious | The number of channels is not in compare with the platform; |
| Software platform | mild | Software platform time and reporting time asynchronous; |
| Gateway | mild | The reporting time subtract acquisition time is larger than 30 minutes; |
| Gateway | mild | The interval between two heart beats is larger than 2 times of cycle |
| Gateway | serious | The acquisition time is the same with the last data |
| Gateway | mild | The gateway voltage is lower than 4.4 volt |
| Gateway | mild | The reset number of gateway increased |
| Transformer | serious | The transformer voltage is the same with the last data |
| Transformer | mild | The transformer voltage is lower than 3.6 volt |
| Transformer | mild | The reset number of transformer increased |
| Sensor | serious | The sensor data is the same with the last data |
| Sensor | serious | The value is out of the upper limit and lower limit |
| Sensor | serious | The change rate is larger than 0.1 |
| Actuator | mild | Illegal operation |

**Fig. 3.** Fault diagnosis rule database

# 5    Design of Fault Diagnosis Flow Chart

I The water quality monitoring system is level clearly demarcated. If the gateway fails, the platform can't get the information below the gateway [8]. In the same way, if the transformer fails, the platform can't get the information below the transformer. The fault diagnosis flow chart is illustrated by Figure 4. The expert system of fault diagnosis for water quality monitoring system follows the flow chart illustrated by Figure 4.

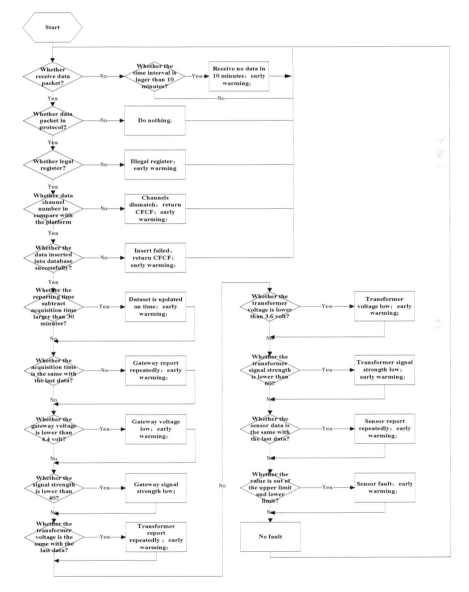

**Fig. 4.** Flowchart for the identification of deficiency symptoms

## 6 System Interface

Fault information management is illustrated by Figure 5. The result of fault diagnosis is stored in the database. For the purpose of being friendly to the users, a web-based system interface has been developed. Users can search the device Id, fault level, fault type, fault state, fault occurring time[9].

首页 》 故障信息管理

根据 设备编号： 故障等级： 请选择…… 故障类型： 请选择…… 故障状态： 请选择……

故障发生时间： 2011-09-10 00:00:00 至 2011-09-10 23:59:59 查询

| 设备编号 | 故障等级 | 故障类型 | 发生故障的时间 | 解决故障的时间 | 编辑 |
|---|---|---|---|---|---|
| 40076 | 严重 | 传感器 | 2011-09-10 11:04:08.0 | | 编辑/详情 |
| 40002 | 严重 | 控制设备 | 2011-09-10 11:02:45.0 | | 编辑/详情 |
| 40002 | 严重 | 控制设备 | 2011-09-10 11:02:43.0 | | 编辑/详情 |
| 40074 | 严重 | 传感器 | 2011-09-10 11:02:22.0 | | 编辑/详情 |
| 40076 | 严重 | 传感器 | 2011-09-10 10:52:16.0 | | 编辑/详情 |
| 40074 | 严重 | 传感器 | 2011-09-10 10:51:35.0 | | 编辑/详情 |
| 40076 | 严重 | 传感器 | 2011-09-10 10:41:09.0 | | 编辑/详情 |
| 40074 | 严重 | 传感器 | 2011-09-10 10:40:49.0 | | 编辑/详情 |
| 40002 | 严重 | 控制设备 | 2011-09-10 10:37:54.0 | | 编辑/详情 |
| 40002 | 严重 | 控制设备 | 2011-09-10 10:37:52.0 | | 编辑/详情 |
| 共87461条记录，每页10条，当前第1页，共8747页 | | | | 首 页 上一页 下一页 尾 页 | |

**Fig. 5.** Fault information management

Fault report is illustrated by Figure 6.The report can statistic the fault information. From this report, we can see the amount of each kind of fault happened in a specified period.

故障发生时间： 2011-09-10 00:00:00 至 2011-09-10 23:59:59 查询

| 场景名称 | 设备地址 | 平台故障 | 网关故障 | 小无线故障 | 传感器故障 | 控制设备故障 | 合计 |
|---|---|---|---|---|---|---|---|
| 史建强-01号池 | 40008 | 0 | 0 | 0 | 0 | 10 | 10 |
| 史建强-02号池 | 40073 | 0 | 15 | 0 | 0 | 0 | 15 |
| 周宝银-01号池 | 40002 | 0 | 0 | 0 | 0 | 44 | 44 |
| 周宝银-02号池 | 40071 | 0 | 5 | 0 | 0 | 0 | 5 |
| 周宝银-03号池 | 40074 | 0 | 5 | 0 | 67 | 0 | 72 |
| 水产模型-01号池 | 40004 | 0 | 5 | 0 | 0 | 0 | 5 |
| 合计 | | 0 | 30 | 0 | 67 | 54 | 151 |

**Fig. 6.** Fault report

## 7 Conclusion

In this paper, we presented an expert system for fault diagnosis of water quality monitoring devices based on rule database. The system allows a user to track the detailed information of the whole monitoring system. The architecture of the system has been described from several points of view and it has shown to have the ability to meet the requirements imposed on early warming of the water quality and monitoring devices and fault diagnosis of the monitoring system.

In the architecture described above, each fault of the water quality monitoring system can be tracked for detailed information. Therefore, the system's stability can be enhanced. The profit of the aquaculture farmers can be ensured. For this reason, our future work will cover the study of artificial intelligence to make the system smarter[10].

# References

1. Avci, E., Avci, D.: An expert system based on fuzzy entropy for automatic threshold selection in image processing. Expert Systems with Applications 36(2, Part 2), 3077–3085 (2009)
2. Avci, D., Varol, A.: An expert diagnosis system for classification of human parasite eggs based on multi-class SVM. Expert Systems with Applications 36(1), 43–48 (2009)
3. Du, Z., Jin, X.: Detection and diagnosis for sensor fault in HVAC systems. Energy Conversion and Management 48(3), 693–702 (2007)
4. Reza, E.: Designing a hierarchical neural network based on fuzzy clustering for fault diagnosis of the Tennessee–Eastman process. Applied Soft Computing 11(1), 1407–1415 (2011)
5. Keleş, A., Keleş, A., Yavuz, U.: Expert system based on neuro-fuzzy rules for diagnosis breast cancer. Expert Systems with Applications 38(5), 5719–5726 (2011)
6. Lee, M., Choi, Y.: Fault detection of wireless sensor networks. Computer Communications 31(14), 3469–3475 (2008)
7. Tsai, N., King, Y., Lee, R.: Fault diagnosis for magnetic bearing systems. Mechanical Systems and Signal Processing 23(4), 1339–1351 (2009)
8. Kang, S., et al.: Development of expert system for extraction of the objects of interest. Expert Systems with Applications 36(3, Part 2), 7210–7218 (2009)
9. Al-Kasassbeh, M., Adda, M.: Network fault detection with Wiener filter-based agent. Journal of Network and Computer Applications 32(4), 824–833 (2009)
10. Barco, R., et al.: Knowledge acquisition for diagnosis model in wireless networks. Expert Systems with Applications 36(3, Part 1), 4745–4752 (2009)

# Preliminary Design of a Recognition System for Infected Fish Species Using Computer Vision

Jing Hu[1], Daoliang Li[2,*], Qingling Duan[2], Guifen Chen[1], and Xiuli Si[1]

[1] College of Information Technology, Jilin Agricultural University, Changchun 130118, China
[2] College of Information and Electrical Engineering, China Agricultural University,
Beijing 100083, China
dliang@cau.edu.cn

**Abstract.** For the purpose of classification of fish species, a recognition system was preliminary designed using computer vision. In the first place, pictures were pre-processed by developed programs, dividing into rectangle pieces. Secondly, color and texture features are extracted for those selected texture rectangle fish skin images. Finally, all the images were classified by multi-class classifier named SVMs. The experiment showed that color and texture are the appropriate features for fish species classification. The multi-class classifier based on SVM will be developed for further work.

**Keywords:** Recognition system, Infected fish, Fish species, Computer vision.

## 1 Introduction

The dramatic and widely spread of fish disease is the driving force in the development of machine vision system to identify these diseases. Our ultimate aim is to develop an image-processing system for identification of common carp in China. Users take a photograph of diseased fish by phone cameras or other move terminal with the ability of taking a picture and sent the photograph to our system, this system identify the disease by image analyzing and send the results to users by wireless network. For an intelligent system of fish diseases recognition based on image processing, the first step must be the recognition of fish species obviously.

So far many different methods of processing images or hydro acoustic techniques for fish recognition, classification and monitoring have been proposed. F Martinez de Dios et al. (2003) [1] used an underwater stereo vision system for estimating the weight of adult fish in sea cages from their length, and an over-the-water stereo system for estimating fish weight in a nursery. D.J.White et al.(2006) [2] described trails of computer vision machine(The Catch Meter) for identifying and measuring different species of fish. The fish are transported along a conveyor underneath a digital camera. Boaz Zion et al.(2007) [3].develop a real-time underwater computer vision system for Common carp (Cyprinus carpio), St. Peter's fish (Oreochromis sp.) and grey mullet

---

\* Corresponding author.

D. Li and Y. Chen (Eds.): CCTA 2011, Part I, IFIP AICT 368, pp. 530–534, 2012.

(Mugil cephalus) in pool in which fish swim through a narrow transparent unidirectional channel. S.Duarte et al.(2009) [4] obtain a quantitative index form measuring flatfish activity using image analysis for studying fish behavior and welfare. Hugo Robotham et al.(2010) [5] classified schools of anchovy, common sardine, and jackmackerel using support vector machines (SVMs) and two types of supervised artificial neural networks (multilayer perceptron, MLP; and probabilistic neural networks, PNNs) during acoustic surveys in south-central Chile by hydro acoustic techniques.

Image analysis is the key techniques before classification for a computer vision. The aim of image analysis is to extract the features of the objects. Texture and color are usually be used as common features for image analysis. Textures are encountered almost in all digital picture from conventional photography to seismic and microscopy images [6-9]. Color is one of the most significant low-level features that can be used to extract homogeneous regions that are most of the time related to objects or part of objects [10].According to extracted features, classification is a procedure for sorting each element of a data set into one of the finite sets of classes utilizing a decision criterion[11].

In this paper, a new system was preliminary designed for recognition of infected fish species, this system refers to color and texture feature extraction and multi-class classifier. In the first step, pictures be pre-processed by developed programs, dividing into some rectangle pieces. Then color and texture features are extracted for those selected texture rectangle fish skin images. Finally, all the images are classified by multi-class classifier named SVMs.

## 2    Materials and Methods

### 2.1    Image Acquisition

Live images are received by a GPRS modem when farms send their infected fish pictures to our system. The computer vision system mainly consists of GPRS modem, image receiver module, image pre-processed module, image analysis module and image recognition module.

Through the GPRS modem, the infected fish images are received, then the image are processed by the pre-processed module to obtain the texture fish skin images as inputs to analysis module. According to the analysis results, the recognition module classified the images by training and studying. Images of six common fish were obtained: grass carp, black fish, chub, wuchang fish, bighead carp, red bellied pacu.

### 2.2    Image Pre-processing

A large number of color images were acquired by GRPS to this computer vision system. All the images were pre-processed. We have the automatic cutting program to cut the infected fish image with 32×32,64×64,128×128,256×256,512×512 window sizes. All the images were manually selected to remove the unqualified ones which are not full of fish body skin.Fig.1 shows one of the original images and one of the processed qualified texture images. . After the selection, images were enhanced by 3×3 media filter which may smooth the noise of the image.

(a)Original image                     (b)Processed image

**Fig. 1.** Original and processed images

## 2.3    Feature Extraction

The texture fish skin images usually have different colors and textures. Therefore, it is difficult to classify them accurately by only one type of feature. Color, shape and texture are commonly used features types in classification problems.

As lighting conditions and environments are easy to be fully controlled, it will be appropriate to use texture and color features as vectors inputs for classification. Fish vary in size and shape, but sometimes for getting a clearly vision for small disease spot, fish photos collected by system users may not be a whole fish, those photos of fish shape cannot be decide. So shape features are desirable to avoid, on the contrary, texture and color features are chosen as the preferable image features.

Texture is the reflection of brightness change of an image in the space. Two different types of statistical texture features are extracted. One is grayscale histograms (GH) based texture and the other is gray level co-occurrence matrices (GLCM) based texture. GH based texture features, including mean intensity, mean contrast, roughness, third-order moment, consistency, and entropy. GLCM based texture features, including second-order moment (energy), entropy, contrast and correlation.

Color is an important feature as well for fish species classification. Eight color features are extracted, i.e., the mean of the R channel of a color image, the mean of the G channel of a color image, the mean of B channel of a color image, the mean of RGB of a image, the mean of H channel of a color image, the mean of S channel of a color image, the mean of I channel of a color image and the mean of HIS of a image.

## 2.4    Classification

As a binary classifier, SVM has the advantage of the generalization ability when limit samples were available. In this research, SVM will be chosen.

The classification of fish species into six categories can be considered as constructing several binary classifiers and combining them into one multi-class classifier. In this study, a MSVM will be constructed to serve for the classification of fish species based on computer vision. A number of methods can be used to construct the MSVM, we used the one-against-one [12] algorithm.

The one-against-one is such a method that constructs k(k-1)/s classifiers where each one is trained on data from two classes. For training data from the jth classes, a binary classification will be solved.

# 3    Experiment and Analysis

All the algorithms used in the research for fish image processing and recognition were programmed in Matlab2010.The test environment was a personal computer with Pentium(R) Dual-Core 2.70 GHZ CPU and 3.24GB SDRAM.

After image pre-processing, totally 540 fish texture images were obtained, including each 90 object s of six fish species. Features were extracted from each image, forming a 22-dimensional feature vector each.

Previous experiment showed that the rotation can hardly affects texture features, thus it is no matter that how the users chose a shooting angle. It will be stable that the image processing system to extract features before classification. Inertia moment and correlation textures remain stable while energy and entropy decreased as window size increased. The next step, we will do some experiment of classification with the obtained feature vectors.

For the theories and some experiment above, the recognition system was preliminary designed as follow (Fig.2).

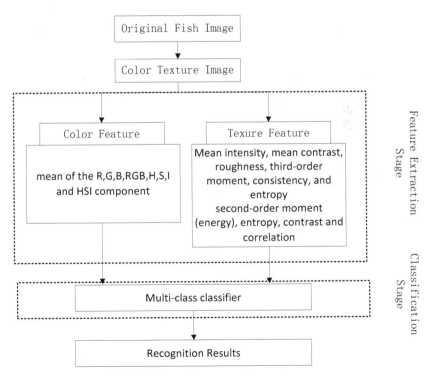

**Fig. 2.** Design of the recognition system

# 4    Conclusion

In this paper, we designed a recognition system for infected fish species. Color and texture features are more effective than any single type of feature to classify species of fish. With the future work of MSVM developing, infected fish species will be classified accurately and quickly.

**Acknowledgments.** This work is support by Beijing Natural Science Fund of "Research on Digital Culture of Intensive Aquatic Product" (4092024); The national science and technology supporting plan of "Integration and Demonstration of Key Technology for overall sense of agricultural field" (2011BAD21B01-1);   Special Grand National Science-technology Project "TD-SCDMA based Development and Demonstration of Rural Informationization Application" (2009ZX03001-019-01); "Remote Diagnosis and Prevention and Control Application of Animal Epidemics " (2009P106) funded by the Translation of Scientific and Technological Achievements in Agriculture into Productive, Tianjin, China.

# References

1. Martinez-de Dios, J.R., Serna, C., Ellero, A.: Computer vision and robotics techniques in fish farms. Robotica 21(3), 233–243 (2003)
2. White, D.J., Svellingen, C., Strachan, N.J.C.: Automated measurement of species and length of fish by computer vision. Fisheries Research 80, 203–210 (2006)
3. Zion, B., Alchanatis, V., Ostrovsky, V., Barki, A., Karplus, I.: Real-time underwater sorting of edible fish species. Computers and Electronics in Agriculture 56(1), 34–45 (2007)
4. Duarte, S., Reig, L., Oca, J.: Measurement of sole activity by digital image analysis. Aquacultural Engineering 41(1), 22–27 (2009)
5. Robotham, H., Bosch, Paul, Gutiérrez-Estrada, J.C., Castillo, J., Pulido–Calvo, I.: Acoustic identification of small pelagic fish species in Chile using support vector machines and neural networks. Fisheries Research 102(1-2), 115–122 (2010)
6. Aydogan, D.B., Hannula, M., Arola, T., Dastidar, B., Hyttinen, J.: 2D texture based classification, segmentation and 3D orientation estimation of tissues using DT-CWT feature extraction methods. Data & Knowledge Engineering 68(12), 1383–1397 (2009)
7. Al-Takrouri, S., Savkin, A.V.: A model validation approach to texture recognition and inpainting. Pattern Recognition 43(6), 2054–2067 (2010)
8. Permuter, H., Francosb, J., Jermync, I.: A study of Gaussian mixture models of color and texture features for image classification and segmentation. Pattern Recognition 39(4), 695–706 (2006)
9. Avci, E., Sengur, A., Hanbay, D.: An optimum feature extraction method for texture classification. Expert Systems with Applications 36(3), 6036–6043 (2009)
10. Tan, K.S., Isa, N.A.M.: Color image segmentation using histogram thresholding – Fuzzy C-means hybrid approach. Pattern Recognition 44(1), 1–15 (2011)
11. Du, C., Sun, D.W.: Multi-classification of pizza using computer vision and support vector machine. Journal of Foos Engineering 86(2), 234–242 (2008)
12. Hsu, C.W., Lin, C.J.: A comparison of methods for Multi-class Support Vector Machines. IEEE Transaction on neural networks 13(2), 415–425 (2002)

# Conservation Based Information System
# for Agrifood Process Network Interoperability

Bela Csukas, Monika Varga, and Sandor Balogh

Kaposvár University, Research Group on Process Informatics,
40 Guba S,7400 Kaposvár, Hungary
{csukas.bela,varga.monika,balogh.sandor}@ke.hu

**Abstract.** Based on the stoichiometric structure of conservational processes, a general methodology has been developed for the computer aided generation and operation of network interoperability services. An appropriate set of unified building elements, having autonomous programs and communicating with a dynamic simulating kernel has been elaborated for the qualitative and quantitative tracing and tracking of trans-sectorial processes. The GNU-Prolog implemented method is scalable and makes possible the ad hoc extension of the models with the actually interesting components to be investigated. The system can also be applied for the identification of hidden resources and wastes, as well as for the analysis of the value chains. This outlines a straightforward cooperative architecture of services between the planned interoperability center and the actors, supervised by the responsible authorities. The method will be illustrated by the example of agrifood processes.

**Keywords:** stoichiometric processes, dynamic simulation, trans-sectorial problem solving, agrifood process networks, interoperability services.

## 1 Introduction

The engineer designed and controlled processes in the almost closed, finite space of resources and reservoirs seem to play an essential role in the solution of the present and forthcoming economical and ecological crisis. The necessary long term, and large scale, hybrid models claim for new, computer oriented frameworks that help to manage extendable simple skeleton of process systems, case specifically.

For example, agrifood processes are built from complex, multiscale, time-varied networks that span many sectors from cultivation, through animal breeding, food industry and food trade to the consumers. Also public health and public administration are interested in agrifood management. Recently, motivated by the food scandals' initiated legislation, many powerful identification and measurement methods, standardized communication protocols have been evolved [1]. The inner traceability of the actors has also been developed, associated with the various ERP systems. However, the sector spanning traceability has not yet been solved, because neither the "one-step backward, one-step forward" passing of IDs, nor the large, central databases, prepared for the numerous possible situations give a feasible solution.

D. Li and Y. Chen (Eds.): CCTA 2011, Part I, IFIP AICT 368, pp. 535–544, 2012.
© IFIP International Federation for Information Processing 2012

A paradox, but powerful concept is that let us solve an apparently more difficult task. This task is the dynamic simulation of the simplified, stoichiometric mass balances that provide us the extendable transparency of the whole network. Agrifood networks can be described by process systems, characterized by the inherent feedback structure between the states and transitions. The general formal models, described by the output and state functions of the process systems, had been developed by Kalman [2], before the powerful Information Technology appeared. The General Net Theory [3] proposes a net model for the description of the respective structure of states and transitions. Many net models, like the early appeared and very innovative Petri Net [4], as well as the various State Transition Nets belong to the above family. The net models do not distinguish between the model specific conservation law based properties and the signs, corresponding to the information processes. State-of-art of process modeling was analyzed by Marquardt [5], who reviewed the methodologies and tools, developed for simulation based problem solving. The significant evolution of process modeling methodologies is determined by the process industries [6].

## 2     Model Specific Conservation Based Stoichiometric Processes

The notion of the measure can be understood simply as an additive quantity. In the scientific context we use Halmos's definition [7] of the measures. Accordingly, *measure* is an extended real valued, non-negative, countable, and additive set function over a ring.

First we define a special class of measures that fulfils the model specific conservation. The only way to interpret this general and plausible, but ill-defined physical notion is the axiomatic approach.

Let C be a measure in the space of the geometric and property co-ordinates that can change in the continuous or discrete time t. Let us denote a finite, closed region in the above space with v. The not necessarily finite and closed "environment" of this region v will be indicated with u\v and called universal complement. Let $C_V(t)$ and $C_{U\backslash V}(t)$ denote the measure C associated with the region v and with its universal complement at time t. The *model specific conservation measures* are characterized by the axiom that the change of the measure in any finite and closed region, v during any time interval $[t_i, t_j]$, is accompanied by the identical change of the same measure in the universal complement with an opposite sign, i.e.

$$\forall_V \forall_{i,j} \{(C_V(t_i) - C_V(t_j)) = -(C_{U\backslash V}(t_i) - C_{U\backslash V}(t_j))\} \qquad (1)$$

Fig. 1 shows an illustration to the notion of the model specific conservational measures.

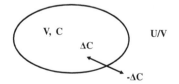

**Fig. 1.** Illustration of model specific conservational measures

Constant conservational measures correspond to the quantities obeying to the conservation laws, existing in the investigated system, within the given model hypothesis. For example, within the model hypothesis of chemistry the number and the mass of the atoms are constant conservational measures. Similarly, there is conservation for the wheels, motors, windscreens, chairs, etc. in an automobile factory. Although all of these model hypotheses have a limited validity, they give a constructive, sound basis for the problem solving within the scope of the given model, because, all of the measures describing the given class of processes can be derived from these model specific conservational measures. The measures that can be derived as the homogeneous linear combinations of the constant conservational measures are called *conservation based stoichiometric measures*.

Thinking about the example of atoms, many chemical compounds can be built from the known atoms. The number and the mass of the molecules do not satisfy the axioms of the conservation measures, because they can transform in chemical reactions. However, we can write balance equations for the reacting systems, with the knowledge of the stoichiometry that determines these secondary measures from the primary, constant ones. Similarly we can speak about the stoichiometries of the cars, or of the animals. Nevertheless, there are special additive measures (like entropy, profit) that cannot be derived from the constant measures without additional source terms.

Consider a finite closed region within a given model hypothesis. The model hypothesis can be characterized by the model specific conservational measures $\underline{C} = \{C_1, C_2, ..., C_m\}$. Designate $\underline{M} = \{M_1, M_2, ..., M_n\}$ the set of measures in the same region. Measures $\underline{M}$ are called the *stoichiometric measures,* derived from the constant measures iff for any time t there is a matrix $\underline{\underline{S}}$ of the stoichiometric coefficients $s_{i,j}(t)$ that satisfies the equation

$$\underline{M}(t) = \underline{\underline{S}}(t)\underline{C}(t) \tag{2}$$

Stoichiometric balance models makes possible to develop a general methodology for the trans-sectorial interoperability for the various (e.g. agrifood) process networks. Accordingly, the essential features of the process network can be described in the special model database of the underlying mass balances in TRUs, i.e. in the unambiguously identifiable and traceable units. The actually investigated intensive parameters (e.g. concentration of the various useful or harmful ingredients, prices, etc.) can be carried with the mass batches or mass flows plausibly. The exact definition of TRU (Traceability Resource Unit) was elaborated by Kim [8] in the language of predicate logic, considering the temporal transportations and transformations, that is familiar with the dynamic processes.

The dynamic mass balance of the input intermediates and output TRUs contains also the necessary and sufficient information about the network structure. Along the simulation of the processes, we can start from the actual states, while the functioning of the processes (i.e. extension of the database) can be solved by stepwise simulation, in line with the data supply.

In this way the various task specific intensive parameters can be carried with the mass flows, e.g. in an associated list. The respective stoichiometries can be derived exactly, or can be estimated by the experts. This solution supports the tracing and tracking of the *ad hoc* appearing problem specific components by the easy extension of the simple mass balances.

The suggested methodology claims for an IT solution, that offers the model generation from unified building elements, helps the scalable storage of the model files in databases, makes possible the case specific extension of the models, and supports the development of the effective multiscale tracing and tracking algorithms.

## 3    Unified Structural Model of Dynamic Processes

The development of the methodology [9] had been motivated by various practical problems [10, 11] that could not be solved with the available tools in that time.

Recently we have been applying the methodology for the sector spanning quantitative tracing and tracking of the agrifood process networks [12].

Quite different process models can be built from the developed toolbox, containing the meta-prototypes of the same building elements. The meta-prototypes (see Fig. 2) are the followings:

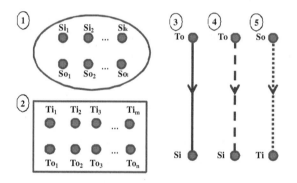

**Fig. 2.** Meta-prototypes of the building element

•1. State elements, characterizing the actual state of the process (ellipses in the graphical representations);

•2. Transition elements, describing the transportations, transformations and rules, corresponding to the time-driven or event-driven changes of the actual state (rectangles in the graphical representation);

•3-5. Connection elements, designating the directed transport of the respective measures or signs between the state and transition elements (different lines correspond to the different changes in the graphical representation).

The state and transition elements contain lists (i.e. arbitrary number) of input (Si or Ti) and output (So or To) slots. The identifier and the type of slots must match to the sending (input) and receiving (output) end of the connections.
The simplified syntax of the state and transition elements is the same, as follows:

```
element(Name,Coord,ProgramName,ParameterList,InputList,
     OutputList,Timing).
```

Both kinds of elements are characterized by the following major attributes: Name: identifying name; Coord: coordinates, determining the scale and place of the given element in the geometrical and parameter space; ProgramName: identifying name of the program; ParameterList: parameter slots, prepared for the storage of the local data, associated with the given elements; InputList: input slots, prepared for receiving data from the containers of the designated connections; OutputList: output slots, prepared for sending data to the containers of the designated connections; Timing: instructions about the temporal behavior of the given element (see later).

The slots of ParameterList, InputList and Outpulist (symbolized by dots in Fig. 2) are described by the following properties: SlotName: determines the local identifier of the given slot; SlotType: gives instructions to the interpretation of the value, associated with the slot; SlotValue: contains the list of data, e.g. in the form of

```
d(DataName,DataValues,Dimension)
```

functors, where DataName: identifies the individual data set; DataValues: is the list of data (numbers or atoms); Dimension: determines the measurement unit or n/a.

The local functionalities of the state and transition elements are described by the program code, identified by the respective ProgramName. Usually many elements use the same program, declared by the prototype of the given subset of elements. In the local execution the elements receive input, execute program and send output.

The programs, referred by ProgramName from the data of InputList and ParameterList calculate the values of OutputList according to the

```
program(ProgramName,InputList,ParameterList,Outputlist):-
ProgramCode.
```

clause, where ProgramCode may be any program in the body of clause that binds the free variables of OutputList with the knowledge of the bound variables of InputList and ParameterList.

In the general case, the state and transition elements may contain both conservational and informational slots. Conservational input slots can receive data only from the increasing and decreasing connections, coming from conservational output slots. Informational input slots can receive data only from the signaling connections, coming from informational output slots. In contrary, conservational output slots can send data only via increasing and decreasing connections to the conservational input slots, as well as informational output slots can send data only via signaling connections to the informational input slots.

There may also be pure conservational and informational state and transition elements, as special cases. The syntactically identical state and transition elements can be distinguished structurally and functionally. The structural difference means that, in the sense of the General Net Theory, only the state → transition and transition → state connections are allowed. The functional difference, in the sense of the State Space Model, is rather semantic than syntactic. Regardless to the fact, that both kinds of elements are associated with programs, at a given point of time the actual state of the process is described by the state elements, alone. In contrary, the dynamic behavior of the process is determined only by the transition elements. Accordingly, the functioning of the state elements is limited to the collection, interpretation and distribution of the static characteristic, while the transportations and transformations are modeled by the transitions.

The syntax of the

```
connection(SendOperator,SendElement,SendCoord,SendSlot,
           ReceiveOperator,ReceiveElement,ReceiveCoord,
           ReceiveSlot,DataType,DataSet,Timing).
```

is general for all increasing, decreasing and signaling connections. All of them carry data in the container of DataSet from a sending slot to a receiving slot and they are characterized by the following major attributes: SendOperator: determines the action to be done at sending slot (e.g. read, etc.); SendElement: identifies the sending element; SendCoord: refers to the (scale and place) coordinates of sending; SendSlot: defines the sending slot of the SendElement at SendCoord; ReceiveOperator: determines the action to be done at receiving slot (e.g. write, decrease, increase, remove, extend, etc.); ReceiveElement: identifies the receiving element; ReceiveCoord: refers to the (scale and place) coordinates of receiving; ReceiveSlot: defines the receiving slot of the ReceiveElement at ReceiveCoord; DataType: gives instructions to the interpretation of the DataSet; DataSet: contains the list of data, e.g. in the form of the functors: d(DataName,DataValues,Dimension); Timing: contains instructions about the temporal behavior of the given connection.

Increasing and decreasing connections transport DataSet from transition to state elements. Signaling connections can transport DataSet both from state to transition elements and *vice versa*. The special reading connections of the conservational substructure transport intensions (intensive parameters) from the output slots of state elements to the input slots of transition elements.

The temporal behavior of the elements and connections is declared by the associated Timing list, containing the

```
t(From,To,[When1,When2,...,WhenM],Step)
```

functors, where From: is a possible starting time; To: is a possible ending time; When1, When2,...,WhenM: are prescribed discrete times of the execution; Step: is the individual time step of the repeated execution.

The multi-scale modeling is supported also by the arbitrary number of integer coordinates given in the lists of Coord. Say, Coord = [3,7,5] refers to the fifth element in scale III, contained by the seventh element in scale II, being in the third element of scale I. The connections can be interpreted both within a scale and between scales. The model is extendable, because the number of functors d(.) on the lists at conservational slots, as well as in the containers of conservational connections isn't prescribed.

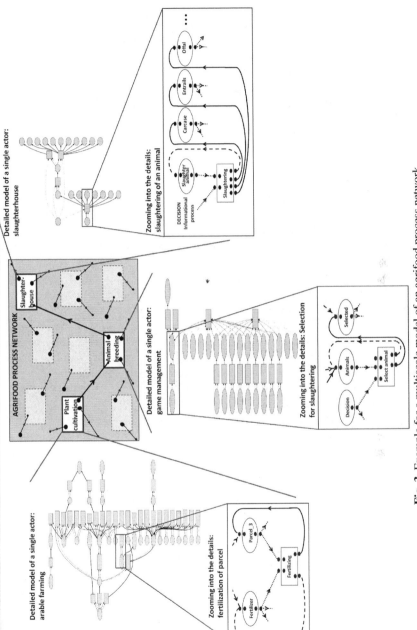

**Fig. 3.** Example for a multiscale model of an agrifood process network

The only convention is that the optionally single first element (first functor) refers to mass, while the following ones refer to the intensions, carried with the given mass batch or mass flow. The conservational state elements receive extensive changes and send intensive properties, while the conservational transition elements receive intensive characteristics and send extensive changes, *vice versa*. The increasing and decreasing of the measures, as well as the extending and removing of functors can be initiated by the increase and decrease, as well as by the extend and remove operators, respectively. The distribution of the investigated new components is calculated by the exactly known or estimated stoichiometries.

The simple example in Fig. 3 illustrates how the multiscale model of an agrifood process network can be built from the above described uniform elements.

The execution of the models consists of four cyclically repeated consecutive steps, as follows: (1) transition elements read the content of the associated state elements through the reading (signaling) connections; (2) brief programs, associated with transition elements calculate the changes; (3) state elements are modified according to the changes carried via modifying connections; (4) brief programs, associated with state elements calculate the new state.

The methodology makes possible the reverse dynamic simulation of conservation based stoichiometric processes, i.e. we can start from any simulated final state and can simulate the process backwards in time. The transitions are calculated causally right, while the increases are replaced for decreases, and *vice versa*. Also the extending and removing of the add-on intensive characteristic can be changed. Consequently, with the knowledge of the stoichiometries, the inverse simulation supports the quantitative tracing of the various problem specific components backwards in space and time.

The recent implementation of the methodology has been written in GNU-Prolog, while the case specific unification of the higher level structures, contained in dynamic partitions, supports the generalized method development. Temporarily an extended GraphViz input interface based model interpreter and a CSV file based Microsoft Excel output interface are used for testing of the methodology. The ongoing new implementation is a platform independent and partly open source tool, with a QT based, interactive GUI. The interface involves a graphical modeling and design environment that allows both the user and the field expert an easy access to the input/output data, while the expert can modify and extend also the field-specific program prototypes.

## 4    Problem Solving Services of Planned Agrifood Interoperability Centres

The effective implementation of the above described methodology can be solved by the cooperative system of the actors in the process network, coordinated by the Interoperability Centre. The schematic architecture of the Agrifood Interoperability Centres is illustrated in Fig. 4. There are three levels of the tasks to be solved, regarding the Interoperability Center, the authorities and the actors.

In the startup phase, the Centre installs communication interfaces both for actors and authorities. The suggested method of stoichiometric mass balances makes possible to generate uniform process models (and interfaces) from the same building blocks for the quite different technologies and activities.

For those actors, who have an appropriate ERP system, the model based interface is adapted to the existing software. It is worth mentioning that the required system of data is very familiar with the capability of the usual ERP modules. For the frequently used ERP systems easily configurable and uniform applications can be generated. For the smallest actors (e.g. minor private companies), who do not have ERP systems, a special user-friendly web application is given by the Interoperability Center.

Having installed the models in the Interoperability Center and the interfaces at the actors and authorities, the systematic data reporting, as well as the in-demand problem solving can start. The data reporting from the actors means the reporting about the new transactions, and the upgrading of process models.

It is to be noted that the majority of the systematically reported process data is limited to the new "connections", describing the up-to-date transportations and transformations. Nevertheless the method supports the assertion, modifying and deletion of state or transition elements, too.

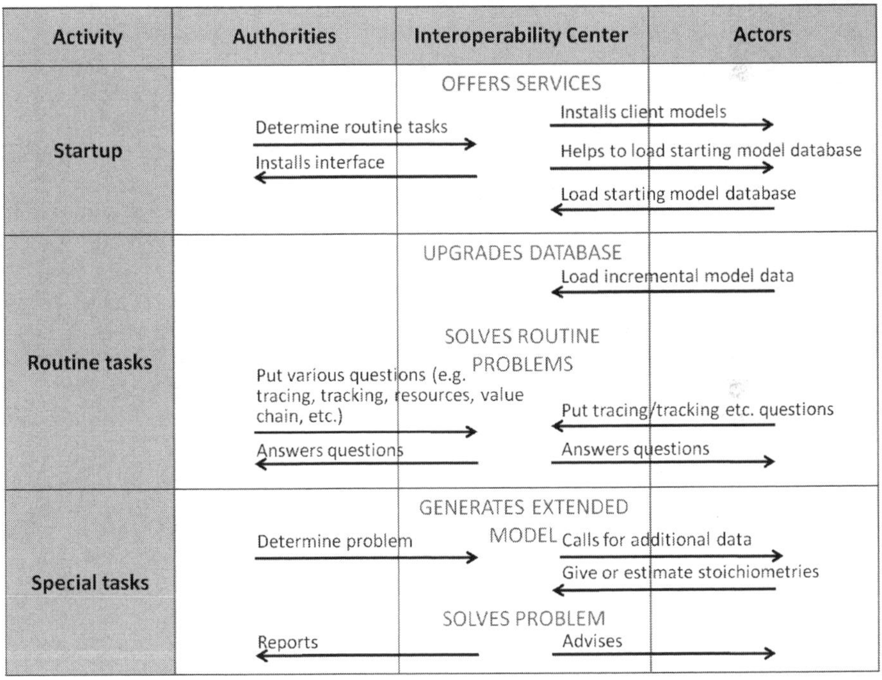

| Activity | Authorities | Interoperability Center | Actors |
|---|---|---|---|
| **Startup** | Determine routine tasks → <br> Installs interface ← | OFFERS SERVICES <br> Installs client models → <br> Helps to load starting model database → <br> Load starting model database ← | |
| **Routine tasks** | Put various questions (e.g. tracing, tracking, resources, value chain, etc.) → <br> Answers questions ← | UPGRADES DATABASE <br> Load incremental model data ← <br> SOLVES ROUTINE PROBLEMS <br> Put tracing/tracking etc. questions ← <br> Answers questions → | |
| **Special tasks** | Determine problem → <br> Reports ← | GENERATES EXTENDED MODEL Calls for additional data → <br> Give or estimate stoichiometries ← <br> SOLVES PROBLEM <br> Advises → | |

**Fig. 4.** Architecture of planned Agrifood Interoperability Centres

In case of special tasks, e.g. when a harmful component appears in the network, the Centre calls for additional data (e.g. for known or estimated stoichiometries) from actors. With the knowledge of dynamic mass balance based "skeleton" of processes and the stoichiometries, regarding the investigated components, Centre runs searching algorithms, and determines possible origins and the suggested measurement points.

The most important tasks, solved by the Centre, are the followings: Qualitative tracking by multiscale search along the forward balance routes; Qualitative tracing by multiscale search along the backward balance routes; Dynamic simulation based quantitative tracking for the concentration of the known or *ad hoc* appearing components to be studied; Backward dynamic simulation based quantitative tracing for the concentration of the known or *ad hoc* appearing components to be studied; Interactive, measurement supported search for the possible origin of the various contaminations (combining the above methods with a genetic algorithm); Reporting about hidden resources or wastes on the basis of balance calculations; Trans-sectorial value chain analysis; Analysis of the basket of typical consumers' groups.

**Acknowledgement.** The project was supported by Baross R&D Project, #REG-DD-09-2-2009-0101.

# References

1. Wolfert, J., Verdouw, C.N., Verloop, C.M., Beulens, A.J.M.: Organizing Information Integration in Agri-food – A Method based on a Service-Oriented Architecture and Living Lab Approach. Computers and Electronics in Agriculture 70(2), 389–405 (2010)
2. Kalman, R., Falb, P., Arbib, M.: Topics in Mathematical System Theory. McGraw Hill (1969)
3. Brauer, W. (ed.): Net Theory and Applications. LNCS, vol. 84. Springer, Heidelberg (1980)
4. Petri, C.A.: Kommunikation mit Automaten (Communication with Automatons). Schriften des Institut für Instrumentelle Mathematik, Nr. 2, Bonn (1962)
5. Marquardt, W.: Trends in Computer-aided Process Modeling. Computers chem. Engng. 20(6/7), 591–609 (1996)
6. Yang, A., Braunschweig, B., Fraga, E.S., Guessoum, Z., Marquardt, W., Nadjemi, O., Paen, D., Pinol, D., Roux, P., Sama, S., Serra, M., Stalker, I.: A Multi-agent System to Facilitate Component-based Process Modeling and Design. Comput. Chem. Engng. 32(10), 2290–2305 (2008)
7. Halmos, P.R.: Mértékelmélet (Measure Theory) Gondolat, Budapest (1984) (in Hungarian)
8. Kim, H.M., Fox, M.S., Gruniger, M.: An Ontology of Quality for Enterprise Modeling. In: IEEE Proceedings of WET-ICE, Los Albamitos, CA, USA, pp. 105–116 (1995)
9. Csukás, B.: Megmaradási és információs folyamatok közvetlen számítógépi leképezése (Direct Computer Mapping of Conservational and Informational Processes) Manuscript of DSc Theses (2001) (in Hungarian)
10. Csukás, B., Balogh, S.: Combining Genetic Programming with Generic Simulation Models in Evolutionary Synthesis. Computers in Industry 36, 181–197 (1998)
11. Csukás, B., Balogh, S., Kováts, S., Aranyi, A., Kocsis, Z., Bartha, L.: Process Design by Controlled Simulation of the Executable Structural Models. Comput. Chem. Engng. 23, 569–572 (1999)
12. Varga, M., Balogh, S., Csukás, B.: Sector Spanning Agrifood Process Transparency with Direct Computer Mapping. Agricultural Informatics Vol 1(2), 73–83 (2010)

# Study of Automatic Test System of Surface Flatness in No-Till Field Based on the PLC Technology[*]

Yanbo Su[1], Hongwen Li[1,**], Yarong Mi[2], Jin He[1], Qingjie Wang[1], Hui Li[1], and Rabi G. Rasaily[1]

[1] Beijing Key Laboratory of Optimized Design for Modern Agricultural Equipment, College of Engineering, China Agricultural University, Beijing 100083, China
[2] College of Mechanical and Electric Engineering, Northwest Agriculture and Forestry University, Yangling 712100, China
lhwen@cau.edu.cn

**Abstract.** In this paper, automatic test system of surface flatness was designed according to the characteristics of the no-till field by combining the PLC (Programmable Logic Controller), laser sensor and stepping motor automatic control technologies. Monitor and Control Generated System (MCGS) configuration software was used to form the interaction interface. Real-time data report and the trend line could be created by accessing PC machine to this system, and then the surface roughness detection was realized automatically. Compared with the traditional test methods, results of the automatic test system showed that the measured value is accordance with the artificial measured value, and the correlation coefficient between them was above 0.95; and the detection efficiency had been improved by 2.3 times. These results proved the effectiveness of the automatic test system in detecting the surface flatness of the no-till field.

**Keywords:** No-till, automatic test system, surface flatness, PLC, MCGS.

## 1 Introduction

Conservation tillage is an advanced agricultural tillage technology, which advocates no tillage or reduced tillage, covering surface with straw, in order to reduce the wind erosion, water erosion and improve drought resistance[1,2]. Surface flatness is one of the significant indexes evaluating the quality of no tillage operations. Currently, the main method to measure the surface flatness is by manually pulling the rope from its ends on the soil surface. Its results are precise, but its efficiency is low and labor intensity is high. Therefore, It is necessary to carry out the research on rapid

---

[*] This work was encouraged by National Natural Science Foundation of China (Grant No. 51175499), the Australian Centre for International Agricultural Research (ACIAR), Beijing Natural Science Foundation (Grant No. 6112015) and the Special Fund for Agro-scientific Research in the Public Interest (Grant No. 200903009).

[**] Corresponding author.

D. Li and Y. Chen (Eds.): CCTA 2011, Part I, IFIP AICT 368, pp. 545–554, 2012.

measurement of the surface flatness to improve the detect efficiency. At present, certain progress has been made in detecting the surface flatness rapidly through automatic detection by domestic and foreign researchers. For example, J. Lee, et al. studied the measurement method of surface height using infrared sensor and ultrasonic sensor[3]. A. M. Mouazen, et al. analyzed the difference of detection performance between the ultrasonic sensor and the linear variable displacement transducer under the field covered with corn straw[4]. Cai Guohua made the comparative study by ultrasonic sensor, infrared sensor and linear variable displacement transducer under the three conditions of wheat broken stalks, residue, both broken stalks and residue respectively[5]. However, infrared sensor and ultrasonic sensor used by these methods can be influenced easily by the moisture content and temperature of soil, and the sensitivity of linear variable displacement transducer to surface deformation is affected. In addition, this method exits a certain delay[5]. In short, the precision and efficiency of surface flatness detection need to be improved. In this paper, the rapid automatic detection under no tillage surface is realized by the principle of laser ranging, combining the PLC and MCGS configuration software. Laser sensor has high precision and less external influence[6], can meet the requirements of precision and speed in detecting the surface flatness.

## 2    Main Structure and Working Principle

No-till surface flatness inspection system mainly composed by control part, the operative part, and the testing part as shown in figure 1. Control part mainly composed by the control box and some of the major PC. The operative part is composed of the test bench, X-axis guidway, Y-axis guidway and the stepping motor. The testing part is composed of LRFS-0040-1 laser sensors and matching circuit. Before testing, first test plots on the grid has to be divided, using laser sensor driven by stepping motor to scan detection line listed by the grid intersection.

While in operations, adjust the height of outrigger, and ensure that the detection system must be in reliable level and in stable state. The surface roughness automatic test system through own structure form the initial space coordinates, and through the manual reset and system in the software of reset control function, ensure the initial operating point for the X-axis, Y-axis intersection.

At the same time, according to detection accuracy and time requirements, set the laser scanning area, X-axis, Y-axis stepper motor stepping distance and speed. After start, the X-axis stepping motor move step by step. When the Y-axis reaches the setting position, PLC receives signal, and then control the stepping motor of X-axis from moving, and drive the Y-axis rail screw rotation through initiating the Y-axis direction movement of stepping motor, thereby stimulating laser sensor stepping a grid distance. After this movement, the alternate detection of flatness scanning is completed. After the scan is complete, through the system reset function can realize reset; adjust the position of the laser sensor. When the Y-axis touches travel switch on the X-axis•PLC control X-axis stepping motor stop the movement. At the same time when laser sensor touches the limit switch of the Y-axis, PLC controls the motor to stop from Y-axis stepping movement, which completes laser sensor reset.

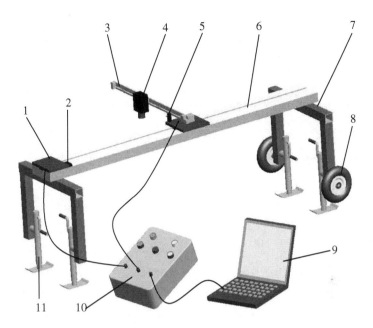

**Fig. 1.** Automatic test system of surface flatness in no-till field
1. Stepping motor of X-axis   2. Limit switch of X-axis   3. Guidway of X-axis   4. laser sensor   5. Limit switch of Y-axis   6. Guidway of Y-axis   7. Bench   8. Wheel   9. PC   10. Control box   11. outrigger

# 3   The Design of Automatic Detection System

## 3.1   The Design of Hardware Part

The hardware part of automatic detection system is mainly made by the control system, the data acquisition system and the test bench. Figure 2 shows the hardware structure of system, noting the wring mean of PLC's each pin that the system used.

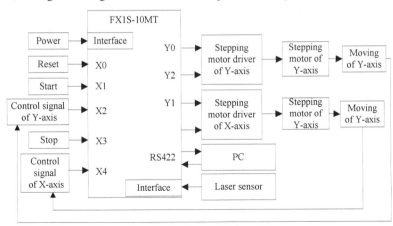

**Fig. 2.** Hardware structure of the system

**The Control System.** The control system consists of PC, slave computer and control devices. PC uses the software of the automatic detection system for surface flatness that developed by MCGS for on-site monitoring. The control of slave computer puts to use Mitsubishi programmable logic. The control system uses PLC as host machine, gathering six electrical signal of reset, start, stop, X-axis limit switch, Y-axis limit switch and laser sensors, and output four electrical signals of stop-start and move for X-axis, Y-axis, to complete position control and detection of surface height in the X-axis and Y axis using the laser sensor.

**The Data Acquisition System.** Data acquisition system uses laser sensors, transmitters, A / D converter through the RS-422 interface to send data to the principal computer, using the software of the automatic detection system for surface flatness monitoring test real-time results.

The system uses LRFS-0040-1-type laser sensors, its main technical parameters shown in Table 1.

**Table 1.** Technical parameters of the laser sensor

| Variable | Parameters | Variable | Parameters |
|----------|------------|----------|------------|
| Measurement Range | 0.2-50m | Measurement Accuracy | ±3mm |
| Output Range | 4-20mA | Testing Rate | 5Hz |
| Resolution | 0.1mm | Radial Dispersion | 0.6mrad |
| Supply Voltage | 10-30VDC | Wavelength | 650nm |

Surface flatness testing for No-till generally be carried out in the field, the solar radiation has a certain influence on detection of the laser[7]. In order to eliminate the deviation caused by sunlight, the paper was calibrated laser range sensor, the methods are as follow:

(1) Install the automatic detection system for surface flatness in the no-till land, and adjust the laser sensor to the level of the state, making the ray of the laser parallel to the X-axis;
(2) Fixed a baffle opposite the laser sensor at 200mm, so that the ray of the laser after reflection by the baffle can be received by the sensor;
(3) Record the initial distance of the sensor to the baffle and the output current of the sensor;
(4) Set stepping distance of X-axis to 10mm, the moving range is 1000mm in MCGS;
(5) Start the system, record the sensor current value when it moves backward 1mm, so you can get 100 groups of distances and corresponding values.
(6) Have a regression analysis for these 100 sets of data, obtain the relation curves between distance and the current, shown in Figure 3.

According to the relation curves between distance and current, we can know the regression equation of the laser sensor:

$$y = 3E - 05x + 3.9931$$

Where x is distance (mm), y is current (mA).

The variance Analysis results show that when the equation of the regression coefficient R> 0.95, linear detection system shows good linearity and a high level of detection accuracy.

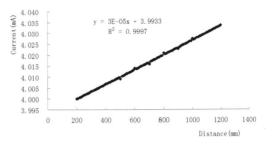

**Fig. 3.** Relation curves between distance and current

**The Test Bench and Hardware.** The test bench mainly includes X-axis guidway, Y-axis guidway, stands leg and land wheel. The distance of X-axis guidway is 2680mm, width is 240mmh and thickness is 85mm. The way of transmission is the ball screw. Because only one end of the Y-axis guidway fixed to the X-axis guidway, in order to ensure Y-axis to maintain the level in the detection process, so determined Y-axis's length is 1000mm, the way of transmission is the lead screw. Test bench leg height adjustable stand, easy to detect in a test station before transfer to the state level. The distance of stands leg on the test bench can adjust, in order to facilitate the test bench to level before the test. Meanwhile, there has a land wheel on each stand leg which is conducive to the movement.

According to the features of no-till surface flatness testing, combined with the need of the detection system, the system employs FX1S-10MT-type PLC made by the Japanese Mitsubishi, which output type is transistor output [8], used 6 inputs and 4 outputs, among them Y0 and Yl port can simultaneously output 100 KHz pulse. Select linear motion unit type WG206 in X-axis direction, stepper motor drives uses SH-2H042MB which is two-phase hybrid stepping motor driver; select 17HS111 type stepper motor in Y-axis, the type of stepper motor drives is 3ND883.

### 3.2    The Design of Software System

The software of this system mainly includes measurement system, data-collection system and configuration monitoring system. The software system development contains, building system project, driving hardware system equipment and connecting with the software, and then user interface edition, variable definition, function set-up and operation strategy development after communication-test normal. The process of the configuration software development is shown in the figure 4.

**Slave Computer.** Slave computer (including intelligent module and PLC) needs to be driven when a configuration project of surface flatness measurement system is built. This system sets up the parameters such as serial port number, signal baud rate, data bits, stop bits, data check mode and data acquisition mode by driving software.

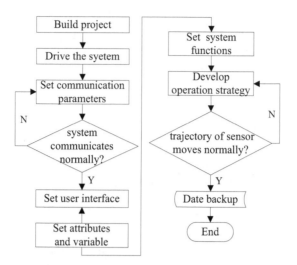

**Fig. 4.** Development process of the configuration software

**PC.** When driving slave computer communication test is normal, the PC configuration is developed in the MCGS configuration software environment[9], such as building monitoring system project, and producing user application system which made up of main control windows, device windows, user windows, real-time databank windows and operation strategy. The main control windows sets up collection range, step distance, step speed of the surface flatness automatic test system X-axis and Y-axis and menu command et al. Device windows, the key of normal equipment operation, is the connection media of the surface flatness automatic test system based on MCGS configuration software and PLC[10-12]. The real-time surface flatness data collected by slave computer sends to the database by building data connection, and the data is output by Excel and reserved permanently in the user windows. The monitoring system could operate real-time database in according to the setting order and condition, control the open and close of user windows, and detect the working state of the device by the definition of operation strategy, so that it will accurately control X-axis, Y-axis and laser sensor working process.

## 4    Experiment Results and Discussion

### 4.1    Experiment Design

The experiment was conducted at the National precision agricultural research station of Xiao Tangshan, Beijing in Sep. 2011. The experimental steps are as follow:

(1) Divide the field into 50 mm x 100 mm grids and install the automatic detection systems on the no-till field. Ensure that the starting point is the junction of the X-axis and Y-axis, and the X, Y axis is adjusted for level.

(2) The stepping distance and measuring range in the X axis direction was set as 50 mm and 1000 mm in the MCGS software, respectively; while in the Y axis direction, the stepping distance and measuring range was set as 100 mm and 300 mm in the MCGS software, respectively. Each value of the marked junctions projected on the field will be measured.

**Fig. 5.** Field experiment

(3) Fix two piles on the field when detecting each junction on the line, and a piece of string should be tied on the two piles and adjusted for lever.
(4) Measure the distance from the marked projecting junctions on the surface of the field to the string.
(5) Conducted 3 groups of the experiment, and record the data of the surface roughness and detecting time measured by the system and manpower, respectively.

## 4.2    Results and Discussion

As shown in table 2, the linear regression between the results detected by the surface flatness automatic test system and manpower was obtained for the 3 groups of results, respectively. The relationship between the two measured values was also shown in Figs. 6(a), 6(c) and 6(e). It was shown obviously in the Figs. that a positive correlation was existed between the surface flatness automatic test system and the artificial measured value in the 3 groups, respectively. Furthermore, the related correlation value for the 3 groups was 0.983, 0.976 and 0.988, respectively, which indicated that the differences between the values detected by the surface flatness automatic test system and manpower were negative.

**Table 2.** Result of linear regression

| | Coefficient of Regression Equation | | $R^2$ | F |
|---|---|---|---|---|
| | k | b | | |
| First | 1.0247 | 567.69 | 0.983 | 2.24E-35 |
| Second | 0.9699 | 604.14 | 0.976 | 1.92E-31 |
| Third | 0.8032 | 654.77 | 0.988 | 4.56E-38 |

After the regression equation was obtained, we put the artificial measured value into the equation, than the trend of the real flatness of the field was acquired. Figs 6 (b), 6 (d) and 6 (f) showed the curves of the trends of the surface flatness in the same line detected by the automatic test system and manpower. The value differences (less than 2mm) between the two measured methods for these 3 groups of experiment were 80%, 80% and 95% respectively of the total measuring point. The differences, especially those more than 2mm, were caused by the existed gap between the straw/blocks with the field surface, such as the differences appeared in the points of 5th, 8th, 12th, 13th in Figs 6 (b), 3rd , 8th, 12th, 20th in Figs 6 (d) and 16th in Figs 6(f).

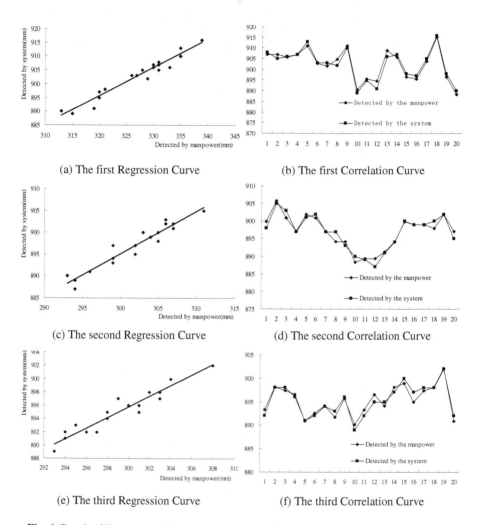

(a) The first Regression Curve

(b) The first Correlation Curve

(c) The second Regression Curve

(d) The second Correlation Curve

(e) The third Regression Curve

(f) The third Correlation Curve

**Fig. 6.** Result of linear regression between system measurements and manual measurements

The average time of detecting the surface flatness in the same line was 18min and 43min, respectively by using the corresponding surface flatness automatically detecting system and manpower. Therefore, the efficiency of the surface flatness automatically detecting system has been improved by 2.3 times compared with the manual measuring method.

## 5     Conclusions

(1) This test system realized the detection of surface flatness based on laser ranging principle by using common PLC technology as the platform and MCGS as a means.

(2) The result of the analysis of the tests showed that the tow lines fit linear correlation and all of their correlation coefficients were over 0.95, which means the regression line fit well with the data points. Using the regression model to predict values, means comparing the predictive value and the measured values of the system, and the points where the error is less than 2mm meet 80% and less than 3mm meet 95%, then we can say that the measured values of the system and the predictive value fit better.

(3) Comparing with traditional manual measurements, this system can improve the test rate more than 2.3 times. So this system can be the better alternative to test Surface Flatness instead of traditional manual measurements in No-Till Field precisely.

## References

1. Zong, J., Liu, X., Liu, H., et al.: Conservation tillage in China. China Agriculture Press (2008) (in Chinese)
2. Chen, Z., Ma, S., Zhao, Y., et al.: Characteristics of drifting sand flux over conservation tillage filed. Transactions of the CSAE 26(1), 118–121 (2010) (in Chinese)
3. Lee, J., Yamazaki, M., Oida, A., et al.: Non contract sensors for distance from ground surface. Journal of Terramechanics 33, 155–165 (1996)
4. Mouazen, A.M., Anthonis, J., Saeys, W., et al.: An automatic depth control system for online measurement of spatial variation in soil compaction, Part 1: Sensor design for measurement of frame height variation from soil surface. Biosystems Engineering 89(2), 139–150 (2004)
5. Cai, G.: Study on automatic opener depth control system for no-till seeder. China Agricultural University (2011) (in Chinese)
6. Tian, Y., Tan, Q.: Parameter optimization of laser triangulation sensor based on PSD. Control & Automation 24(5), 3–7 (2008) (in Chinese)
7. Xie, X., Liu, G., Lang, X., et al.: Laser receiver used for laser-controlled land leveling system. Transactions of the Chinese Society for Agricultural Machinery 40(Supp.), 77–81 (2009) (in Chinese)
8. Wei, J., Sun, J.: Design and implementation of portable testing instrument for PLC. Industrial Control Computer 23(10), 90–92 (2010) (in Chinese)

9. Liang, W., Guo, H.: The development and application of configurable software MCGS. Guangdong Automation & Information Engineering (1), 33–35 (2005) (in Chinese)
10. Yang, Y., Zhang, D.: High-voltage motor test system based on PLC and MCGS configuration software. Electric Power Automation Equipment 28(8), 90–92 (2008) (in Chinese)
11. Shao, L., Wang, X., Niu, X., et al.: Design and experiment on PLC control system of variable rate fertilizer. Transactions of the Chinese Society for Agricultural Machinery 28(8), 90–92 (2008) (in Chinese)
12. Xie, S., Li, X., Yang, S., et al.: Design and implementation of fuzzy control for irrigation system with PLC. Transactions of the CSAE 23(6), 208–210 (2007) (in Chinese)

# Author Index